T0331785

Geometric Spanner Networks

Aimed at an audience of researchers and graduate students in computational geometry and algorithm design, this book uses the Geometric Spanner Network Problem to showcase a number of useful algorithmic techniques, data structure strategies, and geometric analysis techniques with many applications, practical and theoretical.

The authors present rigorous descriptions of the main algorithms and their analyses for different variations of the Geometric Spanner Network Problem. Although the basic ideas behind most of these algorithms are intuitive, very few are easy to describe and analyze. For most of the algorithms, nontrivial data structures need to be designed, and nontrivial techniques need to be developed in order for analysis to take place. Still, there are several basic principles and results that are used throughout the book. One of the most important is the powerful well-separated pair decomposition. This decomposition is used as a starting point for several of the spanner constructions.

Giri Narasimhan earned a B. Tech. in Electrical Engineering from the Indian Institute of Technology in Mumbai, and a Ph.D. in Computer Science from the University of Wisconsin in Madison. He was a member of the faculty at the University of Memphis, Tennessee, and is currently a professor in the School of Computing and Information Sciences at Florida International University in Miami.

Michiel Smid received an M.Sc. degree in Mathematics from the University of Technology in Eindhoven, The Netherlands, and a Ph.D. degree in Computer Science from the University of Amsterdam. He has held teaching positions at the Max-Planck-Institut für Informatik in Saarbrücken, Germany, King's College in London, and the Otto-von-Guericke-Universität in Magdeburg, Germany. Since 2001, he has been at Carleton University, Ottawa, where he is currently a professor of Computer Science.

Geometric Spanner Networks

Giri Narasimhan

Florida International University

Michiel Smid

Carleton University

CAMBRIDGE
UNIVERSITY PRESS

Shaftesbury Road, Cambridge CB2 8EA, United Kingdom

One Liberty Plaza, 20th Floor, New York, NY 10006, USA

477 Williamstown Road, Port Melbourne, VIC 3207, Australia

314–321, 3rd Floor, Plot 3, Splendor Forum, Jasola District Centre, New Delhi – 110025, India

103 Penang Road, #05–06/07, Visioncrest Commercial, Singapore 238467

Cambridge University Press is part of Cambridge University Press & Assessment,
a department of the University of Cambridge.

We share the University's mission to contribute to society through the pursuit of
education, learning and research at the highest international levels of excellence.

www.cambridge.org
Information on this title: www.cambridge.org/9780521815130

First published 2007

A catalogue record for this publication is available from the British Library

Library of Congress Cataloging-in-Publication data
Narasimhan, Giri.
Geometric spanner networks / Giri Narasimhan, Michiel Smid.
p.   cm.
Includes bibliographical references and index.
ISBN-13: 978-0-521-81513-0 (hardback)
ISBN-10: 0-521-81513-4 (hardback)
1. Computer algorithms.   2. Trees (Graph theory) – Data processing.
3. Geometry – Data processing.   I. Smid, Michiel.   II. Title.
QA76.9.A43N37   2007
005.1–dc22   2006028718

ISBN   978-0-521-81513-0   Hardback

To my parents, Kalyani and Narasimhan, who taught me the fundamentals of life and the pursuit of knowledge and excellence, and to Kalai Mathee, with whom I collaborate on the advanced concepts. (G.N.)

To my parents, Nell and Giel, who (unknowingly) convinced me to become a mathematician and theoretical computer scientist. (M.S.)

Contents

Preface

> Philosophy is written in this grand book – I mean universe – which stands continually open to our gaze. But the book cannot be understood unless one first learns to comprehend the language and read the letters in which it is composed. It is written in the language of mathematics, and its characters are triangles, circles, and other geometric figures without which it is humanly impossible to understand a single word of it.
>
> —Galileo, *The Assayer (Il saggiatore)*, 1623

This book started as a collection of personal notes on Geometric Spanner Networks. Over time, these notes grew, and we realized that they could be of value to many researchers in the field. Gautam Das suggested that it be turned into a monograph. It made sense, because the geometric spanner problem is closely related to several fundamental problems in geometric and graph algorithms, including the minimum spanning tree problem, the Steiner minimum tree problem, the traveling salesperson problem, and the shortest path problem. We assume that the reader has had previous exposure to (undergraduate-level) basic concepts of discrete mathematics, data structures, probability and combinatorics, algorithm analysis, fundamental algorithms, and mathematical proof techniques. This book can serve as a reference text and can also be used as a self-study book for anyone interested in research in computational geometry and geometric algorithms.

One of the main features of this book is its attention to detail – detail in the proofs and arguments presented. We have striven to present complete proofs, wherever possible and appropriate, while at the same time peppering it with intuition, so that the reader can understand the underlying train of thought.

While there are numerous examples of the design of efficient algorithms much before that, by 1864 Charles Babbage foresaw rather clearly the development of the field of algorithms when he wrote in *The Life of a Philospher*:

> As soon as an *Analytical Engine* exists, it will necessarily guide the future course of the science. Whenever any result is sought by its aid, the question will then arise – by what course of calculation can these results be arrived at by the machine in the shortest time?

Many of us were drawn to the field of algorithms because of the elegance, subtlety, precision, and clarity of the ideas and arguments. This is especially true of some of the early work in the field, some of which is now part of undergraduate texts. The field has evolved since then. The algorithms and data structures and analysis tools have become more complex and sophisticated. To do research and to keep up with the advances in the field, it is necessary to know how to read papers, focus on their central ideas, and skip unnecessary details that may cloud an elegant argument. But this requires training and skill, and it is particularly challenging for the novice, the beginning graduate student. As academics, we already know that "teaching is not the mere imparting of information but the cultivation of an inquiring mind" (J. Krishnamurthy, *Life Ahead* (1963)). But we face a greater challenge – one of capturing and maintaining students' interest and keeping them challenged. Details, when presented in papers, are often boring and time-consuming, especially when the underlying ideas are new. Details are hard to write down. So, it is with good reason that details are often pushed "under the rug."

Then why should the novice be concerned about understanding details? It takes skill and training to convert good ideas and great intuition into an end result (an algorithm, a proof, etc.). When writing a paper, without the attention to details, one is more prone to errors. It is easier to make wild claims and statements without details, and it is harder to see subtle errors without the attention to details. Many of us have refereed papers for journals and conferences, where this is certainly a critical issue. Also, details help you "take apart" an algorithm or a proof; details help you understand limitations that are not obvious from an overview; details will help you understand the hurdles that must be overcome to make improvements; finally details will help you innovate and dig deeper.

Web site

This book has its own Web site(s); the following are mirror sites:

```
www.scs.carleton.ca/~michiel/SpannerBook.html
www.cis.fiu.edu/~giri/SpannerBook.html
```

They will contain a list of known errors and new developments in Geometric Spanner Networks.

Acknowledgments

We gratefully acknowledge all our "co-conspirators," who have worked with us on spanners and related geometric topics, and from whom we have learned an awful lot. These collaborators include Lyudmil Aleksandrov, Srinivasa Arikati, Estie Arkin, Sunil Arya, Prosenjit Bose, Danny Chen, Paul Chew, Gautam Das, Christian Duncan, Joachim Gudmundsson, Dagmar Handke, Paul Heffernan, Ravi Janardan, Sanjiv Kapoor, Rolf Klein, Christian Knauer, Aaron Lee, Hans-Peter Lenhof, Christos Levcopoulos, Anil Maheshwari, Joe Mitchell, Pat Morin, Jason Morrison, David Mount, Kirk Pruhs, Jeff Salowe, Warren Smith, Petra Specht, Jan Tusch, David Wood, Daming Xu, Martin Zachariasen, Christos Zaroliagis, Norbert Zeh, and Jianlin Zhu.

We thank David Peleg for his perspective on the history of spanners.

We are indebted to several anonymous referees and to people who pointed out errors and sent us feedback on preliminary versions of some of the chapters of this book. They include: Hubert Chan, Rolf Klein, Piyush Kumar, Aaron Lee, Tamas Lukovszki, Joe Mitchell, Marcin Pilat, and Justin Schechter.

Parts of this book were used as lecture notes at the Max-Planck-Institute for Computer Science in Saarbrücken and for courses at the University of Magdeburg and Carleton University. We thank the students in Magdeburg and Ottawa for their enthusiasm and feedback.

The people at Cambridge University Press have been a pleasure to work with. Pooja Jain has been tremendously helpful. We particularly appreciate the patience and the attention to detail of Lauren Cowles, who has worked with us right from the start. Finally, we want to thank Anoop Chaturvedi at TechBooks, Inc., who did an excellent and professional job of taking the book through the publication stage.

Initial ideas for the cover design came from Kalai Mathee. The talent of Namitha Raju helped refine these conceptions and brought them closer to reality. We are grateful to both of them.

A project of this magnitude is never possible without the support and encouragement of friends and family. We are forever indebted to them.

Much of our research on spanners would not have been possible without the resources provided to us by our parent institutions during this period. These include the Max-Planck-Institute, King's College London, University of Magdeburg, Carleton University, University of Memphis, and Florida International University. We also thank København's Universitet, Otto-von-Guericke-Universität in Magdeburg, Lund University, and Florida International University, which hosted several visits, making a lot of this work possible.

We acknowledge the funding provided by the Natural Sciences and Engineering Research Council of Canada (NSERC) and the National Science Foundation (NSF) for some of our personal research reported in this book.

Giri Narasimhan   Michiel Smid
Miami   *Ottawa*

PART I

Preliminaries

1

Introduction

1.1 What is this book about?

In this book, we will consider the following problem:

General network design problem: Given a set S of n points in $\mathbb{R}^d$, how to construct a *good* network that connects these points?

What do we mean by this? A *network connecting the points* of S is a graph $G = (S, E)$ with vertex set S and edge set $E \subseteq S \times S$, such that any two points $p, q \in S$ are connected by a path in G. A *geometric network* is a weighted graph where the vertices correspond to point sites in Euclidean space and the weights on the edges correspond to the distances between the endpoints in the Euclidean metric. Clearly, there are many such networks. For example, the *complete graph*, in which all pairs of distinct points are connected by an edge, is one such network connecting the points of S. The disadvantage, however, is that the number of edges is $\binom{n}{2} = \Theta(n^2)$; it is quadratic in the number of points.

Assume that the goal is to construct networks having only "few" edges. How many edges does a connected graph necessarily contain? The answer is $n - 1$. To prove this, consider an arbitrary network G connecting the points of S, and let m be the number of edges of G. Hence, we have to show that $m \geq n - 1$. Let us do the following: As long as G contains a cycle, take an arbitrary cycle, and remove an arbitrary edge from it.

Removing one edge from a cycle does not destroy the connectivity of the graph. Therefore, repeating this operation over and over again, we obtain an acyclic connected graph G', that is, a *tree*. If m' denotes the number of edges of G', then clearly $m \geq m'$. Hence, it suffices to show that $m' \geq n - 1$.

We claim that in fact $m' = n - 1$. That is, any tree on n points has exactly $n - 1$ edges. The proof is by induction on n. For $n = 1$, the claim is trivial. Let $n \geq 2$, and assume the claim is true for all trees on $n - 1$ points. Now let G' be a tree on n points. Since G' is acyclic, there is a point with degree exactly 1. (This is easy to prove by contradiction: if all degrees are larger than 1, then the graph must contain a cycle.) Remove this point, together with its adjacent edge, from G'. This gives a graph G'' on $n - 1$ points; in fact, G'' is a tree. Hence, by the induction hypothesis, G'' has $n - 2$ edges. Since G' itself has one more edge, the proof is complete.

Property 1.1.1. *Any network connecting a set of n points must have at least n − 1 edges.*

Let us call a network *sparse*, if it has $O(n)$ edges, that is, the number of edges is linear in the number of points. Again, there are many such sparse networks. Later in this chapter, we discuss several of them; each one is *good* in some sense.

The more general network design problem is to connect the set of sites by a network that satisfies a specified set of properties. To measure how *good* a network is, several quality measures have been used in the literature, some of which are listed here:

1. **Size** is defined as the number of edges in the network. In general, it is preferable to have networks with as few edges as possible, perhaps linear in the number of points.

2. **Weight** is defined as the sum of the weights of the edges. Since any network must connect all the points, its weight is bounded from below by the weight of a minimum spanning tree. The weight is a good measure of the cost of building the network; thus, it is often desirable to have networks with small weight.

3. **Stretch Factor** (or **Dilation** or **Distortion**) for two given points is defined as the ratio of the distance between the two points in the network to the metric distance between them. The stretch factor of a network is defined as the maximum stretch factor for any pair of distinct points in the network. It is often required that the stretch factor of the network be bounded by a small constant (which must be at least one). Networks with stretch factor at most t are called t-SPANNERS.

4. **Degree** is the maximum number of edges incident on any point in the network, often required to be bounded by a small constant. For a network, bounded degree implies small size, but not vice versa.

5. **Diameter** is the maximum number of edges along a shortest path connecting any two vertices in the network. It dictates the conciseness with which network paths can be described. A weighted diameter, that is, the total length of the longest path of minimum length could also be used as a quality measure instead. Diameters may be required to be small.

6. **Connectivity** is the vertex or edge connectivity of the network. It is a measure of how fault-tolerant the network is, since it signifies the number of points or links that must fail in order for the network to be disconnected.

7. **Fault Tolerance** is the number of points or links that must fail in order for the network to fail to have some desirable properties. This is slightly more general than the previous property.

8. **Genus:** In many applications, it is desirable for a network to be nearly planar. This is often quantified by its genus; it may also be measured by the size of the largest planar subgraph or the number of crossing edges in a straight-line drawing.

9. **Number of Steiner Points:** Often, better networks can be designed by adding Steiner points (points not in the input set). However, one may be constrained to have very few or no Steiner points in the network.

10. **Load Factor** of an edge can be defined as the number of shortest paths between some pair of vertices that use this edge (many alternate definitions and generalizations exist). The load factor of a network is defined as the load factor of the most "loaded" edge in the network. To prevent bottlenecks, it is desirable that the load factor of a network be small.

Earlier we discussed the property *size*. In general, when designing a network, one would like to impose constraints on a combination of the quality measures mentioned above; when analyzing a network, one would like to understand the properties of the network with respect to these quality measures. A common thread among most of the problems mentioned in this monograph is the study of networks with small stretch factor (in combination with other properties); as mentioned earlier, such networks are called *spanners*. Spanners with small size and/or weight are referred to as *sparse spanners*.

To motivate such problems, we mention a few "concrete" examples. Consider the network of highways connecting n cities, where a road is a straight-line segment connecting two cities. If we want to travel from p to q, then we have to travel at least a distance $|pq|$, the Euclidean distance between p and q. Of course, if there is a direct highway linking p and q, then we travel this distance more or less exactly. Otherwise, it would be nice if there is a path between p and q, whose length is not too large as compared to $|pq|$, thus giving rise to the concept of a spanner. Observe that the *length* of a path is defined as the sum of the lengths of its edges.

Consider the section of the Scandinavian rail network (prior to the year 2000) shown in Figure 1.1. A quick inspection reveals that if one wants to use the rail system to travel from Malmö (marked by a M) in Sweden to Copenhagen (marked by a C) in Denmark, then the distance between these cities in the rail network is more than five times the direct "as-the-crow-flies" distance. Adding a direct link between these two cities would clearly improve the rail network.[1]

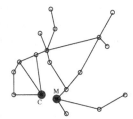

Figure 1.1: A section of the Scandinavian rail network prior to the year 2000.

We consider another example of a network **design** problem that relates to stretch factor: Imagine an existing set of highways connecting a collection of cities, where there is a need to upgrade the highway system in a cost-effective manner. Instead of spending the resources to improve all the existing highways, it would be better to improve only a carefully selected subset of the existing highways. If this subset of highway segments constitute a sparse spanner network (small stretch factor, small size, and small weight) of the highway system, then it is guaranteed that (i) one could drive from any city to any other using only improved highway segments with only a constant factor increase in the driving distance over distances in the original system of highways, and (ii) the amount of resources needed to upgrade the highway system is small since a sparse spanner has small size (number of highway segments) and weight (total length of the highways).

Given an existing system of highways, it is also easy to understand the significance of network **analysis**. Obvious queries include: "What is the size, weight, stretch factor, diameter, degree or connectivity of the network?" or "What is the farthest pair of cities in the network?" or "What is the stretch factor for a given pair of cities (i.e., what is the ratio of the length of the shortest path between two given cities in the network to the Euclidean distance between them?)?" For a federal authority maintaining the highway system, an appropriate query might be: "For which pair of cities in the network is the stretch factor the largest?" If this authority has the resources to build some highway segments, a useful query would be: "Which edge (or k edges) should be added to the network to achieve the greatest decrease in stretch factor and/or load factor?" While budgeting for future improvements to the highway network, a planner may ask: "What is the total length of the edges to be added to the network to achieve a desired fault-tolerance and stretch factor without destroying the planarity?" Planning for emergency situations requires analysis of the fault-tolerance of the network, and this may provoke a query of the type: "What is the maximum increase in stretch factor of the network (assuming it remains connected) if all

---

[1] A 16-km bridge across the Øresund connecting the two cities was opened to traffic during the summer of 2000.

highway segments within a 50-mile radius of some point are unusable due to a natural disaster?"

The list of desirable properties in a "good" network reflects many contradictory needs. For example, if bounded degree networks are desired, then small diameters are not possible; if small stretch factor networks are needed, then arbitrarily small size or weight may not be possible. Thus many network design problems display interesting tradeoffs between the quality measures and they can be thought of as multicriteria optimization problems. It is clear that a versatile software package with a suite of network design and analysis tools can be invaluable in making complex, practical decisions regarding geometric networks.

The network design problem encompasses many interesting and fundamental problems. The *minimum spanning tree* can be thought of as a network with least possible weight and infinite stretch factor; if *Steiner* points can be added, then the network with least possible weight and infinite stretch factor is the *Steiner minimum tree*. As the required stretch factor is decreased and approaches one, the network becomes denser until it ultimately becomes the trivial complete graph. If the degree of each site is required to be 2, then the network with least weight is the *traveling salesperson tour* on the points.

1.1.1 Spanning trees

A tree on a set S of n points is an acyclic connected graph on these points. We also call such a graph a *spanning tree* of S. A spanning tree is good in the sense that it has the minimum number of edges.

A set of points has many spanning trees. Sylvester showed in 1857 – and, independently, Cayley in 1889 – that any set of n points has exactly n^{n-2} spanning trees.

Let T be a spanning tree of the set S. The *weight* $wt(T)$ of T is defined to be the sum of the lengths of its edges, where the *length* of an edge $\{p, q\}$ is the Euclidean distance $|pq|$ between p and q. A *minimum spanning tree* $MST(S)$ of S is a spanning tree of minimum weight. A minimum spanning tree on 13,509 US cities is shown in Figure 1.2.

Property 1.1.2. *A minimum spanning tree of a set S is a* shortest *network connecting the points of S.*

In particular, Property 1.1.2 states the obvious fact that a shortest connected network must be a tree. Thus, a minimum spanning tree is good in the sense that both its number of edges and its weight are minimum. The following property states that it is also good in the sense that it has a small degree. The proof of this property is left as an exercise (see Exercise 4.3).

Property 1.1.3. *In a minimum spanning tree of a set of points in the plane, each point has degree at most six.*

In fact, if S is a finite set of points in $\mathbb{R}^d$, where $d \geq 2$, then the degree of each point of the minimum spanning tree of S is bounded from above by a constant that depends only on d.

The first algorithm for computing a minimum spanning tree (of an arbitrary weighted graph) is due to Borůvka and dates back to 1926. In Section 2.6, we will present two other algorithms for computing a minimum spanning tree.

Figure 1.2: A minimum spanning tree on 13,509 US cities.

1.1.2 Steiner trees

According to Property 1.1.2, a minimum spanning tree is a shortest network that connects a point set S. This is not quite true; it is a shortest graph *with vertex set S* that connects these points.

Assume that we consider connected graphs $G = (V, E)$, whose vertex set V contains the set S. In other words, we allow the graph to contain *additional* vertices. The vertices of $V \setminus S$ are called *Steiner points*. Let $SMT(S)$ be such a graph G of minimum weight, where the weight $wt(G)$ of G is defined to be the sum of the lengths of its edges. This graph is called a *Steiner minimum tree* of S, named after Jakob Steiner – a Swiss mathematician who lived from 1796 until 1863. (Apparently, Steiner had nothing to do with Steiner minimum trees.)

The problem of finding a Steiner minimum tree of the vertices of a triangle is called the *Fermat problem*, named after Pierre de Fermat (1601–65). Gauß (1777–1855) computed the Steiner minimum tree of a set of four German cities. His motivation was to link these cities by railroad.

It is clear that $wt(SMT(S)) \leq wt(MST(S))$. Can a Steiner minimum tree be much smaller than a minimum spanning tree? The following lemma shows that the answer is "no."

Lemma 1.1.4. *Let S be a finite set of points in $\mathbb{R}^d$. Then*

$$wt(MST(S)) \leq 2 \cdot wt(SMT(S)).$$

PROOF Let T be a Steiner minimum tree for S. We will construct a spanning tree T' of S having weight at most twice the weight of T. This will prove the lemma, because the minimum spanning tree of S has weight at most that of T'.

Here is the construction. We double each edge of T. This gives a multigraph W connecting the points of S and the Steiner points of T. The degree of each vertex in W is even. Hence, W contains an *Euler tour*[2] W', which is a tour that visits each edge of W exactly once and that returns to the starting vertex. Observe that this tour may visit vertices more than once. It is clear that the weight of W' is equal to that of W, which in turn is equal to twice the weight of T.

[2] Named after Euler (1707–83), the father of graph theory.

We will construct from W' a spanning tree T' of the points of S. The basic operation is that of *short-cutting*: Assume the Euler tour moves from point a to point b, and then to point c. Then short-cutting means that from point a, we immediately move to point c. By the triangle inequality, such a short-cut operation gives a tour – in general not along all points – having weight at most the weight of W'.

By following the tour W', we repeatedly make short-cuts, in such a way that we (i) remove all Steiner points, and (ii) for each point p of S, remove all visits to p, except the first one. The result is a path that visits each point of S exactly once, and whose weight is at most twice the weight of T. This path is clearly a spanning tree of S; it is the tree T' we were looking for.   ∎

Thus, the weight of a minimum spanning tree is at most twice that of a Steiner minimum tree. Is the factor 2 best possible? We will see in Exercise 1.5 that, for point sets in the two-dimensional plane, a factor smaller than $2/\sqrt{3}$ is not possible. In 1968, Gilbert and Pollack conjectured that $2/\sqrt{3}$ is in fact the best possible factor. That is, they conjectured that for any finite set S of points in $\mathbb{R}^2$,

$$wt(MST(S)) \le \frac{2}{\sqrt{3}} wt(SMT(S)).$$

This remained an open problem for over 20 years until Du and Hwang settled the conjecture in 1990.

We mention that Steiner minimum trees are extremely hard to compute; the problem is known to be **NP**-hard. In fact, it is not known if the decision problem for the Euclidean metric is in **NP**. On the other hand, a minimum spanning tree of n points in the plane can be computed in $O(n \log n)$ time.

1.1.3 The traveling salesperson tour

The *traveling salesperson problem* is an important problem that influenced the blossoming of fields such as operations research, polyhedral combinatorics, probabilistic analysis, and complexity theory. The *traveling salesperson tour TSP(S)* of a finite set S of points is the shortest tour that visits each point of S exactly once, and returns to the starting point. Here the assumption is that the set S of points belongs to a metric space. The problem of computing an optimal length tour is **NP**-hard, even when the points lie in Euclidean space. In terms of approximation algorithms, Rosenkrantz, Stearns, and Lewis showed that a factor 2 approximation to the optimal tour for points in an arbitrary metric space can be obtained from the minimum spanning tree; their argument is basically the one that we presented in the proof of Lemma 1.1.4. By combining minimum spanning trees with minimum weight matchings, Christofides improved the approximation factor to 3/2. In 1996, Arora (and, independently, Mitchell) improved on these results, by designing a polynomial-time approximation scheme for the Euclidean case. An improved polynomial-time approximation scheme by Rao and Smith in 1998 made use of the concept of spanners; details will be given in Chapter 19.

1.1.4 Triangulations

Let S be a set of n points in the plane. A *triangulation* of S is a partition of the convex hull of S into triangles, such that the vertices of these triangles are exactly the points of S.

Since a triangulation is a planar graph, it follows from Euler's theorem that it has at most $3n - 6 = O(n)$ edges. Observe also that a triangulation is a connected graph. Therefore, it is a sparse network connecting the points of S.

In general, a point set can have many triangulations. Santos and Seidel proved in 2003 that any set of n points in the plane has $O(59^n)$ many triangulations. Some triangulations have special properties:

- The Delaunay triangulation, which is the dual of the Voronoi diagram.
- The minimum weight triangulation, which is a triangulation, whose weight is minimum among all triangulations of the point set. In 2006, Mulzer and Rote proved that the problem of computing this triangulation is **NP**-hard.
- The greedy triangulation, which is defined as follows: Sort all $\binom{n}{2}$ edges of the complete graph in increasing order of their lengths. Start with a graph G whose edge set is empty, and consider the edges in sorted order, one after another. Add the current edge to G if and only if it does not intersect any edge already contained in G.

1.2 The topic of this book: Spanners

In this book, we will mainly be concerned with the problem of designing algorithms that compute geometric networks whose stretch factor is bounded. As we have mentioned already, such networks will be referred to as spanners.

Definition 1.2.1 (Spanner). Let S be a set of n points in $\mathbb{R}^d$ and let $t \geq 1$ be a real number. A *t-spanner* for S is an undirected graph G with vertex set S, such that for any two points p and q of S, there is a path in G between p and q, whose length is less than or equal to $t|pq|$. Any path satisfying this condition is called a *t-spanner path* between p and q.

In Figure 1.3, six geometric networks on 532 US cities are shown, each of which is a t-spanner for a different value of t. These spanners were computed by the path-greedy algorithm that will be presented in Section 1.4.

Definition 1.2.1 considers a spanner to be an undirected graph. Sometimes, it is useful to consider *directed* spanners:

Definition 1.2.2 (Directed spanner). Let S be a set of n points in $\mathbb{R}^d$ and let $t \geq 1$ be a real number. A *directed t-spanner* for S is a directed graph G with vertex set S, such that for any two points p and q of S, there is a directed path in G from p to q, whose length is less than or equal to $t|pq|$. Any path satisfying this condition is called a *directed t-spanner path* from p to q.

If G is a t-spanner for the point set S, then obviously, G is also a t'-spanner for any real number t' with $t' > t$. This leads to the following definition:

Definition 1.2.3 (Stretch factor). Let S be a set of n points in $\mathbb{R}^d$ and let G be a Euclidean graph with vertex set S. The *stretch factor* of G is the smallest real number t such that G is a t-spanner of S.

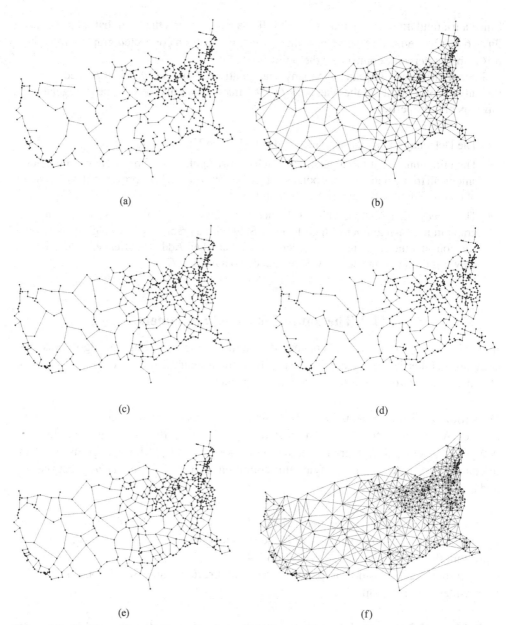

(a)   (b)

(c)   (d)

(e)   (f)

Figure 1.3: Six geometric t-spanner networks on 532 US cities with stretch factors of (a) 10, (b) 5, (c) 3, (d) 2, (e) 1.5, and (f) 1.2, respectively.

Property 1.1.1 and the definition of the minimum spanning tree imply the following property:

Property 1.2.4. *Let S be a set of n points in $\mathbb{R}^d$ and let $t \geq 1$ be a real number. Any t-spanner of S has at least $n - 1$ edges, and weight at least $wt(MST(S))$.*

The complete graph is a 1-spanner, but it has a quadratic number of edges. In fact, if we assume that no three points of S are on a line, then the complete graph is the only 1-spanner for S. Therefore, t-spanners are in general interesting only for values of t that are larger than 1. As you may expect, we are interested in *sparse* spanners, that is, t-spanners with only $O(n)$ edges.

> **Basic spanner problem:** Let S be a set of n points in $\mathbb{R}^d$, and let $t > 1$ be a real number. Does there exist a t-spanner for S having at most $c_{td}n$ edges, where c_{td} is a real number that depends only on t and d? If so, how much time does it take to compute such a t-spanner?

In this book, we will see that the answer to the first question is "yes": Sparse t-spanners exist for values of t that are arbitrarily close to one. Moreover, such t-spanners can be computed in $O(n \log n)$ time, where the constant in the Big-Oh bound depends on the stretch factor t and the dimension d.

In later chapters, we will also consider the existence and construction of sparse t-spanners having one or more of the following additional properties:

> **More spanner problems:** Let S be a set of n points in $\mathbb{R}^d$, and let $t > 1$ be a real number.
>
> 1. Does there exist a t-spanner for S, in which each point has a *degree* that depends only on t and d?
> 2. Does there exist a t-spanner for S, whose *weight* is proportional to the weight of a minimum spanning tree of S?
> 3. Does there exist a sparse t-spanner for S, whose *spanner diameter* is small? Here, the spanner diameter is defined to be the smallest integer D, such that each pair of points is connected by a t-spanner path containing at most D edges.
> 4. Can we construct such t-spanners in $O(n \log n)$ time?

It should be clear that the above properties are conflicting. For example, any t-spanner whose degree is bounded by a constant must have spanner diameter $\Omega(\log n)$. The proof of this claim is left as an exercise; see Exercise 1.11.

In most places in this book, the stretch factor t is a real number that is larger than, but arbitrarily close to, 1. We will always assume that the dimension d is a constant. As such, Big-Oh bounds contain factors that depend on t. On the other hand, factors that involve only d will be omitted in these bounds.

1.3 Using spanners to approximate minimum spanning trees

In this section, we present a first application of spanners. Let S be a set of n points in the plane. Since any minimum spanning tree $MST(S)$ of S is contained in the Delaunay triangulation $DT(S)$ of S, we can compute $MST(S)$ in the following way: First, in $O(n \log n)$ time, compute $DT(S)$. Then, compute the minimum spanning tree of $DT(S)$. This minimum spanning tree is in fact a Euclidean minimum spanning tree of the set S. Since $DT(S)$ contains only a linear number of edges, the entire algorithm has a running time of $O(n \log n)$.

For point sets in $\mathbb{R}^d$, where $d \geq 3$, it is unlikely that the same running time can be obtained. In fact, for $d = 3$, it is even unlikely that an algorithm exists that computes a minimum spanning tree within a time bound that is significantly smaller than $n^{4/3}$. This leads to the natural question of whether there exist fast algorithms that *approximate* a minimum spanning tree. The following theorem shows that this question has a positive answer, provided we have a fast algorithm for computing a spanner.

Theorem 1.3.1. *Let S be a set of n points in $\mathbb{R}^d$, let $t > 1$ be a real number, and let G be an arbitrary t-spanner for S. A minimum spanning tree of G is a t-approximate minimum spanning tree of S, that is, the weight of any minimum spanning tree of G is at most $t \cdot wt(MST(S))$.*

PROOF Let T be a minimum spanning tree of S, and number its edges arbitrarily as $e_1, e_2, \ldots, e_{n-1}$. Consider edge e_i. Since G is a t-spanner for S, there exists a t-spanner path P_i in G between the endpoints of e_i. Thus, the length $wt(P_i)$ of P_i is at most t times the length of edge e_i. It follows that

$$\sum_{i=1}^{n-1} wt(P_i) \leq \sum_{i=1}^{n-1} t \cdot wt(e_i) = t \cdot wt(MST(S)).$$

Let G' be the subgraph of G, whose edge set is the union of the edge sets of the paths P_i, $1 \leq i \leq n - 1$. Then G' is a connected graph with vertex set S, and its weight is at most $t \cdot wt(MST(S))$. Since the weight of a minimum spanning tree of G is less than or equal to the weight of G', the proof is complete. ∎

1.4 A simple greedy spanner algorithm

At this point, it is not clear whether for any set S of n points in $\mathbb{R}^d$, and for any real number $t > 1$, a t-spanner for S having a subquadratic number of edges actually exists. In this section, we present a simple algorithm that, in fact, computes such a spanner.

As discussed before, t-spanners generalize the notion of spanning trees, which require to have paths connecting every pair of points. A t-spanner is required to have reasonably short paths between every pair of points. This observation suggests that an algorithm to construct t-spanners can be obtained by generalizing Kruskal's minimum spanning tree algorithm (which will be discussed in Section 2.6.1). We remark that this spanner algorithm does not necessarily compute a t-spanner of minimum weight.

> **Simple greedy spanner construction:** Generalizing Kruskal's minimum spanning tree algorithm gives a greedy algorithm for constructing spanners. The algorithm starts with a graph G having vertex set S and whose edge set is empty. It considers all pairs of distinct points of S in nondecreasing order of their distances. The decision whether or not to add the current pair $\{p, q\}$ as an edge to G is made as follows: Instead of checking whether the vertices p and q are connected, check whether they have a path of length at most $t|pq|$ that connect them in G.

A formal description of this algorithm is given below.

Algorithm PATHGREEDY(S, t)

Comment: This algorithm takes as input a set S of n points in $\mathbb{R}^d$ and a real number $t > 1$. It returns a t-spanner for S.

> sort the $\binom{n}{2}$ pairs of distinct points in nondecreasing order of their
> distances (breaking ties arbitrarily), and store them in list L;
> $E := \emptyset$;
> $G := (S, E)$;
> **for each** $\{p, q\} \in L$ ($*$ consider pairs in sorted order $*$)
> **do** $\delta :=$ length of a shortest path in G between p and q;
>   **if** $\delta > t|pq|$
>   **then** $E := E \cup \{\{p, q\}\}$;
> $G := (S, E)$
>   **endif**
> **endfor**;
> output the graph G

Algorithm PATHGREEDY(S, t), with the value $t = n - 1$, produces the same output as Kruskal's minimum spanning tree algorithm, when given the complete Euclidean graph on S as input. The proof of this claim is left as an exercise (see Exercise 1.12).

The following lemma states the obvious fact that the path-greedy algorithm computes a t-spanner.

Lemma 1.4.1. *Let S be a set of n points in $\mathbb{R}^d$, and let $t > 1$ be a real number. The output of algorithm* PATHGREEDY(S, t) *is a t-spanner for S.*

Of course, many questions arise from the algorithm given above. Why is it not a minimum-weight t-spanner? Is there a nontrivial bound on the weight of the t-spanner? Is there a nontrivial bound on the number of edges included in the t-spanner? Is there a nontrivial bound on the degree of each vertex in the t-spanner? How can the algorithm be implemented efficiently? All these questions are dealt with in detail in Chapters 14 and 15.

Exercises

1.1. We mentioned in Section 1.1.1 that any set of n points has exactly n^{n-2} spanning trees. Verify this claim for small values of n.

1.2. Prove the following results.

(1) Let T be an arbitrary spanning tree of S. Prove that $wt(T) \leq (n - 1) \cdot wt(MST(S))$.

(2) Let $\epsilon > 0$ be an arbitrarily small constant, and let n be a sufficiently large integer. Give an example of a set S of n points in the plane and a spanning tree T of S for which $wt(T) \geq (n - 1 - \epsilon) \cdot wt(MST(S))$.

1.3. Prove that a Steiner minimum tree really is a tree.

1.4. Consider a triangle with three vertices p, q, and r. Determine the minimum spanning tree and the Steiner minimum tree of these three points. There are two cases to consider, depending on whether or not all angles of the triangle are at most $120°$.

1.5. Let S be the set of vertices of an equilateral triangle. Prove that $wt(MST(S)) = (2/\sqrt{3}) \cdot wt(SMT(S))$.

1.6. Prove that for any finite set S of points in $\mathbb{R}^d$,

$$wt(MST(S)) \leq wt(TSP(S)) \leq 2 \cdot wt(MST(S)).$$

1.7. Let S be a finite set of points in $\mathbb{R}^d$, and let S' be a nonempty subset of S. Prove the following monotonicity properties:

(1) $wt(TSP(S')) \leq wt(TSP(S))$.

(2) $wt(SMT(S')) \leq wt(SMT(S))$.

Prove that, in general, this monotonicity property does not hold for the minimum spanning tree.

1.8. Let S be a set of n points in the plane, not all on a straight line.

(1) Prove that a triangulation of S exists.

(2) Assume that no three points of S are collinear. Let h be the number of points on the convex hull of S. Prove that any triangulation of S has exactly $3n - 3 - h$ edges.

1.9. Get yourself a German dictionary, and find out the meaning of the word *Spanner*.

1.10. Let t be a real number with $1 < t < 2$, and consider an arbitrary t-spanner G for a set S of points in $\mathbb{R}^d$.

(1) Prove that each closest pair in S is connected by an edge in G.

(2) Let $p \in S$, and let q be a nearest neighbor of p in S. Are p and q connected by an edge in G?

(3) Now let $t = 2$. Prove that there is an edge in G, whose endpoints form a closest pair in S.

1.11. Let G be an arbitrary connected graph with n vertices, and let $k \geq 1$ be an integer constant. Assume that each vertex of G has degree at most k. Prove that there are two vertices p and q such that *each* path between p and q contains $\Omega(\log n)$ edges.

1.12. Prove that algorithm PATHGREEDY(S, t) in Section 1.4, with the value $t = n - 1$, is Kruskal's minimum spanning tree algorithm KRUSKAL(G), with G being the complete Euclidean graph on S; see Section 2.6.1.

1.13. Let S be a set of n points in $\mathbb{R}^d$, let $t > 1$ be a real number, and let G be the t-spanner that is computed by algorithm PATHGREEDY(S, t) in Section 1.4. Prove that G contains a minimum spanning tree of S.

1.14. In this exercise, we will introduce a spanner whose size depends on the lengths of the sides of the bounding box of the point set. Let S be a set of n points in the hypercube $[1, W]^d$, and choose real constants α and β such that $\alpha \geq \beta > 1$. Construct a sequence $S_0, S_1, \ldots, S_h$ of subsets of S, such that the following four properties hold:

(1) $S_h \subseteq S_{h-1} \subseteq \ldots \subseteq S_1 \subseteq S_0 = S$.

(2) $|S_h| = 1$ and $h = O(\log W)$.

(3) For each i with $0 \leq i \leq h$, and for any two distinct points p and q in S_i, we have $|pq| \geq \beta^i$.

(4) For each i with $0 \leq i < h$, and for each $p \in S_i$, there exists a point q in S_{i+1}, such that $|pq| \leq \beta^{i+1}$.

For each i with $0 \leq i \leq h$, define

$$E_i := \{\{p, q\} : p, q \in S_i \text{ and } |pq| \leq \alpha\beta^i\}.$$

Let G be the graph with vertex set S and edge set $E := \bigcup_{i=0}^{h} E_i$.

(1) Give an efficient algorithm that constructs the graph G. (Use a grid to compute the subsets $S_0, S_1, \ldots, S_h$.)

(2) Prove a tight upper bound on the number of edges of G.

(3) Assuming that $\alpha > 2\beta/(\beta - 1)$, prove that G is a t-spanner for

$$t = \max\left(\beta \frac{\alpha(\beta - 1) + 2\beta}{\alpha(\beta - 1) - 2\beta}, \frac{\alpha}{\beta}\right).$$

Bibliographic notes

It may be hard to believe, but spanners are known to occur in nature! Many rivers are known to be t-spanners for $t \approx \pi$. That is, the length of a river divided by the Euclidean distance between its source and mouth is roughly equal to π. See Stølum [1996].

History of spanners: While concepts similar to that of a spanner may have appeared in some form in earlier work from other related areas, its first appearance in the Computational Geometry literature can be traced to a paper by Chew [1986]. (The full version of this paper appeared in Chew [1989].) Chew defined the concept only for the complete Euclidean graph, although the word *spanner* was not used in his work. The formal definition of a spanner for an arbitrary graph in the general setting was first introduced about a year later (and, in fact, independently from Chew), in Peleg and Ullman [1987]. (The full version appeared as Peleg and Ullman [1989].) The term *spanners* was coined in this paper. Spanners were further investigated in the follow-up paper by Peleg and Schäffer [1989].

In the literature, stretch factor is also referred to by other terms such as *dilation* (in Peleg and Schäffer [1989]) and *distortion* (in Linial, London, and Rabinovich [1995]).

The field of geometric spanners has been surveyed by Soares [1992], Bern and Eppstein [1997], Eppstein [2000], Mitchell [2000], and Gudmundsson and Knauer [2006].

Related Topics: Much research has been done on spanners in general (i.e., nongeometric) graphs. A good starting point is the book by Peleg [2000]. Without being exhaustive, we also mention the papers by Peleg and Ullman [1987], Peleg and Schäffer [1989], Peleg and Ullman [1989], Cai and Corneil [1992, 1995a,b], Madanlal, Venkatesan, and Rangan [1996], Prisner [1997], Brandstädt, Chepoi, and Dragan [1999], and Le and Le [1999].

With regard to other related topics, excellent overviews of the history of the minimum spanning tree problem can be found in Graham and Hell [1985] and Nešetřil [1997]. The first algorithm for computing a minimum spanning tree was reported in two early papers [Borůvka, 1926a,b]. The most popular minimum spanning tree algorithms are the greedy algorithms by Kruskal [1956], Prim [1957], and Dijkstra [1959]. Many other algorithms exist for the minimum spanning tree problem; see the work of Fredman and Willard [1994], Karger, Klein, and Tarjan [1995], Chazelle [2000b], and Pettie and Ramachandran [2002].

Euclidean variants of the minimum spanning tree problem were studied by Yao [1982a], Vaidya [1988], Agarwal et al. [1991], Callahan and Kosaraju [1993], and Krznaric, Levcopoulos, and Nilsson [1999]. Good expected time algorithms were considered by Bentley and Friedman [1978], Bentley, Weide, and Yao [1980], Clarkson [1989], and Narasimhan and Zachariasen [2001]. The Euclidean minimum spanning tree of a set of n points in the plane can be computed in $O(n \log n)$ time. The fastest known algorithms for computing the minimum spanning tree of a three-dimensional point set have running times that are close to $O(n^{4/3})$; see Agarwal et al. [1991] and Callahan and Kosaraju [1993]. In Erickson [1995], it is argued that it is unlikely that a faster algorithm exists.

Several proofs of the fact that a set of n points has exactly n^{n-2} spanning trees can be found in the books by Aigner and Ziegler [2004] and van Lint and Wilson [1992]; see also Section 2.3.4.6 in Knuth [1997].

For excellent surveys on the topic of Steiner minimum trees, see Du and Hwang [1995] and the book by Hwang, Richards, and Winter [1992] (and the references given therein). The Steiner ratio conjecture was posed by Gilbert and Pollak [1968]. After 20 years, the conjecture was finally settled by Du and Hwang [1990a]; see also Du and Hwang [1990b] and Du and Hwang [1992]. Garey, Graham, and Johnson [1977] showed that computing Steiner minimum trees is **NP**-hard.

A captivating history of the traveling salesperson problem can be found in the book by Lawler et al. [1985], especially in the survey article by Johnson and Papadimitriou [1985]. For points in an arbitrary metric space, the problem of finding an optimal tour was shown to be **NP**-hard by Karp [1972]. For the Euclidean case, this was proved a few years later by Garey, Graham, and Johnson [1977] and Papadimitriou [1977].

The problem of designing good heuristics and approximation algorithms for the traveling salesperson problem has had a long and interesting history. For the general case in which the input does not necessarily satisfy the triangle inequality, Sahni and Gonzalez [1976] showed that computing any approximation to the optimal tour is **NP**-hard. The case when the points are from Euclidean space $\mathbb{R}^d$ was less intractable. A 2-approximation algorithm based on "doubling a minimum spanning tree" was designed by Rosenkrantz, Stearns, and Lewis [1977]; see also Exercise 1.6. For $d = 2$, their algorithm can be implemented to run in $O(n \log n)$ time. However, if the input also includes a planar graph that contains a minimum spanning tree (such as the Delaunay triangulation), then a minimum spanning tree can be computed in linear time using the algorithm of Cheriton and Tarjan [1976]. A $3/2$-approximation algorithm based on minimum spanning trees, Euler tours, and minimum weight matchings was invented by Christofides [1976]. Improving this result was a major open problem for over two decades. Many heuristics and local optimization methods did not help in topping Christofides' result. Many of these heuristics are surveyed in Bentley [1992]. A breakthrough was achieved when Arora [1998] designed the first randomized polynomial-time approximation scheme for the Euclidean traveling salesperson problem, thus achieving a $(1 + \epsilon)$-approximation algorithm with a time complexity of $O(n(\log n)^{(O(\sqrt{d}/\epsilon))^{d-1}})$ for points in $\mathbb{R}^d$. A similar result was discovered independently at about the same time by Mitchell [1999] for points in the plane. Rao and Smith [1998] took this one step further by designing a deterministic $(1 + \epsilon)$-approximation algorithm with a time complexity of $O(n \log n)$ for points in d-dimensional space. More information about the latter result will be given in Chapter 19.

The upper bound on the number of triangulations of any planar point set that was mentioned in Section 1.1.4 appears in Santos and Seidel [2003]. The question of whether or not the minimum weight triangulation problem is in **P** or **NP**-hard appears in the book by Garey and Johnson [1979].This problem was settled only recently by Mulzer and Rote [2006], who showed the problem to be **NP**-hard. Some results about this triangulation and the greedy triangulation can be found in Krznaric [1997]. Triangulations can have small stretch factors. For example, the Delaunay triangulation of a set of points in the plane is a t-spanner for $t = \frac{2\pi}{3\cos \pi/6} \approx 2.42$, see Keil and Gutwin [1992]; it is not known if it is a t-spanner for smaller values of t. It is known that t cannot be smaller than $\pi/2$. See also Section 20.3.

A solution to Exercise 1.14 can be found in Grünewald et al. [2002].

There are many excellent and useful books on computational geometry. These include the following: Mehlhorn [1984a]; Edelsbrunner [1987]; Preparata and Shamos [1988]; Agarwal [1991]; Mulmuley [1994]; de Berg et al. [2000]; Boissonnat and Yvinec [1998]; O'Rourke [1998]; Goodman and O'Rourke [2004]; Sack and Urrutia [2000]; Matoušek [1999]; and Chazelle [2000a].

2
Algorithms and Graphs

The Feynmann problem-solving algorithm: (1) write down the problem; (2) think very hard; (3) write down the answer.

—Attributed to Murray Gell-mann

2.1 Algorithms and data structures

Throughout this book, algorithms will be presented in either plain English or *pseudocode*. Most of our algorithms will be designed for the *algebraic computation-tree model*. In this model, an algorithm works with arbitrary real numbers and can perform the operations of addition $(+)$, subtraction $(-)$, multiplication $(*)$, division $(/)$, and the square root. Each of these operations takes one unit of time. Furthermore, an algorithm can test, again in one unit of time, whether or not any two real numbers, x and y, are equal, whether or not $x < y$, and whether or not $x \leq y$. Operations that are not allowed in our model of computation include the floor and ceiling functions, nonalgebraic functions such as log, sin, cos, and tan, and bitwise operations on bit strings such as XOR. Unless stated otherwise, our algorithms will not use indirect addressing. A formal definition of the algebraic computation-tree model will be given in Chapter 3.

We will use standard data structures such as linked lists, heaps, Fibonacci heaps, balanced binary search trees, and skip lists, and we assume that the reader is familiar with these data structures.

The running time of an algorithm will be expressed as a function of the number n of input elements. This function counts the worst-case number of primitive operations made by the algorithm on any input of length n. Actually, the input will generally be a set of n points in $\mathbb{R}^d$ and, hence, it consists of a sequence of dn real numbers. Since we assume, however, that the dimension d is a constant, it is realistic to consider n to be the length of the input.

We will use the standard asymptotic notation to estimate the running times of algorithms. Let $f : \mathbb{N} \longrightarrow \mathbb{N}$ and $g : \mathbb{N} \longrightarrow \mathbb{N}$ be two functions.

1. $f(n) = O(g(n))$ if there are constants n_0 and C such that $f(n) \leq C \cdot g(n)$ for all $n \geq n_0$.

2. $f(n) = \Omega(g(n))$ if there are constants n_0 and C such that $f(n) \geq C \cdot g(n)$ for all $n \geq n_0$.

3. $f(n) = \Theta(g(n))$ if $f(n) = O(g(n))$ and $f(n) = \Omega(g(n))$.

4. $f(n) = o(g(n))$ if $\lim_{n \to \infty} f(n)/g(n) = 0$. (Here we assume that $g(n) \neq 0$ for all sufficiently large n.)

2.2 Some notions from graph theory

2.2.1 Graphs

An *undirected graph* is a pair $G = (V, E)$, where V is a set whose elements are called
vertices, and E is a set consisting of pairs of vertices. Any element of E is called an *edge*
and has the form $\{u, v\}$ for some distinct vertices u and v in V. We also say that u and
v are *connected by an edge*. Observe that $\{u, v\}$ and $\{v, u\}$ denote the same edge of E.
Throughout this book, we will consider only finite graphs, that is, graphs whose vertex
set is finite.

If u and v are two vertices of an undirected graph $G = (V, E)$, then a *path* between u
and v is a sequence $u_0, u_1, u_2, \ldots, u_k$ of vertices of V for some $k \geq 0$ such that $u = u_0$,
$u_k = v$, and $\{u_i, u_{i+1}\} \in E$, for all i with $0 \leq i < k$. The path is called *simple* if all its
vertices are pairwise distinct. The path is called a *cycle* if all its vertices are pairwise
distinct, except that $u = v$.

Two vertices u and v of an undirected graph $G = (V, E)$ are said to be *connected by
a path* if there is a path in G between u and v. Observe that each vertex is connected
to itself. We say that G is *connected* if each pair of vertices is connected by a path. A
connected component of G is a maximal subset of V, all of whose elements are pairwise
connected by paths.

The *degree* of a vertex u in an undirected graph $G = (V, E)$ is defined as the number
of edges that contain u as a vertex. We denote the degree of u by $\deg(u)$. The *degree* of G
is the maximum degree of any of its vertices.

An undirected graph $G = (V, E)$ is called *weighted* if each of its edges e has a weight
$wt(e)$, which is a real number. If $e = \{u, v\}$, then we write $wt(u, v)$ instead of $wt(\{u, v\})$.
The weight of a path $u_0, u_1, u_2, \ldots, u_k$ is defined as $\sum_{i=0}^{k-1} wt(u_i, u_{i+1})$.

We say that an undirected weighted graph $G = (V, E)$ satisfies the *triangle inequality*
if $wt(u, v) \leq wt(u, w) + wt(w, v)$ for any three edges $\{u, v\}$, $\{u, w\}$, and $\{v, w\}$ of E.

The *complete graph* on a set V is the undirected graph $G = (V, E)$ for which E is the
set of all $\binom{|V|}{2}$ pairs of vertices of V.

A *directed graph* is a pair $G = (V, E)$, where, again, V is a finite set of vertices, but
now, E is a set of directed edges of the form (u, v) for some distinct vertices u and v of
V. We say that u is the *source* and v is the *sink* of the edge. The notions of a path and a
cycle are defined similarly as for undirected graphs, the only difference being that edges
are considered "one-way streets." The *outdegree* of a vertex u is defined as the number of
edges having u as a source, whereas the *indegree* of u is the number of edges having u as
a sink. The *degree* of u is the sum of its indegree and outdegree.

An *embedding* of a directed or undirected graph $G = (V, E)$ is obtained by mapping
each vertex of V to a point in the plane, and each edge of E to a straight-line segment
joining the two vertices of the edge. We require that the vertices are mapped to pairwise
distinct points. The embedding is called *plane* if no two edges in the embedding intersect,
except possibly at their endpoints. The graph G is called *planar* if it admits a plane
embedding. If G is planar then $|E| \leq 3|V| - 6$.

2.2.2 Geometric networks

The *Euclidean distance* $|pq|$ between any two points $p = (p_1, p_2, \ldots, p_d)$ and $q = (q_1, q_2, \ldots, q_d)$ in $\mathbb{R}^d$ is defined as

$$|pq| := \left((q_1 - p_1)^2 + (q_2 - p_2)^2 + \cdots + (q_d - p_d)^2\right)^{1/2}.$$

In this book, we will mainly consider *geometric networks* (or *Euclidean graphs*). Let S be a finite set of points in $\mathbb{R}^d$. A geometric network on S is a graph $G = (S, E)$, in which the weight of each edge is defined as the Euclidean distance between its vertices. The weight of a path in such a graph will also be referred to as its *length*. Hence, if $t > 1$ is a real number, then G is a *t-spanner* for S if any two points p and q of S are connected in G by a path of length at most $t|pq|$.

2.2.3 Trees

An undirected graph $T = (V, E)$ is called a *tree* if T is connected and has no cycles. The vertices of T are also called *nodes*. Observe that T has exactly $|V| - 1$ edges.

Let $T = (V, E)$ be a tree and let r be an arbitrary node that we call the *root* of T. For any node v of T with $v \neq r$, the *parent* of v is defined to be the first node different from v on the (unique) path in T from v to r. If u is a node of T and v is the parent of u, then we say that u is a *child* of v. If v does not have any children, then v is called a *leaf* of the rooted tree T; otherwise, v is called an *internal* node. Any node u on the path between v and r is called an *ancestor* of v; if $u \neq v$, then u is a *proper ancestor* of v. Similarly, any node u for which the path between u and r contains node v is called a *descendent* of v; if $u \neq v$, then u is a *proper descendent* of v. The *subtree* of v is the tree induced by all descendents of v.

A rooted tree T is called a *binary tree* if each node has at most two children. (Observe that a binary tree with more than one node has degree 3.) In case a node v has two children, we call one of them the *left child* and the other one the *right child*.

2.2.4 Representing graphs

Let $G = (V, E)$ be a graph with n vertices and m edges. We assume for simplicity that G is undirected. We number the vertices of V arbitrarily as $v_1, v_2, \ldots, v_n$. There are basically two different ways to store G in a data structure.

The first one uses an *adjacency matrix*. This is an $n \times n$ matrix M, where $M[i, j] = 1$ if $\{v_i, v_j\}$ is an edge of E, and $M[i, j] = 0$ otherwise. The advantage of this representation is that we can decide in constant time if any two vertices v_i and v_j are connected by an edge. (Observe that we need the indirect addressing operation for this.) The disadvantages are that it takes $O(n)$ time to report all edges that are incident to a given vertex of V, and the amount of space used is always $\Theta(n^2)$, irrespective of the size m of E. Since we will mainly consider *sparse* graphs in this book, that is, graphs having $m = O(n)$ edges, we are interested in data structures that need only $O(n + m)$ space.

In an *adjacency lists* representation, we store with each vertex v_i a list containing all vertices that are connected by an edge to v_i. The total amount of space needed is proportional to n plus the sum of the degrees of all vertices, that is, it is $O(n + m)$. Using this representation, we can report all edges that are incident to a given vertex v_i in

$O(\deg(v_i))$ time. The same amount of time is needed to check whether v_i is connected by an edge to any given vertex v_j.

Observe that both representations of undirected graphs can easily be extended to directed graphs.

2.3 Some algorithms on trees

2.3.1 Traversing a binary tree

In many algorithms that operate on trees, it is necessary to traverse the nodes of the tree. The order in which the nodes are visited during this traversal depends on the problem at hand. In this section, we introduce three different orderings. We will see in Section 2.3.2 how they can be used to solve some specific problems.

Let T be a rooted tree. We assume for simplicity that each internal node has exactly two children. We also assume that each internal node has pointers to its two children, and that each node (except the root) has a pointer to its parent.

The three traversals are defined recursively. If T contains only one node, then each of the three traversals is the node itself. Otherwise, the *postorder traversal* is the recursively defined postorder traversal of the left subtree of T's root, followed by the recursively defined postorder traversal of the right subtree of T's root, followed by the root itself. The *inorder traversal* is the recursively defined inorder traversal of the left subtree of T's root, followed by the root, followed by the recursively defined inorder traversal of the right subtree of T's root. Finally, the *preorder traversal* is the root, followed by the recursively defined preorder traversal of the left subtree of T's root, followed by the recursively defined preorder traversal of the right subtree of T's root.

The amount of time needed by each of these three traversals is proportional to the number of nodes of T.

2.3.2 Lowest common ancestors

Let T be a rooted tree. As in the previous section, we assume for simplicity that each internal node has exactly two children. The *lowest common ancestor* of any two nodes u and v is the node that is an ancestor of both u and v, and that is farthest away from the root of T. Equivalently, it is the node in which the two paths from the root to nodes u and v diverge.

In this section and Section 2.3.3, we show how to represent the tree T in such a way that lowest common ancestor queries can be answered efficiently. In such a query, we are given two arbitrary nodes u and v of T, and have to compute their lowest common ancestor. Clearly, we may assume without loss of generality that $u \neq v$.

Let n denote the number of leaves of the tree T. For any node u of T, let $\text{size}(u)$ denote the number of leaves in the subtree of u, and let $\ell(u) := \lfloor \log \text{size}(u) \rfloor$. Observe that $\ell(u)$ is an integer in the range from zero to $\lfloor \log n \rfloor$. Moreover, on the path from any leaf to the root of T, the $\ell(u)$-values form a nondecreasing sequence.

We will use the values $\ell(u)$ to partition the tree T into a collection of pairwise disjoint paths. For any node u of T, let P_u be the subgraph of T consisting of all nodes v for which (i) $\ell(v) = \ell(u)$, and (ii) $\ell(w) = \ell(u)$ for all nodes w on the path in T between u and v. It is not difficult to prove that P_u is a path (see Exercise 2.1).

We extend the tree T by storing with each node u the value of $\text{size}(u)$, and a pointer to the node $gpar(u)$ of P_u that is closest to the root. We call $gpar(u)$ the *group parent* of u.

We denote the parent of node u by $p(u)$. It is easy to prove that if two distinct nodes u and v have the same group parent, then either u is an ancestor of v, or v is an ancestor of u (see Exercise 2.2).

Let u be any node of T, and consider the sequence

$$u, \, gpar(u), \, p(gpar(u)), \, gpar(p(gpar(u))), \, p(gpar(p(gpar(u)))), \, \ldots$$

of nodes, which terminates at the root of T. This sequence consists of at most $2\lfloor \log n \rfloor + 1$ nodes. Hence, we can walk from any node to the root of T in $O(\log n)$ time. We generalize this approach to solve lowest common ancestor queries, as shown in algorithm LCA.

Algorithm LCA(u, v, T)

Comment: This algorithm takes as input two nodes u and v of T, and returns their lowest common ancestor. We assume for simplicity that $u \neq v$, and neither u nor v is the root of T.

Step 1: Compute the sequence $g_0^u, g_1^u, \ldots, g_i^u$ of nodes in T where $g_0^u := u$, $g_1^u := gpar(u)$, $g_k^u := gpar(p(g_{k-1}^u))$ for $2 \leq k \leq i$, and g_i^u is the first node in this sequence that is equal to the root of T. Since u is not the root, we have $i \geq 1$.

Step 2: Compute the sequence $g_0^v, g_1^v, \ldots, g_j^v$ of nodes in T where $g_0^v := v$, $g_1^v := gpar(v)$, $g_k^v := gpar(p(g_{k-1}^v))$ for $2 \leq k \leq j$, and g_j^v is the first node in this sequence that is equal to the root of T. As in Step 1, we have $j \geq 1$.

Step 3: Compute the integer k such that $g_i^u = g_j^v$, $g_{i-1}^u = g_{j-1}^v$, $\ldots$, $g_{i-k+1}^u = g_{j-k+1}^v$, and $g_{i-k}^u \neq g_{j-k}^v$. Since $g_i^u = g_j^v$, we have $k \geq 1$. Obviously, $k \leq \min(i, j)$.

Step 4: There are four possible cases to consider:

   Case 4.1: $i = j = k$.
   Since $g_1^u = g_1^v$, we have $gpar(u) = gpar(v)$ and, hence, one of u and v is an ancestor of the other. Therefore, the algorithm returns u if $size(u) \geq size(v)$, and it returns v otherwise.

   Case 4.2: $i \neq j$ and $k = i$.
   Since $u = g_0^u \neq g_{j-k}^v$ and $gpar(u) = g_1^u = g_{j-k+1}^v$, one of the nodes u and $p(g_{j-k}^v)$ (both are on the path P_u) is the lowest common ancestor of u and v. Therefore, the algorithm returns u if $size(u) \geq size(p(g_{j-k}^v))$, and it returns $p(g_{j-k}^v)$ otherwise.

   Case 4.3: $i \neq j$ and $k = j$.
   This case is symmetric to Case 4.2. The algorithm returns v if $size(v) \geq size(p(g_{i-k}^u))$, and it returns $p(g_{i-k}^u)$ otherwise.

   Case 4.4: $k \neq i$ and $k \neq j$.
   Since $g_{i-k+1}^u = g_{j-k+1}^v$ and $g_{i-k}^u \neq g_{j-k}^v$, one of the nodes $p(g_{i-k}^u)$ and $p(g_{j-k}^v)$ is the lowest common ancestor of u and v. Therefore, the algorithm returns $p(g_{i-k}^u)$ if $size(p(g_{i-k}^u)) \geq size(p(g_{j-k}^v))$, and it returns $p(g_{j-k}^v)$ otherwise.

This completes the description of algorithm LCA for computing the lowest common ancestor of any two nodes of T. It is not difficult to see that the running time is $O(\log n)$. It remains to show how to preprocess the tree T. That is, we have to show how to compute the values $size(u)$ and $\ell(u)$, and the group parents $gpar(u)$.

We start with the computation of the values $size(u)$ and $\ell(u)$. The values $size(u)$ can be computed by traversing the tree T in postorder. From these, we can compute $\ell(u)$ as $\ell(u) = \lfloor \log size(u) \rfloor$. The disadvantage of this approach is that we need the floor and logarithm functions for this. The following observation implies that we can avoid these functions.

Observation 2.3.1. *Let u be an internal node of T and let v and w be the two children of u. Assume that* $\text{size}(v) \leq \text{size}(w)$.

1. *If* $\text{size}(v) + \text{size}(w) \geq 2^{\ell(w)+1}$, *then* $\ell(u) = \ell(w) + 1$.
2. *If* $\text{size}(v) + \text{size}(w) < 2^{\ell(w)+1}$, *then* $\ell(u) = \ell(w)$.

Algorithm SIZEANDLVALUES(u) takes as input a node u of T. It traverses the subtree rooted at u in postorder, and returns the value $2^{\ell(u)}$. After this algorithm has terminated, the values $\text{size}(v)$ and $\ell(v)$ for all nodes v that are in the subtree of u have been computed. Hence, we obtain the values $\text{size}(v)$ and $\ell(v)$ for all nodes v of T, by calling SIZEANDLVALUES(u) with u being the root. The running time for this call is $O(n)$.

Algorithm SIZEANDLVALUES(u)

Comment: This algorithm computes the values $\text{size}(v)$ and $\ell(v)$ for all nodes v that are in the subtree of u, and it returns the value $2^{\ell(u)}$.

```
if u is a leaf
then size(u) := 1;
      ℓ(u) := 0;
      x := 1;
      return x
else v := left child of u;
      w := right child of u;
      x := SizeAndLValues(v);
      y := SizeAndLValues(w);
      (* x = 2^ℓ(v) and y = 2^ℓ(w) *)
      size(u) := size(v) + size(w);
      if size(w) < size(v)
      then swap v and w, and swap x and y
      endif;
      (* size(v) ≤ size(w) *)
      if size(u) ≥ 2y
      then ℓ(u) := ℓ(w) + 1;
            z := 2y;
            return z
      else ℓ(u) := ℓ(w);
            return y
      endif
endif
```

The algorithm that computes the group parents is based on a preorder traversal of the tree T. This algorithm, denoted by GROUPPARENTS(u, x), takes as input two nodes u and x such that $gpar(u) = x$. It computes the group parents of all nodes in the subtree rooted at u. If we denote the root of T by r, then a call to GROUPPARENTS(r, r) computes the group parents of all nodes of the tree. The time for this call is $O(n)$.

Algorithm GROUPPARENTS(u, x)

Comment: This algorithm takes as input two nodes u and x of the tree T, such that $gpar(u) = x$. It computes the group parents of all nodes in the subtree rooted at u.

> $gpar(u) := x$;
> **if** u is not a leaf
> **then** $v :=$ left child of u;
> $w :=$ right child of u;
>   **if** $\ell(u) = \ell(v)$
>   **then** GROUPPARENTS(v, x)
>   **else** GROUPPARENTS(v, v)
>   **endif**;
>   **if** $\ell(u) = \ell(w)$
>   **then** GROUPPARENTS(w, x)
>   **else** GROUPPARENTS(w, w)
>   **endif**
> **endif**

We have described all algorithms for trees in which each internal node has exactly two children. Observe that such a tree with n leaves has exactly $2n - 1$ nodes. We leave it to the reader to generalize the algorithms to arbitrary rooted trees. This gives the following result:

Theorem 2.3.2. *Let T be a rooted tree with n nodes. We can preprocess T in $O(n)$ time such that lowest common ancestor queries can be answered in $O(\log n)$ time.*

2.3.3 A faster algorithm for lowest common ancestor queries

The algorithm in Section 2.3.2 works in the algebraic computation-tree model. In this section, we add the *indirect addressing* operation as a unit time operation to this model. We will show that in this more powerful model, lowest common ancestor queries can be answered in $O(1)$ time, after an $O(n)$–time preprocessing step. This algorithm can in fact be implemented in the algebraic computation-tree model so that after an $O(n)$–time preprocessing, the lowest common ancestor queries can be answered in $O(\log \log n)$ time.

We start by reducing the lowest common ancestor problem on a tree with n nodes to the so-called *range minimum problem* on an array of $O(n)$ real numbers. Then we show how range minimum queries can be answered in $O(1)$ time, after an $O(n)$–time preprocessing of the array.

Reduction to the range minimum problem

Let T be a rooted tree with n nodes. We again assume for simplicity that each internal node has exactly two children. The *level* of any node u of T is the number of edges on the path from the root to u.

We number the nodes of T arbitrarily as $u_1, u_2, \ldots, u_n$. Consider an *Euler tour* of the "double-tree" obtained by doubling each edge of T. This tour starts at the root, visits each edge of T exactly twice, and returns to the root. Let $E[1 .. 2n - 1]$ be the array that stores the nodes of T in the order in which they occur in the Euler tour. To give an example, consider the following tree T with root u_1.

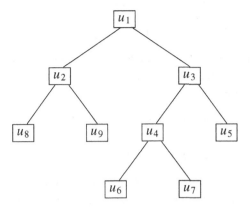

The corresponding array E is shown below with the array indices in the top row and the array entries in the bottom row:

1	2	3	4	5	6	7	8	9	10	11	12	13	14	15	16	17
u_1	u_2	u_8	u_2	u_9	u_2	u_1	u_3	u_4	u_6	u_4	u_7	u_4	u_3	u_5	u_3	u_1

Since we assume that each node has zero or two children, each internal node of T occurs exactly three times in E, whereas each leaf occurs exactly once. Let $L[1 .. 2n - 1]$ be the array where $L[i]$ stores the level of node $E[i]$, $1 \le i \le 2n - 1$. For our example tree, we obtain the following array L, again, with the array indices in the top row:

1	2	3	4	5	6	7	8	9	10	11	12	13	14	15	16	17
0	1	2	1	2	1	0	1	2	3	2	3	2	1	2	1	0

Finally, let $R[1 .. n]$ be the array in which $R[i]$ is equal to the smallest integer ℓ for which $E[\ell] = u_i$, $1 \le i \le n$. In other words, $R[i]$ is equal to the first "time" that node u_i is visited during the Euler tour of T. For our example tree, we get the following array R:

1	2	3	4	5	6	7	8	9
1	2	8	9	15	10	12	3	5

The following lemma explains how the arrays E, L, and R can be used to obtain the lowest common ancestor of any two distinct nodes of the tree T.

Lemma 2.3.3. *Let i and j be distinct integers with $1 \le i \le n$ and $1 \le j \le n$, and assume that $R[i] < R[j]$. Let k be the integer such that $R[i] \le k \le R[j]$ and $L[k]$ is minimum. The lowest common ancestor of the nodes u_i and u_j is equal to $E[k]$.*

PROOF The lowest common ancestor of u_i and u_j is visited during the portion of the Euler tour that starts at the first visit to u_i and ends at the first visit to u_j. Among all nodes visited during this portion, it is that node that is closest to the root of T. This portion of the Euler tour is stored in $E[R[i] .. R[j]]$, and the levels of the nodes of this portion are stored in $L[R[i] .. R[j]]$. ∎

Hence, we can answer lowest common ancestor queries by answering a so-called range minimum query in the array L. We will show later how such queries can be answered in $O(1)$ time after an $O(n)$–time preprocessing step, by using the following property of L.

Observation 2.3.4. *The array L satisfies the* (± 1)-*property, that is,* $L[i + 1]$ *is equal to either* $L[i] + 1$ *or* $L[i] - 1$ *for each i with* $1 \leq i \leq 2n - 2$.

Given the tree T, the arrays E, L, and R can be computed in $O(n)$ time. Moreover, the reduction given above can easily be extended to arbitrary rooted trees. Therefore, we obtain the following result:

Theorem 2.3.5. *Let T be a rooted tree with n nodes. We can preprocess T in* $O(n)$ *time such that lowest common ancestor queries can be answered in* $O(1)$ *time. The algorithms work in the algebraic computation-tree model, extended with indirect addressing.*

The $O(n)$–time preprocessing algorithm can be implemented in the algebraic computation-tree model (i.e., without using indirect addressing). In this weaker model, the query time becomes $O(\log \log n)$. This will imply the following result:

Theorem 2.3.6. *Let T be a rooted tree with n nodes. We can preprocess T in* $O(n)$ *time such that the lowest common ancestor queries can be answered in* $O(\log \log n)$ *time. The algorithms work in the algebraic computation-tree model.*

Solving the range minimum problem

In the *range minimum problem*, we are given an array $A[1 .. n]$ of real numbers. We want to preprocess A such that for any two given integers i and j with $1 \leq i < j \leq n$, we can efficiently compute an integer k with $i \leq k \leq j$, for which $A[k]$ is minimum.

In the application to the lowest common ancestor problem, we have to solve this problem for the array $L[1 .. 2n - 1]$. Observe that for this application, we need the *index* of the minimal element rather than the minimal element itself.

We start by giving two simple solutions to this problem, both of which do not assume any restriction on the array A. These solutions use $O(n^2)$ and $O(n \log n)$ preprocessing time (and space), respectively. Afterward, we show how these solutions can be combined to obtain an $O(n)$–time preprocessing algorithm for arrays that satisfy the (± 1)-property.

A first solution: In this solution to the range minimum problem, we store all $\binom{n}{2}$ possible answers. That is, for each i with $1 \leq i < n$, there is an array $X_i[i + 1 .. n]$, where for each j with $i + 1 \leq j \leq n$, the value of $X_i[j]$ is equal to the integer k with $i \leq k \leq j$, for which $A[k]$ is minimum. It is clear that these arrays can be used to answer a range minimum query in $O(1)$ time. Using the relations

$$X_i[i + 1] = \begin{cases} i & \text{if } A[i] < A[i + 1], \\ i + 1 & \text{otherwise,} \end{cases}$$

for $1 \leq i < n$, and

$$X_i[j] = \begin{cases} X_i[j - 1] & \text{if } A[X_i[j - 1]] < A[j], \\ j & \text{otherwise,} \end{cases}$$

for $1 \leq i < n - 1$ and $i + 2 \leq j \leq n$, all arrays X_i, $1 \leq i < n$, can be computed in $O(n^2)$ time.

A second solution: We improve upon the previous solution, by storing for each i with $1 \leq i < n$, the answers to only $O(\log n)$ different range minimum queries. To be more precise, for each i with $1 \leq i < n$, there is an array $Y_i[1 .. \lfloor \log(n - i + 1) \rfloor]$, in which for each ℓ with $1 \leq \ell \leq \lfloor \log(n - i + 1) \rfloor$, the value of $Y_i[\ell]$ is equal to the integer k with $i \leq k \leq i + 2^\ell - 1$, for which $A[k]$ is minimum.

Let us see how these arrays can be used to answer a range minimum query. Let i and j be two integers with $1 \leq i < j \leq n$ and let $h := \lfloor \log(j - i) \rfloor$. If $h = 0$, then $j = i + 1$ and $Y_i[1]$ is the answer to the query. Assume that $h \geq 1$. We observe that $j - 2^h + 1 \leq i + 2^h$ and, therefore,

$$\{i, i + 1, \ldots, i + 2^h - 1\} \cup \{j - 2^h + 1, j - 2^h + 2, \ldots, j\} = \{i, i + 1, \ldots, j\}.$$

Let $k := Y_i[h]$ and $k' := Y_{j-2^h+1}[h]$. (Observe that h is in the range of both Y_i and Y_{j-2^h+1}.) If $A[k] < A[k']$, then $A[k]$ is a minimal element in the subarray $A[i \mathinner{.\,.} j]$ and, therefore, k is the answer to the query. Otherwise, k' is the answer. Hence, assuming that the value of h can be computed in $O(1)$ time, we can answer a range minimum query in $O(1)$ time.

If we initialize an array $Z[1 \mathinner{.\,.} n]$, where $Z[m] = \lfloor \log m \rfloor$, $1 \leq m \leq n$, then h is obtained in $O(1)$ time by looking up the value $Z[j - i]$. This array can be computed in $O(n)$ time, without using the floor and logarithm functions.

The relations

$$Y_i[1] = \begin{cases} i & \text{if } A[i] < A[i + 1], \\ i + 1 & \text{otherwise,} \end{cases}$$

for $1 \leq i < n$, and

$$Y_i[\ell] = \begin{cases} Y_i[\ell - 1] & \text{if } A[Y_i[\ell - 1]] < A[Y_{i+2^{\ell-1}}[\ell - 1]], \\ Y_{i+2^{\ell-1}}[\ell - 1] & \text{otherwise,} \end{cases}$$

for $1 \leq i < n - 1$ and $2 \leq \ell \leq \lfloor \log(n - i + 1) \rfloor$, imply that all arrays Y_i, $1 \leq i < n$, can be computed in $O(n \log n)$ time.

Hence, we have shown that the array A can be preprocessed in $O(n \log n)$ time, such that range minimum queries can be answered in $O(1)$ time.

An optimal solution: We now assume that the array $A[1 \mathinner{.\,.} n]$ satisfies the (± 1)-property. Furthermore, we assume for simplicity that $\log n$ is an even integer.

We partition A into *blocks* of length $(1/2) \log n$, where the h-th block is the subarray

$$A[((h - 1)/2) \log n + 1, ((h - 1)/2) \log n + 2, \ldots, (h/2) \log n],$$

for $1 \leq h \leq \lceil 2n / \log n \rceil$.

Let $B[1 \mathinner{.\,.} \lceil 2n / \log n \rceil]$ be the array in which $B[h]$ is equal to the minimal element of the h-th block for $1 \leq h \leq \lceil 2n / \log n \rceil$. The array B can be computed in $O(n)$ time. We use our second solution to preprocess B for range minimum queries. This takes $O(n)$ time, after which queries in B can be answered in $O(1)$ time.

We also initialize an array $C[1 \mathinner{.\,.} n]$ in which $C[i] = \lfloor 2i / \log n \rfloor$ for $1 \leq i \leq n$. We will use this array to compute, given any i with $1 \leq i \leq n$, the number of the block that contains $A[i]$. The array C can be computed in $O(n)$ time, without using the floor function.

Let i and j be two integers with $1 \leq i < j \leq n$, let $h := \lceil 2i / \log n \rceil$, and let $h' := \lceil 2j / \log n \rceil$. Hence, $A[i]$ and $A[j]$ are contained in the h-th and h'-th blocks of A, respectively. Let us first consider the case when $h < h'$. The minimal value in the subarray $A[i \mathinner{.\,.} j]$ is equal to the minimum of the following three numbers:

1. the minimum in the portion of the h-th block that starts at position i and ends at the end of this block,

2. the minimum in the portion of the h'-th block that starts at the beginning of this block and ends at position j, and

3. the minimum in the subarray $B[h + 1 .. h' - 1]$. (Let us say that this minimum is ∞ if $h' = h + 1$.)

The third minimum can be computed in $O(1)$ time using the data structure for the array B. To compute the first and second minima, we have to preprocess the blocks so that *in-block* range minimum queries can be answered. If $h = h'$, then $A[i]$ and $A[j]$ are contained in the same block and the query on A reduces to an in-block query.

Let us see how the blocks can be preprocessed for in-block queries. Consider the *normalized* blocks obtained by taking each block and subtracting the first element of the block from each element of the block. The critical point is that even though there are $\lceil 2n/\log n \rceil$ blocks, we will show that the number of distinct normalized blocks is only $O(\sqrt{n})$. To see this, we observe that there are $\lceil 2n/\log n \rceil$ normalized blocks, each

- having length $(1/2)\log n$,
- starting with a zero, and
- satisfying the (± 1)-property.

A normalized block can be uniquely encoded by a string of length $(1/2)\log n - 1$ over the alphabet $\{+1, -1\}$. We observe that relative to the start of a block, the location of the minimal item within that block is dependent only on the string encoding its normalized block and is independent of the value of its first item. Since the number of such strings is only $2^{(1/2)\log n - 1} = (1/2)\sqrt{n}$, it follows that we have to preprocess only up to $(1/2)\sqrt{n}$ many "distinct" blocks.

Our preprocessing proceeds as follows. For each h with $1 \le h \le \lceil 2n/\log n \rceil$, let $s^h := s_1 s_2 \ldots s_{(1/2)\log n - 1}$ be the (± 1)-string corresponding to the h-th block of A, and let the integer x^h be defined by

$$x^h := \sum_{i=1}^{(1/2)\log n - 1} \frac{s_i + 1}{2} 2^i.$$

That is, we replace in s^h each occurrence of -1 by 0, and each occurrence of $+1$ by 1. The resulting binary string is the binary representation of the integer x^h. Each of the $\lceil 2n/\log n \rceil$ integers x^h can be computed in $O(\log n)$ time. Also, we can sort all these integers in $O(n)$ time. After this sorting step, we know the "distinct" blocks of A. For each distinct value of x^h, we preprocess the corresponding normalized block for range minimum queries using our first solution. Since each normalized block has length $O(\log n)$, and since we do this for only $O(\sqrt{n})$ blocks, this part of the preprocessing takes $O(\sqrt{n}\log^2 n) = O(n)$ time.

Finally, for each h with $1 \le h \le \lceil 2n/\log n \rceil$, we store with the h-th block of the array A a pointer to the data structure for the normalized block that corresponds to the integer x^h.

We now present the query algorithm. Given two integers i and j with $1 \le i < j \le n$, we compute $h := \lceil 2i/\log n \rceil$ and $h' := \lceil 2j/\log n \rceil$. If $h < h'$, then we do the following:

1. We follow the pointer to the data structure for the normalized block that corresponds to x^h and compute the index of the minimal element in the portion that starts at position i and ends at the end of this normalized block.

2. We follow the pointer to the data structure for the normalized block that corresponds to $x^{h'}$ and compute the index of the minimal element in the portion that starts at the beginning of this normalized block and ends at position j.

3. If $h < h' - 1$, then we use the data structure for B to compute the index of the minimal element in the subarray $B[h + 1 .. h' - 1]$.

It should be clear that, given this information, the index of the minimal element in the subarray $A[i .. j]$ can be computed in $O(1)$ time. If $h = h'$, then we follow the pointer to the data structure for the normalized block that corresponds to x^h, and answer the query within this normalized block. The answer to this query allows us to find, in $O(1)$ time, the index of the minimal element in the subarray $A[i .. j]$. We have proved the following result:

Theorem 2.3.7. *Let $A[1 .. n]$ be an array of real numbers satisfying the (± 1)-property. We can preprocess A in $O(n)$ time such that range minimum queries can be answered in $O(1)$ time. The algorithms work in the algebraic computation-tree model, extended with indirect addressing.*

In the algorithms given above, indirect addressing is a crucial operation. We claim that these algorithms can be implemented without using indirect addressing, at the expense of an increase in the query time:

Theorem 2.3.8. *Let $A[1 .. n]$ be an array of real numbers satisfying the (± 1)-property. We can preprocess A in $O(n)$ time such that range minimum queries can be answered in $O(\log \log n)$ time. The algorithms work in the algebraic computation-tree model.*

2.3.4 Centroids and separators in trees

Divide-and-conquer is a standard technique in algorithm design. When applying this technique to trees, we have to partition the tree into a small number of pieces such that each piece contains at most a constant fraction of the nodes. In this section, we will introduce the notion of centroid node, centroid edge, and separator node. Each of these can be used to achieve such a partition.

Before we can define centroid nodes, we have to introduce some notation. We denote the number of nodes of any tree T by $\#(T)$. We say that two nodes u and v of T are *neighbors* if they are connected by an edge.

Consider any node u of T. Removing node u (and its incident edges) from T results in a collection of subtrees with one subtree for each neighbor of u. We denote by T_{uv} the subtree that contains neighbor v. Observe that $T_{uv} \neq T_{vu}$. In fact, we have $\#(T_{uv}) + \#(T_{vu}) = \#(T)$.

A node u of the tree T is called a *centroid node* if T_{uv} contains at most $\#(T)/2$ nodes for each neighbor v of u. The following theorem states that such a node always exists and that it can be computed efficiently.

Theorem 2.3.9. *Let $n \geq 2$. Any tree having n nodes contains a centroid node, which can be computed in $O(n)$ time.*

PROOF For each node v of T, we define

$$m_v := \max\{\#(T_{vw}) : w \text{ is a neighbor of } v\}.$$

Let u be a node of T for which m_u is minimum. We will show that u is a centroid node of T.

Let v be a neighbor of u such that the tree T_{uv} contains m_u vertices. Let $u, w_1, w_2, \ldots, w_k$ be the neighbors of v in T. Observe that, by our choice of u, we have $m_v \geq m_u$. Let x be a neighbor of v such that the tree T_{vx} contains m_v nodes. Then

$x \in \{u, w_1, w_2, \ldots, w_k\}$. We claim that $x = u$. To prove this, assume that there is an index i with $1 \le i \le k$, such that $x = w_i$. Then $\#(T_{vw_i}) < \#(T_{uv})$, which is a contradiction, because $\#(T_{vw_i}) = m_v$ and $\#(T_{uv}) = m_u$. It follows that

$$n = \#(T_{uv}) + \#(T_{vu}) = \#(T_{uv}) + \#(T_{vx}) = m_u + m_v \ge 2m_u,$$

that is, we have $m_u \le n/2$. This proves that u is a centroid node. We leave the computation of the centroid node as an exercise (see Exercise 2.12). ■

A similar notion is that of a *centroid edge*, that is, an edge whose removal from the tree T gives two trees having approximately the same size. If the degree of T is bounded by a constant, then such a centroid edge always exists and can be computed in $O(n)$ time. The proof of this claim is left as an exercise (see Exercise 2.14).

Let T be a tree with n nodes. A *separator node* is a node in T whose removal results in two graphs G_1 and G_2 (that are forests), each having at most $2n/3$ nodes. In fact, a centroid node is also a separator node. Given this node, the two graphs G_1 and G_2 can be computed in $O(n)$ time. (The proof of this claim is left as an exercise; see Exercise 2.16.)

2.4 Coloring graphs of bounded degree

For the rest of this chapter, we will discuss several graph algorithms. We start with a simple graph coloring problem. In Chapter 11, we will need an algorithm that gives each vertex of a given graph a color such that any two vertices that are connected by an edge have different colors. In this section, we show that this is always possible using $D + 1$ colors if D is the maximum degree of any vertex.

Let G be an undirected graph with n vertices, let D be the maximum degree of any vertex of G, and let C be a set of $D + 1$ colors. We present a greedy algorithm that colors the vertices of G using the colors of C, such that any two adjacent vertices have different colors.

Let $v_1, v_2, \ldots, v_n$ be the sequence of vertices of G. Our algorithm visits the vertices in this order. For any k with $1 \le k \le n$, if the algorithm has visited $v_1, v_2, \ldots, v_k$, then each of these vertices will have a color of C, such that any two adjacent vertices v_i and v_j, with $1 \le i < j \le k$, have different colors.

Initially, $k = 1$, and the algorithm colors v_1 with an arbitrary element of C. Let $1 \le k < n$, and assume that $v_1, v_2, \ldots, v_k$ have been colored already. The algorithm computes the set C_k of all colors $c \in C$ for which there is an index i, such that $i \le k$, v_i has color c, and $\{v_i, v_{k+1}\}$ is an edge of G. Then the algorithm colors v_{k+1} with an arbitrary element of the set $C \setminus C_k$. Observe that $C \setminus C_k$ is nonempty, because C_k contains at most D elements.

It is clear that this algorithm computes a valid coloring of the vertices of G. Furthermore, the algorithm can be implemented so that its running time is $O(Dn)$. Hence, we have proved the following result:

Theorem 2.4.1. *Let G be an undirected graph with n vertices and let D be a positive integer. Assume that the degree of each vertex of G is less than or equal to D. The vertices of G can be colored using $D + 1$ colors, such that any two adjacent vertices have different colors. Moreover, such a coloring can be computed in $O(Dn)$ time.*

2.5 Dijkstra's shortest paths algorithm

Let $G = (V, E)$ be a weighted undirected graph. Each edge $\{u, v\}$ in E has a weight that we denote by $wt(u, v)$. We assume that these weights are positive real numbers. Since the graph G is undirected, we have $wt(u, v) = wt(v, u)$ for any edge $\{u, v\}$. Recall that the weight of a path in G is defined as the sum of the weights of the edges on this path. For any two vertices u and v of V, we denote by $\delta(u, v)$ the minimum weight of any path in G between u and v. If there is no path between u and v, then $\delta(u, v) := \infty$. Observe that δ satisfies the *triangle inequality*: We have $\delta(u, v) \leq \delta(u, w) + \delta(w, v)$ for any three vertices u, v, and w of V.

In this section, we give an algorithm that solves the following problem:

Problem 2.5.1. Given a weighted undirected graph $G = (V, E)$ in which each edge has a positive real weight, given a vertex $s \in V$, and given a real number $R > 0$, compute all vertices $v \in V$ for which $\delta(s, v) \leq R$, and for each such vertex v, compute the value of $\delta(s, v)$.

If $R = \infty$, then the standard algorithm for solving this problem is *Dijkstra's algorithm*. The idea of this algorithm is as follows. For each vertex v, we maintain a variable $d(v)$, whose value is the smallest weight of any path between s and v encountered so far. Hence, during the algorithm, we always have $\delta(s, v) \leq d(v)$ for all vertices $v \in V$. We also maintain a subset A of V, such that for each $v \in A$, the value of $\delta(s, v)$ has been computed already.

At the start of the algorithm, we set $d(s) := 0$, $d(v) := \infty$ for all vertices $v \in V \setminus \{s\}$, and initialize A to be the empty set. Then we repeatedly select a vertex $u \in V \setminus A$ for which $d(u)$ is minimum. As we will see later, this vertex u has the property that $d(u) = \delta(s, u)$. Therefore, we add u to the set A and update the values $d(v)$ for all vertices $v \in V$ that are connected by an edge to u by assigning $d(v) := \min(d(v), d(u) + wt(u, v))$.

The vertices $v \in V \setminus A$ are maintained in a priority queue PQ with the priority being the value $d(v)$. This priority queue can be implemented, for example, using a binary heap or a Fibonacci heap. In this way, the minimum value $d(u)$ can be selected and deleted efficiently, and the values $d(v)$ that change can be updated efficiently.

It is clear that we can also run this algorithm if R is finite. The disadvantage of this approach is that the running time is at least linear in the number of vertices and edges of the graph G. Our goal is an algorithm whose running time depends only on the number of vertices v for which $\delta(s, v) \leq R$ and the degrees of these vertices.

2.5.1 Algorithm SINGLESOURCE

In our variant of Dijkstra's algorithm, the priority queue PQ stores only those vertices v for which $d(v) \leq R$. For every vertex $v \in V$, the algorithm maintains two Boolean variables *added_to_PQ*(v) and *reported*(v). Initially, all these variables have the value *false*. The algorithm also maintains a set A, which is implemented as a linked list. During the algorithm, the following two properties will be maintained for each vertex v:

1. *added_to_PQ*(v) = *true* if and only if v has ever been inserted into PQ.
2. *reported*(v) = *true* if and only if v is contained in the set A.

As shown later, the set A consists of all vertices v with $\delta(s, v) \leq R$ for which we have computed $\delta(s, v)$. The algorithm terminates as soon as PQ is empty or the current minimum value $d(u)$ in PQ is larger than R.

Algorithm SINGLESOURCE(G, s, R)

Comment: This algorithm takes as input an undirected graph G in which every edge has a positive weight, a vertex s of G, and a real number $R > 0$. It returns the set A of all vertices v for which $\delta(s, v) \leq R$.

Step 1: Initialize $d(s) := 0$, PQ as the priority queue containing s, *added_to_PQ*(s) := *true*, A as the empty list, and *reported*(s) := *false*.

Step 2: If PQ is empty, then go to Step 3. Otherwise, let u be a vertex of PQ for which $d(u)$ is minimum. If $d(u) > R$, then go to Step 3. Otherwise, $d(u) \leq R$, in which case the following Steps 2.1 and 2.2 are made:

Step 2.1: Add u to the list A, set *reported*(u) := *true*, and delete u from PQ.

Step 2.2: For each vertex v for which $\{u, v\}$ is an edge of G and *reported*(v) = *false*, distinguish the following two cases:

Case 2.2.1: If *added_to_PQ*(v) = *false*, then set $d(v) := d(u) + wt(u, v)$ and, if $d(v) \leq R$, insert v into PQ and set *added_to_PQ*(v) := *true*.

Case 2.2.2: If *added_to_PQ*(v) = *true* and $d(u) + wt(u, v) < d(v)$, then set $d(v) := d(u) + wt(u, v)$ and update the priority of v in PQ.

After Steps 2.1 and 2.2 have been made, repeat Step 2.

Step 3: Reset all variables *added_to_PQ*(v) that are *true* to *false*, and reset all variables *reported*(v) with $v \in A$ to *false*.

Step 4: Return the list A.

Remark 2.5.2. In Chapter 15, algorithm SINGLESOURCE(G, s, R) will be run repeatedly on a fixed graph G, for different vertices s. Prior to one call to this algorithm, the values of all variables *added_to_PQ*(v) and *reported*(v) are assumed to be *false*. Because of this, all these variables are reset to *false* in Step 3 of the algorithm. There is no need to reset the values of the variables $d(v)$. Prior to one call to SINGLESOURCE, these variables can have arbitrary values. The proof of this last claim is left as an exercise (see Exercise 2.17).

In Section 2.5.2, we prove that the list A returned in Step 4 indeed consists of all vertices v for which $\delta(s, v) \leq R$. In Section 2.5.3, we analyze the running time of the algorithm.

2.5.2 The correctness proof of algorithm SINGLESOURCE

We start by showing that for each vertex v stored in the priority queue PQ, the value of $d(v)$ is an upper bound on the weight of a shortest path between s and v.

Lemma 2.5.3. *Algorithm* SINGLESOURCE(G, s, R) *maintains the invariant that* $\delta(s, v) \leq d(v)$ *for all vertices v for which added_to_PQ(v) = true.*

PROOF The proof is by induction on the number of times Step 2 has been executed. Immediately after Step 1 (i.e., when Step 2 has not been executed yet), only the variable *added_to_PQ*(s) has the value *true*. At this moment, the variable $d(s)$ has value zero, which is equal to $\delta(s, s)$. Hence, the invariant holds immediately before Step 2 is executed for the first time.

Consider one execution of Step 2, and assume that PQ is not empty at the start of this execution. Consider the vertex u in PQ for which $d(u)$ is minimum and that is chosen in this execution, and assume that $d(u) \leq R$.

Let v be any vertex for which $added\_to\_PQ(v) = true$ at the start of this execution of Step 2. If $d(v)$ does not change during this execution, then we clearly have $\delta(s, v) \leq d(v)$ afterward. Assume that $d(v)$ does change. Then at the end of this execution, we have $d(v) = d(u) + wt(u, v)$. Since $d(u)$ does not change during this execution, we have $\delta(s, u) \leq d(u)$. By the triangle inequality, we have $\delta(s, v) \leq \delta(s, u) + wt(u, v)$. This implies that at the end of this execution of Step 2, we have $\delta(s, v) \leq d(v)$.

Finally, let v be any vertex for which the value of $added\_to\_PQ(v)$ is set to $true$ during this execution of Step 2. Then, $d(v) = d(u) + wt(u, v)$. As in the previous case, we conclude that $\delta(s, v) \leq d(v)$ at the end of this execution.   ■

Next we prove that after the value of a variable $d(v)$ becomes equal to $\delta(s, v)$, it does not change during the rest of the algorithm.

Lemma 2.5.4. *Let v be any vertex of V. Assume that at some moment during the algorithm, $added\_to\_PQ(v) = true$ and the value of $d(v)$ becomes equal to $\delta(s, v)$. Then the value of $d(v)$ does not change during the rest of the algorithm.*

PROOF Since $added\_to\_PQ(v) = true$, we have, by Lemma 2.5.3, $\delta(s, v) \leq d(v)$. It follows from the algorithm that, after $added\_to\_PQ(v)$ has been set to $true$, the value of $d(v)$ does not increase.   ■

Lemma 2.5.5. *The minimum value $d(u)$ stored in the priority queue PQ does not decrease during the algorithm.*

PROOF Consider any execution of Step 2, and let u be the vertex that is inserted into A during this execution. Then $d(u)$ is minimum over all vertices that are stored in PQ. Let v be any vertex such that (i) v is already in PQ and $d(v)$ is decreased during this execution, or (ii) v is inserted into PQ during this execution. Then $d(v) = d(u) + wt(u, v)$, which is larger than $d(u)$. Hence, after deleting u from PQ, the new minimum stored in PQ is not smaller than $d(u)$.   ■

The next lemma is the basis for the correctness proof of algorithm SINGLESOURCE.

Lemma 2.5.6. *Let v be any vertex of V such that $v \neq s$ and $\delta(s, v) \leq R$, and let P be a shortest path between s and v. Let $\{u, v\}$ be the last edge on P. Assume that u is inserted into A during some execution of Step 2, and assume that $d(u) = \delta(s, u)$ at that moment. Then $d(v) = \delta(s, v)$ at any moment after this execution.*

PROOF During the execution of Step 2 in which u is inserted into A, the algorithm considers the edge $\{u, v\}$. We claim that v is not an element of A at that moment, that is, $reported(v) = false$. To prove this, assume that $reported(v) = true$ at the moment when u is inserted into A. It follows from the algorithm that $added\_to\_PQ(v) = true$ at this moment. Also, by Lemma 2.5.5, we have $d(v) \leq d(u)$ at this moment. Combining this with Lemma 2.5.3 and the assumption of the lemma, it follows that

$$\delta(s, v) \leq d(v) \leq d(u) = \delta(s, u). \tag{2.1}$$

On the other hand, since P is a shortest path between s and v, the subpath of P between s and u is a shortest path between s and u. Therefore, $\delta(s, v) = \delta(s, u) + wt(u, v)$.

Combining this with (2.1) implies that $wt(u, v) \leq 0$, which is a contradiction because $u \neq v$ and the edge weights are positive.

Hence, when the algorithm considers the edge $\{u, v\}$, we have $reported(v) = false$. At the end of the execution of Step 2 in which u is inserted into A, we have $d(v) \leq d(u) + wt(u, v)$. Then the assumption of the lemma implies that $d(v) \leq \delta(s, u) + wt(u, v)$ at the end of this execution. We have seen already that $\delta(s, u) + wt(u, v) = \delta(s, v)$. Therefore, we have $d(v) \leq \delta(s, v)$ at the end of this execution. Then Lemmas 2.5.3 and 2.5.4 imply that $d(v) = \delta(s, v)$ at any moment after the execution in which u is inserted into A. ∎

The next lemma states that for each vertex u that is contained in the list A that is returned in Step 4, the algorithm has computed the correct value of $\delta(s, u)$.

Lemma 2.5.7. *Let A be the list that is returned by algorithm* SINGLESOURCE(G, s, R). *We have $d(u) = \delta(s, u)$ for each vertex u in this list.*

PROOF   We claim that for each vertex u of the final list A, we have $d(u) = \delta(s, u)$ at the moment when u is inserted into this list. Since $d(u)$ does not change later, this will prove the lemma.

The proof of the claim is by induction. The vertex s is the first vertex that is inserted into A. For this vertex, the claim clearly holds.

Let u be any vertex of the final list A such that $u \neq s$. Consider the execution of Step 2 in which u is inserted into A. We denote the list A at the beginning of this execution by A'. The inductive hypothesis is that the claim holds for any vertex $x \in A'$. We will show that the claim then also holds for u.

Let P be a shortest path between s and u. (Since $\delta(s, u) \leq d(u) \leq R$, the path P exists.) Observe that $s \in A'$ and $u \notin A'$. Let y be the first[1] vertex on P that is not contained in A' and let x be the predecessor of y. Then $x \in A'$. By the induction hypothesis, we had $d(x) = \delta(s, x)$ at the moment when x was inserted into A. Hence, by Lemma 2.5.6, $d(y) = \delta(s, y)$ at any moment after the execution of Step 2 in which x is inserted into A.

We claim that $y = u$. If this is true, then $d(u) = \delta(s, u)$ at the moment when u is inserted into A, and the proof is complete.

Assume that $y \neq u$. Then $\delta(s, y) < \delta(s, u)$. Hence, at the moment when the algorithm inserts u into A, we have $d(y) < \delta(s, u)$. Vertex u is inserted into A because, at that moment, $d(u)$ is minimum in the priority queue. That is, when u is inserted into A, we have $d(u) \leq d(y)$. Hence, we have $d(u) < \delta(s, u)$ at that moment. This is a contradiction to Lemma 2.5.3 and, therefore, we have shown that $y = u$. ∎

The previous lemma implies that algorithm SINGLESOURCE(G, s, R) computes a subset of the set of all vertices u for which $\delta(s, u) \leq R$. It remains to show that the algorithm computes all such vertices u.

Lemma 2.5.8. *Let A be the list that is returned by algorithm* SINGLESOURCE(G, s, R). *The list A contains all vertices u of V for which $\delta(s, u) \leq R$.*

PROOF   By Lemma 2.5.5, the minimum value of $d(u)$ stored in the priority queue does not decrease over time. This implies that the list A stores the vertices u in nondecreasing order of the value $d(u)$. By Lemma 2.5.7, we have $d(u) = \delta(s, u)$ for each $u \in A$. Therefore, the algorithm can terminate as soon as the minimum value $d(u)$ in the priority queue is larger than R. ∎

---

[1] When following the path P from s to u.

2.5.3 The running time of algorithm SINGLESOURCE

Let n denote the number of vertices of G, and consider the list A that is returned by the algorithm. The running time is dominated by the total time needed to process the following priority queue operations:

1. DELETEMIN: This operation finds and deletes the vertex u in PQ for which $d(u)$ is minimum. It is performed at most $|A| + 1$ times.

2. INSERT(v): This operation inserts the vertex v into PQ, with priority $d(v)$. Since the algorithm inserts v only in case $d(v) \leq R$, this operation is performed $|A|$ times.

3. DECREASEKEY($v, d'(v)$): This operation replaces the priority $d(v)$ of vertex v by the smaller priority $d'(v)$. It is performed at most $|A| + \sum_{v \in A} \deg(v)$ times.

We denote the number of vertices stored in the priority queue by $|PQ|$. If we implement PQ using a Fibonacci heap, then one operation DELETEMIN takes $O(\log |PQ|)$ amortized time, one operation INSERT takes $O(1)$ amortized time, and one operation DECREASEKEY takes $O(1)$ amortized time. Since $|PQ| \leq |A|$ at any moment during the algorithm, we have proved the following result:

Theorem 2.5.9. *Let G be a weighted undirected graph with n vertices, whose edges have positive weights; let s be any vertex of G, and let $R > 0$ be any real number. Algorithm* SINGLESOURCE(G, s, R) *computes*

1. *the set A of all vertices v of G for which $\delta(s, v) \leq R$, and*

2. *for each vertex $v \in A$ the value of $\delta(s, v)$,*

in $O\big(|A| \log |A| + \sum_{v \in A} \deg(v)\big)$ time.

If we run algorithm SINGLESOURCE(G, s, R) with $R = \infty$, then we get for each vertex v the weight $\delta(s, v)$ of a shortest path between s and v. In this case, we have the classical Dijkstra algorithm, which solves the single-source shortest paths problem. Since $|A| \leq n$, and $\sum_{v \in A} \deg(v)$ is equal to twice the number of edges of G, we get the following result:

Corollary 2.5.10. *Let G be a weighted undirected graph with n vertices and m edges, and assume that these edges have positive weights. Let s be any vertex of G. Algorithm* SINGLESOURCE(G, s, ∞) *computes for each vertex v of G the value $\delta(s, v)$ in total time $O(n \log n + m)$.*

2.6 Minimum spanning trees

Let $G = (V, E)$ be a weighted undirected connected graph. Each edge e in E has a weight $wt(e)$, which is a positive real number. The weight of any subgraph $G' = (V, E')$ of G is defined as the sum of the weights of the edges of E'.

In this section, we consider the problem of computing a connected subgraph G' of G having minimum weight. It is not difficult to see that G' must be a tree. Therefore, G' is called a *minimum spanning tree* of G.

We will present two well-known algorithms for computing a minimum spanning tree. Both use a *greedy* strategy to build the tree, and their correctness proofs are based on the following lemma, whose proof is left as an exercise (see Exercise 2.18). We say that two sets A and B of vertices form a partition of the vertex set V if $A \cup B = V$, $A \cap B = \emptyset$, $A \neq \emptyset$, and $B \neq \emptyset$.

Lemma 2.6.1. *Let A and B be two sets of vertices that form a partition of V. Let a and b be vertices of A and B, respectively, such that $\{a, b\}$ is an edge of E and the weight $wt(a, b)$ is minimum. Then the graph G contains a minimum spanning tree in which $\{a, b\}$ is an edge.*

2.6.1 Kruskal's algorithm

Our first minimum spanning tree algorithm is known as Kruskal's algorithm. Let the graph $G = (V, E)$ have n vertices and m edges. Kruskal's algorithm maintains a *forest*, which is a collection of trees. It repeatedly adds an edge of minimum weight that does not create a cycle. To be more precise, the algorithm starts with a forest consisting of n trees, each consisting of a single vertex of V. Then the algorithm combines two trees in the forest, using an edge of minimum weight, and repeats this, until the forest consists of one single tree. This final tree is a minimum spanning tree of the graph G.

The algorithm, which we denote by KRUSKAL(G), is given below. During this algorithm, every tree in the forest has a unique vertex that is chosen as a "leader." When two trees of the forest are combined, one of the two leaders of the two trees is chosen as the leader of the combined tree.

Algorithm KRUSKAL(G)

Comment: This algorithm takes as input a connected weighted undirected graph $G = (V, E)$. It returns the edge set of a minimum spanning tree of G.

> sort the edges of E in nondecreasing order of their weights;
> let $\{u_k, v_k\}$, $1 \leq k \leq |E|$, be the sorted sequence of edges;
> **for each** $u \in V$
> **do** $V_u := \{u\}$;
> $E_u := \emptyset$
> **endfor**;
> **for** $k := 1$ **to** $|E|$
> **do** ($*$ test if the edge $\{u_k, v_k\}$ has to be included $*$)
> $x := $ index such that $u_k \in V_x$;
> $y := $ index such that $v_k \in V_y$;
>   **if** $x \neq y$
>   **then** ($*$ adding edge $\{u_k, v_k\}$ does not introduce a cycle $*$)
> $V_x := V_x \cup V_y$;
> $V_y := \emptyset$;
> $E_x := E_x \cup E_y \cup \{\{u_k, v_k\}\}$;
> $E_y := \emptyset$
>   **endif**
> **endfor**;
> $x := $ index such that $V_x \neq \emptyset$;
> return E_x

We claim that after all edges $\{u_k, v_k\}$ have been tested for inclusion, there is exactly one index x for which $V_x \neq \emptyset$. The corresponding set E_x is the edge set of a minimum spanning tree of the graph G. The correctness proof is based on the following claims, whose proofs are left as an exercise (see Exercise 2.19):

1. At any moment after the edge $\{u_k, v_k\}$ has been tested for inclusion, the vertices u_k and v_k are connected by a path in the graph (V, E'), where $E' := \bigcup_{x \in V} E_x$.
2. During the second for-loop, the following invariant is maintained:
    (a) The nonempty sets V_x form a partition of the vertex set V.

(b) There is a minimum spanning tree of G that contains the edge set $E' := \bigcup_{x \in V} E_x$.

(c) For any two indices x and y, such that $x \neq y$ and V_x and V_y are both nonempty, no vertex of V_x is connected by a path in the graph (V, E') to any vertex of V_y.

To implement Kruskal's algorithm, we have to maintain the nonempty vertex sets V_x under the following three operations:

1. MAKESET(u): Given a vertex u, this operation initializes a new set $V_u := \{u\}$. It has to be processed for each vertex u of V.

2. FIND(u): This operation finds the index x such that vertex u is an element of the set V_x. It has to be processed $2m$ times.

3. UNION(V_x, V_y): This operation assigns $V_x := V_x \cup V_y$ and $V_y := \emptyset$. It has to be processed $n - 1$ times.

The problem of designing a data structure that supports these three operations is called the *union-find* problem. In Exercise 2.20, you are asked to design a data structure in which each MAKESET and UNION operation takes $O(1)$ time and each FIND operation takes $O(\log n)$ time. Therefore, we obtain the following result:

Theorem 2.6.2. *Given a connected weighted undirected graph G with n vertices and m edges, algorithm KRUSKAL(G) computes a minimum spanning tree of G in $O(m \log n)$ time.*

2.6.2 Prim's algorithm

The second algorithm for computing a minimum spanning tree is known as Prim's algorithm. As before, we denote the number of vertices and edges of the graph $G = (V, E)$ by n and m, respectively. Prim's algorithm starts with a set A containing an arbitrary vertex of G, and an empty set E' of edges. Then, it repeatedly adds to the edge set E' an edge of minimum weight between a vertex of A and a vertex of $V \setminus A$. If $\{u, v\}$ is such an edge, with $u \in A$, then the vertex v "moves" to the set A. The algorithm terminates as soon as $A = V$. At that moment, the graph (V, E') is a minimum spanning tree of G.

Algorithm PRIM(G)

Comment: This algorithm takes as input a connected weighted undirected graph $G = (V, E)$. It returns the edge set of a minimum spanning tree of G.

$r :=$ arbitrary vertex of G;
$A := \{r\}$;
$E' := \emptyset$;
while $A \neq V$
do find a vertex $u \in A$ and a vertex $v \in V \setminus A$ such that
    $\{u, v\} \in E$ and $wt(u, v)$ is minimum;
    $A := A \cup \{v\}$;
    $E' := E' \cup \{\{u, v\}\}$
endwhile;
return E'

The correctness proof of this minimum spanning tree algorithm is left as an exercise (see Exercise 2.21). If we implement the algorithm using a Fibonacci heap, then we get the following result:

Theorem 2.6.3. *Given a connected weighted undirected graph G with n vertices and m edges, algorithm* PRIM(G) *computes a minimum spanning tree of G in $O(n \log n + m)$ time.*

Exercises

2.1. Prove that the subgraph P_u in Section 2.3.2 is a path.

2.2. In Section 2.3.2, we defined the notion of a *group parent*. Prove that if two distinct nodes u and v have the same group parent, then either u is an ancestor of v, or v is an ancestor of u.

2.3. Prove the correctness of algorithm LCA in Section 2.3.2.

2.4. Prove Observation 2.3.1.

2.5. Algorithm GROUPPARENTS(u, x) in Section 2.3.2 is based on a preorder traversal of the tree T. Design an algorithm that is based on a postorder traversal and that computes the group parents of all nodes of T.

2.6. Let T be a rooted binary tree with n nodes. Assume that each internal node of T stores pointers to its left and right children, but no node stores a pointer to its parent. Design an $O(n)$–time algorithm that stores with each node of T (except for the root) a pointer to its parent.

2.7. We have proved Theorem 2.3.2 for binary trees. Extend the proof to arbitrary rooted trees.

2.8. Let $T = (V, E_V)$ be a tree with n nodes, and let $G = (V, E)$ be an undirected graph that contains T, that is, $E_V \subseteq E$. Let u and v be any two distinct nodes of V, and let $P = (u = x_0, x_1, x_2, \ldots, x_\ell = v)$ be the unique path in T between u and v. A path $Q = (u = x_{i_0}, x_{i_1}, x_{i_2}, \ldots, x_{i_k} = v)$ in the graph G between u and v is called a *T-monotone path*, if $0 = i_0 < i_1 < i_2 < \cdots < i_k = \ell$. The *T-monotone diameter* of G is defined as the smallest integer k, such that for any two distinct nodes u and v of V, there is a T-monotone path in G between u and v that contains at most k edges.

Design an $O(n)$–time algorithm that computes, when given any tree T with n nodes as input, a graph having $O(n)$ edges and whose T-monotone diameter is $O(\log n)$. (*Hint:* Use the paths P_u that were defined in Section 2.3.2.)

2.9. Prove Theorems 2.3.6 and 2.3.8.

2.10. Let T be a rooted tree with n nodes. For any two distinct nodes u and v of T, let w be their lowest common ancestor, and let w_u and w_v be the children of w that contain u and v in their subtrees, respectively. Extend the results of Section 2.3.3 such that, when given u and v, not only their lowest common ancestor w, but also w_u and w_v are returned.

2.11. We have proved Theorems 2.3.7 and 2.3.8 for arrays that satisfy the (± 1)-property. Prove that these theorems hold for arbitrary arrays. (*Hint:* Reduce the range minimum problem for an arbitrary array to the lowest common ancestor problem.)

2.12. Design an algorithm that computes, in $O(n)$ time, a centroid node of any given tree with n nodes.

2.13. Can a tree have more than one centroid node? Can it have more than two centroid nodes?

2.14. Let n and D be integers such that $n \geq 2$ and $2 \leq D < n$. Let T be a tree with n nodes in which each node has degree at most D. Prove that T contains a *centroid edge*, that is, an edge e, such that removing e from T gives two trees, each of which contains at least $(n - 1)/D$, and at most $((D - 1)n + 1)/D$ nodes. Design an $O(n)$–time algorithm that computes such a centroid edge.

2.15. Let P be a simple polygon with n vertices. A *diagonal* is a line segment joining two nonadjacent vertices of P that is completely contained in P. Such a diagonal cuts P into two disjoint simple polygons P_1 and P_2. Prove that there is a diagonal such that both P_1 and P_2 have at least $1 + n/3$ and at most $1 + 2n/3$ vertices. (*Hint:* The dual of any triangulation of P is a tree.)

2.16. Let $n \geq 2$ and let T be a tree with n vertices. Prove that G contains a separator node v, that is, a node whose removal gives two graphs G_1 and G_2 – that are not necessarily trees – each having at most $2n/3$ vertices. Moreover, design an algorithm that computes such a vertex v and the corresponding graphs G_1 and G_2 in $O(n)$ time.

2.17. Consider algorithm SINGLESOURCE(G, s, R) of Section 2.5.1. Assume that, prior to running this algorithm, the variable $d(v)$ of each vertex v of G has some arbitrary value. Prove that the algorithm still correctly solves Problem 2.5.1.

2.18. Prove Lemma 2.6.1.

2.19. Use Lemma 2.6.1 to prove the correctness of Kruskal's minimum spanning tree algorithm.

2.20. Design a data structure for the union-find problem on a set of n elements (see Section 2.6.1), in which each MAKESET and UNION operation takes $O(1)$ time, and each FIND operation takes $O(\log n)$ time.

2.21. Use Lemma 2.6.1 to prove the correctness of Prim's minimum spanning tree algorithm.

2.22. Prove that the vertices of any planar graph can be colored using six colors, such that no two adjacent vertices have the same color. (*Hint:* First prove that in any planar graph, there is a vertex whose degree is less than or equal to five.)

Bibliographic notes

Good and thorough introductions to algorithms can be found in the books by Manber [1989] and Cormen et al. [2001]. Much deeper treatments of graph theory can be found in the books by Bollobás [1998], Diestel [2000], Even [1979], and Harary [1972].

The technique that we used in Section 2.3.2 to partition a tree T into pairwise disjoint paths is due to Cole and Vishkin [1988].

Harel and Tarjan were the first to show that lowest common ancestor queries in a tree with n nodes can be answered in $O(1)$ time (using indirect addressing) after an $O(n)$–time preprocessing; see Harel and Tarjan [1984]. They also proved an $\Omega(\log \log n)$ lower bound for pointer machine algorithms. The algorithm of Harel and Tarjan was simplified in Schieber and Vishkin [1988] (see also Chapter 8 of the book by Gusfield [1997]). The simple algorithm given in Section 2.3.3 is from Bender and Farach-Colton [2000]; this paper also contains a solution to Exercise 2.11.

Jordan [1869] was the first to show that every tree contains a centroid node; see Theorem 2.3.9. The proof given in Section 2.3.4 is from Bodlaender, Tel, and Santoro [1994]. The existence of a separator node in a tree is a special case of Lipton and Tarjan's separator theorem for planar graphs, see Lipton and Tarjan [1979, 1980].

Dijkstra's single-source shortest paths algorithm appeared in Dijkstra [1959]. Fibonacci heaps are due to Fredman and Tarjan [1987]. Kruskal's minimum spanning tree algorithm appeared in Kruskal [1956], whereas Prim's algorithm was discovered independently by Jarník [1930], Prim [1957], and Dijkstra [1959]. Good descriptions of the algorithms of Dijkstra, Kruskal, and Prim, as well as Fibonacci heaps and data structures for the union-find problem can be found in the book by Cormen et al. [2001]. The currently fastest known algorithm for computing a minimum spanning tree appears in Chazelle [2000b].

The *Euclidean minimum spanning tree MST(S)* of a set S of n points in $\mathbb{R}^d$ is a minimum spanning tree of the complete Euclidean graph whose vertex set is S. Prim's algorithm computes this tree in $O(n^2)$ time. By exploiting geometry, we can do better. Let us assume that the dimension d is equal to two. It is known that $MST(S)$ is a subgraph of the Delaunay triangulation $DT(S)$ of S. That is, the minimum spanning tree of $DT(S)$ is a Euclidean minimum spanning tree of the point set S. Since $DT(S)$ is a planar graph with n vertices, it has at most $3n - 6$ edges. Therefore, given $DT(S)$, we can use either Kruskal's or Prim's algorithm to compute $MST(S)$ in $O(n \log n)$ time. In fact, Cheriton and Tarjan [1976] have shown that $MST(S)$ can be computed in $O(n)$ time from $DT(S)$. Several algorithms are know for computing $DT(S)$ in $O(n \log n)$ time (see Shamos and Hoey [1975], Lee and Schachter [1980], or any of the books on computational geometry mentioned in the bibliographic notes at the end of Chapter 1).

In dimensions $d \geq 3$, the Euclidean minimum spanning tree problem becomes considerably harder. For example, if $d = 3$, a Euclidean minimum spanning tree can be computed in a time that is roughly proportional to $n^{4/3}$ (see Agarwal et al. [1991] and Callahan and Kosaraju [1993]). In Chapter 10, we will show how spanners can be used to compute an approximate Euclidean minimum spanning tree of any set of n points in $\mathbb{R}^d$ in $O(n \log n)$ time.

3

The Algebraic Computation-Tree Model

> My intelligence is bewildered by Your equivocal instructions. Therefore, please tell me decisively which will be most beneficial for me.
>
> —*The Bhagavad Gita*

In this chapter, we formalize the model of computation that will be used throughout most of this book. This model, called the *algebraic computation-tree model*, captures algorithms that perform exact arithmetic on arbitrary real numbers, and that use the following primitive operations: comparison of two real numbers, and the arithmetic operations of addition ($+$), subtraction ($-$), multiplication ($\times$), division ($/$), and the square root. Algorithms in this model take sequences of real numbers as input. The worst-case running time of such an algorithm depends only on the *number* of elements in the input sequence. Hence, it does *not* depend on the number of bits needed to specify the input.

We start in Section 3.1 with a formal definition of computation problems, and algebraic computation-trees as devices for solving such problems. In Section 3.2, we introduce a restricted type of algebraic computation-trees, called *algebraic decision trees*, that solve decision problems (i.e., their output is either YES or NO). In Section 3.3, we present a general technique for proving lower bounds on the time complexity for solving decision problems. Since a given computation problem often "contains" a related decision problem, this also gives a general approach for proving lower bounds on the time complexity for solving computation problems. In Section 3.4, we apply this approach and prove that the time complexity of computing a t-spanner of a set of n points in $\mathbb{R}^d$ is $\Omega(n \log n)$.

3.1 Algebraic computation-trees

Informally, an algorithm is a procedure that transforms an input consisting of n real numbers (i.e., a point in $\mathbb{R}^n$) to an output (e.g., a real number or a combinatorial structure) belonging to some *solution space* $\mathcal{S}$. In other words, an algorithm solves a *computation problem*, which is a function

$$\mathcal{P} : \mathbb{R}^n \to \mathcal{S}.$$

An example of a computation problem is the *sorting problem*, in which $\mathcal{S}$ is the set of all nondecreasing sequences of n real numbers.

Definition 3.1.1. Let n be a positive integer, and let $\mathcal{S}$ be a solution space. An *algebraic computation-tree* on a sequence $s_1, s_2, \ldots, s_n$ of n variables is a finite tree T in which each node has at most two children, and that satisfies the following three conditions:

1. Each leaf is labeled with the combinatorial description, in terms of the variables $s_1, s_2, \ldots, s_n$, of an element in $\mathcal{S}$.

41

2. Each node u having one child is labeled with a variable $Z(u)$ and an assignment of the form

    (a) $Z(u) := A_1 \& A_2$, where $\& \in \{+, -, *, /\}$, or

    (b) $Z(u) := \sqrt{A_1}$,

    where, for $i = 1, 2$, (i) $A_i = Z(u')$ for some proper ancestor u' of u in T, (ii) $A_i \in \{s_1, s_2, \ldots, s_n\}$, or (iii) A_i is a real number constant.

3. Each node u having two children is labeled with a comparison of the form $A \bowtie 0$, where (i) $A = Z(u')$ for some proper ancestor u' of u in T, or (ii) $A \in \{s_1, s_2, \ldots, s_n\}$. The two outgoing edges leading to the left and right children of u are labeled with $\leq$ and $>$, respectively.

An algebraic computation-tree T corresponds to an algorithm $\mathcal{A}_T$ that solves a computation problem $\mathcal{P} : \mathbb{R}^n \to \mathcal{S}$. Given an input sequence $s_1, s_2, \ldots, s_n$ of n real numbers, algorithm $\mathcal{A}_T$ traverses a path down the tree T starting at the root. If the current node u has one child, then $\mathcal{A}_T$ performs the corresponding arithmetic operation, assigns the result to the variable $Z(u)$, and proceeds to the child of u. If the current node u has two children, then the corresponding comparison is made and, depending on the outcome, $\mathcal{A}_T$ proceeds to the left or right child of u. When $\mathcal{A}_T$ reaches a leaf, say w, it takes the label stored at w, replaces all variables in this label by the values of the real numbers $s_1, s_2, \ldots, s_n$, returns the resulting label and terminates. The returned label is the solution to the problem $\mathcal{P}$ on input sequence $s_1, s_2, \ldots, s_n$, that is, the value of $\mathcal{P}(s_1, s_2, \ldots, s_n)$.

We require that no computation leads to a division by 0 or taking the square root of a negative number. Hence, for any sequence of n real numbers, algorithm $\mathcal{A}_T$ is well-defined. We also require that for each leaf w of T, there exists an input sequence of length n, on which algorithm $\mathcal{A}_T$ terminates in w.

Thus, a specific algebraic computation-tree can represent only an algorithm on all inputs of a specific length. In this sense, the algebraic computation-tree represents all possible behaviors of an algorithm over all input sequences consisting of n real numbers. We remark that an algebraic computation-tree is used only to *analyze* an algorithm; the tree is *not* explicitly constructed. As we will see, algebraic computation-trees are a convenient tool to prove lower bounds for computation problems.

An algorithm $\mathcal{A}$ that makes only comparisons and the arithmetic operations $+, -, *, /$, and $\sqrt{}$, is called an *algebraic computation-tree algorithm*, if there is an algebraic computation-tree T such that $\mathcal{A} = \mathcal{A}_T$. In Exercise 3.6, you will be asked to prove that *not* every such algorithm $\mathcal{A}$ is an algebraic computation-tree algorithm.

Definition 3.1.2. Let $\mathcal{P} : \mathbb{R}^n \to \mathcal{S}$ be a computation problem. We say that $\mathcal{P}$ is *solvable in the algebraic computation-tree model* if there exists an algebraic computation-tree T such that, for any $(s_1, s_2, \ldots, s_n) \in \mathbb{R}^n$, the corresponding algorithm $\mathcal{A}_T$ returns the value of $\mathcal{P}(s_1, s_2, \ldots, s_n)$. We say then that T *solves* the computation problem $\mathcal{P}$.

Intuitively, the worst-case running time of an algebraic computation-tree algorithm $\mathcal{A}_T$ is the maximum number of comparisons and arithmetic operations that are made on any input sequence of length n. Hence, each comparison and each of the elementary operations $+, -, *, /$, and $\sqrt{}$ takes unit time. The following definition expresses this in terms of the tree T.

Definition 3.1.3. Let T be an algebraic computation-tree. The *time complexity* of the corresponding algorithm $\mathcal{A}_T$ is defined as the height of the tree T.

Having defined the time complexity of an algorithm, we can define the time complexity of a computation problem:

Definition 3.1.4. Let $\mathcal{P} : \mathbb{R}^n \to \mathcal{S}$ be a computation problem that is solvable in the algebraic computation-tree model. The *time complexity* of $\mathcal{P}$ is defined as the minimum height of any algebraic computation-tree that solves $\mathcal{P}$.

3.2 Algebraic decision trees

A computation problem $\mathcal{P} : \mathbb{R}^n \to \mathcal{S}$ is called a *decision problem* if $\mathcal{S} = \{\text{YES,NO}\}$. An example is the *element uniqueness problem*, in which we are given a sequence $s_1, s_2, \ldots, s_n$ of n real numbers and have to decide if these elements are pairwise distinct. In this case, we have

$$\mathcal{P}(s_1, s_2, \ldots, s_n) = \begin{cases} \text{YES} & \text{if } s_i \neq s_j \text{ for all } i \neq j, \\ \text{NO} & \text{otherwise.} \end{cases}$$

Throughout this book, we will mainly consider computation problems. As we will see, however, lower bounds for decision problems are generally easier to prove than lower bounds for computation problems. Fortunately, it is often the case that a computation problem implicitly "contains" a related decision problem. For example, any algorithm that computes the minimum distance in a set of n points also solves the element uniqueness problem. As a result, any lower bound for the latter decision problem immediately implies a lower bound for the corresponding computation problem.

An algebraic computation-tree that solves a decision problem is called a *algebraic decision tree*. This restricted type of decision tree is formally defined by replacing Condition 1 in Definition 3.1.1 by the following condition:

- Each leaf is labeled with either YES or NO.

Let $\mathcal{P} : \mathbb{R}^n \to \{\text{YES,NO}\}$ be a decision problem. A point $(s_1, s_2, \ldots, s_n)$ in $\mathbb{R}^n$ is called a *YES-instance* for $\mathcal{P}$, if the value of $\mathcal{P}(s_1, s_2, \ldots, s_n)$ is YES. We associate with $\mathcal{P}$ the subset $V_{\mathcal{P}}$ of $\mathbb{R}^n$ consisting of all YES-instances. Conversely, for any subset V of $\mathbb{R}^n$, there is a decision problem $\mathcal{P}$ for which $V_{\mathcal{P}} = V$. Hence, we can identify decision problems with subsets of $\mathbb{R}^n$. As an example, if $\mathcal{P}$ is the element uniqueness problem, then we have

$$V_{\mathcal{P}} = \left\{ (s_1, s_2, \ldots, s_n) \in \mathbb{R}^n : \prod_{1 \leq i < j \leq n} (s_i - s_j) \neq 0 \right\}.$$

A decision problem $\mathcal{P} : \mathbb{R}^n \to \{\text{YES,NO}\}$ is called *decidable in the algebraic decision tree model*, if there exists an algebraic decision tree T such that, for any $(s_1, s_2, \ldots, s_n) \in \mathbb{R}^n$, the corresponding algorithm $\mathcal{A}_T$ returns YES if $(s_1, s_2, \ldots, s_n) \in V_{\mathcal{P}}$, and NO if $(s_1, s_2, \ldots, s_n) \notin V_{\mathcal{P}}$. We say then that T *decides* the decision problem $\mathcal{P}$.

Definition 3.2.1. Let V be a subset of $\mathbb{R}^n$, and let $\mathcal{P}$ be the corresponding decision problem. If $\mathcal{P}$ is decidable in the algebraic decision tree model, then we define the *time complexity* of V as the minimum height of any algebraic decision tree that decides $\mathcal{P}$.

3.3 Lower bounds for algebraic decision tree algorithms

In this section, we will show that the topological structure of a set $V \subseteq \mathbb{R}^n$ yields a lower bound on the time complexity of V.

Basic Idea: A lower bound on the time complexity of a decision problem $\mathcal{P}$ can be obtained by inspecting the topological structure of $V_{\mathcal{P}}$. If the number of connected components of $V_{\mathcal{P}}$ is $CC(V_{\mathcal{P}})$, then the following is true: In the linear decision tree model, its time complexity is lower bounded by $\log(CC(V_{\mathcal{P}}))$; in the algebraic decision tree model, its time complexity is lower bounded by $\frac{\log(CC(V_{\mathcal{P}})) - n \log 3}{1 + 2 \log 3}$.

3.3.1 Linear decision trees

In order to introduce the basic approach, we first consider a restricted class of algorithms. We consider algorithms that can perform only the following unit-time operations: First, quantities that can be added or substracted are either constants, input elements, or values that have been previously computed. Second, any input element and any previously computed value can be multiplied by a constant. Finally, any input element and any previously computed value can be compared with zero with an outcome of either "$\leq$" or "$>$."

This restricted class of algorithms is formally defined by replacing Condition 2 in Definition 3.1.1 by the following condition:

- Each node u having one child is labeled with a variable $Z(u)$ and an assignment $Z(u) := A_1 \& A_2$, having one of the following two forms:

  1. $\& \in \{+, -\}$ and, for $i = 1, 2$, (i) $A_i = Z(u')$ for some proper ancestor u' of u in T, (ii) $A_i \in \{s_1, s_2, \ldots, s_n\}$, or (iii) A_i is a real constant.
  2. $\& \in \{*, /\}$ and
     (a) $A_1 = Z(u')$ for some proper ancestor u' of u in T, or $A_1 \in \{s_1, s_2, \ldots, s_n\}$, or A_1 is a real constant, whereas
     (b) A_2 is a real constant.

Observe that two input elements (or previously computed values) cannot be multiplied or divided, thus avoiding nonlinear functions of the input elements. Hence, each variable that occurs during the execution of the corresponding algorithm is a linear function of the input variables, such as $4 + 3s_1 + s_2/7 - 8s_3 + 2s_4 - s_5$. Therefore, we call these algorithms *linear decision tree algorithms*.

Consider a decision problem $\mathcal{P}$ that is decidable in this linear model, and let $V := V_{\mathcal{P}} \subseteq \mathbb{R}^n$ be the corresponding set of YES-instances. Let T be an arbitrary linear decision tree that decides $\mathcal{P}$. Hence, the algorithm $\mathcal{A}_T$ corresponding to T returns YES if and only if it gets an element of V as input.

For any leaf w of T, we denote by $R(w)$ the set of those inputs on which algorithm $\mathcal{A}_T$ terminates in leaf w. To give a formal definition of this set, consider the path $u_1, u_2, \ldots, u_\ell$ from the root u_1 to $u_\ell = w$. Let $v_1, v_2, \ldots, v_k$ be all nodes on this path that have two children. For each i with $1 \leq i \leq k$, algorithm $\mathcal{A}_T$ makes a comparison in node v_i, which can be written as

$$F_i(s_1, s_2, \ldots, s_n) \bowtie 0,$$

where F_i is a linear function of the n input variables $s_1, s_2, \ldots, s_n$. Then $R(w)$ is the set consisting of all points $(s_1, s_2, \ldots, s_n) \in \mathbb{R}^n$, such that for all i with $1 \leq i \leq k$,

1. $F_i(s_1, s_2, \ldots, s_n) \leq 0$ if the path in T to w proceeds from v_i to its left child, and
2. $F_i(s_1, s_2, \ldots, s_n) > 0$ if the path in T to w proceeds from v_i to its right child.

The following lemma states the main property of the sets $R(w)$ that we will use to prove a lower bound on the time complexity of the decision problem $\mathcal{P}$.

Lemma 3.3.1. *The set $R(w)$ is connected, i.e., for any two points p and q in $R(w)$, there is a continuous curve in $\mathbb{R}^n$ between p and q that is completely contained in $R(w)$.*

PROOF   The inequality at node v_i, given by $F_i(s_1, s_2, \ldots, s_n) \bowtie 0$, defines a closed or open halfspace in $\mathbb{R}^n$. The set $R(w)$ is the intersection of the halfspaces defined by the inequalities at nodes $v_1, \ldots, v_k$. Hence, since each halfspace is convex, $R(w)$ is also convex and, therefore, connected. ∎

The set V consists of one or more *connected components*. Let A and B be two distinct connected components of V, and let $p = (s_1, s_2, \ldots, s_n)$ and $q = (t_1, t_2, \ldots, t_n)$ be points in A and B, respectively. Let w_p be the leaf of T in which algorithm $\mathcal{A}_T$ terminates on input p. Define w_q similarly with respect to input q.

Lemma 3.3.2. *The leaves w_p and w_q are distinct.*

PROOF   Assume that $w_p = w_q$, and denote this leaf by w. Observe that p and q are both contained in the set $R(w)$. We saw in the proof of Lemma 3.3.1 that $R(w)$ is convex. Therefore, the line segment pq is completely contained in $R(w)$. Hence, for each point $x = (x_1, x_2, \ldots, x_n)$ that is on pq, algorithm $\mathcal{A}_T$, when given x as input, terminates in w. Since $p \in V$, leaf w is labeled with YES. This proves that each point x on pq belongs to the set V. As a result, points p and q are connected by a continuous curve (viz. the line segment pq) that is completely inside V. This is a contradiction because these points are in different connected components of V. ∎

Lemma 3.3.2 immediately implies the following lower bound. For any subset V of $\mathbb{R}^n$, we denote the number of its connected components by $CC(V)$.

Theorem 3.3.3. *Let $\mathcal{P}$ be a decision problem that is decidable in the linear decision tree model and let $V_{\mathcal{P}} \subseteq \mathbb{R}^n$ be the corresponding set of YES-instances. The time complexity of $V_{\mathcal{P}}$ in the linear decision tree model is greater than or equal to $\log(CC(V_{\mathcal{P}}))$.*

PROOF   Let T be an arbitrary linear decision tree that decides $V_{\mathcal{P}}$. By Lemma 3.3.2, T has at least $CC(V_{\mathcal{P}})$ leaves. Hence, the height of this tree is greater than or equal to $\log(CC(V_{\mathcal{P}}))$. ∎

Let us apply this result to the element uniqueness problem, in which case we have

$$V_{\mathcal{P}} = \left\{ (s_1, s_2, \ldots, s_n) \in \mathbb{R}^n : \prod_{1 \leq i < j \leq n} (s_i - s_j) \neq 0 \right\}.$$

In order to get a lower bound on this problem for linear decision tree algorithms, we need to estimate the number of connected components of $V_{\mathcal{P}}$.

Let π and ρ be two distinct permutations of $1, 2, \ldots, n$, and consider the points $p := (\pi(1), \pi(2), \ldots, \pi(n))$ and $r := (\rho(1), \rho(2), \ldots, \rho(n))$ in $\mathbb{R}^n$. Clearly, both p and r belong to the set $V_{\mathcal{P}}$. We will show that these two points belong to different connected components of $V_{\mathcal{P}}$. This will prove that $CC(V_{\mathcal{P}}) \geq n!$.

Because π and ρ are distinct, there are indices i and j with $1 \leq i \leq n$ and $1 \leq j \leq n$, such that $\pi(i) < \pi(j)$ and $\rho(i) > \rho(j)$. Hence, the points p and r are on different sides of the hyperplane $x_i = x_j$. Any continuous curve in $\mathbb{R}^n$ between p and r must pass through this hyperplane. That is, any such curve contains a point $q := (q_1, q_2, \ldots, q_n)$ for which $q_i = q_j$. As a result, this curve is not completely contained in the set $V_{\mathcal{P}}$. Therefore, p and r belong to different connected components of $V_{\mathcal{P}}$.

Theorem 3.3.3 immediately implies the following lower bound.

Theorem 3.3.4. *The time complexity of the element uniqueness problem for n real numbers in the linear decision tree model is greater than or equal to $\lceil \log n! \rceil = n \log n - O(n)$.*

This theorem states that using comparisons, the arithmetic operations of addition and subtraction, and multiplication and division by constants, it is not possible to solve the element uniqueness problem in $o(n \log n)$ time. It does not rule out, however, $o(n \log n)$–time algorithms that can multiply and divide input elements and take square roots. In the next section, we will show that these operations do not significantly reduce the time complexity of the element uniqueness problem.

3.3.2 The general lower bound

The proof of Theorem 3.3.3 heavily depends on the fact that the set $R(w)$ associated with a leaf w is connected. For an algebraic decision tree, this set is, in general, not connected. For example, for $n = 2$, let $R(w)$ be defined by the two inequalities $s_1^2 + s_2^2 - 1 \leq 0$ and $-8s_1^2 + s_2 + 2 \leq 0$. That is, $R(w)$ is the set of those points that are inside the unit circle and below the parabola $s_2 = 8s_1^2 - 2$. This set clearly consists of two connected components.

In this section, we will prove that the arguments of Section 3.3.1 can, nevertheless, be generalized. As we will see, the number of connected components of the set $V_{\mathcal{P}}$ of YES-instances still gives a lower bound on the time complexity of the (decidable) decision problem $\mathcal{P}$. The proof will be based on the following result from algebraic topology.

Theorem 3.3.5. *Let k and g be positive integers, and let $F_1, F_2, \ldots, F_k$ be polynomials in n variables, each having degree less than or equal to g. Let*

$$W := \{(x_1, x_2, \ldots, x_n) \in \mathbb{R}^n : F_i(x_1, x_2, \ldots, x_n) = 0 \text{ for all } 1 \leq i \leq k\}.$$

The set W has at most $g(2g - 1)^{n-1}$ connected components.

For a proof of this theorem, which is highly nontrivial, the reader is referred to the references given in the bibliographic notes at the end of this chapter. Observe that the upper bound on the number of connected components of the set W depends only on the number of variables and the degrees of the polynomials; it does not depend on the number of polynomials.

Consider an arbitrary algebraic decision tree T, and let w be any leaf of T. Later in this section, we will show that the set $R(w) \subseteq \mathbb{R}^n$ of all inputs on which algorithm $\mathcal{A}_T$ terminates in w can be described by a system of polynomial equations and inequalities, each having degree less than or equal to 2. Our goal is to derive an upper bound on the number of connected components of $R(w)$. This will be done by transforming the system of equations and inequalities that describe $R(w)$ into a system containing polynomial equations only and then applying Theorem 3.3.5. The details of this transformation are given in the following theorem.

Theorem 3.3.6. *Let a, b and c be nonnegative integers, and let $E_1, \ldots, E_a, N_1, \ldots, N_b,$ $P_1, \ldots, P_c$ be polynomials in n variables, each having degree less than or equal to 2. Let W be the set of all points $(x_1, \ldots, x_n)$ in $\mathbb{R}^n$ such that the following is true:*

1. $E_i(x_1, \ldots, x_n) = 0$ *for all i with $1 \leq i \leq a$,*

2. $N_i(x_1, \ldots, x_n) \leq 0$ *for all i with $1 \leq i \leq b$, and*

3. $P_i(x_1, \ldots, x_n) > 0$ *for all i with $1 \leq i \leq c$.*

The set W has at most 3^{n+b+c} connected components.

PROOF   It can be shown that the number $CC(W)$ of connected components of W is finite. Let $d := CC(W)$. For each j with $1 \leq j \leq d$, let $p_j \in \mathbb{R}^n$ be an arbitrary point in the j-th connected component of W. Define

$$\epsilon := \min\{P_i(p_j) : 1 \leq i \leq c, 1 \leq j \leq d\}.$$

Clearly, $\epsilon > 0$. Let W_ϵ be the set of all points $(x_1, \ldots, x_n) \in \mathbb{R}^n$, such that

- $E_i(x_1, \ldots, x_n) = 0$ for all i with $1 \leq i \leq a$,
- $N_i(x_1, \ldots, x_n) \leq 0$ for all i with $1 \leq i \leq b$, and
- $P_i(x_1, \ldots, x_n) \geq \epsilon$ for all i with $1 \leq i \leq c$.

Then, $W_\epsilon \subseteq W$ and W_ϵ contains the points $p_1, p_2, \ldots, p_d$.

We transform the equations and inequalities that define W_ϵ into a system of polynomial equations by introducing $b + c$ new variables $x_{n+1}, \ldots, x_{n+b+c}$. Let W' be the set of all points $(x_1, \ldots, x_{n+b+c}) \in \mathbb{R}^{n+b+c}$ such that

- $E_i(x_1, \ldots, x_n) = 0$ for all i with $1 \leq i \leq a$,
- $N_i(x_1, \ldots, x_n) + x_{n+i}^2 = 0$ for all i with $1 \leq i \leq b$, and
- $P_i(x_1, \ldots, x_n) - x_{n+b+i}^2 - \epsilon = 0$ for all i with $1 \leq i \leq c$.

The projection of W' onto the first n coordinates is exactly the set W_ϵ, that is,

$$W_\epsilon = \{(x_1, \ldots, x_n) : \exists x_{n+1}, \ldots, x_{n+b+c} \in \mathbb{R}, (x_1, \ldots, x_{n+b+c}) \in W'\}.$$

For each j with $1 \leq j \leq d$, let p'_j be a point in W' such that its projection onto the first n coordinates is the point p_j. Since the points $p_1, p_2, \ldots, p_d$ are in pairwise distinct connected components of W and since $W_\epsilon \subseteq W$, it follows that the points $p'_1, p'_2, \ldots, p'_d$ are in pairwise distinct connected components of W'. Hence, $CC(W') \geq d$.

The set W' is defined by polynomial equations in $n + b + c$ variables, each having degree less than or equal to 2. Therefore, by Theorem 3.3.5, we have

$$CC(W') \leq 2 \cdot 3^{n+b+c-1} \leq 3^{n+b+c}.$$

This completes the proof.   ■

Now we are ready to prove the lower bound for algebraic decision tree algorithms.

Theorem 3.3.7. *Let $\mathcal{P}$ be a decision problem that is decidable in the algebraic decision tree model, and let $V_{\mathcal{P}} \subseteq \mathbb{R}^n$ be the corresponding set of YES-instances. The time complexity of $V_{\mathcal{P}}$ in the algebraic decision tree model is greater than or equal to*

$$\frac{\log(CC(V_{\mathcal{P}})) - n \log 3}{1 + 2 \log 3}.$$

PROOF Let T be an arbitrary algebraic decision tree that decides $V_{\mathcal{P}}$, and let w be any leaf of T. Let $R(w)$ be the set of all points $(s_1, s_2, \ldots, s_n) \in \mathbb{R}^n$, such that the computation in T on input $s_1, s_2, \ldots, s_n$ terminates in w. We will derive an upper bound on the number of connected components of $R(w)$.

Consider the path $u_1, u_2, \ldots, u_{k+1}$ in T from the root u_1 to $u_{k+1} = w$. Let r be the number of nodes on this path that have exactly one child, and let s be the number of such nodes that are labeled with a $\sqrt{}$-assignment. We will define a system of $k + s$ polynomial equations and inequalities in the variables $x_1, \ldots, x_{n+k}$. The variables $x_1, \ldots, x_n$ represent the input variables $s_1, \ldots, s_n$, whereas the variables $x_{n+1}, \ldots, x_{n+k}$ represent the program variables of the nodes $u_1, \ldots, u_k$.

Let i be any integer with $1 \leq i \leq k$, and consider node u_i. There are two possible cases.

Case 1: u_i has one child, that is, u_i is a computation node.

Node u_i is labeled with an assignment of the form $Z(u_i) := A_1 \& A_2$ or $Z(u_i) := \sqrt{A_1}$, where $\& \in \{+, -, *, /\}$, and, for $m = 1, 2$, (i) $A_m = Z(u_j)$ for some index j with $1 \leq j < i$, (ii) $A_m \in \{s_1, s_2, \ldots, s_n\}$, or (iii) $A_m = c$ for some real constant c. (See Definition 3.1.1.)

We add one equation to our system for this computation node u_i. Furthermore, depending on the form of the assignment, we may add one $\leq$-inequality to our system. In Table 3.1, all possibilities are listed. For example, if the assignment is $Z(u_i) := s_a/Z(u_\ell)$, then we add the equation $x_{n+i} x_{n+\ell} - x_a = 0$. Here, x_{n+i} represents the program variable $Z(u_i)$, $x_{n+\ell}$ represents $Z(u_\ell)$, and x_a represents the input variable s_a. If the assignment is $Z(u_i) := \sqrt{s_a}$, then we add the equation $x_{n+i}^2 - x_a = 0$ and the inequality $-x_{n+i} \leq 0$. (Observe that $x_{n+i} = \sqrt{x_a}$ if and only if $x_{n+i}^2 = x_a$ and $x_{n+i} \geq 0$.)

Case 2: u_i has two children, that is, u_i is a comparison node.

Node u_i is labeled with a comparison of the form $A \bowtie 0$, where (i) $A = Z(u_j)$ for some index j with $1 \leq j < i$, or (ii) $A \in \{s_1, s_2, \ldots, s_n\}$.

In case the path in T to w proceeds from u_i to its left child, we do the following: If the comparison in u_i has the form $Z(u_j) \bowtie 0$, then we add the inequality $x_{n+j} \leq 0$ to our system. Otherwise, the comparison in u_i has the form $s_a \bowtie 0$, in which case we add the inequality $x_a \leq 0$.

In case the path to w proceeds from u_i to its right child, we do the following: If the comparison in u_i has the form $Z(u_j) \bowtie 0$, then we add the inequality $x_{n+j} > 0$. Otherwise, the comparison in u_i has the form $s_a \bowtie 0$, in which case we add the inequality $x_a > 0$.

Recall that r denotes the number of computation nodes on the path to w, and s denotes the number of computation nodes on this path that are labeled with a $\sqrt{}$-assignment. Let t be the number of times this path proceeds from a comparison node to its left child. Then we have obtained a system of r polynomial equations, $s + t$ polynomial $\leq$-inequalities, and $k - r - t$ polynomial $>$-inequalities, in the variables $x_1, \ldots, x_{n+k}$. Each of these polynomials has degree less than or equal to 2. Let $W \subseteq \mathbb{R}^{n+k}$ be the set of all points that satisfy these equations and inequalities. Then, by Theorem 3.3.6, W has at most $3^{n+2k+s-r}$ connected components.

Table 3.1: *The equations and inequalities corresponding to all possible assignments of computation node u_i. The indices j and ℓ satisfy $1 \leq j < i$ and $1 \leq \ell < i$; the indices a and b satisfy $1 \leq a \leq n$ and $1 \leq b \leq n$; and c and d are real constants.*

Assignment	Equation/inequality
$Z(u_i) := Z(u_j) + Z(u_\ell)$	$x_{n+i} - x_{n+j} - x_{n+\ell} = 0$
$Z(u_i) := Z(u_j) - Z(u_\ell)$	$x_{n+i} - x_{n+j} + x_{n+\ell} = 0$
$Z(u_i) := Z(u_j) * Z(u_\ell)$	$x_{n+i} - x_{n+j}x_{n+\ell} = 0$
$Z(u_i) := Z(u_j)/Z(u_\ell)$	$x_{n+i}x_{n+\ell} - x_{n+j} = 0$
$Z(u_i) := \sqrt{Z(u_j)}$	$x_{n+i}^2 - x_{n+j} = 0$ and $-x_{n+i} \leq 0$
$Z(u_i) := s_a + Z(u_\ell)$	$x_{n+i} - x_a - x_{n+\ell} = 0$
$Z(u_i) := s_a - Z(u_\ell)$	$x_{n+i} - x_a + x_{n+\ell} = 0$
$Z(u_i) := Z(u_\ell) - s_a$	$x_{n+i} - x_{n+\ell} + x_a = 0$
$Z(u_i) := s_a * Z(u_\ell)$	$x_{n+i} - x_a x_{n+\ell} = 0$
$Z(u_i) := s_a/Z(u_\ell)$	$x_{n+i}x_{n+\ell} - x_a = 0$
$Z(u_i) := Z(u_\ell)/s_a$	$x_{n+i}x_a - x_{n+\ell} = 0$
$Z(u_i) := s_a + s_b$	$x_{n+i} - x_a - x_b = 0$
$Z(u_i) := s_a - s_b$	$x_{n+i} - x_a + x_b = 0$
$Z(u_i) := s_a * s_b$	$x_{n+i} - x_a x_b = 0$
$Z(u_i) := s_a/s_b$	$x_{n+i}x_b - x_a = 0$
$Z(u_i) := \sqrt{s_a}$	$x_{n+i}^2 - x_a = 0$ and $-x_{n+i} \leq 0$
$Z(u_i) := c + Z(u_\ell)$	$x_{n+i} - c - x_{n+\ell} = 0$
$Z(u_i) := c - Z(u_\ell)$	$x_{n+i} - c + x_{n+\ell} = 0$
$Z(u_i) := Z(u_\ell) - c$	$x_{n+i} - x_{n+\ell} + c = 0$
$Z(u_i) := c * Z(u_\ell)$	$x_{n+i} - cx_{n+\ell} = 0$
$Z(u_i) := c/Z(u_\ell)$	$x_{n+i}x_{n+\ell} - c = 0$
$Z(u_i) := Z(u_\ell)/c$	$cx_{n+i} - x_{n+\ell} = 0$
$Z(u_i) := c + s_b$	$x_{n+i} - c - x_b = 0$
$Z(u_i) := c - s_b$	$x_{n+i} - c + x_b = 0$
$Z(u_i) := s_b - c$	$x_{n+i} - x_b + c = 0$
$Z(u_i) := c * s_b$	$x_{n+i} - cx_b = 0$
$Z(u_i) := c/s_b$	$x_{n+i}x_b - c = 0$
$Z(u_i) := s_b/c$	$cx_{n+i} - x_b = 0$
$Z(u_i) := c + d$	$x_{n+i} - c + d = 0$
$Z(u_i) := c - d$	$x_{n+i} - c + d = 0$
$Z(u_i) := c * d$	$x_{n+i} - cd = 0$
$Z(u_i) := c/d$	$dx_{n+i} - c = 0$
$Z(u_i) := \sqrt{c}$	$x_{n+i}^2 - c = 0$ and $-x_{n+i} \leq 0$

The projection of W onto the first n coordinates is equal to the set $R(w)$. This implies that $CC(R(w)) \leq CC(W)$ and, hence, $CC(R(w)) \leq 3^{n+2k+s-r}$. Let h be the height of our algebraic decision tree T. Then, since $k \leq h$ and $s \leq r$, we have proved that $CC(R(w)) \leq 3^{n+2h}$.

Now we can complete the proof of the theorem. Recall that $V_{\mathcal{P}} \subseteq \mathbb{R}^n$ is the set of YES-instances for the decision problem $\mathcal{P}$. A leaf w of T is called a *YES-leaf*, if its label is YES. Since

$$V_{\mathcal{P}} = \bigcup_{w:\text{YES-leaf of } T} R(w),$$

we have

$$CC(V_{\mathcal{P}}) \leq \sum_{w:\text{YES-leaf of } T} CC(R(w)).$$

Hence, the number of connected components of $V_{\mathcal{P}}$ is less than or equal to 3^{n+2h} times the number of YES-leaves of T. Since T has height h, it has at most 2^h leaves. Therefore,

$$CC(V_{\mathcal{P}}) \leq 3^{n+2h} \cdot 2^h.$$

Taking logarithms and rewriting this inequality, we obtain

$$h \geq \frac{\log(CC(V_{\mathcal{P})}) - n \log 3}{1 + 2 \log 3},$$

which is exactly what we wanted to show. ∎

Remark 3.3.8. Let $\mathcal{P}$ be a decision problem that is decidable in the algebraic decision tree model, and let $V \subseteq \mathbb{R}^n$ be the corresponding set of YES-instances. It follows from the proof of Theorem 3.3.7 that the number of connected components of V is finite.

3.3.3 Some applications

Let us again consider the element uniqueness problem. As we have seen already in Section 3.3.1, the corresponding subset V of $\mathbb{R}^n$ has at least $n!$ connected components. Hence, Theorem 3.3.7 gives a lower bound of

$$\frac{\log n! - n \log 3}{1 + 2 \log 3} = \Omega(n \log n)$$

on the time complexity of this problem.

Theorem 3.3.9. *The time complexity of the element uniqueness problem for n real numbers in the algebraic decision tree model is $\Omega(n \log n)$.*

Using simple reductions, this theorem implies other interesting lower bounds.

Corollary 3.3.10. *The following two problems have time complexity $\Omega(n \log n)$ in the algebraic computation-tree model:*

1. *the sorting problem for n real numbers, and*

2. *the closest pair problem, that is, given a set S of n points in $\mathbb{R}^d$, compute two distinct points of S, whose distance is minimum.*

PROOF Let $\mathcal{A}$ be an arbitrary algebraic computation-tree algorithm that solves the sorting problem, and let $T(n)$ be its time complexity. The following algebraic decision tree algorithm $\mathcal{B}$ solves the element uniqueness problem: On an input consisting of n real numbers $s_1, s_2, \ldots, s_n$, $\mathcal{B}$ first uses algorithm $\mathcal{A}$ to sort them. Then, $\mathcal{B}$ compares all pairs of elements that are neighbors in the sorted sequence. Algorithm $\mathcal{B}$ returns YES if no two equal elements are encountered; otherwise, it returns NO.

Algorithm $\mathcal{B}$ has time complexity $T(n) + O(n)$, which, by Theorem 3.3.9, must be $\Omega(n \log n)$. It follows that $T(n) = \Omega(n \log n)$.

The lower bound for the closest pair problem follows immediately from Theorem 3.3.9 because the input sequence contains two equal elements if and only if the distance of the closest pair is zero. ∎

We now give an example of a problem that is not decidable in the algebraic decision tree model. Consider a decision problem $\mathcal{P}$, and let $V \subseteq \mathbb{R}^n$ be the corresponding set of YES-instances. If V has an infinite number of connected components, then it follows from Remark 3.3.8 that $\mathcal{P}$ is not decidable in the algebraic decision tree model. Hence, by taking $V := \mathbb{N} = \{0, 1, 2, \ldots\}$, we obtain the following result:

Theorem 3.3.11. *There is no algebraic decision tree algorithm that, when given an arbitrary real number x as input, returns YES if $x \in \mathbb{N}$, and NO if $x \notin \mathbb{N}$.*

3.4 A lower bound for constructing spanners

In this section, we will use Theorem 3.3.7 to prove an $\Omega(n \log n)$ lower bound for constructing t-spanners. We try to make this lower bound as strong as possible, that is, it should hold for a very general class of spanner graphs. To be more precise, the lower bound that we will prove holds for any value of $t > 1$, that is, t may even depend on the number n of input points. Also, it holds for spanners that include additional vertices that were not part of the input. We formally define these spanners as follows.

Let S be a multiset of n points in $\mathbb{R}^d$. We consider graphs $G = (V, E)$, such that V is a finite multiset of points in $\mathbb{R}^d$ that contains all points of S. Let $t > 1$ be a real number. Consider a graph $G = (V, E)$ that satisfies these two conditions. Assume that for any two points p and q of S, there is a path in G between p and q whose length is less than or equal to $t|pq|$. Hence, if $V = S$, then G is a t-spanner for S. If the size of V is larger than that of S, then we call G a *Steiner t-spanner* for S. In this case, the points of V that are not in S are called the *Steiner points* of G.

To be as general as possible, the graph G may have multiple vertices that represent the same point: There may be points u and v in S that are distinct as elements of S, but that represent the same point in $\mathbb{R}^d$. Similarly, there may be a point u of S and a Steiner point v that represent the same point in $\mathbb{R}^d$. Finally, there may be Steiner points u and v that are distinct as vertices of G, but that represent the same point. Hence, graph G may have edges of length zero.

Throughout this section, we consider algebraic computation-tree algorithms that construct Steiner t-spanners with $o(n \log n)$ edges. (Clearly, any algorithm that constructs Steiner t-spanners with $\Omega(n \log n)$ edges takes $\Omega(n \log n)$ time.) Moreover, we will focus on algorithms that construct Steiner t-spanners for one-dimensional multisets, that is, multisets of real numbers. We will prove that even this one-dimensional case has an $\Omega(n \log n)$ lower bound. Of course, this implies the same lower bound for any dimension $d \geq 1$.

3.4.1 A reduction from the element uniqueness problem

Let $s_1, s_2, \ldots, s_n, t$ be a sequence of $n + 1$ real numbers, such that $t > 1$. The main observation is encapsulated in the following key idea.

> **Key Idea:** If $s_i = s_j$ for some i and j with $i \neq j$, then any Steiner t-spanner for $s_1, s_2, \ldots, s_n$ contains a path between s_i and s_j, whose length is less than or equal to $t|s_i - s_j| = 0$. In particular, each edge on this path has length zero.

We have to be careful in formalizing this, however, because the spanner may contain Steiner points.

Let $\mathcal{A}$ be an arbitrary algebraic computation-tree algorithm that, when given a sequence of n real numbers $s_1, s_2, \ldots, s_n$ and a real number $t > 1$, constructs a Steiner t-spanner for the multiset $S = \{s_1, s_2, \ldots, s_n\}$ of n points on the one-dimensional real line. We may assume that each vertex of the spanner graph constructed by $\mathcal{A}$ is labeled as either being an element of S or being a Steiner point.

We will show how algorithm $\mathcal{A}$ can be used to solve the element uniqueness problem. Consider the following algorithm that takes as input a sequence $S = (s_1, s_2, \ldots, s_n)$ of n real numbers:

Step 1: Choose an arbitrary real number $t > 1$, and run algorithm $\mathcal{A}$ on the input sequence $s_1, s_2, \ldots, s_n, t$. Let G be the resulting Steiner t-spanner.

Step 2: Construct the subgraph G' of G such that G' contains the same vertices as G, and G' contains all edges of G having length zero.

Step 3: Compute the connected components of the graph G'.

Step 4: For each connected component of G', check whether it contains two or more distinct elements (i.e., elements having distinct indices) of S among its vertices. If this is the case for some connected component, return NO. Otherwise, return YES.

It is not difficult to see that this algorithm correctly solves the element uniqueness problem. Hence, given the Steiner t-spanner G, we can solve the element uniqueness problem in a time that is proportional to the number of edges of G, which we assumed to be $o(n \log n)$. Therefore, it follows from Theorem 3.3.9 that the worst-case running time of algorithm $\mathcal{A}$ is $\Omega(n \log n)$.

Theorem 3.4.1. *Let $d \geq 1$ be an integer constant. In the algebraic computation-tree model, any algorithm that, when given a multiset S of n points in $\mathbb{R}^d$, and a real number $t > 1$, constructs a Steiner t-spanner for S, takes $\Omega(n \log n)$ time in the worst case.*

This lower bound proof is unsatisfying, in the sense that most existing algorithms to construct t-spanners, assume implicitly that all input points are pairwise distinct. When the inputs are thus constrained, the above proof does not work: If the points are known to be pairwise distinct, then the element uniqueness problem can be solved in $O(1)$ time, because the output is always YES. In the next section, we will consider algorithms that construct Steiner spanners for inputs consisting of pairwise distinct points.

3.4.2 A lower bound for a set of pairwise distinct points

The main result of this section is encapsulated below.

> **Main Result:** In the algebraic computation-tree model, the lower bound of $\Omega(n \log n)$ for the Steiner t-spanner construction problem holds even if the input is known to consist of pairwise distinct *points*. The proof effectively uses a lower bound of $\Omega(n \log n)$ for the mingap problem.

As in the previous section, we will consider only algorithms that compute Steiner t-spanners for one-dimensional point sets, that is, sets of real numbers.

Throughout this section, we fix an integer n. Moreover, $\mathcal{A}$ denotes an arbitrary algebraic computation-tree algorithm that, when given a set S of n pairwise distinct real numbers, and a real number $t > 1$, constructs a Steiner t-spanner for S with $o(n \log n)$ edges. Hence, the output of $\mathcal{A}$ is a graph having as its vertices the elements of S and (possibly) some additional Steiner points. We assume that each vertex of this graph is labeled as either being an element of S or being a Steiner point. If two input elements of S are equal, then algorithm $\mathcal{A}$ is not defined.

Our goal is to prove that the worst-case running time of $\mathcal{A}$ is $\Omega(n \log n)$. First observe that $\mathcal{A}$ solves a computation problem. Therefore, in order to apply Theorem 3.3.7, we have to define an appropriate algorithm $\mathcal{D}$, such that

1. $\mathcal{D}$ solves a decision problem; that is, it returns YES or NO;

2. $\mathcal{D}$ has a running time that is within a constant factor of $\mathcal{A}$'s running time; and

3. the set of YES-instances of $\mathcal{D}$, considered as a subset of $\mathbb{R}^n$, consists of many (at least $n!$, in our case) connected components.

Roughly stated, algorithm $\mathcal{D}$ takes the input to algorithm $\mathcal{A}$ and returns YES if the length of the shortest edge in the spanner returned by $\mathcal{A}$ is greater than a specified length. Consequently, proving a lower bound of $\Omega(n \log n)$ for algorithm $\mathcal{D}$ implies the same lower bound for algorithm $\mathcal{A}$.

However, the above strategy faces the following hurdle: Since algorithm $\mathcal{A}$ (and, consequently, algorithm $\mathcal{D}$) accepts only pairwise distinct real numbers, it is not defined on all points in $\mathbb{R}^n$. In fact, the subset of $\mathbb{R}^n$ on which it is defined trivially contains at least $n!$ connected components. Thus we cannot apply Theorem 3.3.7 to these algorithms.

To emphasize the point that Theorem 3.3.7 cannot be applied here, consider, for example, an algorithm $\mathcal{X}$ that takes as input any sequence of n pairwise distinct real numbers, and simply returns YES (therefore, it runs in $O(1)$ time). Since algorithm $\mathcal{X}$ is not defined if two input elements are equal, the subset of $\mathbb{R}^n$ accepted by this algorithm has at least $n!$ connected components.

Therefore, in order to apply Theorem 3.3.7, we carefully define algorithm $\mathcal{D}$ so that it can take *any* point of $\mathbb{R}^n$ as input and that its set of YES-instances still has $\Omega(n!)$ connected components. We will define algorithm $\mathcal{D}$ in three steps.

1. First, we define an algorithm $\mathcal{B}$ that takes pairwise distinct real numbers as input. This algorithm runs algorithm $\mathcal{A}$ on this input, and returns the length L of a shortest edge of nonzero length in the graph that $\mathcal{A}$ computes.

2. Next, we use algorithm $\mathcal{B}$ to define a positive real number L^*. Algorithm $\mathcal{C}$ takes pairwise distinct real numbers as input. It runs algorithm $\mathcal{B}$ on this input, and returns YES if and only if the output L of $\mathcal{B}$ is greater than or equal to L^*.

3. Finally, we change algorithm $\mathcal{C}$, such that it is well-defined on *any* input sequence of real numbers. The resulting algorithm is the algebraic decision tree algorithm $\mathcal{D}$ we are looking for.

In the rest of this section, we will fill in the details.

Algorithm $\mathcal{B}$

Algorithm $\mathcal{B}$ does the following on an input consisting of n pairwise distinct real numbers $s_1, s_2, \ldots, s_n$ and a real number $t > 1$: It first runs algorithm $\mathcal{A}$ on the input $s_1, s_2, \ldots, s_n, t$.

Let G be the Steiner t-spanner that is computed by $\mathcal{A}$. By considering all edges of G, algorithm $\mathcal{B}$ selects a shortest edge of nonzero length and returns the length L of this edge.

The following lemma relates the output L of algorithm $\mathcal{B}$ to the minimum distance of its input sequence. For real numbers $s_1, s_2, \ldots, s_n$, we define

$$\text{mingap}(s_1, s_2, \ldots, s_n) := \min\{|s_i - s_j| : 1 \leq i < j \leq n\}.$$

Lemma 3.4.2. *The real number L that is returned by algorithm $\mathcal{B}$ satisfies*

$$0 < L \leq t \cdot \text{mingap}(s_1, s_2, \ldots, s_n).$$

PROOF   Let i and j be two indices, such that $|s_i - s_j| = \text{mingap}(s_1, s_2, \ldots, s_n)$. Observe that since the input elements are pairwise distinct, we have $|s_i - s_j| > 0$. The graph G constructed by algorithm $\mathcal{A}$ contains a path between s_i and s_j, whose length is less than or equal to $t|s_i - s_j|$. The length of each edge on this path is obviously less than or equal to $t|s_i - s_j|$. The claim follows because this path contains at least one edge of nonzero length. ∎

Let $T_{\mathcal{A}}(n, t)$ and $T_{\mathcal{B}}(n, t)$ denote the worst-case running times of algorithms $\mathcal{A}$ and $\mathcal{B}$, respectively. Then, the fact that the graph G has $o(n \log n)$ edges implies that

$$T_{\mathcal{B}}(n, t) \leq T_{\mathcal{A}}(n, t) + o(n \log n).$$

Algorithm $\mathcal{C}$

We fix a real number $t > 1$. Before we define algorithm $\mathcal{C}$, we use algorithm $\mathcal{B}$ to define a positive real number L^* as follows: For each permutation π of the integers $1, 2, \ldots, n$, let L_{π} be the output of algorithm $\mathcal{B}$ when given as input the sequence $\pi(1), \pi(2), \ldots, \pi(n), t$. Among all these $n!$ outputs, let L^* be one that has the minimum value.

Now we can define algorithm $\mathcal{C}$. It takes only input sequences of our fixed length n, consisting of n pairwise distinct real numbers. On input $s_1, s_2, \ldots, s_n$, algorithm $\mathcal{C}$ does the following: It first runs algorithm $\mathcal{B}$ on the input sequence $s_1, s_2, \ldots, s_n, t$. Let L be the output of $\mathcal{B}$. Algorithm $\mathcal{C}$ returns YES if $L \geq L^*$, and NO otherwise.

We remark that it is not necessary to compute L^*, which would take a lot of time. For our proof, it is sufficient that algorithm $\mathcal{C}$ *exists*. In other words, since algorithm $\mathcal{C}$ takes only inputs of our fixed length n, and since we also fixed t, we may assume that it "knows" the value L^*.

It is clear that the running time of algorithm $\mathcal{C}$ is within a constant factor of $\mathcal{B}$'s running time.

Algorithm $\mathcal{D}$

Algorithm $\mathcal{C}$ is defined only for inputs consisting of n pairwise distinct real numbers. As a result, $\mathcal{C}$ can safely perform operations such as $z := x/(s_i - s_j)$ and $z := \sqrt{y}$, without having to worry whether the denominator $s_i - s_j$ is zero, or whether $y \geq 0$. Our final algorithm $\mathcal{D}$ will take any sequence $s_1, s_2, \ldots, s_n$ of n real numbers as input. On such an input, $\mathcal{D}$ performs the same computation as $\mathcal{C}$ does on the same input, except that each operation of the form $z := x/y$ is performed by $\mathcal{D}$ as

```
if y ≠ 0
then z := x/y
else return YES and terminate
endif
```

and each operation of the form $z := \sqrt{y}$ is performed by $\mathcal{D}$ as

> **if** $y \geq 0$
> **then** $z := \sqrt{y}$
> **else** return YES and terminate
> **endif**

Since $\mathcal{C}$ is a well-defined algorithm for inputs consisting of n pairwise distinct real numbers, it will always be the case that $y \neq 0$ when the operation $z := x/y$ is performed. When two input elements are equal, it may still be true that $y \neq 0$, although this is not necessarily the case. Similarly, if the input elements are pairwise distinct, it will always be the case that $y \geq 0$ when the operation $z := \sqrt{y}$ is performed. When two input elements are equal, y may still be nonnegative, although, again, this is not necessarily the case.

It is clear that $\mathcal{C}$ and $\mathcal{D}$ give the same output when given, as input, the same sequence of n pairwise distinct real numbers. If these numbers are not pairwise distinct, then $\mathcal{C}$ is not defined, whereas $\mathcal{D}$ is, although its output may not have a meaning at all. Finally, observe that the running time of $\mathcal{D}$ is within a constant factor of that of $\mathcal{C}$.

Analysis of algorithm $\mathcal{D}$

We now prove that the worst-case running time of algorithm $\mathcal{D}$ is $\Omega(n \log n)$. This will imply the same lower bound on the running time of our target algorithm $\mathcal{A}$.

Let W be the set of all points $(s_1, s_2, \ldots, s_n) \in \mathbb{R}^n$ such that algorithm $\mathcal{D}$ returns YES on the input sequence $s_1, s_2, \ldots, s_n$. The lower bound will follow from the following lemma:

Lemma 3.4.3. *The set W has at least $n!$ connected components.*

PROOF Let π and ρ be two distinct permutations of $1, 2, \ldots, n$. We will show that the points

$$p := (\pi(1), \pi(2), \ldots, \pi(n))$$

and

$$r := (\rho(1), \rho(2), \ldots, \rho(n))$$

belong to different connected components of W. (Observe that both these points are elements of W.) This will prove the lemma.

Since π and ρ are distinct permutations, there are indices i and j with $1 \leq i \leq n$ and $1 \leq j \leq n$, such that $\pi(i) < \pi(j)$ and $\rho(i) > \rho(j)$.

Consider an arbitrary continuous curve C in $\mathbb{R}^n$ that connects p and r. We will show that C contains a point q, which does not belong to the set W. From this, it will follow that p and r are in different connected components of W. In order to guarantee that $q \notin W$, the point $q = (q_1, q_2, \ldots, q_n)$ must have the property that $L < L^*$, where L is the output of algorithm $\mathcal{B}$ on input $q_1, q_2, \ldots, q_n, t$. Moreover, we have to take care that the coordinates of q are pairwise distinct.

Since the curve C passes through the hyperplane $x_i = x_j$, it contains points for which the absolute difference between the i-th and j-th coordinates is positive but arbitrarily small. However, for such points $q = (q_1, q_2, \ldots, q_n)$, there may be two distinct indices k and ℓ, such that $q_k = q_\ell$. We do not have any control over algorithm $\mathcal{D}$ when given such a point q as input. Therefore, we proceed as follows: We take for q the first point on the curve C, such that

$$\text{mingap}(q_1, q_2, \ldots, q_n) \leq L^*/(2t).$$

We will see below that the coordinates of q are pairwise distinct. If we run algorithm $\mathcal{B}$ on input $q_1, q_2, \ldots, q_n, t$, then, by Lemma 3.4.2, the output L satisfies $L \leq t \cdot L^*/(2t) < L^*$. Hence, point q is not contained in the set W. In the rest of the proof, we will formalize this.

We parameterize the curve C as $C(\tau)$, $0 \leq \tau \leq 1$, where $C(0) = p$ and $C(1) = r$. For each k with $1 \leq k \leq n$, we write the k-th coordinate of the point $C(\tau)$ as $C(\tau)_k$. We define

$$\tau_0 := \min\{0 \leq \tau \leq 1 : \text{mingap}(C(\tau)_1, C(\tau)_2, \ldots, C(\tau)_n) \leq L^*/(2t)\}.$$

Observe that τ_0 exists because the curve C passes through the hyperplane $x_i = x_j$ and the function mingap is continuous along C.

Let $q := C(\tau_0)$. We write this point as $q = (q_1, q_2, \ldots, q_n)$. Clearly, we have

$$\text{mingap}(q_1, q_2, \ldots, q_n) \leq L^*/(2t).$$

Also, by Lemma 3.4.2, and since $C(0) = p \in W$, we have

$$\text{mingap}(C(0)_1, C(0)_2, \ldots, C(0)_n) \geq L^*/t > L^*/(2t).$$

The value of τ_0 is the first "time" at which the mingap-function is less than or equal to $L^*/(2t)$. Since this function is continuous along C, we have mingap $(q_1, q_2, \ldots, q_n) > 0$. Hence $(q_1, q_2, \ldots, q_n)$ is a sequence of n pairwise distinct real numbers.

Consider what happens when we run algorithm $\mathcal{D}$ on the input sequence $q_1, q_2, \ldots, q_n$. First, algorithm $\mathcal{B}$ is run on the input sequence $q_1, q_2, \ldots, q_n, t$. Let L be the output of $\mathcal{B}$. By Lemma 3.4.2, we have

$$L \leq t \cdot \text{mingap}(q_1, q_2, \ldots, q_n).$$

Hence, $L \leq t \cdot L^*/(2t) < L^*$ and, therefore, algorithm $\mathcal{D}$ returns NO. This implies that point q does not belong to the set W. This completes the proof. ∎

Recall that we denote the number of connected components of the set W by $CC(W)$. Lemma 3.4.3 and Theorem 3.3.7 imply that the running time of any algebraic decision tree algorithm that decides the set W is bounded from below by

$$\Omega\left(\log(CC(W)) - n\right) = \Omega\left(n \log n\right).$$

Since $\mathcal{D}$ is such an algorithm, it follows that for our fixed values of n and t, the worst-case running time of $\mathcal{D}$ is greater than or equal to $cn \log n$, where c is a positive constant independent of n and t. This, in turn, implies that there is an input on which algorithm $\mathcal{A}$ takes time at least $c'n \log n$, for some constant $c' > 0$. Since c' does not depend on n and t, this implies that the lower bound holds for all values of n and t. Hence, we have proved the following theorem.

Theorem 3.4.4. *Let $d \geq 1$ be an integer constant. In the algebraic computation-tree model, any algorithm that, when given a set S of n pairwise distinct points in $\mathbb{R}^d$ and a real number $t > 1$, constructs a Steiner t-spanner for S, takes $\Omega(n \log n)$ time in the worst case.*

Our lower bound proof of Theorem 3.4.4 holds for inputs consisting of pairwise distinct points. In computational geometry, we often make stronger assumptions on the input, for example, no three points are on a line, no four points are in a two-dimensional plane, etc. We say that a set S of points in $\mathbb{R}^d$ is in *general position*, if for each k with $3 \leq k \leq d+1$, no k points of S are contained in a $(k-2)$-dimensional subspace of $\mathbb{R}^d$. For such general position inputs, our lower bound proof does not hold; the proof heavily uses the fact that the points are on a line.

Open problem: Let $d \geq 2$ be an integer constant. Prove that, in the algebraic computation-tree model, any algorithm that, when given a set S of n points in $\mathbb{R}^d$ that are in general position and a real number $t > 1$, constructs a Steiner t-spanner for S, takes $\Omega(n \log n)$ time in the worst case.

Exercises

3.1. Prove that $\log n! = n \log n - O(n)$.

3.2. Prove Theorem 3.3.5 for $n = 1$.

3.3. In the proof of Theorem 3.3.7, it is mentioned that the projection of the set W onto the first n coordinates is equal to the set $R(w)$. Prove this claim.

3.4. Prove that, in the algebraic computation-tree model, the following problems have time complexity $\Omega(n \log n)$:

- Constructing the convex hull of a set of n points in the plane. (The convex hull vertices should be reported in clockwise or counterclockwise order.)

- Constructing the Voronoi diagram of a set of n points in the plane.

- Constructing an arbitrary triangulation of a set of n points in the plane.

3.5. It is known that the sorting problem for a set of n arbitrary *integers* has an $\Omega(n \log n)$ lower bound in the algebraic computation-tree model. Use this fact to prove that the sorting problem for n pairwise distinct integers has the same lower bound in this model.

3.6. In Figure 3.1, an algorithm is given that takes an arbitrary real number x as input, and returns YES if and only if $x \in \mathbb{N}$. Does this contradict Theorem 3.3.11?

3.7. Prove that there is no algebraic computation-tree algorithm that, on an arbitrary input $x \in \mathbb{R}$, computes the value $\lfloor x \rfloor$. (*Hint:* Use Theorem 3.3.11.)

```
Algorithm NATURALNUMBER(x)
(* x is a real number *)
if x < 0
then return NO
else k := 0;
     while k ≤ x
     do k := k + 1
     endwhile;
     ℓ := k - 1;
     if x > ℓ
     then return NO
     else return YES
     endif
endif
```

Figure 3.1: An algorithm that decides the set $\mathbb{N} = \{0, 1, 2, \ldots\}$.

3.8. Prove that there is no algebraic computation-tree algorithm that, on an arbitrary input $x \in \mathbb{R}$, computes the value of $\sin x$.

3.9. We have seen in Remark 3.3.8 that any set $V \subseteq \mathbb{R}^n$, having an infinite number of connected components, is not decidable in the algebraic decision tree model. Give an example of a set $V \subseteq \mathbb{R}^2$ with a finite number of connected components that is not decidable in this model. (In fact, there is such a set V consisting of only one connected component.)

3.10. In the algebraic computation-tree model, square roots can be computed in unit time. Prove that Theorem 3.3.7 also holds (with different constant factors) if k-th roots can be computed in unit time, where k is any element from a finite set of positive integers. (The size of this set is a constant that does not depend on n.)

3.11. Let $A[1 .. n]$ and $B[1 .. m]$ be arrays, and assume that $B[i] \in \{1, 2, \ldots, n\}$ for all i with $1 \leq i \leq m$. An assignment of the form $x := A[B[i]]$ is called an *indirect addressing assignment*. Algorithms that use such assignments as unit-cost operations do not work in the algebraic computation-tree model. Explain why this is the case. Observe that this implies that the lower bound proofs that have been presented in this chapter are not valid for such algorithms.

3.12. For any sequence $s_1, s_2, \ldots, s_n$ of real numbers, we define a *gap* to be the absolute value of the difference of two elements s_i and s_j (with $i \neq j$) that are consecutive in the sorted sequence. The *uniformgap*-problem is defined as follows: Given a sequence $s_1, s_2, \ldots, s_n$ of real numbers, and given a real number g, decide whether all $n - 1$ gaps are equal to g. Prove an $\Omega(n \log n)$ lower bound on the time complexity of the *uniformgap*-problem in the algebraic decision tree model.

3.13. The *maxgap*-problem is defined as follows: Given a sequence $s_1, s_2, \ldots, s_n$ of real numbers, compute the *maximum gap* in this sequence, which is the largest absolute value of the difference of any two elements s_i and s_j (with $i \neq j$) that are consecutive in the sorted sequence. Use Exercise 3.12 to prove an $\Omega(n \log n)$ lower bound on the time complexity of the *maxgap*-problem in the algebraic computation-tree model.

3.14. Consider the algebraic computation-tree model in which, additionally, any indirect addressing operation takes unit time, and in which the floor-function can be computed in unit time. Prove that in this model, the *maxgap*-problem can be solved in $O(n)$ time.

Bibliographic notes

Sections 3.1, 3.2, and 3.3 are based on the books by Mehlhorn [1984b] and Preparata and Shamos [1988].

Ford and Johnson [1959] introduced decision trees as a model to study comparison-based sorting algorithms. In 1966, Rabin generalized decision trees to the more general class of algebraic computation-trees; see Rabin [1972] and Reingold [1972]. Dobkin and Lipton [1979] introduced the linear decision tree model and proved Theorem 3.3.3. Theorems 3.3.6 and 3.3.7 are due to Ben-Or [1983], who extended earlier work by Steele and Yao [1982]. Theorem 3.3.5 was proved independently by Milnor [1964] and Thom [1965]. In the proof of Theorem 3.3.6, it is mentioned that the set W has a finite number of connected components. This was proved by Milnor [1968]. A wealth of information about algebraic algorithms can be found in the book by Bürgisser, Clausen, and Shokrollahi [1997].

The lower bound for constructing spanners that is presented in Section 3.4 is due to Chen, Das, and Smid [2001].

The $\Omega(n \log n)$ lower bound for sorting n integers in the algebraic computation-tree model that is mentioned in Exercise 3.5 is due to Yao [1991]. A solution to this exercise can be found in Chen, Das, and Smid [2001].

The $\Omega(n \log n)$ lower bounds for the *uniformgap-* and *maxgap*-problems in Exercises 3.12 and 3.13 are due to Lee and Wu [1986]. Earlier, these lower bounds were proved in Manber and Tompa [1985] for the linear decision tree model. The $O(n)$–time algorithm in the more powerful model in Exercise 3.14 is due to Gonzalez [1975]; see also Preparata and Shamos [1988].

We have considered only deterministic algebraic algorithms. In Yao [1977], a general technique for proving lower bounds on the expected running time of *randomized* algorithms is presented. This technique is also described in the books by Mehlhorn [1984b] and Motwani and Raghavan [1995].

PART II
Spanners Based on Simplicial Cones

4

Spanners Based on the Θ-Graph

> It is not always by plugging away at a difficulty and sticking to it that one overcomes it; often it is by working on the one next to it. Some things and some people have to be approached obliquely, at an angle.
> —Andre Gide, *Journals*, 26 October, 1924

If you want to drive from Dallas to Washington, DC, then you are most likely to set out on Interstate highway 30 East. Why? Because, among the many higways leading out of Dallas, it is the only major highway that is headed in the northeasterly direction from Dallas, and is therefore headed in the general direction of your destination.

In this chapter, we introduce the Θ-graph, which insists on adding an edge in each of κ different directions for each of the n input points. Thus, to find a short path from one vertex in the graph to another, one would simply "follow one's nose," that is, pick an edge in the general direction of the destination.

We also show that the Θ-graph is a sparse t-spanner for any arbitrarily small given real number $t > 1$. As we will see, this graph may have large degree, large weight, and a large spanner diameter. Nevertheless, we will use the Θ-graph to efficiently construct a sparse t-spanner whose degree is bounded from above by a function that depends only on t, and a sparse spanner whose spanner diameter is $O(\log n)$.

All results for Θ-graphs and its variants are presented for two-dimensional point sets. In Chapter 5, we will show how these results can be extended to d-dimensional point sets, for any $d \geq 2$.

4.1 The Θ-graph

Let S be a set of points in the plane. Assume that we have an undirected graph G with the property that for any two distinct points p and q in S, G contains an edge $\{p, r\}$ such that

1. the vector $\overrightarrow{pr}$ points "in the general direction" of q, and

2. following this edge from p to r does not take us "too far" beyond q.

Then, we can (attempt to) construct a path in G between p and q as follows: Start at $p_0 := p$. Let $i \geq 0$, and assume we have already constructed a path $p_0, p_1, \ldots, p_i$. If $p_i = q$, then we have reached our destination. Otherwise, if $p_i \neq q$, but $\{p_i, q\}$ is an edge of G, then we follow this edge, and arrive at our destination. Assume that $p_i \neq q$, and $\{p_i, q\}$ is not an edge of G. Let p_{i+1} be a point of S such that $\{p_i, p_{i+1}\}$ is an edge of G that satisfies 1. and 2. above. That is, $\{p_i, p_{i+1}\}$ takes us in the general direction of q, but not too far beyond q. Then p_{i+1} is the next point on our path. The Θ-graph, which will be defined below, is based on this idea. The notion of an edge taking us "in the general direction" of a point or a set of points is based on cones.

63

> **The Θ-graph:** For each $p \in S$, among all "nearly-parallel" edges incident on p in the complete graph, the Θ-graph retains only the "shortest" one. These graphs are t-spanners for an appropriate value of t. The stretch factor t is determined by the condition for edges to be considered "nearly parallel."

A *cone* is the region in the plane between two rays that emanate from the same point, called the *apex* of the cone.

Let $\kappa \geq 2$, and define $\theta := 2\pi/\kappa$. If we rotate the positive x-axis by angles $i\theta$, $0 \leq i < \kappa$, then we get κ rays. Each pair of successive rays defines a cone whose apex is at the origin. We denote the collection of these κ cones by $\mathcal{C}_\kappa$. It is clear that the cones of $\mathcal{C}_\kappa$ partition the plane. Also, the two bounding rays of any cone of $\mathcal{C}_\kappa$ make an angle θ.

For each cone $C \in \mathcal{C}_\kappa$, let ℓ_C be a fixed ray that emanates from the origin and that is contained in C. The ray ℓ_C can be chosen arbitrarily; as a concrete example, we can choose it to be the bisector of C. In other words, for the set of directions in cone C, ℓ_C is a representative direction.

Let C be any cone of $\mathcal{C}_\kappa$ and let p be any point in the plane. We define $C_p := C + p := \{x + p : x \in C\}$; that is, C_p is the cone obtained by translating C such that its apex is at p. Similarly, we define $\ell_{C,p} := \ell_C + p$. Hence, $\ell_{C,p}$ is the ray that emanates from p, that is contained in the translated cone C_p, and that is parallel to ℓ_C.

We are now ready to define the Θ-graph; refer to Figure 4.1.

Definition 4.1.1 (Θ-graph). Let $\kappa \geq 2$ be an integer, let $\theta = 2\pi/\kappa$, and let S be a set of points in the plane. The undirected graph $\Theta(S, \kappa)$ is defined as follows:

1. The vertices of $\Theta(S, \kappa)$ are the points of S.

2. For each point p of S and for each cone C of $\mathcal{C}_\kappa$, such that the translated cone C_p contains one or more points of $S \setminus \{p\}$, the graph $\Theta(S, \kappa)$ contains one edge $\{p, r\}$, where r is a point in $C_p \cap S \setminus \{p\}$, whose orthogonal projection onto $\ell_{C,p}$ is closest to p.

An example of a Θ-graph for 30 points is given in Figure 4.2. In this example, the number κ of cones is equal to 9, and for each cone C, the ray ℓ_C is the bisector of C. In Section 4.1.1, we will present a technique that can be used to prove that this graph is a t-spanner for $t = 1/(1 - 2\sin(\pi/9)) \approx 3.165$; see also Exercise 4.4. In fact, the true stretch factor of this graph is approximately equal to 1.496.

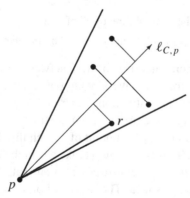

Figure 4.1: The graph $\Theta(S, \kappa)$ contains an edge between p and r, since, among all points in the cone C_p, the projection of point r onto $\ell_{C,p}$ is closest to p.

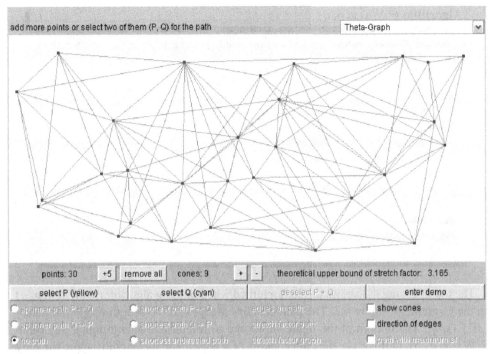

Figure 4.2: A Θ-graph for 30 points based on 9 cones. For each cone C, the ray ℓ_C is the bisector of C.

Remark 4.1.2. If we take for r a point in $C_p \cap S \setminus \{p\}$ that is closest to p, in the Euclidean metric, then we obtain a graph that is called the *geographic neighborhood graph*. It can be shown that this graph has properties similar to that of a Θ-graph and is a sparse t-spanner, for some real number t that depends on the angle θ. (The proof is left as an exercise; see Exercise 4.5.) Moreover, this graph can be constructed in $O(n \log n)$ time. As we will see in Section 4.1.2, defining the edges as in the Θ-graph definition (Definition 4.1.1) has the advantage that there is a simple $O(n \log n)$–time algorithm for constructing $\Theta(S, \kappa)$. Moreover, a direct generalization of this graph to an arbitrary – but constant – dimension can be constructed in $O(n \log^{O(1)} n)$ time. For dimensions larger than 2, it is not known if the geographic neighborhood graph can be constructed within this time bound.

Before we prove an upper bound on the stretch factor of $\Theta(S, \kappa)$, let us mention the obvious fact that the Θ-graph is sparse:

Lemma 4.1.3. *If S is a set of n points in the plane, and $\kappa \geq 2$ is a constant, then the graph $\Theta(S, \kappa)$ contains at most $\kappa n = (2\pi/\theta)n = O(n)$ edges.*

4.1.1 Bounding the stretch factor of the Θ-graph

We start by presenting an obvious algorithm that constructs a path in $\Theta(S, \kappa)$ between two points p and q of S. Later in this section, we will prove an upper bound on the length of the path constructed by this algorithm.

Algorithm Θ-WALK(p, q)

Comment: This algorithm takes as input two points p and q in S, and returns a path in $\Theta(S, \kappa)$ between p and q.

$p_0 := p$;
$i := 0$;
while $p_i \neq q$
do (* $p = p_0, p_1, \ldots, p_i$ is a path in $\Theta(S, \kappa)$ *)
    $C :=$ cone of $\mathcal{C}_\kappa$ such that $q \in C_{p_i}$;
    $p_{i+1} :=$ point of $C_{p_i} \cap S \setminus \{p_i\}$ such that $\{p_i, p_{i+1}\}$
            is an edge of $\Theta(S, \kappa)$;
    $i := i + 1$
endwhile;
return the path $p_0, p_1, \ldots, p_i$

The top of Figure 4.3 shows the path returned when running algorithm Θ-WALK(p, q) on the Θ-graph of Figure 4.2. The path contains 5 edges and its length is approximately $1.071 \cdot |pq|$. The bottom of the figure shows the path returned when running algorithm Θ-WALK(q, p). In this case, the path consists of 4 edges, and its length is approximately $1.037 \cdot |pq|$.

Below, we prove a geometric lemma that is valid for all $\kappa \geq 8$. If $\kappa \geq 9$, it will enable us to determine an upper bound on the stretch factor of $\Theta(S, \kappa)$. To be more precise, this lemma will imply that for $\kappa \geq 9$ (i) algorithm Θ-WALK(p, q) terminates, that is, the path constructed indeed reaches point q, and (ii) the length of this path is at most a constant factor times the Euclidean distance between p and q, where the constant depends on κ.

Lemma 4.1.4. *Let $\kappa \geq 8$ be an integer, let $\theta = 2\pi/\kappa$, let p and q be two distinct points in the plane, and let C be the cone of $\mathcal{C}_\kappa$ such that $q \in C_p$. Let r be a point in C_p such that the orthogonal projection of r onto the ray $\ell_{C,p}$ is at least as close to p as the orthogonal projection of q onto $\ell_{C,p}$. Then,*

1. $|pr| \leq |pq|/\cos\theta$, and

2. $|rq| \leq |pq| - (\cos\theta - \sin\theta)|pr|$.

PROOF   If $r = q$, then both claims hold. We assume in the rest of the proof that $r \neq q$. Let q' be the orthogonal projection of q onto $\ell_{C,p}$ and let α be the angle between the segments pq and pq'. Observe that $0 \leq \alpha \leq \theta$. We have

$$|pq'| = |pq|\cos\alpha \leq |pq|.$$

Similarly, let r' be the orthogonal projection of r onto $\ell_{C,p}$, and let β be the angle between pr and pr'. Then $0 \leq \beta \leq \theta$ and

$$|pr'| = |pr|\cos\beta \geq |pr|\cos\theta.$$

Our assumption implies that $|pr'| \leq |pq'|$. Therefore,

$$|pr|\cos\theta \leq |pr'| \leq |pq'| \leq |pq|,$$

which proves the first claim in the lemma.

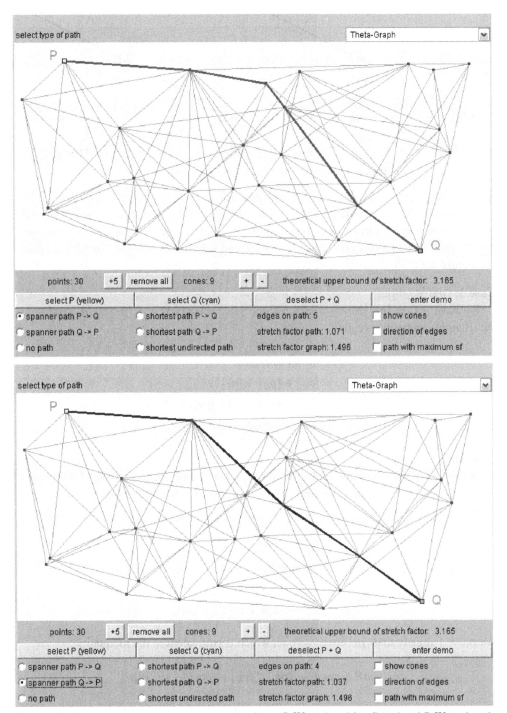

Figure 4.3: The paths computed when running algorithms Θ-WALK(p, q) (top figure) and Θ-WALK(q, p) (bottom figure) on the Θ-graph of Figure 4.2.

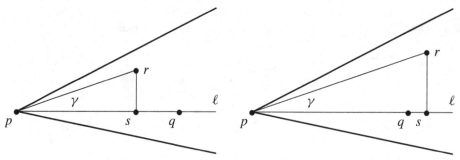

Figure 4.4: Cases 1 and 2 in the proof of Lemma 4.1.4.

To prove the second claim, let ℓ be the line through p and q, and let s be the orthogonal projection of r onto ℓ. Finally, let γ be the angle between the segments pq and pr. We have $0 \leq \gamma \leq \theta$. We distinguish two cases depending on whether $|ps| \leq |pq|$ or $|ps| > |pq|$; see Figure 4.4.

Case 1: $|ps| \leq |pq|$.

We have $|rs| = |pr| \sin \gamma \leq |pr| \sin \theta$ and $|ps| = |pr| \cos \gamma \geq |pr| \cos \theta$. Applying the triangle inequality, we get

$$\begin{aligned}
|rq| &\leq |rs| + |sq| \\
&= |rs| + |pq| - |ps| \\
&\leq |pr| \sin \theta + |pq| - |pr| \cos \theta \\
&= |pq| - (\cos \theta - \sin \theta)|pr|.
\end{aligned}$$

Case 2: $|ps| > |pq|$.

We have $|rs| = |pr| \sin \gamma$ and $|ps| = |pr| \cos \gamma$. Applying the triangle inequality and using the fact that the function $\sin x + \cos x$ is nondecreasing for $0 \leq x \leq \pi/4$, we get

$$\begin{aligned}
|rq| &\leq |rs| + |sq| \\
&= |rs| + |ps| - |pq| \\
&= |pr|(\sin \gamma + \cos \gamma) - |pq| \\
&\leq |pr|(\sin \theta + \cos \theta) - |pq|.
\end{aligned}$$

We proved already that $|pr| \cos \theta \leq |pq|$, which is equivalent to the inequality

$$|pr|(\sin \theta + \cos \theta) - |pq| \leq |pq| - (\cos \theta - \sin \theta)|pr|.$$

Therefore, even in this case, we have $|rq| \leq |pq| - (\cos \theta - \sin \theta)|pr|$.   ∎

Let $\kappa \geq 9$, so that $0 < \theta < \pi/4$. Let p and q be two distinct points of S, and consider the path $p = p_0, p_1, p_2, \ldots$ that is constructed by algorithm Θ-WALK(p, q). Let $i \geq 0$, and assume that $p_i \neq q$. Then point p_{i+1} exists; that is, the algorithm extends the path by one more point. Consider the three points p_i, q, and p_{i+1}. Let C be the cone such that $q \in C_{p_i}$. By the definition of $\Theta(S, \kappa)$, the orthogonal projection of p_{i+1} onto the ray ℓ_{C,p_i}

is at least as close to p_i as the orthogonal projection of q onto ℓ_{C,p_i}. Hence, we can apply Lemma 4.1.4, and obtain

$$|p_{i+1}q| \leq |p_iq| - (\cos\theta - \sin\theta)|p_ip_{i+1}| < |p_iq|, \tag{4.1}$$

where the strict inequality follows from the fact that $0 < \theta < \pi/4$.

Hence we have shown that the points p_0, p_1, p_2, ... on the path starting at p are pairwise distinct; each successive point on this path takes us strictly closer to our destination q. Since the set S is finite, this implies that algorithm Θ-WALK(p, q) terminates. That is, this algorithm indeed constructs a path between p and q.

We now prove an upper bound on the length of this path. Let m be the index such that $p_m = q$. Rearranging the leftmost inequality in (4.1), yields

$$|p_ip_{i+1}| \leq \frac{1}{\cos\theta - \sin\theta}(|p_iq| - |p_{i+1}q|)$$

for each i with $0 \leq i < m$. Therefore, the length of the path between p and q has length

$$\sum_{i=0}^{m-1}|p_ip_{i+1}| \leq \frac{1}{\cos\theta - \sin\theta}\sum_{i=0}^{m-1}(|p_iq| - |p_{i+1}q|)$$

$$= \frac{1}{\cos\theta - \sin\theta}(|p_0q| - |p_mq|)$$

$$= \frac{1}{\cos\theta - \sin\theta}|pq|.$$

We have shown that the graph $\Theta(S, \kappa)$ is a t-spanner of S for $t = 1/(\cos\theta - \sin\theta)$.

The stretch factor of the Θ-graph: When we are at p_i, we are a distance $|p_iq|$ from our destination. When following edge $\{p_i, p_{i+1}\}$, we travel a distance $|p_ip_{i+1}|$ and, by (4.1), this takes us closer to our destination by at least $\cos\theta - \sin\theta$ times this distance, implying that the stretch factor of $\Theta(S, \kappa)$ is at most $1/(\cos\theta - \sin\theta)$.

The following theorem summarizes the results obtained so far.

Theorem 4.1.5. *Let $\kappa \geq 9$ be an integer, let $\theta = 2\pi/\kappa$, and let S be a set of points in the plane. The graph $\Theta(S, \kappa)$ is a t-spanner for S, for $t = 1/(\cos\theta - \sin\theta)$. It contains at most κn edges.*

Remark 4.1.6. For each $t > 1$, there is a $\kappa \geq 9$ such that $1 < 1/(\cos\theta - \sin\theta) \leq t$ holds for $\theta = 2\pi/\kappa$. Hence, for each real constant $t > 1$, there exists a sparse t-spanner. Let us consider what happens if $t > 1$ and $t \to 1$. We obtain the best result if we choose the minimum κ for which $1/(\cos\theta - \sin\theta) \leq t$. If $t \to 1$, then $\theta \to 0$ and $t \sim 1 + \theta = 1 + 2\pi/\kappa$. Hence, Theorem 4.1.5 gives a t-spanner for S having $O((1/(t-1))n)$ edges. In Section 4.1.2, we will see that this spanner can be computed in $O((1/(t-1))n\log n)$ time.

4.1.2 Constructing the Θ-graph

We now turn to the problem of constructing the Θ-graph. Let S be a set of n points in the plane, and let $\kappa \geq 2$ be an integer. Recall that C_κ is a set of cones that partition the plane

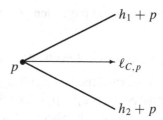

Figure 4.5: The translated cone C_p.

and have the origin as their apex. Let C be a fixed cone of $\mathcal{C}_\kappa$. We will give an algorithm that computes all edges of $\Theta(S, \kappa)$ that correspond to C, that is, edges of the form $\{p, r\}$, where $p \in S$ and $r \in C_p \cap S \setminus \{p\}$. Repeating this for all κ cones of $\mathcal{C}_\kappa$, we obtain the entire graph $\Theta(S, \kappa)$.

We have to introduce some notation; refer to Figure 4.5. Let h_1 and h_2 be the two lines through the origin containing the bounding rays of C. Thus, $h_1 + p$ and $h_2 + p$ are lines through point p containing the bounding rays of C_p. We assume without loss of generality that the ray ℓ_C coincides with the positive x-axis, and that h_1 (resp. h_2) contains the upper (resp. lower) bounding ray of C. Figure 4.5 illustrates this scenario.

The following observation characterizes the point r, which defines the edge $\{p, r\}$ in $\Theta(S, \kappa)$.

Observation 4.1.7. *Let p be a point of S, and assume that the translated cone C_p contains one or more points of $S \setminus \{p\}$. Let $\{p, r\}$ be the edge of $\Theta(S, \kappa)$ for which $r \in C_p \cap S \setminus \{p\}$. The point r has the property that it has the least x-coordinate among all points of S that are (i) below $h_1 + p$, and (ii) above $h_2 + p$.*

The question is how to compute this point r efficiently for each point p of S. We will solve this problem using a simple *plane sweep* algorithm. We start by considering a simpler dynamic query problem.

Finding the leftmost point in a translated query halfplane

Our algorithm for computing all edges of $\Theta(S, \kappa)$ that correspond to the fixed cone C will use a solution to the following problem:

Problem 4.1.8 (FIND-LEFTMOST-IN-TRANSLATED-HALFPLANE). Let h be a fixed nonvertical line through the origin. Maintain a set S of n points in a data structure that supports the following operations:

> MINABOVE(p): Given a query point $p \in S$, compute a point with the minimum x-coordinate among all points in S that are above $h + p$.
>
> INSERT(p): Insert an arbitrary point $p \in \mathbb{R}^2$ into S.
>
> DELETE(p): Delete point p from S.

Let D be the directed line through the origin that is orthogonal to the line h. This line is directed to point toward the halfplane consisting of all points in $\mathbb{R}^2$ that are above h.

We use the directed line D to define the following order relation on the points of S: Let p and q be two points of S, and let p' and q' be their orthogonal projections onto D, respectively. Then, p is smaller than q in the order relation, if the vector from p' to q' has the same direction as D. We call this relation the *order induced by D*.

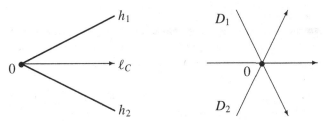

Figure 4.6: The cone C and the directed lines D_1 and D_2.

To solve the problem FIND-LEFTMOST-IN-TRANSLATED-HALFPLANE (Problem 4.1.8), we store the points of S at the leaves of a balanced binary search tree T, sorted according to the order induced by D. Each internal node u of T contains information to guide searching (e.g., the point stored at the rightmost leaf in the left subtree rooted at u). Also, each node u of T contains as additional information a point z_u stored in the subtree of u whose x-coordinate is minimum. This tree T can be built in $O(n \log n)$ time; the proof of this claim is left as an exercise (see Exercise 4.10).

Given the tree T, we can answer a query MINABOVE(p), where $p \in S$, as follows: Initialize an empty set M. Then follow the path in T from the root to the leaf storing p. Each time this path proceeds from a node v to its left child, add the right child of v to M. After the path has been completely traversed, the set M contains $O(\log n)$ nodes, having the following property. The subsets of S stored in the subtrees rooted at the nodes of M partition the set of all points of S that are larger (according to the order induced by D) than p. These are exactly the points that are above the line $h + p$. Recall that each node u stores a point z_u from its subtree having minimum x-coordinate. Therefore, if we take that point among the points z_u, $u \in M$, having minimum x-coordinate, then we get exactly the point that we want to compute. It is not difficult to see that the time of this query algorithm is $O(\log n)$.

If we take T from, say, the class of red-black trees, then the operations INSERT and DELETE can also be performed in $O(\log n)$ time. (The details of the update algorithms are left as Exercise 4.10.) We obtain the following result:

Lemma 4.1.9. *The above tree T solves the problem* FIND-LEFTMOST-IN-TRANSLATED-HALFPLANE *(Problem 4.1.8). It supports each of the operations* MINABOVE, INSERT, *and* DELETE *in $O(\log n)$ time. This data structure has size $O(n)$ and can be built in $O(n \log n)$ time.*

Computing all edges of $\Theta(S, \kappa)$ corresponding to a cone

We are now ready to present the plane sweep algorithm that computes the edges of $\Theta(S, \kappa)$ that correspond to the fixed cone C. Recall that h_1 and h_2 are the lines through the upper and lower bounding rays of C, respectively, and that we assume that the ray ℓ_C coincides with the positive x-axis.

Let D_1 and D_2 be the lines through the origin that are orthogonal to h_1 and h_2, respectively. We direct D_1 such that it points toward the halfplane consisting of all points in $\mathbb{R}^2$ that are below h_1, and we direct D_2 such that it points toward the halfplane consisting of all points in $\mathbb{R}^2$ that are above h_2. Figure 4.6 illustrates this scenario.

Algorithm BUILDΘGRAPH(S, C)

Comment: This algorithm takes as input a set S of n points in the plane and a cone C of $\mathcal{C}_\kappa$. It returns the set of all edges of $\Theta(S, \kappa)$ that correspond to C. The algorithm makes the following three steps:

Step 1: Sort the points of S according to the order induced by the directed line D_1. Let $p_1, p_2, \ldots, p_n$ be the sorted sequence of points.

Step 2: Initialize an empty data structure T for solving problem FIND-LEFTMOST-IN-TRANSLATED-HALFPLANE (Problem 4.1.8) using $h := h_2$.

Step 3: Visit the points of S one after another, starting at p_n. Assume the algorithm has already visited the points $p_n, p_{n-1}, \ldots, p_{i+1}$. Also, assume that T stores these $n - i$ points (and no other points). The next point to be visited is p_i. The algorithm does the following:

- It inserts p_i into T; that is, it performs the operation INSERT(p_i).

- It finds the point r_i in T that is above the line $h_2 + p_i$ and whose x-coordinate is minimum; that is, it answers the query MINABOVE(p_i).

Observe that point r_i is one of the points $p_n, p_{n-1}, \ldots, p_{i+1}$. These are exactly the points of S that are below the line $h_1 + p_i$. Therefore, $\{p_i, r_i\}$ is the edge of $\Theta(S, \kappa)$ that corresponds to cone C.

After all points of S have been visited in Step 3, all edges of $\Theta(S, \kappa)$ that correspond to the cone C have been computed.

We analyze the running time of algorithm BUILDΘGRAPH(S, C). The initial sorting of the points in Step 1 takes $O(n \log n)$ time. Clearly, Step 2 takes $O(1)$ time. By Lemma 4.1.9, the total time for Step 3 is $O(n \log n)$. Hence, the entire algorithm takes $O(n \log n)$ time.

The complete graph $\Theta(S, \kappa)$ is obtained by running algorithm BUILDΘGRAPH(S, C) κ times, once for each cone C of $\mathcal{C}_\kappa$. We have proved the following result:

Theorem 4.1.10. *Let $\kappa \geq 2$ be an integer, let $\theta = 2\pi/\kappa$, and let S be a set of n points in the plane. The graph $\Theta(S, \kappa)$ can be constructed in $O(\kappa n \log n)$ time, using $O(n)$ space.*

Remark 4.1.11. In Chapters 2 and 3, we made the convention that the running time of an algorithm is expressed as a function of the number, say N, of input elements. Algorithm BUILDΘGRAPH takes as input a set of n points in the plane (where each point is specified by its x- and y-coordinates), and an integer κ. Hence, we have $N = 2n + 1$. The time complexity in Theorem 4.1.10, however, is not a function of N only, but also depends on the size of the parameter κ. In other words, algorithm BUILDΘGRAPH does not work in the algebraic computation-tree model, if κ is considered to be an input variable. If κ is a constant, however, then the result in Theorem 4.1.10 is valid in this model.

Most algorithms in the rest of this book take as input a set of n points, together with some additional parameters that specify the degree of approximation in the output. Running times will always be expressed as functions that depend on n and the values of these additional parameters. We allow that algorithms compute nonalgebraic functions (such as the floor and ceiling functions, and log, sin, cos, and tan) of these parameters. For example, to compute a t-spanner for a given set of n points in the plane, the algorithm may start by computing an integer κ such that $1/(\cos(2\pi/\kappa) - \sin(2\pi/\kappa)) \leq t$, and then use algorithm BUILDΘGRAPH to compute the t-spanner $\Theta(S, \kappa)$. If each of these additional parameters is considered to be a constant, then the algorithms will work in the algebraic computation-tree model and, therefore, the results will not contradict Theorem 3.3.11 and Exercises 3.6, 3.7, and 3.8.

> **Constructing the Θ-graph:** For any $p \in S$, let r be the point such that $\{p, r\}$ is the edge of $\Theta(S, \kappa)$ corresponding to the cone C. Then r is the solution to a minimization query subject to two linear constraints. Using the plane sweep technique, the number of constraints is reduced to one. On the other hand, these one-constraint minimization queries have to be answered for a dynamically changing set of points.

4.1.3 Is the Θ-graph a good spanner?

We have seen that for any real number $t > 1$, there is an integer κ such that the graph $\Theta(S, \kappa)$ is a sparse t-spanner for S. What can we say about the other measures that were mentioned in Section 1.2? That is, is the degree of $\Theta(S, \kappa)$ "small"? Does $\Theta(S, \kappa)$ have "low" weight? Finally, what can we say about the spanner diameter of $\Theta(S, \kappa)$?

Let S consist of the origin and $n - 1$ points that are on the unit circle. Assume that these $n - 1$ points are the vertices of a regular $(n - 1)$-gon. If $\kappa \geq 9$, then $\Theta(S, \kappa)$ contains an edge between each of the $n - 1$ points on the circle and the origin. Hence, the vertex at the origin has degree $n - 1$ in $\Theta(S, \kappa)$. If n is sufficiently large, then the weight of a minimum spanning tree of S is approximately equal to $2\pi + 1$. On the other hand, if $\kappa \geq 9$, then the weight of $\Theta(S, \kappa)$ increases linearly with n, proving that the Θ-graphs may have neither low weight nor low degree.

Now let S be a set of n points on the x-axis. Then $\Theta(S, \kappa)$ is basically the sequence of points, sorted from left to right. The unique path between the leftmost and rightmost point is a 1-spanner path consisting of $n - 1$ edges. Therefore, $\Theta(S, \kappa)$ has spanner diameter $n - 1$, proving that the Θ-graphs may not have low spanner diameter.

Hence, the Θ-graph is good only in the sense that it is sparse and has a small stretch factor. In Sections 4.2 and 4.3, we will show how the Θ-graph can be transformed into spanners of bounded degree and $O(\log n)$ spanner diameter, respectively. To obtain a spanner of low weight, new techniques are needed. These will be dealt with in Chapters 6, 7, 14, and 15.

4.2 A spanner of bounded degree

In this section, we will give an $O(n \log n)$–time algorithm that constructs a t-spanner, for any given constant $t > 1$, in which each vertex has a degree that is bounded by a constant. The basic idea is given below.

> **Basic Idea:** Start with a Θ-graph that is a $\sqrt{t}$-spanner. Direct all the edges in such a way that the outdegree is bounded for every vertex. To take care of vertices with high indegree, replace each "star" subgraph consisting of edges pointing into a vertex by a structure that is a bounded degree "sink spanner." This is done in a way that can increase the stretch factor by a multiplicative factor of $\sqrt{t}$, thus resulting in a bounded degree t-spanner.

To be more precise, we will prove the following result. Let S be a set of n points in the plane, let $t' > 1$ be a constant, and let G be an arbitrary undirected t'-spanner for S. Assume that, in $O(n \log n)$ time, the edges of G can be directed such that each vertex has an *outdegree* that is bounded by a constant. Let t be an arbitrary constant larger than t'. We will then show how to transform G into an undirected t-spanner in which the degree of each vertex is bounded by a constant. This transformation takes $O(n \log n)$ time.

By *directing* the edges of G, we mean the following. We replace each edge $\{p, q\}$ of G by either the directed edge (p, q) or the directed edge (q, p). We remark that this is a purely conceptual notion that is needed in the transformation. In particular, we do not require that a t'-spanner path in G be a directed path in the directed graph.

To give an example, replace in Definition 4.1.1 the edge $\{p, r\}$ of $\Theta(S, \kappa)$ by the directed edge (p, r). Then it is easy to see that in the resulting directed graph, the outdegree of each vertex is less than or equal to $\kappa = 2\pi/\theta$.

Our transformation uses the notion of a sink spanner, which will be introduced in Section 4.2.1. In Section 4.2.2, we will present the transformation itself. We tie it all up in Section 4.2.3.

4.2.1 Sink spanners

Definition 4.2.1 (Sink spanner). *Let S be a set of n points in the plane, let q be a point of S, and let $t > 1$ be a real number. A directed graph having the points of S as its vertices is called a q-sink t-spanner for S, if for every point p of S there is a directed t-spanner path from p to q in this graph.*

We show how to construct a q-sink t-spanner in which (i) each vertex has an indegree that is bounded from above by an integer that depends only on t, (ii) the outdegree of q is zero, and (iii) each other vertex has outdegree one. The construction is similar to that of the Θ-graph.

Let $\kappa \geq 9$ be an integer, and let $\theta = 2\pi/\kappa$. Consider the collection $\mathcal{C}_\kappa$ of cones that was defined in Section 4.1. For each cone C of $\mathcal{C}_\kappa$, let ℓ_C be a fixed ray that emanates from the origin and that is contained in C. As introduced in Section 4.1, we will use the notation C_p to represent the cone C translated so that its apex is at the point p, and $\ell_{C,p}$ to be the ray ℓ_C translated to emanate from point p.

Consider the set S and the point q of S. Let n be the number of points of S. We recursively define a graph $\Theta(S, q, \kappa)$ having the points of S as its vertices. Later, we will see that $\Theta(S, q, \kappa)$ is indeed a q-sink spanner for the set S.

If $n = 1$, then $\Theta(S, q, \kappa)$ is the graph consisting of the single vertex q. Assume that $n \geq 2$. For each $C \in \mathcal{C}_\kappa$, let S_C be the set of all points of $S \setminus \{q\}$ that are contained in the cone C_q. If a subset S_C contains more than $n/2$ points, then we partition it (arbitrarily) into two subsets $S_{C,1}$ and $S_{C,2}$, each of size at most $n/2$. Since there can be at most one subset S_C of size more than $n/2$, we get a partition of $S \setminus \{q\}$ into at most $\kappa + 1$ nonempty subsets, each of size at most $n/2$.

For each nonempty subset S_C or, in case this set contains more than $n/2$ points, for each subset $S_{C,i}$, $i = 1, 2$, let r be the point in this subset whose orthogonal projection onto the ray $\ell_{C,q}$ is closest to q. The graph $\Theta(S, q, \kappa)$ contains

1. the directed edge (r, q), and
2. a recursively defined graph $\Theta(A, r, \kappa)$ for the subset $A := S_C$ (respectively $A := S_{C,i}$).

Lemma 4.2.2. *In the graph* $\Theta(S, q, \kappa)$*, the indegree of each vertex is less than or equal to* $\kappa + 1$*, the outdegree of* q *is zero, while the outdegree of all the other vertices is one. The graph* $\Theta(S, q, \kappa)$ *can be constructed in* $O(\kappa + n \log n \log \kappa)$ *time.*

PROOF The bounds on the outdegree and indegree follow easily from the definition of $\Theta(S, q, \kappa)$. Also, this definition immediately implies a recursive algorithm for constructing $\Theta(S, q, \kappa)$. It takes $O(\kappa)$ time to construct the collection $\mathcal{C}_\kappa$ of cones. Let $T(n)$ denote the time needed by the algorithm to construct the graph $\Theta(S, q, \kappa)$ for a set S of size n. Then $T(1)$ is a constant and for $n \geq 2$, we have

$$T(n) = O(n \log \kappa) + \sum_A T(|A|), \tag{4.2}$$

where A ranges over the (at most $\kappa + 1$) nonempty subsets S_C (resp. $S_{C,i}$). (The $\log \kappa$ term is the time for distributing the points over the κ cones.) Since each subset A has size at most $n/2$, and these subsets partition the set S, this recurrence solves to $T(n) = O(n \log n \log \kappa)$. ∎

It remains to prove that $\Theta(S, q, \kappa)$ is a q-sink t-spanner, for an appropriate value of t. Let p be a point of S. The algorithm that computes a spanner path from p to q is basically the same as algorithm Θ-WALK in Section 4.1.1.

The path from p to q is constructed recursively, in a backward order. We define $q_0 := q$. Let $i \geq 0$, and assume that we have already constructed a directed path $q_i, q_{i-1}, \ldots, q_0$, in $\Theta(S, q, \kappa)$. If $q_i = p$, then we stop the construction. Otherwise, let C be the cone of $\mathcal{C}_\kappa$ such that $p \in C_{q_i}$. The graph $\Theta(S, q, \kappa)$ contains a subgraph $\Theta(A, q_i, \kappa)$, for some subset A of S, in which p is a vertex. (The proof of this claim is left as an exercise; see Exercise 4.13.) This subgraph contains an edge (r, q_i), where

1. r is contained in C_{q_i},
2. the orthogonal projection of r onto the ray ℓ_{C,q_i} is at least as close to q_i as the orthogonal projection of p onto this ray, and
3. p and r are in the same subset S_C (or $S_{C,1}$ resp. $S_{C,2}$).

We define $q_{i+1} := r$; that is, r is the next vertex on our path.

Consider the reversed sequence $q = q_0, q_1, q_2, \ldots$, that is constructed in this way. For each $i \geq 0$, there is a cone C in $\mathcal{C}_\kappa$ such that p and q_{i+1} are both contained in C_{q_i}, and the orthogonal projection of q_{i+1} onto ℓ_{C,q_i} is at least as close to q_i as the orthogonal projection of p onto this ray. Therefore, by Lemma 4.1.4, we have

$$|q_{i+1}p| \leq |q_i p| - (\cos \theta - \sin \theta)|q_i q_{i+1}|.$$

It follows (in exactly the same way as in Section 4.1.1) that there is an index m such that $q_m = p$, and the path $p = q_m, q_{m-1}, \ldots, q_1, q_0 = q$, which is a directed path in $\Theta(S, q, \kappa)$, has length at most $t|pq|$ for $t = 1/(\cos \theta - \sin \theta)$. That is, we have shown that the graph $\Theta(S, q, \kappa)$ is a q-sink t-spanner for this value of t. We have proved the following result.

Theorem 4.2.3. *Let S be a set of n points in the plane, let q be a point of S, let $\kappa \geq 9$ be an integer, and let $\theta = 2\pi/\kappa$ and $t = 1/(\cos \theta - \sin \theta)$. The graph $\Theta(S, q, \kappa)$ is a q-sink t-spanner for S. It can be constructed in $O(\kappa + n \log n \log \kappa)$ time. In $\Theta(S, q, \kappa)$, the indegree of each vertex is less than or equal to $\kappa + 1$, the outdegree of q is 0, and the outdegree of each other vertex is 1.*

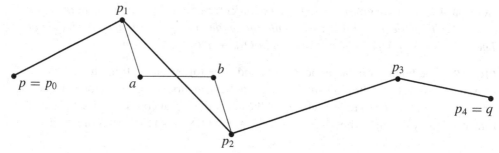

Figure 4.7: G contains the t'-spanner path $p = p_0, p_1, p_2, p_3, p_4 = q$. Edge $\{p_1, p_2\}$ on this path is approximated by the (t/t')-spanner path p_1, a, b, p_2 in G_0.

Remark 4.2.4. There exists a much simpler algorithm than the recursive one described above to construct a spanner path from p to q. Since the graph $\Theta(S, q, \kappa)$ is a tree rooted at q, there is a unique path from p to q. This path is obtained by starting at p and following outgoing edges until the root q has been reached.

4.2.2 The transformation

We are now ready to present the transformation to obtain a bounded degree spanner, but with a possible increase in the stretch factor. Let S be a set of n points in the plane, and let t and t' be real numbers such that $t > t' > 1$. Let G be a t'-spanner for S whose edges can be directed such that each vertex has outdegree at most D, for some integer D. We denote the directed version of G by $\vec{G}$, and the time for computing $\vec{G}$ from G by $T(n)$. We show that by making local changes to $\vec{G}$, we can transform it into a t-spanner for S of bounded degree. We remind the reader once again that the Θ-graph satisfies the above condition; that is, its edges can be directed to make the outdegree of each of its vertices to be bounded by a constant. Hence, as discussed in Section 4.2.3, this transformation is well-suited for Θ-graphs.

Let $\kappa \geq 9$ be an integer such that $1/(\cos\theta - \sin\theta) \leq t/t'$ for $\theta = 2\pi/\kappa$. For each point q of S, we do the following. Let V_q be the set of all points $r \in S$ for which (r, q) is an edge of $\vec{G}$. In the graph $\vec{G}$, we replace all edges (r, q), with $r \in V_q$, by the edges of the q-sink (t/t')-spanner $\Theta(V_q \cup \{q\}, q, \kappa)$.

Let $\vec{G}_0$ be the directed graph that is obtained in this way. We replace each edge (p, q) of $\vec{G}_0$ by the undirected edge $\{p, q\}$, and denote the resulting undirected graph by G_0. We claim that G_0 is a t-spanner for S in which each vertex has bounded degree.

Let us first prove that G_0 is a t-spanner; refer to Figure 4.7. Let p and q be any two points of S. The graph G contains a path

$$Q = (p = p_0, p_1, p_2, \ldots, p_m = q)$$

between p and q of length at most $t'|pq|$. Let i be any integer with $0 \leq i < m$, and consider the edge $\{p_i, p_{i+1}\}$ on this path. Assume that in $\vec{G}$, this edge is directed from p_i to p_{i+1}. (The case when the edge is directed from p_{i+1} to p_i can be handled similarly.) The directed graph $\vec{G}_0$ contains the p_{i+1}-sink (t/t')-spanner $\Theta(V_{p_{i+1}} \cup \{p_{i+1}\}, p_{i+1}, \kappa)$, in which p_i is a vertex. Hence, in the graph G_0 there is a path Q_i between p_i and p_{i+1} of length at most $(t/t')|p_i p_{i+1}|$.

The concatenation of the paths Q_i, $0 \leq i < m$, is a path in G_0 between the points p and q. This path has length at most

$$\sum_{i=0}^{m-1} (t/t')|p_i p_{i+1}|,$$

which is (t/t') times the length of the path Q. This, in turn, is bounded from above by $(t/t')t'|pq| = t|pq|$, completing the proof that G_0 is a t-spanner for S.

To bound the degrees of the vertices in G_0, we first consider the directed graph $\vec{G}_0$. Let p be an arbitrary point of S, and let W_p be the set of all points $q \in S$ for which (p, q) is an edge of $\vec{G}$.

We start by estimating the outdegree of p in $\vec{G}_0$. Let r be any point of S for which (p, r) is an edge of $\vec{G}_0$. There is a point q in S such that (p, r) is an edge of the sink spanner $\Theta(V_q \cup \{q\}, q, \kappa)$. Observe that $q \neq p$. Since p is a vertex of $\Theta(V_q \cup \{q\}, q, \kappa)$, we have $p \in V_q$; that is, (p, q) is an edge of $\vec{G}$. Hence, we have shown that each edge of $\vec{G}_0$ having p as a source is contained in one of the sink spanners $\Theta(V_q \cup \{q\}, q, \kappa)$, $q \in W_p$. Since p has outdegree one in any of these sink spanners, and since W_p contains at most D elements, it follows that the outdegree of p in $\vec{G}_0$ is less than or equal to D.

Next we consider the indegree of p in $\vec{G}_0$. Let r be any point of S for which (r, p) is an edge of $\vec{G}_0$. As above, there is a point q in S such that (r, p) is an edge of $\Theta(V_q \cup \{q\}, q, \kappa)$. Now either $q = p$ or (p, q) is an edge of $\vec{G}$. Hence, each edge of $\vec{G}_0$ having p as a sink is contained in one of the sink spanners $\Theta(V_q \cup \{q\}, q, \kappa)$, $q \in W_p \cup \{p\}$. Since p has indegree at most $\kappa + 1$ in any of these sink spanners, we have shown that the indegree of p in $\vec{G}_0$ is less than or equal to $(D + 1)(\kappa + 1)$.

In the (undirected) t-spanner G_0, the degree of a vertex is less than or equal to the sum of its outdegree and its indegree in $\vec{G}_0$. That is, in G_0, each vertex has a degree that is bounded from above by $D + (D + 1)(\kappa + 1)$.

Finally, let us consider the time needed to construct the t-spanner G_0 from the original t'-spanner G. It takes $O(\kappa)$ time to construct the collection C_κ of cones that are used for the various sink (t/t')-spanners. By our assumption, it takes $T(n)$ time to construct the directed graph $\vec{G}$. Let q be any point of S, and consider the set V_q. By Theorem 4.2.3, we can build the q-sink spanner $\Theta(V_q \cup \{q\}, q, \kappa)$ in $O((|V_q| + 1) \log(|V_q| + 1) \log \kappa)$ time, which is $O(|V_q| \log n \log \kappa)$. Therefore, the time needed to construct G_0 is

$$O\left(\kappa + T(n) + \sum_{q \in S} |V_q| \log n \log \kappa\right).$$

Since each edge in $\vec{G}$ has outdegree at most D, the number of edges of G is less than or equal to Dn. Hence, $\sum_{q \in S} |V_q|$, which exactly counts the number of edges of G, is bounded from above by Dn. This shows that we can construct G_0 from G in $O(\kappa + T(n) + Dn \log n \log \kappa)$ time. We have proved the following result.

Theorem 4.2.5. *Let S be a set of n points in the plane, let t and t' be real numbers with $t > t' > 1$, and let $\kappa \geq 9$ be an integer such that $1/(\cos \theta - \sin \theta) \leq t/t'$, where $\theta = 2\pi/\kappa$. Let G be a t'-spanner for S, whose edges can be directed in $T(n)$ time, such that each vertex has outdegree at most D, for some integer D. In $O(\kappa + T(n) + Dn \log n \log \kappa)$ time, we can transform G into a t-spanner for S in which each vertex has degree at most $D + (D + 1)(\kappa + 1)$.*

> **The transformation:** For each $q \in S$, we replace in the directed version $\vec{G}$ of the spanner G, each "star" subgraph consisting of all edges pointing to q by a q-sink spanner. Since the directed version of each edge e of G is contained in some star subgraph of $\vec{G}$, it follows that e is replaced by a spanner path between the endpoints of e.

4.2.3 Applying the transformation

Let S be a set of n points in the plane, and let $t > 1$ be a real number. We show how Theorem 4.2.5 can be applied to obtain a bounded degree t-spanner for S.

Let $\kappa \geq 9$ be an integer such that $1/(\cos\theta - \sin\theta) \leq \sqrt{t}$, where $\theta = 2\pi/\kappa$. Let G be the graph $\Theta(S, \kappa)$, which is a $\sqrt{t}$-spanner for S; see Theorem 4.1.5. Given the point set S, we can construct this graph in $O(\kappa n \log n)$ time; see Theorem 4.1.10. We saw already at the beginning of Section 4.2 that the edges of G can be directed, in $O(\kappa n)$ time, such that each vertex has outdegree at most κ.

Thus, Theorem 4.2.5, applied with $t' = \sqrt{t}$, $T(n) = O(\kappa n)$, and $D = \kappa$, shows that we can, in $O((\kappa \log \kappa)n \log n)$ time, transform G into a t-spanner for S in which each vertex has degree at most $\kappa + (\kappa + 1)^2$. This proves the following theorem:

Theorem 4.2.6. *Let S be a set of n points in the plane, let $t > 1$ be a real number, and let $\kappa \geq 9$ be an integer such that $1/(\cos\theta - \sin\theta) \leq \sqrt{t}$, where $\theta = 2\pi/\kappa$. In $O((\kappa \log \kappa)n \log n)$ time, we can construct a t-spanner for S in which each vertex has a degree that is less than or equal to $\kappa^2 + 3\kappa + 1$.*

Remark 4.2.7. Let us consider what happens if $t > 1$ and $t \to 1$. If we choose κ as small as possible such that $1/(\cos\theta - \sin\theta) \leq \sqrt{t}$, then we have $\theta \to 0$, $\sqrt{t} \sim 1 + \theta$, $t \sim 1 + 2\theta = 1 + 4\pi/\kappa$, and $\kappa \sim 4\pi/(t - 1)$. Theorem 4.2.6 guarantees the construction of a t-spanner for S, such that the spanner

1. can be constructed in

$$O\left(\frac{\log(1/(t-1))}{t-1} n \log n\right)$$

    time, and

2. the degree of each vertex is $O(1/(t-1)^2)$.

4.3 Generalizing skip lists: A spanner with logarithmic spanner diameter

We now turn to the problem of constructing a spanner whose spanner diameter is "small." We will show that by generalizing *skip lists*, we get a *randomized* algorithm that constructs a sparse spanner whose *expected* spanner diameter is $O(\log n)$. In Section 4.3.1, we review skip lists. As we will see, for any set of n real numbers, this randomized data structure is a sparse 1-spanner whose spanner diameter has an expected value of $O(\log n)$. In Section 4.3.2, we present the generalization to the planar case.

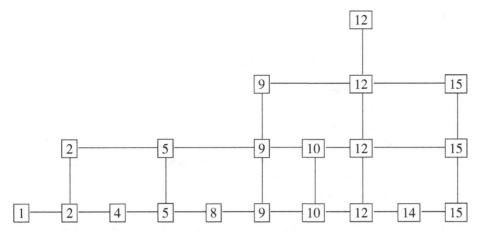

Figure 4.8: A skip list for the set $S = \{1, 2, 4, 5, 8, 9, 10, 12, 14, 15\}$. There are four nonempty subsets S_1, S_2, S_3, and S_4. The value of h is equal to 4.

4.3.1 Skip lists

Let S be a set of n real numbers. We construct a nested sequence of subsets of S, as follows. Initialize by setting $S_1 := S$ and $i := 1$. As long as $S_i \neq \emptyset$, construct a random subset S_{i+1} of S_i, in the following way. For each element of S_i, flip a coin that comes up heads with probability $1/2$ and that is independent of the coin flips for the other elements of S_i. Set S_{i+1} to be the subset of all elements from S_i whose coin flips came up heads. Finally, set $i := i + 1$ and iterate.

Let h be the number of iterations of this construction. Then we obtain the sequence

$$\emptyset = S_{h+1} \subseteq S_h \subseteq S_{h-1} \subseteq S_{h-2} \subseteq \cdots \subseteq S_2 \subseteq S_1 = S$$

of subsets of S, where $S_h \neq \emptyset$.

Definition 4.3.1. Consider the subsets S_i, $1 \leq i \leq h$, of S that are constructed by the above coin flipping process. The *skip list* for S is defined as follows:

1. For each i, with $1 \leq i \leq h$, there is a doubly linked list L_i storing the elements of S_i in sorted order. We say that the elements of S_i are at *level i* of the skip list.

2. For each i, with $1 < i \leq h$, and each $p \in S_i$, the occurrences of p in L_i and L_{i-1} are connected by pointers.

An example of a skip list is given in Figure 4.8.

Observe that the value of h and the sizes of the subsets S_i are random variables. The following lemma, which we state without proof, gives some basic properties of these variables.

Lemma 4.3.2. *Consider the subsets S_i, $1 \leq i \leq h$, produced by the given random process, and let M be the total size of the corresponding skip list.*

1. *The expected value of h is $O(\log n)$.*

2. *There is a positive constant c such that for all sufficiently large real numbers s, we have*

$$\Pr(h \geq s \log n) \leq 1/n^{cs}.$$

3. *The value of M is proportional to $\sum_{i=1}^{h} |S_i|$, and the expected value of this summation is $O(n)$.*

4. *There is a positive constant c' such that for all sufficiently large real numbers s, we have*

$$\Pr(M \geq sn) = e^{-c'sn}.$$

Let p and q be two elements of S with $p < q$, and assume that we want to construct a path in the skip list between p and q. Of course, we can walk along the bottom list L_1. This may lead, however, to a path having up to $n-1$ edges.

Therefore, we do the following. We start at the occurrence of p in L_1, and walk along this list to the right, until we reach our destination q or encounter an element that occurs at level 2. If we reach q, then we are done with the construction. Otherwise, let p_1 be the first element encountered that occurs at level 2. Now we start at the occurrence of q in L_1, and walk along this list to the left, until we reach p_1 or encounter an element that occurs at level 2. If we reach p_1, then we are done; otherwise, let q_1 be the first element encountered that occurs at level 2. Then we "move" with p_1 and q_1 to level 2, and recursively construct a path between p_1 and q_1.

In this way, we construct two paths, one starting at p and extending "to the right," and the other starting at q and extending "to the left." These paths are extended alternately, and the construction stops as soon as the paths meet.

If we use this algorithm to construct a path in the skip list of Figure 4.8 between elements 4 and 14, then we get the following result (j_i denotes the occurrence of element j at level i):

$$4_1, 5_1, 5_2, 9_2, 9_3, 12_3, 12_2, 12_1, 14_1 \tag{4.3}$$

Below we give the *intuition* why the expected number of steps made by our algorithm when it constructs a path between p and q is $O(\log n)$. By Lemma 4.3.2, the expected number of levels in the skip list is $O(\log n)$. Consider any level i, and let p_i and q_i be the elements of L_i such that, at level i, our algorithm starts at p_i (resp. q_i) and walks along L_i to the right (resp. left). What is the expected number of steps made at level i? Consider the subpath at level i that starts at p_i, and let x be an arbitrary element on this subpath. If x is not the last element on this subpath, then x does not occur at level $i+1$. Hence, since every element at level i occurs at level $i+1$ with probability $1/2$, the expected number of elements on this subpath should be bounded by a constant. Similarly, the expected number of elements on the subpath at level i that starts in q_i should be bounded by a constant. Hence, the expected number of steps made by the algorithm at any level of the skip list should be $O(1)$. As a result, the expected number of steps made by the algorithm, when constructing the path between p and q, should be $O(\log n)$. We remark here that this argument does *not* constitute a proof.

Remark 4.3.3. For a set of real numbers, we can also define the skip list by including every second element of the sorted subset S_i in the subset S_{i+1}. This gives a deterministic data structure with the same performance. Using randomization has three advantages. First, it leads to simple update algorithms; that is, elements can be inserted and deleted in a simple and efficient way. Second, for the deterministic version, an adversary can design a set of inserts and deletes that can make later search operations very expensive ($O(n)$). In contrast, the adversary would have to know the results of the coin flips in order to have the same damaging effect on the randomized version of the data structure. Third, it is easy to generalize to the case when the elements are points in the plane. (Observe that for points in the plane, there is no natural notion of "every second" element.)

By "flattening" the vertices of the skip list, we can regard this data structure as a graph G having the elements of S as its vertices. This graph has, expected, $O(n)$ edges, and for any two elements p and q of S, there is a path in G between p and q having length $|pq|$, which is the absolute value of the difference between p and q, and containing an expected number of $O(\log n)$ edges. To illustrate this, consider the path (4.3) in our example skip list. In the corresponding graph G, this becomes the path 4, 5, 9, 12, 14.

Hence, the skip list can be regarded as a 1-spanner for S. (In fact, even the list L_1, the first level list from the data structure is itself a 1-spanner for S.) What can we say about its expected spanner diameter? To answer this question, we have to bound the *expected maximum* number of edges on the shortest[1] 1-spanner path between any pair of elements. We know that for any two fixed elements p and q of S, the expected number of edges on a shortest path between p and q is $O(\log n)$. This does not imply, however, that the expected spanner diameter is $O(\log n)$. The reason is that, in general, the expected value of the maximum of random variables is *not* equal to the maximum of the expected values of these variables. (See also Exercise 4.16.)

Fortunately, it can be shown that for any two fixed elements p and q of S, the number $N(p, q)$ of edges on the shortest 1-spanner path between p and q is $O(\log n)$, *with high probability*. That is, there exists a positive constant c such that for all sufficiently large real numbers s, we have

$$\Pr(N(p, q) \geq s \log n) \leq 1/n^{cs}.$$

Since the spanner diameter N_0 is equal to $\max_{p,q \in S} N(p, q)$, it follows that

$$\Pr(N_0 \geq s \log n) \leq \binom{n}{2} \cdot 1/n^{cs} \leq n^{2-cs}.$$

From this, it can be shown that the expected spanner diameter of the skip list is $O(\log n)$. In fact, the spanner diameter is $O(\log n)$ with high probability. More details about these claims will be given in Section 4.3.3. We summarize our results.

Theorem 4.3.4. *Let S be a set of n real numbers. The skip list of S can be regarded as a graph which is a 1-spanner for S. With high probability, the number of edges of this graph is $O(n)$ and its spanner diameter is $O(\log n)$.*

4.3.2 The skip list spanner

The generalization of the results of Section 4.3.1 to the two-dimensional case should be clear. Let S be a set of n points in the plane. We use the same random process as in Section 4.3.1, to obtain a nested sequence

$$\emptyset = S_{h+1} \subseteq S_h \subseteq S_{h-1} \subseteq S_{h-2} \subseteq \cdots \subseteq S_2 \subseteq S_1 = S$$

of subsets of S, where $S_h \neq \emptyset$. As before, every element of S_i has a probability of 1/2 of being incuded in S_{i+1}.

---

[1] With respect to the number of edges.

Definition 4.3.5. Let $\kappa \geq 2$ be an integer, and consider the subsets S_i, $1 \leq i \leq h$, that are constructed by the coin flipping process. The *skip list spanner* $SLS(S, \kappa)$ for S is defined as follows:

1. For each i with $1 \leq i \leq h$, the points of S_i are stored in the graph $\Theta(S_i, \kappa)$; see Definition 4.1.1. We say that the points of S_i are at *level i* of the skip list spanner.

2. For each i with $1 < i \leq h$ and each $p \in S_i$, the occurrences of p at level i and level $i - 1$ are connected by pointers.

If all points of S lie on a line, then each graph $\Theta(S_i, \kappa)$ is basically a list containing the points of S_i in sorted order, in which case, the skip list spanner is a standard skip list.

We regard $SLS(S, \kappa)$ as a graph with vertex set S and edge set the union of the edge sets of the graphs $\Theta(S_i, \kappa)$, $1 \leq i \leq h$. The pointers that connect the Θ-graphs of consecutive levels are not considered to be edges of the graph.

Lemma 4.3.6. *Let $\kappa \geq 9$ be an integer, let $\theta = 2\pi/\kappa$, and let S be a set of n points in the plane. The skip list spanner $SLS(S, \kappa)$ is a t-spanner for S with $t = 1/(\cos\theta - \sin\theta)$. With high probability, this graph contains $O(\kappa n)$ edges and can be constructed in $O(\kappa n \log n)$ time.*

PROOF The skip list spanner contains $\Theta(S, \kappa)$, which, by Theorem 4.1.5, is a t-spanner. Therefore, $SLS(S, \kappa)$ is also a t-spanner. By Theorem 4.1.5, the number of edges of $SLS(S, \kappa)$ is at most $\sum_{i=1}^{h} \kappa|S_i|$. Lemma 4.3.2 implies that, with high probability, the value of this summation is $O(\kappa n)$. The bound on the construction time follows in a similar way. ∎

Hence, the skip list spanner is a t-spanner. In order to construct a t-spanner path between two points p and q of S that contains few edges, we use the following algorithm. (Recall our notation C_κ for the collection of κ cones of angle $\theta = 2\pi/\kappa$, that have their apex at the origin, and that partition the plane; see Section 4.1.)

Just as with the one-dimensional case, we grow two partial paths, one starting from p, referred to as the p-path, and one starting from q, referred to as the q-path. When the paths intersect, the process stops.

We start at the occurrence of p at level 1 of the skip list spanner and construct a path in the graph $\Theta(S_1, \kappa)$ from p toward q. Suppose that we have already constructed a path from p to x. If $x = q$, then we have reached our destination, and the construction stops. If $x \neq q$, then we check if x occurs at level 2. If this is not the case, then we extend the path as follows. Let C be the cone of C_κ such that $q \in C_x$. Let x' be the point of $C_x \cap S_1$ such that $\{x, x'\}$ is an edge of $\Theta(S_1, \kappa)$. Then x' is the next point on the path from p toward q, i.e., we set $x := x'$. We keep on extending this path until $x = q$ or the point x occurs at level 2 of the skip list spanner.

Assume that the path has reached a point x that occurs at level 2. Then we start constructing a path in $\Theta(S_1, \kappa)$ from q toward x. Suppose that we have already constructed a path from q to y. We stop extending this path if y is equal to one of the points on the path from p to x, or y occurs at level 2. Let us first assume that y is equal to the point, say, p' on the path from p to x. Then we return the path in $\Theta(S_1, \kappa)$ from p to p', followed by the reverse of the path in $\Theta(S_1, \kappa)$ from q to p'. In this case, the construction stops. Otherwise, y occurs at level 2, and we move with x and y to the second level of the skip list spanner and use the same algorithm to compute a path between x and y. The formal algorithm is given below.

Algorithm *SLS*-WALK(p, q)

Comment: This algorithm takes as input two points p and q in S, and returns a t-spanner path between p and q in the skip list spanner $SLS(S, \kappa)$.

$p_0 := p; q_0 := q; a := 0; b := 0; r := 0; s := 0; i := 1;$
$(* \ p = p_0, p_1, \ldots, p_r, \ldots, p_a$ and $q = q_0, q_1, \ldots, q_s, \ldots, q_b$ are
$\quad$ paths in $SLS(S, \kappa), r = \min\{j : p_j \in S_i\}, s = \min\{j : q_j \in S_i\},$
$\quad$ and $p_r, p_{r+1}, \ldots, p_a, q_s, q_{s+1}, \ldots, q_b \in S_i \ *)$
stop := *false*;
while *stop* = *false*
do while $p_a \neq q_b$ and $p_a \notin S_{i+1}$
$\quad$ **do** $C :=$ cone of $\mathcal{C}_\kappa$ such that $q_b \in C_{p_a}$;
$\qquad p_{a+1} :=$ point of $C_{p_a} \cap S_i$ such that $\{p_a, p_{a+1}\}$ is
$\qquad\qquad$ an edge of $\Theta(S_i, \kappa)$;
$\qquad a := a + 1$
endwhile;
$(* \ p_a = q_b$ or $p_a \in S_{i+1} \ *)$
while $q_b \notin \{p_r, p_{r+1}, \ldots, p_a\}$ and $q_b \notin S_{i+1}$
do $C :=$ cone of $\mathcal{C}_\kappa$ such that $p_a \in C_{q_b}$;
$\quad q_{b+1} :=$ point of $C_{q_b} \cap S_i$ such that $\{q_b, q_{b+1}\}$ is
$\qquad$ an edge of $\Theta(S_i, \kappa)$;
$\quad b := b + 1$
endwhile;
$(* \ q_b \in \{p_r, p_{r+1}, \ldots, p_a\}$ or both p_a and q_b occur in $S_{i+1} \ *)$
if $q_b \in \{p_r, p_{r+1}, \ldots, p_a\}$
then $\ell :=$ index such that $q_b = p_\ell$;
$\qquad$ return the path $p = p_0, p_1, \ldots, p_\ell, q_{b-1}, q_{b-2}, \ldots, q_0 = q$;
$\qquad$ *stop* := *true*
else $i := i + 1; r := a; s := b$
endif
endwhile

We first prove the correctness of this algorithm. The idea of the proof is the same as in Section 4.1.1.

Lemma 4.3.7. *Let $\kappa \geq 9$ be an integer, and let $\theta = 2\pi/\kappa$. For any two points p and q of S, algorithm SLS-WALK(p, q) constructs a t-spanner path in $SLS(S, \kappa)$ between p and q, for $t = 1/(\cos\theta - \sin\theta)$.*

PROOF In this proof, we use the notation of algorithm *SLS*-WALK. Consider the two partial paths $p = p_0, p_1, p_2, \ldots$ and $q = q_0, q_1, q_2, \ldots$ that are constructed by the algorithm. As mentioned above, these are referred to as the p-path and q-path, respectively. First observe that if $p_a \neq q_b$, $p_a \notin S_{i+1}$, and the two paths do not intersect, then the p-path is extended by a point $p_{a+1} \in S_i$. A similar remark holds for the q-path.

The proof of the lemma is by induction on the number of levels of the skip list spanner. To prove the base case, assume that $SLS(S, \kappa)$ consists of only one level. Consider what happens during the first iteration of the outer while-loop. In the first inner while-loop, a path $p = p_0, p_1, p_2, \ldots$ is constructed. This inner while-loop terminates if and only if the last point on this path is equal to q. Let $a \geq 0$ and consider the points p_a and p_{a+1}. Then $p_a \neq q$. Let C be the cone such that $q \in C_{p_a}$, and consider the ray ℓ_C that emanates from the origin and that is contained in C; see Section 4.1. It follows from the algorithm and the definition of the graph $\Theta(S_1, \kappa)$ that (i) $\{p_a, p_{a+1}\}$ is an edge of the skip list spanner, (ii) $p_{a+1} \in C_{p_a}$, and (iii) the orthogonal projection of p_{a+1} onto the ray ℓ_{C,p_a} is at least as close to p_a as the orthogonal projection of q onto ℓ_{C,p_a}. Therefore, by Lemma 4.1.4, we have

$$|p_{a+1}q| \leq |p_a q| - (\cos\theta - \sin\theta)|p_a p_{a+1}| < |p_a q|. \tag{4.4}$$

This proves that during each iteration of the first inner while-loop, the Euclidean distance between p_a and q becomes strictly smaller. As a result, this inner while-loop terminates. Let z be the number of iterations made. Then the algorithm has constructed a path $p = p_0, p_1, p_2, \ldots, p_z = q$. The second inner while-loop is not executed at all since the test fails right at the start. Since the points $p_0, p_1, \ldots, p_z$ are pairwise distinct, the variable ℓ is assigned the value z. Hence, the algorithm returns the path $p = p_0, p_1, p_2, \ldots, p_z = q$ and terminates. The length of this path is equal to

$$\sum_{a=0}^{z-1} |p_a p_{a+1}| \leq t \sum_{a=0}^{z-1} (|p_a q| - |p_{a+1} q|)$$
$$= t(|p_0 q| - |p_z q|)$$
$$= t|pq|.$$

Hence, the algorithm has constructed a t-spanner path between p and q. This proves the base case of the induction.

Let $h > 1$, and consider a skip list spanner consisting of h levels. Also, assume the lemma holds for all skip list spanners with less than h levels.

Consider again the first iteration of the outer while-loop. During the first inner while-loop, a path $p = p_0, p_1, p_2, \ldots, p_z$ is constructed such that $p_z = q$ or $p_z \in S_2$. Also, (4.4) holds for all a, $0 \leq a \leq z - 1$.

If $p_z = q$, then the path $p = p_0, p_1, p_2, \ldots, p_z$ is returned and the algorithm terminates. In exactly the same way as above, it follows that this path is a t-spanner path between p and q.

Assume that $p_z \neq q$. Then $p_z \in S_2$. Observe that the points $p_0, p_1, \ldots, p_z$ are pairwise distinct. During the second inner while-loop, a path $q = q_0, q_1, q_2, \ldots$ is constructed. Using Lemma 4.1.4, it follows that

$$|q_{b+1} p_z| \leq |q_b p_z| - (\cos\theta - \sin\theta)|q_b q_{b+1}| < |q_b p_z| \tag{4.5}$$

for all b such that q_b and q_{b+1} are defined. The second inner while-loop terminates if and only if the last point on the q-path is (i) equal to one of the p_i's or (ii) occurs at level 2 of the skip list spanner. Since during each iteration, the Euclidean distance between q_b and p_z becomes strictly smaller, this while-loop terminates. Let y be the number of iterations made. Then the algorithm has constructed a path $q = q_0, q_1, q_2, \ldots, q_y$. It follows from (4.5) that the points on this path are pairwise distinct. The termination condition implies that all points $p_0, p_1, \ldots, p_z, q_0, q_1, \ldots, q_{y-1}$ are pairwise distinct. There are two possible cases.

The first case is when $q_y \in \{p_0, p_1, \ldots, p_z\}$. Let ℓ be such that $q_y = p_\ell$. Then the algorithm returns the path $p = p_0, p_1, \ldots, p_\ell = q_y, q_{y-1}, \ldots, q_0 = q$, having length

$$\sum_{a=0}^{\ell-1} |p_a p_{a+1}| + \sum_{b=0}^{y-1} |q_b q_{b+1}|$$

$$\leq \sum_{a=0}^{z-1} |p_a p_{a+1}| + \sum_{b=0}^{y-1} |q_b q_{b+1}|$$

$$\leq t \sum_{a=0}^{z-1} (|p_a q| - |p_{a+1} q|) + t \sum_{b=0}^{y-1} (|q_b p_z| - |q_{b+1} p_z|)$$

$$= t(|p_0 q| - |p_z q| + |q_0 p_z| - |q_y p_z|)$$

$$= t(|pq| - |q_y p_z|) \leq t|pq|.$$

Hence, in this case the algorithm has constructed a t-spanner path between p and q.

The second case is when $q_y \notin \{p_0, p_1, \ldots, p_z\}$. Now, $q_y \in S_2$ and the algorithm moves to level 2 of the skip list spanner. The rest of the algorithm "takes place" at levels $2, \ldots, h$. These levels constitute a skip list spanner $SLS(S_2, \kappa)$ consisting of $h - 1$ levels. Therefore, by the induction hypothesis, a t-spanner path between p_z and q_y is constructed during the rest of the algorithm. At termination, the algorithm returns the concatenation of the path $p_0, p_1, \ldots, p_z$, the t-spanner path between p_z and q_y, and the path $q_y, q_{y-1}, \ldots, q_0$. The length of this path is bounded from above by

$$\sum_{a=0}^{z-1} |p_a p_{a+1}| + t|p_z q_y| + \sum_{b=0}^{y-1} |q_b q_{b+1}|$$

$$\leq t \sum_{a=0}^{z-1} (|p_a q| - |p_{a+1} q|) + t|p_z q_y| + t \sum_{b=0}^{y-1} (|q_b p_z| - |q_{b+1} p_z|)$$

$$= t(|p_0 q| - |p_z q| + |p_z q_y| + |q_0 p_z| - |q_y p_z|)$$

$$= t|pq|.$$

Hence, in this case too, the algorithm has constructed a t-spanner path between p and q. This completes the proof. ∎

Remark 4.3.8. Consider the t-spanner path $p = p_0, p_1, \ldots, p_\ell = q_b, q_{b-1}, \ldots, q_0 = q$ that is returned by algorithm SLS-WALK(p, q). Let i be any integer such that $1 \leq i \leq h$. Consider the points that are added to the p-path and the q-path during the iteration of the outer while-loop that "takes place" at level i of the skip list spanner. It follows from the proof of Lemma 4.3.7 that these points are pairwise distinct. This property will be used later in the analysis of the expected spanner diameter.

Remark 4.3.9. In the skip list spanner $SLS(S, \kappa)$, a t-spanner path is obtained by concatenating t-spanner paths in Θ-graphs for different point sets. At first sight, one may think that a skip list spanner can be based on any t-spanner. This is, however, not the case. The proof that the path constructed by algorithm SLS-WALK is a t-spanner path heavily depends on the properties of the Θ-graph, and, more specifically, on Lemma 4.1.4. There exist t-spanners that do *not* result in a t-spanner when they are used for constructing the skip list spanner. The proof of this claim is left as an exercise (see Exercise 4.15).

4.3.3 Bounding the spanner diameter of the skip list spanner

In this section, we analyze the expected behavior of algorithm SLS-WALK. That is, we consider two points p and q, and estimate the expected number of edges on the t-spanner path between p and q that is constructed by algorithm SLS-WALK(p, q).

Let N denote the number of edges on the t-spanner path between p and q that is constructed by algorithm SLS-WALK(p, q). Observe that N is a random variable; its value depends on the coin flips that determine the levels of the skip list spanner. We will prove that the expected value of N is $O(\log n)$. In fact, $N = O(\log n)$ with high probability.

Roughly speaking, vertices in Θ-graphs are connected to their closest neighbors in each of the cones. Intuitively, edges in Θ-graphs at higher levels are expected to have greater lengths on the average than the ones at lower levels. This is because every successive level is expected to have about half as many vertices as that in the previous level. Consequently, the nearest neighbor is also expected to be farther away in each cone. Therefore, to decrease the number of edges on a path, it is advantageous to do the traversal at a higher level whenever possible.

Consider the paths $p = p_0, p_1, p_2, \ldots$ and $q = q_0, q_1, q_2, \ldots$ that are constructed by algorithm SLS-WALK(p, q). We will again refer to these as the p-path and q-path, respectively. Let i, $1 \leq i \leq h$, be fixed. We estimate the expected number of points that are added to these two paths at level i of the skip list spanner.

Intuitively, the expected number of points added at level i is bounded by a constant: During the first inner while-loop, the p-path is extended until (i) it meets the q-path, or (ii) a point has been reached that occurs at level $i + 1$. Since each point of S_i occurs at level $i + 1$ with probability $1/2$, we expect that – at level i – at most a constant number of points are added to the p-path. During the second inner while-loop, the q-path is extended. By a similar argument, we expect that – at level i – at most a constant number of points are added to this path.

To make this rigorous, we have to show that each point added to one of these paths *indeed occurs at level $i + 1$ with probability $1/2$*. Put it differently, we have to convince ourselves of the following fact: It is *not* the case that the coin flips that are used to build the skip list spanner cause algorithm SLS-WALK(p, q) to visit points at level i for which it is likely (i.e., with probability more than $1/2$) that they do not occur at level $i + 1$. In the rest of this section, we will give a rigorous proof of this fact.

Analyzing one level of the skip list spanner

Our proof will use *conditional probabilities*. Recall that we have fixed level i of the skip list spanner. The subsets of S that determine the first i levels of the skip list spanner depend on coin flips. Let us fix subsets

$$S_i \subseteq S_{i-1} \subseteq \cdots \subseteq S_2 \subseteq S_1 = S.$$

We will analyze the expected number of points added to the p- and q-paths at level i, given that the subsets $S_1, S_2, \ldots, S_i$ were produced by the coin flipping process. As we see later, our upper bound on this expectation does not depend on these subsets.

Let r and s be the smallest indices such that $p_r \in S_i$ and $q_s \in S_i$, respectively. Observe that r and s do not depend on any coin flips, because we have fixed p, q, and $S_1, \ldots, S_i$.

Assume – for the *sake of analysis* only – that we have not yet flipped our coin for determining the set S_{i+1}. Consider the path $p'_r = p_r, p'_{r+1}, p'_{r+2}, \ldots, p'_m = q_s$ that our algorithm *would have* constructed if all points of S_i did not occur at level $i + 1$. (It follows from the proof of Lemma 4.3.7 that the algorithm indeed would have constructed a path between p_r and q_s. Moreover, the points on this path are pairwise distinct.) Now let z be the number of points that are added – at level i – to the p-path by the *actual* algorithm. Observe that z is a random variable.

Let ℓ be an integer with $0 \leq \ell \leq m - r$, and assume that $z = \ell$. It is easy to see that $p'_r = p_r, p'_{r+1} = p_{r+1}, \ldots, p'_{r+\ell} = p_{r+\ell}$. It follows from the actual algorithm that $p'_a \notin S_{i+1}$ for all $a, r \leq a \leq r + \ell - 1$. Therefore,

$$\Pr(z = \ell) \leq \Pr\left(\bigwedge_{a=r}^{r+\ell-1} (p'_a \notin S_{i+1})\right).$$

Since the path $p'_r, p'_{r+1}, \ldots, p'_m$ is completely determined by the points p and q, and by the sets $S_1, \ldots, S_i$, each of the points on this path is contained in S_{i+1} with probability $1/2$. Therefore, using the fact that all coin flips are independent, it follows that

$$\Pr(z = \ell) \leq \prod_{a=r}^{r+\ell-1} \Pr(p'_a \notin S_{i+1}) = (1/2)^\ell.$$

That is, the random variable z has a geometric distribution with parameter $1/2$. This is not quite true: z is bounded from above by a random variable z' having a geometric distribution with parameter $1/2$.

Again for the *sake of analysis* only, we consider the following experiment. Assume that we have not yet flipped our coin for determining the set S_{i+1}. Now we flip the coin for the points $p'_r, p'_{r+1}, \ldots, p'_m$, in this order, stopping (i) the first time we obtain heads, or (ii) after having obtained $m - r$ times tails. The number of times we obtain tails has the same distribution as the random variable z above.

Let $\ell, 0 \leq \ell \leq m - r$, be fixed and assume that $z = \ell$. If $\ell = m - r$, then the p-path constructed by the *actual* algorithm has reached point q_s and the algorithm terminates. So assume that $\ell < m - r$. Then, at this moment, we know that (i) $p'_r, p'_{r+1}, \ldots, p'_{r+\ell-1}$ do not occur at level $i + 1$, (ii) $p'_{r+\ell}$ occurs at level $i + 1$, and (iii) for all points of $S'_i :=$ $S_i \setminus \{p'_r, p'_{r+1}, \ldots, p'_{r+\ell}\}$ we have not yet flipped the coin. Let $q'_s = q_s, q'_{s+1}, q'_{s+2}, \ldots$ be the path that *would have been* constructed during the second inner while-loop if none of the points of S'_i occurred at level $i + 1$. Let y be the number of points of S_i that are added to the q-path – at level i – by the *actual* algorithm.

Let $u \geq 0$ and assume that $y = u$. Then, $q'_s = q_s, q'_{s+1} = q_{s+1}, \ldots, q'_{s+u} = q_{s+u}$. By Remark 4.3.8, all points $p'_r, p'_{r+1}, \ldots, p'_{r+\ell}, q'_s, q'_{s+1}, \ldots, q'_{s+u-1}$ are pairwise distinct. In particular, $q'_b \in S'_i$ for all $b, s \leq b \leq s + u - 1$. As a result, in the actual skip list spanner, each point q'_b, with $s \leq b \leq s + u - 1$, occurs at level $i + 1$, independently, with probability $1/2$. Since $q'_b \notin S_{i+1}$ for all $b, s \leq b \leq s + u - 1$, it follows that

$$\Pr(y = u) \leq \Pr\left(\bigwedge_{b=s}^{s+u-1} (q'_b \notin S_{i+1})\right) = \prod_{b=s}^{s+u-1} \Pr(q'_b \notin S_{i+1}) = (1/2)^u.$$

What have we proved? Conditional on the fixed subsets $S_1, S_2, \ldots, S_i$ and a fixed value of the random variable z, the random variable y is bounded from above by a random variable y' having a geometric distribution with parameter $1/2$. Since the distribution of y' does not depend on z, the random variable y' also has a geometric distribution with parameter $1/2$, conditional on $S_1, \ldots, S_i$ only.

Altogether, conditional on fixed subsets $S_1, S_2, \ldots, S_i$, the random variables z and y that count the number of points that are added – by the actual algorithm at level i – to the

p- and q-paths are bounded by random variables z' and y', respectively, both of which have a geometric distribution with parameter $1/2$. Since the distributions of z' and y' do not depend on the subsets $S_1, \ldots, S_i$, this statement holds unconditionally as well.

Completing the proof

Now we can analyze the expected behavior of algorithm SLS-$\text{WALK}(p, q)$ in exactly the same way as for standard skip lists. Recall that the value of the random variable N is equal to the number of edges on the t-spanner path that is computed by algorithm SLS-$\text{WALK}(p, q)$.

For any i, $1 \leq i \leq h$, let z_i and y_i be the random variables whose values are equal to the number of edges that are added, at level i, to the p-path and q-path, respectively. Then $N = \sum_{i=1}^{h}(z_i + y_i)$. We have seen above that each of the random variables z_i and y_i, $1 \leq i \leq h$, is bounded from above by a random variable z_i' and y_i', respectively, that is distributed according to a geometric distribution with parameter $1/2$. The $2h$ random variables z_i' and y_i' are mutually independent. (Observe that h itself is also a random variable.) Using Chernoff bounds and the fact that $h = O(\log n)$ with high probability, it can be shown that $N = O(\log n)$ with high probability.

At this moment, we know that for any two fixed points p and q of S, algorithm SLS-$\text{WALK}(p, q)$ constructs a t-spanner path between p and q that contains $O(\log n)$ edges with high probability. What does this imply for the spanner diameter of the skip list spanner? To answer this question, let $N(p, q)$ be the random variable whose value is equal to the number of edges on the t-spanner path that is computed by algorithm SLS-$\text{WALK}(p, q)$. Then $N(p, q) = O(\log n)$ with high probability, and we are interested in the expected value of the random variable $N_0 := \max_{p,q \in S} N(p, q)$.

Using Chernoff bounds, it can be shown that there is a positive constant c such that for any two points p and q of S, and for any sufficiently large real number s, we have

$$\Pr(N(p, q) \geq s \log n) \leq n^{-cs}.$$

If the value of N_0 is greater than or equal to $s \log n$, then there are two distinct points p and q in S such that $N(p, q) \geq s \log n$. Since the number of such pairs is $\binom{n}{2} \leq n^2$, it follows that for sufficiently large values of s,

$$\Pr(N_0 \geq s \log n) \leq n^2 \cdot n^{-cs} \leq n^{-cs/2}.$$

This proves that, with high probability, the spanner diameter of the skip list spanner is $O(\log n)$. In particular, the expected spanner diameter is $O(\log n)$.

The next theorem summarizes the results of Section 4.3.

Theorem 4.3.10. *Let $\kappa \geq 9$ be an integer, let $\theta = 2\pi/\kappa$, and let S be a set of n points in the plane. Then the following is true:*

1. *The skip list spanner $SLS(S, \kappa)$ is a t-spanner for $t = 1/(\cos\theta - \sin\theta)$. With high probability, it contains $O(\kappa n)$ edges.*

2. *The skip list spanner can be constructed in $O(\kappa n \log n)$ time, with high probability.*

3. *With high probability, the spanner diameter of the skip list spanner is $O(\log n)$.*

4. *All these bounds are with respect to the coin flips that are used to build the skip list spanner.*

> **The skip list spanner:** Construct a nested sequence S_i, $i \geq 1$, of subsets of S, where $S_1 = S$ and S_{i+1} is a random subset of S_i for $i \geq 1$. Construct a Θ-graph for each S_i. The expected number of levels is $O(\log n)$.
>
> When computing a spanner path between p and q, use a two-way algorithm that computes two paths starting at p and q, respectively. Extend these paths alternately, always trying to move up one level in the skip list spanner. The randomized construction of the subsets implies that the expected number of points added to the paths at any level is bounded by a constant. Thus the spanner path between any pair of points is expected to have $O(\log n)$ edges.

The above theorem shows that there is an efficient randomized algorithm for constructing a sparse t-spanner with *expected* spanner diameter $O(\log n)$. In particular, it implies that for any set S of n points in the plane and any real constant $t > 1$, there *exists* a t-spanner for S having $O(n)$ edges and $O(\log n)$ spanner diameter.

Exercises

4.1. What can you prove about the stretch factor of $\Theta(S, \kappa)$ if $\kappa \leq 8$? In particular, is $\Theta(S, \kappa)$ connected for such values of κ?

4.2. Algorithm Θ-WALK(p, q) in Section 4.1.1 computes a t-spanner path in the graph $\Theta(S, \kappa)$ between the points p and q. Is this path necessarily the shortest path in $\Theta(S, \kappa)$ between p and q?

4.3. Use Lemma 4.1.4 to prove that in a minimum spanning tree of a set of points in the plane, each point has degree at most eight. Use a direct geometric argument to prove that each point has in fact degree at most six.

4.4. In Section 4.1, we chose for every cone $C \in \mathcal{C}_\kappa$, an arbitrary ray ℓ_C emanating from the origin and that is contained in C. Now let ℓ_C be the bisector of C. Prove that the second inequality in Lemma 4.1.4 can be improved as follows:

$$|rq| \leq |pq| - (1 - 2\sin(\theta/2))|pr|.$$

Prove that the graph $\Theta(S, \kappa)$ defined by using these bisectors is a t-spanner for $t = 1/(1 - 2\sin(\theta/2))$. This result is marginally better than that of Theorem 4.1.5. For large values of κ, however, we have $1/(\cos\theta - \sin\theta) \sim 1 + \theta$, and $1/(1 - 2\sin(\theta/2)) \sim 1 + \theta$.

4.5. Consider the geographic neighborhood graph that was defined in Remark 4.1.2. Prove that for a sufficiently small cone angle θ, this graph is a t-spanner for $t = 1/(\cos\theta - \sin\theta)$. Prove that for a sufficiently small cone angle θ, this graph contains the minimum spanning tree of the point set.

4.6. We call a Euclidean graph $G = (S, E)$ a *strong t-spanner* for the point set S, if for any two points p and q of S, there exists a t-spanner path between p and q in G, all of whose edges have length at most $|pq|$. Consider the geographic neighborhood graph on a set S of n points in the plane (see Remark 4.1.2), and let $t = 1/(\cos\theta - \sin\theta)$. Prove that this graph is a strong t-spanner for S.

4.7. Let S be a set of n points in the plane, let $E = \{\{p, q\} : p \in S, q \in S, 0 < |pq| \leq 1\}$, and let $U = (S, E)$. The graph U is called the *unit disk graph* of S. Let G be the graph consisting of all edges in the geographic neighborhood graph of S (see Remark 4.1.2) having length at most 1. Prove that G is a t-spanner of U, for $t = 1/(\cos\theta - \sin\theta)$. That is, prove that for any two points p and q of S, the graph G contains a path between p and q, whose length is less than or equal to t times the length of a shortest path between p and q in U. (*Hint*: Use Exercise 4.6.)

4.8. Let S be a set of n points in the plane, and let $t > 1$ be a real number. Prove that there exists a t-spanner of the unit disk graph U of S, in which the degree of every vertex is bounded by a function that depends only on t. (Refer to Exercise 4.7 for the definition of U.)

4.9. Let S be a set of n points in the plane. In Exercise 4.7, we defined the unit disk graph U of S. Observe that U can have up to $\binom{n}{2}$ edges. Design an algorithm that computes the connected components of U in $O(n \log n)$ time. Prove that the time complexity of computing the connected components of U is $\Omega(n \log n)$ in the algebraic computation-tree model.

4.10. Prove that the data structure of Lemma 4.1.9 can be built in $O(n \log n)$ time. Give the details of the insertion and deletion algorithms for this data structure. In particular, explain how the variables z_u can be updated in $O(\log n)$ time during the insertion or deletion of a point.

4.11. Algorithm BUILDΘGRAPH(S, C), as presented in Section 4.1.2, computes the set of all edges of $\Theta(S, \kappa)$ corresponding to the cone C, by performing only the operations MINABOVE and INSERT in the data structure of Lemma 4.1.9. In other words, the operation DELETE is not used by this algorithm. Design a variant of algorithm BUILDΘGRAPH(S, C), which returns the same set of edges, and which performs, besides building the data structure from scratch for a given set of points, only the operations MINABOVE and DELETE in the data structure. Show that the running time of the new algorithm is still $O(n \log n)$.

4.12. Prove that the solution $T(n)$ of the recurrence given by (4.2) is $O(n \log n \log \kappa)$.

4.13. Consider the algorithm for constructing a spanner path from p to q that was given after the proof of Lemma 4.2.2. Prove that $\Theta(S, q, \kappa)$ indeed contains a subgraph $\Theta(A, q_i, \kappa)$, for some subset A of S, in which p is a vertex.

4.14. Prove that the sink spanner $\Theta(S, q, \kappa)$ of Section 4.2.1 is a tree.

4.15. Argue why the skip list spanner cannot be based on an arbitrary spanner; see Remark 4.3.9.

4.16. Consider a skip list for a set S of n real numbers. For any $p \in S$, let h_p be the random variable whose value is equal to the number of levels of the skip list at which p occurs. Prove that the expected value $\mathbb{E}(h_p)$ of h_p is equal to 2. Prove that $\mathbb{E}(\max_{p \in S} h_p) = \Theta(\log n)$.

4.17. Let S be a set of n points in the plane, let $\kappa \geq 9$ be an integer, and let $\theta = 2\pi/\kappa$ and $t = 1/(\cos \theta - \sin \theta)$. Let $\sigma = (p_1, p_2, \ldots, p_n)$ be an arbitrary permutation of the points of S. The *ordered Θ-graph* with respect to σ, denoted by $\Theta(S, \kappa, \sigma)$, is defined as follows:

- The vertices of $\Theta(S, \kappa, \sigma)$ are the points of S.
- For each i with $1 \leq i \leq n$ and for each cone C of C_κ, such that the translated cone C_{p_i} contains one or more points of $\{p_1, p_2, \ldots, p_{i-1}\}$, the graph $\Theta(S, \kappa, \sigma)$ contains one edge $\{p_i, p_j\}$, where p_j is a point in $C_{p_i} \cap \{p_1, p_2, \ldots, p_{i-1}\}$ whose orthogonal projection onto ℓ_{C, p_i} is closest to p_i.

(1) Prove that for every permutation σ of the points of S, the graph $\Theta(S, \kappa, \sigma)$ is a t-spanner for S.

(2) Design an algorithm that computes the graph $\Theta(S, \kappa, \sigma)$ in $O(\kappa n \log n)$ time.

(3) Let σ be a *random* permutation of S. Prove that the expected spanner diameter of $\Theta(S, \kappa, \sigma)$ is $O(\log n)$.

(4) Give an example of a point set S that contains a point p, such that the following is true: For a *random* permutation σ of S, the expected degree of p in $\Theta(S, \kappa, \sigma)$ is linear in n.

(5) Prove that for every point set S, there exists a permutation σ of S such that the degree of every vertex in $\Theta(S, \kappa, \sigma)$ is less than or equal to $\kappa(1 + \sum_{i=1}^{n-1} 1/i) = O(\kappa \log n)$. (It is not known if a permutation σ exists for which the degree of every vertex is bounded by a function of κ only. Also, it is not known if a permutation σ exists for which $\Theta(S, \kappa, \sigma)$ has both "small" degree and spanner diameter $O(\log n)$.)

Bibliographic notes

The Θ-graph was discovered independently by Clarkson [1987] and Keil [1988]; see also Keil and Gutwin [1992]. In fact, Clarkson defined these graphs for points in two- and three-dimensional spaces, whereas Keil considered only the two-dimensional case. Althöfer et al. [1993] and Ruppert and Seidel [1991] defined the Θ-graph for arbitrary dimensions. See also Arya, Mount, and Smid [1994] and Arya, Mount, and Smid [1999]. A solution to Exercise 4.4 can be found in Ruppert and Seidel [1991].

Figures 4.2 and 4.3 are from an applet implemented by Petra Specht. The applet can be accessed through the Web site: http://isgnw2.cs.uni-magdeburg.de/ ~petra/spanner.html

The geographic neighborhood graph that was mentioned in Remark 4.1.2 is due to Yao [1982a]. Chang, Huang, and Tang [1990] present an algorithm that constructs this graph in $O(n \log n)$ time.

The plane sweep technique that we used in Section 4.1.2 to construct the Θ-graph is one of the most powerful techniques in computational geometry. Nievergelt and Preparata [1982] were probably the first to describe it as a general algorithmic paradigm. General descriptions of this paradigm can be found in the books Preparata and Shamos [1988], and de Berg et al. [2000].

The results of Section 4.2 are due to Arya et al. [1995].

Skip lists were introduced in Pugh [1990] as an alternative to balanced binary search trees. A detailed description and analysis of this elegant data structure can be found in the books Mulmuley [1994], and Motwani and Raghavan [1995]. Chernoff introduced his technique for analyzing tail estimates for sums of random variables in Chernoff [1952]. Good expositions of this technique are given in Mulmuley [1994], Motwani and Raghavan [1995], and Mitzenmacher and Upfal [2005].

The skip list spanner of Section 4.3 is due to Arya, Mount, and Smid [1994] and Arya, Mount, and Smid [1999]. The ordered Θ-graph of Exercise 4.17 is due to Bose, Gudmundsson, and Morin [2004a].

5

Cones in Higher Dimensional Space and Θ-Graphs

To the inhabitants of space in general and H. C. in particular this work is dedicated by a humble native of Flatland in the hope that even as he was initiated into the mysteries of THREE dimensions having been previously conversant with ONLY TWO so the citizens of that celestial region may aspire yet higher and higher to the secrets of FOUR FIVE OR EVEN SIX dimensions thereby contributing to the enlargement of THE IMAGINATION and the possible developement of that most rare and excellent gift of MODESTY among the superior races of SOLID HUMANITY.
—From the Dedication in *Flatland: A romance of many dimensions* by Edwin A. Abbott, 1884

In Chapter 4, we used the collection $\mathcal{C}_\kappa$ of cones to define the Θ-graph $\Theta(S, \kappa)$ for two-dimensional point sets. Each cone C in $\mathcal{C}_\kappa$ is defined by two infinite rays emanating from the origin and making an angle of $\theta = 2\pi/\kappa$. As a result, the cone C can be written as the intersection of two halfplanes in $\mathbb{R}^2$. The lines orthogonal to the rays bounding C (that is, D_1 and D_2 in Figure 4.6) define a coordinate system that we used in algorithm BUILDΘGRAPH(S, C) of Section 4.1.2 to compute all edges of $\Theta(S, \kappa)$ that correspond to C.

In this chapter, we will generalize the Θ-graph and its variants to the d-dimensional case, for any integer constant $d \geq 2$. In order to obtain this generalization, we start in Sections 5.1 and 5.2 with showing how the d-dimensional analogue of the collection $\mathcal{C}_\kappa$ can be constructed. In Section 5.3, we will present some applications of $\mathcal{C}_\kappa$ that will be used at several places in the rest of this book. In order to generalize algorithm BUILDΘGRAPH(S, C), we need orthogonal range trees, which will be presented in Section 5.4. Finally, in Section 5.5, we will present the d-dimensional analogues of all results in Chapter 4.

5.1 Simplicial cones and frames

For a point $p \in \mathbb{R}^d$ and a set $V = \{v^1, v^2, \ldots, v^k\}$ of points in $\mathbb{R}^d$, we define the *cone with apex p* that is *generated by V* to be the set

$$cone(p, V) := \left\{ p + \sum_{j=1}^{k} \lambda_j v^j : \lambda_j \geq 0 \text{ for all } j = 1, 2, \ldots, k \right\}.$$

If $p = 0$, that is, p is the origin, then we write $cone(V)$ instead of $cone(0, V)$. Thus $cone(V)$ is the set of all points obtained by linear combinations with nonnegative coefficients of points in V, and $cone(p, V)$ is $cone(V)$ translated to point p.

Definition 5.1.1. Let $p \in \mathbb{R}^d$, let V be a finite set of points in $\mathbb{R}^d$, and let $C = cone(p, V)$ be the cone with apex p that is generated by V. We say that C is a *simplicial cone*, if $|V| = d$ and the d points $v - p$, with $v \in V$, are linearly independent.

Let C be a simplicial cone with apex p that is generated by a set V of d points in $\mathbb{R}^d$. For any subset V' of V of size $d - 1$, there is a unique hyperplane H through p and the points of V'. Moreover, C is completely contained in one of the (closed) halfspaces defined by H. Since V consists of d elements, the number of such subsets V' is equal to d. Hence, C can be written as the intersection of d halfspaces in $\mathbb{R}^d$. Since the points $v - p$, with $v \in V$, are linearly independent, the directed lines orthogonal to these halfspaces can be used as a coordinate system in $\mathbb{R}^d$. Observe also that C is equal to the convex hull of the d infinite rays emanating from p and going through the points of the translated set $V + p$.

Let $q = (q_1, q_2, \ldots, q_d)$ and $r = (r_1, r_2, \ldots, r_d)$ be two points in $\mathbb{R} \setminus \{0\}$. The *angle* between q and r, denoted by angle (q, r), is defined to be the unique real number α, with $0 \leq \alpha \leq \pi$, that satisfies the equation

$$q \cdot r = \|q\| \times \|r\| \cos \alpha,$$

where $q \cdot r = \sum_{i=1}^{d} q_i r_i$ is the *inner product* of q and r, and $\|q\| = \left(\sum_{i=1}^{d} q_i^2\right)^{1/2}$ and $\|r\| = \left(\sum_{i=1}^{d} r_i^2\right)^{1/2}$ are the lengths of the vectors $\vec{q}$ and $\vec{r}$ from the origin to the points q and r, respectively. Equivalently, we can define angle(q, r) to be the angle between $\vec{q}$ and $\vec{r}$ in the two-dimensional plane through q, r, and the origin.

If $p \in \mathbb{R}^d$ and V is a finite set of points in $\mathbb{R}^d$, then we define the *angular diameter* of $cone(p, V)$ as

$$\max \{\text{angle}(q - p, r - p) : q, r \in cone(p, V) \setminus \{p\}\}.$$

Having defined all concepts that are needed, we can now define the notion of a frame:

Definition 5.1.2. Let θ be a real number, such that $0 < \theta < \pi$. A θ-*frame* is a collection $\mathcal{C}$ of cones, having the following properties:

1.   Each cone in $\mathcal{C}$ has its apex at the origin.
2.   The cones in $\mathcal{C}$ cover $\mathbb{R}^d$; that is, $\cup_{C \in \mathcal{C}} C = \mathbb{R}^d$.
3.   The angular diameter of each cone in $\mathcal{C}$ is at most θ.
4.   Each cone in $\mathcal{C}$ is a simplicial cone.

5.2 Constructing a θ-frame

In this section, we will show how a θ-frame, consisting of $O(d^{(3d-1)/2}(\pi/\theta)^{d-1})$ simplicial cones, can be constructed. We start in Section 5.2.1 by proving this claim for the case when the cones are not required to be simplicial. In Section 5.2.2, we show how to construct a triangulation of a hypercube. Then, in Section 5.2.3, we use this triangulation to refine the cones of Section 5.2.1 to simplicial cones.

5.2.1 Covering $\mathbb{R}^d$ by cones

Let θ be a real number, such that $0 < \theta < \pi$. In the two-dimensional case, we obtain a θ-frame, by subdividing the unit circle into segments of angle θ. Each of these segments defines a simplicial cone, and the collection of all these cones clearly satisfies the requirements in Definition 5.1.2. We can generalize this construction, by subdividing the boundary of the unit ball in $\mathbb{R}^d$ into "small pieces." Since this process is difficult to describe and analyze, we will use the boundary of a d-dimensional hypercube instead of the unit ball.

A *d-dimensional hypercube* is defined to be the Cartesian product of d closed intervals, all having the same length. This length is called the *side length* of the hypercube. Hence, a hypercube with side length ℓ can be written as

$$[a_1, a_1 + \ell] \times [a_2, a_2 + \ell] \times \cdots \times [a_d, a_d + \ell],$$

for some real numbers $a_1, a_2, \ldots, a_d$.

Consider the hypercube $B := [-1, 1]^d$ in $\mathbb{R}^d$. This hypercube is bounded by $2d$ hyperplanes, each one given by one of the equations $x_1 = 1, x_1 = -1, x_2 = 1, x_2 = -1, \ldots, x_d = 1, x_d = -1$.

In the rest of this section, we will partition each of the $2d$ faces of B into $(d-1)$-dimensional hypercubes, each one having a small diameter. These small hypercubes will then be used to define a collection of cones that cover $\mathbb{R}^d$ and whose angular diameters are at most θ.

Let F be a face of the hypercube B. For ease of notation, we assume that this face is contained in the hyperplane with equation $x_d = 1$. Hence, F is the $(d-1)$-dimensional hypercube

$$F = [-1, 1]^{d-1} \times \{1\}.$$

Define

$$m := \left\lceil \sqrt{\frac{2(d-1)}{1 - \cos\theta}} \right\rceil \text{ and } \ell := 2/m. \tag{5.1}$$

We partition F into m^{d-1} $(d-1)$-dimensional hypercubes, called *subhypercubes*, each one having side length ℓ. These subhypercubes are

$$\prod_{j=1}^{d}[-1 + i_j\ell, -1 + (i_j + 1)\ell] \times \{1\},$$

where $i_1, i_2, \ldots, i_d$ range over all elements of the set $\{0, 1, \ldots, m-1\}$.

In Lemma 5.2.2 below, we will prove that angle$(q, r) \leq \theta$, for any two points q and r that are contained in the same subhypercube. Before we can prove this claim, we need the following result, which relates angle(q, r) to the Euclidean distance $|qr|$:

Lemma 5.2.1. *Let q and r be two points in F, and let $\alpha = $ angle(q, r). We have*

$$\cos\alpha \geq 1 - |qr|^2/2.$$

PROOF   Using elementary linear algebra, we have

$$\begin{aligned}
|qr|^2 &= \|q - r\|^2 \\
&= (q - r) \cdot (q - r) \\
&= q \cdot q + r \cdot r - 2(q \cdot r) \\
&= \|q\|^2 + \|r\|^2 - 2\|q\| \times \|r\| \cos\alpha.
\end{aligned}$$

Using the inequality $a^2 + b^2 \geq 2ab$, which is valid for all real numbers a and b, it follows that

$$|qr|^2 \geq 2(1 - \cos\alpha)\|q\| \times \|r\|.$$

Since q and r are both contained in the hyperplane with equation $x_d = 1$, we have $\|q\| \geq 1$ and $\|r\| \geq 1$. Therefore,

$$|qr|^2 \geq 2(1 - \cos\alpha),$$

which is equivalent to the inequality in the lemma. ∎

Lemma 5.2.2. *Let q and r be two points that are contained in the same subhypercube. Then* angle$(q, r) \leq \theta$.

PROOF We denote angle(q, r) by α. Since q and r are in the same subhypercube, $|qr|$ is at most $\sqrt{d-1}$ times the side length ℓ of this subhypercube. This, together with Lemma 5.2.1, implies that

$$\cos\alpha \geq 1 - |qr|^2/2 \geq 1 - (d-1)\ell^2/2.$$

Since $m^2 \geq 2(d-1)/(1 - \cos\theta)$, we have $\ell^2 = 4/m^2 \leq 2(1 - \cos\theta)/(d-1)$. By combining these inequalities, it follows that $\cos\alpha \geq \cos\theta$. Thus, $\alpha \leq \theta$, because $0 < \theta < \pi$. ∎

If we apply the above construction to each of the $2d$ faces of the hypercube B, then we obtain a collection of subhypercubes, each one being a $(d-1)$-dimensional hypercube. Denote the total number of subhypercubes by k, and let $\mathcal{B} = \{B_1, B_2, \ldots, B_k\}$ be the collection of cones, where B_i is the cone with apex 0 that is generated by the vertex set of the i-th subhypercube. Observe that $k = 2dm^{d-1}$.

The cones in $\mathcal{B}$ cover $\mathbb{R}^d$, because each ray emanating from the origin intersects at least one subhypercube. It follows from Lemma 5.2.2 that the angular diameter of each cone in $\mathcal{B}$ is at most θ. Finally, since $1 - \cos\theta \geq 2\theta^2/\pi^2$ for all θ with $0 < \theta < \pi$, we have $m \leq \lceil (\pi/\theta)\sqrt{d} \rceil$, and, therefore, $k = O(d^{(d+1)/2}(\pi/\theta)^{d-1})$. We have proved the following result:

Lemma 5.2.3. *The collection $\mathcal{B}$ consists of $k = O(d^{(d+1)/2}(\pi/\theta)^{d-1})$ cones, for which the following properties hold:*

1. *Each cone in $\mathcal{B}$ has its apex at the origin.*

2. *The cones in $\mathcal{B}$ cover $\mathbb{R}^d$.*

3. *The angular diameter of each cone in $\mathcal{B}$ is at most θ.*

5.2.2 Triangulating a hypercube

The cones in Lemma 5.2.3 are not simplicial, because they are defined by subhypercubes having 2^{d-1} vertices. In order to refine these cones to simplicial cones, we will partition each subhypercube into a collection of simplices. In this section, we show how such a partition can be obtained. We will describe the construction for a hypercube in $\mathbb{R}^d$, and apply it in Section 5.2.3 with d replaced by $d-1$.

Definition 5.2.4. Let j be an integer with $0 \leq j \leq d$, and let $V = \{v^0, v^1, \ldots, v^j\}$ be a set of $j + 1$ points in $\mathbb{R}^d$. If the points $v^i - v^0$, $1 \leq i \leq j$, are linearly independent, then the convex hull $\Delta(V)$ of V is called a *j-simplex*.

We will show how a d-dimensional hypercube U can be partitioned into a collection of d-simplices, all having vertices that are vertices of U. This partition is called a *triangulation* of U. For ease of notation, we will assume that U is the *unit hypercube*; that is, $U = [0, 1]^d$.

The triangulation of U is obtained as follows. For each permutation σ of $\{1, 2, \ldots, d\}$, define the following $d + 1$ points $v_\sigma^0, v_\sigma^1, \ldots, v_\sigma^d$ in $\mathbb{R}^d$:

1. v_σ^0 is the origin.

2. For each i with $1 \leq i \leq d$, v_σ^i is obtained from v_σ^{i-1} by changing the $\sigma(i)$-th coordinate from 0 to 1.

In other words, v_σ^i is the vertex of U such that the line through v_σ^{i-1} and v_σ^i is parallel to the $\sigma(i)$-th coordinate axis. Observe that v_σ^d is the point $(1, 1, \ldots, 1)$.

To give an example, if $d = 4$ and $\sigma = (3, 1, 4, 2)$, then we obtain the points

$$v_\sigma^0 = (0, 0, 0, 0),$$
$$v_\sigma^1 = (0, 0, 1, 0),$$
$$v_\sigma^2 = (1, 0, 1, 0),$$
$$v_\sigma^3 = (1, 0, 1, 1),$$
$$v_\sigma^4 = (1, 1, 1, 1).$$

We define Δ_σ to be the d-simplex

$$\Delta_\sigma := \Delta(\{v_\sigma^0, v_\sigma^1, \ldots, v_\sigma^d\}).$$

Let

$$\mathcal{S} := \{\Delta_\sigma : \sigma \text{ is a permutation of } \{1, 2, \ldots, d\}\}$$

be the resulting collection of d-simplices. Clearly, $|\mathcal{S}| = d!$. In the next two lemmas, we prove that the d-simplices in $\mathcal{S}$ form a triangulation of the hypercube U.

Lemma 5.2.5. *The collection $\mathcal{S}$ of d-simplices cover the d-dimensional unit hypercube U, i.e.,*

$$\bigcup_\sigma \Delta_\sigma = U.$$

PROOF   Since each d-simplex Δ_σ is the convex hull of $d + 1$ vertices of U, it is clear that $\cup_\sigma \Delta_\sigma \subseteq U$.

To prove that $U \subseteq \cup_\sigma \Delta_\sigma$, let y be an arbitrary point in U. Let σ be a permutation of $\{1, 2, \ldots, d\}$, such that $y_{\sigma(1)} \geq y_{\sigma(2)} \geq \ldots \geq y_{\sigma(d)}$, and consider the vertices $v_\sigma^0, v_\sigma^1, \ldots, v_\sigma^d$ of the d-simplex Δ_σ. We will prove that the point y can be written as a convex combination of these vertices. This will imply that y is contained in Δ_σ.

Define the real numbers $\lambda_0 := 1 - y_{\sigma(1)}$, $\lambda_i := y_{\sigma(i)} - y_{\sigma(i+1)}$ for $1 \leq i \leq d - 1$, and $\lambda_d := y_{\sigma(d)}$. Then, $\lambda_i \geq 0$ for each i with $0 \leq i \leq d$, and $\sum_{i=0}^d \lambda_i = 1$. We claim that

$$y = \sum_{i=0}^d \lambda_i v_\sigma^i, \tag{5.2}$$

which can be verified by comparing the $\sigma(j)$-th coordinates of the points on both sides of this equation, for $j = 1, 2, \ldots, d$. This proves that y is indeed a convex combination of the vertices of Δ_σ.   ∎

Lemma 5.2.6. *The interiors of any two distinct d-simplices in $\mathcal{S}$ are disjoint.*

PROOF Let σ be a permutation of $\{1, 2, \ldots, d\}$, and consider the vertices $v_\sigma^i, 0 \leq i \leq d$, of the d-simplex Δ_σ in $\mathcal{S}$. Let A be the $d \times d$ matrix having the points $v_\sigma^i, 1 \leq i \leq d$, as its rows. Since v_σ^0 is the origin, the volume of Δ_σ is equal to $1/d!$ times the absolute value of the determinant of A. By permuting the columns of A appropriately, we obtain the matrix

$$A' = \begin{pmatrix} 1 & 0 & 0 & 0 & \ldots & 0 \\ 1 & 1 & 0 & 0 & \ldots & 0 \\ 1 & 1 & 1 & 0 & \ldots & 0 \\ & & & \vdots & & \\ 1 & 1 & 1 & 1 & \ldots & 1 \end{pmatrix},$$

whose determinant is equal to ± 1 times the determinant of A. Since the determinant of A' is equal to 1, it follows that the volume of Δ_σ is equal to $1/d!$.

By Lemma 5.2.5, we have $\cup_\sigma \Delta_\sigma = U$. Since the volume of U is equal to 1, and since $|\mathcal{S}| = d!$, the lemma follows. ∎

We summarize the results obtained in this section:

Theorem 5.2.7. *A d-dimensional hypercube can be triangulated into $d!$ d-simplices with disjoint interiors.*

5.2.3 Refining the cones in $\mathcal{B}$ to simplicial cones

Having shown how to triangulate a hypercube, we are now able to give the final step in our construction of the θ-frame.

Consider the collection $\mathcal{B} = \{B_1, B_2, \ldots, B_k\}$ of cones in Lemma 5.2.3, where $k = 2dm^{d-1}$, and m is as in (5.1). Each cone B_i in $\mathcal{B}$ is of the form $B_i = cone(V_i)$, where V_i is the vertex set of a $(d-1)$-dimensional hypercube that is contained in one of the $2d$ hyperplanes $x_1 = 1, x_1 = -1, x_2 = 1, x_2 = -1, \ldots, x_d = 1, x_d = -1$. By Theorem 5.2.7, we can triangulate this hypercube into $(d-1)!$ many $(d-1)$-simplices $\Delta_i^1, \Delta_i^2, \ldots, \Delta_i^{(d-1)!}$, that are all contained in the same hyperplane as V_i. For each j with $1 \leq j \leq (d-1)!$, we define C_i^j to be the cone with apex 0 that is generated by the vertex set of Δ_i^j. Let

$$\kappa_{d\theta} := k(d-1)! = 2d! \left\lceil \sqrt{2(d-1)/(1-\cos\theta)} \right\rceil^{d-1}. \tag{5.3}$$

We will write κ as a short-hand for $\kappa_{d\theta}$, and define

$$\mathcal{C}_\kappa := \{C_i^j : 1 \leq i \leq k, 1 \leq j \leq (d-1)!\}.$$

Since $k = O(d^{(d+1)/2}(\pi/\theta)^{d-1})$, the collection $\mathcal{C}_\kappa$ consists of

$$\kappa \leq kd^{d-1} = O\left(d^{(3d-1)/2}(\pi/\theta)^{d-1}\right)$$

simplicial cones that cover $\mathbb{R}^d$, and that all have their apex at the origin. Since C_i^j is contained in B_i, it follows from Lemma 5.2.3 that the angular diameter of each cone in $\mathcal{C}_\kappa$ is at most θ. Hence, we have proved the following result:

Theorem 5.2.8. *Let $d \geq 2$ be an integer, let θ be a real number such that $0 < \theta < \pi$, and let $\kappa = \kappa_{d\theta}$ be as in (5.3). The collection $\mathcal{C}_\kappa$ constitutes a θ-frame in $\mathbb{R}^d$, consisting of $\kappa = O(d^{(3d-1)/2}(\pi/\theta)^{d-1})$ simplicial cones. If d is a constant, then $\mathcal{C}_\kappa$ can be constructed in $O(1/\theta^{d-1})$ time and consists of $\kappa = O(1/\theta^{d-1})$ cones with disjoint interiors.*

5.3 Applications of θ-frames

In our first application, we use Theorem 5.2.8 to prove an upper bound on the size of any set of points for which the minimum angle is at least some given real number θ:

Theorem 5.3.1. *Let $d \geq 2$ be an integer constant, let θ be a real number such that $0 < \theta < \pi$, and let S be a set of points in $\mathbb{R}^d \setminus \{0\}$, such that angle$(q, r) > \theta$ for any two distinct points q and r in S. The size of S is $O(1/\theta^{d-1})$.*

PROOF Consider the θ-frame $\mathcal{C}_\kappa$ in Theorem 5.2.8. For each cone C in $\mathcal{C}_\kappa$, let S_C be the set of all points in S that are contained in C. If a point is contained in more than one cone, then we put it in exactly one subset S_C. In this way, we obtain a partition of S into $\kappa = O(1/\theta^{d-1})$ subsets. Since the angular diameter of each cone in $\mathcal{C}_\kappa$ is at most θ, each subset S_C contains at most one element of S. Therefore, $|S| \leq \kappa = O(1/\theta^{d-1})$. ■

The cones in the θ-frame $\mathcal{C}_\kappa$ of Theorem 5.2.8 cover $\mathbb{R}^d$. This leads to the question of how to compute, when given an arbitrary query point q in $\mathbb{R}^d$, a cone $C \in \mathcal{C}_\kappa$ for which $q \in C$. The following theorem shows that the special structure of $\mathcal{C}_\kappa$ can be used to answer such a *point location* query in $O(\log \kappa)$ time.

Theorem 5.3.2. *Let $d \geq 2$ be an integer constant, let θ be a real number such that $0 < \theta < \pi$, and let $\mathcal{C}_\kappa$ be the θ-frame in Theorem 5.2.8. In $O(1/\theta^{d-1})$ time, we can preprocess $\mathcal{C}_\kappa$ into a data structure of size $O(1/\theta^{d-1})$, such that for any query point $q \in \mathbb{R}^d$, a cone in $\mathcal{C}_\kappa$ that contains q can be computed in $O(\log(1/\theta))$ time.*

PROOF Recall how we constructed the θ-frame $\mathcal{C}_\kappa$: We started in Section 5.2.1 by partitioning each of the $2d$ faces of the hypercube $B = [-1, 1]^d$ into m^{d-1} subhypercubes, where m is defined in (5.1). Then, in Section 5.2.3, we triangulated each of the resulting $2dm^{d-1}$ subhypercubes into $(d-1)!$ many $(d-1)$-simplices. Finally, the θ-frame $\mathcal{C}_\kappa$ was defined as the collection of cones that are generated by the vertex sets of these simplices.

The data structure that supports point location queries in $\mathcal{C}_\kappa$ is obtained as follows: For each face F of B, we store the subhypercubes in the partition of F in a balanced binary search tree T_F, sorted, for example, by the lexicographically smallest vertex of each subhypercube. With each subhypercube in T_F, we store a list consisting of all $(d-1)$-simplices in the triangulation of this subhypercube.

Each such tree T_F can be constructed in $O(m^{d-1}) = O(1/\theta^{d-1})$ time, because we can obtain the sorted order of the subhypercubes in the partition of F in this amount of time. Hence, the entire data structure can be constructed in $O(1/\theta^{d-1})$ time.

To answer a point location query for a point $q \in \mathbb{R}^d$, we do the following: If q is the origin, then we return an arbitrary cone in $\mathcal{C}_\kappa$. Assume that q is not the origin. We shoot a ray from the origin toward q, and determine a face F of B that is hit by this ray. Then we compute the point q' on F that is hit by this ray. Next, we search with q' in the tree T_F for a subhypercube H in F that contains q'. Finally, we search for a $(d-1)$-simplex Δ in H that contains q'. The cone generated by the vertex set of Δ is a cone in $\mathcal{C}_\kappa$ that contains q. Since d is a constant, the time for a point location query is logarithmic in the size of T_F. ■

At several places in this book, we are given a set of directed edges in $\mathbb{R}^d$, and want to partition this set into subsets, such that the edges within each subset are "nearly parallel." The theorem below states that there exists an efficient algorithm that computes such a partition. The notion of being "nearly parallel" is formalized using the angle between two directed edges, which we define now.

Let p, q, r, and s be points in $\mathbb{R}^d$ such that $p \neq q$ and $r \neq s$, and consider the two directed edges (p, q) and (r, s). The *angle* between (p, q) and (r, s), denoted by angle(pq, rs), is defined as

$$\text{angle}(pq, rs) := \text{angle}(q - p, s - r).$$

In other words, if we translate the two edges (p, q) and (r, s) such that their sources are at the origin, then angle(pq, rs) is the angle between the two translates.

Theorem 5.3.3. *Let $d \geq 2$ be an integer constant, let θ be a real number such that $0 < \theta < \pi$, and let E be a set of directed edges in $\mathbb{R}^d$. In $O(1/\theta^{d-1} + |E| \log(1/\theta))$ time, we can partition E into $O(1/\theta^{d-1})$ subsets, such that* angle$(pq, rs) \leq \theta$ *for any two edges (p, q) and (r, s) that are in the same subset.*

PROOF The algorithm does the following: Compute the θ-frame $\mathcal{C}_\kappa$ of Theorem 5.2.8, and preprocess it for point location queries; see Theorem 5.3.2. For each cone C in $\mathcal{C}_\kappa$, initialize an empty edge list E_C. For each edge (p, q) in E, compute a cone $C \in \mathcal{C}_\kappa$ that contains the point $q - p$, and add (p, q) to E_C.

The resulting edge sets E_C, with $C \in \mathcal{C}_\kappa$, form the required partition. The claim on the running time follows from Theorems 5.2.8 and 5.3.2. ∎

5.4 Range trees

A *d-dimensional hyperrectangle* is defined to be the Cartesian product of d closed intervals. Hence, such a hyperrectangle Q can be written as

$$Q = [a_1, b_1] \times [a_2, b_2] \times \cdots \times [a_d, b_d],$$

where a_i and b_i are real numbers with $a_i \leq b_i$, $1 \leq i \leq d$.

In this section, we design an efficient data structure that solves the following problem:

Problem 5.4.1 (ORTHOGONAL RANGE SEARCHING). *Let $d \geq 1$ be an integer. Preprocess a set S of n points in $\mathbb{R}^d$ into a data structure that supports the following operation:*

RANGEQUERY(S, d, Q). Given a d-dimensional query hyperrectangle $Q = \prod_{i=1}^d [a_i, b_i]$, report all points $p \in S$ that are contained in Q; that is, all points $p = (p_1, p_2, \ldots, p_d) \in S$ for which $a_1 \leq p_1 \leq b_1$, $a_2 \leq p_2 \leq b_2$, $\ldots$, $a_d \leq p_d \leq b_d$.

The data structure that we will use to solve the orthogonal range searching problem is the *range tree*. It consists of a nested collection of balanced binary search trees. Each tree T in this collection stores a subset of the point set S at its leaves, sorted by the j-th coordinates of the points, for some j with $1 \leq j \leq d$. For any node v in T, we denote by S_v the set of all points of S that are stored in the subtree rooted at v. Each node v in T stores information to guide searches. For example, we can store at v the two points that are stored at the leftmost and rightmost leaves in the subtree rooted at v. Using this search information, we can find, in $O(\log |S_v|) = O(\log n)$ time, the leftmost leaf in T that stores a point whose j-th coordinate is greater than or equal to some given value. Similarly, we can find, again in $O(\log n)$ time, the rightmost leaf in T that stores a point whose j-th coordinate is less than or equal to some given value.

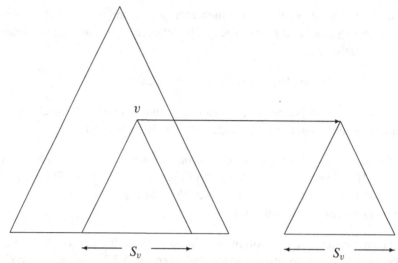

Figure 5.1: A two-dimensional range tree. The tree on the left is the main tree, storing the points of S, sorted by their first coordinates. Each node v of the main tree stores a pointer to its associated structure, which is the tree on the right. The associated structure of v stores the point set S_v, sorted by their second coordinates.

Definition 5.4.2 (Range Tree). Let $d \geq 1$ be an integer, and let S be a set of n points in $\mathbb{R}^d$. A *d-dimensional range tree* for S is the data structure $RT_d(S)$ that is defined as follows:

1. If $d = 1$, then $RT_d(S)$ is a balanced binary search tree storing the points of S in sorted order at its leaves.

2. If $d > 1$, then $RT_d(S)$ consists of a balanced binary search tree, called the *main tree*, that stores the points of S at its leaves, sorted by their first coordinates. For any node v of the main tree, let $S'_v \subseteq \mathbb{R}^{d-1}$ be the set obtained by deleting the first coordinate from each point in S_v. Each node v of the main tree stores a pointer to an *associated structure*, which is a $(d-1)$-dimensional range tree $RT_{d-1}(S'_v)$ for the point set S'_v.

For example, the main tree of a two-dimensional range tree $RT_2(S)$ is a balanced binary search tree, storing the points of S at its leaves, sorted by their first coordinates. Each node v of the main tree stores a pointer to an associated structure, which is a balanced binary search tree storing the point set S_v at its leaves, sorted by their second coordinates; see Figure 5.1.

Lemma 5.4.3. *Let $d \geq 1$ be an integer constant, and let S be a set of n points in $\mathbb{R}^d$. The range tree $RT_d(S)$ for S has size $O(n \log^{d-1} n)$, and can be built in $O(n \log n + n \log^{d-1} n)$ time.*

PROOF   We assume for simplicity that n is a power of 2. Let $M_d(n)$ denote the size of a d-dimensional range tree storing a set of n points. For $d = 1$, we clearly have $M_d(n) = O(n)$. Assume that $d \geq 2$. A d-dimensional range tree storing n points consists of (i) the root of the main tree, (ii) a $(d-1)$-dimensional range tree storing n points (this is the associated structure of the root), and (iii) two d-dimensional range trees (which are the left and right substructures of the root), each storing $n/2$ points. Hence, we have

$$M_d(n) = \begin{cases} O(n) & \text{if } d = 1, \\ O(1) + M_{d-1}(n) + 2M_d(n/2) & \text{if } d \geq 2. \end{cases}$$

By a double induction on d and n, it follows that $M_d(n) = O(n \log^{d-1} n)$.

Let $P_d(n)$ denote the time needed to build a d-dimensional range tree for a set of n points, which are sorted by their d-th coordinates. Then

$$P_d(n) = \begin{cases} O(n) & \text{if } d = 1, \\ O(n) + P_{d-1}(n) + 2P_{d-1}(n/2) & \text{if } d \geq 2. \end{cases}$$

Again, a double induction on d and n shows that $P_d(n) = O(n \log^{d-1} n)$. Since pre-sorting the points of the set S (according to their d-th coordinates), takes $O(n \log n)$ time, the total time to build a d-dimensional range tree for a set of n points is $O(n \log n) + P_d(n)$. ■

5.4.1 Answering range queries

Before we can show how range trees can be used to perform RANGEQUERY operations, we have to introduce the notion of *canonical nodes*. Consider a d-dimensional range tree $RT_d(S)$ for a set S of n points in $\mathbb{R}^d$, and let a and b be two real numbers with $a \leq b$. Let ℓ_a be the leftmost leaf in the main tree of $RT_d(S)$ that stores a point whose first coordinate is greater than or equal to a, let ℓ_b be the rightmost leaf in the main tree that stores a point whose first coordinate is less than or equal to b, and let u be the lowest common ancestor of ℓ_a and ℓ_b. We define a set C of nodes in the main tree, as follows:

1. The leaves ℓ_a and ℓ_b are both elements of C.
2. For each node v on the path from the left child of u to ℓ_a and for which this path proceeds to the left child of v, the set C contains the right child of v.
3. For each node v on the path from the right child of u to ℓ_b and for which this path proceeds to the right child of v, the set C contains the left child of v.

The nodes in C are called the *canonical nodes* with respect to the real numbers a and b. The following lemma implies that the canonical nodes can be used to reduce a RANGEQUERY operation in $\mathbb{R}^d$ to $O(\log n)$ RANGEQUERY operations in $\mathbb{R}^{d-1}$. The proof is left as an exercise; see Exercise 5.8.

Lemma 5.4.4. *Consider a range tree $RT_d(S)$ for a set S of n points in $\mathbb{R}^d$, and let a and b be two real numbers such that $a \leq b$. The set C of canonical nodes with respect to a and b can be computed in $O(\log n)$ time. The set C has the property that*

$$\{p \in S : a \leq p_1 \leq b\} = \bigcup_{w \in C} S_w,$$

where the sets in the union on the right-hand side are pairwise disjoint.

We are now ready to present the algorithm for answering range queries.

Algorithm RANGEQUERY(r, d, Q)

Comment: This algorithm takes as input a pointer to the root r of the main tree of a range tree $RT_d(S)$, and a query hyperrectangle $Q = \prod_{i=1}^{d}[a_i, b_i]$. It returns the set of all points in S that are contained in Q.

$C :=$ the set of canonical nodes with respect to a_1 and b_1;
$A := \emptyset$;
if $d = 1$
then for each $w \in C$
    do $A := A \cup S_w$
    endfor
else for each $w \in C$
    do $r' :=$ the root of the associated structure of r;
        $Q' := \prod_{i=2}^{d}[a_i, b_i]$;
        $A := A \cup$ RANGEQUERY($r', d - 1, Q'$)
    endfor
endif;
return A

In the following lemma, we prove the correctness of this algorithm and analyze its running time.

Lemma 5.4.5. *Let $d \geq 1$ be an integer constant, let S be a set of n points in $\mathbb{R}^d$, let r be the root of the main tree of a range tree $RT_d(S)$ for S, let Q be a hyperrectangle in $\mathbb{R}^d$, and let A be the set of all points in S that are contained in Q. Algorithm RANGEQUERY(r, d, Q) returns the set A in $O(\log^d n + |A|)$ time.*

PROOF It follows from Lemma 5.4.4 that each point in A is reported exactly once by algorithm RANGEQUERY(r, d, Q). Let $T_d(n)$ denote the running time of this algorithm. By Lemma 5.4.4, the set C of canonical nodes can be computed in $O(\log n)$ time. Therefore, we obtain the following recurrence:

$$T_d(n) = \begin{cases} O(\log n + |A|) & \text{if } d = 1, \\ O(\log n) + \sum_{w \in C} T_{d-1}(|S_w|) & \text{if } d \geq 2. \end{cases}$$

Since the size of C is $O(\log n)$, it follows that $T_d(n) = O(\log^d n + |A|)$. ∎

Remark 5.4.6. Using a technique called *layering*, the range tree data structure can be extended such that RANGEQUERY operations can be performed in $O(\log n + \log^{d-1} n + |A|)$ time. The proof of this claim is left as an exercise; see Exercise 5.10.

5.4.2 Supporting deletions

Until now, we have considered range trees as a static data structure. When inserting or deleting a point, the main difficulty is to rebalance the binary search trees that constitute the data structure. It is possible to maintain a range tree under insertions and deletions, in polylogarithmic time per update operation. In this book, however, it is sufficient to have a simpler dynamic range tree that supports only deletions; see Sections 5.5 and 7.4.

Consider a range tree $RT_d(S)$ for a point set S. Deleting a point p from $RT_d(S)$ is simply done by removing all information that is related to p from the data structure. To be more precise, we delete the leaves in all binary search trees that store p, and we update all search information in which p is "involved." When deleting a point, we do not rebalance any of the binary search trees. Since the initial data structure is balanced, at any moment during the sequence of delete operations, each binary search tree in the range tree will have height $O(\log n)$, where n is the initial size of S.

Algorithm DELETE(r, d, p)

Comment: This algorithm takes as input a pointer to the root r of the main tree of a range tree $RT_d(S)$, and a point p of S. It returns a pointer to the root of the main tree of a range tree $RT_d(S \setminus \{p\})$.

Step 1: Follow the path P in the main tree from the root r to the parent of the leaf ℓ_p that stores p.

Step 2: Delete the leaf ℓ_p from the main tree, and update the search information at the nodes on the path P.

Step 3: If $d \geq 2$, then for each node v on P, call algorithm DELETE$(r'_v, d - 1, p)$, where r'_v is the root of the associated structure of v.

Step 4: Return a pointer to the root of the main tree.

If we assume that the initial range tree $RT_d(S)$ is balanced and stores a set of n points, then at any moment during a sequence of delete operations, each binary tree that is part of the range tree has height $O(\log n)$. An analysis similar to the one in the proof of Lemma 5.4.5 shows that the running time of algorithm DELETE(r, d, p) is $O(\log^d n)$.

The following theorem summarizes our main results on range trees.

Theorem 5.4.7. *Let $d \geq 1$ be an integer constant.*

1. *Let S be a set of n points in $\mathbb{R}^d$. A range tree $RT_d(S)$ for S in which each binary search tree has height $O(\log n)$ has size $O(n \log^{d-1} n)$. Such a range tree can be built in $O(n \log n + n \log^{d-1} n)$ time.*

2. *Given a set S of n points in $\mathbb{R}^d$, and given a range tree $RT_d(S)$ for S in which each binary search tree has height $O(\log n)$, we can perform any sequence of RANGEQUERY and DELETE operations, such that at any moment during this sequence,*

   (a) the data structure has size $O(n \log^{d-1} n)$,

   (b) each DELETE operation takes $O(\log^d n)$ time, and

   (c) each RANGEQUERY operation takes $O(\log^d n + |A|)$ time, where A is the set of all points in the current point set that are contained in the query hyperrectangle.

5.5 Higher-dimensional Θ-graphs

In Chapter 4, we have seen several algorithms that construct spanners that are based on two-dimensional Θ-graphs. In this section, we will use the θ-frame of Theorem 5.2.8 and the range tree of Theorem 5.4.7 to generalize all these results to the d-dimensional case, where $d \geq 2$ is a constant. Since these generalizations are obtained in a straightforward manner, we will omit most of the details.

5.5.1 The d-dimensional Θ-graph

Let θ be a real number such that $0 < \theta < \pi$, let $\kappa = \kappa_{d\theta}$ be as in (5.3), and let $\mathcal{C}_\kappa$ be the θ-frame of Theorem 5.2.8. Recall that (i) each cone in $\mathcal{C}_\kappa$ has its apex at the origin, (ii) the angular diameter of each cone in $\mathcal{C}_\kappa$ is at most θ, (iii) each cone in $\mathcal{C}_\kappa$ is a simplicial cone; that is, it is the intersection of d halfspaces, (iv) the cones in $\mathcal{C}_\kappa$ cover $\mathbb{R}^d$, and (v) the number of cones in $\mathcal{C}_\kappa$ is $\kappa = O(1/\theta^{d-1})$.

As in Section 4.1, we fix, for each cone $C \in \mathcal{C}_\kappa$, a ray ℓ_C that emanates from the origin and that is contained in C. For any point $p \in \mathbb{R}^d$, we define $C_p := C + p = \{x + p : x \in C\}$ and $\ell_{C,p} := \ell_C + p$.

Definition 5.5.1 (Θ-graph). Let S be a set of n points in $\mathbb{R}^d$. The d-dimensional Θ-*graph* $\Theta(S, \kappa)$ is defined as follows:

1. The vertices of $\Theta(S, \kappa)$ are the points of S.
2. For each point p of S and for each cone C of $\mathcal{C}_\kappa$, such that the translated cone C_p contains one or more points of $S \setminus \{p\}$, the graph $\Theta(S, \kappa)$ contains one edge $\{p, r\}$, where r is a point in $C_p \cap S \setminus \{p\}$ whose orthogonal projection onto $\ell_{C,p}$ is closest to p.

Let C be a cone of $\mathcal{C}_\kappa$. We have seen in Section 5.1 that C can be written as the intersection of d halfspaces in $\mathbb{R}^d$. Let $D_1, D_2, \ldots, D_d$ be the lines through the origin that are orthogonal to the hyperplanes bounding these halfspaces. These lines define a coordinate system that can be used to compute all edges of $\Theta(S, \kappa)$ that correspond to C. The algorithm is a straightforward generalization of algorithm BUILDΘGRAPH(S, C) in Section 4.1.2 and Exercise 4.11. It uses a variant of a $(d-1)$-dimensional range tree, where we take into account only the $d - 1$ orders induced by the lines $D_2, D_3, \ldots, D_d$. By sweeping over all points of S according to the order induced by D_1, we obtain all edges of $\Theta(S, \kappa)$ that correspond to the cone C, in $O(n \log^{d-1} n)$ time.

We obtain the following result, which generalizes Theorems 4.1.5 and 4.1.10.

Theorem 5.5.2. *Let S be a set of n points in $\mathbb{R}^d$, let θ be a real number such that $0 < \theta < \pi/4$, and let $\kappa = \kappa_{d\theta}$ be as in (5.3).*

1. *The graph $\Theta(S, \kappa)$ is a t-spanner for S, for $t = 1/(\cos\theta - \sin\theta)$.*
2. *The graph $\Theta(S, \kappa)$ contains at most $\kappa n = O(n/\theta^{d-1})$ edges.*
3. *The graph $\Theta(S, \kappa)$ can be constructed in $O((n/\theta^{d-1}) \log^{d-1} n)$ time, using $O(n/\theta^{d-1} + n \log^{d-2} n)$ space.*

5.5.2 The d-dimensional sink spanner

Let S be a set of n points in $\mathbb{R}^d$, let q be a point of S, and let $t > 1$ be a real number. A q-*sink t-spanner* for S is defined as in Definition 4.2.1: It is a directed graph having the points of S as its vertices and that contains, for every $p \in S$, a directed t-spanner path from p to q.

A q-sink t-spanner for S can be constructed using a straightforward generalization of the algorithm given in Section 4.2.1. This generalized algorithm uses a θ-frame $\mathcal{C}_\kappa$, where θ is a real number such that $t \leq 1/(\cos\theta - \sin\theta)$ and κ is the number of cones in $\mathcal{C}_\kappa$ as given in (5.3). We denote the resulting q-sink t-spanner by $\Theta(S, q, \kappa)$. When constructing this graph, Theorem 5.3.2 is used to distribute the points over the cones of $\mathcal{C}_\kappa$. In this way, we obtain the following generalization of Theorem 4.2.3:

Theorem 5.5.3. *Let S be a set of n points in $\mathbb{R}^d$, let q be a point of S, let θ be a real number such that $0 < \theta < \pi/4$, and let $\kappa = \kappa_{d\theta}$ be as in (5.3).*

1. *The graph $\Theta(S, q, \kappa)$ is a q-sink t-spanner for S, for $t = 1/(\cos\theta - \sin\theta)$.*

2. *In $\Theta(S, q, \kappa)$, the indegree of each vertex is less than or equal to $\kappa + 1 = O(n/\theta^{d-1})$, the outdegree of q is 0, and the outdegree of each other vertex is 1.*

3. *The graph $\Theta(S, q, \kappa)$ can be constructed in $O(1/\theta^{d-1} + \log(1/\theta)n \log n)$ time.*

5.5.3 Transforming a spanner of bounded outdegree to a spanner of bounded degree

Given Theorem 5.5.3, the results of Section 4.2.2 immediately generalize to the higher-dimensional case:

Theorem 5.5.4. *Let S be a set of n points in $\mathbb{R}^d$, let t and t' be real numbers such that $t > t' > 1$, and let θ be a real number such that $0 < \theta < \pi/4$ and $1/(\cos\theta - \sin\theta) \leq t/t'$. Let G be a t'-spanner for S, whose edges can be directed in $T(n)$ time, such that each vertex has outdegree at most D, for some integer D. In*

$$O\left(1/\theta^{d-1} + T(n) + D\log(1/\theta)n \log n\right)$$

time, we can transform G into a t-spanner for S in which each vertex has degree $O(D/\theta^{d-1})$.

5.5.4 A d-dimensional spanner of bounded degree

We now show how Theorems 5.5.2 and 5.5.4 can be combined to obtain a t-spanner in which the degree of each vertex is bounded by a function that depends only on t.

Let S be a set of n points in $\mathbb{R}^d$, and let $t > 1$ be a real number. We choose a real number θ such that $0 < \theta < \pi/4$ and $1/(\cos\theta - \sin\theta) \leq \sqrt{t}$. Let $\kappa = \kappa_{d\theta}$ be as in (5.3), and consider the θ-frame $\mathcal{C}_\kappa$ of Theorem 5.2.8, where $\kappa = O(1/\theta^{d-1})$.

Let G be the Θ-graph $\Theta(S, \kappa)$. By Theorem 5.5.2, G is a $\sqrt{t}$-spanner for S, which contains at most κn edges, and which can be constructed in $O(\kappa n \log^{d-1} n)$ time. It follows from the definition of $\Theta(S, \kappa)$ that the edges of G can be directed in $O(\kappa n)$ time, such that the outdegree of each vertex is less than or equal to κ. Therefore, by applying Theorem 5.5.4, with $t' = \sqrt{t}$, $T(n) = O(\kappa n)$, and $D = \kappa$, we can transform G, in $O(\kappa \log(1/\theta)n \log n)$ time, into a t-spanner G_0 for S in which each vertex has degree $O(\kappa/\theta^{d-1})$.

If we choose θ as large as possible, and assume that $t > 1$ and $t \to 1$, then $\theta \sim (t-1)/2$. Since $\kappa = O(1/\theta^{d-1})$, we have $\kappa = O(1/(t-1)^{d-1})$. We obtain the following generalization of Theorem 4.2.6:

Theorem 5.5.5. *Let S be a set of n points in $\mathbb{R}^d$, and let $t > 1$ be a real number. In*

$$O\left(\frac{1}{(t-1)^{d-1}} n \log^{d-1} n + \frac{\log(1/(t-1))}{(t-1)^{d-1}} n \log n\right)$$

time, we can construct a t-spanner for S in which each vertex has degree $O(1/(t-1)^{2d-2})$.

5.5.5 The d-dimensional skip list spanner

Using Theorem 5.5.2, the skip list spanner of Section 4.3.2 generalizes to the higher-dimensional case in a straightforward way. We denote the d-dimensional version of this spanner by $SLS(S, \kappa)$. The following theorem is the generalization of Theorem 4.3.10:

Theorem 5.5.6. *Let S be a set of n points in $\mathbb{R}^d$, let θ be a real number such that $0 < \theta < \pi/4$, and let $\kappa = \kappa_{d\theta}$ be as in (5.3). Then the following is true:*

1. *The skip list spanner $SLS(S, \kappa)$ is a t-spanner for S, for $t = 1/(\cos\theta - \sin\theta)$. With high probability, it contains $O(n/\theta^{d-1})$ edges.*

2. *The graph $SLS(S, \kappa)$ can be constructed in $O((n/\theta^{d-1})\log^{d-1} n)$ time, using $O(n/\theta^{d-1} + n\log^{d-2} n)$ space, with high probability.*

3. *With high probability, the spanner diameter of $SLS(S, \kappa)$ is $O(\log n)$.*

4. *All these bounds are with respect to the coin flips that are used to build the skip list spanner.*

Exercises

5.1. Let V be a finite set of points in $\mathbb{R}^d$, let CH be the convex hull of V, let $p \in \mathbb{R}^d$, and consider $cone(p, V)$; that is, the cone with apex p that is generated by V. Prove that $cone(p, V)$ is equal to the set of all points $x \in \mathbb{R}^d$ for which a point y in CH exists such that x is on the ray emanating from p and going through $y + p$.

5.2. Let $0 \le j \le d$, and let $V = \{v^0, v^1, \ldots, v^j\}$ be a set of points in $\mathbb{R}^d$. In the definition of a j-simplex $\Delta(V)$, see Definition 5.2.4, we require that the points $v^i - v^0$, $1 \le i \le j$, are linearly independent. Prove that if this is the case, then for any k, the points $v^i - v^k$ with $0 \le i \le j$ and $i \ne k$, are also linearly independent.

5.3. Let σ be a permutation of $\{1, 2, \ldots, d\}$, and consider Δ_σ as defined in Section 5.2.2. Prove that Δ_σ is a d-simplex. Also, prove that

$$\Delta_\sigma = \{y \in \mathbb{R}^d : 0 \le y_{\sigma(d)} \le y_{\sigma(d-1)} \le \ldots \le y_{\sigma(1)} \le 1\}.$$

5.4. Prove the equation in (5.2) in the proof of Lemma 5.2.5.

5.5. In Section 5.2.2, we have shown that a three-dimensional cube U can be partitioned into $3! = 6$ tetrahedra (i.e., 3-simplices). Prove that U can in fact be partitioned into 5 tetrahedra.

5.6. Give an example of a set V of d points in $\mathbb{R}^d \setminus \{0\}$, such that $\Delta(V)$ is a $(d-1)$-simplex, but $cone(V)$ is not a simplicial cone.

5.7. Prove that the cones in the θ-frame $\mathcal{C}_\kappa$ in Theorem 5.2.8 are simplicial cones (i.e., satisfy the requirements in Definition 5.1.1). Also, prove that the interiors of any two distinct cones in $\mathcal{C}_\kappa$ are disjoint.

5.8. Prove Lemma 5.4.4.

5.9. In Lemmas 5.4.3 and 5.4.5, we have analyzed the complexity of range trees assuming that the dimension d is a constant. By analyzing the recurrences in the proofs of these lemmas more carefully, prove that the constant factors in the Big-Oh bounds are in fact proportional to $1/(d-1)!$.

5.10. Extend the range tree data structure such that RANGEQUERY operations can be performed in $O(\log n + \log^{d-1} n + |A|)$ time. (*Hint*: First, prove this claim for the case when $d = 2$. For any two nodes v and w in the main tree, such that w is a child of v, connect their associate structures by pointers. This technique is called *layering*.)

5.11. Work out the details for Section 5.5.

Bibliographic notes

Sections 5.2.1 and 5.2.3 are due to Lukovszki [1999b]. Alternative constructions of θ-frames appear in Yao [1982a] and Ruppert and Seidel [1991]; these constructions produce more cones than the construction that we presented.

The triangulation presented in Section 5.2.2 is known as *Kuhn's triangulation* and appears in Kuhn [1960]. According to Kuhn, this triangulation was used earlier by A. W. Tucker. The earliest reference seems to be Freudenthal [1942].

It is possible to construct triangulations of a hypercube in $\mathbb{R}^d$ that consist of less than $d!$ simplices. Determining the smallest number of simplices in any triangulation of a hypercube is an extremely difficult problem, which has been solved only for dimensions $d \leq 7$. More information about this triangulation problem can be found in Chapter 17 of Goodman and O'Rourke [2004].

The orthogonal range searching problem of Section 5.4 was introduced in Knuth [1973]. The range tree data structure was discovered independently by Bentley [1979], Lee and Wong [1980], Lueker [1978], and Willard [1979]. Lueker [1978] shows that range trees can be maintained under insertions and deletions, in $O(\log^d n)$ time per update operation. The layering technique that improves the time for answering range queries (see Remark 5.4.6 and Exercise 5.10) is due to Lueker [1978] and Willard [1978]. A generalization of this technique, called *fractional cascading*, appears in Chazelle and Guibas [1986a] and Chazelle and Guibas [1986b]. The layered range tree is more difficult to maintain under insertions and deletions. Mehlhorn and Näher [1990] give a dynamic version of fractional cascading, and show that it can be used to maintain range trees in $O(\log^{d-1} n \log \log n)$ time per update operation. A detailed discussion about range trees can be found in Willard and Lueker [1985], and in the books Preparata and Shamos [1988] and de Berg et al. [2000]. Comprehensive surveys on geometric range searching problems can be found in Agarwal and Erickson [1999] and Agarwal [2004]. A solution to Exercise 5.9 can be found in Monier [1980].

6

Geometric Analysis: The Gap Property

> In attempting to understand the elements out of which mental phenomena are compounded, it is of the greatest importance to remember that from the protozoa to man there is nowhere a very wide gap either in structure or in behaviour.
>
> —Bertrand Russell, *The Analysis of Mind*, 1921

In Chapters 4 and 5, we have seen how sparse spanners, spanners of bounded degree, and spanners having a logarithmic spanner diameter can be computed. Even though the algorithms were nontrivial, the arguments that were used in the analysis of each of these spanners were straightforward. In Section 1.2, we also mentioned the weight of a spanner as a measure to be optimized. To analyze the weight, we need tools for estimating the weight of Euclidean graphs that satisfy a certain property.

> **Geometric analysis:** Let S be a set of n points in $\mathbb{R}^d$, and let E be a set of (directed or undirected) edges whose endpoints belong to S and that satisfy some property $\mathcal{P}$. Find a good upper bound on the weight $wt(E)$ of E, being the sum of the lengths of its edges.

How does this relate to the problem of computing a spanner of low weight? We will follow a two-step approach:

Step 1: Devise a property $\mathcal{P}$ for which we can prove a good upper bound for $wt(E)$.

Step 2: Design an algorithm that computes a spanner whose edge set satisfies property $\mathcal{P}$.

In this chapter, we will introduce and analyze one such property $\mathcal{P}$, the so-called *gap property*. We will prove that the weight of any set of edges satisfying this property is $O(\log n)$ times the weight of a minimum spanning tree of their n endpoints. In Chapter 7, we will show that there is an efficient algorithm that computes a spanner, for any point set S, whose edges satisfy the gap property. Hence, the results of the current chapter immediately imply that the weight of this spanner is $O(\log n)$ times the weight of a minimum spanning tree of S. In Section 6.2, we show a lower bound on the maximum possible weight of any set of edges satisfying the gap property.

The gap property is not only useful to analyze the weight of spanners. In Section 6.5, we will show that it can be applied in a worst-case analysis of the 2-Opt algorithm for the traveling salesperson problem.

6.1 The gap property

For technical reasons, we will consider sets of directed edges.

The gap property: A set of directed edges satisfies the gap property, if the sources of any two distinct edges are "far" apart (relative to the length of the shorter of the two edges). If this condition also holds for the sinks of any two distinct edges, then the edge set satisfies the strong gap property.

These properties are formally defined as follows (see Figure 6.1):

Definition 6.1.1 (Gap Property). Let $w \geq 0$ be a real number, and let E be a set of directed edges in $\mathbb{R}^d$.

1. We say that E satisfies the *w-gap property* if for any two distinct edges (p, q) and (r, s) in E, we have

$$|pr| > w \cdot \min(|pq|, |rs|).$$

2. We say that E satisfies the *strong w-gap property* if for any two distinct edges (p, q) and (r, s) in E, we have

$$|pr| > w \cdot \min(|pq|, |rs|)$$

and

$$|qs| > w \cdot \min(|pq|, |rs|).$$

The *Gap Theorem* below bounds the total length of any set of edges that satisfies the gap property. Recall that for any directed edge (p, q), p is called the *source*, and q is called the *sink*.

Theorem 6.1.2 (Gap Theorem). *Let S be a set of n points in $\mathbb{R}^d$, and let $E \subseteq S \times S$ be a set of directed edges that satisfies the w-gap property.*

1. *If $w \geq 0$, then each point of S is the source of at most one edge of E.*
2. *If $w > 0$, then*

$$wt(E) < (1 + 2/w) \cdot wt(MST(S)) \log n,$$

where $MST(S)$ denotes a minimum spanning tree of S.

3. *If $w \geq 0$, and E satisfies the strong w-gap property, then each point of S is the sink of at most one edge of E.*

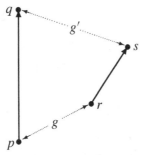

Figure 6.1: Illustrating the strong w-gap property for the two directed edges (p, q) and (r, s). The distance g between the two sources p and r is larger than w times the length of the shorter edge (r, s). Similarly, the distance g' between the two sinks q and s is larger than $w|rs|$.

PROOF　Let (p, q) and (r, s) be two distinct edges of E. The lower bound on $|pr|$, which is the distance between the source vertices, in Definition 6.1.1 immediately implies that $|pr| > 0$. Therefore, $p \neq r$, which proves the first claim. The third claim follows in a similar way, by applying the argument to the sink vertices.

In the rest of the proof, we will prove the second of the three claims. So assume that $w > 0$. Let m be the number of edges in E. First observe that the second claim holds if $m = 1$. Henceforth, we assume that $m \geq 2$.

Let us first assume that m is even. We make an additional claim that E contains a subset E' of size $m/2$, such that $wt(E') < (2/w) \cdot wt(MST(S))$. To prove this claim, we consider a shortest traveling salesperson tour $TSP(S)$ of S, and number the points of S such that $TSP(S) = (p_1, p_2, \ldots, p_n, p_1)$. Now we walk along this tour, starting at p_1, and consider the order in which we visit the *sources* of the edges of E. (We know that all sources are distinct. Hence, this order is uniquely defined.) We number the edges of E according to this order as $e_1, e_2, \ldots, e_m$. For each i with $1 \leq i \leq m$, let $|e_i|$ denote the length of e_i, and let k_i be the index such that edge e_i has point p_{k_i} as its source. Observe that $1 \leq k_1 < k_2 < \cdots < k_m \leq n$.

Let i be an integer with $1 \leq i \leq m/2$, and consider the edges e_{2i-1} and e_{2i}. Let T_i be the portion of $TSP(S)$ that starts at $p_{k_{2i-1}}$ and ends at $p_{k_{2i}}$, that is,

$$T_i = (p_{k_{2i-1}}, p_{k_{2i-1}+1}, \ldots, p_{k_{2i}}).$$

The triangle inequality implies that

$$|p_{k_{2i-1}} p_{k_{2i}}| \leq wt(T_i).$$

On the other hand, since e_{2i-1} and e_{2i} satisfy the w-gap property, we have

$$|p_{k_{2i-1}} p_{k_{2i}}| > w \cdot \min(|e_{2i-1}|, |e_{2i}|).$$

Combining these two inequalities, we get

$$\min(|e_{2i-1}|, |e_{2i}|) < \frac{1}{w} \cdot wt(T_i).$$

Since the portions T_i, $1 \leq i \leq m/2$, are pairwise disjoint, the latter inequality implies that

$$\sum_{i=1}^{m/2} \min(|e_{2i-1}|, |e_{2i}|) < \frac{1}{w} \sum_{i=1}^{m/2} wt(T_i) \leq \frac{1}{w} \cdot wt(TSP(S)).$$

It should be clear how the subset E' is obtained: For each i with $1 \leq i \leq m/2$, E' contains the shorter of the two edges e_{2i-1} and e_{2i}. (Ties are broken arbitrarily.) This set E' has size $m/2$, and its weight is less than $(1/w) \cdot wt(TSP(S))$. Since $wt(TSP(S)) \leq 2 \cdot wt(MST(S))$, see Exercise 1.6, it follows that $wt(E') < (2/w) \cdot wt(MST(S))$.

If m is an odd integer with $m \geq 3$, then a similar argument implies that E contains a subset E' of size $(m + 1)/2$ such that $wt(E') < (1 + 2/w) \cdot wt(MST(S))$.

Now we can prove the second claim in the lemma. We will show by induction on m that

$$wt(E) < (1 + 2/w) \cdot wt(MST(S)) \log m. \tag{6.1}$$

This will imply the second claim, because $m \leq n$.

To start the induction, assume that $m = 2$. Since m is even, the set E contains an edge whose length is less than $(2/w) \cdot wt(MST(S))$. The length of the other edge of E is clearly less than or equal to $wt(MST(S))$. Hence, (6.1) holds in this case.

Let $m \geq 3$, and assume that (6.1) holds for all sets of edges that have less than m elements and satisfy the w-gap property. Let E' be a subset of E containing at least $m/2$ elements such that $wt(E') < (1 + 2/w) \cdot wt(MST(S))$. We have proved above that E' exists. The set $E \setminus E'$ has size at most $m/2$ and satisfies the w-gap property. Hence, by the induction hypothesis, we have $wt(E \setminus E') < (1 + 2/w) \cdot wt(MST(S)) \log(m/2)$. Since $wt(E) = wt(E') + wt(E \setminus E')$, it follows that (6.1) holds for the set E. ■

> **Proof of the Gap Theorem:** The optimal TSP tour is used in the proof. The lengths of the edges in E are "charged" to the TSP tour edges. The edges of E are numbered according to the order in which their sources are visited by an optimal traveling salesperson tour $TSP(S)$. For a given positive real number w, the shorter of any two consecutive edges has length less than $1/w$ times the portion of $TSP(S)$ that is bounded by their sources. Therefore, E contains a subset E' of size about half the size of E, such that $wt(E') = O(wt(TSP(S))) = O(wt(MST(S)))$. Applying this argument recursively to $E \setminus E'$ proves that $wt(E) = O(wt(MST(S)) \log n)$.

Remark 6.1.3. Besides the triangle inequality, we did not use any geometric properties in the proof of the Gap Theorem. Consequently, this theorem also holds for the case when E is a set of edges with weights from an arbitrary metric space.

Remark 6.1.4. In the proof, the lengths of the edges in E are "charged" to the TSP tour edges. However, the proof does not need the tour to be explicitly computed. It merely requires its existence.

6.2 A lower bound

The Gap Theorem gives an upper bound on the weight of any set of edges that satisfy the gap property. The following theorem proves that this upper bound is tight:

Theorem 6.2.1. *Let w be a real number with $0 < w < 1$, let $k \geq 2$ be an integer, and let $n = 3^k - 1$. There exists a set S of n points on the real line and a set $E \subseteq S \times S$ of directed edges, such that E satisfies the strong w-gap property, and*

$$wt(E) = \Omega(wt(MST(S)) \log n).$$

PROOF For each i with $0 \leq i < k$, we partition the interval $[0, 1]$ into 3^i intervals, each having length $1/3^i$. Thus, for $j = 0, 1, \ldots, 3^i - 1$, the j-th interval in this partition is $[j/3^i, (j+1)/3^i]$. For each such j, we divide the j-th interval into three subintervals of equal length, and define e_{ij} to be the middle of these three subintervals. Thus,

$$e_{ij} = [j/3^i + 1/3^{i+1}, j/3^i + 2/3^{i+1}].$$

We consider e_{ij} to be an edge on the real line, and define

$$E_i := \{e_{ij} : j = 0, 1, \ldots, 3^i - 1\}.$$

Finally, we define

$$E := E_0 \cup E_1 \cup E_2 \cup \cdots \cup E_{k-1}$$

and $S \subseteq \mathbb{R}$ to be the set of endpoints of the edges in E.

The number of edges in E is equal to

$$\sum_{i=0}^{k-1} 3^i = \frac{3^k - 1}{2}.$$

Let n denote the number of elements in S. Since the endpoints of all edges in E are pairwise distinct, we have $n = 3^k - 1$. We leave it as an exercise to verify that E satisfies the strong w-gap property, for *any* assignment of directions to the edges in E; see Exercise 6.2.

In order to prove the second part of the claim, we need to analyze the weight of E and the weight of a minimum spanning tree of S. Since the total weight of all edges in E_i is equal to $1/3$, we have

$$wt(E) = k/3 = \frac{1}{3} \log_3(n + 1) = \Omega(\log n).$$

The minimum spanning tree of S basically consists of the sorted sequence of the elements of S. Since the minimum and maximum elements of S are equal to $1/3^k$ and $1 - 1/3^k$, respectively, it follows that

$$wt(MST(S)) = 1 - \frac{2}{3^k} < 1.$$

By combining these bounds, it follows that

$$wt(E)/wt(MST(S)) > wt(E) = \Omega(\log n),$$

completing the proof of the theorem.   ∎

6.3 An upper bound for points in the unit cube

The Gap Theorem compares the weight of a set of edges satisfying the gap property to the weight of a minimum spanning tree on the endpoints of these edges. In this section, we consider the case when these endpoints are in the d-dimensional unit cube $[0, 1]^d$. It is well known that the weight of a minimum spanning tree of such a point set is $O(n^{1-1/d})$, and that this upper bound is tight (up to constant factors). The theorem below states that the same upper bound holds for the weight of a set of edges that satisfies the gap property. Let

$$c_d := \frac{\pi^{d/2}}{\Gamma(d/2 + 1)}, \tag{6.2}$$

where Γ denotes Euler's gamma-function. For large values of d, we have

$$c_d \sim \frac{1}{\sqrt{\pi d}} \left(\frac{2e\pi}{d} \right)^{d/2}.$$

Recall that a d-dimensional ball of radius R has volume $c_d R^d$.

Theorem 6.3.1. *Let S be a set of n points in the d-dimensional unit cube $[0, 1]^d$, where $d \geq 2$. Let w be a real number with $0 < w \leq 2/\sqrt{d}$, and let $E \subseteq S \times S$ be a set of directed edges that satisfies the w-gap property. Then*

$$wt(E) \leq c_{dw} n^{1-1/d},$$

where

$$c_{dw} = 1 + \frac{2^{2d+2}}{c_d w^d}.$$

For large dimensions d, we have

$$c_{dw} \sim 1 + \frac{2^{3d/2+2} \, d^{(d+1)/2}}{w^d \, e^{d/2} \, \pi^{(d-1)/2}}.$$

PROOF   We know from Theorem 6.1.2 that each point of S is the source of at most one edge of E. Therefore, the set E contains at most n edges.

We partition the edges of E into two subsets. An edge (p, q) is called *long*, if $|pq| > n^{-1/d}$, and *short* otherwise. Let E_ℓ be the set containing all long edges of E, and let E_s be the set containing all short edges of E. Clearly, we have

$$wt(E_s) \leq |E_s| n^{-1/d} \leq n^{1-1/d}.$$

In the rest of the proof, we will bound the weight of the long edges.

For any integer j, we define the interval $I_j \subseteq \mathbb{R}$ by

$$I_j := \left(\frac{2^j}{n^{1/d}}, \frac{2^{j+1}}{n^{1/d}} \right].$$

Using these intervals, we further partition the set E_ℓ into subsets

$$F_j := \{(p, q) \in E_\ell : |pq| \in I_j\}.$$

Since long edges are of length more than $n^{-1/d}$ and at most $\sqrt{d}$ (the diameter of the unit cube), we need to consider only sets F_j for integers j in the range

$$\left[0, \left\lfloor \log \left(\sqrt{d} n^{1/d} \right) \right\rfloor \right].$$

Let j be any index such that the set F_j is nonempty. We will prove an upper bound on the weight of F_j. Let k be the number of edges in F_j. We denote these edges by (p_i, q_i), $1 \leq i \leq k$. Let $L := 2^j/n^{1/d}$. Then for any i with $1 \leq i \leq k$, we have $L < |p_i q_i| \leq 2L$. Moreover, since the edges of E satisfy the w-gap property, we have

$$|p_i p_{i'}| > w \cdot \min(|p_i q_i|, |p_{i'} q_{i'}|) > wL$$

for any two distinct indices i and i'. Hence, if we draw a d-dimensional ball B_i of radius $wL/2$ around each point p_i, $1 \leq i \leq k$, then these balls are pairwise disjoint. Since $wL/2 \leq w\sqrt{d}/2 \leq 1$, at least a fraction $(1/2)^d$ of each ball B_i is contained in the unit cube.

Recall that we defined c_d to be $\pi^{d/2}/\Gamma(d/2 + 1)$, and that a d-dimensional ball of radius R has volume $c_d R^d$. It follows that the total volume of all portions of the balls B_i inside the unit cube is greater than or equal to

$$k \left(\frac{1}{2} \right)^d c_d \left(\frac{wL}{2} \right)^d.$$

This quantity must obviously be less than or equal to 1. Therefore,

$$k \leq \frac{2^{2d}}{c_d w^d L^d}.$$

Since each edge of F_j has length at most $2L$, we get the upper bound

$$wt(F_j) \leq 2Lk \leq 2L \frac{2^{2d}}{c_d w^d L^d} = \frac{2^{2d+1}}{c_d w^d 2^{j(d-1)}} n^{1-1/d}.$$

Define $m := \lfloor \log(\sqrt{d} n^{1/d}) \rfloor$. Then summing the weights of all sets F_j, we get

$$wt(E_\ell) = \sum_{j=0}^{m} wt(F_j)$$

$$\leq \sum_{j=0}^{m} \frac{2^{2d+1}}{c_d w^d 2^{j(d-1)}} n^{1-1/d}$$

$$\leq \frac{2^{2d+2}}{c_d w^d} n^{1-1/d},$$

where the last inequality follows from the fact that $d \geq 2$. Since $wt(E) = wt(E_s) + wt(E_\ell)$, the proof is complete.   ∎

6.4 A useful geometric lemma

In this section, we generalize Lemma 4.1.4; the reader may recall that it proved that in order to go from vertex p to vertex q, it is worthwhile to head for any vertex that is (approximately) at most as far as q and that is in the general direction of q. The more technical, yet stronger, lemma presented in this section will be used at several places in this book, for example in the analysis in Section 6.5 of the 2-OPT algorithm for the traveling salesperson problem, in the proof in Section 7.1 that the output of the gap-greedy algorithm is a spanner, and in the analysis in Section 15.1.1 of the output of the path-greedy algorithm.

In Section 5.3, we defined the angle between two directed edges. We recall the definition: Let p, q, r, and s be four points in $\mathbb{R}^d$ such that $p \neq q$ and $r \neq s$. The angle between the directed edges (p, q) and (r, s), denoted by angle(pq, rs), is defined as follows: Translate the two edges (p, q) and (r, s) such that their sources are at the origin. Then angle(pq, rs) is the angle between these two translates; it is a real number in the interval $[0, \pi]$.

Lemma 6.4.1. *Let t, θ, and w be real numbers, such that $0 < \theta < \pi/4$, $0 \leq w < (\cos\theta - \sin\theta)/2$, and $t \geq 1/(\cos\theta - \sin\theta - 2w)$. Let $p, q, r,$ and s be points in $\mathbb{R}^d$, such that*

1. $p \neq q, r \neq s$,
2. angle$(pq, rs) \leq \theta$,
3. $|rs| \leq |pq|/\cos\theta$, and
4. $|pr| \leq w|rs|$.

Then $|pr| < |pq|, |sq| < |pq|,$ and $t|pr| + |rs| + t|sq| \leq t|pq|$.

PROOF   Since $|rs| \leq |pq|/\cos\theta$ and $0 < \theta < \pi/4$, we have $|rs| < \sqrt{2}|pq|$. Also, since $w < 1/2$ and $|pr| \leq w|rs|$, we have $|pr| < |rs|/2$. Combining these two inequalities gives $|pr| < \sqrt{2}|pq|/2 < |pq|$.

Let ℓ be the ray that emanates from r and that has the same direction as the vector $\vec{pq}$. Let v be the point on ℓ, such that $|rv| = |pq|$. Observe that $|pr| = |vq|$. Let u be the orthogonal projection of s onto ℓ, and let α be the angle between $\vec{rs}$ and ℓ. Then $\alpha = $ angle$(pq, rs) \leq \theta$, $\sin\alpha = |su|/|rs|$ and $\cos\alpha = |ru|/|rs|$. We distinguish two cases, depending on whether $|ru| \leq |rv|$ or $|ru| > |rv|$; see Figure 6.2.

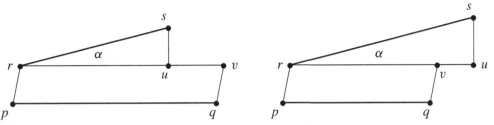

Figure 6.2: Cases 1 and 2 in the proof of Lemma 6.4.1.

Case 1: $|ru| \leq |rv|$.

To show that $|sq| < |pq|$, we apply the triangle inequality and simplify:

$$
\begin{aligned}
|sq| &\leq |su| + |uv| + |vq| \\
&= |su| + |rv| - |ru| + |vq| \\
&= |su| + |pq| - |ru| + |pr| \\
&= |rs|(\sin\alpha - \cos\alpha) + |pq| + |pr| \\
&\leq |rs|(\sin\theta - \cos\theta) + |pq| + w|rs| \\
&= |pq| - |rs|(\cos\theta - \sin\theta - w).
\end{aligned}
\tag{6.3}
$$

Since $w < (\cos\theta - \sin\theta)/2$ and $r \neq s$, we conclude that $|sq| < |pq|$.

To prove the third claim, we use (6.3) and the assumptions of the lemma, and obtain

$$
\begin{aligned}
t|pr| + |rs| + t|sq| &\leq t|pr| + |rs| + t|pq| - t|rs|(\cos\theta - \sin\theta - w) \\
&\leq tw|rs| + |rs| + t|pq| - t|rs|(\cos\theta - \sin\theta - w) \\
&= (1 - t(\cos\theta - \sin\theta - 2w))\,|rs| + t|pq| \\
&\leq t|pq|.
\end{aligned}
$$

Case 2: $|ru| > |rv|$.

As in Case 1, we apply the triangle inequality and simplify:

$$
\begin{aligned}
|sq| &\leq |su| + |uv| + |vq| \\
&= |su| + |ru| - |rv| + |vq| \\
&= |rs|(\sin\alpha + \cos\alpha) - |pq| + |pr| \\
&\leq |rs|(\sin\theta + \cos\theta) - |pq| + w|rs| \\
&= |rs|(\sin\theta + w) + |rs|\cos\theta - |pq| \\
&\leq |rs|(\sin\theta + w) \\
&\leq \frac{|pq|}{\cos\theta}\left(\sin\theta + \frac{\cos\theta - \sin\theta}{2}\right) \\
&= \frac{1}{2}|pq|(1 + \tan\theta).
\end{aligned}
\tag{6.4}
$$

Since $0 < \theta < \pi/4$, we have $\tan\theta < 1$. Therefore, $|sq| < |pq|$.

We complete the proof by using (6.4) and the assumptions of the lemma. We have

$$
\begin{aligned}
t|pr| + |rs| + t|sq| &\leq t|pr| + |rs| + t|rs|(\sin\theta + w) \\
&\leq tw|rs| + |rs| + t|rs|(\sin\theta + w)
\end{aligned}
$$

$$= (1 + t(\sin\theta + 2w)) |rs|$$
$$= t|pq| - t|pq| + (1 + t(\sin\theta + 2w)) |rs|$$
$$\leq t|pq| - t|rs|\cos\theta + (1 + t(\sin\theta + 2w)) |rs|$$
$$= t|pq| - (t(\cos\theta - \sin\theta - 2w) - 1) |rs|$$
$$\leq t|pq|.$$

This completes the proof. ∎

An application: Assume that we want to travel from vertex p to vertex q. Moreover, assume that there is a directed edge (r, s), such that (i) (r, s) is almost parallel to (p, q), (ii) $|rs|$ is not much larger than $|pq|$, and (iii) r is close to p. Then Lemma 6.4.1 states that we obtain a short path between p and q, by first traveling from p to r, then following the edge (r, s), and finally traveling from s to q. We remark that Lemma 6.4.1 states that the two edges (p, q) and (r, s) do *not* satisfy the *leapfrog property* that will be defined in Section 14.1.

6.5 Worst-case analysis of the 2-OPT algorithm for the traveling salesperson problem

In this section, we show the following surprising application of the Gap Theorem: The 2-OPT algorithm for the Euclidean traveling salesperson problem outputs a set of edges that can be partitioned into a constant number of subsets, each of which satisfies the gap property. Hence, the 2-OPT algorithm computes, for a given set S of n points in $\mathbb{R}^d$, a tour of length $O(\log n)$ times the length of an optimal traveling salesperson tour of S.

Let S be a set of n points in $\mathbb{R}^d$. Recall that in the traveling salesperson problem, we want to find a shortest tour that visits each point of S and returns to its starting point. Such a shortest tour is denoted by $TSP(S)$. Since this problem is **NP**-hard, *heuristics* have been developed that are fast and compute tours that are reasonably short on practical instances. One such heuristic is the 2-OPT algorithm.

In the 2-OPT algorithm, we start with an arbitrary initial tour, and improve it by making small local changes. To be more precise, let T be the current tour along the points of S. We assume that the edges of T are directed. As long as T contains distinct edges (p, q) and (r, s), such that

$$|pr| + |qs| < |pq| + |rs|, \tag{6.5}$$

the 2-OPT algorithm improves T by replacing the two edges (p, q) and (r, s) by the edges (p, r) and (q, s), and reversing the direction of the edges on the path from q to r; the situation is shown in Figure 6.3, where the original tour is shown as straight lines, and the replacement edges are shown as dotted lines.

The 2-OPT algorithm results in a tour T_0 such that (6.5) does not hold for any pair of distinct edges. Such a tour is called 2-*optimal*. Computing the worst-case value for the approximation factor $wt(T_0)/wt(TSP(S))$ was a long-standing open problem. As mentioned above, we use the gap property to show that this approximation factor is $O(\log n)$.

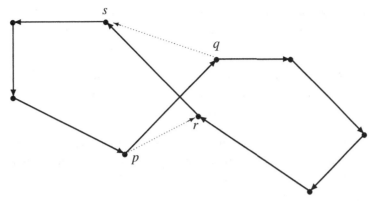

Figure 6.3: The 2-OPT algorithm replaces the two edges (p, q) and (r, s) by the edges (p, r) and (q, s). Reversing the direction of the edges on the path from q to r results in a shorter (directed) tour.

To prove this claim, let T_0 be a tour along the points of S that is 2-optimal. Then for any two distinct edges (p, q) and (r, s) of T_0, we have

$$|pr| + |qs| \geq |pq| + |rs|. \tag{6.6}$$

The following lemma states that any two distinct edges of T_0 that are approximately parallel satisfy the gap property. We choose real numbers θ and w such that $0 < \theta < \pi/4$ and $0 < w < (\cos\theta - \sin\theta)/2$.

Lemma 6.5.1. *Let (p, q) and (r, s) be two distinct edges of T_0, and assume that* angle$(pq, rs) \leq \theta$. *Then*

$$|pr| > w \cdot \min(|pq|, |rs|),$$

i.e., (p, q) and (r, s) satisfy the w-gap property.

PROOF We may assume without loss of generality that $|rs| \leq |pq|$. The proof is by contradiction. So assume that $|pr| \leq w|rs|$. Let $t := 1/(\cos\theta - \sin\theta - 2w)$. Then, by Lemma 6.4.1, we have

$$t|pr| + |rs| + t|sq| \leq t|pq|.$$

Since the tour T_0 is 2-optimal, inequality (6.6) implies that $|pq| \leq |pr| + |sq| - |rs|$. Therefore, we have

$$t|pr| + |rs| + t|sq| \leq t|pr| + t|sq| - t|rs|,$$

which rewrites to $(1 + t)|rs| \leq 0$. This is clearly a contradiction, because $r \neq s$. ∎

We partition the edges of T_0 into $O(1/\theta^{d-1})$ subsets, such that any two edges within the same subset make an angle of at most θ; see Theorem 5.3.3. It follows from Lemma 6.5.1 and Theorem 6.1.2 that the weight of the edges within each subset is less than $(1 + 2/w) \cdot wt(MST(S)) \log n$. Hence, by using the fact that $wt(MST(S)) \leq wt(TSP(S))$ (see Exercise 1.6), it follows that

$$wt(T_0) = O\left(\frac{1}{w\theta^{d-1}} \cdot wt(TSP(S)) \log n\right). \tag{6.7}$$

Observe that this upper bound holds for all real numbers θ and w for which $0 < \theta < \pi/4$ and $0 < w < (\cos\theta - \sin\theta)/2$. Choosing θ and w to be constants implies the following theorem.

Theorem 6.5.2. *Let $d \geq 2$ be an integer constant, and let S be a set of n points in $\mathbb{R}^d$. The 2-OPT algorithm computes a tour along the points of S, whose length is $O(\log n)$ times the length of an optimal traveling salesperson tour of S.*

Hence, the worst-case approximation ratio of the 2-OPT algorithm is $O(\log n)$. It can be shown that there are infinitely many integers n for which this ratio is greater than or equal to $c \log n / \log \log n$, for some fixed constant c.

> **Open problem:** What is the largest possible value of the ratio $wt(T_0)/wt(TSP(S))$, over all sets S of n points in $\mathbb{R}^d$ and all 2-optimal tours T_0 of S?

Exercises

6.1. Let $w > 0$ be a real number, let S be finite set of points in $\mathbb{R}^d$, and let $E \subseteq S \times S$ be a set of directed edges, such that for any two distinct edges (p, q) and (r, s) in E,

$$|pr| > w \cdot \max(|pq|, |rs|).$$

Prove that

$$wt(E) = O((1 + 1/w) \cdot wt(MST(S))).$$

6.2. Prove that the edge set E defined in the proof of Theorem 6.2.1 satisfies the strong w-gap property, for any real number w with $0 < w < 1$ and for any assignment of directions to the edges in E.

6.3. Let S be a set of n points in the d-dimensional unit cube $[0, 1]^d$. Prove that the weight of a minimum spanning tree of S is less than or equal to $c'_d n^{1-1/d}$, where c'_d is a real number that depends only on d. Prove that this upper bound is tight (to within a constant factor), if d is a constant.

6.4. Prove that Lemma 4.1.4 is a special case of Lemma 6.4.1.

6.5. Let S be a finite set of points in the plane, and let T_0 be a traveling salesperson tour that is 2-optimal. Prove that no two edges of T_0 cross.

6.6. Give an example of a noncrossing tour along a set of points in the plane that is not 2-optimal.

6.7. We have seen that the 2-OPT algorithm computes a tour T_0 along the point set S whose length is

$$O\left(\frac{1}{w\theta^{d-1}} \cdot wt(TSP(S)) \log n\right)$$

for any two real numbers θ and w for which $0 < \theta < \pi/4$ and $0 < w < (\cos\theta - \sin\theta)/2$; see (6.7). Determine θ and w for which this upper bound is as small as possible.

6.8. Prove the following claim: For infinitely many positive integers n, there exists a set S of n points in the plane and a tour T_0 along the points of S, such that T_0 is 2-optimal and

$$wt(T_0) \geq c \cdot wt(TSP(S)) \frac{\log n}{\log \log n},$$

for some fixed constant c.

Bibliographic notes

The gap property was introduced by Chandra et al. [1995]. They also proved the Gap Theorem. Section 6.3 is based on Chandra [1994], whereas Section 6.4 is based on Arya and Smid [1997].

The 2-OPT algorithm for the traveling salesperson problem is due to Lin [1965]; see also Lin and Kernighan [1973]. The analysis given in Section 6.5 is based on Chandra, Karloff, and Tovey [1999]; see also Alon and Azar [1993]. A solution to Exercise 6.8 can be found in Chandra, Karloff, and Tovey [1999].

The upper bound in Exercise 6.3 was originally shown by Few [1955]. The dependence on the dimension d was subsequently improved by Smith [1988] and Steele and Snyder [1989]; see also the book Hwang, Richards, and Winter [1992].

7

The Gap-Greedy Algorithm

> The point is, ladies and gentlemen, that greed, for lack of a better word, is good. Greed is right. Greed works.
> —Gordon Gecko (played by Michael Douglas), *Wall Street*, 1987

In Chapter 6, we defined the *gap property* (Definition 6.1.1). The Gap Theorem (Theorem 6.1.2) proved that any set E of directed edges whose endpoints belong to a set S of n points in $\mathbb{R}^d$ and that satisfies the w-gap property for some constant $w > 0$ has weight $O(wt(MST(S)) \log n)$. We also proved that if E satisfies the strong w-gap property, then both the indegree and outdegree of each point of S are at most one in the graph (S, E).

In this chapter, we present the so-called gap-greedy algorithm. This algorithm computes a spanner whose edge set can be partitioned into a constant number of subsets, each satisfying the strong gap property. Thus, Theorem 6.1.2 immediately gives upper bounds on the degree and the weight of this spanner.

We will give only the details for the planar case. In Section 7.5, we will indicate how the algorithm can be generalized to an arbitrary dimension $d \geq 2$.

In Section 7.2, we start with a simple and inefficient version of the gap-greedy algorithm. A geometric lemma, proved in Section 7.1, shows that this graph has a small stretch factor. Hence, this algorithm, when given any set S of n points in the plane, constructs a spanner of bounded degree and having weight $O(wt(MST(S)) \log n)$. Its running time, however, is $\Theta(n^3)$. In Sections 7.3 and 7.4, we design a variant of this algorithm, and show how to implement it such that its running time is $O(n \log^2 n)$.

It turns out to be convenient to describe the algorithm so that it computes a directed spanner. Therefore, all edges in this chapter are directed edges. Recall that the degree of a vertex in a directed graph is defined to be the sum of its indegree and outdegree.

7.1 A sufficient condition for "spannerhood"

In this section, we prove a geometric lemma, which will be used later to prove that the graph constructed by the gap-greedy algorithm has a small stretch factor.

> **When does a directed graph G have a small stretch factor:** Assume that for any two distinct points p and q of a point set S, there is an edge (r, s) in G such that (i) the vectors $\overrightarrow{pq}$ and $\overrightarrow{rs}$ have approximately the same direction, (ii) $|rs|$ is not much larger than $|pq|$, and (iii) at least one of the distances $|pr|$ and $|qs|$ is small (relative to the length of (r, s)). Then G has a small stretch factor.

We will use the notation angle (pq, rs) for the angle between the directed edges (p, q) and (r, s); see Section 5.3.

Lemma 7.1.1. *Let* θ, w, *and* t *be real numbers such that* $0 < \theta < \pi/4$, $0 \le w < (\cos\theta - \sin\theta)/2$, *and* $t \ge 1/(\cos\theta - \sin\theta - 2w)$. *Let* S *be a set of* n *points in the plane, and let* $G = (S, E)$ *be a directed graph, such that the following holds: For any two distinct points* p *and* q *of* S, *there is an edge* $(r, s) \in E$, *such that*

1. angle $(pq, rs) \le \theta$,
2. $|rs| \le |pq|/\cos\theta$, *and*
3. $|pr| \le w|rs|$ *or* $|qs| \le w|rs|$.

Then, the graph G *is a* t-*spanner for* S.

PROOF Let p and q be any two points of S. We will show that G contains a (directed) t-spanner path from p to q. The proof is by induction on the rank of the distance $|pq|$ in the sorted sequence of distances determined by all ordered pairs of points. If $|pq| = 0$, then $p = q$ and G clearly contains a t-spanner path from p to q. Assume that $|pq| > 0$. Furthermore, assume that for any two points x and y of S with $|xy| < |pq|$, the graph G contains a t-spanner path from x to y.

Let (r, s) be any edge of E for which all three premises of this lemma hold. We will consider the case only when $|pr| \le w|rs|$. (The case when $|qs| \le w|rs|$ can be treated by a symmetric argument.) Since the premises of Lemma 6.4.1 from the previous chapter are satisfied, it follows from that lemma that $|pr| < |pq|$, $|sq| < |pq|$, and

$$t|pr| + |rs| + t|sq| \le t|pq|. \tag{7.1}$$

Hence, by the induction hypothesis, there are t-spanner paths in G from p to r, and from s to q. Consider the path in G that starts in p, follows the t-spanner path to r, then takes the edge from r to s, and finally follows the t-spanner path from s to q. The length of this path is bounded from above by $t|pr| + |rs| + t|sq|$, which, by (7.1), is less than or equal to $t|pq|$. Hence, G contains a t-spanner path from p to q. ■

7.2 The gap-greedy algorithm

In this section, we give a simple greedy algorithm for constructing a spanner. We call it the *gap-greedy* algorithm, in order to distinguish it from the *path-greedy* algorithm that will be given in Chapter 15.

Recall the strong gap property of Section 6.1: If $w \ge 0$ is a real number, then a set E of directed edges satisfies the strong w-gap property, if for any two distinct edges (p, q) and (r, s) in E, we have

$$|pr| > w \cdot \min(|pq|, |rs|)$$

and

$$|qs| > w \cdot \min(|pq|, |rs|).$$

The gap-greedy algorithm: The algorithm starts with an empty set E of edges, and considers all ordered pairs of distinct points in nondecreasing order of their distances. Let p and q form the current pair of points. The algorithm adds the edge (p, q) to E if it does not violate the strong gap property. That is, the decision whether or not edge (p, q) is added to E is based on Lemma 7.1.1: Edge (p, q) is added if and only if there is no edge (r, s) in the current edge set E such that (i) (p, q) and (r, s) have approximately the same direction, and (ii) at least one of the distances $|pr|$ and $|qs|$ is small. If there is such an edge (r, s), then Lemma 7.1.1 implies that we do not need to add the edge (p, q) in order to get a graph with a small stretch factor.

Algorithm GapGreedy(S, θ, w)

Comment: This algorithm takes as input a set S of n points in the plane, and two real numbers θ and w such that $0 < \theta < \pi/4$ and $0 \leq w < (\cos\theta - \sin\theta)/2$. The algorithm returns a directed t-spanner $G = (S, E)$, for $t = 1/(\cos\theta - \sin\theta - 2w)$.

sort the $2\binom{n}{2}$ ordered pairs of distinct points in non-decreasing order
of their distances (ties are broken arbitrarily), and store them in a
list L;
$E := \emptyset$;
for each ordered pair $(p, q) \in L$ (* consider pairs in sorted order *)
do $add := true$;
   for each edge $(r, s) \in E$
   do if angle$(pq, rs) \leq \theta$.
     then $add := add \wedge (|pr| > w|rs|) \wedge (|qs| > w|rs|)$
    endif
   endfor;
   if $add = true$ **then** $E := E \cup \{(p, q)\}$ **endif**
endfor;
return the graph $G = (S, E)$

Lemma 7.2.1. *Let θ and w be real numbers such that $0 < \theta < \pi/4$ and $0 \leq w < (\cos\theta - \sin\theta)/2$, and let S be a set of n points in the plane. The graph $G = (S, E)$ that is returned by algorithm GapGreedy(S, θ, w) is a t-spanner for S, for $t = 1/(\cos\theta - \sin\theta - 2w)$.*

PROOF It is sufficient to show that the set E satisfies the three conditions of Lemma 7.1.1, since this implies that the graph G is a t-spanner for S.

Let p and q be any two distinct points of S. If (p, q) is an edge of E, then the three conditions of Lemma 7.1.1 hold with $r = p$ and $s = q$. Assume that (p, q) is not an edge of E. Consider the iteration of the outer for-loop during which the pair (p, q) was inspected. The algorithm did not add (p, q) to E because this set contained an edge (r, s), such that (i) angle$(pq, rs) \leq \theta$, and (ii) at least one of $|pr|$ and $|qs|$ is less than or equal to $w|rs|$. Since (r, s) was contained in E at the moment when the algorithm inspected the pair (p, q), we have $|rs| \leq |pq|$. In particular, $|rs| \leq |pq|/\cos\theta$. Therefore, the three conditions of Lemma 7.1.1 are satisfied. ∎

Lemma 7.2.2. *Let θ and w be real numbers such that $0 < \theta < \pi/4$ and $0 \leq w < (\cos\theta - \sin\theta)/2$, and let S be a set of n points in the plane.*

1. *Algorithm* GapGreedy(S, θ, w) *computes a graph in which each vertex has degree at most $2\lceil 2\pi/\theta \rceil$.*

2. *If $w > 0$, then the weight of this graph is less than $\lceil 2\pi/\theta \rceil(1 + 2/w)\log n$ times the weight of a minimum spanning tree of S.*

PROOF Consider any two distinct edges (p, q) and (r, s) in the graph $G = (S, E)$ that is constructed by algorithm GapGreedy(S, θ, w), and assume that angle $(pq, rs) \leq \theta$. We may assume without loss of generality that (r, s) was added to E before (p, q). It follows from the algorithm that $|rs| \leq |pq|$, $|pr| > w|rs|$, and $|qs| > w|rs|$. Hence, the strong w-gap property holds for the edges (p, q) and (r, s).

Consider a collection $\mathcal{C}$ of $\lceil 2\pi/\theta \rceil$ cones of angle θ that have their apex at the origin and that cover the plane. Number the cones of $\mathcal{C}$ as $C_1, C_2, \ldots, C_{\lceil 2\pi/\theta \rceil}$. For each i with $1 \leq i \leq \lceil 2\pi/\theta \rceil$, define

$$E_i := \{(p, q) \in E : q - p \in C_i\}.$$

Since $E_i \subseteq E$ for $1 \leq i \leq \lceil 2\pi/\theta \rceil$, it is clear that E_i satisfies the strong w-gap property. Furthermore, Theorem 6.1.2 implies that no two distinct edges of E_i share a source, and no two distinct edges of E_i share a sink. Since the sets E_i, $1 \leq i \leq \lceil 2\pi/\theta \rceil$, partition E, it follows that each point p of S has indegree and outdegree at most $\lceil 2\pi/\theta \rceil$ in G; that is, the degree of p in G is less than or equal to $2\lceil 2\pi/\theta \rceil$. Also, if $w > 0$, then Theorem 6.1.2 implies that the weight of E is less than

$$\lceil 2\pi/\theta \rceil(1 + 2/w) \cdot wt(MST(S))\log n.$$

This completes the proof. ∎

Let us examine the quality of the output of algorithm GapGreedy, as a function of the upper bound t on the stretch factor.

Let $\epsilon > 0$ be a real number and let $t = 1 + \epsilon$. We assume that ϵ is close to zero. How should we choose θ and w so as to achieve the best bound on the weight of the t-spanner? In order to minimize the weight, we have to minimize the expression $(2\pi/\theta)(1 + 2/w)$. Since $t = 1 + \epsilon = 1/(\cos\theta - \sin\theta - 2w)$, we have

$$w = \frac{1}{2}\left(\cos\theta - \sin\theta - \frac{1}{1 + \epsilon}\right).$$

Since ϵ is close to zero, θ is close to zero as well, and we can approximate the expression for w by

$$w \sim \frac{1}{2}(1 - \theta - (1 - \epsilon)) = \frac{1}{2}(\epsilon - \theta).$$

Hence, we have to minimize

$$\frac{2\pi}{\theta}\left(1 + \frac{2}{w}\right) \sim \frac{2\pi}{\theta}\frac{4}{\epsilon - \theta};$$

that is, we have to maximize $\theta(\epsilon - \theta)$. The latter expression is maximum for $\theta = \epsilon/2$, which gives $w = \epsilon/4$. The corresponding $(1 + \epsilon)$-spanner has degree at most $8\pi/\epsilon$, and weight at most $(32\pi/\epsilon^2)\log n$ times the weight of a minimum spanning tree of S. Hence, we have proved the following result.

Theorem 7.2.3. *Let S be a set of n points in the plane, and let $t > 1$ be a real number. Algorithm GAPGREEDY$(S, (t-1)/2, (t-1)/4)$ computes a t-spanner for S,*

1. in which the degree of each point is $O(1/(t-1))$ and

2. whose weight is $O((1/(t-1)^2) \cdot wt(MST(S)) \log n)$.

7.3 Toward an efficient implementation

A direct implementation of algorithm GAPGREEDY has running time $\Theta(n^3)$. One of the obstacles in designing an $o(n^2)$–time implementation of this algorithm is the fact that all pairs of points are considered. In this section, we discuss several modifications to the algorithm with the goal of improving the time complexity. As we will see in the next section (Section 7.4), this modified version can be implemented such that its running time is $O(n \log^2 n)$.

Throughout this section, we fix a real number θ with $0 < \theta < \pi/4$. Let $\kappa = \lceil 2\pi/\theta \rceil$, and let $\mathcal{C}_\kappa$ be a collection of κ cones of angle θ that have their apex at the origin and that cover the plane. As always, we denote the Euclidean distance between the points p and q by $|pq|$. The L_∞-distance between $p = (p_1, p_2)$ and $q = (q_1, q_2)$ will be denoted by $|pq|_\infty$, i.e.,

$$|pq|_\infty = \max(|p_1 - q_1|, |p_2 - q_2|).$$

It is easy to see that

$$|pq|_\infty \leq |pq| \leq \sqrt{2}|pq|_\infty.$$

We will make three major modifications to algorithm GAPGREEDY. Consider the formal description of the algorithm as given in Section 7.2.

Modification 1: We replace the condition "angle$(pq, rs) \leq \theta$" by "$q - p$ and $s - r$ are contained in the same cone of $\mathcal{C}_\kappa$." It is clear that the latter condition implies the former although the converse need not be true.

Modification 2: As prescribed in the pseudocode, after algorithm GAPGREEDY has added an edge (r, s) to the graph, it does not add any edge (p, q) that has approximately the same direction as (r, s), and for which p is "close" to r or q is "close" to s. Consider this condition for the points p and r. In the algorithm, p is "close" to r, if p is contained in a circle that is centered at r and that has radius $w|rs|$. Since it is not clear how to efficiently find all points p of S that are in this circle, we modify the notion of p being "close" to r, in the following way.

In algorithm GAPGREEDY, we replace the inequality "$|pr| > w|rs|$" by "$|pr|_\infty > (w/\sqrt{2})|rs|$," and the inequality "$|qs| > w|rs|$" by "$|qs|_\infty > (w/\sqrt{2})|rs|$." That is, for the points p and r (and for the points q and s), we switch from the Euclidean metric to the L_∞-metric. Observe that all points p for which $|pr|_\infty \leq (w/\sqrt{2})|rs|$ are contained in the axes-parallel square that is centered at r and that has sides of length $2(w/\sqrt{2})|rs|$. Using range trees, see Section 5.4, we can find these points p efficiently. A similar remark holds for the points q and s.

Modification 3: Algorithm GAPGREEDY considers all pairs of points in nondecreasing order of their Euclidean distances. If (r, s) is an edge of the current graph, and (p, q) is the current pair to be tested for inclusion, then we know that $|rs| \leq |pq|$. By Lemma 7.1.1,

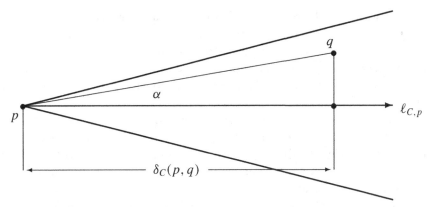

Figure 7.1: The approximate distance $\delta_C(p, q)$.

however, it suffices that $|rs| \leq |pq|/\cos\theta$, that is, $|rs|$ can be slightly larger than $|pq|$. (See also the proof of Lemma 7.2.1.)

Our third modification is as follows. Instead of considering all pairs of points in nondecreasing order of their distances, we consider them in nondecreasing order of their *approximate* distances, to be defined below. As we will see later, this avoids having to explicitly consider all pairs of points.

The approximate distances that we will use are based on the cones of $\mathcal{C}_\kappa$. For each cone $C \in \mathcal{C}_\kappa$, let ℓ_C be a fixed ray that emanates from the origin and that is contained in C. For example, we can think of ℓ_C as being the bisector of cone C. Recall the notation $C_p := C + p := \{x + p : x \in C\}$ and $\ell_{C,p} := \ell_C + p$ introduced in Section 4.1.

For any cone $C \in \mathcal{C}_\kappa$, and any two points p and q in the plane, we define (refer to Figure 7.1)

$$\delta_C(p, q) := \begin{cases} \text{the Euclidean distance between } p \text{ and} \\ \text{the orthogonal projection of } q \text{ onto } \ell_{C,p} & \text{if } q \in C_p, \\ \infty & \text{if } q \notin C_p. \end{cases}$$

Observe that δ_C is not a metric; in particular, it is not a symmetric function. The following lemma states that $\delta_C(p, q)$ is a good approximation for the Euclidean distance between p and q, if $q \in C_p$.

Lemma 7.3.1. *Let C be a cone of $\mathcal{C}_\kappa$, and let p and q be two distinct points in the plane, such that $q \in C_p$. Then*

$$|pq| \cos\theta \leq \delta_C(p, q) \leq |pq|.$$

PROOF Let α be the angle between $\ell_{C,p}$ and (p, q); see Figure 7.1. Then, $0 \leq \alpha \leq \theta$ and $\cos\alpha = \delta_C(p, q)/|pq|$. Hence, $\delta_C(p, q) = |pq| \cos\alpha \geq |pq| \cos\theta$ and $\delta_C(p, q) = |pq| \cos\alpha \leq |pq|$.   ∎

Now we are ready to present the modified version of algorithm GapGreedy. For each cone C of $\mathcal{C}_\kappa$, this modified algorithm computes a set E_C of edges (p, q) such that $q - p \in C$. The union of these sets will be the edge set of our final spanner.

Consider a cone C of $\mathcal{C}_\kappa$. The algorithm initializes E_C to the empty set. Then it computes two distinct points r and s for which $\delta_C(r, s)$ is minimum, and adds the edge (r, s) to E_C. Lemma 7.1.1 implies that, having added this edge, one may discard from further consideration for addition to E_C, all edges (p, q) for which (i) $q - p \in C$, and (ii) the distance between p and r is "small." That is, after having added (r, s), each point p that is "close" to r should not occur as the source of any edge that is added to E_C later during the algorithm. Similarly, after having added the edge (r, s) to E_C, each point q that is "close" to s should not occur as the sink of any edge that is added to E_C afterward. That is, the addition of edge (r, s) to E_C causes certain points to become *forbidden* as a source or a sink.

After having added the edge (r, s) to E_C, the algorithm computes two distinct points r' and s' such that r' is not forbidden as a source, s' is not forbidden as a sink, and $\delta_C(r', s')$ is minimum. It adds the edge (r', s') to E_C, and makes the appropriate points forbidden as a source or forbidden as a sink. The algorithm repeats this, as long as there are nonforbidden points having a finite δ_C-distance.

The algorithm uses variables *dist* to keep track of the points that are forbidden as source or sink vertices. Initially, $dist(r, s) = \delta_C(r, s)$, for any two points r and s in S. If an edge (r, s) is added to E_C, then the algorithm finds all points p that are "close" to r, and, for each such p, assigns $dist(p, q) := \infty$, for all $q \in S$. Similarly, the algorithm finds all points q that are "close" to s, and, for each such q, assigns $dist(p, q) := \infty$, for all $p \in S$.

Interpretation of the *dist*-variables: If $p \neq q$, then $dist(p, q)$ is finite if and only if, (i) $dist(p, q) = \delta_C(p, q)$, (ii) $q - p \in C$ (i.e., (p, q) may still be included in the edge set E_C), (iii) p is not forbidden (yet) as a source, and (iv) q is not forbidden (yet) as a sink.

Algorithm MODGAPGREEDY(S, θ, w)

Comment: This algorithm takes as input a set S of n points in the plane, and two real numbers θ and w such that $0 < \theta < \pi/4$ and $0 \leq w < (\cos\theta - \sin\theta)/2$. The algorithm returns a directed t-spanner $G = (S, E)$, for $t = 1/(\cos\theta - \sin\theta - 2w)$.

> **for each** cone C of $\mathcal{C}_\kappa$
> **do for each** $r \in S$ and $s \in S$ **do** $dist(r, s) := \delta_C(r, s)$ **endfor;**
> $E_C := \emptyset$;
>   **while** there are distinct points r and s such that $dist(r, s) < \infty$
>   **do** choose r and s $(r \neq s)$ such that $dist(r, s)$ is minimum;
> $E_C := E_C \cup \{(r, s)\}$;
>   **for each** $p \in S$ such that $|pr|_\infty \leq (w/\sqrt{2})|rs|$
>   **do for each** $q \in S$ **do** $dist(p, q) := \infty$ **endfor**
>   **endfor;**
>   **for each** $q \in S$ such that $|qs|_\infty \leq (w/\sqrt{2})|rs|$
>   **do for each** $p \in S$ **do** $dist(p, q) := \infty$ **endfor**
>   **endfor**
>   **endwhile**
> **endfor;**
> return the graph $G = (S, E)$, where $E := \bigcup_C E_C$

Lemma 7.3.2. *Let θ and w be real numbers such that $0 < \theta < \pi/4$ and $0 \leq w < (\cos\theta - \sin\theta)/2$, and let S be a set of n points in the plane. The graph $G = (S, E)$*

that is returned by algorithm MODGAPGREEDY(S, θ, w) *is a t-spanner for S, for* $t = 1/(\cos\theta - \sin\theta - 2w)$.

PROOF   The proof is similar to that of Lemma 7.2.1. Let p and q be two distinct points of S. If $(p, q) \in E$, then the three conditions of Lemma 7.1.1 hold. So assume that (p, q) is not contained in E. Let C be the cone of $\mathcal{C}_\kappa$ such that $q - p \in C$. Consider the iteration of the outer for-loop during which the edge set E_C is constructed. At the start of this iteration, $dist(p, q)$ is initialized to $\delta_C(p, q)$, which is finite. Since (p, q) is not added to E_C, the value of $dist(p, q)$ changes to ∞ during one of the iterations of the while-loop. Let (r, s) be the edge that is added to E_C during the iteration in which $dist(p, q)$ is set to ∞. At the start of this iteration, we have (i) $dist(r, s) \leq dist(p, q) < \infty$, (ii) $dist(r, s) = \delta_C(r, s)$ and (iii) $dist(p, q) = \delta_C(p, q)$. Moreover, we have $|pr|_\infty \leq (w/\sqrt{2})|rs|$ or $|qs|_\infty \leq (w/\sqrt{2})|rs|$. We consider these two cases separately.

Case 1: $|pr|_\infty \leq (w/\sqrt{2})|rs|$.
   In this case, we have $|pr| \leq \sqrt{2}|pr|_\infty \leq w|rs|$. Since $s - r$ and $q - p$ are both contained in C, we have angle $(pq, rs) \leq \theta$. By Lemma 7.3.1, we have $|rs| \leq \delta_C(r, s)/\cos\theta$ and $\delta_C(p, q) \leq |pq|$. Since $\delta_C(r, s) \leq \delta_C(p, q)$, we conclude that $|rs| \leq |pq|/\cos\theta$. Hence, the three conditions of Lemma 7.1.1 hold for the points p and q.

Case 2: $|qs|_\infty \leq (w/\sqrt{2})|rs|$.
   It follows in the same way as in Case 1 that $|qs| \leq w|rs|$, angle$(qp, sr) \leq \theta$ and $|rs| \leq |pq|/\cos\theta$. Hence also in this case, the three conditions of Lemma 7.1.1 hold for the points p and q.

We have shown that for any two distinct points p and q of S, the three conditions of Lemma 7.1.1 are satisfied. Therefore, the graph G is a t-spanner for S.   ∎

Lemma 7.3.3. *Let θ and w be real numbers such that $0 < \theta < \pi/4$ and $0 \leq w < (\cos\theta - \sin\theta)/2$, and let S be a set of n points in the plane.*

1.   *Algorithm* MODGAPGREEDY(S, θ, w) *computes a graph in which each vertex has degree at most $2\lceil 2\pi/\theta \rceil$.*

2.   *If $w > 0$, then the weight of this graph is less than $\lceil 2\pi/\theta \rceil (1 + 2\sqrt{2}/w) \log n$ times the weight of a minimum spanning tree of S.*

PROOF   Consider an arbitrary cone C of $\mathcal{C}_\kappa$. We will prove that the edges of E_C satisfy the strong $(w/\sqrt{2})$-gap property. Having proved this, the lemma follows from Theorem 6.1.2.
   Consider any two distinct edges (p, q) and (r, s) of E_C. We may assume without loss of generality that (r, s) was added to E_C before (p, q). We have $|pr|_\infty > (w/\sqrt{2})|rs|$ and $|qs|_\infty > (w/\sqrt{2})|rs|$. (Otherwise, the algorithm would have set $dist(p, q)$ to ∞ immediately after (r, s) was added to E_C and, as a result, p and q would never have been chosen as a pair with finite and minimal $dist$-value. In particular, the edge (p, q) would not have been added to E_C.) This immediately implies that

$$|pr| \geq |pr|_\infty > (w/\sqrt{2})|rs| \geq (w/\sqrt{2}) \cdot \min(|pq|, |rs|)$$

and

$$|qs| \geq |qs|_\infty > (w/\sqrt{2})|rs| \geq (w/\sqrt{2}) \cdot \min(|pq|, |rs|),$$

that is, the strong $(w/\sqrt{2})$-gap property holds.   ∎

> **The modified gap-greedy algorithm:** For each cone C, set $E_C := \emptyset$ and $dist(r, s) := \delta_C(r, s)$ for all $r \in S$ and $s \in S$. Repeatedly choose two distinct points r and s for which $dist(r, s)$ is minimum (and finite). Add (r, s) to E_C, and set $dist(p, q) := \infty$ for (i) all p that are "close" to r, and all $q \in S$, and (ii) all q that are "close" to s, and all $p \in S$. The region of "closeness" for r (resp. s) is the square centered at r (resp. s) and having sides of length $2(w/\sqrt{2})|rs|$. The algorithm adds edges to E_C in nondecreasing order of their δ_C-distances, which is in "approximately nondecreasing" order of their Euclidean distances. By Lemma 7.1.1, the resulting graph has a small stretch factor. Moreover, each set E_C satisfies the strong gap property.

7.4 An efficient implementation of the gap-greedy algorithm

Let C be a cone of $\mathcal{C}_\kappa$, and consider the iteration of the outer for-loop of algorithm MODGAPGREEDY during which the edge set E_C is constructed. As stated, the algorithm starts by computing a quadratic number of $dist$-values. Then, during each iteration of the while-loop, it selects two distinct points r and s for which $dist(r, s)$ is minimum (and finite), adds the edge (r, s) to E_C, and sets the appropriate $dist$-values to ∞. Since the final set E_C contains $O(n)$ edges, the while-loop makes only a linear number of iterations.

In this section, we show how to implement algorithm MODGAPGREEDY such that its running time is bounded by $O(n \log^2 n)$.

> **The main ingredients:** The first ingredient is a data structure based on range trees (see Section 5.4) that implicitly stores all finite $dist$-values, together with the minimum value among them. The second ingredient consists of two standard range trees that are used to find those points p and q for which $|pr|_\infty \leq (w/\sqrt{2})|rs|$ and $|qs|_\infty \leq (w/\sqrt{2})|rs|$, respectively.

Before we can define these data structures, we have to introduce some notation. The cone C is the intersection of two halfplanes. Let h_1 and h_2 be the two lines that bound these halfplanes, and let D_1 and D_2 be the lines through the origin that are orthogonal to h_1 and h_2, respectively. We give the lines D_1 and D_2 directions, as indicated in Figure 7.2. Let L be the line that contains the ray ℓ_C. We give L the same direction as ℓ_C. As in Section 7.3, we use the notation $\ell_{C,p}$ to be the ray ℓ_C translated to emanate from point p.

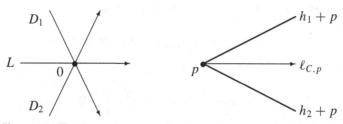

Figure 7.2: The directed lines D_1, D_2 and L, and the translated cone C_p.

Our data structures will store points with respect to different coordinate axes. Let p be any point in the plane.

1. We write the coordinates of p with respect to the *standard* (orthogonal) coordinate axes as p_1 and p_2.
2. For each $i \in \{1, 2\}$, we denote by p'_i the coordinate of p with respect to the axis D_i. That is, p'_i is the signed Euclidean distance between the origin and the orthogonal projection of p onto D_i, where the sign is positive or negative according to whether this projection is to the "right" or "left" of the origin.
3. We denote by p'_3 the coordinate of p with respect to the axis L. That is, p'_3 is the signed Euclidean distance between the origin and the orthogonal projection of p onto L.

Using this notation, we can write the cone C as

$$C = \{x \in \mathbb{R}^2 : x'_i \geq 0, i = 1, 2\}.$$

Similarly, for any $p \in \mathbb{R}^2$, we can write the translated cone C_p as

$$C_p = \{x \in \mathbb{R}^2 : x'_i \geq p'_i, i = 1, 2\}.$$

We define $-C_p := -C + p = \{-y + p : y \in C\}$. Then we have

$$-C_p = \{x \in \mathbb{R}^2 : x'_i \leq p'_i, i = 1, 2\}.$$

Finally, we have

$$\delta_C(p, q) = \begin{cases} q'_3 - p'_3 & \text{if } q \in C_p, \\ \infty & \text{if } q \notin C_p. \end{cases}$$

We assume for simplicity that the p_1-coordinates of all points of S are pairwise distinct. We make similar assumptions about the p_2-, p'_1-, p'_2-, and p'_3-coordinates.

7.4.1 The main data structure

Let S be a set of n points in the plane, and let C be any cone of $\mathcal{C}_\kappa$. The main data structure used by our algorithm maintains the minimal finite *dist*-value, under the following two operations:

FORBIDSOURCE(p): Given any point $p \in S$, this operation makes p forbidden as a source; that is, it sets *dist*(p, q) to ∞ for all $q \in S$.

FORBIDSINK(q): Given any point $q \in S$, this operation makes q forbidden as a sink; that is, it sets *dist*(p, q) to ∞ for all $p \in S$.

The data structure that supports these two operations will be referred to as the *mindist-structure*; we will denote it by T. This data structure has the form of a 3-layered range tree; it depends on the cone C. We start by describing this data structure in detail; refer to Figure 7.3. Later, we will show how the operations FORBIDSOURCE and FORBIDSINK can be implemented.

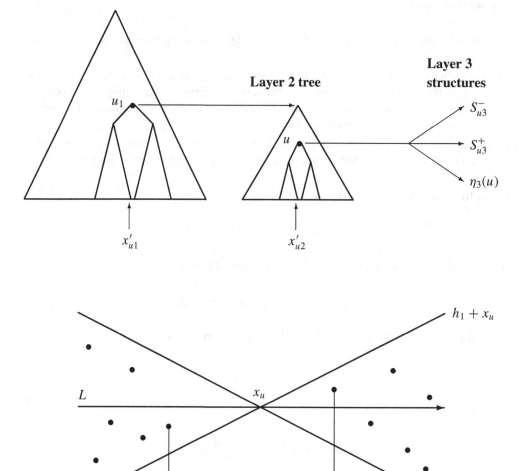

Figure 7.3: Illustration of the *mindist*-structure. Node u_2 is equal to u. The points in the cone $-C_{x_u}$ belong to the list S_{u3}^-, while those in the cone C_{x_u} belong to the list S_{u3}^+.

> **The *mindist*-structure T:** We use a 2-layered range tree, based on the p_1'- and p_2'-coordinates, to partition the set $\{(r,s) : r \in S, s \in S, r \neq s, \delta_C(r,s) < \infty\}$ into $O(n \log n)$ subsets. Each subset is a Cartesian product of the form $A \times B$, for two sets A and B that can be separated by a line orthogonal to L. Since A is to the "left" of B, we have $\min\{\delta_C(a,b) : a \in A, b \in B\} = \delta_C(r,s)$, where r is the point of A for which r_3' is maximum and s is the point of B for which s_3' is minimum. We add a third layer to the range tree, storing the sets A and B sorted by their p_3'-coordinates.

The layer 1 tree

There is a balanced binary search tree, called the *layer 1 tree*, storing the points of S at its leaves, sorted in nondecreasing order of their p_1'-coordinates. Internal nodes of this tree contain information to guide searches, as in Section 5.4. For any node v of the layer 1 tree, we denote by S_{v1} the subset of S that is stored in the subtree of v.

The layer 2 trees

Each node v of the layer 1 tree contains a pointer to the root of a balanced binary search tree, called a *layer 2 tree*, storing the points of S_{v1} at its leaves, sorted in nondecreasing order of their p_2'-coordinates. Again, internal nodes contain information to guide searches.

Before we can define the third layer of the data structure, we introduce some notation. Let u be any node of a layer 2 tree. We define two nodes u_1 and u_2, as follows. First, $u_2 := u$. To define u_1, start at node u, and walk to the root of the layer 2 tree that contains u. Then u_1 is defined as that node of the layer 1 tree that contains a pointer to this root.

For each $i \in \{1, 2\}$, we denote by x_{ui}' the maximal p_i'-coordinate that is stored in the left subtree of node u_i (as indicated in Figure 7.3). The point with coordinates x_{u1}' and x_{u2}' is denoted by x_u. (These coordinates are with respect to the axes D_1 and D_2. In general, x_u is not an element of S.)

The third layer of the data structure

Each node u of any layer 2 tree contains pointers to data structures that form the third layer. Consider any such node u. We denote by S_{u2} the subset of S that is stored in the subtree of u. Consider the point x_u as defined above.

Let S_{u3}^- be a subset of $\{p \in S_{u2} : p_i' \leq x_{ui}', i = 1, 2\}$ and let S_{u3}^+ be a subset of $\{p \in S_{u2} : p_i' \geq x_{ui}', i = 1, 2\}$. Observe that the points of S_{u3}^- and S_{u3}^+ are contained in the cones $-C_{x_u}$ and C_{x_u}, respectively. (During the algorithm, S_{u3}^- and S_{u3}^+ will be the subsets of $S_{u2} \cap (-C_{x_u})$ and $S_{u2} \cap C_{x_u}$ consisting of those points that are not forbidden as a source and a sink, respectively. For the description of the data structure, we assume that they are arbitrary subsets.) Node u of the layer 2 tree contains pointers to:

1. a list storing the points of S_{u3}^-, sorted in nondecreasing order of their p_3'-coordinates (for simplicity, we let S_{u3}^- denote both the set and the sorted list),

2. a list storing the points of S_{u3}^+, sorted in nondecreasing order of their p_3'-coordinates (for simplicity, we let S_{u3}^+ denote both the set and the sorted list),

3. a variable $\eta_3(u)$ whose value is

$$\eta_3(u) = \min\{\delta_C(p, q) : p \in S_{u3}^-, q \in S_{u3}^+\},$$

4. and, in case, $\eta_3(u) < \infty$, a pair (p, q) of points such that $p \in S_{u3}^-$, $q \in S_{u3}^+$ and $\eta_3(u) = \delta_C(p, q)$.

The lists S_{u3}^- and S_{u3}^+ are called *layer 3 lists*. If S_{u3}^- or S_{u3}^+ is empty, then $\eta_3(u) = \infty$. (In particular, this is the case if u is a leaf.) Otherwise, $\eta_3(u) = \delta_C(p, q) = q_3' - p_3'$, where p and q are the maximal and minimal elements that are stored in the lists S_{u3}^- and S_{u3}^+, respectively.

The reader is urged to prove the following lemma before reading on (see Exercise 7.2).

Lemma 7.4.1. *Assume that $S_{u3}^- = S_{u2} \cap (-C_{x_u})$ and $S_{u3}^+ = S_{u2} \cap C_{x_u}$ for all nodes u of any layer 2 tree. Then $\{(r, s) : r \in S, s \in S, r \neq s, \delta_C(r, s) < \infty\}$ is the disjoint union of the Cartesian products $S_{u3}^- \times S_{u3}^+$. Hence, the minimal δ_C-value is equal to the minimal η_3-value.*

Additional information stored in the nodes of layer 1 and layer 2 trees

In order to maintain the minimal η_3-value efficiently, we need the following additional information.

We store with each node u of any layer 2 tree a variable $\eta_2(u)$, whose value is defined as follows. If u is a leaf, then $\eta_2(u) = \infty$. Otherwise, let u_l and u_r be the left and right children of u, respectively. The variable $\eta_2(u)$ has value

$$\eta_2(u) = \min(\eta_2(u_l), \eta_2(u_r), \eta_3(u)). \tag{7.2}$$

In case $\eta_2(u) < \infty$, we also store with node u a corresponding pair of points that realizes $\eta_2(u)$.

In the same way, we store with each node v of any layer 1 tree a variable $\eta_1(v)$. If v is a leaf, then $\eta_1(v) = \infty$. Otherwise, let v_l and v_r be the left and right children of v, respectively, and let u_v be the root of the layer 2 tree to which v has a pointer. Then

$$\eta_1(v) = \min(\eta_1(v_l), \eta_1(v_r), \eta_2(u_v)). \tag{7.3}$$

In case $\eta_1(v) < \infty$, we also store with node v a pair of points that realizes $\eta_1(v)$.

Observe that the value $\eta_1(v)$, where v is the root of the layer 1 tree, is equal to the minimum of $\eta_3(u)$, where u ranges over all nodes of all layer 2 trees.

The dictionary

In order to speed up searching during the algorithm, we store all points of S in a *dictionary*, for example, a balanced binary search tree, where we can use any ordering of the points. Hence, we can in $O(\log n)$ time, search for an arbitrary point of S in this dictionary. With each point p in the dictionary, we store the following:

1. a list of pointers to all occurrences of p in the lists S_{u3}^- and
2. a list of pointers to all occurrences of p in the lists S_{u3}^+.

This concludes the description of the *mindist*-structure T. Recall that this structure depends on the cone C. We state the following lemma without proof.

Lemma 7.4.2. *The mindist-structure T, together with the dictionary and its lists of pointers, has size $O(n \log^2 n)$ and can be built in $O(n \log^2 n)$ time.*

The operations FORBIDSOURCE and FORBIDSINK

At the start of the iteration in which the efficient implementation of algorithm MODGAPGREEDY computes the edge set E_C corresponding to the cone C, layer 3 lists S_{u3}^- and S_{u3}^+ store the sets $\{p \in S_{u2} : p_i' \leq x_{ui}', i = 1, 2\}$ and $\{p \in S_{u2} : p_i' \geq x_{ui}', i = 1, 2\}$, respectively. During the algorithm, points will be made forbidden as a source or a sink, which corresponds to deleting the point from these lists (based on their proximities to the endpoints of other edges added to E_C).

> **Making a point forbidden as a source or a sink:** If a point p is deleted from a list S_{u3}^-, then it will not "contribute" anymore to the value $\eta_3(u)$. Therefore, deleting p from all lists S_{u3}^- in which it occurs corresponds to making p forbidden as a source (i.e., setting $dist(p, q)$ to ∞ for all $q \in S$). Similarly, deleting a point q from all lists S_{u3}^+ in which it occurs corresponds to making q forbidden as a sink.

Algorithm FORBIDSOURCE(T, p)

Comment: This algorithm takes as input a point p of S. It makes p forbidden as a source, by deleting p from all lists S_{u3}^- in which it occurs. After these deletions, the algorithm updates the *mindist*-structure T.

Step 1: Search for p in the dictionary, and follow the pointers to the positions of all occurrences of p in the lists S_{u3}^-. For each such list S_{u3}^-, carry out Steps 2 and 3.

Step 2: Delete p from S_{u3}^-. If the list S_{u3}^+ is empty, then we are done; otherwise, let q be the minimal element of S_{u3}^+. Go to Step 3.

Step 3: If p was not the maximal element of S_{u3}^-, then we are done. Otherwise, if p was the only element in S_{u3}^-, then set $\eta_3(u) := \infty$. Finally, if p was the maximal, but not the only element in S_{u3}^-, then let r be the new maximal element of S_{u3}^-. In this case, set $\eta_3(u) := \delta_C(r, q) = q_3' - r_3'$, and store the pair (r, q) with node u.

Step 4: At this moment, all layer 3 lists and all η_3-variables have been updated correctly. In this final step, the rest of the data structure is updated.

  Search for p in the layer 1 tree. For each node v on the search path, search for p in the layer 2 tree of v. Let ℓ_v be the leaf of this layer 2 tree in which the search ends. (Observe that $\eta_2(\ell_v) = \infty$.) Then, starting at ℓ_v, walk back to the root of the layer 2 tree of v, and for each node u on the path, recompute the value of $\eta_2(u)$ using (7.2), and update the pair of points realizing $\eta_2(u)$.

  Having done this for all nodes v, all η_2-variables have the correct values. The η_1-variables are updated in a similar fashion: Let ℓ be the leaf of the layer 1 tree that stores p. Then, starting at ℓ, walk back to the root of the layer 1 tree, and for each node v on the path, recompute $\eta_1(v)$ using (7.3), and update the pair of points realizing $\eta_1(v)$.

We remark that algorithm FORBIDSOURCE(T, p) does *not* delete p from the layer 1 and layer 2 trees, because this is not necessary for our final implementation of the gap-greedy algorithm. Hence, the layer 1 and layer 2 trees do not change during a deletion, except that the values of the η_1- and η_2-variables are updated. Point p has been deleted from all layer 3 lists S_{u3}^- and, therefore, cannot contribute any more to any η_3-variable. Point p may be deleted from the dictionary, but this is not necessary.

In a completely symmetric way, we obtain algorithm FORBIDSINK(T, q), which deletes the point q from all lists S_{u3}^+ in which it occurs, and updates the *mindist*-structure. We state the following lemma without proof.

Lemma 7.4.3. *The following two claims hold.*

1. *Given a point p of S, algorithm* FORBIDSOURCE(T, p) *deletes p from all lists S_{u3}^- in which it occurs, and updates the entire mindist-structure, in $O(\log^2 n)$ time.*

2. *Given a point q of S, algorithm* FORBIDSINK(T, q) *deletes q from all lists S_{u3}^+ in which it occurs, and updates the entire mindist-structure, in $O(\log^2 n)$ time.*

7.4.2 The final algorithm

We are now ready to present an efficient implementation of algorithm MODGAPGREEDY. As before, all cones of $\mathcal{C}_\kappa$ are considered separately. If C is the current cone, then our algorithm maintains the following information:

1. The *mindist*-structure T, consisting of the 3-layered data structure, together with the dictionary and its lists of pointers.

2. A 2-dimensional range tree (see Section 5.4), denoted by RT_{source}, storing a subset of S according to their standard coordinates p_1 and p_2. A point of S is contained in this range tree if and only if it has not been forbidden as a source.

3. A 2-dimensional range tree, denoted by RT_{sink}, storing a subset of S according to their standard coordinates p_1 and p_2. A point of S is contained in this range tree if and only if it has not been forbidden as a sink.

Recall that the range trees RT_{source} and RT_{sink} can be used to find, for any two given points r and s, all points p and q such that $|pr|_\infty \leq (w/\sqrt{2})|rs|$ and $|qs|_\infty \leq (w/\sqrt{2})|rs|$, respectively; see algorithm RANGEQUERY in Section 5.4.1. Also recall algorithm DELETE in Section 5.4.2 for deleting a point p from a range tree (without rebalancing the data structure). We denote this algorithm by DELETE(RT_{source}, p) and DELETE(RT_{sink}, p), respectively.

Algorithm FASTGAPGREEDY(S, θ, w)

Comment: This algorithm takes as input a set S of n points in the plane, and two real numbers θ and w such that $0 < \theta < \pi/4$ and $0 \leq w < (\cos\theta - \sin\theta)/2$. The algorithm returns a directed t-spanner $G = (S, E)$, for $t = 1/(\cos\theta - \sin\theta - 2w)$.

for each cone C of $\mathcal{C}_\kappa$
do store the points of S in the *mindist*-structure T, such that
    for each node u of each layer 2 tree, the layer 3 lists S_{u3}^-
    and S_{u3}^+ store the sets $\{p \in S_{u2} : p_i' \leq x_{ui}', i = 1, 2\}$ and
    $\{p \in S_{u2} : p_i' \geq x_{ui}', i = 1, 2\}$, respectively;
    store the points of S in the 2-dimensional range tree RT_{source};
    store the points of S in the 2-dimensional range tree RT_{sink};
    $E_C := \emptyset$;
    $\eta := \eta_1$-value stored with the root of the layer 1 tree of T;
    while $\eta < \infty$
    do let (r, s) be the pair such that $\eta = \delta_C(r, s)$;
        $E_C := E_C \cup \{(r, s)\}$;
        for each $p \in RT_{\text{source}}$ such that $|pr|_\infty \leq (w/\sqrt{2})|rs|$
        do DELETE(RT_{source}, p);
            FORBIDSOURCE(T, p)
        endfor;
        for each $q \in RT_{\text{sink}}$ such that $|qs|_\infty \leq (w/\sqrt{2})|rs|$
        do DELETE(RT_{sink}, q);
            FORBIDSINK(T, q)
        endfor;
        $\eta := \eta_1$-value stored with the root of the layer 1 tree of T
    endwhile
endfor;
return the graph $G = (S, E)$, where $E := \bigcup_C E_C$

We mentioned already that the η_1-value stored with the root of the layer 1 tree of T is equal to the minimal finite *dist*-value of algorithm MODGAPGREEDY. The following lemma gives the precise statement of this claim.

Lemma 7.4.4. *Let $C \in \mathcal{C}_\kappa$, and consider the iteration of the outer for-loop of algorithm* FASTGAPGREEDY(S, θ, w) *during which the edge set E_C is constructed. At the start of any iteration of the while-loop, we have*

$$\eta = \min\{\delta_C(p, q) : p \in RT_{\text{source}}, q \in RT_{\text{sink}}, p \neq q\}.$$

PROOF   First observe that $\eta < \infty$. Since the value of each η_i-variable, $1 \leq i \leq 3$, is either ∞ or $\delta_C(p, q)$ for some $p \in RT_{\text{source}}$ and $q \in RT_{\text{sink}}$, it is clear that

$$\eta \geq \min\{\delta_C(p, q) : p \in RT_{\text{source}}, q \in RT_{\text{sink}}, p \neq q\}. \tag{7.4}$$

If at least one of RT_{source} and RT_{sink} is empty, then $\eta = \infty$. Hence, both these range trees are nonempty. Let $r \in RT_{\text{source}}$ and $s \in RT_{\text{sink}}$ be two distinct points such that

$$\delta_C(r, s) = \min\{\delta_C(p, q) : p \in RT_{\text{source}}, q \in RT_{\text{sink}}, p \neq q\}.$$

We will show that there is a node u in some layer 2 tree of T such that $\eta_3(u) = \delta_C(r, s)$. Since $\eta \leq \eta_3(u)$, this will imply that

$$\eta \leq \min\{\delta_C(p, q) : p \in RT_{\text{source}}, q \in RT_{\text{sink}}, p \neq q\}$$

and, therefore, complete the proof of the lemma.

Let u_1 be the lowest common ancestor of the leaves storing r and s in the layer 1 tree of T. Similarly, let u_2 be the lowest common ancestor of the leaves storing r and s in the layer 2 tree that is attached to node u_1. We will prove that $\eta_3(u_2) = \delta_C(r, s)$.

Let $u := u_2$, and consider the point $x_u \in \mathbb{R}^2$ as defined in the description of the layer 2 trees of T. (The nodes u_1 and u_2 defined in that description are exactly the nodes that we defined in the preceding paragraph.) Since $\eta < \infty$, inequality (7.4) implies that $\delta_C(r, s) < \infty$ and, hence, $s \in C_r$. Therefore, $s_1' \geq r_1'$ and $s_2' \geq r_2'$, that is, both in the layer 1 tree and in the layer 2 tree pointed to by u_1, the leaf storing r is to the left of the leaf storing s. Then, the definitions of x_{u1}' and x_{u2}' immediately imply that $r_1' \leq x_{u1}' \leq s_1'$ and $r_2' \leq x_{u2}' \leq s_2'$. (See also Exercise 7.6.) Since $r \in RT_{\text{source}}$ and $s \in RT_{\text{sink}}$, the points r and s are contained in the lists S_{u3}^- and S_{u3}^+, respectively. But then, since all points of S_{u3}^- are stored in RT_{source}, all points of S_{u3}^+ are stored in RT_{sink}, and $\delta_C(r, s)$ is minimum, r and s must be the maximal and minimal elements in their lists, respectively. Then, the definition of $\eta_3(u)$ implies that $\eta_3(u) = \delta_C(r, s)$. Hence the result. ∎

We claim that algorithms MODGAPGREEDY and FASTGAPGREEDY compute the *same* graph (S, E). Once we have proved this, Lemmas 7.3.2 and 7.3.3 imply upper bounds on the stretch factor, the degree and, if $w > 0$, the weight of this graph. To prove this claim, we run, for the sake of analysis, both algorithms in parallel, and show that during each iteration of their while-loops, they add the *same* edge to E.

Let C be a cone of $\mathcal{C}_\kappa$, and consider the corresponding outer for-loops of both algorithms. Immediately before the while-loops of both algorithms, we have,

$$\{dist(r, s) : r \in S, s \in S, r \neq s, dist(r, s) < \infty\}$$
$$= \{\delta_C(r, s) : r \in RT_{\text{source}}, s \in RT_{\text{sink}}, r \neq s, \delta_C(r, s) < \infty\}. \tag{7.5}$$

Assume that Eq. (7.5) holds at the start of a specific iteration of both the algorithms.

Algorithm MODGAPGREEDY takes a pair (r', s') for which $dist(r', s')$ is a minimal element in the set on the left-hand side of (7.5). By Lemma 7.4.4, algorithm FASTGAPGREEDY takes a pair (r'', s'') for which $\delta_C(r'', s'')$ is a minimal element in the set on the right-hand side of (7.5). Hence, we have $dist(r', s') = \delta_C(r'', s'')$. Observe that the sets in (7.5) may have several minimal elements. In that case, we force algorithm MODGAPGREEDY to choose the pair that is chosen by algorithm FASTGAPGREEDY. We denote the chosen pair by (r, s). Both algorithms add the edge (r, s) to their edge sets E_C. Then MODGAPGREEDY updates certain $dist$-values, while FASTGAPGREEDY updates the structures T, RT_{source}, and RT_{sink}. By comparing the algorithms, it follows that (7.5) continues to hold at the end of that iteration in both algorithms. This proves that algorithms MODGAPGREEDY and FASTGAPGREEDY, indeed, compute the same edge set E.

Finally, let us analyze the running time of algorithm FASTGAPGREEDY(S, θ, w). Consider a fixed cone C of C_κ. By Lemma 7.4.2, the $mindist$-structure T has size $O(n \log^2 n)$, and can be built in $O(n \log^2 n)$ time. By Theorem 5.4.7, the range trees RT_{source} and RT_{sink} have size $O(n \log n)$, and can be built in $O(n \log n)$ time. Using these range trees, all points contained in an axes-parallel query square can be reported in time proportional to $\log^2 n$ plus the number of points in this square. Furthermore, a point can be deleted from a range tree in $O(\log^2 n)$ time.

We estimate the running time of the while-loop of algorithm FASTGAPGREEDY(S, θ, w). Any point p of S is deleted from a range tree at the moment when it is reported as being contained in a "query" square. Hence, the total time spent for all these queries and deletions in the range trees is $O(n \log^2 n)$.

Consider any point p of S. It is deleted at most once from RT_{source}. At the moment when it is deleted from this range tree, algorithm FORBIDSOURCE(T, p) deletes p from all lists S_{u3}^- in which it occurs, and updates T. By Lemma 7.4.3, this takes $O(\log^2 n)$ time. Similarly, when p is deleted from RT_{sink}, algorithm FORBIDŠINK(T, p) spends $O(\log^2 n)$ time for updating T. Hence for each point p of S, $O(\log^2 n)$ time is spent for updating the $mindist$-structure T.

We have shown that algorithm FASTGAPGREEDY(S, θ, w) spends $O(n \log^2 n)$ time for each cone C in C_κ. Since there are κ such cones, the total running time of the algorithm is $O(\kappa n \log^2 n)$. We have proved the main result of this chapter:

Theorem 7.4.5. *Let θ and w be real numbers such that $0 < \theta < \pi/4$ and $0 \le w < (\cos \theta - \sin \theta)/2$, and let S be a set of n points in the plane. In $O((1/\theta)n \log^2 n)$ time and using $O(n \log^2 n + (1/\theta)n)$ space, algorithm FASTGAPGREEDY(S, θ, w) computes a t-spanner for S, such that*

1. *$t = 1/(\cos \theta - \sin \theta - 2w)$,*

2. *each vertex in the spanner has degree at most $2\lceil 2\pi/\theta \rceil$, and*

3. *if $w > 0$, the weight of the spanner is less than $\lceil 2\pi/\theta \rceil (1 + 2\sqrt{2}/w) \log n$ times the weight of a minimum spanning tree of S.*

If we assume that $t > 1$ and $t \to 1$, then, as indicated just before Theorem 7.2.3, we obtain the best result by taking $\theta \sim (t - 1)/2$ and $w \sim (t - 1)/4$. For these values, the degree of the t-spanner is $O(1/(t - 1))$ and its weight is $O((1/(t - 1)^2) \cdot wt(MST(S)) \log n)$.

7.5 Generalization to higher dimensions

In the previous sections, we have presented the gap-greedy algorithm for two-dimensional point sets. We now indicate how algorithm FASTGAPGREEDY(S, θ, w) can be generalized to the higher dimensional case.

Let $d \geq 2$ be an integer constant, and let S be a set of n points in $\mathbb{R}^d$. We choose two arbitrary real numbers θ and w such that $0 < \theta < \pi/4$ and $0 \leq w < (\cos\theta - \sin\theta)/2$. Observe that Lemma 7.1.1 remains valid. Let $\kappa = \kappa_{d\theta}$ be as in (5.3), and let $\mathcal{C}_\kappa$ be the θ-frame of Theorem 5.2.8. Recall that $\kappa = O(1/\theta^{d-1})$.

Let C be a cone in $\mathcal{C}_\kappa$. We fix a ray ℓ_C that emanates from the origin and that is contained in C. Since C is a simplicial cone, it can be written as the intersection of d halfspaces. Let $D_1, D_2, \ldots, D_d$ be the lines through the origin that are orthogonal to the hyperplanes bounding these halfspaces. Furthermore, let D_{d+1} be the line through ℓ_C.

For any point p in $\mathbb{R}^d$, we write the coordinates of p with respect to the standard (orthogonal) coordinate axes as $p_1, p_2, \ldots, p_d$. For each i with $1 \leq i \leq d+1$, we denote by p_i' the coordinate of p with respect to the line D_i. That is, p_i' is the signed Euclidean distance between the origin and the orthogonal projection of p onto D_i. Using these coordinates, we can write the translated cone C_p as

$$C_p = \{x \in \mathbb{R}^d : x_i' \geq p_i', i = 1, 2, \ldots, d\}.$$

The approximate distance function δ_C of Section 7.3 generalizes to

$$\delta_C(p, q) = \begin{cases} q_{d+1}' - p_{d+1}' & \text{if } q \in C_p, \\ \infty & \text{if } q \notin C_p. \end{cases}$$

The *mindist*-structure T of Section 7.4.1 becomes a $(d+1)$-layered data structure. The first d layers form a d-dimensional range tree, using the coordinate system defined by $D_1, D_2, \ldots, D_d$. The $(d+1)$-st layer is defined using the coordinates p_{d+1}' defined by D_{d+1}.

The algorithm, denoted by FASTGAPGREEDYDDIM(S, θ, w), is a direct generalization of the corresponding algorithm in Section 7.4.2. Besides the *mindist*-structure T, it uses two d-dimensional range trees RT_{source} and RT_{sink}, each storing a subset of S according to their standard coordinates $p_1, p_2, \ldots, p_d$. The output of algorithm FASTGAPGREEDYDDIM(S, θ, w) consists of a directed t-spanner $G = (S, E)$, for $t = 1/(\cos\theta - \sin\theta - 2w)$. The following theorem generalizes Theorem 7.4.5.

Theorem 7.5.1. *Let θ and w be real numbers such that $0 < \theta < \pi/4$ and $0 \leq w < (\cos\theta - \sin\theta)/2$, and let S be a set of n points in $\mathbb{R}^d$. In $O((1/\theta^{d-1})n \log^d n)$ time and using $O(n \log^d n + (1/\theta^{d-1})n)$ space, algorithm FASTGAPGREEDYDDIM(S, θ, w) computes a t-spanner for S, such that*

1. *$t = 1/(\cos\theta - \sin\theta - 2w)$,*
2. *each vertex in the spanner has degree $O(1/\theta^{d-1})$, and*
3. *the weight of this graph is $O((1/\theta^{d-1})(1 + 1/w)\log n)$ times the weight of a minimum spanning tree of S.*

Let us assume that $t > 1$ and $t \to 1$. Then, using an analysis that is similar to the one just before Theorem 7.2.3, it can be shown that we obtain the best result by taking $\theta \sim \frac{d-1}{d}(t-1)$ and $w \sim (t-1)/(2d)$. For these values, the degree of the t-spanner is $O(1/(t-1)^{d-1})$ and its weight is $O((1/(t-1)^d) \cdot wt(MST(S))\log n)$.

Exercises

7.1. Prove that the while-loop of algorithm MODGAPGREEDY (see Section 7.3) terminates.

7.2. Prove Lemma 7.4.1.

7.3. Consider the *mindist*-structure that was defined in Section 7.4.1. Let v be the root of the layer 1 tree. Convince yourself of the fact that

$$\eta_1(v) = \min\{\eta_3(u) : u \text{ is a node of a layer 2 tree}\}.$$

7.4. Prove Lemma 7.4.2.

7.5. Prove Lemma 7.4.3.

7.6. In the description of the *mindist*-structure in Section 7.4.1, we assumed that all p_i'-coordinates are pairwise distinct, $1 \leq i \leq 3$. Give the details of this data structure for arbitrary point sets. (*Hint:* The main difficulty is to guarantee that the proof of Lemma 7.4.4 remains valid.)

7.7. Let S be a set of n points in the plane, let θ be a sufficiently small positive real number, let $\kappa = \lceil 2\pi/\theta \rceil$, and let C_κ be a collection of κ cones of angle θ that have their apex at the origin and that cover the plane. Let $\{p, q\}$ be an edge of a minimum spanning tree of S, and let C be the cone of C_κ such that $q - p \in C$. Consider the *mindist*-structure of Section 7.4.1, for the special case as in Lemma 7.4.1. Prove that there is a node u in one of the layer 2 trees such that $p \in S_{u3}^-$, $q \in S_{u3}^+$ and $|pq|$ is the minimum distance between any point in S_{u3}^- and any point in S_{u3}^+.

7.8. Work out the details for Section 7.5.

Bibliographic notes

The results of this chapter are due to Arya and Smid [1997]. Algorithm GAPGREEDY(S, θ, w), with $w = 0$, was discovered by Salowe [1994] and, according to Vaidya [1991], also by Feder and Nisan.

The *mindist*-structure of Section 7.4 is closely related to the data structure of Agarwal et al. [1991], who used it to establish a relationship between computing minimum spanning trees and bichromatic closest pairs. (A solution to Exercise 7.7 can be found in their paper.) Smid [1992] uses a similar data structure for maintaining the closest pair in a set of points under insertions and deletions. Datta et al. [1995] present a variant of this data structure that can be used to maintain the "smallest" k-point cluster in a dynamically changing set of points.

The algorithm of this chapter belongs to the class of *greedy algorithms*. More information about this powerful class of algorithms can be found in the book by Cormen et al. [2001].

8

Enumerating Distances Using Spanners
of Bounded Degree

> Only a fraction of a man's virtues should be enumerated in his presence.
>
> —*The Talmud*

In this chapter, we show that spanners of bounded degree can be used to solve a basic problem in computational geometry, that is, the problem of enumerating, in nondecreasing order, the k smallest distances among the $\binom{n}{2}$ distances in a set of n points.

Let S be a set of n points in $\mathbb{R}^d$, and let k be an integer such that $1 \leq k \leq \binom{n}{2}$. A sequence $\{a_1, b_1\}, \{a_2, b_2\}, \ldots, \{a_k, b_k\}$ of pairwise distinct pairs of points of S is called a sequence of k *closest pairs*, if

1. $|a_1 b_1| \leq |a_2 b_2| \leq \cdots \leq |a_k b_k|$ and
2. the distances $|a_i b_i|, 1 \leq i \leq k$, are the k smallest elements in the multiset $\{|pq| : \{p, q\} \subseteq S, p \neq q\}$.

In Section 8.1, we start by showing that any bounded-degree spanner can be used to enumerate the k *approximate* closest pairs in $O(n + k \log k)$ time. Then, in Section 8.2, we show how to modify the algorithm of Section 8.1 to obtain the k exact closest pairs, in $O((n + k) \log n)$ time. Finally, in Section 8.3, we show that by using the gap-greedy spanner of Chapter 7, the time bound for exact enumeration can be improved to $O(n + k \log k)$. (All these time bounds do not include the time to construct the spanner.)

All spanners in this chapter are undirected.

8.1 Approximate distance enumeration

Let S be a set of n points in $\mathbb{R}^d$, let k be an integer such that $1 \leq k \leq \binom{n}{2}$, and let $t > 1$ be a real number.

Let $\{a_i, b_i\}, 1 \leq i \leq \binom{n}{2}$, be the sequence of all pairs of points of S, sorted in non-decreasing order of their Euclidean distances. We say that a sequence $\{p_i, q_i\}, 1 \leq i \leq k$, of pairwise distinct pairs of points of S is a sequence of k t-*approximate closest pairs*, if

$$|a_i b_i|/t \leq |p_i q_i| \leq t |a_i b_i|,$$

for all i with $1 \leq i \leq k$.

Let D be a positive integer, and let $G = (S, E)$ be an arbitrary t-spanner for S, such that the degree of each point of S is less than or equal to D. In this section, we give an algorithm that uses the t-spanner G to compute a sequence of k t-approximate closest pairs in S. The idea is to run Dijkstra's single-source shortest paths algorithm (see Section 2.5) simultaneously from all points of S. The algorithm uses a priority queue PQ that stores, at any moment, at most k pairs of points. In the priority queue PQ, the priority value associated with a pair $\{p, q\}$ is denoted by $priority(\{p, q\})$, and is equal to the length of the shortest path in G between p and q found so far.

Algorithm APPROXDISTENUM(G, k)

Comment: This algorithm takes as input a t-spanner $G = (S, E)$ and an integer k such that $1 \leq k \leq \binom{n}{2}$. It returns a sequence of k t-approximate closest pairs in S.

At the start of the algorithm, the priority queue PQ contains the $\min(k, |E|)$ shortest edges of E; the priority $priority(\{p, q\})$ of any such edge $\{p, q\}$ is equal to the Euclidean distance between p and q. Then a sequence of k iterations is carried out.

In one iteration, the algorithm finds a pair $\{p, q\}$ with smallest priority in PQ, deletes this pair from PQ, and reports it. Then for each edge $\{q, r\}$ of G (and, in a completely symmetric way, for each edge $\{p, s\}$ of G), the algorithm does the following:

1.   If the pair $\{p, r\}$ has not already been reported and does not occur in PQ, then the algorithm sets $priority(\{p, r\}) := priority(\{p, q\}) + |qr|$, and inserts $\{p, r\}$ into PQ. If PQ contains $k + 1$ pairs at this moment, then the pair with the highest priority is deleted.

2.   If the pair $\{p, r\}$ has not already been reported, but occurs in PQ with a priority that is larger than $priority(\{p, q\}) + |qr|$, then the algorithm decreases $priority(\{p, r\})$ to $priority(\{p, q\}) + |qr|$, and updates PQ accordingly.

The analysis of Dijkstra's algorithm in Section 2.5.2 shows that algorithm APPROXDISTENUM(G, k) reports, in nondecreasing order, the k smallest shortest-path distances in G. Below, we show that, in fact, the k pairs reported form a sequence of k t-approximate closest pairs.

As before, let $\{a_i, b_i\}$, $1 \leq i \leq \binom{n}{2}$, be the sequence of all pairs of points of S, sorted in nondecreasing order of their Euclidean distances. For each i with $1 \leq i \leq \binom{n}{2}$, let $w_i := |a_i b_i|$, and let w'_i be the length of a shortest path between a_i and b_i in the t-spanner G. Observe that

$$w_1 \leq w_2 \leq w_3 \leq \cdots \leq w_{\binom{n}{2}}.$$

Let π be a permutation of $\{1, 2, \ldots, \binom{n}{2}\}$ such that

$$w'_{\pi(1)} \leq w'_{\pi(2)} \leq w'_{\pi(3)} \leq \cdots \leq w'_{\binom{n}{2}}.$$

Hence, algorithm APPROXDISTENUM(G, k) reports k pairs of points whose final *priority*-values are equal to $w'_{\pi(1)}, w'_{\pi(2)}, \ldots, w'_{\pi(k)}$.

Lemma 8.1.1. *For each i with $1 \leq i \leq \binom{n}{2}$, we have*

$$w_i \leq w'_{\pi(i)} \leq tw_i, \tag{8.1}$$

and

$$w_i/t \leq w_{\pi(i)} \leq tw_i. \tag{8.2}$$

PROOF   Let i be any integer in the range $\left[1, \binom{n}{2}\right]$. Since G is a t-spanner for S, we have $w_i \leq w'_i \leq tw_i$. By replacing i by $\pi(i)$, we get

$$w_{\pi(i)} \leq w'_{\pi(i)} \leq tw_{\pi(i)}. \tag{8.3}$$

First observe that (8.1) and (8.3) together imply (8.2). Therefore, it remains to show that (8.1) holds.

We first show that $w_i \leq w'_{\pi(i)}$. We distinguish two cases. The first case is when $\pi(i) \geq i$. Then, $w_{\pi(i)} \geq w_i$, which, when combined with the first part of inequality (8.3), implies the desired result. The second case is when $\pi(i) < i$. Since π is a permutation, there is an integer j, such that $1 \leq j < i$ and $\pi(j) \geq i$. Since $j < i$, we have $w'_{\pi(j)} \leq w'_{\pi(i)}$. Also, since $\pi(j) \geq i$, we have $w_{\pi(j)} \geq w_i$. Since (8.3) implies that $w_{\pi(j)} \leq w'_{\pi(j)}$, it follows that $w_i \leq w'_{\pi(i)}$.

To show that $w'_{\pi(i)} \leq tw_i$, we again consider two cases. The first case is when $\pi(i) \leq i$. Then, $w_{\pi(i)} \leq w_i$. Multiplying this inequality by t and combining it with the second part of inequality (8.3) implies the claim. The second case is when $\pi(i) > i$. There is an integer j, such that $i < j \leq \binom{n}{2}$ and $\pi(j) \leq i$. Since $i < j$, we have $w'_{\pi(i)} \leq w'_{\pi(j)}$. Also, since $\pi(j) \leq i$, we have $w_{\pi(j)} \leq w_i$. Since the second part of inequality (8.3) implies that $w'_{\pi(j)} \leq tw_{\pi(j)}$, the claim follows. ■

Let $\{p_i, q_i\}$, $1 \leq i \leq k$, be the k pairs of points that are reported by algorithm APPROXDISTENUM(G, k). To prove that these pairs form a sequence of k t-approximate closest pairs, we have to show that for each i with $1 \leq i \leq k$, we have

$$w_i/t \leq |p_i q_i| \leq tw_i. \tag{8.4}$$

First observe that the length of a shortest path in G between p_i and q_i is equal to $w'_{\pi(i)}$. If $w_{\pi(i)} = |p_i q_i|$, then (8.4) follows from (8.2). Since the permutation π need not be unique, it may happen that $w_{\pi(i)}$ and $|p_i q_i|$ are not equal. Therefore, we proceed as follows. Let δ be the length of a shortest path in G between p_i and q_i. Then $\delta = w'_{\pi(i)}$ and, since G is a t-spanner, we have $|p_i q_i| \leq \delta \leq t|p_i q_i|$. Combining this with (8.1) gives

$$|p_i q_i| \leq \delta = w'_{\pi(i)} \leq tw_i,$$

and

$$|p_i q_i| \geq \delta/t = w'_{\pi(i)}/t \geq w_i/t,$$

proving (8.4). The following theorem summarizes our result.

Theorem 8.1.2. *Let S be a set of n points in $\mathbb{R}^d$, let $t > 1$ be a real number, let D be a positive integer, and let G be a t-spanner for S of degree D. Given any integer k with $1 \leq k \leq \binom{n}{2}$, algorithm APPROXDISTENUM(G, k) computes a sequence of k t-approximate closest pairs in S, in $O(Dn + Dk \log k)$ time.*

PROOF We have already proved the correctness of the algorithm. The proof of the running time is left as an exercise (see Exercise 8.1). ■

Approximate distance enumeration: Run Dijkstra's algorithm from all points simultaneously. Use one priority queue that contains the k smallest distances in G found so far. The algorithm enumerates the k smallest distances in the spanner G, which are k approximately smallest Euclidean distances in S.

8.2 Exact distance enumeration

As in the previous section, let $G = (S, E)$ be a t-spanner for point set S, such that its maximum degree is D. We show that, by making two modifications to algorithm APPROXDISTENUM(G, k) of Section 8.1, we can enumerate the k exact closest pairs.

Algorithm EXACTDISTENUM(G, k)

Comment: This algorithm takes as input a t-spanner $G = (S, E)$ and an integer k such that $1 \leq k \leq \binom{n}{2}$. It returns a sequence of k exact closest pairs in S.

The algorithm is obtained by making the following two modifications to algorithm APPROXDISTENUM(G, k) of Section 8.1:

1. The priority queue PQ is maintained at full size; that is, it is not pruned to keep only k pairs of points.

2. The algorithm does not report pairs at the moment when they have minimum priority in PQ. Instead, it keeps track of the k closest pairs (in the Euclidean sense) among all pairs that were ever inserted into PQ. The algorithm terminates as soon as the smallest priority in PQ is larger than t times the Euclidean distance of the k-th closest pair found so far. At termination, the k closest pairs that have been found are reported.

To implement algorithm EXACTDISTENUM(G, k), a second priority queue is maintained that contains the same pairs as PQ, and in which the priority of any pair $\{p, q\}$ is equal to the Euclidean distance $|pq|$. (Recall that the priority of any pair $\{p, q\}$ in PQ is the length of the shortest path in G between p and q found so far.)

We first prove the correctness of algorithm EXACTDISTENUM(G, k). Let x be the Euclidean distance of the k-th pair reported by the algorithm, and let p and q be any two distinct points of S such that the pair $\{p, q\}$ is never inserted into PQ. We claim that $|pq| > x$. To prove this claim, let $\{r, s\}$ be the pair that causes the algorithm to terminate. Then, at the moment the algorithm terminates, we have $priority(\{r, s\}) > tx$. Also, at that moment $priority(\{r, s\})$ is equal to the length of a shortest path in G between r and s. At termination, all shortest paths in G having length less than $priority(\{r, s\})$ have been found already. (This follows from general properties of Dijkstra's algorithm, see Section 2.5.2.) Hence, if we denote the length of a shortest path in G between p and q by δ, then $\delta \geq priority(\{r, s\})$. Since G is a t-spanner, we have $|pq| \geq \delta/t$. It follows that $|pq| > x$.

Hence, we have shown that each pair $\{p, q\}$, with $|pq| \leq x$, is inserted into PQ during some iteration of the algorithm. Since the distance of a k-th closest pair in S is less than or equal to x, it follows that algorithm EXACTDISTENUM(G, k) enumerates the k closest pairs in S.

The analysis of the running time is based on the following claim: let w_k be the k-th smallest Euclidean distance in S, let $\{p, q\}$ be the current pair with minimum priority in PQ that is selected by the algorithm, and assume that $\{p, q\}$ is the first pair for which $|pq| > tw_k$. We claim that algorithm EXACTDISTENUM(G, k) terminates at the moment when it selects $\{p, q\}$.

To prove this claim, let δ be the length of a shortest path in G between p and q, and let x be the k-th smallest Euclidean distance found by the algorithm at the moment when it selects $\{p, q\}$. Since $priority(\{p, q\}) = \delta$ at this moment, we have to show that $\delta > tx$.

First observe that $\delta \geq |pq|$ and, therefore, $\delta > tw_k$. Also, any pair $\{r, s\}$ whose distance in G is less than δ has already occurred as minimal element in PQ. Let r and s be any two distinct points of S such that $|rs| \leq w_k$, and let δ' be the length of a shortest path in G between r and s. Then $\delta' \leq t|rs| \leq tw_k < \delta$. Hence, at the moment when the algorithm selects the pair $\{p, q\}$ as a minimal element in PQ, all pairs of distinct points of S having Euclidean distance at most w_k have been inserted into PQ. This implies that $x = w_k$ and, therefore, $\delta > tx$.

Let I be the number of iterations made by algorithm EXACTDISTENUM(G, k). Then the total running time is $O(Dn + ID \log n)$. We have just shown that I is less than or equal to the number of pairs of distinct points of S having distance at most tw_k. The following lemma gives an upper bound on I.

Lemma 8.2.1. *Let w_k be the k-th smallest Euclidean distance in S, let $t > 1$ be a real number, and let M be the number of pairs of distinct points of S having distance at most tw_k. Then*

$$M < \left(2\lceil t\sqrt{d}\rceil + 1\right)^d (n + 2k).$$

PROOF Let $w := w_k$ and let $\mathcal{G}$ be the d-dimensional grid with cells of side lengths $w/\sqrt{d}$. Each cell of this grid has the form

$$\left[i_1 w/\sqrt{d}, (i_1 + 1)w/\sqrt{d}\right) \times \cdots \times \left[i_d w/\sqrt{d}, (i_d + 1)w/\sqrt{d}\right),$$

for some integers $i_1, i_2, \ldots, i_d$. In other words, a cell is the Cartesian product of d intervals, which are closed on the left and open on the right.

We call a cell of $\mathcal{G}$ *nonempty*, if it contains at least one point of S. Let g be the number of nonempty cells. We number these cells arbitrarily as $1, 2, \ldots, g$. For each i with $1 \leq i \leq g$, let n_i denote the number of points of S that are contained in the i-th nonempty cell. We define

$$Z := \sum_{i=1}^{g} \binom{n_i}{2};$$

that is, Z is the total number of pairs $\{x, y\}$ of points such that x and y are contained in the same cell of $\mathcal{G}$. If two points of S are in the same cell, then their distance is less than $\sqrt{d} \cdot w/\sqrt{d} = w$. Hence, since w is the k-th smallest distance in S, we have

$$Z < k. \tag{8.5}$$

Let $\beta := \lceil t\sqrt{d}\rceil$, and let

$$C := \left[i_1 w/\sqrt{d}, (i_1 + 1)w/\sqrt{d}\right) \times \cdots \times \left[i_d w/\sqrt{d}, (i_d + 1)w/\sqrt{d}\right)$$

be an arbitrary cell of the grid $\mathcal{G}$. We define the *neighborhood* of C in the following way. Consider the d-dimensional hypercube

$$C' := \left[(i_1 - \beta)w/\sqrt{d}, (i_1 + 1 + \beta)w/\sqrt{d}\right) \times \cdots \times \left[(i_d - \beta)w/\sqrt{d}, (i_d + 1 + \beta)w/\sqrt{d}\right).$$

Hence, the side lengths of C' are equal to $(2\beta + 1)w/\sqrt{d}$, and C' contains the cell C in its center. The neighborhood of C is defined as the set of all nonempty cells of $\mathcal{G}$ that overlap C'. For each i with $1 \leq i \leq g$, we denote by N_i the set of all indices j, such that the j-th nonempty cell is in the neighborhood of the i-th nonempty cell. It is clear that $|N_i| \leq (2\beta + 1)^d$.

Let p and q be any two distinct points of S such that $|pq| \leq tw$. Let i and j be the indices such that p and q are contained in the i-th and j-th nonempty cells of $\mathcal{G}$, respectively. We claim that $j \in N_i$. Indeed, if this were not the case, then

$$|pq| > \beta \cdot w/\sqrt{d} \geq t\sqrt{d} \cdot w/\sqrt{d} = tw,$$

which is a contradiction.

Now we can prove the upper bound on M, that is, the number of distances in S that are less than or equal to tw. We have

$$M \leq \frac{1}{2} \sum_{i=1}^{g} n_i \sum_{j \in N_i} n_j$$

$$\leq \frac{1}{2} \sum_{i=1}^{g} \sum_{j \in N_i} \left(\max(n_i, n_j) \right)^2$$

$$\leq \sum_{\ell=1}^{g} |N_\ell| n_\ell^2 \tag{8.6}$$

$$\leq (2\beta + 1)^d \sum_{\ell=1}^{g} n_\ell^2$$

$$= (2\beta + 1)^d \sum_{\ell=1}^{g} \left(n_\ell + 2 \binom{n_\ell}{2} \right)$$

$$\leq (2\beta + 1)^d (n + 2Z)$$

$$< (2\beta + 1)^d (n + 2k),$$

where the last inequality follows from (8.5). We leave it as an exercise to show the validity of inequality (8.6) (see Exercise 8.3).   ■

The following theorem summarizes the results of this section.

Theorem 8.2.2. *Let S be a set of n points in $\mathbb{R}^d$, let $t > 1$ be a real number, let D be a positive integer, and let G be a t-spanner for S of degree D. Given any integer k with $1 \leq k \leq \binom{n}{2}$, algorithm* EXACTDISTENUM(G, k) *computes a sequence of k exact closest pairs in S, in $O(Dt^d(n + k) \log n)$ time.*

8.3 Using the gap-greedy spanner

Theorem 8.2.2 holds for any spanner G of bounded degree. In this section, we show that the running time for exact distance enumeration can be improved, if G is taken as the gap-greedy spanner of Chapter 7.

Let θ be a real number such that $0 < \theta < \pi/4$ and $\cos\theta - \sin\theta > 1/2$, and let G_0 be the directed graph that is constructed by algorithm FASTGAPGREEDYDDIM(S, θ, w), with $w = 0$; see Section 7.5 and Theorem 7.5.1. Let $G = (S, E)$ be the graph obtained from G_0 by replacing each directed edge (p, q) by the undirected edge $\{p, q\}$. The graph G is a t-spanner for S, for $t = 1/(\cos\theta - \sin\theta)$. Let D be the degree of G. Then $D = O(1/\theta^{d-1})$.

Algorithm GAPEXACTDISTENUM(G, k)

Comment: This algorithm takes as input the undirected gap-greedy t-spanner $G = (S, E)$ and an integer k such that $1 \leq k \leq \binom{n}{2}$. It returns a sequence of k exact closest pairs in S.

The algorithm is obtained by running algorithm APPROXDISTENUM(G, k) of Section 8.1, with the following modification: set the priority value of each pair $\{p, q\}$ in the priority queue PQ to $|pq|$.

The running time of algorithm GAPEXACTDISTENUM(G, k) is clearly the same as that of algorithm APPROXDISTENUM(G, k).

We prove by induction that algorithm GAPEXACTDISTENUM(G, k) reports a sequence of k exact closest pairs. Let $w_1 \leq w_2 \leq \cdots \leq w_k$ be the k smallest distances in the multiset $\{|pq| : \{p, q\} \subseteq S, p \neq q\}$.

To start the induction, consider two points p and q of S, with $|pq| = w_1$. Since we chose θ, such that $\cos\theta - \sin\theta > 1/2$, we have $t < 2$. Therefore, p and q are connected by an edge in G; see Exercise 1.10. Hence, in the initialization step, all pairs having distance w_1 (or k of them in case there are more than k pairs having distance w_1) are inserted into PQ. It follows that the first pair reported by the algorithm has distance w_1.

Let i be such that $2 \leq i \leq k$, and assume that the algorithm has already reported $i - 1$ pairs of points, having distances $w_1, w_2, \ldots, w_{i-1}$. We show that the next pair to be reported has distance w_i. Let p and q be two points of S with $|pq| = w_i$. If $\{p, q\}$ is an edge of G, then we are done, because the pair $\{p, q\}$ was inserted into PQ in the initialization step. So assume that p and q are not connected by an edge in G. Since the directed graph G_0 satisfies the conditions of Lemma 7.1.1, we know that (i) there is a point $s \in S$ such that $\{p, s\} \in E$, angle$(pq, ps) \leq \theta$ and $|ps| \leq |pq|/\cos\theta$, or (ii) there is a point $r \in S$ such that $\{r, q\} \in E$, angle$(pq, rq) \leq \theta$ and $|rq| \leq |pq|/\cos\theta$. We consider the case only when (i) holds. (The case when (ii) holds can be treated similarly.) By Lemma 6.4.1, we have $|sq| < |pq|$. Hence, the algorithm has already reported the pair $\{s, q\}$. At the moment this pair was reported, the algorithm inserted the pair $\{p, q\}$ into PQ. Hence, after the algorithm has reported $i - 1$ pairs, the minimum priority in PQ is equal to w_i. This completes the correctness proof.

Theorem 8.3.1. *Let S be a set of n points in $\mathbb{R}^d$, let θ be a real number such that $0 < \theta < \pi/4$ and $\cos\theta - \sin\theta > 1/2$, let G_0 be the directed graph that is constructed by algorithm* FASTGAPGREEDYDDIM$(S, \theta, 0)$, *and let G be the undirected version of G_0. Given any integer k with $1 \leq k \leq \binom{n}{2}$, algorithm* GAPEXACTDISTENUM(G, k) *computes a sequence of k exact closest pairs in S, in $O((1/\theta^{d-1})n + (1/\theta^{d-1})k \log k)$ time.*

In Section 10.3.2, we will present a completely different algorithm for computing a sequence of k closest pairs.

Exercises

8.1. Prove the time bound in Theorem 8.1.2. In particular, explain how to implement the priority queue PQ, and how to test whether the pair $\{p, r\}$ has been reported already.

8.2. Throughout this chapter, we assumed that the value of k is part of the input, that is, the number k of (exact or approximate) closest pairs to be reported is known at the start of the algorithm. Consider the case when this number is not known to start with. Such a situation would occur, for example, if the algorithm is required to use some other criteria to terminate. Prove that Theorems 8.1.2, 8.2.2, and 8.3.1 still hold, where k is the number of pairs reported.

8.3. Prove that the summation in (8.6) is greater than or equal to the double-summation immediately above it.

8.4. In Section 8.3, we chose θ such that $0 < \theta < \pi/4$ and $\cos\theta - \sin\theta > 1/2$, and took for G the undirected version of the directed graph computed by algorithm FASTGAPGREEDYDDIM(S, θ, w), with $w = 0$. Do the results of Section 8.3 hold if $\cos\theta - \sin\theta = 1/2$ and/or if $w > 0$?

8.5. Do the results of Section 8.3 hold if we take for G the Θ-graph of Section 4.1?

8.6. Given a Delaunay triangulation of a set of n points in the plane, show that a sequence of k closest pairs can be computed in $O(n + k \log k)$ time. What is the time complexity if the points are from $\mathbb{R}^d$, for $d > 2$?

8.7. Given any set S of n points in $\mathbb{R}^d$, show that a set $S' \subset \mathbb{R}^d$ of size $O(n)$ can be computed in $O(n \log n)$ time, such that the Delaunay triangulation of $S \cup S'$ has bounded degree and, therefore, has $O(n)$ edges.

8.8. Prove that the problem of computing k closest pairs in a set of n points in $\mathbb{R}^d$ has a lower bound of $\Omega(n \log n + k)$ in the algebraic computation-tree model, even if the pairs are not required to be output in nondecreasing order of distance.

Bibliographic notes

Salowe [1992] was the first to solve the problem of computing k closest pairs, not necessarily in sorted order, in $O(n \log n + k)$ time. Observe that this is optimal in the algebraic computation-tree model (see Exercise 8.8). Alternative algorithms, having the same running time, were given by Lenhof and Smid [1995] (their algorithm uses indirect addressing), Dickerson and Eppstein [1996] (their algorithm is discussed below), Callahan [1995] (this algorithm will be presented in Section 10.3.2), and Chan [2001]. A comprehensive overview of results on closest pair problems can be found in Smid [2000].

The results of this chapter are due to Arya and Smid [1997]. The algorithms were inspired by Dickerson, Drysdale, and Sack [1992], who showed that, given the Delaunay triangulation of a set of n points in the plane, a sequence of k closest pairs can be computed in $O(n + k \log k)$ time (see Exercise 8.6). Arya and Smid [1997] showed that the algorithm in Dickerson, Drysdale, and Sack [1992] also works if the Delaunay triangulation is replaced by a spanner of bounded degree.

The efficiency of the algorithm in Dickerson, Drysdale, and Sack [1992] depends heavily on the fact that the Delaunay triangulation of a set of n points in the plane has $O(n)$ edges. In dimensions larger than 2, this does not hold. Dickerson and Eppstein [1996], however, circumvent this by using the following result of Bern, Eppstein, and Gilbert [1994]: Given any set S of n points in $\mathbb{R}^d$, a set $S' \subset \mathbb{R}^d$ of size $O(n)$ can be computed in $O(n \log n)$ time, such that the Delaunay triangulation DT' of $S \cup S'$ is of bounded degree and, hence, has $O(n)$ edges. Moreover, given S, DT' can be computed in $O(n \log n)$ time (see Exercise 8.7). Dickerson and Eppstein show that DT' can be used to compute a sequence of k closest pairs in S, in $O(n \log n + k \log k)$ time. They also present a variant of their algorithm that computes k closest pairs, in no particular order, in $O(n \log n + k)$ time.

The proof of Lemma 8.2.1 uses ideas from Salowe [1992] and Lenhof and Smid [1995]. A solution to Exercise 8.2 can be found in Arya and Smid [1997].

PART III

The Well-Separated Pair Decomposition and Its Applications

9

The Well-Separated Pair Decomposition

We introduce the *well-separated pair decomposition*, which is a data structure that can be used to efficiently solve a large variety of proximity problems. We will show that, using this data structure, a t-spanner with $O(n)$ edges, for any given set of n points in $\mathbb{R}^d$, and any given constant $t > 1$, can be computed in $O(n \log n)$ time. In this chapter, we present an algorithm that computes the well-separated pair decomposition in $O(n \log n)$ time. Applications of this powerful data structure are given in Chapter 10. Moreover, the spanner constructions in several of the later chapters in this book will be based on this data structure.

9.1 Definition of the well-separated pair decomposition

We start by defining the notion of two sets being well-separated.

Well-separated pair: As shown in Figure 9.1, two point sets A and B form a well-separated pair if they can be enclosed in two balls of equal radius that are "far" apart, relative to their radius. The first consequence of this property is that the distance between any point in A and any point in B is "large" compared to the distances between points within A (and within B). The second consequence is that all distances between a point in A and a point in B are "approximately" equal.

Before we can formally define this notion, we have to introduce the following notation. If X is a bounded subset of $\mathbb{R}^d$, then we denote by $R(X)$ the smallest axes-parallel d-dimensional hyperrectangle that contains X. We call $R(X)$ the *bounding box* of X. The *distance between two disjoint balls* C and C' in $\mathbb{R}^d$ is defined to be the minimum of the Euclidean distances $|xy|$, over all points $x \in C$ and $y \in C'$. This minimum distance is attained for the points x and y on the boundaries of C and C', respectively, that are on the line segment joining the centers of C and C'.

Definition 9.1.1 (Well-Separated Pair). Let $s > 0$ be a real number, and let A and B be two finite sets of points in $\mathbb{R}^d$. We say that A and B are *well-separated with respect to s* if there are two disjoint d-dimensional balls C_A and C_B, such that

1. C_A and C_B have the same radius,
2. C_A contains the bounding box $R(A)$ of A,

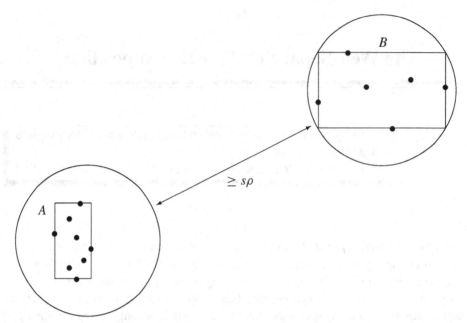

Figure 9.1: Two planar point sets A and B that are well-separated. Both circles have radius ρ, and their distance is greater than or equal to $s\rho$.

3. C_B contains the bounding box $R(B)$ of B, and

4. the distance between C_A and C_B is greater than or equal to s times the radius of C_A.

Refer to Figure 9.1 for an illustration. The real number s will be called the *separation ratio*. Observe that two sets A and B that are well-separated must be disjoint, because the two balls C_A and C_B are required to be disjoint. In Definition 9.1.1, the centers of the two balls C_A and C_B can be at arbitrary locations; they are *not* required to be at the centers of the two bounding boxes $R(A)$ and $R(B)$. Strictly speaking, $R(A)$ and $R(B)$ are not needed in Definition 9.1.1. We include these boxes in this definition, because they can be used to test in $O(1)$ time whether A and B are well-separated. This claim is left as an exercise (see Exercise 9.1).

We now come to an important property of well-separated sets, which will be used repeatedly throughout the rest of this book. Consider two sets A and B that are well-separated with respect to a large separation ratio s. Then (i) the distance between any two points in A is much smaller than the distance between any point in A and any point in B, and (ii) all distances between a point in A and a point in B are approximately equal. The following lemma formalizes this.

Lemma 9.1.2. *Let $s > 0$ be a real number, let A and B be two finite sets of points that are well-separated with respect to s, let p and p' be any two points in A, and let q and q' be any two points in B. Then*

1. $|pp'| \leq (2/s)|pq|$, *and*

2. $|p'q'| \leq (1 + 4/s)|pq|$.

PROOF By Definition 9.1.1, there are two disjoint balls C_A and C_B that contain the points of A and B, respectively, that have the same radius, say ρ, and whose distance is greater than or equal to $s\rho$. Clearly, we have $|pp'| \leq 2\rho$ and $|pq| \geq s\rho$. These two inequalities immediately imply that $|pp'| \leq (2/s)|pq|$, proving the first claim. By a symmetric argument, we can prove that $|qq'| \leq (2/s)|pq|$. By combining these inequalities and applying the triangle inequality, we get

$$\begin{aligned} |p'q'| &\leq |p'p| + |pq| + |qq'| \\ &\leq (2/s)|pq| + |pq| + (2/s)|pq| \\ &= (1 + 4/s)|pq|, \end{aligned}$$

which proves the second claim. ∎

> **Approximating a well-separated pair:** The second inequality in Lemma 9.1.2 implies that the distance between an arbitrary point p in A and an arbitrary point q in B approximates all the $|A| \cdot |B|$ distances between the pairs in the Cartesian product $A \times B$.

Definition 9.1.3 (Well-Separated Pair Decomposition). Let S be a set of n points in $\mathbb{R}^d$, and let $s > 0$ be a real number. A *well-separated pair decomposition* (WSPD) for S, with respect to s, is a sequence

$$\{A_1, B_1\}, \{A_2, B_2\}, \ldots, \{A_m, B_m\}$$

of pairs of nonempty subsets of S, for some integer m, such that

1. for each i with $1 \leq i \leq m$, A_i and B_i are well-separated with respect to s, and
2. for any two distinct points p and q of S, there is exactly one index i with $1 \leq i \leq m$, such that

    (a) $p \in A_i$ and $q \in B_i$, or

    (b) $p \in B_i$ and $q \in A_i$.

The integer m is called the *size* of the WSPD.

> **Well-separated pair decomposition:** Intuitively, a WSPD for S is a partition of the $\binom{n}{2}$ edges of the complete graph on S into a collection of m well-separated pairs.

Does a WSPD exist for any set S? The answer is "yes": Let any two distinct points p and q of S form a pair $\{\{p\}, \{q\}\}$. Then Condition 2. in Definition 9.1.3 clearly holds. To prove that Condition 1. also holds, observe that the bounding box $R(X)$ of a set X consisting of a single point has sides of length zero. For the sets $A := \{p\}$ and $B := \{q\}$, we can take for C_A and C_B the balls of radius zero centered at p and q, respectively. (Alternatively, we can take the radius to be $|pq|/(s + 2)$, which is strictly positive.) Hence, we indeed have a WSPD for S. Its size, however, is equal to $\binom{n}{2}$, which is quadratic in n.

The main result of this chapter will be an algorithm that constructs, in $O(n \log n)$ time, a WSPD of size $O(n)$, for any set S of n points in $\mathbb{R}^d$, and for any constant separation ratio $s > 0$.

We remark that the size m of a WSPD is *not* the same as the total size $\sum_{i=1}^{m}(|A_i| + |B_i|)$ of all subsets that constitute the WSPD. In fact, in Exercise 9.2, we will see that there are sets S of n points such that for *any* WSPD for S, this summation is larger than $\binom{n}{2}$. Still, we will see later that the WSPD computed by our algorithm can be represented implicitly using $O(m)$ space.

9.2 Spanners based on the well-separated pair decomposition

Before we present the algorithm that computes a WSPD, let us show how it can be used to obtain a spanner.

> **Basic spanner construction:** Construct a well-separated pair decomposition with separation ratio $s > 4$, and take one (arbitrary) edge for each pair of the decomposition. This results in a t-spanner with $t = (s + 4)/(s - 4)$.

In order to prove this, let S be a set of n points in $\mathbb{R}^d$, and let $t > 1$ be a real number. Consider an arbitrary WSPD

$$\{A_1, B_1\}, \{A_2, B_2\}, \ldots, \{A_m, B_m\}$$

for S, with separation ratio $s := 4(t + 1)/(t - 1)$. For each i with $1 \leq i \leq m$, let a_i be an arbitrary point of A_i and let b_i be an arbitrary point of B_i. We call these points the *representatives* of A_i and B_i, respectively. We claim that the undirected graph $G = (S, E)$, where $E := \{\{a_i, b_i\} : 1 \leq i \leq m\}$, is a t-spanner for S. This claim can be proved using Lemma 7.1.1; this proof is left as an exercise, see Exercise 9.3. Below, we give a more direct proof that uses Lemma 9.1.2.

We will show by induction on the rank of the distance $|pq|$ in the sorted sequence of distances in S, that the graph G contains a t-spanner path between p and q. To start the induction, this claim clearly holds if $|pq| = 0$. Assume that $|pq| > 0$ and, moreover, assume that for any two points x and y of S with $|xy| < |pq|$, the graph (S, E) contains a t-spanner path between x and y. By Definition 9.1.3, there is a pair $\{A_i, B_i\}$ in the WSPD such that (i) $p \in A_i$ and $q \in B_i$, or (ii) $p \in B_i$ and $q \in A_i$. We may assume without loss of generality that (i) holds. Consider the representatives a_i and b_i of the sets A_i and B_i, respectively. By Lemma 9.1.2, we have $|pa_i| \leq (2/s)|pq|$, which is less than $|pq|$, because $s > 4$. Therefore, by the induction hypothesis, there is a t-spanner path P_1 in G between p and a_i. Similarly, since $|b_iq| < |pq|$, there is a t-spanner path P_2 in G between b_i and q. Let P be the path between p and q, obtained by concatenating the path P_1, the edge $\{a_i, b_i\}$, and the path P_2, and let L denote the length of P. First observe that

$$L \leq t|pa_i| + |a_ib_i| + t|b_iq|. \tag{9.1}$$

By Lemma 9.1.2, we have $|a_ib_i| \leq (1 + 4/s)|pq|$. Combining this inequality with (9.1) and the two inequalities $|pa_i| \leq (2/s)|pq|$ and $|b_iq| \leq (2/s)|pq|$, we get

$$L \leq \left(\frac{4(t + 1)}{s} + 1\right)|pq|,$$

which is equal to $t|pq|$, by our choice of the separation ratio s. We have thus proved the following result.

Theorem 9.2.1 (WSPD-Spanner). *Let S be a set of n points in $\mathbb{R}^d$, let $t > 1$ be a real number, and let $s = 4(t + 1)/(t - 1)$. Given an arbitrary WSPD for S, with respect to s, we can construct a t-spanner for S consisting of m edges, where m is the size of the WSPD.*

Having thus shown the motivation for the WSPD, we return to the details of the WSPD construction.

9.3 The split tree

Let S be a set of n points in $\mathbb{R}^d$, and let $s > 0$ be a real number. The algorithm for computing a WSPD for S, with respect to s, consists of the following two stages:

1. In the first stage, a binary tree, called the *split tree*, is constructed. This tree does *not* depend on s.
2. In the second stage, the split tree is used to construct the WSPD itself.

In this section, we will introduce the split tree and show how to construct it in $O(n \log n)$ time. The second stage will be considered in Section 9.4.

A *hyperrectangle*, or more precisely, a d-dimensional axes-parallel hyperrectangle, is the Cartesian product of d closed intervals. Hence, such a hyperrectangle R can be written as

$$R = [\ell_1, r_1] \times [\ell_2, r_2] \times \cdots \times [\ell_d, r_d],$$

where ℓ_i and r_i are real numbers with $\ell_i \leq r_i$, $1 \leq i \leq d$. We call $L_i(R) := r_i - \ell_i$ the *side length* of R along the i-th dimension. Furthermore, we define $L_{\max}(R)$ and $L_{\min}(R)$ as the maximum and minimum side lengths of R along any dimension, respectively. Let j be the index such that $L_{\max}(R) = L_j(R)$. We define $h(R) := (\ell_j + r_j)/2$; that is, $h(R)$ is the center of the largest interval of R. If all values $L_i(R)$, $1 \leq i \leq d$, are equal, then we call R a *hypercube*.

9.3.1 Definition of the split tree

Recall that $R(S)$ is the bounding box of the set S. The split tree for S is a rooted binary tree containing the points of S in its leaves.

> **The split tree:** If S consists of only one point, then the split tree consists of one single node that stores that point. Assume that $|S| \geq 2$. Split $R(S)$ into two hyperrectangles by cutting its longest interval into two equal parts. Let S_1 and S_2 be the subsets of S that are contained in these two new hyperrectangles. The split tree for S consists of a root having two subtrees, which are recursively defined split trees for S_1 and S_2.

This informal description immediately leads to the following recursive algorithm for computing the split tree:

Algorithm SPLITTREE(S, R)

Comment: This algorithm takes as input a set S of n points in $\mathbb{R}^d$, and a hyperrectangle R that contains the bounding box $R(S)$ of S. It returns the root of the split tree for S.

> **if** $|S| = 1$
> **then** create a new node u;
> $R(u) := R(S)$;
> $R_0(u) := R$;
>   store with u the only point of S, and the two hyperrectangles
> $R(u)$ and $R_0(u)$, and set its two children pointers to be nil;
>   return node u
> **else** compute the bounding box $R(S)$ of S;
>   compute i such that $L_{\max}(R(S)) = L_i(R(S))$;
>   let H be the hyperplane with equation $x_i = h(R(S))$;
>   using H, split R into two hyperrectangles R_1 and R_2;
> $S_1 := S \cap R_1$; $(* \ S_1 \neq \emptyset$ and R_1 contains $R(S_1)$ $*)$
> $S_2 := S \setminus S_1$; $(* \ S_2 \neq \emptyset$ and R_2 contains $R(S_2)$ $*)$
> $v := $ SPLITTREE(S_1, R_1);
> $w := $ SPLITTREE(S_2, R_2);
>   create a new node u;
> $R(u) := R(S)$;
> $R_0(u) := R$;
>   store with u the two hyperrectangles $R(u)$ and $R_0(u)$, and
>   set its left and right child pointers to v and w, respectively;
>   return node u
> **endif**

Each node u of the tree that is computed by algorithm SPLITTREE(S, R) stores the following information; see also Figure 9.2.

1. The bounding box, denoted by $R(u)$, of the points stored in the subtree rooted at u.

2. A hyperrectangle $R_0(u)$ that contains $R(u)$.

3. If u is a leaf, then u also stores a point of S.

In Section 9.4, we will use the bounding boxes $R(u)$ to decide in constant time whether the subsets of S that are contained in any two subtrees are well-separated. In an actual implementation, the hyperrectangles $R_0(u)$ (and, hence, the initial hyperrectangle R) are *not* needed; they are used only in the analysis in Section 9.4.1.

Since each internal node of the split tree has exactly two children, and since the tree has n leaves, it has $2n - 1$ nodes. The *height* of the split tree, however, may be linear in n. As a result, a direct implementation of algorithm SPLITTREE has a worst-case running

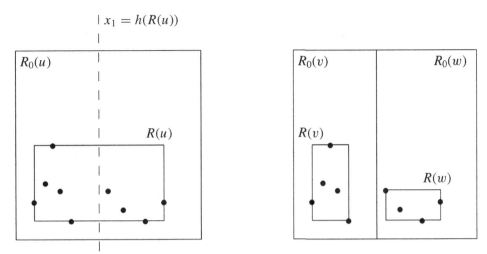

Figure 9.2: An illustration of algorithm SPLITTREE for a planar point set. Because the longest side of $R(u)$ is horizontal, the algorithm uses the vertical line $x_1 = h(R(u))$ to split $R(u)$ into two rectangles of equal size. This line splits $R_0(u)$ into two rectangles $R_0(v)$ and $R_0(w)$. The split tree contains a node u having v and w as its left and right children, respectively.

time of $\Theta(n^2)$. In Section 9.3.2, we will give an improved algorithm that constructs the split tree in $O(n \log n)$ time.

For any node u of the split tree (except for the root), we denote the parent of u by $\pi(u)$. As seen from the algorithm, $R_0(u)$ is the hyperrectangle obtained when the hyperrectangle $R_0(\pi(u))$ of its parent node was split into 2. Before we present the improved algorithm, we prove a property of the hyperrectangles $R_0(u)$ that will be crucial in the analysis in Section 9.4.1. The lemma states that even though the bounding boxes of the children may be considerably smaller than that of the parent, the hyperrectangle $R_0(u)$ associated with u is sufficiently large compared to the bounding box $R(\pi(u))$ of its parent.

Lemma 9.3.1. *Let R be a hypercube that contains the bounding box $R(S)$ of the set S and that has sides of length $L_{\max}(R(S))$. Let T be the tree that is computed by algorithm* SPLITTREE(S, R), *and let u be any node of T. If u is not the root of T, then*

$$L_{\min}(R_0(u)) \geq \frac{1}{2} \cdot L_{\max}(R(\pi(u))).$$

PROOF   The proof is by induction. First assume that u is a child of the root of T. Then $R(\pi(u)) = R(S)$ and $L_{\max}(R(\pi(u)))$ is equal to the side length of the hypercube R. It follows from the algorithm that $L_{\min}(R_0(u))$ is half the side length of R. Hence, the lemma holds for u.

Let u be a node of T such that $\pi(u)$ is not the root of T, and assume that the lemma holds for $\pi(u)$, that is,

$$L_{\min}(R_0(\pi(u))) \geq \frac{1}{2} \cdot L_{\max}(R(\pi(\pi(u)))).$$

We distinguish two cases.

Case 1: $L_{\min}(R_0(u)) = L_{\min}(R_0(\pi(u)))$.

Since the hyperrectangle $R(\pi(u))$ is contained in the hyperrectangle $R(\pi(\pi(u)))$, we have $L_{\max}(R(\pi(\pi(u)))) \geq L_{\max}(R(\pi(u)))$. Therefore, we get

$$
\begin{aligned}
L_{\min}(R_0(u)) &= L_{\min}(R_0(\pi(u))) \\
&\geq \frac{1}{2} \cdot L_{\max}(R(\pi(\pi(u)))) \\
&\geq \frac{1}{2} \cdot L_{\max}(R(\pi(u))).
\end{aligned}
$$

Case 2: $L_{\min}(R_0(u)) \neq L_{\min}(R_0(\pi(u)))$.

Then we must have

$$L_{\min}(R_0(u)) < L_{\min}(R_0(\pi(u))). \tag{9.2}$$

Let i be the index such that $L_{\max}(R(\pi(u))) = L_i(R(\pi(u)))$. We claim that

$$L_i(R_0(u)) = L_{\min}(R_0(u)). \tag{9.3}$$

In other words, for this case, we claim that the dimension along which $R_0(u)$ has its smallest side is the dimension along which the parent was split. Assume that this claim is false. Then there is an index j with $j \neq i$, such that $L_j(R_0(u)) = L_{\min}(R_0(u)) < L_i(R_0(u))$. The algorithm has split the hyperrectangle $R(\pi(u))$ along dimension i. Therefore, we must have $L_j(R_0(u)) = L_j(R_0(\pi(u)))$. That is, we have

$$L_{\min}(R_0(\pi(u))) \leq L_j(R_0(\pi(u))) = L_j(R_0(u)) = L_{\min}(R_0(u)),$$

which contradicts (9.2).

The fact that

$$L_i(R_0(u)) \geq \frac{1}{2} \cdot L_i(R(\pi(u))),$$

and equation (9.3) imply that

$$L_{\min}(R_0(u)) = L_i(R_0(u)) \geq \frac{1}{2} \cdot L_i(R(\pi(u))) = \frac{1}{2} \cdot L_{\max}(R(\pi(u))),$$

which is exactly what we wanted to show. ∎

9.3.2 Computing the split tree in $O(n \log n)$ time

If the split tree is "balanced," in the sense that each split of a hyperrectangle splits the point set contained in it evenly, then its height will be $O(\log n)$, and it is not hard to see that it can be computed in $O(n \log n)$ time. However, the splits may be very uneven. In fact, in the worst case, even after $\Theta(n)$ splits, there may be one node with $\Theta(n)$ points in its corresponding bounding box. Thus, as mentioned before, a direct implementation of algorithm SPLITTREE has a quadratic worst-case running time. In this section, we will show that by doing the splits in a specific order, we can build the entire split tree in $O(n \log n)$ time.

Let a *partial split tree* be defined in the same way as the split tree, except that subsets represented by the leaves may have size larger than 1.

> **Computing the split tree efficiently:** There are several key ingredients that con-
> tribute to the efficiency of the algorithm: (a) The algorithm starts by computing d
> sorted lists, where the i-th list, $1 \leq i \leq d$, contains the points of S in nondecreas-
> ing order of their i-th coordinates. Doing this initially avoids resorting in later
> recursive calls. (b) The algorithm computes a partial split tree for S, such that
> for each leaf u, the set S_u has size at most $n/2$. As we will see, using the sorted
> lists, this can be done in $O(n)$ time. Finally, for each leaf u of the partial split
> tree, the algorithm recursively computes a split tree for the set S_u. (c) At each
> node u, the algorithm splits the corresponding bounding box into two equal-sized
> hyperrectangles. The corresponding point set S_u is to be partitioned into point
> sets S_v and S_w corresponding to the point sets of the children nodes v and w. It
> is critical that the time complexity of this split be proportional to the smaller of
> $|S_v|$ and $|S_w|$, and not to $|S_u|$.

Clearly, the main problem is to compute, in $O(n)$ time, a partial split tree, such that each
leaf corresponds to a subset of size at most $n/2$. We give a specification of the algorithm
that accomplishes this task.

Algorithm PARTIALSPLITTREE(S, R, $(LS_i)_{1 \leq i \leq d}$)

Comment: The algorithm specification is provided here. The algorithm itself consists of
Steps 1 through 6, which are given after this specification.

Input

I.1: A set S of n points in $\mathbb{R}^d$, and a hyperrectangle R that contains the bounding box $R(S)$.

I.2: A collection of doubly-linked lists LS_i, $1 \leq i \leq d$, where LS_i contains the points of S,
sorted in nondecreasing order of their i-th coordinates.

I.3: The d lists LS_i are connected by *cross-pointers*. That is, for each point p of S, the
occurrences of p in all these lists are connected by pointers such that the following
holds. For each i and j, given the position of p in the list LS_i, we can find p's position
in LS_j in $O(1)$ time.

Output

O.1: A partial split tree T for S, such that each leaf u corresponds to a subset S_u of size
at most $n/2$.

O.2: Each node u of T stores two hyperrectangles $R(u)$ and $R_0(u)$, which are the same
hyperrectangles as in algorithm SPLITTREE.

O.3: Each leaf u of T stores the following additional information.

   O.3.1: A collection of doubly-linked lists LS_i^u, $1 \leq i \leq d$, where LS_i^u contains the points
   of S_u, sorted in nondecreasing order of their i-th coordinates.

   O.3.2: The d lists LS_i^u are connected by cross-pointers.

The algorithm that meets this specification makes the following six steps.

Step 1: Make copies CLS_i of the lists LS_i, $1 \leq i \leq d$, and their cross-pointers. For each i
with $1 \leq i \leq d$, add cross-pointers between LS_i and CLS_i. Set size $:= n$. Create a node

u, which will be the root of the final partial split tree. Set $R_0(u) := R$, rename S as S_u and, for each i with $1 \leq i \leq d$, rename the list LS_i as LS_i^u. Go to Step 2.

Step 2: If size $\leq n/2$, then for each i with $1 \leq i \leq d$, walk along the list LS_i^u. For each point z in this list, follow the cross-pointer to the occurrence of z in CLS_i and store with this occurrence a pointer to node u. Then go to Step 6. Otherwise (i.e., if size $> n/2$), go to Step 3.

Step 3: Using the lists LS_i^u, $1 \leq i \leq d$, compute the bounding box $R(S_u)$ of the set S_u, and set $R(u) := R(S_u)$. Compute an index i such that $L_{\max}(R(u)) = L_i(R(u))$, and let H be the hyperplane with equation $x_i = h(R(u))$. Run the following procedure:

> $p :=$ first point of LS_i^u;
> $p' :=$ successor of p in LS_i^u;
> $q :=$ last point of LS_i^u;
> $q' :=$ predecessor of q in LS_i^u;
> size$' := 1$;
> **while** $p_i' \leq h(R(u))$ and $q_i' \geq h(R(u))$
> **do** $p := p'$;
> $p' :=$ successor of p in LS_i^u;
> $q := q'$;
> $q' :=$ predecessor of q in LS_i^u;
>   size$' :=$ size$' + 1$;
> **endwhile**;

Immediately after this procedure, the following holds. If $p_i' > h(R(u))$, then (i) p is the rightmost point in LS_i^u whose i-th coordinate is less than or equal to $h(R(u))$, and (ii) the value of size$'$ is equal to the number of points in LS_i^u that are strictly to the left of p'. Similarly, if $q_i' < h(R(u))$, then (i) q is the leftmost point in LS_i^u whose i-th coordinate is greater than or equal to $h(R(u))$, and (ii) the value of size$'$ is equal to the number of points in LS_i^u that are strictly to the right of q'. In both cases, we have size$' \leq n/2$. Observe that size$'$ is the size of the smaller of the two sets into which S_u is partitioned, and in general, may be much smaller than $|S_u|$.

If $p_i' > h(R(u))$, then proceed with Step 4. Otherwise (i.e., if $q_i' < h(R(u))$), proceed with Step 5.

Step 4: Create new nodes v and w, and make them the left and right children of u, respectively. Using the hyperplane H, split hyperrectangle R into two hyperrectangles R_1 and R_2, where R_1 is to the "left" of R_2. Set $R_0(v) := R_1$ and $R_0(w) := R_2$.
Starting at the first element, walk along the list LS_i^u, until point p is reached. For each point z encountered (including point p itself), do the following.

4.1: From the occurrence of z in LS_i^u, follow cross-pointers to its occurrences in all lists CLS_j, $1 \leq j \leq d$. With the occurrence of z in each list CLS_j, store a pointer to node v.

4.2: Follow the cross-pointers from the occurrence of z in LS_i^u to its occurrences in all lists LS_j^u, $j \neq i$, and delete z from these lists.

4.3: Delete z from LS_i^u.

Finally, set $u := w$, size $:=$ size $-$ size$'$, and go to Step 2.

After Step 4.3, the following holds. First, each list LS_j^u, $1 \leq j \leq d$, contains the points of the subset S_w, sorted in nondecreasing order of their j-th coordinates. Second, these lists are connected by cross-pointers. Finally, the time for executing Steps 3 and 4 is proportional to $|S_v|$, which is the size of the *smaller* of the two subsets S_v and S_w. Node v will be a leaf in the final partial split tree.

Step 5: This step is symmetric to Step 4. Create new nodes v and w, and make them the left and right children of u, respectively. Using the hyperplane H, split hyperrectangle R into two hyperrectangles R_1 and R_2, where R_1 is to the "left" of R_2. Set $R_0(v) := R_1$ and $R_0(w) := R_2$.

Starting at the last element, walk backward along the list LS_i^u, until point q is reached. For each point z encountered (including point q itself), do the following.

5.1: From the occurrence of z in LS_i^u, follow cross-pointers to its occurrences in all lists CLS_j, $1 \le j \le d$. With the occurrence of z in each list CLS_j, store a pointer to node w.

5.2: Follow the cross-pointers from the occurrence of z in LS_i^u to its occurrences in all lists LS_j^u, $j \ne i$, and delete z from these lists.

5.3: Delete z from LS_i^u.

Finally, set $u := v$, size $:=$ size $-$ size$'$, and go to Step 2.

Immediately before Step 6 is carried out, the following holds. The tree that has been constructed so far satisfies conditions O.1 and O.2, except that the hyperrectangles $R(u)$ for the leaves u are still missing. Hence, what remains to be done is computing these missing hyperrectangles, and establishing conditions O.3.1 and O.3.2. This is done in Step 6. Denote the tree constructed so far by T.

Step 6: For each leaf u of T, initialize empty lists LS_j^u, $1 \le j \le d$. Then, for each j with $1 \le j \le d$, walk along the copy CLS_j of the original list LS_j, and for each point z in this copy, follow the pointer to the leaf u of T for which $z \in S_u$, and add this point to the end of the list LS_j^u. Moreover, establish cross-pointers between the lists LS_j^u, $1 \le j \le d$. Finally, for each leaf u of T, compute the bounding box $R(S_u)$, and assign it to $R(u)$. Observe that this bounding box is easily computed by looking at the first and last items in the lists LS_j^u, $1 \le j \le d$.

This concludes the description of algorithm PARTIALSPLITTREE. The next lemma proves the correctness of this algorithm and analyzes its running time.

Lemma 9.3.2. *Algorithm* PARTIALSPLITTREE$(S, R, (LS_i)_{1 \le i \le d})$ *computes a partial split tree that satisfies conditions O.1, O.2, O.3.1, and O.3.2. The running time of the algorithm is $O(n)$.*

PROOF The correctness of the algorithm follows from the discussion above. The running time of Steps 1–5 is proportional to $n + \Sigma_u |S_u|$, where the summation is taken over all leaves u of the partial split tree. Since the sets S_u that occur in this summation form a partition of S, the summation is exactly equal to n. Finally, Step 6 clearly takes $O(n)$ time. ∎

> **Time complexity of algorithm** PARTIALSPLITTREE: In the partial split tree T, each internal node u has two children, and at least one of these is a leaf. Let u_c be such a leaf. The algorithm spends $O(|S_{u_c}|)$ time to process node u (in Steps 3–5). For each leaf u of T, the algorithm spends $O(|S_u|)$ time (in Steps 2 and 6).

Having described the algorithm that computes a partial split tree, we can now present the $O(n \log n)$–time algorithm that computes the complete split tree.

Algorithm FASTSPLITTREE(S, R)

Comment: This algorithm takes as input a set S of n points in $\mathbb{R}^d$, and a hyperrectangle R that contains the bounding box $R(S)$ of S. It returns the root of the split tree for S.

If $n = 1$, then proceed as in algorithm SPLITTREE(S, R). Assume that $n > 1$. In a preprocessing step, sort the points d times, once for each coordinate, and store them in the lists LS_i, $1 \leq i \leq d$, together with the cross-pointers. Now the actual algorithm starts. Run algorithm PARTIALSPLITTREE(S, R, $(LS_i)_{1 \leq i \leq d}$), that computes, in $O(n)$ time, a partial split tree satisfying conditions O.1, O.2, O.3.1, and O.3.2. Then, for each leaf u of this tree, recursively call algorithm FASTSPLITTREE(S_u, $R_0(u)$). (Observe that in recursive calls, preprocessing is not necessary.)

This recursive algorithm FASTSPLITTREE(S, R) computes the same tree as algorithm SPLITTREE(S, R). We denote its running time (after the preprocessing step, which can be performed in $O(n \log n)$ time) by $T(n)$. This function satisfies the recurrence

$$T(n) = O(n) + \sum_u T(|S_u|),$$

where the summation is over all leaves u of the partial split tree. Since each subset S_u has size at most $n/2$, and since these subsets partition the set S, it follows that $T(n) = O(n \log n)$. Hence, we have proved the following result.

Theorem 9.3.3. *Let S be a set of n points in $\mathbb{R}^d$. The split tree for S can be computed in $O(n \log n)$ time.*

9.4 Computing the well-separated pair decomposition

Let S be a set of n points in $\mathbb{R}^d$, and let $s > 0$ be a real number. In this section, we will give an algorithm that uses the split tree and computes a WSPD for S with respect to the separation ratio s.

Let R be a hypercube that contains the bounding box $R(S)$ of S and that has sides of length $L_{\max}(R(S))$. Let T be the tree computed by algorithm FASTSPLITTREE(S, R) in Section 9.3.2 (or, equivalently, by algorithm SPLITTREE(S, R) in Section 9.3.1.) Recall that each node u of T stores two hyperrectangles $R(u)$ and $R_0(u)$, where (i) $R(u)$ is the bounding box of the subset S_u of S that is stored in the subtree of u, (ii) $R(u) \subseteq R_0(u)$, and (iii) $R_0(u)$ is determined by algorithm FASTSPLITTREE(S, R).

Computing the WSPD: For each internal node u of the split tree, run algorithm FINDPAIRS(v, w), where v and w are the children of u. This algorithm tests whether S_v and S_w are well-separated. If they are, it reports the node pair $\{v, w\}$. Otherwise, it tests whether $L_{\max}(R(v)) \leq L_{\max}(R(w))$ or $L_{\max}(R(v)) > L_{\max}(R(w))$. In the first case, FINDPAIRS(v, w) generates two recursive calls FINDPAIRS(v, w_l) and FINDPAIRS(v, w_r), where w_l and w_r are the two children of w. In the second case, FINDPAIRS(v, w) generates two recursive calls FINDPAIRS(v_l, w) and FINDPAIRS(v_r, w), where v_l and v_r are the two children of v.

The formal algorithms, denoted by COMPUTEWSPD(T, s) and FINDPAIRS(v, w), are given below. The latter algorithm tests whether the sets S_v and S_w are well-separated with respect to s. Since the bounding boxes $R(v)$ and $R(w)$ of S_v and S_w are stored at v and w, respectively, this test can be done in $O(1)$ time.

Algorithm COMPUTEWSPD(T, s)

Comment: This algorithm takes as input the split tree T for the point set S, and a real number $s > 0$. It returns a WSPD for S with respect to the separation ratio s.

> **for each** internal node u of T
> **do** $v :=$ left child of u;
> $\quad$ $w :=$ right child of u;
> $\quad$ FINDPAIRS(v, w)
> **endfor**

Algorithm FINDPAIRS(v, w)

Comment: This algorithm takes as input two nodes v and w of the split tree T for S, whose subtrees are disjoint. It returns a collection of well-separated pairs $\{A, B\}$, where A is stored in the subtree of v, and B is stored in the subtree of w.

> **if** S_v and S_w are well-separated with respect to s
> **then** return the node pair $\{v, w\}$
> **else if** $L_{\max}(R(v)) \leq L_{\max}(R(w))$
> $\quad$ **then** ($* |S_w| > 1$, hence w is not a leaf $*$)
> $\quad\quad$ $w_l :=$ left child of w;
> $\quad\quad$ $w_r :=$ right child of w;
> $\quad\quad$ FINDPAIRS(v, w_l);
> $\quad\quad$ FINDPAIRS(v, w_r)
> $\quad$ **else** $v_l :=$ left child of v;
> $\quad\quad$ $v_r :=$ right child of v;
> $\quad\quad$ FINDPAIRS(v_l, w);
> $\quad\quad$ FINDPAIRS(v_r, w)
> $\quad$ **endif**
> **endif**

Let us first prove that algorithm FINDPAIRS(v, w) terminates. Assume without loss of generality that $L_{\max}(R(v)) \leq L_{\max}(R(w))$. Since $|S_v| \cdot |S_{w_l}| < |S_v| \cdot |S_w|$ and $|S_v| \cdot |S_{w_r}| < |S_v| \cdot |S_w|$, the product of the number of points in the subtrees of the two nodes involved becomes smaller in each recursive call. If this product is equal to 1, then both nodes are leaves, and the corresponding two sets are well-separated with respect to s.

Next we prove that algorithm COMPUTEWSPD(T, s) computes a WSPD for S.

Lemma 9.4.1. *Let $\{v_i, w_i\}$, $1 \leq i \leq m$, be the sequence of node pairs returned by algorithm* COMPUTEWSPD(T, s). *The sequence*

$$\{S_{v_1}, S_{w_1}\}, \{S_{v_2}, S_{w_2}\}, \ldots, \{S_{v_m}, S_{w_m}\}$$

is a WSPD for the set S with respect to s.

PROOF   Let i be an integer with $1 \leq i \leq m$. It follows immediately from the algorithm that S_{v_i} and S_{w_i} are nonempty and well-separated with respect to s.

It remains to prove that the second condition in Definition 9.1.3 is satisfied. Let p and q be any two distinct points of S. We will show that there is an index i with $1 \leq i \leq m$, such that (i) $p \in S_{v_i}$ and $q \in S_{w_i}$, or (ii) $p \in S_{w_i}$ and $q \in S_{v_i}$. The uniqueness of this index is left as an exercise (see Exercise 9.8).

Let u be the lowest common ancestor of the two leaves in T that store the points p and q, and let v and w be the left and right children of u, respectively. We may assume without loss of generality that p is in the subtree of v and q is in the subtree of w. Algorithm COMPUTEWSPD(T, s) calls FINDPAIRS(v, w). We claim that this call eventually results in a pair $\{v_i, w_i\}$ such that $p \in S_{v_i}$ and $q \in S_{w_i}$.

The proof of this claim is by induction on the number N of recursive calls generated by FINDPAIRS(v, w). If $N = 0$, then the pair $\{v, w\}$ is returned, and we have $p \in S_v$ and $q \in S_w$. Assume that $N > 0$. We may assume without loss of generality that $L_{\max}(R(v)) \leq L_{\max}(R(w))$. Let w_l and w_r be the left and right children of w, respectively, and assume without loss of generality that $q \in S_{w_l}$. Then one of the two recursive calls generated by FINDPAIRS(v, w) is FINDPAIRS(v, w_l). Since the number of recursive calls generated by FINDPAIRS(v, w_l) is less than N, it follows by induction that the call FINDPAIRS(v, w_l) results in a pair $\{v_i, w_i\}$ such that $p \in S_{v_i}$ and $q \in S_{w_i}$.   ∎

The proof of the following lemma is left as an exercise (see Exercise 9.10).

Lemma 9.4.2. *Let m be the size of the WSPD for S that is computed by algorithm* COMPUTEWSPD(T, s). *The running time of this algorithm is $O(m)$. (This does not include the time to compute the split tree T.)*

Representation of the WSPD: For each pair $\{A, B\}$ in the WSPD, there are two nodes v and w in the split tree T such that $A = S_v$ and $B = S_w$. Hence, the WSPD can be represented by m pairs of nodes of T.

9.4.1 The analysis of algorithm COMPUTEWSPD

We have seen in Lemmas 9.4.1 and 9.4.2 that algorithm COMPUTEWSPD(T, s) computes a WSPD for the set S, in time proportional to the number m of pairs in the decomposition. The main problem that remains is proving an upper bound on m.

One of the difficulties is the fact that there may be nodes a in the split tree T that are "involved" in many pairs of the WSPD. That is, there may be $\Theta(n)$ nodes b in T for which $\{S_a, S_b\}$ is a pair in the WSPD. (See Exercise 9.11.) To overcome this difficulty, we use the idea encapsulated below. Recall that for any node u of T (except for the root), $\pi(u)$ denotes the parent of u.

> **The main idea:** Make every well-separated pair an ordered pair (i.e., give it a direction). Then, use a packing argument to show that every node is involved in at most a small number (dependent only on s) of directed pairs.
>
> To apply the packing argument, we make the following critical observation: Let a and b be two nodes of the split tree T, and assume that $\{S_a, S_b\}$ is a pair in the WSPD that is computed by algorithm COMPUTEWSPD(T, s). Then, the sets $S_{\pi(a)}$ and S_b, or the sets S_a and $S_{\pi(b)}$, are *not* well-separated.

The consequence of the above observation is as follows. Let $\{S_a, S_{b_i}\}$, $1 \le i \le k$, be all pairs in the WSPD that contain the set S_a as a component. Then, the sets S_{b_i}, with $1 \le i \le k$, are pairwise disjoint. Intuitively, since for each i, the sets $S_{\pi(a)}$ and S_{b_i}, or the sets S_a and $S_{\pi(b_i)}$, are not well-separated, each set S_{b_i} is not "too far" away from S_a. In order to apply a packing argument, we have to associate pairwise disjoint regions Z_{b_i} in $\mathbb{R}^d$ to the sets S_{b_i}, $1 \le i \le k$, such that each region Z_{b_i} is "large" and "close" to S_a. These regions will be obtained by using the R_0-hyperrectangles and the fact that the initial hyperrectangle R is a hypercube containing $R(S)$ and having sides of length $L_{max}(R(S))$ (hence, we can apply Lemma 9.3.1). The packing argument (see Lemmas 9.4.3 and 9.4.5) states that there cannnot be too many "large" regions "close" to S_a.

We start the detailed analysis with the following lemma, which states the conditions under which a packing argument can be applied.

Lemma 9.4.3. *Let C be a hypercube in $\mathbb{R}^d$, let ℓ be the side length of C, and let α be a positive real number. Let $b_1, b_2, \ldots, b_k$ be nodes of the split tree T such that*

1. b_i *is not the root of T for all i with $1 \le i \le k$,*

2. *the sets S_{b_i}, $1 \le i \le k$, are pairwise disjoint,*

3. $L_{max}(R(\pi(b_i))) \ge \ell/\alpha$ *for all i with $1 \le i \le k$, and*

4. $R(b_i) \cap C \ne \emptyset$ *for all i with $1 \le i \le k$.*

Then $k \le (2\alpha + 2)^d$.

PROOF By Lemma 9.3.1, we have

$$L_{min}(R_0(b_i)) \ge \frac{1}{2} \cdot L_{max}(R(\pi(b_i))).$$

Then the third assumption implies that $L_{min}(R_0(b_i)) \ge \ell/(2\alpha)$. Also, since $R_0(b_i)$ contains $R(b_i)$, the fourth assumption implies that $R_0(b_i) \cap C \ne \emptyset$. For each i with $1 \le i \le k$, let C_i be a hypercube with sides of length $\ell/(2\alpha)$ such that $C_i \subseteq R_0(b_i)$ and $C \cap C_i \ne \emptyset$. It follows from the second assumption and the description of algorithm SPLITTREE that the interiors of the hyperrectangles $R_0(b_i)$, $1 \le i \le k$, are pairwise disjoint. Hence, the interiors of the hypercubes C_i, $1 \le i \le k$, are pairwise disjoint as well.

We have shown that there exist k hypercubes $C_1, C_2, \ldots, C_k$, all having sides of length $\ell/(2\alpha)$ and whose interiors are pairwise disjoint, such that $C \cap C_i \ne \emptyset$ for all i with $1 \le i \le k$.

Let C' be the hypercube having sides of length $\ell + 2\ell/(2\alpha)$ and that contains C in its "center." Then all hypercubes C_i, $1 \le i \le k$, are contained in C'. Since the volumes of $\cup_{i=1}^k C_i$ and C' are equal to $k(\ell/(2\alpha))^d$ and $(\ell(1 + 1/\alpha))^d$, respectively, it follows that $k(\ell/(2\alpha))^d \le (\ell(1 + 1/\alpha))^d$. This implies that $k \le (2\alpha + 2)^d$. ∎

We mentioned already that we will represent each pair $\{S_a, S_b\}$ in the WSPD as a directed pair. Whether the pair is represented as (S_a, S_b) or (S_b, S_a) will be based on the following lemma.

Lemma 9.4.4. *Let a and b be two nodes of the split tree T, and assume that $\{S_a, S_b\}$ is a pair in the WSPD constructed by algorithm* COMPUTEWSPD(T, s). *Then at least one of the following two claims holds.*

1. *$S_{\pi(a)}$ and S_b are not well-separated, $L_{\max}(R(b)) \leq L_{\max}(R(\pi(a)))$ and $L_{\max}(R(\pi(a))) \leq L_{\max}(R(\pi(b)))$.*

2. *$S_{\pi(b)}$ and S_a are not well-separated, $L_{\max}(R(a)) \leq L_{\max}(R(\pi(b)))$ and $L_{\max}(R(\pi(b))) \leq L_{\max}(R(\pi(a)))$.*

PROOF   The intuition is as follows. If $\{S_a, S_b\}$ is a pair in the WSPD, then this pair must have been returned by the call FINDPAIRS(a, b). If this call was a result of a recursive call from FINDPAIRS$(\pi(a), b)$, then the lemma shows that the longest side of $R(\pi(a))$ lies between those of $R(b)$ and $R(\pi(b))$. On the other hand, if it was a result of a recursive call from FINDPAIRS$(a, \pi(b))$, then the longest side of $R(\pi(b))$ lies between those of $R(a)$ and $R(\pi(a))$. Finally, if a and b are siblings, then both conditions are true.

More formally, let u be the lowest common ancestor of the nodes a and b. Furthermore, let v and w be the left and right children of u, respectively. We may assume without loss of generality that a is in the subtree of v and b is in the subtree of w. The pair $\{a, b\}$ was returned by algorithm FINDPAIRS(v, w) or by one of the recursive calls generated by FINDPAIRS(v, w).

First assume that FINDPAIRS(v, w) does not generate any recursive calls. Then $a = v$ and $b = w$, and since $\pi(a) = \pi(b)$, both claims in the lemma hold. In the rest of the proof, we assume that FINDPAIRS(v, w) does generate recursive calls. Hence $a \neq v$ or $b \neq w$. The recursive call FINDPAIRS(a, b) (which returns the pair $\{a, b\}$) is generated either by FINDPAIRS$(\pi(a), b)$ or by FINDPAIRS$(a, \pi(b))$. We assume that FINDPAIRS(a, b) is generated by FINDPAIRS$(\pi(a), b)$, and we will prove that the first claim in the lemma holds. (By a symmetric argument, the other case implies that the second claim holds.) Observe that $a \neq v$.

It follows immediately from algorithm FINDPAIRS that $S_{\pi(a)}$ and S_b are not well-separated and $L_{\max}(R(b)) \leq L_{\max}(R(\pi(a)))$. Therefore, it remains to show that $L_{\max}(R(\pi(a))) \leq L_{\max}(R(\pi(b)))$. We distinguish two cases.

Case 1: $b = w$.

In this case, $\pi(a)$ is contained in the subtree of $\pi(b)$, which implies that $L_{\max}(R(\pi(a))) \leq L_{\max}(R(\pi(b)))$.

Case 2: $b \neq w$.

We define $\pi^0(a) := a$, and $\pi^{k+1}(a) := \pi(\pi^k(a))$ for $k \geq 0$. Recall that we assumed that FINDPAIRS(a, b) is generated by FINDPAIRS$(\pi(a), b)$. Since $b \neq w$, there is an integer $k \geq 1$, such that

1. FINDPAIRS$(\pi^k(a), b)$ is generated by FINDPAIRS$(\pi^k(a), \pi(b))$, and

2. for each i with $0 \leq i \leq k - 1$, FINDPAIRS$(\pi^{k-i-1}(a), b)$ is generated by FINDPAIRS$(\pi^{k-i}(a), b)$.

(This claim can be proved by analyzing the recursive calls backward, starting with FINDPAIRS(a, b).) The first property implies that $L_{\max}(R(\pi^k(a))) \leq L_{\max}(R(\pi(b)))$.

Since $k \geq 1$, node $\pi(a)$ is in the subtree rooted at $\pi^k(a)$. Hence, $L_{\max}(R(\pi(a))) \leq L_{\max}(R(\pi^k(a)))$. It follows that $L_{\max}(R(\pi(a))) \leq L_{\max}(R(\pi(b)))$. This completes the proof. ∎

We are now ready to prove an upper bound on the size of the WSPD that is computed by algorithm COMPUTEWSPD(T, s). Consider any pair $\{S_a, S_b\}$ in this decomposition. If the first claim in Lemma 9.4.4 holds, i.e., $S_{\pi(a)}$ and S_b are not well-separated and $L_{\max}(R(b)) \leq L_{\max}(R(\pi(a))) \leq L_{\max}(R(\pi(b)))$, then we represent this pair as the *directed* pair (S_a, S_b). Otherwise, we represent it as the directed pair (S_b, S_a). The following lemma bounds the number of directed well-separated pairs that a node is "involved" in.

Lemma 9.4.5. *Let a be any node of the split tree T. There are at most $((2s + 4)\sqrt{d} + 4)^d$ nodes b in T such that (S_a, S_b) is a directed pair in the WSPD computed by algorithm* COMPUTEWSPD(T, s).

PROOF In this proof, we will denote the distance between any two (finite or infinite) bounded and closed sets X and Y in $\mathbb{R}^d$ by $|XY|$. That is,

$$|XY| = \min\{|xy| : x \in X, y \in Y\}.$$

Let b be any node in T such that (S_a, S_b) is a directed pair in the WSPD. Then $L_{\max}(R(b)) \leq L_{\max}(R(\pi(a)))$. Let C_a and C_b be the balls of radius $(\sqrt{d}/2) \cdot L_{\max}(R(\pi(a)))$ that are centered at the centers of $R(\pi(a))$ and $R(b)$, respectively. Then $R(\pi(a)) \subseteq C_a$ and $R(b) \subseteq C_b$. Let x and y be the centers of the balls C_a and C_b, respectively. Then $|R(\pi(a))R(b)| \leq |xy|$. We claim that

$$|R(\pi(a))R(b)| < (s/2 + 1)\sqrt{d} \cdot L_{\max}(R(\pi(a))). \tag{9.4}$$

To prove this claim, first assume that C_a and C_b are not disjoint. Then $|xy| \leq \sqrt{d} \cdot L_{\max}(R(\pi(a)))$, from which (9.4) follows. If C_a and C_b are disjoint, then

$$|C_aC_b| = |xy| - \sqrt{d} \cdot L_{\max}(R(\pi(a)))$$
$$\geq |R(\pi(a))R(b)| - \sqrt{d} \cdot L_{\max}(R(\pi(a))). \tag{9.5}$$

Since the sets $S_{\pi(a)}$ and S_b are not well-separated, we have

$$|C_aC_b| < s(\sqrt{d}/2) \cdot L_{\max}(R(\pi(a))). \tag{9.6}$$

By combining (9.5) and (9.6), we obtain (9.4).

Let C be the hypercube that is centered at x and that has sides of length $((s + 2)\sqrt{d} + 1) \cdot L_{\max}(R(\pi(a)))$. If $R(b) \cap C = \emptyset$, then $|R(\pi(a))R(b)|$ is larger than half the side length of C minus $L_{\max}(R(\pi(a)))/2$, contradicting (9.4). Hence, $R(b) \cap C \neq \emptyset$.

Next, since the first claim in Lemma 9.4.4 holds, we have $L_{\max}(R(\pi(a))) \leq L_{\max}(R(\pi(b)))$. Hence, if we denote the side length of C by ℓ, then

$$L_{\max}(R(\pi(b))) \geq \frac{\ell}{(s + 2)\sqrt{d} + 1}.$$

Now consider all directed pairs $(S_a, S_{b_1}), (S_a, S_{b_2}), \ldots, (S_a, S_{b_k})$ in our WSPD that contain S_a as their first component. Since S_a is common to all these k pairs and since every pair of points must be in a unique pair (property 2. in Definition 9.1.3), it is clear that the sets S_{b_i}, $1 \leq i \leq k$, are pairwise disjoint. Moreover, none of the nodes $b_1, b_2, \ldots, b_k$

are the root of T. Finally, we have just shown that for each i with $1 \leq i \leq k$,

$$L_{max}(R(\pi(b_i))) \geq \frac{\ell}{(s+2)\sqrt{d}+1}$$

and that $R(b_i) \cap C \neq \emptyset$. Therefore, by Lemma 9.4.3, we have $k \leq ((2s+4)\sqrt{d}+4)^d$. ∎

Consider again the WSPD that is computed by our algorithm. Each pair in this decomposition has the form $\{S_a, S_b\}$, for some nodes a and b in the split tree T, neither of them being the root of T. Such a pair is directed either as (S_a, S_b) or as (S_b, S_a). Since T has $2n - 2$ nonroot nodes, it follows from Lemma 9.4.5 that the size of the WSPD, i.e., the number of its pairs, is less than or equal to $(2n - 2)((2s+4)\sqrt{d}+4)^d$. We have proved the following result.

Theorem 9.4.6 (WSPD Theorem). *Let S be a set of n points in $\mathbb{R}^d$ and let $s > 0$ be a real number.*

1. *The split tree for S can be computed in $O(n \log n)$ time. This tree has size $O(n)$ and does not depend on the value of s.*
2. *Given the split tree, we can compute in $O(s^d n)$ time, a WSPD for S with respect to s of size $O(s^d n)$. This WSPD can be represented implicitly in $O(s^d n)$ space.*

Theorems 9.4.6 and 9.2.1 immediately imply the following result.

Corollary 9.4.7 (WSPD-Spanner). *Let S be a set of n points in $\mathbb{R}^d$ and let $t > 1$ be a real number. In $O(n \log n + n/(t-1)^d)$ time, we can construct a t-spanner for S having $O(n/(t-1)^d)$ edges.*

Thus, the WSPD-spanner has $O(n)$ edges and can be constructed in $O(n \log n)$ time. Let us consider the other quality measures for spanners that we have seen before:

1. There is no nontrivial bound on the degree of the WSPD-spanner. However, we will show in Section 10.1.1 that the technique of Section 5.5.3 can be used to transform the WSPD-spanner to a spanner of bounded degree.
2. There is no nontrivial bound on the spanner diameter of the WSPD-spanner. However, we will show in Section 10.2 that for a special choice of the representatives for each well-separated pair $\{A_i, B_i\}$, the WSPD-spanner has spanner diameter $O(\log n)$.
3. By combining the Gap Theorem (Theorem 6.1.2) of Chapter 6 with the so-called dumbbell trees that will be introduced in Chapter 11, it can be shown that the weight of the WSPD-spanner is $O(\log n)$ times the weight of a minimum spanning tree of the point set S; see Exercises 9.12 and 11.6.

9.5 Finding the pair that separates two points

For a given set S of n points in $\mathbb{R}^d$, let $\{A_i, B_i\}$, $1 \leq i \leq m$, be a WSPD with respect to a separation ratio $s > 0$. By definition, for any two distinct points p and q of S, there exists a unique well-separated pair in the decomposition that contains this pair of points. In several applications of the WSPD, we need an efficient algorithm that computes such a well-separated pair from the decomposition. In this section, we consider the problem of answering such *pair queries*.

Problem 9.5.1 (PAIR QUERY). Given a WSPD $\{A_i, B_i\}$, $1 \leq i \leq m$, for a set S of n points in $\mathbb{R}^d$, and given two distinct points p and q in S, compute the index i for which $p \in A_i$ and $q \in B_i$, or $p \in B_i$ and $q \in A_i$.

In general, it is not clear how a pair query can be answered efficiently. In this section, we will present two algorithms that use the special structure of the WSPD that is computed by algorithm COMPUTEWSPD(T, s), to answer such a query in $O(\log n)$ time.

9.5.1 Answering pair queries using centroid edges

Consider the split tree T for the set S. Recall that each node u of T stores the bounding box $R(u)$ of the subset S_u. Also recall that algorithm COMPUTEWSPD(T, s) (see Section 9.4) uses T to compute the WSPD. For each internal node u of T, this algorithm calls the recursive algorithm FINDPAIRS(v, w) (see Section 9.4), where v and w are the two children of u. The recursive calls generated by FINDPAIRS(v, w) define a binary *recursion tree* $RT(v, w)$ in a natural way. Formally, this tree is defined as follows. If the sets S_v and S_w are well-separated, then $RT(v, w)$ consists of a single node storing the bounding boxes $R(v)$ and $R(w)$, and two pointers to the nodes v and w in the split tree T. Otherwise, assume without loss of generality that $L_{\max}(R(v)) \leq L_{\max}(R(w))$. Let w_l and w_r be the two children of w. Then $RT(v, w)$ consists of a root storing the bounding boxes $R(v)$ and $R(w)$. This root has pointers to two recursively defined recursion trees $RT(v, w_l)$ and $RT(v, w_r)$.

Observe that each pair in the WSPD corresponds to a unique leaf in exactly one of the recursion trees. Conversely, any leaf in any recursion tree corresponds to exactly one pair in the WSPD.

Let us see how these recursion trees can be used to answer a pair query. Let p and q be two distinct points of S, and let i be the index such that $p \in A_i$ and $q \in B_i$, or $p \in B_i$ and $q \in A_i$. Let a and b be the nodes of T such that $S_a = A_i$ and $S_b = B_i$, or $S_a = B_i$ and $S_b = A_i$. Hence, our goal is to find the two nodes a and b. Let u be the lowest common ancestor of the leaves of T storing the points p and q. Then it is not difficult to see that (pointers to) a and b are stored with one of the leaves of the recursion tree $RT(v, w)$, where v and w are the two children of u. Let us denote this leaf by ℓ.

We find the leaf ℓ by walking down the tree $RT(v, w)$. We start at the root, which stores the hyperrectangles $R(v)$ and $R(w)$. Observe that (i) $p \in R(v)$ and $q \in R(w)$, or (ii) $p \in R(w)$ and $q \in R(v)$. We may assume without loss of generality that (i) holds. If $RT(v, w)$ consists of one single node, then this node is the leaf ℓ we are looking for and, hence, we are done. Otherwise, assume without loss of generality that $L_{\max}(R(v)) \leq L_{\max}(R(w))$, and let w_l and w_r be the two children of w. If $q \in R(w_l)$, then ℓ is a leaf in the tree $RT(v, w_l)$; hence, we proceed our search recursively in this tree. Otherwise, $q \in R(w_r)$ and we continue our search for ℓ in the tree $RT(v, w_r)$.

The correctness of this algorithm is clear. To analyze its running time, first observe that the lowest common ancestor u can be computed in $O(\log n)$ time, see Theorem 2.3.2. (There is even a faster algorithm, see Theorem 2.3.6. A logarithmic bound is, however, good enough for our purposes.) Given u, the search in the corresponding recursion tree $RT(v, w)$ takes time proportional to the height of this tree. Unfortunately, this height may be linear in n.

To improve the time to search in the recursion tree $RT(v, w)$, we observe that it is not necessary to start at its root. Recall that $p \in R(v)$ and $q \in R(w)$. Let x be an arbitrary internal node of $RT(v, w)$, and let a_x and b_x be the two nodes of T that correspond to x, where $R(a_x) \subseteq R(v)$ and $R(b_x) \subseteq R(w)$. If $p \in R(a_x)$ and $q \in R(b_x)$, then the leaf ℓ we want to find is contained in the subtree of $RT(v, w)$ rooted at x. Otherwise, ℓ is contained in the tree obtained from $RT(v, w)$ by deleting the subtree rooted at x.

Let e be a centroid edge of $RT(v, w)$ (see Exercise 2.14), and let x be the endpoint of e that is furthest away from the root of $RT(v, w)$. Deleting e from $RT(v, w)$ results in two trees having approximately the same number of nodes. Hence, if we start our search for ℓ in node x, then in one "step," we reduce the size of the tree in which we continue the search by a constant factor. By continuing the search in a recursive manner, we find the leaf ℓ in a time that is logarithmic in the number of nodes of $RT(v, w)$. Since the number of nodes of the tree $RT(v, w)$ is polynomial in n, we find ℓ in $O(\log n)$ time.

In the preprocessing needed to answer pair queries, we preprocess the split tree for lowest common ancestor queries (see Section 2.3.2), compute the recursion trees, and use centroid edges to represent them in a balanced form (this is left as an exercise; see Exercise 9.13). Since a centroid edge of a tree can be computed in time that is linear in the size of the tree (see Exercise 2.14), we have proved the following result:

Theorem 9.5.2. *Let S be a set of n points in $\mathbb{R}^d$, and let $s > 0$ be a real number. The WSPD of Theorem 9.4.6 can be represented in $O(s^d n)$ space, such that for any two distinct points p and q in S, a pair query can be answered in $O(\log n)$ time. This representation can be computed in $O(s^d n \log n)$ time.*

9.5.2 Answering pair queries using a path decomposition

The second data structure for answering pair queries improves the preprocessing time in Theorem 9.5.2 from $O(s^d n \log n)$ to $O(n)$. (This does not include the time needed to compute the split tree and the WSPD.)

We will need the following lemma, which states that the longest side of the bounding box of the subset of S contained in the subtree of a node in the split tree T decreases by a factor of at least 2 if we descend T by d levels.

Lemma 9.5.3. *Let b and b' be two nodes in the split tree T such that b is in the subtree of b' and the path between them contains at least d edges. Then*

$$L_{\max}(R(b)) \leq \frac{1}{2} \cdot L_{\max}(R(b')).$$

PROOF Let i be an integer with $1 \leq i \leq d$. It is sufficient to prove that

$$L_i(R(b)) \leq \frac{1}{2} \cdot L_{\max}(R(b')).$$

Let b'' be the child of b' such that b is in the subtree of b''. First assume that there is a node u on the path between b and b'' such that algorithm SPLITTREE splits $R(\pi(u))$ along dimension i. Then

$$
\begin{aligned}
L_i(R(b)) &\leq L_i(R(u)) \\
&\leq \frac{1}{2} \cdot L_i(R(\pi(u))) \\
&\leq \frac{1}{2} \cdot L_i(R(b')) \\
&\leq \frac{1}{2} \cdot L_{\max}(R(b')).
\end{aligned}
$$

We are left with the case when for each node u on the path between b and b'', algorithm SPLITTREE splits $R(\pi(u))$ along a dimension different from i. Since the path between b and b'' contains at least d nodes, there is an index j with $j \neq i$, and two distinct nodes u and v on this path, such that both $R(\pi(u))$ and $R(\pi(v))$ are split along dimension j. Assume without loss of generality that u is in the subtree of v. Then

$$
\begin{aligned}
L_i(R(b)) &\leq L_i(R(\pi(u))) \\
&\leq L_j(R(\pi(u))) \\
&\leq L_j(R(v)) \\
&\leq \frac{1}{2} \cdot L_j(R(\pi(v))) \\
&\leq \frac{1}{2} \cdot L_j(R(b')) \\
&\leq \frac{1}{2} \cdot L_{\max}(R(b')).
\end{aligned}
$$

This completes the proof. ∎

The data structure for answering pair queries that will be discussed in the rest of this section is based on several properties of well-separated pairs and the split tree. These properties are stated in the following two lemmas. We define

$$
\alpha := \frac{2}{(s+4)\sqrt{d}}.
$$

The proof of the following lemma is left as an exercise. (See Exercise 9.14.)

Lemma 9.5.4. *Let A and B be two bounded subsets of $\mathbb{R}^d$, let p be a point in A, let q be a point in B, and let $s > 0$ be a real number.*

1. *If A and B are well-separated with respect to s, then both $L_{\max}(R(A))$ and $L_{\max}(R(B))$ are less than or equal to $(2/s)|pq|$.*
2. *If both $L_{\max}(R(A))$ and $L_{\max}(R(B))$ are less than or equal to $\alpha|pq|$, then A and B are well-separated with respect to s.*

Let $s > 0$ be a real number, and let $\{A_i, B_i\}$, $1 \leq i \leq m$, be the WSPD of S, with separation ratio s, that is computed by algorithm COMPUTEWSPD(T, s) in Section 9.4. Recall that, by Theorem 9.4.6, we have $m = O(s^d n)$. Every node u of the split tree T stores the bounding box $R(u)$ of the set of all points that are stored in the subtree rooted at u. For any ordered pair (p, q) of distinct points in the point set S, we define the following two nodes in T:

- u_{pq} is the highest node u on the path in T from the leaf storing p to the root, such that $L_{\max}(R(u)) \leq (2/s)|pq|$.
- u'_{pq} is the highest node u on the path in T from the leaf storing p to the root, such that $L_{\max}(R(u)) \leq \alpha|pq|$.

For each i with $1 \leq i \leq m$, let v_i and w_i be the nodes in T such that $A_i = S_{v_i}$ and $B_i = S_{w_i}$.

Lemma 9.5.5. *Let p and q be two distinct points of S, and let i be the index such that (i) $p \in A_i$ and $q \in B_i$, or (ii) $p \in B_i$ and $q \in A_i$. Assume without loss of generality that (i) holds.*

1. *If we follow the path in T from the leaf storing p to the root, then we encounter, in this order, the nodes u'_{pq}, v_i, and u_{pq}.*

2. *If we follow the path in T from the leaf storing q to the root, then we encounter, in this order, the nodes u'_{qp}, w_i, and u_{qp}.*

3. *The path in T between u'_{pq} and u_{pq} contains $O(1/s)$ nodes.*

4. *The path in T between u'_{qp} and u_{qp} contains $O(1/s)$ nodes.*

5. *Given pointers to the nodes u_{pq} and u_{qp}, we can compute the nodes v_i and w_i in $O(1/s)$ time.*

PROOF   By the construction of the split tree, we know that the sizes of the bounding boxes of the corresponding nodes increases as we traverse from any node in the split tree to its root. Thus, the first claim follows from the definition of the nodes u'_{pq} and u_{pq}, from Lemma 9.5.4, and from algorithm FINDPAIRS of Section 9.4. The second claim follows by a symmetric argument. The third and fourth claims follow from Lemma 9.5.3. The last claim follows from the third and fourth claims, and from algorithm FINDPAIRS.   ■

The previous lemma implies that, in order to answer a pair query for two points p and q, it is sufficient to compute the two nodes u_{pq} and u_{qp}.

We are now ready to describe the data structure that will allow us to efficiently answer a pair query. We use the construction of Section 2.3.2 to partition the split tree T into pairwise disjoint paths. Recall that these paths have the property that we can walk from any node in T to the root, in $O(\log n)$ time. For each path P in the partition of T, let T_P be a balanced binary search tree storing the nodes on the path P. The search information stored with each node u in T_P is the value of $L_{max}(R(u))$. When given the split tree T, its partition into paths, as well as the collection of all trees T_P, can be computed in $O(n)$ time.

Given two distinct points p and q of S, let i be the index such that (i) $p \in A_i$ and $q \in B_i$, or (ii) $p \in B_i$ and $q \in A_i$. As usual, we assume without loss of generality that (i) holds. Answering the pair query for p and q (i.e., finding the two nodes v_i and w_i) is done in the following way. First, in $O(\log n)$ time, find the path P in the partition of T that contains the node u_{pq}. Then, use the binary search tree T_P to find, again in $O(\log n)$ time, the node u_{pq} on P. Finally, in $O(1/s)$ time, find the node v_i. In a symmetric way, we find the node w_i in $O(\log n + 1/s)$ time.

Theorem 9.5.6. *Let S be a set of n points in $\mathbb{R}^d$, and let $s > 0$ be a real number. The WSPD of Theorem 9.4.6 can be represented in $O(s^d n)$ space, such that for any two distinct points p and q in S, a pair query can be answered in $O(\log n + 1/s)$ time. Given the split tree T and this WSPD, this representation can be computed in $O(n)$ time.*

In Section 16.3.3, we will show that the solution given above can be extended to answer a restricted type of pair queries more efficiently.

9.6 Extension to other metrics

We have introduced the well-separated pair decomposition for point sets in $\mathbb{R}^d$, under the Euclidean metric. A natural question is whether the WSPD can be generalized to other metrics. This is meaningful, because in many applications the underlying metric is non-Euclidean.

A *metric space* is a pair (S, δ), where S is a (finite or infinite) set, whose elements are called points, and $\delta : S \times S \longrightarrow \mathbb{R}$ is a function that assigns a *distance* $\delta(p, q)$ to any two points p and q in S, and that satisfies the following three conditions:

1. For all points p and q in S, $\delta(p, q) \geq 0$.
2. For all points p and q in S, $\delta(p, q) = 0$ if and only if $p = q$.
3. For all points p and q in S, $\delta(p, q) = \delta(q, p)$.
4. For all points p, q, and r in S, $\delta(p, q) \leq \delta(p, r) + \delta(r, q)$.

The fourth condition is called the *triangle inequality*.

Let (S, δ) be an arbitrary metric space, where S is a finite set. Before we can define the WSPD based on the metric δ, we have to define the notion of two sets being well-separated. The *diameter* $D(A)$ of a subset A of S is defined as

$$D(A) := \max\{\delta(a, b) : a, b \in A\}.$$

The *distance* $\delta(A, B)$ of two subsets A and B of S is defined as

$$\delta(A, B) := \min\{\delta(a, b) : a \in A, b \in B\}.$$

For a real number $s > 0$, we say that the subsets A and B of S are *well-separated with respect to s* if

$$\delta(A, B) \geq s \cdot \max(D(A), D(B)).$$

Using this generalized notion of being well-separated, we define a well-separated pair decomposition (WSPD) for S, with respect to the separation ratio s, as in Definition 9.1.3. As before, we define the *size* of a WSPD to be the number of pairs in the decomposition.

For every metric space (S, δ), and for every real number $s > 0$, there exists a WSPD of size $\binom{n}{2}$. Unfortunately, there exist metric spaces for which no WSPD of smaller size exists; see Exercise 9.17. Below, we give two examples of metric spaces that do have a WSPD of subquadratic size.

9.6.1 The unit disk metric

Let S be a set of n points in $\mathbb{R}^d$. Recall the *unit disk graph* $U = (S, E)$ of S, that was defined in Exercise 4.7. The edge set E of this graph is defined as

$$E = \{\{p, q\} : p \in S, q \in S, 0 < |pq| \leq 1\}.$$

For any two points p and q in S, we define $\delta(p, q)$ to be the length of a shortest path between p and q in the graph U. Then, (S, δ) is a metric space. We state the following theorem without proof.

Theorem 9.6.1. *Let S be a set of n points in $\mathbb{R}^d$ such that the unit disk graph of S is connected, and let $s > 1$ be a real number. Consider the metric space (S, δ) as defined above.*

1. *If $d = 2$, then a WSPD for S, with respect to s, having size $O(s^4 n \log n)$, can be computed in $O(s^4 n \log n)$ time.*
2. *If $d = 3$, then a WSPD for S, with respect to s, having size $O(n^{4/3})$, can be computed in $O(n^{4/3} \log^{O(1)} n)$ time.*
3. *If $d \geq 4$, then a WSPD for S, with respect to s, having size $O(n^{2-2/d})$, can be computed in $O(n^{2-2/d})$ time.*

9.6.2 Doubling metrics

Several natural extensions to the concept of dimension in Euclidean spaces have been defined and studied. One such concept is that of the *doubling dimension* of a metric space. Let (S, δ) be a metric space, where S is a finite set. The doubling dimension of this space is defined to be the smallest positive real number λ, such that the following holds: For every real number $\rho > 0$, every ball of radius ρ can be covered by 2^λ balls of radius $\rho/2$. We say that (S, δ) is a *doubling metric*, if its doubling dimension does not depend on the size of S. We state the following theorem without proof.

Theorem 9.6.2. *Let (S, δ) be a metric space with doubling dimension λ, let n be the size of S, and let $s > 1$ be a real number. There exists a WSPD for S, with respect to s, consisting of $O(n/s^{O(\lambda)})$ pairs. There exists a randomized algorithm that computes such a WSPD in*

$$O\left(2^{O(\lambda)} n \log n + n/s^{O(\lambda)}\right)$$

expected time.

Observe that this result is weaker than the deterministic results presented in this chapter for Euclidean metrics.

> **Open problem:** Which metric spaces (S, δ) admit a WSPD of subquadratic size? Design efficient algorithms that compute such a WSPD.

Exercises

9.1. Let A and B be two finite sets of points in $\mathbb{R}^d$, and assume that we know their bounding boxes $R(A)$ and $R(B)$. Give an algorithm that decides in $O(1)$ time if A and B are well-separated with respect to some given real number $s > 0$.

9.2. Let $s > 0$ be a real number, let $x := 2/s + 1$, and let S be the set consisting of the n real numbers x^i, $0 \le i \le n - 1$. Let $\{A_i, B_i\}$, $1 \le i \le m$, be an arbitrary WSPD for S with separation ratio s. Prove that

$$\sum_{i=1}^{m}(|A_i| + |B_i|) = \binom{n}{2} + m.$$

(*Hint:* For each i, at least one of the sets A_i and B_i contains only one element.)

9.3. Use Lemma 7.1.1 to prove that the graph $G = (S, E)$ of Section 9.2 is a t-spanner for S.

9.4. In Section 9.2, we pick arbitrary representatives in the sets A_i and B_i to define the t-spanner G. Choose the representatives a_i in A_i and b_i in B_i such that $|a_i b_i|$ is minimum. Prove that the resulting graph has the *strong* spanner property of Exercise 4.6: For any two points p and q of the point set S, there is a path between p and q whose length is less than or equal to $t|pq|$ and all of whose edges have length at most $|pq|$.

9.5. Let S be a set of n points in $\mathbb{R}^d$, let p be a point of S, and let q be a nearest neighbor of p in S, i.e., $q \in S$ and $|pq| = \min\{|pr| : r \in S, r \ne p\}$. Consider an arbitrary WSPD for S, with separation ratio $s > 2$. Let $\{A, B\}$ be the pair in this decomposition such that $p \in A$ and $q \in B$. Prove that the set A is a singleton set containing only the point p.

9.6. Let S be a set of n points in $\mathbb{R}^d$, and let $\{p, q\}$ be an arbitrary closest pair in S, that is, $|pq| = \min\{|ab| : a, b \in S, a \ne b\}$. Consider an arbitrary WSPD for S, with separation ratio $s > 2$. Prove that this decomposition contains the pair $\{\{p\}, \{q\}\}$.

9.7. Let S be a set of n points in $\mathbb{R}^d$.

    (1) Use Exercise 9.5 to prove that the size of any WSPD for S, with separation ratio $s > 2$, is greater than or equal to $n/2$.

    (2) Use the results from Section 9.2 to prove that the size of any WSPD for S, with separation ratio $s > 4$, is greater than or equal to $n - 1$. (See also Exercise 10.7.)

9.8. Prove that the index i in the proof of Lemma 9.4.1 is unique.

9.9. Use algorithm COMPUTEWSPD to compute a WSPD for the set S of Exercise 9.2.

9.10. Prove Lemma 9.4.2.

9.11. Let S be the set of n real numbers defined as

$$S := \{2^i : 1 \leq i \leq n - 2\} \cup \{-1, -2^{n-2}\},$$

and let $s > 3$ be a real number. Let T be the split tree for S, and consider the WSPD that is computed by algorithm COMPUTEWSPD(T, s). Prove that for each i with $1 \leq i \leq n - 2$, the pair $\{\{-1\}, \{2^i\}\}$ is contained in this WSPD.

9.12. Let S be the set consisting of the n integers $1, 2, \ldots, n$, let $s > 1$ be a real number, and let $\{A_i, B_i\}$, $1 \leq i \leq m$, be an arbitrary WSPD for S with separation ratio s. Prove that the weight of the spanner of Section 9.2 for this WSPD, for any choice of the representatives, is $\Omega(\frac{s-1}{s+1} n \log n)$. Thus, there exist point sets S in $\mathbb{R}^d$, such that the WSPD-spanner for S has weight $\Omega(\log n)$ times the weight of a minimum spanning tree of S. (In Exercise 11.6, we will see that this lower bound is tight.)

9.13. In Section 9.5.1, we sketched an algorithm that uses centroid edges to search in a recursion tree $RT(v, w)$. Fill in the details of this algorithm. In particular, explain how centroid edges are used to compute a balanced representation of $RT(v, w)$ in $O(n' \log n')$ time, where n' is the number of nodes of $RT(v, w)$.

9.14. Prove Lemma 9.5.4.

9.15. Let S be a set of n points in $\mathbb{R}^d$ and let $s > 0$ be a real number. Let $\{A_i, B_i\}$, $1 \leq i \leq m$, be the WSPD for S with separation ratio s, as referred to in Theorem 9.4.6. Prove that

$$\sum_{i=1}^{m} \min(|A_i|, |B_i|) = O(s^d n \log n).$$

9.16. Let S be a set of n points in $\mathbb{R}^d$ and let $s > 0$ be a real number. Give an algorithm that computes, in $O(s^d n \log n)$ time, a WSPD for S with separation ratio s, consisting of $O(s^d n \log n)$ pairs of the form $\{A, B\}$, where at least one of A and B contains only one element.

9.17. Let S be a set of n elements, and define the function $\delta : S \times S \longrightarrow \mathbb{R}$ by

$$\delta(p, q) := \begin{cases} 0 & \text{if } p = q, \\ 1 & \text{if } p \neq q. \end{cases}$$

    (1) Prove that (S, δ) is a metric space.

    (2) Let $s > 1$ be a real number. Prove that for the metric space (S, δ), every WSPD for S, with respect to the separation ratio s, consists of exactly $\binom{n}{2}$ pairs.

9.18. In Section 9.6.2, we have defined the doubling dimension of a metric space. Determine the doubling dimension of the metric space (S, δ), where S is a finite set of points in $\mathbb{R}^d$ and δ is the Euclidean distance function.

Bibliographic notes

The well-separated pair decomposition was introduced by Callahan and Kosaraju [1992, 1995b]; see also Callahan [1995]. Their motivation was to adapt the *fast multipole method* (see Greengard [1988]) for the efficient computation of n-body potential fields. The algorithm of Greengard makes certain assumptions about the distribution of the input points. Callahan and Kosaraju devised the WSPD to show that this algorithm can be adapted so that its running time does not depend on the bit representation of the input points. The term "well-separated" is taken from Greengard.

The results of Sections 9.1, 9.3, and 9.4 are due to Callahan [1995] and Callahan and Kosaraju [1992, 1995b]. Previously, algorithms for computing spanners, nearest neighbors, and closest pairs, that are based on similar ideas, were given by Salowe [1991, 1992] and Vaidya [1988, 1989, 1991]. Section 9.2 is based on Callahan and Kosaraju [1993].

The algorithm in Section 9.5.1 for answering pair queries is due to Arya, Mount, and Smid [1994]. The improved algorithm in Section 9.5.2 is based on Gudmundsson, Narasimhan, and Smid [2005].

A solution to Exercise 9.2 can be found in Callahan and Kosaraju [1995b]. Solutions to Exercises 9.15 and 9.16 can be found in Callahan [1995].

The algorithm for computing the WSPD, as presented in this chapter, is based on the split tree. There are other trees that can be used instead of the split tree. We mention the *balanced box-decomposition tree* of Arya et al. [1998] (see also Arya and Mount [2000]), and the *balanced aspect ratio tree* of Duncan, Goodrich, and Kobourov [2001] (see also Duncan [1999]).

Callahan [1995], Narasimhan, Zhu, and Zachariasen [2000], Narasimhan and Zachariasen [2001], and Tate and Xu [2000] present experimental work on (variants of) the split tree and the WSPD.

Varadarajan [1998] defines the *semi-separated decomposition* (which is a variant of the WSPD), and uses it to compute the minimum-cost perfect matching of a set of points in the plane.

It is natural to ask whether any theory developed for Euclidean metrics can be extended to more general metric spaces. In Section 9.6, we stated that the WSPD can be generalized to unit disk and doubling metric spaces. Theorem 9.6.1 for the unit disk metric is due to Gao and Zhang [2005]. Clearly, a good candidate for an extension is any metric space that can be isometrically embedded (i.e., embedded while preserving distances faithfully) into a low-dimensional Euclidean space. For some applications, it may be sufficient to find low-distortion embeddings (instead of isometric embeddings). For a fixed real number $c > 1$, the *metric dimension* of a finite metric space (X, δ) is defined to be the least dimension of a real normed space $(Y, \| \cdot \|)$, such that there is an embedding ϕ of X into Y, where every two points $x_1, x_2 \in X$ satisfy

$$\delta(x_1, x_2) \geq \|\phi(x_1) - \phi(x_2)\| \geq \frac{1}{c} \cdot \delta(x_1, x_2).$$

Bourgain [1985] showed that it is possible to embed an arbitrary metric space with n elements into a $O(\log n)$-dimensional Euclidean space, but with a logarithmic distortion, i.e., distances suffer a distortion of at most a logarithmic factor in the embedding. The seminal work of Linial, London, and Rabinovich [1995] showed that there exist metric spaces (constant-degree expanders) for which every embedding into a Euclidean space (of any dimension) has a distortion of $\Omega(\log n)$, thus showing that Bourgain's result cannot be improved for general metric spaces. (See also the book by Matoušek [2002].) Small distortions are not possible even for the case of the doubling metrics (see Section 9.6.2), as shown by Semmes [1996] and Laakso [2002].

For many applications (such as nearest neighbor problems), often the underlying metric is non-Euclidean. This motivated attempts to define "Euclidean-like" metrics that extended the concepts of a Euclidean metric. While embedding problems are of interest for these extended metrics, the focus was on bypassing the embedding step and designing algorithms for these metrics directly. The *growth-restricted metrics* were introduced by Karger and Ruhl [2002]. These metrics satisfy the property that for any point q and any real number $\rho > 0$, the number of points within distance 2ρ of q is at most a constant factor larger than the number of points within distance ρ. Karger and Ruhl [2002] designed algorithms for nearest neighbor problems under these metrics. These algorithms are useful in networking applications, such as the Internet or peer-to-peer networks, and vector quantization applications, where feature vectors fall into low-dimensional manifolds within high-dimensional vector spaces.

The doubling metrics of Section 9.6.2 were defined by Assouad [1983] (see also Heinonen [2001] and Gupta, Krauthgamer, and Lee [2003]). For doubling metrics, Talwar [2004] showed the existence of an efficiently computable well-separated pair decomposition, as well as quasi-polynomial time $(1 + \epsilon)$-approximation algorithms for various optimization problems such as TSP, k-median, and facility location. However, Talwar's results depended on the aspect ration of the points, which is defined as the ratio of the maximum to the minimum interpoint distance for the points in the set. Har-Peled and Mendel [2006] eliminated the dependence on the aspect ratio in Talwar's results, and obtained Theorem 9.6.2. They showed how to construct in linear expected time a hierarchical net for doubling metrics. Using this data structure, they devised improved algorithms for many problems including approximate nearest neighbor, well-separated pair decomposition, spanners, compact representation schemes, and computation of quantities such as the doubling dimension and the (approximate) Lipschitz constant of a function.

Other related papers include those by Hildrum et al. [2004], Krauthgamer and Lee [2004a,b], and Krauthgamer et al. [2005].

10

Applications of Well-Separated Pairs

"Then you must be sure to require the citizens of your ideal state not to neglect geometry. It has considerable incidental advantages too."

"What are they?" he asked.

"Its usefulness for war, which you have already mentioned," I replied; "and there is a certain facility for learning all other subjects in which we know that those who have studied geometry lead the field."

"They are miles ahead," he agreed.

"So shall we make this the second subject our young men must study?"

"Yes."

—from *The Republic* depicted as dialogues of Plato (*c.* 427–347 BC) with Socrates

In this chapter, we will present several applications of the well-separated pair decomposition (WSPD) that was introduced in the previous chapter. In Section 10.1, we will give two $O(n \log n)$ – time algorithms that compute, for any set of n points in $\mathbb{R}^d$, a t-spanner in which the degree of each vertex is bounded by a constant. Observe that these results improve Theorem 5.5.5. In Section 10.2, we show that a t-spanner with $O(n)$ edges and $O(\log n)$ spanner diameter can be computed in $O(n \log n)$ time, improving the result of Theorem 5.5.6. Finally, in Section 10.3, we show that the WSPD can be used to obtain efficient algorithms for the closest pair problem, the k closest pairs problem, the all-nearest neighbors problem, and the problem of computing an approximate minimum spanning tree.

10.1 Spanners of bounded degree

In this section, we give two $O(n \log n)$-time algorithms for constructing bounded degree t-spanners for a set S of n points in $\mathbb{R}^d$. The first algorithm combines the transformation of Section 5.5.3 (which takes a high-degree "star" subgraph at a vertex and transforms it into a sink spanner) with the technique used in Section 9.4.1 (which directs the WSPD pairs computed by algorithm COMPUTEWSPD from Section 9.4). The second construction computes a subgraph of the WSPD-spanner of Corollary 9.4.7. We show that this subgraph satisfies the conditions of Lemma 7.1.1, thus guaranteeing that it is a spanner. We also show that this subgraph has bounded outdegree, and therefore, applying the transformation of Section 5.5.3 gives us the required bounded degree spanner.

10.1.1 The first construction

Let S be a set of n points in $\mathbb{R}^d$ and let $t > 1$ be a real number. Consider the WSPD,

$$\{A_1, B_1\}, \{A_2, B_2\}, \ldots, \{A_m, B_m\}$$

for S, with separation ratio $s := 4(\sqrt{t} + 1)/(\sqrt{t} - 1)$, which is computed by algorithm COMPUTEWSPD. By Theorem 9.4.6, this WSPD has size $m = O(s^d n)$ and can be computed in $O(n \log n + s^d n)$ time.

For each i with $1 \leq i \leq m$, let a_i be an arbitrary element of A_i and let b_i be an arbitrary element of B_i. We showed in Section 9.2 that the undirected graph $G = (S, E)$, where $E := \{\{a_i, b_i\} : 1 \leq i \leq m\}$, is a $\sqrt{t}$-spanner for S. The construction in the current section chooses the representatives a_i and b_i in a careful way, so that the degrees of the vertices of G can be carefully controlled.

Consider the split tree T that gave rise to our WSPD. For each leaf u of T, let $r(u)$ be the point of S that is stored in u. Moreover, for each internal node u of T, let $r(u)$ be the point of S that is stored in the rightmost leaf of the left subtree of u. Since every internal node of T has two children, $r(u)$ is distinct for every internal node. Also, observe that this rightmost leaf immediately precedes u in an inorder traversal of T. Hence, in $O(n)$ total time, we can compute, for each node u of T, the point $r(u)$, and store it with u.

Let i be an integer with $1 \leq i \leq m$, and consider the well-separated pair $\{A_i, B_i\}$. This pair is represented implicitly by two nodes, say u_i and v_i, of T. Hence, A_i and B_i are the sets of points stored in the subtrees of u_i and v_i, respectively. We take the point $a_i := r(u_i)$ to be the representative of A_i. Similarly, we take the point $b_i := r(v_i)$ to be the representative of B_i. Observe that $a_i \in A_i$ and $b_i \in B_i$. The following two lemmas explain why we choose the representatives in this way.

Lemma 10.1.1. *Let p be any point of S. There are at most two nodes u in T for which $r(u) = p$.*

PROOF The proof follows from the way in which we defined the representatives.   ∎

For each i with $1 \leq i \leq m$, we direct the pair $\{A_i, B_i\}$ as described after the proof of Lemma 9.4.4, and direct the edge $\{a_i, b_i\}$ accordingly. We denote the directed version of G by $\vec{G}$.

Lemma 10.1.2. *The outdegree of each vertex of $\vec{G}$ is less than or equal to $2((2s + 4)\sqrt{d} + 4)^d$.*

PROOF Let p be an arbitrary vertex of $\vec{G}$. By Lemma 10.1.1, there are at most two nodes u in T such that $r(u) = p$. Consider such a node u. For each directed pair (A_i, B_i), where A_i is the set of points stored in u's subtree, p has one outgoing edge in $\vec{G}$. Moreover, all outgoing edges of p are obtained in this way. The claim now follows from Lemma 9.4.5, which bounds the number of directed pairs in which any set is involved in.   ∎

Let θ be a real number such that $0 < \theta < \pi/4$ and $1/(\cos \theta - \sin \theta) \leq \sqrt{t}$. By applying Theorem 5.5.4 to the graph G, with $t' = \sqrt{t}$ and $D = O(s^d)$, we transform G, in

$$O\left(1/\theta^{d-1} + D \log(1/\theta) n \log n\right)$$

time, into an undirected t-spanner for S, in which each vertex has degree $O(D/\theta^{d-1})$.

Let us assume that $t > 1$ and $t \to 1$. Then, s is proportional to $1/(t - 1)$, and θ is proportional to $t - 1$. We have proved the following theorem.

Theorem 10.1.3. *Let S be a set of n points in $\mathbb{R}^d$, and let $t > 1$ be a real number. In*

$$O\left(\frac{\log(1/(t - 1))}{(t - 1)^d} n \log n\right)$$

time, we can construct a t-spanner for S, in which each vertex has degree $O(1/(t-1)^{2d-1})$.

> **First construction of a bounded-degree spanner:** For each internal node in the split tree, pick the point stored in its inorder predecessor as a representative; for each leaf, pick the point stored in it as the representative. For each pair in the WSPD, add an edge connecting the two representatives. Direct the edges of the resulting graph using Lemma 9.4.4. This yields a graph of bounded outdegree. Use the construction of Section 5.5.3 to transform this graph into an undirected spanner of bounded degree.

10.1.2 The second construction

It turns out to be convenient to describe the second construction for directed graphs. We will use the following special case of Lemma 7.1.1 (where the last condition was simplified).

Lemma 10.1.4. *Let θ, w, and t be real numbers such that $0 < \theta < \pi/4$, $0 \leq w < (\cos\theta - \sin\theta)/2$, and $t \geq 1/(\cos\theta - \sin\theta - 2w)$. Let S be a set of n points in $\mathbb{R}^d$, and let $G = (S, E)$ be a directed graph, such that the following holds: For any two distinct points p and q of S, there is an edge $(x, y) \in E$, such that*

- $\text{angle}(pq, xy) \leq \theta$, $|xy| \leq |pq|/\cos\theta$, *and* $|px| \leq w|xy|$.

Then, the graph G is a t-spanner for S.

Let S be a set of n points in $\mathbb{R}^d$, and let $t > 1$ be a real number. We choose a real number θ such that $0 < \theta < \pi/4$ and $\cos\theta - \sin\theta > 1/t$, and define

$$s := \max\left(\frac{4\cos\theta}{1-\cos\theta}, \frac{4}{\sin(\theta/2)}, \frac{4}{\cos\theta - \sin\theta - 1/t}\right)$$

and $w := 2/s$. The proof of the following lemma is straightforward.

Lemma 10.1.5. *We have*

1. $1 + 4/s \leq 1/\cos\theta$,
2. $4/s \leq \sin(\theta/2)$,
3. $t \geq 1/(\cos\theta - \sin\theta - 2w)$, *and*
4. $0 < w < (\cos\theta - \sin\theta)/2$.

We now present our second construction. We first compute the split tree T, together with the corresponding WSPD

$$\{A_1, B_1\}, \{A_2, B_2\}, \ldots, \{A_m, B_m\}$$

for S, with separation ratio s. By Theorem 9.4.6, this tree and the WSPD can be computed in $O(n \log n + s^d n)$ time. Moreover, we have $m = O(s^d n)$.

For each node u of T, let S_u be the set of all points of S that are stored in the subtree of u. For each i with $1 \leq i \leq m$, let u_i and v_i be the nodes of T such that $S_{u_i} = A_i$ and $S_{v_i} = B_i$. We choose the representatives $a_i \in A_i$ and $b_i \in B_i$, $1 \leq i \leq m$, as in Section 10.1.1 (i.e., by picking the rightmost leaf of the left subtree). Let $G_0 = (S, E_0)$ be the directed graph with edge set

$$E_0 := \{(a_i, b_i) : 1 \leq i \leq m\} \cup \{(b_i, a_i) : 1 \leq i \leq m\}.$$

We number the edges of E_0 arbitrarily, from one to $|E_0|$.

Let $\kappa := \kappa_{d,\theta/2}$ be as in equation (5.3) in Section 5.2.3 (where we have replaced θ by $\theta/2$), and let $\mathcal{C}_\kappa$ be the $(\theta/2)$-frame of Theorem 5.2.8, consisting of $\kappa = O(1/\theta^{d-1})$ cones. Recall that $\mathcal{C}_\kappa$ is a collection of κ simplicial cones of angular diameter $\theta/2$, having their apex at the origin, and that cover $\mathbb{R}^d$. For each cone $C \in \mathcal{C}_\kappa$, let

$$E_0(C) := \{(p, q) \in E_0 : q - p \in C\}.$$

We *mark* a subset of the edges of E_0 by performing the following for each cone C of $\mathcal{C}_\kappa$, and for each point p of S. For a fixed cone $C \in \mathcal{C}_\kappa$ and a fixed point $p \in S$, do the following: Consider all nodes u of the split tree T such that

1. u is on the path from the root to the leaf storing p,
2. there is a node v in T, such that
    (a) $\{S_u, S_v\}$ is a pair in our WSPD, and
    (b) if x_u and y_v are the representatives of S_u and S_v, respectively, then edge (x_u, y_v) is contained in $E_0(C)$.

Assume that there exists at least one node u, for which Conditions 1. and 2. are satisfied. Then, among all edges (x_u, y_v) obtained in this way, we mark the *shortest* one. In case of ties, we mark the shortest edge whose index is minimum.

Let E be the set of all marked edges. We will prove that the directed graph $G = (S, E)$ is a t-spanner for S. We need the following lemma.

Lemma 10.1.6. *Let A and B be two finite sets of points in $\mathbb{R}^d$ that are well-separated with respect to a separation ratio $s > 0$. Let p and x be two points in A, and let q and y be two points in B. Then,*

$$\sin(\text{angle}(pq, xy)) \leq 4/s.$$

PROOF If $s \leq 4$, then the claim clearly holds. So assume that $s > 4$. Let $\alpha := \text{angle}(pq, xy)$. Observe that $\alpha \geq 0$. Let ℓ be the ray emanating from x that is parallel to pq, and let z be the point on ℓ such that $|xz| = |pq|$. Then, $|px| = |qz|$, and $\alpha = \text{angle}(xz, xy)$. Let y' be the orthogonal projection of y onto ℓ. Then

$$\sin \alpha = \frac{|yy'|}{|xy|} \leq \frac{|yz|}{|xy|} \leq \frac{|yq| + |qz|}{|xy|} = \frac{|yq| + |px|}{|xy|}.$$

Since A and B are well-separated, Lemma 9.1.2 implies that $|yq| \leq (2/s)|xy|$ and $|px| \leq (2/s)|xy|$. This implies that $\sin \alpha \leq 4/s$. ∎

Lemma 10.1.7. *The graph $G = (S, E)$ is a t-spanner for S.*

PROOF We will show that the edges of E satisfy the condition of Lemma 10.1.4. First observe that, by Lemma 10.1.5, $0 < w < (\cos \theta - \sin \theta)/2$ and $t \geq 1/(\cos \theta - \sin \theta - 2w)$.

Let p and q be any two distinct points of S, and let i be the integer such that (i) $p \in A_i$ and $q \in B_i$, or (ii) $p \in B_i$ and $q \in A_i$. We may assume without loss of generality that (i) holds. Consider the representatives a_i and b_i of A_i and B_i, respectively. Then, by

Lemma 10.1.6, we have $\sin(\text{angle}(pq, a_i b_i)) \leq 4/s$, which, by Lemma 10.1.5, is less than or equal to $\sin(\theta/2)$. Hence, $\text{angle}(pq, a_i b_i) \leq \theta/2$.

Let C be the cone of $\mathcal{C}_\kappa$ such that $(a_i, b_i) \in E_0(C)$. Recall that u_i is the node of the split tree T for which $S_{u_i} = A_i$. It is clear that u_i is on the path from the root to the leaf storing p. Therefore, when we considered the cone C and the point p, (a_i, b_i) was one of the edges that satisfied conditions 1. and 2. above. Let (x, y) be the edge of $E_0(C)$ that was marked when we considered C and p. Then (x, y) is an edge of E, and $|xy| \leq |a_i b_i|$. We have

$$\text{angle}(pq, xy) \leq \text{angle}(pq, a_i b_i) + \text{angle}(a_i b_i, xy) \leq \theta/2 + \theta/2 = \theta.$$

Since A_i and B_i are well-separated, we know from Lemma 9.1.2 that $|a_i b_i| \leq (1 + 4/s)|pq|$. Then, Lemma 10.1.5 implies that $|a_i b_i| \leq |pq|/\cos\theta$. In particular, we have $|xy| \leq |pq|/\cos\theta$.

Finally, let j be the integer such that (i) $x \in A_j$ and $y \in B_j$, or (ii) $x \in B_j$ and $y \in A_j$. We may assume without loss of generality that (i) holds. When we considered the cone C and the point p, we marked (x, y). Therefore, u_j is on the path in T from the root to the leaf storing p and, hence, $p \in A_j$. Since A_j and B_j are well-separated, Lemma 9.1.2 implies that $|px| \leq (2/s)|xy| = w|xy|$. Since all the premises of Lemma 10.1.4 are satisfied, we have proved that G is a t-spanner.   ∎

Lemma 10.1.8. *The outdegree of each vertex of the graph $G = (S, E)$ is less than or equal to $2|\mathcal{C}_\kappa| = O(1/\theta^{d-1})$.*

PROOF   Let x be a point of S, and let C be a cone of $\mathcal{C}_\kappa$. Clearly, it is sufficient to show that, in G, x is the source of at most two edges in cone C. Assume that the edge set E contains three pairwise distinct edges (x, y), (x, y'), and (x, y'') that are all contained in $E_0(C)$. We may assume without loss of generality that $|xy| \leq |xy'| \leq |xy''|$. Moreover, in case $|xy| = |xy'|$, we may assume without loss of generality that (x, y) has a lower index than (x, y'). Similarly, in case $|xy'| = |xy''|$, we may assume without loss of generality that (x, y') has a lower index than (x, y'').

Let p be the point of S, such that we marked edge (x, y) when we considered the cone C and the point p. Consider the nodes u and v of T such that $(x_u, y_v) = (x, y)$. (Refer to conditions 1. and 2. for the notation.)

Let p' be the point of S, such that we marked edge (x, y') when we considered the cone C and the point p'. Furthermore, let u' and v' be the nodes of T such that $(x_{u'}, y_{v'}) = (x, y')$. Observe that u' is on the path from the root to the leaf storing p'. Define the point p'' of S, and the nodes u'' and v'' of T similarly with respect to the edge (x, y'').

Assume that $u = u'$. Then u is on the path from the root to the leaf storing p'. Since $|xy| \leq |xy'|$, we could not have marked edge (x, y') when we considered C and p', which is a contradiction. Therefore, $u \neq u'$. By symmetric arguments, it follows that $u \neq u''$ and $u' \neq u''$. Hence the set

$$\{u_i \in T : 1 \leq i \leq m, a_i = x\} \cup \{v_i \in T : 1 \leq i \leq m, b_i = x\}$$

contains at least three nodes. This contradicts Lemma 10.1.1.   ∎

We now show how to efficiently compute the edges of E from the edge set E_0. First, we compute the subsets $E_0(C)$, $C \in \mathcal{C}_\kappa$. By Theorem 5.3.2, this takes $O(1/\theta^{d-1} + m \log(1/\theta))$ time. Then we run the following algorithm for each cone C of $\mathcal{C}_\kappa$ separately.

We may assume that each edge $(x, y) \in E_0(C)$ has a pointer to the node u_i (or v_i) of the split tree T such that x is the representative of A_i (or B_i). Hence, by following these pointers, we can store with each node u of T, a list L_u containing all edges $(x, y) \in E_0(C)$ such that x is the representative of S_u, for some pair $\{S_u, S_v\}$ in our WSPD. By considering all nodes u of T, we compute the shortest edge, which we denote by e_u, in the list L_u. (Ties are broken by using the index of the edge. If L_u is the empty list, then $e_u = nil$.)

Finally, we compute for each node u the shortest edge among all edges e_v, where v ranges over the ancestors of u. Denote this shortest edge by e'_u. (Again, ties are broken by using the index of the edge. If there is no such edge e_v, then $e'_u = nil$.) This final step can easily be implemented by a preorder traversal of the nodes of T.

At the end of this algorithm, the edges e'_u that are stored at the leaves of T are exactly the marked edges for this cone C. Thus, given the subsets $E_0(C)$, $C \in \mathcal{C}_\kappa$, we can compute the marked edge set E, in $O(\kappa n + m) = O(n/\theta^{d-1} + m)$ time.

In summary, the running time of the entire algorithm is the sum of the following expressions:

1. $O(n \log n + m)$, where $m = O(s^d n)$. This is the time for computing the split tree and the WSPD.
2. $O(n + m) = O(m)$. This is the time for computing the graph $G_0 = (S, E_0)$.
3. $O(1/\theta^{d-1} + m \log(1/\theta))$. This is the time for computing the subsets $E_0(C)$, $C \in \mathcal{C}_\kappa$.
4. $O(n/\theta^{d-1} + m)$. This is the time for computing the set E of marked edges.

Recall from Lemma 10.1.8 that the outdegree of the t-spanner G depends on θ. To obtain the smallest outdegree, we must choose θ as large as possible, subject to the condition $\cos\theta - \sin\theta > 1/t$, which was made in the beginning of this section. Let us assume that $t > 1$ and $t \to 1$. Then, we obtain a value for θ that is proportional to $t - 1$. This, in turn, implies that the separation ratio s is proportional to $1/(t-1)^2$. We have proved the following theorem.

Theorem 10.1.9. *Let S be a set of n points in $\mathbb{R}^d$, and let $t > 1$ be a real number. In*

$$O\left(n \log n + \frac{\log(1/(t-1))}{(t-1)^{2d}} n\right)$$

time, we can construct a directed t-spanner for S, in which each vertex has outdegree $O(1/(t-1)^{d-1})$.

In order to obtain a spanner of bounded degree, we apply the transformation of Theorem 5.5.4 to the spanner in Theorem 10.1.9 (with t replaced by $\sqrt{t}$). This gives the following result:

Theorem 10.1.10. *Let S be a set of n points in $\mathbb{R}^d$, and let $t > 1$ be a real number. In*

$$O\left(\frac{\log(1/(t-1))}{(t-1)^d} n \log n + \frac{\log(1/(t-1))}{(t-1)^{2d}} n\right)$$

time, we can construct a t-spanner for S, in which each vertex has degree $O(1/(t-1)^{2d-1})$.

> **Second construction of a bounded-degree spanner:** In the basic WSPD-spanner (see Section 9.2), a graph is constructed by adding an edge for every well-separated pair in the WSPD. However, this spanner construction tends to add more edges than necessary. A single point can be part of many sets involved in well-separated pairs, and each of these pairs results in an edge. The second construction keeps only the shortest edge for each of the cone directions. The resulting spanner is of bounded outdegree. By applying the transformation of Theorem 5.5.4, we obtain a spanner of bounded degree.

10.2 A spanner with logarithmic spanner diameter

In Section 4.3 and its generalization to higher dimensions in Section 5.5.5, we have seen a randomized construction of a spanner having logarithmic spanner diameter. In this section, we will show that the WSPD can be used to obtain the same result with a deterministic construction.

Let S be a set of n points in $\mathbb{R}^d$, and let $t > 1$ be a real number. Consider the split tree T and the corresponding WSPD

$$\{A_1, B_1\}, \{A_2, B_2\}, \ldots, \{A_m, B_m\}$$

for S, with separation ratio $s := 4(t + 1)/(t - 1)$. The spanner of logarithmic spanner diameter will be obtained by carefully selecting the representatives of A_i and B_i, for all i with $1 \le i \le m$.

We label the edges of T as being *heavy* or *light*, according to the following scheme. Let u be any internal node of T, and let u_l and u_r be the left and right children of u, respectively. Let e_l and e_r be the edges of T that connect u and u_l, and u and u_r, respectively. Finally, let n_l and n_r be the number of leaves in the subtrees rooted at u_l and u_r, respectively. If $n_l \ge n_r$, then we label e_l heavy and e_r light. Otherwise, if $n_l < n_r$, we label e_l light and e_r heavy.

Since each internal node is connected by exactly one heavy edge to one of its children, there is a unique maximal chain of heavy edges leading up from each leaf of T. These chains partition the nodes of T into n subsets, one associated with each leaf. For each node u of T, let $\ell(u)$ be the leaf whose chain contains u, and let $r(u)$ be the point of S that is stored at $\ell(u)$.

For each i with $1 \le i \le m$, consider the pair $\{A_i, B_i\}$ in our WSPD. Let u_i and v_i be the nodes of T such that the subtrees of u_i and v_i store the points of A_i and B_i, respectively. Then we define the representative a_i of A_i to be the point $r(u_i)$. Similarly, we define the representative b_i of B_i to be the point $r(v_i)$. Observe that $a_i \in A_i$ and $b_i \in B_i$. Let $E := \{\{a_i, b_i\} : 1 \le i \le m\}$, and consider the graph $G = (S, E)$.

Lemma 10.2.1. *For each i with $1 \le i \le m$, and for each point $p \in A_i$, there is a t-spanner path in G between p and the representative a_i of A_i, that contains at most $\log |A_i|$ edges.*

PROOF It follows from the results in Section 9.2 that the following algorithm constructs a t-spanner path between the points p and a_i. If $p = a_i$, then return the empty path Q; otherwise, let j be the index such that (i) $p \in A_j$ and $a_i \in B_j$ or (ii) $p \in B_j$ and $a_i \in A_j$. Assume that (i) holds. (Otherwise, interchange A_j and B_j.) Recursively construct a path

Q_1 between p and the representative a_j of A_j, and recursively construct a path Q_2 between a_i and the representative b_j of B_j. Return the path Q obtained by concatenating the path Q_1, the edge $\{a_j, b_j\}$, and the path Q_2.

We will show that the number of edges on Q is less than or equal to $\log |A_i|$, if $p \in A_i$. The proof is by induction on the size of the set A_i. To start the induction, let i be an index for which $|A_i|$ is minimum. We know that A_i has size 1; that is, $A_i = \{a_i\}$; see Exercise 9.6. For this case, the claim follows trivially.

Let i be an index such that $|A_i|$ is not minimum. Furthermore, assume that for all k such that $|A_k| < |A_i|$, and for all $x \in A_k$, the algorithm above constructs a t-spanner path between x and the representative a_k of A_k, with the condition that it contains at most $\log |A_k|$ edges.

Let p be any point of A_i. We will show that our algorithm constructs a t-spanner path between p and a_i that contains at most $\log |A_i|$ edges. If $p = a_i$, then this path contains no edges, and the claim clearly holds, because $|A_i| \geq 1$. Assume that $p \neq a_i$. Let j be the index such that (i) $p \in A_j$ and $a_i \in B_j$, or (ii) $p \in B_j$ and $a_i \in A_j$. We may assume without loss of generality that (i) holds. Consider the representatives a_j and b_j of A_j and B_j, respectively. Our algorithm computes the concatenation Q of a path Q_1 between p and a_j, the edge $\{a_j, b_j\}$, and a path Q_2 between b_j and a_i.

Let u_i, u_j, and v_j be the nodes of the split tree T, whose subtrees store the sets A_i, A_j, and B_j, respectively. The facts that (i) u_i is a common ancestor of the leaves storing p and a_i, (ii) u_j lies on the path from the root to the leaf storing p, (iii) v_j lies on the path from the root to the leaf storing a_i, and (iv) the sets A_j and B_j are disjoint, imply that u_j and v_j are both in the subtree of u_i, and neither is an ancestor of the other.

We claim that $a_i = b_j$. Indeed, a_i is representative of A_i, because node u_i belongs to the maximal chain associated with the leaf storing a_i. This chain also contains v_j. Therefore, a_i is also representative of B_j; that is, $a_i = b_j$. This implies that Q_2 is the empty path.

Next, we claim that $|A_j| \leq |A_i|/2$. The reason is that otherwise, all edges on the path in T between u_i and u_j would be heavy. But then the representative a_i of A_i would be an element of A_j, contradicting the disjointness of A_j and B_j.

By the induction hypothesis, the path Q_1 between p and a_j contains at most $\log |A_j|$ edges, which is less than or equal to $\log |A_i| - 1$. Adding to this the single edge $\{a_j, b_j\}$ gives a total number of at most $\log |A_i|$ edges for the path Q. ∎

We are now ready to prove that the graph G is a t-spanner, having spanner diameter $O(\log n)$.

Lemma 10.2.2. *The graph G is a t-spanner for S whose spanner diameter is less than or equal to $2 \log n - 1$.*

PROOF Let p and q be two distinct points of S. We will show that there is a t-spanner path in G between p and q that contains at most $2 \log n - 1$ edges.

Let i be the index such that (i) $p \in A_i$ and $q \in B_i$, or (ii) $p \in B_i$ and $q \in A_i$. We may assume without loss of generality that (i) holds. The results of Section 9.2 imply an algorithm that recursively computes a path P_1 between p and the representative a_i of A_i, and a path P_2 between q and the representative b_i of B_i. This algorithm returns the concatenation P of P_1, the edge $\{a_i, b_i\}$, and P_2. This path P is a t-spanner path between p and q.

It follows from Lemma 10.2.1 that the path P_1 contains at most $\log |A_i|$ edges. By a symmetric argument, the path P_2 contains at most $\log |B_i|$ edges. Hence, the number of edges on the path P between p and q is less than or equal to $1 + \log |A_i| + \log |B_i|$. Since the sets A_i and B_i are disjoint, we have $|A_i| + |B_i| \leq n$. This, together with the fact that the function $-\log x$ is convex, implies that

$$\log |A_i| + \log |B_i| \leq \log |A_i| + \log(n - |A_i|) \leq 2 \log(n/2) = 2 \log n - 2.$$

Hence, P contains at most $2 \log n - 1$ edges.   ∎

It is not difficult to see that, given the split tree T and the WSPD, we can compute all representatives in $O(m)$ time, where m is the number of pairs in the WSPD. Therefore, we have proved the following result.

Theorem 10.2.3. *Let S be a set of n points in $\mathbb{R}^d$, and let $t > 1$ be a real number. In $O(n \log n + n/(t-1)^d)$ time, we can construct a t-spanner for S having $O(n/(t-1)^d)$ edges and whose spanner diameter is less than or equal to $2 \log n - 1$.*

> **Spanner of logarithmic spanner diameter:** For each node u in the split tree, follow the path down the tree by always moving to the larger subtree. The point stored at the leaf in which the path ends is the representative of u. For each pair in the WSPD, add an edge connecting the two representatives.

Remark 10.2.4. If $t > 1$ and $t \to 1$, then Theorems 9.5.6 and 10.2.3 imply that a t-spanner path having at most $2 \log n - 1$ edges can be computed in $O(\log^2 n)$ time. The amount of space needed to represent the spanner is $O(n/(t-1)^d)$. Using $O(n \log n + n/(t-1)^d)$ space, this path can even be computed in $O(\log n)$ time. The proof of the latter claim is left as an exercise; see Exercise 10.2.

10.3 Applications to other proximity problems

In the rest of this chapter, we discuss a variety of applications of the WSPD. In particular, these problems are not spanner problems, although they may be broadly classified as proximity problems.

10.3.1 The closest pair problem

In this problem, we are given a set S of n points in $\mathbb{R}^d$, and want to compute a pair of distinct points of S, whose distance is minimum. Such a pair is called a *closest pair*. It should be no surprise that the WSPD can be used to solve this problem.

> **Algorithm** CLOSESTPAIR(S)
>
> **Comment:** This algorithm takes as input a set S of n points in $\mathbb{R}^d$. It returns a closest pair in S.
>
> Let $t = 2$. In $O(n \log n)$ time, we compute the WSPD t-spanner of Corollary 9.4.7. This spanner consists of $O(n)$ edges. We know from Exercise 1.10 that in this spanner, some closest pair is connected by an edge. Hence, given the spanner, we find a closest pair in S in $O(n)$ time.

Theorem 10.3.1. *Given a set S of n points in $\mathbb{R}^d$, algorithm* CLOSESTPAIR(S) *computes a closest pair in S in $O(n \log n)$ time.*

Closest pair: The WSPD contains a pair of singleton sets representing a closest pair of points. Thus the basic WSPD spanner contains an edge between the closest pair of points.

We extend this idea to prove a lower bound for constructing a WSPD for S. Let $s > 2$ be a real number, and let

$$\{A_1, B_1\}, \{A_2, B_2\}, \ldots, \{A_m, B_m\}$$

be an arbitrary WSPD for S with separation ratio s. According to Exercise 9.6, there is an index i such that (i) the sets A_i and B_i both have size one, and (ii) the points contained in A_i and B_i form a closest pair in S. Hence, we can consider all pairs $\{A_i, B_i\}$, $1 \leq i \leq m$, and for each pair consisting of two singleton sets, compute the distance between the two points. The smallest distance found in this way gives us the closest pair.

If $T(n)$ denotes the worst-case time for computing the WSPD for any set S of n points, then we can compute the closest pair of this set in $T(n) + O(m)$ time. Clearly, $T(n) \geq m$, which implies that the time to compute the closest pair is $O(T(n))$. By Corollary 3.3.10, the closest pair problem has an $\Omega(n \log n)$ lower bound in the algebraic computation-tree model. Therefore, we have $T(n) = \Omega(n \log n)$.

Theorem 10.3.2. *Any algebraic computation-tree algorithm that, when given a set S of n points in $\mathbb{R}^d$ and a real number $s > 2$, computes a WSPD for S with separation ratio s, has a worst-case running time of $\Omega(n \log n)$.*

10.3.2 Computing k closest pairs

We have seen this problem already in Chapter 8. Let S be a set of n points in $\mathbb{R}^d$, and let k be an integer such that $1 \leq k \leq \binom{n}{2}$. A sequence $\{p_i, q_i\}$, $1 \leq i \leq k$, of pairwise distinct pairs, where $p_i, q_i \in S$ and $p_i \neq q_i$ for all i, is called a sequence of k *closest pairs* of S, if the distances $|p_i q_i|$, $1 \leq i \leq k$, are the k smallest elements in the multiset $\{|xy| : \{x, y\} \subseteq S, x \neq y\}$. In this section, we show that the well-separated pair decomposition can be used to compute such a sequence of k closest pairs. Recall that for any bounded and closed set $X \subseteq \mathbb{R}^d$, we denote by $R(X)$ the bounding box of X, that is, the smallest axes-parallel d-dimensional hyperrectangle that contains X.

Let $s > 0$ be a real number. Consider the split tree T, and the corresponding WSPD

$$\{A_1, B_1\}, \{A_2, B_2\}, \ldots, \{A_m, B_m\}$$

for the set S with separation ratio s, where $m = O(s^d n)$; see Theorem 9.4.6. For any i with $1 \leq i \leq m$, we denote the minimum distance between the bounding boxes $R(A_i)$ and $R(B_i)$ by $|R(A_i)R(B_i)|$. We assume without loss of generality that the pairs are numbered, such that

$$|R(A_1)R(B_1)| \leq |R(A_2)R(B_2)| \leq |R(A_3)R(B_3)| \leq \cdots \leq |R(A_m)R(B_m)|.$$

Algorithm KCLOSESTPAIRS(S, k)

Comment: This algorithm takes as input a set S of n points in $\mathbb{R}^d$ and an integer k such that $1 \leq k \leq \binom{n}{2}$. It assumes that a WSPD for S has been computed already. The algorithm returns a sequence of k closest pairs in S.

Step 1: Compute the smallest integer $\ell \geq 1$, such that

$$\sum_{i=1}^{\ell} |A_i| \cdot |B_i| \geq k.$$

Step 2: Let $r := |R(A_\ell)R(B_\ell)|$. Compute the integer ℓ', which is defined as the number of indices i with $1 \leq i \leq m$, such that

$$|R(A_i)R(B_i)| \leq (1 + 4/s)r.$$

Compute the set L consisting of all pairs $\{p, q\}$ for which there is an index i with $1 \leq i \leq \ell'$, such that $p \in A_i$ and $q \in B_i$, or $q \in A_i$ and $p \in B_i$.

Step 3: Compute and return the k smallest distances determined by the pairs in the set L.

The correctness of algorithm KCLOSESTPAIRS(S, k) follows from the following lemma, which shows that the pairs $\{A_i, B_i\}$, $1 \leq i \leq \ell'$, must determine all the k closest pairs.

Lemma 10.3.3. *Let p and q be two distinct points of S, and let j be the index such that $p \in A_j$ and $q \in B_j$, or $q \in A_j$ and $p \in B_j$. If $j > \ell'$, then $\{p, q\}$ is not one of the k closest pairs of the set S.*

PROOF For any index i with $1 \leq i \leq m$, let $x_i \in R(A_i)$ and $y_i \in R(B_i)$ be two points such that $|x_i y_i| = |R(A_i)R(B_i)|$. (In general, x_i and y_i are not points of S.)

Let i be any index such that $1 \leq i \leq \ell$, let a be any point of A_i, and let b be any point of B_i. By Lemma 9.1.2, we have $|ab| \leq (1 + 4/s)|x_i y_i|$. It follows that

$$|ab| \leq (1 + 4/s)|R(A_i)R(B_i)| \leq (1 + 4/s)|R(A_\ell)R(B_\ell)| = (1 + 4/s)r.$$

By Step 1 of algorithm KCLOSESTPAIRS(S, k), the pairs $\{A_i, B_i\}$, $1 \leq i \leq \ell$, satisfy

$$\sum_{i=1}^{\ell} |A_i| \cdot |B_i| \geq k,$$

and thus determine at least k distances, all of which are less than or equal to $(1 + 4/s)r$. On the other hand, since $j > \ell'$, we have

$$|pq| \geq |R(A_j)R(B_j)| > (1 + 4/s)r.$$

This proves the lemma.   ■

In the rest of this section, we will analyze the running time of algorithm KCLOSESTPAIRS(S, k). We first remark that the ordering of the pairs of the WSPD by the distances between their bounding boxes is used only in the analysis of the algorithm. This ordering is *not* computed by the algorithm.

Consider Step 1. By traversing the split tree T in postorder, we can compute for each node u, the number of leaves in the subtree of u. Using this information, we can compute for each i with $1 \leq i \leq m$, the value of $|A_i| \cdot |B_i|$, in $O(m)$ total time. Then, the integer ℓ can be computed in $O(m)$ time, using a weighted version of a linear-time selection algorithm; see Exercise 10.3. Hence, Step 1 of algorithm KCLOSESTPAIRS(S, k) takes $O(m)$ time.

To bound the running time for Step 2, observe that each node u of the split tree T stores the bounding box of all points that are stored in the subtree of u. Hence, the integer ℓ' can be computed in $O(m)$ time, by considering the pairs $\{A_i, B_i\}$, $1 \leq i \leq m$, one after another. Given ℓ', the set L can be computed in time

$$O \left(\sum_{i=1}^{\ell'} |A_i| \cdot |B_i| \right). \tag{10.1}$$

Step 3 can be implemented as follows. First, using a linear-time selection algorithm, we compute the k-th smallest distance δ determined by the pairs in the set L. Then, by considering all pairs of L, we select those pairs, whose distance is less than or equal to δ. Hence, the time for Step 3 is bounded from above by the summation in (10.1).

It follows that the total running time of algorithm KCLOSESTPAIRS(S, k) is

$$O \left(m + \sum_{i=1}^{\ell'} |A_i| \cdot |B_i| \right). \tag{10.2}$$

It remains to give an upper bound on the summation in (10.2). We will derive such an upper bound through the following two lemmas. The first lemma relates the value of r of Step 2 to the k-th smallest distance in S.

Lemma 10.3.4. *Let δ be the k-th smallest distance in the set S, and let $r = |R(A_\ell)R(B_\ell)|$ be the value computed in Step 2 of algorithm KCLOSESTPAIRS(S, k). Then, $r \leq \delta$.*

PROOF The proof is by contradiction. So assume that $\delta < r$. For any index i with $i \geq \ell$, for any point $p \in A_i$, and for any point $q \in B_i$, we have

$$|pq| \geq |R(A_i)R(B_i)| \geq |R(A_\ell)R(B_\ell)| = r > \delta.$$

Hence, the pairs $\{A_i, B_i\}$, $1 \leq i \leq \ell - 1$, "contain" the k closest pairs. This contradicts the choice of ℓ in Step 1 of the algorithm. ∎

The next lemma gives an upper bound on the distances that are considered in Step 3 of algorithm KCLOSESTPAIRS(S, k).

Lemma 10.3.5. *Let δ be the k-th smallest distance in the set S, and let $\{p, q\}$ be any pair of points that is contained in the set L, as computed in Step 2 of algorithm KCLOSESTPAIRS(S, k). Then, we have*

$$|pq| \leq (1 + 4/s)^2 \delta.$$

PROOF Let i be the index such that (i) $p \in A_i$ and $q \in B_i$, or (ii) $q \in A_i$ and $p \in B_i$. We assume without loss of generality that (i) holds. Observe that $1 \leq i \leq \ell'$. Let $x_i \in R(A_i)$ and $y_i \in R(B_i)$ be two points such that $|x_i y_i| = |R(A_i)R(B_i)|$. (In general, x_i and y_i are not points of S.)

By Lemma 9.1.2, we have $|pq| \leq (1 + 4/s)|x_i y_i|$. Also, since $1 \leq i \leq \ell'$, we have $|R(A_i)R(B_i)| \leq (1 + 4/s)r$. It follows that

$$
\begin{aligned}
|pq| &\leq (1 + 4/s)|x_i y_i| \\
&= (1 + 4/s)|R(A_i)R(B_i)| \\
&\leq (1 + 4/s)^2 r \\
&\leq (1 + 4/s)^2 \delta,
\end{aligned}
$$

where the last inequality follows from Lemma 10.3.4. ∎

Let M denote the number of distances in the set S that are less than or equal to $(1 + 4/s)^2 \delta$. Then (10.2) and Lemma 10.3.5 imply that the total running time of algorithm KClosestPairs(S, k) is $O(m + M)$. Given that there are at most k pairs of points with distance at most δ, recall that Lemma 8.2.1 bounds the number of pairs of points with distance at most $(1 + 4/s)^2 \delta$. Using this lemma, we have

$$ M < \left(2\lceil (1 + 4/s)^2 \sqrt{d} \rceil + 1 \right)^d (n + 2k). \tag{10.3} $$

Theorem 10.3.6. *Given a set S of n points in $\mathbb{R}^d$, and an integer k such that $1 \leq k \leq \binom{n}{2}$, algorithm KClosestPairs(S, k) computes a sequence of k closest pairs in S, in $O(n \log n + k)$ time.*

PROOF We choose a small separation ratio s, for example $s = 1$. By Theorem 9.4.6, a WSPD for S of size $m = O(n)$ can be computed in $O(n \log n)$ time. We have seen above that, given this WSPD, algorithm KClosestPairs(S, k) computes the k closest pairs in S, in $O(m + M)$ time. An upper bound on M is given in (10.3). Hence the result. ∎

Computing k closest pairs using a WSPD: The algorithm orders the well-separated pairs according to their "separation" and then picks the first ℓ pairs that determine k pairs of points (Step 1). Since there may be other well-separated pairs with nearly the same separation as the last one, the algorithm picks a "few" extra pairs (Step 2) that are separated by a distance fractionally larger than that of the largest of the first ℓ pairs; this brings the total to ℓ' pairs. Lemma 10.3.3 shows that ℓ' pairs are sufficient. In order to show the time complexity, it is necessary to show that the ℓ' well-separated pairs do not determine too many pairs of points. Lemma 10.3.5 shows that all pairs of points in the ℓ' well-separated pairs have a distance that is not much larger than the k-th smallest distance. Lemma 8.2.1, the most critical lemma, shows that if there are k pairs of points with interpoint distance δ, then the number of pairs of points with interpoint distance at most $c\delta$ is $O(n + k)$. This is also a bound on the number of pairs of points from the ℓ' well-separated pairs selected in Step 2 of the algorithm, and is also a key to ensuring the $O(n \log n + k)$ time complexity.

10.3.3 The all-nearest neighbors problem

In this problem, we are given a set S of n points in $\mathbb{R}^d$, and want to compute for each point p of S a *nearest neighbor* in S, that is, a point $q \in S \setminus \{p\}$ for which $|pq|$ is minimum.

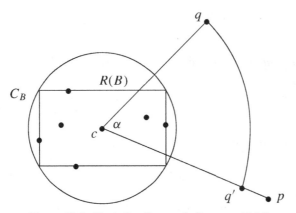

Figure 10.1: Illustrating the proof of Lemma 10.3.7.

The analysis of the algorithm that we will present in this section uses a generalization of the fact that any point can be the nearest neighbor of at most a constant number of other points. Lemmas 10.3.7 and 10.3.8, given below, help prove this fact.

Lemma 10.3.7. *Let B be a finite set of points in $\mathbb{R}^d$, let C_B be the smallest ball that contains the bounding box $R(B)$ of B, let c be the center of C_B, and let $s > 1$ be a real number. Let p and q be two distinct points in $\mathbb{R}^d$ such that both $\{p\}$ and B, and $\{q\}$ and B are well-separated with respect to s. Furthermore, assume that $|pC_B| \leq |pq|$ and $|qC_B| \leq |pq|$. Finally, let $\alpha := \text{angle}(cp, cq)$. Then, we have $\alpha \geq (s-1)/s$.*

PROOF If $\alpha \geq 1$, then the claim is true, because $(s-1)/s \leq 1$. So assume that $\alpha < 1$. Denote the radius of C_B by r, and let $x := |pc|$ and $y := |qc|$. We may assume without loss of generality that $x \geq y$.

Let q' be the point on the line segment cp such that $|cq| = |cq'|$; see Figure 10.1. The circular arc with center c that joins q and q' has length $\alpha|cq| = \alpha y$. Also, $|pq'| = x - y$. Hence, the triangle inequality implies that

$$|pq| \leq |pq'| + |q'q| \leq (x - y) + \alpha y = x - (1 - \alpha)y. \tag{10.4}$$

Since $\{q\}$ and B are well-separated, there are two balls C_1 and C_2, having the same radius, say ρ, such that C_1 contains q, C_2 contains $R(B)$, and $|C_1 C_2| \geq s\rho$. Since the center c of C_B is contained in $R(B)$, it is also contained in C_2. Also, since C_B is the smallest ball that contains $R(B)$, we have $\rho \geq r$. It follows that

$$y = |qc| \geq |C_1 C_2| \geq s\rho \geq sr. \tag{10.5}$$

Combining this inequality with (10.4), and using the fact that $\alpha < 1$, we obtain

$$|pq| \leq x - (1 - \alpha)y \leq x - (1 - \alpha)sr. \tag{10.6}$$

Next, we claim that $x = |pc| \geq sr$, the proof of which is the same as that of (10.5). Since $s > 1$, this implies that p is outside the ball C_B. Therefore,

$$x = |pc| = |pC_B| + r \leq |pq| + r.$$

Combining this with (10.6) yields

$$|pq| \leq (|pq| + r) - (1 - \alpha)sr,$$

which rewrites to $\alpha \geq (s-1)/s$. $\blacksquare$

Next we prove that there cannot be more than a constant number of points satisfying the conditions of Lemma 10.3.7.

Lemma 10.3.8. *Let A and B be two finite sets of points in $\mathbb{R}^d$, let C_B be the smallest ball that contains $R(B)$, and let $s > 1$ be a real number. Assume that for all $p \in A$, the sets $\{p\}$ and B are well-separated with respect to s. Also, assume that $|pC_B| \leq |pq|$, for any two distinct points p and q of A. Then, the set A contains $O((s/(s-1))^d)$ elements.*

PROOF Let c be the center of C_B. Then, by Lemma 10.3.7, we have

$$\text{angle}(cp, cq) \geq \frac{s-1}{s}$$

for any two distinct points p and q of A. The lemma follows from Theorem 5.3.1, which bounds the size of any set of points for which the minimum angle is at least some given real number. ∎

Now the stage is set, and we are ready to present the algorithm that solves the all-nearest neighbors problem for the point set S. We choose a real number $s > 2$, and compute the split tree T and the corresponding WSPD

$$\{A_1, B_1\}, \{A_2, B_2\}, \ldots, \{A_m, B_m\}$$

for S with separation ratio s, where $m = O(s^d n)$; see Theorem 9.4.6.

Let p be a point of S, and let q be a nearest neighbor of p. Let i be the index such that (i) $p \in A_i$ and $q \in B_i$, or (ii) $p \in B_i$ and $q \in A_i$. Assume without loss of generality that (i) holds. According to Exercise 9.5, the set A_i consists only of the point p. Hence, in order to solve the all-nearest neighbors problem, we have to consider only pairs of the WSPD, for which at least one of their sets is a singleton. Unfortunately, this observation does not lead to an efficient algorithm yet, because although the number of such sets is linear in n, the number of pairs of points to consider may be large.

Recall that for any node u of the split tree T, S_u denotes the set of all points of S that are stored in the subtree rooted at u. For any node u, we define $F(u)$ to be the set of all points $p \in S$ such that the pair $\{\{p\}, S_v\}$ is contained in our WSPD for some ancestor v of u. (Node u is considered to be an ancestor of itself.) Moreover, we define $N(u)$ to be the set of all points $p \in F(u)$, such that the distance from p to the smallest ball containing $R(S_u)$ is less than or equal to the smallest distance between p and any other point of $F(u)$. Observe that $N(u) \subseteq F(u)$.

Lemma 10.3.9. *For any node u of T, the size of the set $N(u)$ is $O((s/(s-1))^d)$.*

PROOF Let $A := N(u)$ and $B := S_u$. We will show that these two sets satisfy the conditions of Lemma 10.3.8. From this, the claim will follow.

Let C_B be the smallest ball that contains $R(B)$, and let $p \in A$. Then $p \in F(u)$ and, hence, there is an ancestor v of u such that the sets $\{p\}$ and S_v are well-separated. Since S_u is a subset of S_v, the sets $\{p\}$ and $S_u = B$ are well-separated as well.

Now let p and q be two distinct points of A. Then, by the definition of $N(u)$, the distance between p and C_B is less than or equal to the smallest distance between p and any other point of $F(u)$. In particular, since $q \in F(u)$, we have $|pC_B| \leq |pq|$. ∎

Assume from now on that the separation ratio s is a small constant such that $s > 2$. The sets $N(u)$ can be computed in a top-down fashion, in $O(n)$ total time. (The proof of this claim is left as an exercise; see Exercise 10.5.) At this moment, it is still unclear how we can use these sets. Here is the answer. Let p be a point of S, let q be a nearest neighbor of p, and let u be the leaf of T that contains q. We know that there is an index i, such that (i) $A_i = \{p\}$ and $q \in B_i$, or (ii) $B_i = \{p\}$ and $q \in A_i$. We may assume without loss of generality that (i) holds. Hence, there is an ancestor v of u such that $B_i = S_v$. Therefore, $p \in F(u)$. Also, since $S_u = \{q\}$, the distance between p and the smallest ball containing $R(S_u)$ is just $|pq|$, which is clearly less than or equal to the distance between p and any other point of $F(u)$. This proves that $p \in N(u)$.

The discussion above leads to the following algorithm.

Algorithm ALLNEARESTNEIGHBORS(S)

Comment: This algorithm takes as input a set S of n points in $\mathbb{R}^d$. It returns for each point in S its nearest neighbor.

Step 1: Choose a constant $s > 2$, and compute the split tree T and the corresponding WSPD for S, with respect to s, having size $O(n)$.

Step 2: Compute the sets $N(u)$, for all nodes u of T.

Step 3: Compute a list L consisting of all pairs $\{p, q_u\}$ of points, where u ranges over all leaves of the split tree, q_u is the point of S stored at u, and p ranges over all points of $N(u)$.

Step 4: For each $p \in S$, compute a point q_p such that $\{p, q_p\} \in L$ and $|pq_p|$ is minimum.

Step 5: Return the pairs $\{p, q_p\}$, where p ranges over all points of S.

We have proved the following result.

Theorem 10.3.10. *Given a set S of n points in $\mathbb{R}^d$, algorithm* ALLNEARESTNEIGHBORS(S) *computes for each point in S its nearest neighbor, in $O(n \log n)$ time.*

Computing all nearest neighbors: If $x \in S$ and y is a nearest neighbor of x, then the pair in the WSPD that separates x and y contains the singleton set $\{x\}$. For any leaf u of the split tree T, storing, say, the point q, let $F(u)$ be the set of all $p \in S$ for which there is a node v in T such that $q \in S_v$ and $\{\{p\}, S_v\}$ is a pair in the WSPD. Furthermore, let $N(u)$ be the set of all $p \in F(u)$ for which q is a nearest neighbor of p in the set $F(u) \cup \{p\}$. The size of each such set $N(u)$ is bounded by a constant. Moreover, the split tree can be used to compute these sets in $O(n)$ time. Finally, if w is the leaf of T that stores y, then $x \in N(w)$.

10.3.4 Computing an approximate minimum spanning tree

Let S be a set of n points in $\mathbb{R}^d$, and let $t > 1$ be a real number. A tree T connecting the points of S is called a *t-approximate minimum spanning tree* of S, if the weight of T is less than or equal to $t \cdot wt(MST(S))$. The following algorithm computes such a tree.

Algorithm APPROXMST(S, t)

Comment: This algorithm takes as input a set S of n points in $\mathbb{R}^d$, and a real number $t > 1$. It returns a t-approximate minimum spanning tree of S.

Step 1: Compute the WSPD t-spanner G of Corollary 9.4.7.

Step 2: Using algorithm PRIM(G), see Section 2.6.2, compute a minimum spanning tree T of G.

Step 3: Return the tree T.

Step 1 takes $O(n \log n + n/(t - 1)^d)$ time (see Corollary 9.4.7), whereas Step 2 takes $O(n \log n + m)$ time, where m denotes the number of edges of G (see Theorem 2.6.3). By Corollary 9.4.7, we have $m = O(n/(t - 1)^d)$. By Theorem 1.3.1, the tree T returned by the algorithm is a t-approximate minimum spanning tree of S. Thus, we have proved the following result.

Theorem 10.3.11. *Let S be a set of n points in $\mathbb{R}^d$, and let $t > 1$ be a real number. A t-approximate minimum spanning tree of S can be computed in $O(n \log n + n/(t - 1)^d)$ time.*

Exercises

10.1. Consider the directed spanner $G = (S, E)$ of Section 10.1.2. Does this spanner satisfy the gap property of Definition 6.1.1?

10.2. Assume that $t > 1$ is a real constant. In Theorem 10.2.3, we have seen a t-spanner that can be represented in $O(n)$ space such that for any two points, a t-spanner path between them having $O(\log n)$ edges can be computed in $O(\log^2 n)$ time. Give a representation using $O(n \log n)$ space that can be used to compute such a path in $O(\log n)$ time.

10.3. Let $x_1, x_2, \ldots, x_n$ be a sequence of n real numbers, and let every element x_i have a weight w_i, which is a positive integer. Let k be any positive integer. Element x_i is called a *weighted k-th smallest element* if

$$\sum_{j:x_j < x_i} w_j < k \text{ and } \sum_{j:x_j \leq x_i} w_j \geq k.$$

Give an algorithm that computes a weighted k-th smallest element in $O(n)$ time.

10.4. Let S be a set of n points in $\mathbb{R}^d$ and let p be a point of S. Prove that p can be the nearest neighbor of at most a constant number of points of S, where the constant depends only on the dimension d.

10.5. Prove that the sets $N(u)$ that were used in algorithm ALLNEARESTNEIGHBORS(S) in Section 10.3.3 can be computed in $O(n)$ total time.

10.6. Let S be a set of n points in $\mathbb{R}^d$, and let $s > 2$ be a real number. Consider an arbitrary WSPD

$$\{A_1, B_1\}, \{A_2, B_2\}, \ldots, \{A_m, B_m\}$$

for S, with separation ratio s. For each i with $1 \leq i \leq m$, let a_i and b_i be points in A_i and B_i, respectively, such that

$$|a_i b_i| = \min\{|xy| : x \in A_i, y \in B_i\}.$$

Let $G = (S, E)$ be the graph with edge set $E := \{\{a_i, b_i\} : 1 \leq i \leq m\}$. Prove that any minimum spanning tree of G is a minimum spanning tree of S.

10.7. Let S be a set of n points in $\mathbb{R}^d$. Use Exercise 10.6 to prove that every WSPD for S, with any separation ratio $s > 2$, has size greater than or equal to $n - 1$.

10.8. (APPROXIMATE FARTHEST PAIR PROBLEM) Let S be a set of n points in $\mathbb{R}^d$, and let $\epsilon > 0$ be a real constant. A pair $\{p, q\}$ of points of S is called a $(1 + \epsilon)$-diametrical pair, if $|xy| \leq (1 + \epsilon)|pq|$ for all points x and y in S. Give an algorithm that computes a $(1 + \epsilon)$-diametrical pair in $O(n \log n)$ time.

10.9. Let S be a set of n points in $\mathbb{R}^d$. For each point $p \in S$, define

$$w(p) := \sum_{q \in S} |pq|.$$

Let $\epsilon > 0$ be a real constant. Give an algorithm that computes, in $O(n \log n)$ time, for each $p \in S$, a $(1 + \epsilon)$-approximation to $w(p)$, that is, a real number $w'(p)$, such that

$$w(p)/(1 + \epsilon) \leq w'(p) \leq (1 + \epsilon)w(p).$$

10.10. Let S be a set of n points in $\mathbb{R}^d$, and let k be a positive integer, such that $1 \leq k \leq n$. Extend the results of section 10.3.3 to compute, for each point $p \in S$, the k nearest neighbors in S.

Bibliographic notes

The construction of the spanner in Section 10.1.2 is due to Arya et al. [1995]. Their claims that the directed spanner of Theorem 10.1.9 has bounded indegree and that its weight is proportional to the weight of a minimum spanning tree of the points are unfortunately wrong.

The construction of a spanner with logarithmic spanner diameter in Section 10.2 is due to Arya, Mount, and Smid [1994]. This reference also contains a solution to Exercise 10.2.

The observation that the WSPD can be used to solve the closest pair problem (see Section 10.3.1) is due to Callahan and Kosaraju [1993]. The algorithm of Section 10.3.2 for computing k closest pairs is due to Callahan [1995]. See the bibliographical notes at the end of Chapter 8 for an overview of results for the k closest pairs problem.

Blum et al. [1973] gave a linear-time algorithm for computing the k-th smallest element in a set of real numbers; see also the book by Cormen et al. [2001]. The generalization to the weighted case (see Exercise 10.3) can be found in Johnson and Mizoguchi [1978].

Vaidya [1989] was the first who solved the all-nearest neighbors problem, in any fixed dimension d, in $O(n \log n)$ time. The algorithm presented in Section 10.3.3 is based on Callahan and Kosaraju [1992], who also provide a solution to Exercise 10.5. The journal version Callahan and Kosaraju [1995b] extends the all-nearest neighbors algorithm to one that computes, in $O(n \log n + kn)$ time, for each point its k nearest neighbors.

Vaidya [1988] and Salowe [1991] showed that approximate minimum spanning trees, in any fixed dimension d, can be computed in $O(n \log n)$ time. Our presentation in Section 10.3.4 is based on Callahan and Kosaraju [1993], who also give a variant of the algorithm having a smaller dependence on the approximation factor t. The result of Theorem 10.3.11 is optimal in the algebraic computation-tree model, if $t \leq n^{1-\epsilon}$ for some constant $\epsilon > 0$. In fact, Das, Kapoor, and Smid [1997] have shown that the complexity of computing a t-approximate minimum spanning tree is $\Theta(n \log(n/t))$ in the algebraic computation-tree model. Exercise 1.6 implies that computing a t-approximate traveling salesperson tour has the same complexity.

Exercise 10.4 follows immediately from Lemma 10.3.8. Day and Edelsbrunner [1984] have shown that a point can be the nearest neighbor of at most $3^d - 1$ points.

More applications of the WSPD can be found in Bespamyatnikh and Segal [2002], Callahan [1993, 1995], and Callahan and Kosaraju [1993, 1995a,b], and in Chapters 11, 13, and 18.

11

The Dumbbell Theorem

Man was put on this earth to eat meat . . . The Bible says so dumbbell . . . I mean look it up will ya? All them old bible peoples, they was always eating meat; soon as they found out eating apples was wrong . . . It's true, on special occasions: goats and lambs. Who the hell ever hear of sacrificing a head of lettuce? You?
—Archie Bunker (played by Carroll O'Connor), *All in the Family*

In Chapter 9, we introduced the well-separated pair decomposition (WSPD). For a set S of n points in $\mathbb{R}^d$, the WSPD consists of well-separated pairs $\{A_i, B_i\}$, $1 \le i \le m$. In Section 9.2, we showed that by taking an arbitrary edge $\{a_i, b_i\}$ from each pair in the WSPD, we obtain a spanner for S. We also showed that a spanner path can be computed between any two distinct points p and q of S, in the following way: First, find the index i such that $p \in A_i$ and $q \in B_i$. Then, recursively compute a spanner path P_1 between p and a_i, and recursively compute a spanner path P_2 between b_i and q. The path P obtained by concatenating P_1, edge $\{a_i, b_i\}$, and P_2 is a spanner path between p and q.

It follows from the results in Section 9.2 that in order for P to be a spanner path, P_1 and P_2 do not have to be spanner paths. Rather, it is sufficient if the lengths of both P_1 and P_2 are bounded by a small constant times the distance between the bounding boxes $R(A_i)$ and $R(B_i)$. In this chapter, we use this observation to construct a spanner for S that is represented by a constant number of rooted trees.

Throughout this chapter, we assume familiarity with Chapter 9.

11.1 Chapter overview

Let S be a set of n points in $\mathbb{R}^d$. Consider the split tree and a corresponding WSPD, $\{A_i, B_i\}$, $1 \le i \le m$, as computed by the algorithms of Chapter 9. Recall that $R(A_i)$ and $R(B_i)$ denote the bounding boxes of A_i and B_i, respectively. For each pair $\{A_i, B_i\}$, we consider the geometric object consisting of the *heads* $R(A_i)$ and $R(B_i)$, and the line segment joining their centers. This object will be called a *dumbbell* and will be formally defined in Section 11.2. The *length* of a dumbbell will be defined as the distance between the centers of its two heads. In Section 11.3, we prove a packing result for dumbbells whose lengths are approximately equal. This packing result is used later in the chapter.

In Sections 11.4 and 11.5, we partition the set of all dumbbells into a small number of subsets, such that the following holds for any two distinct dumbbells D and D' that are in the same subset. Let ℓ and ℓ' be the lengths of D and D', respectively, and assume that $\ell \le \ell'$.

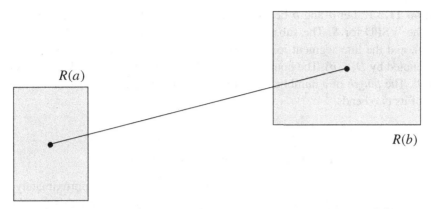

Figure 11.1: The dumbbell $D(a, b)$ consists of the two bounding boxes $R(a)$ and $R(b)$, and the line segment joining their centers. Since $\{S_a, S_b\}$ is a pair in the WSPD for S, this line segment is "long" compared to the side lengths of $R(a)$ and $R(b)$. The centers of $R(a)$ and $R(b)$ are not necessarily points of S.

Length-grouping property: Either $\ell' \leq 2\ell$ or $\ell' \geq \ell/\beta$, where β is a fixed real number such that $0 < \beta < 1/2$. That is, D and D' either have approximately the same lengths or their lengths differ by a large amount.

Empty-region property: If $\ell' \leq 2\ell$, then the distance between any head of D and any head of D' is larger than $\gamma\ell$, where γ is a fixed positive real number. That is, any head of D and any head of D' are disjoint and separated by a large amount.

Consider any two distinct dumbbells D and D' that are in the same subset of the partition and whose heads are close together. Then, by the two properties above, D and D' differ in lengths by a large amount. This property implies a *hierarchy* on the dumbbells within each subset. In Section 11.6, we show how this hierarchy can be stored in a *dumbbell tree*. This tree stores, besides the dumbbells of the subset, the points of S at its leaves. In Section 11.7, we show how the dumbbell trees can be constructed, whereas in Section 11.8, we prove that these trees constitute a spanner for the point set S. Finally, in Section 11.9, we summarize the entire construction and state the final result as the *Dumbbell Theorem*.

11.2 Dumbbells

Throughout this chapter, we fix a set S of n points in $\mathbb{R}^d$ and a real number $s > 1$. Moreover, T denotes the split tree for S, as computed by algorithm FASTSPLITTREE of Section 9.3.2, and $\{A_i, B_i\}$, $1 \leq i \leq m$, denotes the WSPD for S, with respect to the separation ratio s, as computed by algorithm COMPUTEWSPD(T, s) of Section 9.4.

Recall that each node u of T stores the bounding box $R(u)$ of S_u, where S_u is the set of all points of S that are stored at the leaves of the subtree rooted at u. The length of the longest side of $R(u)$ is denoted by $L_{\max}(R(u))$. The parent of u is denoted by $\pi(u)$. Finally, each pair in the WSPD is specified by two nodes of T. That is, for each i with $1 \leq i \leq m$, there are two nodes a and b in T such that $A_i = S_a$ and $B_i = S_b$.

We now formalize the notion of a *dumbbell*, which will be the building block for the results in the rest of this chapter. For an illustration of a dumbbell, see Figure 11.1.

Definition 11.2.1. Let a and b be two nodes of the split tree T such that $\{S_a, S_b\}$ is a pair in the WSPD for S. The subset of $\mathbb{R}^d$ consisting of the two bounding boxes $R(a)$ and $R(b)$, and the line segment joining the centers of these boxes is called a *dumbbell*, and is denoted by $D(a, b)$. The bounding boxes $R(a)$ and $R(b)$ are called the *heads* of the dumbbell. The *length* of a dumbbell is defined to be the Euclidean distance between the centers of its two heads.

11.3 A packing result for dumbbells

Given a positive real number ℓ and a dumbbell D whose length is approximately equal to ℓ, we will need an upper bound on the number of dumbbells of length approximately equal to ℓ and that are close to D. As we will prove in Lemma 11.3.4, this upper bound depends only on the separation ratio s. Before we can prove this lemma, we need some preliminary results. The first of these states that for any dumbbell $D(a, b)$, the length of the longest side of the bounding box $R(\pi(a))$ is at least proportional to the length of $D(a, b)$.

Lemma 11.3.1. *Let $D(a, b)$ be a dumbbell and let ℓ be its length. We have*

$$L_{\max}(R(\pi(a))) \geq \frac{2}{\sqrt{d}(s + 4)} \ell,$$

and

$$L_{\max}(R(\pi(b))) \geq \frac{2}{\sqrt{d}(s + 4)} \ell.$$

PROOF Assume, without loss of generality, that $L_{\max}(R(\pi(b))) \geq L_{\max}(R(\pi(a)))$. Therefore, it clearly suffices to prove the first inequality. Let u be the lowest common ancestor of a and b in the split tree T, and let v and w be the two children of u, respectively. We may assume without loss of generality that a is in the subtree of v and, hence, b is in the subtree of w.

First assume that $a = v$. Then $\pi(a) = u$, $R(a) \subseteq R(u)$, and $R(b) \subseteq R(u)$. Hence, $D(a, b)$ is contained in $R(u)$, which implies that the length of $D(a, b)$ is less than or equal to the diameter of $R(u)$. It follows that

$$\ell \leq \sqrt{d} \cdot L_{\max}(R(u)) = \sqrt{d} \cdot L_{\max}(R(\pi(a))),$$

from which the first inequality in the lemma follows.

In the rest of the proof, we assume that $a \neq v$. Define $\pi^0(a) := a$, and $\pi^k(a) := \pi(\pi^{k-1}(a))$ for $k \geq 1$. Consider algorithm COMPUTEWSPD(T, s) of Section 9.4, which computes the WSPD. It calls FINDPAIRS(v, w), which eventually outputs the pair $\{S_a, S_b\}$. Let $k \geq 0$ be an integer such that FINDPAIRS$(a, \pi^k(b))$ is a recursive call generated by the recursive call FINDPAIRS$(\pi(a), \pi^k(b))$. (Observe that such a k exists.) Then, the sets $S_{\pi(a)}$ and $S_{\pi^k(b)}$ are not well-separated, and

$$L_{\max}(R(\pi^k(b))) \leq L_{\max}(R(\pi(a))).$$

Assume that

$$L_{max}(R(\pi(a))) < \frac{2}{\sqrt{d}(s+4)}\,\ell.$$

Let x and y be the centers of $R(a)$ and $R(b)$, respectively, and let x' and y' be the centers of $R(\pi(a))$ and $R(\pi^k(b))$, respectively. Observe that the length ℓ of dumbbell $D(a,b)$ is equal to $|xy|$. Furthermore, since x is contained in $R(\pi(a))$, we have

$$|xx'| \le \frac{1}{2}\sqrt{d}\cdot L_{max}(R(\pi(a))) < \frac{\ell}{s+4}.$$

Similarly, since y is contained in $R(\pi^k(b))$, we have

$$|yy'| \le \frac{1}{2}\sqrt{d}\cdot L_{max}(R(\pi^k(b))) \le \frac{1}{2}\sqrt{d}\cdot L_{max}(R(\pi(a))) < \frac{\ell}{s+4}.$$

By the triangle inequality, we have $\ell = |xy| \le |xx'| + |x'y'| + |y'y|$, which implies that

$$|x'y'| > \ell - \frac{2\ell}{s+4} = \left(1 - \frac{2}{s+4}\right)\ell.$$

Let C_1 and C_2 be the balls of radius $\rho := \ell/(s+4)$ that are centered at x' and y', respectively. Since

$$|x'y'| - 2\rho > \left(1 - \frac{4}{s+4}\right)\ell = s\rho > 0,$$

these two balls are disjoint, and we have

$$|C_1 C_2| = |x'y'| - 2\rho > s\rho.$$

Also observe that C_1 and C_2 contain $R(\pi(a))$ and $R(\pi^k(b))$, respectively. But this implies that the sets $S_{\pi(a)}$ and $S_{\pi^k(b)}$ are well-separated, which is a contradiction. ∎

Consider two dumbbells $D(a,b)$ and $D(a',b')$ of approximately the same length such that b is in the subtree of b'. The next lemma gives an upper bound on the number of edges on the path in the split tree between b and b'.

Lemma 11.3.2. *Let $\ell > 0$ be a real number, and let $D(a,b)$ and $D(a',b')$ be two dumbbells whose lengths are in the interval $[\ell, 2\ell]$. Assume that, in the split tree, b is in the subtree of b', and let h be the number of edges on the path between b and b'. Then*

$$h \le 1 + d + d\log\left(\frac{2\sqrt{d}(s+4)}{s}\right).$$

PROOF We may assume that $h \ge 1$, since otherwise, the lemma clearly holds. Recall Lemma 9.5.3, which states that the longest side of the bounding box of the subset of S contained in the subtree of a node in the split tree T decreases by a factor of at least 2 if we descend T by d levels. It follows from this lemma that

$$L_{max}(R(\pi(b))) \le (1/2)^{\lfloor (h-1)/d \rfloor}\cdot L_{max}(R(b')).$$

Also, it can be shown that $L_{\max}(R(b'))$ is less than or equal to $2/s$ times the length of dumbbell $D(a', b')$; see Exercise 11.1. Therefore,

$$L_{\max}(R(b')) \leq 4\ell/s.$$

Combining these two inequalites gives

$$L_{\max}(R(\pi(b))) \leq (1/2)^{\lfloor(h-1)/d\rfloor} \cdot 4\ell/s. \tag{11.1}$$

By Lemma 11.3.1, we have

$$L_{\max}(R(\pi(b))) \geq \frac{2}{\sqrt{d}(s+4)}\,\ell. \tag{11.2}$$

The lemma follows by combining (11.1) and (11.2) and observing that $(h - 1)/d - 1 \leq \lfloor (h-1)/d \rfloor$. ∎

The next lemma gives an upper bound on the number of dumbbells having a fixed head and whose lengths are approximately equal.

Lemma 11.3.3. *Let a be a node of the split tree T and let $\ell > 0$ be a real number. The number of dumbbells having $R(a)$ as a head and whose lengths are in the interval $[\ell, 2\ell]$ is less than or equal to $(4\sqrt{d}(s+4) + 2)^d$.*

PROOF Recall that in Lemma 9.4.3, we showed a bound on the number of large and pairwise disjoint bounding boxes corresponding to nodes of the split tree that intersect a hypercube of a specified size. We will use this result to prove the lemma.

Let b be any node of T such that $D(a, b)$ is a dumbbell whose length is in the interval $[\ell, 2\ell]$. Let x and y be the centers of $R(a)$ and $R(b)$, respectively. Then $|xy| \leq 2\ell$. Let C be the hypercube centered at x and having sides of length 4ℓ. Then $R(b) \cap C \neq \emptyset$. By Lemma 11.3.1, we have

$$L_{\max}(R(\pi(b))) \geq \frac{2}{\sqrt{d}(s+4)}\,\ell = \frac{1}{2\sqrt{d}(s+4)}\,4\ell.$$

Applying Lemma 9.4.3, with 4ℓ instead of ℓ, and with $\alpha = 2\sqrt{d}(s+4)$, proves an upper bound of $(4\sqrt{d}(s+4) + 2)^d$ on the number of nodes b, thus completing the proof. ∎

We are now ready to prove the main property of dumbbells.

Lemma 11.3.4. *Let γ and ℓ be positive real numbers, and let $D(u, v)$ be a dumbbell whose length is in the interval $[\ell, 2\ell]$. The number of dumbbells $D(a, b)$ such that*

1. *the length of $D(a, b)$ is in the interval $[\ell, 2\ell]$ and*
2. *at least one of $R(a)$ and $R(b)$ is within distance $\gamma\ell$ of some head of $D(u, v)$*

is less than or equal to

$$c_{s\gamma} := 2^{2d+3}(4\sqrt{d}(s+4) + 2)^d \left(\frac{2\sqrt{d}(s+4)(\gamma s + 2)}{s} + 2 \right)^d \left(\frac{\sqrt{d}(s+4)}{s} \right)^d$$

$$= O\left(s^d (1 + \gamma s)^d \right).$$

PROOF Consider the set $\mathcal{D}$ of all dumbbells whose lengths are in the interval $[\ell, 2\ell]$, and for which at least one of their heads is within distance $\gamma\ell$ of $R(u)$. For each dumbbell $D(a, b) \in \mathcal{D}$, we may assume without loss of generality that $R(b)$ is within distance $\gamma\ell$ of $R(u)$. For each node b of the split tree T, let $\mathcal{D}_b$ be the set of all dumbbells in $\mathcal{D}$ involving b, i.e.,

$$\mathcal{D}_b := \{D(a, b) : a \text{ is a node in } T \text{ and } D(a, b) \in \mathcal{D}\}.$$

Let k be the number of nodes b of T for which $\mathcal{D}_b$ is nonempty, and let $b_1, b_2, \ldots, b_k$ be the nodes of T such that $\mathcal{D}$ is the disjoint union of $\mathcal{D}_{b_i}$, $1 \le i \le k$. By Lemma 11.3.3, we have

$$|\mathcal{D}_{b_i}| \le (4\sqrt{d}(s + 4) + 2)^d,$$

for each i with $1 \le i \le k$. Therefore,

$$|\mathcal{D}| = \sum_{i=1}^{k} |\mathcal{D}_{b_i}| \le (4\sqrt{d}(s + 4) + 2)^d k. \tag{11.3}$$

In the rest of the proof, we will derive an upper bound on k. Let $\ell' := (2\gamma + 4/s)\ell$. By Lemma 11.3.1, we have

$$L_{\max}(R(\pi(b_i))) \ge \frac{2}{\sqrt{d}(s + 4)}\ell = \frac{s}{\sqrt{d}(s + 4)(\gamma s + 2)}\ell',$$

for each i with $1 \le i \le k$. Let x and y be the centers of $R(u)$ and $R(v)$, respectively. By Exercise 11.1, we have

$$L_{\max}(R(u)) \le (2/s)|xy| \le (4/s)\ell.$$

Let C be the hypercube centered at x and having sides of length ℓ'. Then $R(b_i) \cap C \ne \emptyset$ for each i with $1 \le i \le k$.

We would like to apply Lemma 9.4.3 to obtain an upper bound on k. Unfortunately, this is not possible, because the sets S_{b_i}, $1 \le i \le k$, are not necessarily pairwise disjoint. Therefore, we proceed as follows.

Let $b'_1, b'_2, \ldots, b'_{k'}$ be the subsequence of $b_1, b_2, \ldots, b_k$ such that (i) each b_i, $1 \le i \le k$, is in the subtree of a node b'_j for some j with $1 \le j \le k'$, and (ii) the sets $S_{b'_j}$, $1 \le j \le k'$, are pairwise disjoint. By Lemma 9.4.3, applied with ℓ' and $\alpha = \sqrt{d}(s + 4)(\gamma s + 2)/s$, we have

$$k' \le \left(\frac{2\sqrt{d}(s + 4)(\gamma s + 2)}{s} + 2\right)^d. \tag{11.4}$$

For each j with $1 \le j \le k'$, define

$$I_j := \{i : 1 \le i \le k \text{ and } b_i \text{ is in the subtree of } b'_j\}.$$

If b_i is in the subtree of b'_j, then, by Lemma 11.3.2, the path in T between b_i and b'_j contains at most

$$1 + d + d\log\left(\frac{2\sqrt{d}(s + 4)}{s}\right)$$

edges. If we denote this quantity by h, then it follows that for each j with $1 \leq j \leq k'$, we have

$$|I_j| \leq 2^{h+1} - 1 \leq 2^{2d+2} \left(\frac{\sqrt{d}(s+4)}{s} \right)^d. \tag{11.5}$$

Since $k = \sum_{j=1}^{k'} |I_j|$, the value of k is less than or equal to the product of the quantities in (11.4) and (11.5). By combining this upper bound with (11.3), it follows that

$$|\mathcal{D}| \leq 2^{2d+2}(4\sqrt{d}(s+4) + 2)^d \left(\frac{2\sqrt{d}(s+4)(\gamma s+2)}{s} + 2 \right)^d \left(\frac{\sqrt{d}(s+4)}{s} \right)^d.$$

The same upper bound holds for the number of dumbbells whose lengths are in the interval $[\ell, 2\ell]$ and for which at least one of their heads is within distance $\gamma\ell$ of $R(v)$. Since the dimension d is a constant, and since we assume that $s > 1$, it follows that $c_{s\gamma} = O(s^d(1 + \gamma s)^d)$. ■

We summarize the results of Lemmas 11.3.1 through 11.3.4 in the following capsule.

Properties of dumbbells: We have shown the following:

1. For any dumbbell D, the bounding boxes of the parents of the heads of D are not too small as compared to the length of D.

2. If the head of a dumbbell contains the head of another dumbbell, and if they are of similar length, then the nodes in the split tree that correspond to these heads are within a bounded number of levels apart.

3. There is a bound on the number of dumbbells of similar length sharing one head.

4. There is a bound on the number of dumbbells of similar length all of which have one of their heads within a small distance of some head of another fixed dumbbell of a similar length.

11.4 Establishing the length-grouping property

In this section, we show how the set of dumbbells can be partitioned into subsets such that, within each subset, the length-grouping property of Section 11.1 holds. We fix real numbers β and δ, such that $0 < \beta < \delta < 1$. In fact, we will show a more general result; that is, we will show how to partition the set of dumbbells into subsets, such that any two dumbbells within the same subset have either lengths within a factor of $1/\delta$ from each other or lengths that are different from each other by a factor of at least $1/\beta$.

Recall that m denotes the number of pairs in our WSPD. Hence, we have exactly m dumbbells. Let M be the multiset consisting of the lengths of all dumbbells. We will present an algorithm that partitions M into $O(\log_{1/\delta}(1/\beta))$ subsets, such that for any two elements ℓ and ℓ' that are in the same subset and for which $\ell \leq \ell'$, we either have $\ell' \leq \ell/\delta$ or $\ell' \geq \ell/\beta$. We say that such a subset satisfies the (β, δ)-*length-grouping property*. Clearly, by setting $\delta = 1/2$, this partition of M implies a partition of the dumbbells for which the length-grouping property of Section 11.1 holds. (In Chapter 14, we will need the (β, δ)-length-grouping property for the general case.)

> **Achieving the length-grouping property:** The goal is to partition the multi-set of lengths into a constant number of subsets, such that any two lengths in the same subset are either similar or considerably different. This is achieved by a *preliminary* partition step, which consists of partitioning the lengths into (a potentially unbounded number of) intervals whose widths increase geometrically by a factor of $1/(\beta\delta)$. A *refined* partition of each of the intervals is made, where each interval is partitioned into a constant number of subintervals whose widths increase geometrically by a factor of $1/\delta$. Thus the refined partition is "orthogonal" to the preliminary partition. The final partition is obtained by collecting together corresponding subsets from the refined partition.

The preliminary and refined partitionings are done in a way that can be implemented in the algebraic computation-tree model. The following algorithm produces the preliminary partition of M.

Algorithm PRELIMPARTITION(M, β, δ)

Comment: This algorithm takes as input a multiset M consisting of m real numbers, and two real numbers β and δ such that $0 < \beta < \delta < 1$. The algorithm returns the preliminary partition of M.

Step 1: Sort the elements of M, and denote the sorted sequence by $\ell_1 \le \ell_2 \le \ldots \le \ell_m$.

Step 2: Run the following while-loop:

$L := \ell_1; P_1 := \{\ell_1\}; k := 1; i := 1;$
while $i < m$
do if $\ell_{i+1} < L/(\beta\delta)$
    then $P_k := P_k \cup \{\ell_{i+1}\}$
    else $P_{k+1} := \{\ell_{i+1}\}; L := \ell_{i+1}; k := k+1$
    endif;
    $i := i+1$
endwhile

Step 3: Return the sequence $P_1, P_2, \ldots, P_k$ of sorted sets.

Consider the sequence $P_1, P_2, \ldots, P_k$ of sorted and nonempty subsets of M that is returned by algorithm PRELIMPARTITION(M, β, δ). We denote the minimum and maximum elements of any subset P_i by $\min(P_i)$ and $\max(P_i)$, respectively. The next lemma follows immediately from the algorithm.

Lemma 11.4.1. *Let i and i' be two integers, such that $1 \le i \le k$ and $1 \le i' \le k$.*

1. *For every element $\ell \in P_i$, we have $\min(P_i) \le \ell < \min(P_i)/(\beta\delta)$.*
2. *If $i < i'$, then $\min(P_{i'}) \ge \min(P_i)/(\beta\delta)$.*

This lemma implies that, if $i < i'$,

$$\max(P_i) < \min(P_i)/(\beta\delta) \le \min(P_{i'}),$$

i.e., the intervals $[\min(P_i), \max(P_i))$, $1 \le i \le k$, are pairwise disjoint. However, observe that in this preliminary partition, the number of sets may not be bounded by a function that depends only on β and δ. This motivates the next partitioning step.

Algorithm REFINEDPARTITION$(M, \beta, \delta, (P_i)_{1 \le i \le k})$

Comment: This algorithm takes as input a multiset M consisting of m real numbers, two real numbers β and δ such that $0 < \beta < \delta < 1$, and the preliminary partition $P_1, P_2, \ldots, P_k$ of M, as computed by algorithm PRELIMPARTITION(M, β, δ). The algorithm returns a partition of M into subsets, each of which satisfies the (β, δ)-length-grouping property.

Step 1: For each i with $1 \le i \le k$, partition the set P_i into subsets P_{ij}, $1 \le j \le 2 + \log_{1/\delta}(1/\beta)$, where

$$P_{ij} := \{\ell \in P_i : \min(P_i)/\delta^{j-1} \le \ell < \min(P_i)/\delta^j\}.$$

Step 2: For each j with $1 \le j \le 2 + \log_{1/\delta}(1/\beta)$, compute the set

$$M_j := \bigcup_{i=1}^{k} P_{ij}.$$

Step 3: Return the sequence M_j, $1 \le j \le 2 + \log_{1/\delta}(1/\beta)$, of sets.

Thus, the set M_j contains the j-th subset P_{ij} of set P_i, for all i with $1 \le i \le k$. Even though k, the number of subsets in the preliminary partition, may not be bounded, the number of sets M_j is bounded by $2 + \log_{1/\delta}(1/\beta)$.

It is not difficult to see that it is sufficient for the index j to be in the range from 1 to $2 + \log_{1/\delta}(1/\beta)$. As a result, the output of algorithm REFINEDPARTITION is indeed a partition of M. The following lemma states that each subset M_j in this partition satisfies the (β, δ)-length-grouping property.

Lemma 11.4.2. *Let j be an integer with $1 \le j \le 2 + \log_{1/\delta}(1/\beta)$, and let ℓ and ℓ' be two elements of M_j such that $\ell \le \ell'$. Then $\ell' \le \ell/\delta$ or $\ell' \ge \ell/\beta$.*

PROOF Let i and i' be the two indices such that $\ell \in P_{ij}$ and $\ell' \in P_{i'j}$. Since $\ell \le \ell'$, we have $i \le i'$. If $i = i'$, then, by the definition of P_{ij}, we have $\ell' \le \ell/\delta$. Assume that $i < i'$. Since, again by the definitions of P_{ij} and $P_{i'j}$, $\ell < \min(P_i)/\delta^j$ and $\ell' \ge \min(P_{i'})/\delta^{j-1}$, it follows that

$$\ell'/\ell > \delta \cdot \min(P_{i'})/\min(P_i) \ge 1/\beta,$$

where the last inequality follows from Lemma 11.4.1. ∎

It remains to analyze the total running time of algorithms PRELIMPARTITION and REFINEDPARTITION. Recall that in Step 1 of algorithm PRELIMPARTITION, the elements of M are sorted, which takes $O(m \log m)$ time. Steps 2 and 3 of this algorithm clearly take $O(m)$ time. Consider algorithm REFINEDPARTITION. Since the elements of P_i are sorted, Step 1 in this algorithm spends $O(|P_i| + \log_{1/\delta}(1/\beta))$ time for the set P_i. Hence, the total time for Step 1 is

$$O\left(m + k \log_{1/\delta}(1/\beta)\right) = O\left((m \log_{1/\delta}(1/\beta)\right).$$

Steps 2 and 3 of algorithm REFINEDPARTITION can be performed within this time bound. We have proved the following result.

Lemma 11.4.3. *Let β and δ be real numbers, such that $0 < \beta < \delta < 1$. In*

$$O\left(m \log m + m \log_{1/\delta}(1/\beta)\right)$$

time, the set of m dumbbells that correspond to the WSPD can be partitioned into at most $2 + \log_{1/\delta}(1/\beta)$ subsets, such that each subset satisfies the (β, δ)-length-grouping property. That is, within each subset, the lengths of any two dumbbells either are within a factor of $1/\delta$ or differ by a factor of at least $1/\beta$. By choosing $\delta = 1/2$, the length-grouping property of Section 11.1 holds.

11.5 Establishing the empty-region property

Let β and γ be positive real numbers, such that $\beta < 1/2$. In this section, we show how any set of dumbbells satisfying the length-grouping property can be partitioned into subsets, each of which satisfies the empty-region property with parameter γ. Thus, for any two distinct dumbbells D and D' that are in the same subset, whose lengths are ℓ and ℓ', respectively, and for which $\ell \leq \ell' \leq 2\ell$, the distance between any head of D and any head of D' is larger than $\gamma \ell$. We say that such a subset satisfies the γ-*empty-region property*.

In fact, we will take each set M_j obtained from the previous section to obtain this partition. We start in Section 11.5.1 by considering only dumbbells whose lengths are within a factor of 2 of each other. The general case is considered in Section 11.5.2.

11.5.1 Dumbbells of approximately the same length

In this section, we fix a real number $\ell > 0$, and consider a set $\mathcal{E}$ of dumbbells whose lengths are in the interval $[\ell, 2\ell]$. Recall the number $c_{s\gamma}$ that was defined in Lemma 11.3.4. We will show how to partition the set $\mathcal{E}$ into at most $1 + c_{s,2\gamma}$ subsets, each of which satisfies the γ-empty-region property.

> **Achieving the empty-region property:** We define a graph with vertex set $\mathcal{E}$, in which two vertices are connected by an edge if the corresponding dumbbells have heads that are within distance $2\gamma \ell$ of each other. By Lemma 11.3.4, this graph is of degree at most $c_{s,2\gamma}$ and, therefore, its vertices can be colored using $1 + c_{s,2\gamma}$ colors, such that any two adjacent vertices have different colors. Our partition is obtained by putting all dumbbells with the same color in one subset.

We define the following graph G. The vertex set of G is the set $\mathcal{E}$ of dumbbells. Any two distinct vertices D and D' are connected by an edge in G, if some head of D and some head of D' have distance at most $2\gamma \ell$.

By Lemma 11.3.4, the degree of each vertex of G is less than or equal to $\lfloor c_{s,2\gamma} \rfloor$. Hence, by Theorem 2.4.1, the vertices of G can be colored using $1 + \lfloor c_{s,2\gamma} \rfloor$ colors, such that adjacent vertices have different colors. For each color κ that is used in the coloring of G, let $\mathcal{E}_\kappa$ be the subset of $\mathcal{E}$ consisting of all dumbbells whose color is κ. Then, it is clear that the sets $\mathcal{E}_\kappa$ form the desired partition of $\mathcal{E}$. Given the graph G, the coloring can be computed in $O(c_{s,2\gamma}|\mathcal{E}|)$ time; see Theorem 2.4.1. So it remains to show how the graph G can be constructed efficiently.

Let $D(u, v)$ be a dumbbell in $\mathcal{E}$, and consider one of its heads, say $R(u)$. Let x be the center of $R(u)$, and let C be the hypercube centered at x and having sides of length $L_{\max}(R(u)) + 4\gamma\ell$. To compute all vertices in G that are connected by an edge to $D(u, v)$ "because of" $R(u)$, we have to find all dumbbells $D(a, b)$ in $\mathcal{E}$, such that $R(a) \cap C \neq \emptyset$ or $R(b) \cap C \neq \emptyset$. Consider such a dumbbell $D(a, b)$, and assume that $R(b) \cap C \neq \emptyset$. Let y be the center of $R(b)$. Then,

$$|xy| \leq \sqrt{d}\left(\frac{1}{2} \cdot L_{\max}(R(u)) + 2\gamma\ell\right) + \frac{1}{2}\sqrt{d} \cdot L_{\max}(R(b)).$$

Since, by Exercise 11.1, $L_{\max}(R(u)) \leq 4\ell/s$ and $L_{\max}(R(b)) \leq 4\ell/s$, it follows that

$$|xy| \leq \sqrt{d}\,(2\gamma + 4/s)\,\ell.$$

Thus, if we compute all centers y of the heads of the dumbbells in $\mathcal{E}$ for which $|xy| \leq \sqrt{d}(2\gamma + 4/s)\ell$, then we obtain a subset $\mathcal{E}'$ of $\mathcal{E}$ that contains all dumbbells that are connected (in G) by an edge to $D(u, v)$ "because of" $R(u)$. Each dumbbell in $\mathcal{E}'$ contains a head whose distance to $R(u)$ is less than or equal to $\sqrt{d}(2\gamma + 4/s)\ell$. Hence, by Lemma 11.3.4 (applied with $\sqrt{d}(2\gamma + 4/s)$ instead of γ), we have

$$|\mathcal{E}'| = O\left(s^d\,(1 + \gamma s)^d\right).$$

The problem of constructing the graph G has been reduced to the following problem: Given the set S' of centers of the heads of the dumbbells in $\mathcal{E}$, compute all pairs x and y of points in S' for which $|xy| \leq \sqrt{d}(2\gamma + 4/s)\ell$. We can compute these pairs in the following way: First, construct a τ-spanner G' for S' (where, say, $\tau = 2$) having bounded degree; by Theorem 10.1.3, this can be done in $O(|S'| \log |S'|) = O(|\mathcal{E}| \log |\mathcal{E}|)$ time. Then, for each vertex x, traverse G' and report all vertices y such that $|xy| \leq \sqrt{d}(2\gamma + 4/s)\ell$. Observe that for such a vertex y, the distance in G' between x and y is less than or equal to $\tau \cdot \sqrt{d}(2\gamma + 4/s)\ell$. In this way, we obtain the graph G in time

$$O\left(|\mathcal{E}| \log |\mathcal{E}| + |\mathcal{E}|s^d\,(1 + \gamma s)^d\right).$$

We summarize our result.

Lemma 11.5.1. *Let $\ell > 0$ be a real number and let $\mathcal{E}$ be a set of dumbbells whose lengths are in the interval $[\ell, 2\ell]$. In*

$$O\left(|\mathcal{E}| \log |\mathcal{E}| + |\mathcal{E}|s^d\,(1 + \gamma s)^d\right)$$

time, we can partition $\mathcal{E}$ into $O(s^d(1 + \gamma s)^d)$ subsets, each of which satisfies the γ-empty-region property.

11.5.2 The general case

We are now ready to show how the set $\mathcal{D}$ of all m dumbbells can be partitioned into subsets, each of which satisfies both the length-grouping property and the γ-empty-region property.

Using algorithms PRELIMPARTITION and REFINEDPARTITION of Section 11.4, where we take $\delta = 1/2$, we partition the set $\mathcal{D}$ into subsets $\mathcal{E}_{ij}$, where $1 \leq i \leq k$ and $1 \leq j \leq 2 + \log(1/\beta)$, such that the following holds. Let D and D' be any two distinct dumbbells in $\cup_{i=1}^{k}\mathcal{E}_{ij}$, for some j. Let i and i' be the indices such that $D \in \mathcal{E}_{ij}$ and $D' \in \mathcal{E}_{i'j}$, respectively, let ℓ and ℓ' be the lengths of D and D', respectively, and assume that $\ell \leq \ell'$. If $i = i'$, then $\ell' \leq 2\ell$, whereas $\ell' \geq \ell/\beta$ if $i < i'$.

For each i and j, with $1 \leq i \leq k$ and $1 \leq j \leq 2 + \log(1/\beta)$, we use the algorithm of Section 11.5.1 to partition $\mathcal{E}_{ij}$ into subsets $\mathcal{E}_{ij}^{\kappa}$, where $\kappa \in \{1, 2, \ldots, 1 + \lfloor c_{s,2\gamma} \rfloor\}$, such that the following holds. For any two distinct dumbbells D and D' that are in the same subset $\mathcal{E}_{ij}^{\kappa}$, the distance between any head of D and any head of D' is larger than γ times the length of the shorter of D and D'.

For each j and κ with $1 \leq j \leq 2 + \log(1/\beta)$ and $1 \leq \kappa \leq 1 + c_{s,2\gamma}$, let

$$\mathcal{D}_j^{\kappa} := \bigcup_{i=1}^{k} \mathcal{E}_{ij}^{\kappa}.$$

These subsets $\mathcal{D}_j^{\kappa}$ form a partition of $\mathcal{D}$ into subsets, each of which satisfies both the length-grouping property and the γ-empty-region property. Using Lemmas 11.4.3 and 11.5.1, we obtain the following result.

Lemma 11.5.2. *Let $\mathcal{D}$ be the set of m dumbbells that correspond to the WSPD, and let β and γ be positive real numbers such that $\beta < 1/2$. In*

$$O\left(m \log m + \left(s^d (1 + \gamma s)^d + \log(1/\beta)\right) m\right)$$

time, we can partition $\mathcal{D}$ into subsets $\mathcal{D}_1, \mathcal{D}_2, \ldots, \mathcal{D}_k$, where

$$k = O\left(s^d (1 + \gamma s)^d \log(1/\beta)\right),$$

such that for each j with $1 \leq j \leq k$, the subset $\mathcal{D}_j$ satisfies the length-grouping property and the γ-empty-region property.

11.6 Dumbbell trees

In this section, we choose positive real numbers β and γ, such that $\beta < 1/2$. Consider the partition of the set $\mathcal{D}$ of all m dumbbells into subsets $\mathcal{D}_1, \mathcal{D}_2, \ldots, \mathcal{D}_k$, where $k = O(s^d(1 + \gamma s)^d)$, as given by Lemma 11.5.2.

Let R_0 be a large hypercube that contains all the dumbbells in $\mathcal{D}$. We define a "dummy" dumbbell D_0 that contains R_0 and a translated copy of R_0 as its heads, and whose length is equal to $1/\beta$ times the maximum length of any dumbbell in $\mathcal{D}$. Furthermore, for the root r of the split tree T, we define $R(r) := R_0$.

Dumbbell tree: For each j with $1 \leq j \leq k$, the following two properties hold:

1. For each dumbbell D in $\mathcal{D}_j$, there is a unique shortest dumbbell D' in $\mathcal{D}_j \cup \{D_0\}$, such that at least one head of D' is close to some head of D, and the length of D' is at least $1/\beta$ times the length of D.

2. For each point p in S, there is a deepest node a in the split tree, such that $p \in R(a)$ and $R(a)$ is the head of some dumbbell in $\mathcal{D}_j \cup \{D_0\}$.

These properties imply a hierarchy on the dumbbells in $\mathcal{D}_j \cup \{D_0\}$ and the points in S, which will be stored in a dumbbell tree DT_j.

We fix an index j with $1 \leq j \leq k$. Let γ' be a real number, such that $0 < \gamma' \leq \gamma$ and

$$\gamma \geq \beta \left(1 + 2\gamma' + 2\sqrt{d}/s\right).$$

The following lemma implies the hierarchy on the dumbbells in $\mathcal{D}_j \cup \{D_0\}$.

Lemma 11.6.1. *Let D be a dumbbell in $\mathcal{D}_j$, and let ℓ be its length. There is a unique dumbbell D' of minimum length in $\mathcal{D}_j \cup \{D_0\}$, such that*

1. *the length of D' is larger than ℓ, and*

2. *at least one of the heads of D' is within distance $\gamma'\ell$ of some head of D.*

If we denote the length of D' by ℓ', then $\ell' \geq \ell/\beta$.

PROOF First observe that the dummy dumbbell D_0 satisfies 1. and 2. above. Therefore, there exists a dumbbell of minimum length that satisfies these two requirements. Let D' be such a dumbbell, and let ℓ' be its length. We first show that $\ell' \geq \ell/\beta$. By the second requirement, we have $\ell < \ell'$. Assume that $\ell' \leq 2\ell$. Then, since $\gamma' \leq \gamma$, D and D' do not satisfy the γ-empty-region property, which is a contradiction. Thus, $\ell' > 2\ell$. Then, it follows from the length-grouping property that $\ell' \geq \ell/\beta$.

It remains to show that D' is unique. Assume, to the contrary, that there is another dumbbell D'' of length ℓ', such that at least one of the heads of D'' is within distance $\gamma'\ell$ of some head of D.

By Exercise 11.1, both heads of D have sides of length at most $2\ell/s$. Let R' be a head of D' and let R_1 be a head of D, such that R' is within distance $\gamma'\ell$ of R_1. Let R'' be a head of D'' and let R_2 be a head of D, such that R'' is within distance $\gamma'\ell$ of R_2. Let x_1 and x_2 be the centers of R_1 and R_2, respectively. Then $|x_1x_2| \leq \ell$, and the distance between R' and R'' is less than or equal to

$$\gamma'\ell + \frac{1}{2}\sqrt{d} \cdot L_{\max}(R_1) + |x_1x_2| + \frac{1}{2}\sqrt{d} \cdot L_{\max}(R_2) + \gamma'\ell,$$

which is less than or equal to

$$\left(2\gamma' + 1 + 2\sqrt{d}/s\right)\ell.$$

Since $\ell' \geq \ell/\beta$, the latter quantity is less than or equal to

$$\beta\left(2\gamma' + 1 + 2\sqrt{d}/s\right)\ell' \leq \gamma\ell'.$$

This implies that D' and D'' do not satisfy the γ-empty-region property, which is a contradiction. Hence, we have shown that D' is unique. ∎

We are now ready to define the dumbbell tree DT_j for the set $\mathcal{D}_j$ of dumbbells. This tree is a rooted tree, consisting of *dumbbell nodes*, *head nodes*, and *leaves*.

1. For each dumbbell D in $\mathcal{D}_j \cup \{D_0\}$, there is a dumbbell node that stores D. This dumbbell node has two children, which are head nodes storing the two heads of D.

2. The dumbbell node storing the dummy dumbbell D_0 is the root of DT_j.

3. For each dumbbell D in $\mathcal{D}_j$, let D' be the dumbbell in $\mathcal{D}_j \cup \{D_0\}$ that satisfies the conditions in Lemma 11.6.1. Let ℓ be the length of D, and let R' be a head of D' that is within distance $\gamma'\ell$ of some head of D. Then the dumbbell node storing D is a child of the head node storing R'.

4. For each point p in S, there is a leaf that stores p. Let a be the deepest node in the split tree T, such that $p \in R(a)$ and $R(a)$ is the head of some dumbbell in $\mathcal{D}_j \cup \{D_0\}$. Let D be the dumbbell in $\mathcal{D}_j \cup \{D_0\}$ of minimum length that has $R(a)$ as a head, let v be the dumbbell node that stores D, and let u be the child of v that stores $R(a)$. Then, the leaf storing p is a child of u. (Observe that, by the length-grouping and empty-region properties, the dumbbell D is uniquely defined.)

5. Each node v of DT_j stores one point of S, which is called the *representative* of v. These representatives are chosen in the following way:

   (a) If v is a leaf, then the representative of v is the point of S that is stored at v.

   (b) If v is a head node, then the representative of v is an arbitrary point of S that is contained in the head stored at v.

   (c) If v is a dumbbell node, then the representative of v is an arbitrary point of S that is contained in one of the heads of the dumbbell stored at v.

This concludes the definition of the dumbbell tree DT_j. Since this tree has $1 + |\mathcal{D}_j|$ dumbbell nodes, $2 + 2|\mathcal{D}_j|$ head nodes, and n leaves, it is obvious that the size of DT_j is $O(n + |\mathcal{D}_j|)$. The next lemma states that, even though DT_j may have nodes with only one child, the size of DT_j is in fact $O(n)$. The proof is left as an exercise; see Exercise 11.3.

Lemma 11.6.2. *For each j with $1 \leq j \leq k$, the size of the dumbbell tree DT_j is $O(n)$.*

11.7 Constructing the dumbbell trees

Let j be any index with $1 \leq j \leq k$, and consider the set $\mathcal{D}_j$ of dumbbells. We will show how the dumbbell tree DT_j can be constructed. The main difficulty is computing the parents of the dumbbell nodes.

Let $D = D(a, b)$ be any dumbbell in $\mathcal{D}_j$, and let ℓ be its length. We need to compute the dumbbell D' in $\mathcal{D}_j \cup \{D_0\}$ of minimum length, such that (i) the length of D' is larger than ℓ, and (ii) the distance between some head of D' and some head of D is less than or equal to $\gamma'\ell$. We know from Lemma 11.6.1 that the length of D' is in fact at least ℓ/β. Condition (ii) leads to two different possibilities. We fix one of these: Given the head $R(a)$ of D, we want to compute the dumbbell D' in $\mathcal{D}_j \cup \{D_0\}$ of minimum length, such that

1. the length of D' is at least ℓ/β, and

2. the distance between $R(a)$ and some head of D' is less than or equal to $\gamma'\ell$.

Consider this dumbbell D'. Recall that $L_{\max}(R(a)) \leq 2\ell/s$. Let x be the center of $R(a)$, and let C be the hypercube centered at x and having sides of length $2(\gamma' + 1/s)\ell$. Then, one of the heads of D' has a nonempty intersection with C. Let u and v be the nodes of the split tree, such that $D' = D(u, v)$, and assume without loss of generality that $R(u) \cap C \neq \emptyset$.

Consider the grid on C, consisting of $O(\beta^d (1 + \gamma's)^d)$ cells, where each cell is a hypercube having sides of length $\ell/(\beta\sqrt{d}(s + 4))$. Consider the hyperrectangle $R_0(u)$ that is associated with $R(u)$; see Section 9.3.1. Using Lemmas 9.3.1 and 11.3.1, we obtain

$$L_{\min}(R_0(u)) \geq \frac{1}{2} \cdot L_{\max}(R(\pi(u))) \geq \frac{1}{\beta\sqrt{d}(s + 4)} \ell.$$

Thus, the length of *every* side of $R_0(u)$ is at least $\ell/(\beta\sqrt{d}(s + 4))$. It follows that $R_0(u)$ contains at least one grid point. Let z be a grid point such that $z \in R_0(u)$. Recall from Section 9.3.1 that the hyperrectangles $R_0(w)$, where w ranges over all leaves of the split tree T, partition the bounding box of S. Let w be the leaf in T, such that $z \in R_0(w)$. Then, u is the deepest node in T on the path from the root to w, such that

1. $R(u)$ is the head of some dumbbell D' in $\mathcal{D}_j$,

2. the length of D' is at least ℓ/β, and

3. the distance between $R(u)$ and $R(a)$ is less than or equal to $\gamma'\ell$.

We have reduced the problem of computing the parent in DT_j of the dumbbell node storing $D(a, b)$, to the following query problem: Given a grid point z of the grid on the hypercube C,

1. compute the leaf w in T, such that $z \in R_0(w)$, and
2. compute the deepest node u in T on the path from the root to w, such that
   (a) $R(u)$ is the head of some dumbbell D' in $\mathcal{D}_j$,
   (b) the length of D' is at least ℓ/β, and
   (c) the distance between $R(u)$ and $R(a)$ is less than or equal to $\gamma'\ell$.

We obtain the parent of the dumbbell node storing $D(a, b)$, by answering $O(\beta^d(1 + \gamma's)^d)$ such queries (for the grid corresponding to the head $R(a)$ and for the grid corresponding to the head $R(b)$).

Given a grid point z, the leaf w in T for which $z \in R_0(w)$ can be computed in $O(\log n)$ time, using a balanced representation of T based on centroid edges (see Section 9.5.1 and Exercise 9.13). Given this leaf w, we can answer the second query (in which we compute the node u) in $O(\log n)$ time, using the path decomposition of T (see Sections 2.3.2 and 9.5.2). The details of this query algorithm are left as an exercise; see Exercise 11.4.

We have shown that, given any dumbbell D in $\mathcal{D}_j$, the parent in DT_j of the dumbbell node storing D can be computed in time

$$O\left(\beta^d \left(1 + \gamma's\right)^d \log n\right).$$

Using the split tree T, the parents in DT_j of all leaves (which store the points of S) can be computed in $O(n)$ total time. Again in $O(n)$ total time, we can store with each node of T, an arbitrary point of S from its subtree. Using this, the representatives for all nodes in DT_j can be computed in $O(n)$ time. Thus, we have shown that each dumbbell tree DT_j can be constructed in time

$$O\left(n \log n + \beta^d \left(1 + \gamma's\right)^d |\mathcal{D}_j| \log n\right).$$

The total time for constructing all $k = O(s^d(1 + \gamma s)^d \log(1/\beta))$ dumbbell trees is

$$O\left(kn \log n + \beta^d \left(1 + \gamma's\right)^d m \log n\right).$$

We have proved the following result:

Lemma 11.7.1. *Let β, γ, and γ' be positive real numbers, such that $\beta < 1/2$, $\gamma' \leq \gamma$, and*

$$\gamma \geq \beta \left(1 + 2\gamma' + 2\sqrt{d}/s\right).$$

Consider the partition of the set $\mathcal{D}$ of all m dumbbells into subsets $\mathcal{D}_j$, $1 \leq j \leq k$, where $k = O(s^d(1 + \gamma s)^d \log(1/\beta))$, as given by Lemma 11.5.2. In

$$O\left(kn \log n + \beta^d \left(1 + \gamma's\right)^d m \log n\right)$$

total time, we can compute, for each j with $1 \leq j \leq k$, the dumbbell tree DT_j for $\mathcal{D}_j$.

11.8 The dumbbell trees constitute a spanner

In this section, we consider the dumbbell trees DT_j, $1 \leq j \leq k$, and show how they can be used to obtain a spanner path between any two points of S. We assume that the parameters β, γ, and γ' are chosen such that the inequalities in Lemma 11.7.1 are satisfied. Additionally, we assume that $\gamma' < 1$.

Let j be an index with $1 \le j \le k$, and let u and v be two nodes of DT_j. Let $u = u_1, u_2, \ldots, u_f = v$ be the path in this tree between u and v, and for each i with $1 \le i \le f$, let p_i be the representative of u_i. Observe that the points p_i, $1 \le i \le f$, are not necessarily pairwise distinct. Let P be the (possibly nonsimple) path $p_1, p_2, \ldots, p_f$, and let Q be the simple path obtained by removing cycles from P. We call Q the *geometric path between u and v*. By the triangle inequality, the length of Q is less than or equal to the length of P.

A geometric path between two leaf nodes can be thought of as consisting of two subpaths; that is, it starts at the first leaf node, goes up the dumbbell tree to an ancestor, and then goes down the tree to the other leaf node. Each of the subpaths traverses through dumbbells, where successive dumbbells are "close" to each other and have lengths differing by a factor of at least $1/\beta$. As we will show, this property implies that, for any two distinct points p and q of S, there is a dumbbell tree DT_j, such that the geometric path between the leaves that store p and q is a t-spanner path, where t depends only on the parameters s, β, γ, and γ'. Before we can prove this strong property, we need to prove the following weak spanner property.

> **Weak spanner property:** The length of the geometric path between any leaf u of DT_j and any head node v in DT_j that is an ancestor of u, is bounded by a constant times the length of the dumbbell stored at the parent of v.

This property relates the length of a geometric path and the length of a related dumbbell. It is called the "weak spanner property," because instead of guaranteeing a t-spanner path between the representatives p and q of u and v (i.e., a path of length at most $t|pq|$), it guarantees only a path whose length is at most proportional to the length of the related dumbbell.

Lemma 11.8.1. *Let u and v be nodes in a dumbbell tree DT_j, such that u is a leaf, v is a head node, and u is in the subtree of v. Let ℓ be the length of the dumbbell stored at the parent of v. Then, the length of the geometric path between u and v is less than or equal to $c\ell$, where*

$$c = 6\beta + 8\sqrt{d}/s.$$

PROOF We write the path in DT_j between u and v as $u = u_1, u_2, \ldots, u_f = v$. Observe that f is an even integer. For each i with $1 \le i \le f$, let p_i be the representative of node u_i. The lemma will follow from the claim that

$$\sum_{i=1}^{f-1} |p_i p_{i+1}| \le c\ell. \tag{11.6}$$

We define u_{f+1} to be the parent of v. Observe that u_1 is a leaf, $u_2, u_4, \ldots, u_f$ are head nodes, and $u_3, u_5, \ldots, u_{f+1}$ are dumbbell nodes. For each $i = 3, 5, \ldots, f+1$, let ℓ_i be the length of the dumbbell stored at u_i.

We start by analyzing the first term $|p_1 p_2|$ in (11.6). Let a be the node of the split tree such that $R(a)$ is stored at the head node u_2. Since p_1 and p_2 are both contained in $R(a)$, we have

$$|p_1 p_2| \le \sqrt{d} \cdot L_{\max}(R(a)) \le \frac{2\sqrt{d}}{s} \ell_3. \tag{11.7}$$

Let i be an index with $1 \leq i \leq f/2 - 1$. We analyze the distance between p_{2i} and p_{2i+1}. Let $D(a, b)$ be the dumbbell stored at u_{2i+1}, and assume without loss of generality that the head node u_{2i} stores $R(a)$. Observe that p_{2i} is contained in $R(a)$, and p_{2i+1} is contained in either $R(a)$ or $R(b)$. Hence, if we denote the centers of $R(a)$ and $R(b)$ by x and y, respectively, then $|xy| = \ell_{2i+1}$ and

$$
\begin{aligned}
|p_{2i} p_{2i+1}| &\leq \frac{1}{2}\sqrt{d} \cdot L_{\max}(R(a)) + |xy| + \frac{1}{2}\sqrt{d} \cdot L_{\max}(R(b)) \\
&\leq \frac{2\sqrt{d}}{s} \ell_{2i+1} + \ell_{2i+1} \\
&= \left(1 + \frac{2\sqrt{d}}{s}\right) \ell_{2i+1}.
\end{aligned}
\tag{11.8}
$$

We next analyze the distance between p_{2i-1} and p_{2i}, where i is any index with $2 \leq i \leq f/2$. Let $D(a, b)$ be the dumbbell stored at u_{2i-1}, and let $D(a', b')$ be the dumbbell stored at u_{2i+1}. We may assume without loss of generality that (i) the head node u_{2i} stores $R(a')$, and (ii) $R(a')$ is within distance $\gamma' \ell_{2i-1}$ of $R(a)$. Observe that p_{2i-1} is contained in either $R(a)$ or $R(b)$, and p_{2i} is contained in $R(a')$. Hence, if we denote the centers of $R(a)$ and $R(b)$ by x and y, respectively, then $|xy| = \ell_{2i-1}$ and

$$
\begin{aligned}
|p_{2i-1} p_{2i}| &\leq \frac{1}{2}\sqrt{d} \cdot L_{\max}(R(b)) + |xy| + \frac{1}{2}\sqrt{d} \cdot L_{\max}(R(a)) \\
&\quad + \gamma' \ell_{2i-1} + \sqrt{d} \cdot L_{\max}(R(a')) \\
&\leq \frac{\sqrt{d}}{s} \ell_{2i-1} + \ell_{2i-1} + \frac{\sqrt{d}}{s} \ell_{2i-1} + \gamma' \ell_{2i-1} + \frac{2\sqrt{d}}{s} \ell_{2i+1} \\
&= \left(\frac{2\sqrt{d}}{s} + 1 + \gamma'\right) \ell_{2i-1} + \frac{2\sqrt{d}}{s} \ell_{2i+1}.
\end{aligned}
$$

Since, by Lemma 11.6.1, $\ell_{2i-1} \leq \beta \ell_{2i+1}$, it follows that

$$
|p_{2i-1} p_{2i}| \leq \left(\frac{2(1+\beta)\sqrt{d}}{s} + \beta(1 + \gamma')\right) \ell_{2i+1}.
\tag{11.9}
$$

By combining (11.7), (11.8), and (11.9), it follows that

$$
\begin{aligned}
\sum_{i=1}^{f-1} |p_i p_{i+1}| = |p_1 p_2| &+ \sum_{i=1}^{f/2-1} |p_{2i} p_{2i+1}| + \sum_{i=2}^{f/2} |p_{2i-1} p_{2i}| \\
&\leq \left(\frac{2(1+\beta)\sqrt{d}}{s} + \beta(1 + \gamma')\right) \ell_{f+1} \\
&\quad + \left(\frac{2(2+\beta)\sqrt{d}}{s} + 1 + \beta(1 + \gamma')\right) \sum_{i=1}^{f/2-1} \ell_{2i+1}.
\end{aligned}
\tag{11.10}
$$

It follows from Lemma 11.6.1 that, for each i with $1 \leq i \leq f/2 - 1$,

$$
\ell_{2i+1} \leq \beta \ell_{2i+3} \leq \beta^2 \ell_{2i+5} \leq \cdots \leq \beta^{f/2-i} \ell_{f+1} = \beta^{f/2-i} \ell.
$$

Therefore,

$$
\sum_{i=1}^{f/2-1} \ell_{2i+1} \leq \ell \sum_{i=1}^{f/2-1} \beta^{f/2-i} \leq \frac{\beta}{1-\beta} \ell \leq 2\beta \ell,
$$

because $\beta < 1/2$. This, together with (11.10) and our assumption that $\gamma' \leq 1$, completes the proof of the inequality in (11.6). ∎

Consider the head R of some dumbbell in $\mathcal{D}_j$, and let p be a point of S that is contained in R. Let v be the head node of the dumbbell tree DT_j that stores R, and let u be the leaf in DT_j that stores p. Since the path in DT_j between v and any leaf in its subtree may contain dumbbells that have a nonempty intersection with R, it is not clear whether the leaf u is in the subtree of v. The following lemma states that, for appropriate choices of the parameters β and γ', u must be in the subtree of v.

Lemma 11.8.2. *Assume that $\beta < s/(\sqrt{d}(s+4))$, $c \leq \gamma'$, and $c < s/(s+4)$, where c is as in Lemma 11.8.1. Let be p be a point in S, let u be the leaf in a dumbbell tree DT_j that stores p, and let v be a head node in DT_j, such that p is contained in the head stored at v. Then, u is in the subtree of v.*

PROOF Let v' be the parent of u. Then, v' is a head node and p is contained in the head stored at v'. If $v = v'$, then the lemma holds. Assume that $v \neq v'$.

Let D be the dumbbell that is stored at the parent of v, let ℓ be the length of D, let D' be the dumbbell that is stored at the parent of v', and let ℓ' be the length of D'.

Assume that $D = D'$. Then v and v' have the same parent. Since p is contained in both the head stored at v and the head stored at v', it follows that $v = v'$, a contradiction. Therefore, D and D' are distinct dumbbells.

We first show that $\ell' \leq \ell$. The proof is by contradiction, so we assume that $\ell < \ell'$. Let a be the node of the split tree T, such that the head node v stores $R(a)$, and let a' be the node of T, such that the head node v' stores $R(a')$. Since p is contained in both $R(a)$ and $R(a')$, it follows from basic properties of the split tree that a is in the subtree of a', or a' is in the subtree of a. Since p is stored at u, which is a child of v', the definition of the dumbbell tree DT_j implies that a' is in the subtree of a. It also follows from the definition of DT_j, and the assumption that $\ell < \ell'$, that $a \neq a'$. This, together with Lemma 11.3.1, implies that

$$L_{\max}(R(a)) \geq L_{\max}(R(\pi(a'))) \geq \frac{2}{\sqrt{d}(s+4)} \ell'.$$

On the other hand, since $R(a)$ and $R(a')$ have a nonempty intersection, and since $D \neq D'$, the length-grouping and empty-region properties imply that $\ell \leq \beta \ell'$. Therefore, we have

$$L_{\max}(R(a)) \leq 2\ell/s \leq 2\beta \ell'/s.$$

Thus,

$$\frac{2}{\sqrt{d}(s+4)} \ell' \leq \frac{2\beta}{s} \ell',$$

contradicting our assumption that $\beta < s/(\sqrt{d}(s+4))$.

Hence, we have shown that $\ell' \leq \ell$. We next show that, in fact, $\ell' < \ell$. The proof is again by contradiction. So we assume that $\ell' = \ell$. Let p' be the representative of v'. Since $|pp'|$ is less than or equal to the length of the geometric path between u and v', it follows from Lemma 11.8.1 that $|pp'| \leq c\ell$. This, together with the facts that (i) p is in one of the heads of D, (ii) p' is in one of the heads of D', and (iii) $c \leq \gamma' \leq \gamma$, implies that the dumbbells D and D' do not satisfy the γ-empty-region property. This is a contradiction and, thus, we have shown that $\ell' < \ell$.

Let v'' be the highest head node on the path in DT_j from u to the root, such that the dumbbell stored at the parent of v'' has length at most ℓ. Observe that v'' exists. We will prove that $v'' = v$, which implies the lemma. The proof is by contradiction, so we assume that $v'' \neq v$.

Let D'' be the dumbbell stored at the parent of v'', let ℓ'' be the length of D'', and let p'' be the representative of v''. Since $|pp''|$ is less than or equal to the length of the geometric path between u and v'', it follows from Lemma 11.8.1 that $|pp''| \leq c\ell''$.

We prove, by contradiction, that $D'' \neq D$. Thus, we assume that $D'' = D$. Then, $|pp''| \leq c\ell$. Since $v \neq v''$, the points p and p'' are in different heads of D. Let x and y be the centers of the two heads of D. Then, using Lemma 9.1.2, we have

$$\ell = |xy| \leq (1 + 4/s)|pp''| \leq c(1 + 4/s)\ell < \ell,$$

which is a contradiction.

By our choice of v'', we have $\ell'' \leq \ell$. Therefore, by the length-grouping property, we have either (i) $\ell \leq 2\ell''$ or (ii) $\ell \geq \ell''/\beta$. We will prove that (ii) holds. In order to prove this, assume that (i) holds. Then, the dumbbells D and D'' do not satisfy the γ-empty-region property, because (i) p is in one of the heads of D, (ii) p'' is in one of the heads of D'', (iii) $|pp''| \leq c\ell''$, and (iv) $c \leq \gamma' \leq \gamma$. This is a contradiction and, therefore, we have shown that (ii) holds; that is, $\ell'' \leq \beta\ell$.

Since $|pp''| \leq c\ell'' \leq \gamma'\ell''$, some head of D and some head of D'' are within distance $\gamma'\ell''$ of each other. Since $\ell > \ell''$, D satisfies conditions 1. and 2. in Lemma 11.6.1 (when applying this lemma to the dumbbell D''). Thus, the dumbbell node storing D is a candidate for being the grandparent of the dumbbell node storing D''. In particular, this grandparent stores a dumbbell D''' whose length is less than or equal to that of D. But, by our choice of v'', the length of D''' is larger than ℓ. This is a contradiction. Thus, we have shown that $v'' = v$. This completes the proof of the lemma. ∎

We are now ready to prove the spanner property of the dumbbell trees.

Lemma 11.8.3. *Assume that $\beta < s/(\sqrt{d}(s + 4))$, $c \leq \gamma'$, and $c < s/(s + 4)$, where c is as in Lemma 11.8.1. Let p and q be two distinct points of S, let D be the dumbbell that contains p in one of its heads and q in its other head, let j be the index such that the dumbbell tree DT_j stores D, and let u and u' be the leaves in DT_j that store p and q, respectively. Then, the length of the geometric path between u and u' is less than or equal to $t|pq|$, where*

$$t = 1 + 10c + 6/s.$$

PROOF Let w be the dumbbell node in DT_j that stores D, and let v and v' be the children of w. It follows from Lemma 11.8.2 that (i) u is in the subtree of v and u' is in the subtree of v', or (ii) u is in the subtree of v' and u' is in the subtree of v. We may assume without loss of generality that (i) holds.

Let ℓ be the length of the dumbbell D, let x be the representative of v, let y be the representative of w, and let z be the representative of v'. Let P_1 be the geometric path between u and v, and let P_2 be the geometric path between v' and u'. Then, the path P obtained by concatenating P_1, the edges $\{x, y\}$ and $\{y, z\}$, and P_2, is the geometric path between u and u'. By Lemma 11.8.1, the length of both P_1 and P_2 is less than or equal to $c\ell$. Observe that (i) p and q are in different heads of D, (ii) x and z are in different heads of D, and (iii) y is in one of the heads of D. Then, using Lemma 9.1.2, we obtain

$$|xy| + |yz| \leq (2/s)|pq| + (1 + 4/s)|pq| = (1 + 6/s)|pq|.$$

We also have $\ell \leq (1 + 4/s)|pq|$, which follows again from Lemma 9.1.2. Thus, the length of P is less than or equal to

$$2c\ell + (1 + 6/s)|pq| \leq (2c(1 + 4/s) + 1 + 6/s)|pq| \leq (1 + 10c + 6/s)|pq|,$$

where the last inequality follows from our assumption that $s \geq 1$. ∎

11.9 The Dumbbell Theorem

We summarize how the dumbbell trees were obtained. Let S be a set of n points in $\mathbb{R}^d$. Choose positive real numbers s, β, γ, and γ', and define

$$c = 6\beta + 8\sqrt{d}/s$$

and

$$t = 1 + 10c + 6/s.$$

These parameters are chosen such that $s > 1$, $\beta < 1/2$, $\beta < s/(\sqrt{d}(s + 4))$, $\gamma' < 1$, $c \leq \gamma' \leq \gamma$, $c < s/(s + 4)$, and

$$\gamma \geq \beta\left(1 + 2\gamma' + 2\sqrt{d}/s\right).$$

1. Compute the split tree T and the corresponding WSPD, $\{A_i, B_i\}$, $1 \leq i \leq m$, with respect to s. Assign representatives for each node of T. By Theorem 9.4.6, we have $m = O(s^d n)$, and it takes $O(n \log n + s^d n)$ time to compute T and the WSPD.

2. Consider the set of m dumbbells corresponding to the WSPD. Partition this set into k subsets, such that within each subset, both the $(\beta, 1/2)$-length-grouping property and the γ-empty-region property hold. By Lemma 11.5.2, we have $k = O(s^d(1 + \gamma s)^d \log(1/\beta))$, and it takes

$$O\left(s^d n \log n + \left(s^{2d}(1 + \gamma s)^d + s^d \log(1/\beta)\right) n\right)$$

   time to compute this partition.

3. Store each of the k subsets of dumbbells in a dumbbell tree. Assign representatives for each leaf, head node and dumbbell node. By Lemma 11.7.1, this takes

$$O\left(\left(s^d(1 + \gamma s)^d \log(1/\beta) + \beta^d s^d(1 + \gamma' s)^d\right) n \log n\right)$$

   time.

Given the point set S, the entire algorithm computes the k dumbbell trees in time

$$O\left(s^d(1 + \gamma s)^d(\log(1/\beta))n \log n + s^{2d}(1 + \gamma s)^d n\right).$$

Let G be the graph with vertex set S and whose edge set consists of all pairs $\{p, q\}$ of distinct points of S for which there is a dumbbell tree and two nodes u and v in this tree such that (i) u is a child of v, (ii) p is the representative of u, and (iii) q is the representative of v. Then G consists of $O(kn + m) = O(s^d(1 + \gamma s)^d(\log(1/\beta))n)$ edges and, by Lemma 11.8.3, G is a t-spanner for S, where

$$t = 1 + O(c + 1/s).$$

If we choose $s \geq 32\sqrt{d}$,

$$\beta < \min\left(\frac{1}{24}, \frac{s}{2\sqrt{d}(s + 4)}\right),$$

and

$$\gamma = \gamma' = 6\beta + 8\sqrt{d}/s,$$

then all requirements on the parameters are satisfied, and

$$t = 1 + O(\beta + 1/s).$$

Hence, in order to obtain a t-spanner, where t is close to 1, we choose $\beta = c'(t-1)$, for some small positive constant c', and $s = 1/\beta$. We have proved the main result of this chapter.

Theorem 11.9.1 (Dumbbell Theorem). *Let S be a set of n points in $\mathbb{R}^d$ and let $t > 1$ be a real number. In*

$$O\left(\frac{\log(1/(t-1))}{(t-1)^d} n \log n + \frac{1}{(t-1)^{2d}} n\right)$$

time, a t-spanner for S, consisting of

$$O\left(\frac{\log(1/(t-1))}{(t-1)^d} n\right)$$

edges, can be computed. This t-spanner is represented by

$$O\left(\frac{\log(1/(t-1))}{(t-1)^d}\right)$$

dumbbell trees. Each dumbbell tree is a rooted tree with n leaves and $O(n)$ nodes, each leaf stores a unique point of S, and each node stores a representative point of S. For any two distinct points p and q of S, there is a dumbbell tree DT, such that the geometric path between p and q that corresponds to the leaves of DT that store p and q, is a t-spanner path.

How do we actually compute a t-spanner path in this spanner between two distinct points p and q of S? A first solution is to compute, for each dumbbell tree, the geometric path corresponding to the leaves that store p and q. The shortest path obtained in this way is a t-spanner path between p and q. The time spent to find the t-spanner path is bounded from above by the number of dumbbell trees times the maximum number of edges visited in any dumbbell tree. A second solution is to use Theorem 9.5.2 or Theorem 9.5.6 to find the dumbbell tree that "contains" a t-spanner path between p and q, and then to find this path in this tree. In this way, the time spent is $O(\log n)$ plus the number of edges on the path visited in this dumbbell tree. In both solutions, the time to find a t-spanner path can be linear in n. In Chapter 12, we will "shortcut" the dumbbell trees such that the number of edges on a t-spanner path is drastically reduced.

The main result of this chapter is capsuled below.

Dumbbell trees and the Dumbbell Theorem: Given a set S of n points in $\mathbb{R}^d$, it is possible to build, in $O(n \log n)$ time, a data structure consisting of $k = O(1)$ dumbbell trees, with the property that for any two points p and q of S, one of the k dumbbell trees has a geometric path, which is a t-spanner path between p and q. The structure gives a t-spanner for S with $O(n)$ edges.

Exercises

11.1. Let $D(a, b)$ be a dumbbell and let ℓ be its length. Prove that

$$L_{\max}(R(a)) \leq 2\ell/s$$

and

$$L_{\max}(R(b)) \leq 2\ell/s.$$

11.2. The algorithms in Section 11.4 work in the algebraic computation-tree model. Assume that we add indirect addressing, the floor function, and the logarithm function as unit time operations. Show that, in this more powerful model, the (β, δ)-length property can be established in $O(m)$ time.

11.3. Prove Lemma 11.6.2.

11.4. Work out the details for Section 11.7. In particular, show how the parent of any given dumbbell node can be computed in $O(\beta^d(1 + \gamma's)^d \log n)$ time.

11.5. Let S be a set of n points in $\mathbb{R}^d$, and let $t > 1$ be a constant. Use the dumbbell trees to show how to construct, in $O(n \log n)$ time, a t-spanner for S, whose spanner diameter is $O(\log n)$ and that consists of $O(n)$ edges. (*Hint:* Use Exercise 2.8.)

11.6. Let S be a set of n points in $\mathbb{R}^d$, let $t > 1$ be a real constant, and let G be the t-spanner of Section 9.2 that uses the WSPD for S, as computed by algorithm COMPUTEWSPD of Section 9.4. Use the dumbbell trees and the gap property of Chapter 6 to show that the weight of G is $O(\log n)$ times the weight of a minimum spanning tree of S. (By Exercise 9.12, this upper bound is tight.)

11.7. Let S be a set of n points in $\mathbb{R}^d$, and let $t > 1$ be a constant. Show how to construct, in $O(n \log n)$ time, a t-spanner for S whose spanner diameter is $O(\log n)$, that consists of $O(n)$ edges, and whose weight is $O(\log n)$ times the weight of a minimum spanning tree of S. (*Hint:* Use the construction of Section 10.2.)

Bibliographic notes

The notion of dumbbells first appeared in Das, Heffernan, and Narasimhan [1993]. They also introduced the length-grouping property, the empty-region property, and the nesting of dumbbells. Their purpose was to analyze the weight of a set of edges satisfying the so-called leapfrog property; see Chapter 14.

This chapter is based on Arya et al. [1995] and on Mount's unpublished notes (Mount [1994]). Section 11.3 also uses results from Zeh [2002].

In Arya et al. [1995] and Mount [1994], it is shown how dumbbell trees can be combined with the topology trees of Frederickson [1997] to obtain a t-spanner whose degree and spanner diameter are less than or equal to c_t and $c_t' \log n$, respectively, where c_t and c_t' depend only on t.

Solutions to Exercises 11.6 and 11.7 can be found in Arya et al. [1995]. Exercise 11.7 shows that a sparse spanner exists, whose spanner diameter is $O(\log n)$ and whose weight is $O(\log n)$ times the weight of a minimum spanning tree of the points. Agarwal, Wang, and Yin [2005] prove the following lower bound: Let S be the set consisting of the integers $1, 2, \ldots, n$, and let $t > 1$ be a real constant. Then, every t-spanner for S with spanner diameter $O(\log n)$ has weight $\Omega(\log n / \log \log n)$ times the weight of a minimum spanning tree of S. This leads us to the following open problem.

> **Open problem:** Does there exist a set S of n points in $\mathbb{R}^d$, such that for any real constant $t > 1$, every t-spanner for S with spanner diameter $O(\log n)$ has weight $\Omega(\log n)$ times the weight of a minimum spanning tree of S?

12

Shortcutting Trees and Spanners with Low Spanner Diameter

> I think that I shall never see a billboard lovely as a tree. Perhaps, unless the billboards fall, I'll never see a tree at all.
>
> —Ogden Nash

In this chapter, we consider the problem of constructing spanners with low spanner diameter. Recall that in Sections 4.3, 5.5.5, and 10.2, we gave algorithms that construct, for any set of n points in $\mathbb{R}^d$, and for any constant $t > 1$, a t-spanner having $O(n)$ edges, and whose spanner diameter is $O(\log n)$. In this chapter, we will see that these results can be improved considerably.

We start in Section 12.1 by considering a *shortcutting problem* on trees. In this problem, we are given a tree T with n vertices, and we want to add a "small" number of edges to it, such that for any two vertices u and v of T, there exists a path Q between u and v, such that (i) Q contains a "small" number of edges, and (ii) Q is a "subpath" of the path in T between u and v. It turns out that this problem leads to the Ackermann function and its inverse $\alpha(n)$ in a natural way. The main result will be that, by adding $O(n)$ edges to T, the path Q consists of only $O(\alpha(n))$ edges.

In Section 12.2, we will use solutions to the shortcutting problem, together with the Dumbbell Theorem of the previous chapter (Theorem 11.9.1), to construct spanners with low spanner diameter. In particular, we will see how to construct a spanner with $O(n)$ edges and spanner diameter $O(\alpha(n))$.

Throughout this chapter, we will encounter several recurrences, which will be analyzed using induction. For these analyses, it turns out to be convenient to define $\log 0 := 0$.

12.1 Shortcutting trees

Let V be a finite set of vertices, and let $T = (V, E_V)$ be a tree. We will consider undirected graphs that contain T. Let $G = (V, E)$ be such a graph (hence, $E_V \subseteq E$), and let u and v be any two vertices of V. Let

$$P = (u = x_0, x_1, x_2, \ldots, x_\ell = v)$$

be the unique path in T between u and v. A path

$$Q = \left(u = x_{i_0}, x_{i_1}, x_{i_2}, \ldots, x_{i_k} = v\right)$$

in G between u and v is called a *T-monotone path* if

$$0 = i_0 < i_1 < i_2 < \ldots < i_k = \ell.$$

In other words, Q is a path between u and v, that is obtained from the path P by taking shortcuts.

Definition 12.1.1. Let V be a set of n vertices, let $T = (V, E_V)$ be a tree, and let $G = (V, E)$ be a graph, such that $E_V \subseteq E$. The T-*monotone diameter* of G is defined to be the smallest integer k, such that for any two vertices u and v of V, there exists a T-monotone path in G between u and v, that consists of at most k edges.

In this section, we consider the following shortcutting problem.

Problem 12.1.2 (SHORTCUTTING TREE). Given a tree $T = (V, E_V)$, and given a positive integer k, compute a graph $G = (V, E)$, with $E_V \subseteq E$, whose T-monotone diameter is k, and for which the size of E is as small as possible.

12.1.1 Monotone diameters 1 and 2

Any graph G having T-monotone diameter 1 is clearly the complete graph. So let us turn to the problem of computing a graph having T-monotone diameter 2.

We denote the number of vertices of any tree T by $|T|$. Let T be a tree and let u be a vertex of T. The *components* of u are the trees that are obtained by removing u, together with its incident edges, from T. Recall that the vertex u is called a *centroid vertex* of T if each component of u contains at most $|T|/2$ vertices (see Section 2.3.4). By Lemma 2.3.9, a centroid vertex always exists and can be computed in $O(|T|)$ time.

Monotone diameter 2: Consider the tree T with n vertices, and let u be a centroid vertex of T. We connect each vertex of T to u. By removing u from T, we obtain a collection of components (which are trees again), each having at most $n/2$ vertices. For each of these components, we recursively compute a graph having monotone diameter 2. Since $O(n)$ edges are added at each level of the recursion, and since the recursion depth is $O(\log n)$, the final graph will have $O(n \log n)$ edges.

Algorithm TREEMONODIAM2(T, n)

Comment: This algorithm takes as input a tree T having n vertices. It returns a graph whose T-monotone diameter is at most 2.

If $1 \leq n \leq 3$, then the algorithm returns the edge set E of T. Assume that $n \geq 4$.

Step 1: Compute a centroid vertex u of T, and compute the edge set

$$E' := \{\{v, u\} : v \text{ is a vertex of } T, v \neq u\}.$$

Step 2: Let g be the degree of u in T, and let T_i, $1 \leq i \leq g$, be the components of u. For each i with $1 \leq i \leq g$, recursively call TREEMONODIAM2$(T_i, |T_i|)$, and let E_i be the edge set returned by this call.

Step 3: Return the edge set $E := E' \cup E_1 \cup E_2 \cup \ldots \cup E_g$.

The following theorem analyzes algorithm TREEMONODIAM2.

Theorem 12.1.3. *Let T be a tree having n vertices. Algorithm* TREEMONODIAM2(T, n) *computes, in $O(n \log n)$ time, a graph on the vertices of T, having at most $n \log n$ edges, and whose T-monotone diameter is less than or equal to 2.*

PROOF Let V be the vertex set of T, and let $G = (V, E)$ be the graph that is returned by algorithm TREEMONODIAM2(T, n). We first prove that the T-monotone diameter of G is less than or equal to 2. The proof is by induction on n. If $1 \leq n \leq 3$, then this is clearly the case. So let $n \geq 4$, and assume that for any tree T' with less than n vertices, algorithm TREEMONODIAM2$(T', |T'|)$ returns a graph having T'-monotone diameter less than or equal to 2.

Let v and w be any two distinct vertices of V. Consider the centroid vertex u of T that is computed by algorithm TREEMONODIAM2(T, n). If one of v and w is equal to u, then v and w are connected by an edge from E' and this edge forms a T-monotone path between v and w. If v and w are in different components of u, then they are connected by the path Q in G consisting of the two edges $\{v, u\}$ and $\{u, w\}$. Since the unique path in T between v and w passes through the centroid vertex u, the path Q is T-monotone. Finally, assume that v and w are contained in the same component, say T_i, of u. Note that the path in G consisting of the two edges $\{v, u\}$ and $\{u, w\}$ is not T-monotone. But, by the induction hypothesis, the recursive call TREEMONODIAM2$(T_i, |T_i|)$ returns a graph in which v and w are connected by a T_i-monotone path consisting of at most two edges. This path is also a path in G, and it is T-monotone.

Next we prove that the graph G contains at most $n \log n$ edges. If $1 \leq n \leq 3$, then G contains exactly $n - 1$ edges, which is less than or equal to $n \log n$. Let $n \geq 4$, and assume that for any tree T' with less than n vertices, algorithm TREEMONODIAM2$(T', |T'|)$ returns a graph having at most $|T'| \log |T'|$ edges. Consider again the centroid vertex u of T, let g be its degree in T, and consider the components T_i, $1 \leq i \leq g$, of u. Observe that $|T_i| \leq n/2 < n$ for all i with $1 \leq i \leq g$, and $n = 1 + \sum_{i=1}^{g} |T_i|$. It follows from the algorithm and the induction hypothesis that the number of edges of G is bounded from above by

$$
\begin{aligned}
n - 1 + \sum_{i=1}^{g} |T_i| \log |T_i| &\leq n + \sum_{i=1}^{g} |T_i| \log(n/2) \\
&= n + (n - 1) \log(n/2) \\
&\leq n + n \log(n/2) \\
&= n \log n.
\end{aligned}
$$

Since, by Lemma 2.3.9, a centroid vertex in a tree with n vertices can be computed in $O(n)$ time, it follows in a similar way that the running time of algorithm TREEMONODIAM2(T, n) is $O(n \log n)$. ∎

12.1.2 Monotone diameter 3

We now turn to the problem of constructing a graph having T-monotone diameter 3. The construction is a generalization of the previous algorithm TREEMONODIAM2(L, n).

Monotone diameter 3: Given the tree T with n vertices, we remove approximately $\sqrt{n}$ vertices, together with their incident edges, such that each of the resulting components contains less than $\sqrt{n}$ vertices. The vertices that are removed are called *cut vertices*. We connect these cut vertices by a complete graph. Each vertex v of T that is not a cut vertex is connected by an edge to each of the cut vertices that is on the "boundary" of the component containing v. Finally, we run the algorithm recursively on each of the components. As we will see, $O(n)$ edges are added at each level of the recursion. Since the recursion depth is $O(\log \log n)$, the final graph will have $O(n \log \log n)$ edges.

Existence of cut vertices

The first question is whether cut vertices having the property mentioned above exist. We will show that such vertices indeed exist, and that they can be computed by a simple recursive algorithm that is based on Lemma 2.3.9. That is, we compute a *centroid tree* $CT(T)$ of T, in the following way. First, we compute a centroid vertex u of T, which we store with the root of $CT(T)$. Then we recursively compute a centroid tree of each of the components of u. The roots of all these recursively computed centroid trees are made children of the root of $CT(T)$. A formal description of this algorithm is given below.

Algorithm CENTROIDDECOMP(T, n)

Comment: This algorithm takes as input a tree T with n vertices. It returns the root of the centroid tree $CT(T)$ of T.

```
create a new node x;
if n = 1
then store the only vertex of T with node x
else u := centroid vertex of T;
      store vertex u with node x;
      g := degree of u in T;
      let T_i, 1 ≤ i ≤ g, be the components of u;
      for i := 1 to g
      do x_i := CENTROIDDECOMP(T_i, |T_i|);
          make x_i a child of x
      endfor
endif
return node x
```

Lemma 12.1.4. *Let T be a tree with n vertices. The running time of algorithm* CENTROIDDECOMP(T, n) *is* $O(n \log n)$.

PROOF The proof follows from the facts that (i) a centroid vertex in a tree with m vertices can be computed in $O(m)$ time, and (ii) the recursion depth of algorithm CENTROIDDECOMP(T, n) is $O(\log n)$. ∎

The next lemma tells us how the desired cut vertices can be obtained from the centroid tree $CT(T)$. Before we can state this lemma, we have to introduce some terminology.

First observe that each node of the centroid tree stores a unique vertex of the tree T. Each node of $CT(T)$ *represents* a subtree of T in a natural way: Let x be any node of $CT(T)$, and let T_x be the subtree of T on those vertices that are stored with the nodes in the subtree of x. (Observe that T_x is connected and, therefore, indeed a tree.) We will say that node x *represents* the subtree T_x.

Let n and ℓ be positive integers, let T be a tree with n vertices, and let $CT(T)$ be the centroid tree that is computed by algorithm CENTROIDDECOMP(T, n). We define

$$R_\ell := \{x \ : \ x \text{ is a node of } CT(T) \text{ that represents a subtree of } T \text{ having at least } \ell \text{ vertices}\},$$

and

$$CV_\ell := \{u \ : \ u \text{ is a vertex of } T \text{ and there is a node } x \in R_\ell \text{ such that } u \text{ is stored with } x\}.$$

The following lemma implies that the vertices of the set CV_ℓ can be used as cut vertices.

Lemma 12.1.5. *Using the notation introduced above, the following holds.*

1. *By removing all vertices of CV_ℓ, together with their incident edges, from the tree T, we get a collection of trees, each having less than ℓ vertices.*

2. *The set CV_ℓ consists of at most $2n/\ell$ vertices of T.*

PROOF The first claim follows immediately from the definition of the sets R_ℓ and CV_ℓ. In the rest of the proof, we will prove the second claim. If $\ell = 1$, then CV_ℓ is equal to the set of all vertices of T. In this case, the second claim clearly holds. Assume from now on that $\ell \geq 2$.

Let $CT_\ell(T)$ be the tree obtained from $CT(T)$ by removing all nodes that are not in R_ℓ. Observe that $CT_\ell(T)$ may have nodes with only one child. We denote the number of nodes of $CT_\ell(T)$ by $|CT_\ell(T)|$. We will show that

$$|CT_\ell(T)| \leq \max(0, 2n/\ell - 1). \tag{12.1}$$

Since $|CV_\ell| = |R_\ell| = |CT_\ell(T)|$, this will prove the second claim.

The proof of (12.1) is by induction on n. If $1 \leq n < \ell$, then $CT_\ell(T)$ is empty. In this case, we have $|CT_\ell(T)| = 0 \leq \max(0, 2n/\ell - 1)$.

Let $n \geq \ell$ and assume that for any tree T' with less than n vertices, algorithm CENTROIDDECOMP$(T', |T'|)$ computes a centroid tree $CT(T')$ for which the corresponding tree $CT_\ell(T')$ has at most $\max(0, 2|T'|/\ell - 1)$ nodes. Consider the centroid vertex u of T that is computed by algorithm CENTROIDDECOMP(T, n). Let g be the degree of u in T, and let $T_1, T_2, \ldots, T_g$ be the components of u, that is, the trees obtained by removing u, together with its incident edges, from T. We may assume without loss of generality that $|T_1| \geq |T_2| \geq \ldots \geq |T_g|$.

First assume that $|T_1| < \ell$. Then the tree $CT_\ell(T)$ consists of exactly one node (viz. the node that stores the vertex u) and, therefore, $|CT_\ell(T)| = 1 \leq 2n/\ell - 1 = \max(0, 2n/\ell - 1)$.

Assume from now on that $|T_1| \geq \ell$. Let h be the index such that $1 \leq h \leq g$ and

$$|T_1| \geq |T_2| \geq \ldots \geq |T_h| \geq \ell > |T_{h+1}| \geq |T_{h+2}| \geq \ldots \geq |T_g|.$$

We distinguish two cases. The first case is when $h \geq 2$. Then we have

$$|CT_\ell(T)| = 1 + \sum_{i=1}^{h} |CT_\ell(T_i)|.$$

The induction hypothesis implies that for each i with $1 \leq i \leq h$,

$$|CT_\ell(T_i)| \leq \max(0, 2|T_i|/\ell - 1) = 2|T_i|/\ell - 1.$$

Therefore,

$$|CT_\ell(T)| \leq 1 + \sum_{i=1}^{h} (2|T_i|/\ell - 1)$$

$$= 1 - h + \frac{2}{\ell} \sum_{i=1}^{h} |T_i|$$

$$\leq -1 + 2n/\ell$$

$$= \max(0, 2n/\ell - 1).$$

We are left with the case when $h = 1$. In this case,

$$|CT_\ell(T)| = 1 + |CT_\ell(T_1)|.$$

By the induction hypothesis, we have

$$|CT_\ell(T_1)| \leq \max(0, 2|T_1|/\ell - 1) = 2|T_1|/\ell - 1.$$

Combining this with the fact that $|T_1| \leq n/2$, we get

$$|CT_\ell(T)| \leq 1 + 2|T_1|/\ell - 1 \leq n/\ell \leq 2n/\ell - 1 = \max(0, 2n/\ell - 1).$$

This completes the proof. ∎

Connecting the vertices of T to the cut vertices

At this moment, we know that the vertices of CV_ℓ can be used as cut vertices. According to our earlier description, all the cut vertices get connected by edges to form a complete subgraph. The next question is how to connect the other vertices of T to these cut vertices. Of course, we want to do this, using only $O(n)$ edges.

Let n and ℓ be positive integers such that $n \geq \ell$, let T be a tree with n vertices, and let $CT(T)$ be the centroid tree of T. Let V be the vertex set of T, and consider the set CV_ℓ of cut vertices of Lemma 12.1.5. Let $T_1, T_2, \ldots, T_g$ be the collection of subtrees obtained by removing all vertices of CV_ℓ, together with their incident edges, from T. For each i with $1 \leq i \leq g$, we define the *border* of T_i as the set of all vertices $u \in CV_\ell$ that are connected by an edge (in T) to some vertex of T_i. We also say that u is a *border vertex* of T_i (even though it is not strictly in T_i).

We connect the vertices of $V \setminus CV_\ell$ to the cut vertices in the following way. Each vertex $v \in V \setminus CV_\ell$ is connected by an edge to each border vertex of the subtree that contains v. In the algorithm that will be given later, the set of edges obtained in this way is denoted by E''. Hence,

$$E'' := \{\{v, u\} : v \notin CV_\ell, u \in CV_\ell, u \text{ is a border vertex of the subtree that has } v \text{ as a vertex}\}.$$

The following lemma states that the set E'', indeed, consists of $O(n)$ edges.

Lemma 12.1.6. *Let n and ℓ be positive integers, such that $n \geq \ell$, and consider the set E'' defined above. Then,*

1. *the set E'' contains at most $3n$ edges, and*
2. *given the centroid tree $CT(T)$, the set E'' can be computed in $O(n)$ time.*

PROOF Consider the subtrees $T_1, T_2, \ldots, T_g$ that we get by removing the vertices of CV_ℓ from T. We fix an arbitrary vertex r of CV_ℓ. Using this vertex, we divide the edges of E'' into two groups. Let $\{v, u\}$ be any edge of E'' and assume without loss of generality that $v \notin CV_\ell$ and $u \in CV_\ell$. Let T_i be the subtree that contains v. Since u is a border vertex of T_i, each vertex on the path in T between u and v, except for u, is a vertex of T_i, thus ruling out the possibility that r is on this path. This implies that either (i) u is on the path in T between r and v or (ii) v is on the path in T between r and u. We call edge $\{v, u\}$ of E'' an *upstream edge* if (i) holds. Otherwise, (ii) holds, in which case $\{v, u\}$ is called a *downstream edge*. We will count the upstream and downstream edges separately.

Each vertex $v \notin CV_\ell$ is incident on exactly one upstream edge. (Otherwise, the tree T would contain a cycle.) Conversely, each upstream edge of E'' is incident on exactly one vertex that is not in CV_ℓ. Therefore, the set E'' contains exactly $n - |CV_\ell|$ upstream edges.

Let u be any vertex of $CV_\ell \setminus \{r\}$ and consider two distinct downstream edges $\{v, u\}$ and $\{v', u\}$. Hence, neither of v and v' is a vertex of CV_ℓ. Let i and j be the indices such that v and v' are vertices of T_i and T_j, respectively. Then, we have $i = j$, because otherwise, the tree T would contain a cycle. It follows that each downstream edge of E'' that is incident on u, is incident on a vertex of T_i. Since T_i has less than ℓ vertices, this implies that there are less than ℓ downstream edges that are incident on u. Since each downstream edge is incident on exactly one vertex of $CV_\ell \setminus \{r\}$, this proves that the number of downstream edges in E'' is bounded from above by $(|CV_\ell| - 1)(\ell - 1)$.

We know from Lemma 12.1.5 that CV_ℓ contains at most $2n/\ell$ vertices. Therefore, the number of edges in E'' is bounded from above by

$$(n - |CV_\ell|) + (|CV_\ell| - 1)(\ell - 1) \leq n + |CV_\ell|\ell \leq 3n.$$

This proves the first claim. The proof of the second claim is left as an exercise (see Exercise 12.4). ∎

We are now ready to present the algorithm that constructs a graph whose T-monotone diameter is at most 3.

Algorithm TREEMONODIAM3(T, n, x)

Comment: This algorithm takes as input a tree T with n vertices, and the root x of the centroid tree $CT(T)$. It returns a graph whose T-monotone diameter is at most 3.

If $1 \leq n \leq 4$, then the algorithm returns the edge set E of T. Assume that $n \geq 5$.

Step 1: Let $\ell := \lceil \sqrt{n} \rceil$. Use the centroid tree $CT(T)$ to compute the set CV_ℓ of cut vertices of T (see Lemma 12.1.5). Compute the set E' as the edge set of the complete graph on CV_ℓ.

Step 2: Compute the subtrees $T_1, T_2, \ldots, T_g$ obtained by removing the vertices of CV_ℓ from T, and compute the edge set

$$E'' := \{\{v, u\} : \; v \notin CV_\ell, u \in CV_\ell, \; u \text{ is a border vertex of the}$$
$$\text{subtree that has } v \text{ as a vertex}\}.$$

For each i with $1 \leq i \leq g$, let x_i be the node of $CT(T)$ that represents T_i, run algorithm TREEMONODIAM3$(T_i, |T_i|, x_i)$, and let E_i be the edge set returned by this algorithm.

Step 3: Return the edge set $E := E' \cup E'' \cup E_1 \cup E_2 \cup \ldots \cup E_g$.

Theorem 12.1.7. *Let T be a tree with n vertices. In $O(n \log n)$ time, we can compute a graph on these vertices, having at most $6n \log \log n + 1$ edges, and whose T-monotone diameter is less than or equal to 3.*

PROOF   Given the tree T, we first use algorithm CENTROIDDECOMP(T, n) to compute a centroid tree $CT(T)$ of T. By Lemma 12.1.4, this can be done in $O(n \log n)$ time. Let x be the root of this centroid tree. We claim that algorithm TREEMONODIAM3(T, n, x) gives the desired graph.

Let V be the vertex set of T, and let $G = (V, E)$ be the graph that is returned by algorithm TREEMONODIAM3(T, n, x). We first prove that the T-monotone diameter of this graph is less than or equal to 3. If $1 \leq n \leq 4$, then this is clearly the case. Let $n \geq 5$ and assume that for any tree T' with less than n vertices, algorithm TREEMONODIAM3 computes a graph whose T'-monotone diameter is less than or equal to 3.

Let $\ell := \lceil \sqrt{n} \rceil$, let CV_ℓ be the set of cut vertices of T that are computed by the algorithm, and let $T_1, T_2, \ldots, T_g$ be the trees obtained by removing these cut vertices from T. Let u and v be any two distinct vertices of V. First assume that u and v are both cut vertices. Then, u and v are connected by an edge in G, and this edge forms a T-monotone path between u and v. Next assume that $u \in CV_\ell$ and $v \notin CV_\ell$. Let w be the first vertex of CV_ℓ on the path in T from v to u. If $u = w$, then $\{v, u\}$ is an edge in G, which forms a T-monotone path between u and v. If $u \neq w$, then $\{v, w\}$ and $\{w, u\}$ are edges in G. These two edges form a T-monotone path between u and v. The case when $v \in CV_\ell$ and $u \notin CV_\ell$ is symmetric. The next case is when neither u nor v is a cut vertex and these two vertices are in different subtrees. Let w and w' be the first and last vertices of CV_ℓ on the path in T from u to v, respectively. If $w \neq w'$, then the three edges $\{u, w\}$, $\{w, w'\}$, and $\{w', v\}$, which are edges in G, form a T-monotone path between u and v. If $w = w'$, then the two edges $\{u, w\}$ and $\{w, v\}$ are edges in G and form a T-monotone path between u and v. The final case is when u and v are contained in the same subtree, say T_i. By the induction hypothesis, the recursive call TREEMONODIAM3$(T_i, |T_i|, x_i)$ computes a graph in which u and v are connected by a T_i-monotone path, consisting of at most three edges. This path is also a path in G, and it is T-monotone.

Next we prove an upper bound on the number of edges of the graph G. If $1 \leq n \leq 4$, then G contains $n - 1$ edges, which is less than or equal to $6n \log \log n + 1$. Let $n \geq 5$, and assume that for any tree T' with less than n vertices, algorithm TREEMONODIAM3 constructs a graph having at most $6|T'| \log \log |T'| + 1$ edges.

Consider again the set CV_ℓ of cut vertices in T, and the corresponding subtrees $T_1, T_2, \ldots, T_g$. Observe that, by Lemma 12.1.5, $|T_i| \leq \lceil \sqrt{n} \rceil - 1 < \sqrt{n} < n$ for each i with $1 \leq i \leq g$, and $\sum_{i=1}^{g} |T_i| \leq n$. Again by Lemma 12.1.5, we have

$$|CV_\ell| \leq 2n/\ell = 2n/\lceil \sqrt{n} \rceil \leq 2\sqrt{n}.$$

Therefore, the size of the edge set E' of the complete graph on CV_ℓ satisfies

$$|E'| = \binom{|CV_\ell|}{2} \leq |CV_\ell|^2/2 \leq 2n.$$

Lemma 12.1.6 implies that the size of the edge set E'' that is computed by the algorithm satisfies

$$|E''| \leq 3n.$$

Let i be any integer with $1 \leq i \leq g$, and consider the edge set E_i that is computed by the recursive call TREEMONODIAM3$(T_i, |T_i|, x_i)$. By the induction hypothesis, we have

$$|E_i| \leq 6|T_i| \log \log |T_i| + 1 \leq 6|T_i| \log \log \sqrt{n} + 1.$$

It follows that

$$\sum_{i=1}^{g} |E_i| \leq g + \sum_{i=1}^{g} 6|T_i| \log \log \sqrt{n} \leq n + 6n \log \log \sqrt{n}.$$

Putting everything together, we get the following upper bound on the size of the edge set E:

$$|E| = |E'| + |E''| + \sum_{i=1}^{g} |E_i|$$
$$\leq 6n + 6n \log \log \sqrt{n}$$
$$= 6n \log \log n$$
$$\leq 6n \log \log n + 1.$$

It remains to analyze the running time of the algorithm. Let $n \geq 5$, and assume that we have already computed the centroid tree of T. Then, by Lemma 12.1.6, the algorithm spends $O(n)$ time at each level of the recursion. Since the recursion depth is $O(\log \log n)$, it follows that the total running time of algorithm TREEMONODIAM3(T, n, x) is $O(n \log \log n)$. Hence, the entire algorithm for computing the graph G, when only given T as input, takes $O(n \log n)$ time. ∎

12.1.3 Generalization to larger monotone diameters

Our goal is to generalize the results of Theorems 12.1.3 and 12.1.7 to monotone diameters that are larger than 3. We first introduce the general idea before getting into the details.

> **General approach:** Given the tree T with n vertices, and given an integer $k \geq 4$, we choose an integer ℓ_k and remove approximately n/ℓ_k cut vertices, together with their incident edges, such that each of the resulting components contains less than ℓ_k vertices. As in Section 12.1.2, we connect each vertex v of T that is not a cut vertex by an edge to each of the cut vertices that is a border vertex of the component containing v. Then we run the algorithm recursively, with the same value of k, on each of the components. We would like to run the algorithm, with k replaced by $k - 2$, on the cut vertices. For this, we have to connect the cut vertices into a tree. We will see that this can be done by "inheriting" the tree structure of T. The disadvantage is that the T-monotone diameter of the resulting graph will be $2k$ instead of k. We will choose ℓ_k such that (i) the number of edges that are added at each level of the recursion is $O(n)$, and (ii) the recursion depth is as small as possible. It turns out that the "correct" value of ℓ_k is related to the inverse of the Ackermann function.

The next section is devoted to the understanding of the details of the Ackermann function and its inverse.

12.1.4 The Ackermann function and its inverse

The set of nonnegative integers will be denoted by $\mathbb{N}$. We will use the following notation. For any function $f : \mathbb{N} \longrightarrow \mathbb{N}$ and any $s \in \mathbb{N}$, we denote the s-fold iteration of f by $f^{(s)}$. That is, the functions $f^{(s)} : \mathbb{N} \longrightarrow \mathbb{N}$ are inductively defined as follows:

$$f^{(0)}(n) := n, \text{ for all } n \geq 0,$$

and

$$f^{(s)}(n) := f(f^{(s-1)}(n)), \text{ for all } n \geq 0 \text{ and } s \geq 1.$$

Definition 12.1.8. For each $k \geq 0$, the functions $A_k : \mathbb{N} \longrightarrow \mathbb{N}$ and $B_k : \mathbb{N} \longrightarrow \mathbb{N}$ are recursively defined as follows:

$$A_0(n) := 2n, \text{ for all } n \geq 0,$$

$$A_k(n) := \begin{cases} 1 & \text{if } k \geq 1 \text{ and } n = 0, \\ A_{k-1}(A_k(n-1)) & \text{if } k \geq 1 \text{ and } n \geq 1, \end{cases}$$

$$B_0(n) := n^2, \text{ for all } n \geq 0,$$

$$B_k(n) := \begin{cases} 2 & \text{if } k \geq 1 \text{ and } n = 0, \\ B_{k-1}(B_k(n-1)) & \text{if } k \geq 1 \text{ and } n \geq 1. \end{cases}$$

The following lemma gives an alternative way for computing the functions A_k and B_k. The claims can be proved by a straightforward induction on n.

Lemma 12.1.9. *For all $k \geq 1$ and $n \geq 0$, we have*

1. $A_k(n) = A_{k-1}^{(n)}(1)$, *and*
2. $B_k(n) = B_{k-1}^{(n)}(2)$.

Let us consider some examples. Using Definition 12.1.8 or Lemma 12.1.9, it can be verified that for all $n \geq 0$,

- $A_1(n) = 2^n$,
- $A_2(n) = \underbrace{2^{2^{\cdot^{\cdot^{\cdot^{2}}}}}}_{n}$,
- $B_1(n) = 2^{2^n}$,
- $B_2(n) = \underbrace{2^{2^{\cdot^{\cdot^{\cdot^{2}}}}}}_{2n+1}$.

It should be clear from these examples that, for $k \geq 2$, the functions A_k and B_k are extremely fast growing. The next four lemmas state some useful monotonicity properties of these functions.

Lemma 12.1.10. *For all $k \geq 0$ and $n \geq 0$, we have*
1. $A_k(n) \geq 2n$ *and*
2. $B_k(n) \geq n^2$.

PROOF The claims can be proved by double inductions on k and n. ∎

Lemma 12.1.11. *For all $k \geq 0$, the functions A_k and B_k are nondecreasing.*

PROOF It follows immediately from the definition of A_0 that this function is nondecreasing. Let $k \geq 1$ and $n \geq 1$. We have

$$A_k(n) = A_{k-1}(A_k(n-1)) \geq 2A_k(n-1) \geq A_k(n-1),$$

where the equality holds by definition, and the first of the two inequalities is due to Lemma 12.1.10. Thus, the function A_k is nondecreasing. The proof that each of the functions $B_k, k \geq 0$, is nondecreasing is similar. ∎

Lemma 12.1.12. *For all $k \geq 0$ and $n \geq 0$, we have $A_{k+1}(n) \geq A_k(n)$.*

PROOF The claim can be proved using Lemmas 12.1.10 and 12.1.11. ∎

Lemma 12.1.13. *For all $k \geq 0$ and $n \geq 3$, we have $A_k(n+1) \leq A_{k+1}(n)$.*

PROOF First observe that, by Lemma 12.1.12,

$$A_{k+1}(n-1) \geq A_0(n-1) = 2n - 2 \geq n + 1.$$

Since the function A_k is nondecreasing, it follows that

$$A_{k+1}(n) = A_k(A_{k+1}(n-1)) \geq A_k(n+1),$$

which is what we wanted to show. ∎

We now define the functional inverses of the functions A_k and B_k.

Definition 12.1.14. For each $k \geq 0$, we define the functions $\alpha_{2k} : \mathbb{N} \longrightarrow \mathbb{N}$ and $\alpha_{2k+1} : \mathbb{N} \longrightarrow \mathbb{N}$ as follows:

1. $\alpha_{2k}(n) := \min\{s \geq 0 : A_k(s) \geq n\}$, for all $n \geq 0$, and

2. $\alpha_{2k+1}(n) := \min\{s \geq 0 : B_k(s) \geq n\}$, for all $n \geq 0$.

Observe that, by Lemma 12.1.10, these functions are well-defined. Let us look at some examples. For each $n \geq 0$, we define

$$\log^* n := \min\{s \geq 0 : \underbrace{\log \log \ldots \log}_{s} n \leq 1\}.$$

(Observe that $\log^* 0 = \log^* 1 = 0$.) For all $n \geq 0$, we have

- $\alpha_0(n) = \lceil n/2 \rceil$,
- $\alpha_1(n) = \lceil \sqrt{n} \rceil$,
- $\alpha_2(n) = \lceil \log n \rceil$,
- $\alpha_3(n) = \lceil \log \log n \rceil$,
- $\alpha_4(n) = \log^* n$,
- $\alpha_5(n) = \lfloor \frac{1}{2} \log^* n \rfloor$.

Lemma 12.1.15. *For each $k \geq 0$, the function α_k is nondecreasing.*

PROOF   We will prove the claim for even values of k. (For odd values of k, the proof is similar.) For simplicity, we write $2k$ instead of k. Let m and n be two nonnegative integers such that $m < n$. We will prove that $\alpha_{2k}(m) \leq \alpha_{2k}(n)$.

Let $s := \alpha_{2k}(n)$. By the definition of the function α_{2k}, we have $A_k(s) \geq n$. Since $m < n$, we also have $A_k(s) \geq m$. Then, the definition of α_{2k} implies that $\alpha_{2k}(m) \leq s$, i.e., $\alpha_{2k}(m) \leq \alpha_{2k}(n)$. ∎

In Lemma 12.1.18 below, we will state a useful characterization of the functions α_k. Before we can prove it, we need two more lemmas.

Lemma 12.1.16. *For each $k \geq 1$, we have*

1. $\alpha_{2k}(n) = 1 + \alpha_{2k}(\alpha_{2k-2}(n))$, *for all $n \geq 2$, and*

2. $\alpha_{2k+1}(n) = 1 + \alpha_{2k+1}(\alpha_{2k-1}(n))$, *for all $n \geq 3$.*

PROOF   Let $k \geq 1$ and $n \geq 2$. Since the function A_{k-1} is nondecreasing, it follows from the definition of the function α_{2k-2} that, for all $m \geq 0$,

$$A_{k-1}(m) \geq n \text{ if and only if } m \geq \alpha_{2k-2}(n).$$

By using this equivalence, we get the following chain of equalities:

$$
\begin{aligned}
\alpha_{2k}(n) &= \min\{s \geq 0 : A_k(s) \geq n\} \\
&= \min\{s \geq 1 : A_k(s) \geq n\} \\
&= \min\{s \geq 1 : A_{k-1}(A_k(s-1)) \geq n\} \\
&= \min\{s \geq 1 : A_k(s-1) \geq \alpha_{2k-2}(n)\} \\
&= 1 + \min\{s' \geq 0 : A_k(s') \geq \alpha_{2k-2}(n)\} \\
&= 1 + \alpha_{2k}(\alpha_{2k-2}(n)),
\end{aligned}
$$

proving the first claim. The second claim can be proved in a similar way. ∎

Lemma 12.1.17. *Let $k \geq 0$.*

1. *For each $n \geq 2$, there is an $s \geq 1$, such that $\alpha_{2k}^{(s)}(n) \leq 1$.*

2. *For each $n \geq 3$, there is an $s \geq 1$, such that $\alpha_{2k+1}^{(s)}(n) \leq 2$.*

PROOF We will prove the first claim, and leave the proof of the second claim to the reader. By Lemma 12.1.10, we have $A_k(m-1) \geq 2(m-1) \geq m$, for all $m \geq 2$. Then, the definition of the function α_{2k} implies that

$$\alpha_{2k}(m) \leq m - 1, \text{ for all } m \geq 2. \tag{12.2}$$

Assume that $\alpha_{2k}^{(s)}(n) \geq 2$ for all $s \geq 1$. For $s = n$, this reads $\alpha_{2k}^{(n)}(n) \geq 2$. On the other hand, by repeatedly applying (12.2), we obtain

$$\begin{aligned}
\alpha_{2k}^{(n)}(n) &= \alpha_{2k}(\alpha_{2k}^{(n-1)}(n)) \\
&\leq \alpha_{2k}^{(n-1)}(n) - 1 \\
&\leq \alpha_{2k}^{(n-2)}(n) - 2 \\
&\;\;\vdots \\
&\leq \alpha_{2k}^{(1)}(n) - (n-1) \\
&= \alpha_{2k}(n) - (n-1) \\
&\leq 0,
\end{aligned}$$

which is a contradiction. ∎

Lemma 12.1.18. *For all $k \geq 1$ and $n \geq 0$, we have*

1. $\alpha_{2k}(n) = \min\{s \geq 0 : \alpha_{2k-2}^{(s)}(n) \leq 1\}$, *and*

2. $\alpha_{2k+1}(n) = \min\{s \geq 0 : \alpha_{2k-1}^{(s)}(n) \leq 2\}$.

PROOF We prove only the first claim. The second claim can be proved in a similar way. If $n \in \{0, 1\}$, then the first claim follows from the fact that $\alpha_{2k}(n) = 0$. Assume that $n \geq 2$. Let $s \geq 1$ be the smallest integer such that $\alpha_{2k-2}^{(s)}(n) \leq 1$. By Lemma 12.1.17, s is well-defined. Observe that $\alpha_{2k-2}^{(j)}(n) \geq 2$ for all j with $0 \leq j < s$. By applying Lemma 12.1.16 twice, we get

$$\begin{aligned}
\alpha_{2k}(n) &= 1 + \alpha_{2k}(\alpha_{2k-2}(n)) \\
&= 2 + \alpha_{2k}(\alpha_{2k-2}(\alpha_{2k-2}(n))) \\
&= 2 + \alpha_{2k}(\alpha_{2k-2}^{(2)}(n)).
\end{aligned}$$

Repeating this, we get

$$\begin{aligned}
\alpha_{2k}(n) &= 3 + \alpha_{2k}(\alpha_{2k-2}^{(3)}(n)) \\
&= 4 + \alpha_{2k}(\alpha_{2k-2}^{(4)}(n)) \\
&\;\;\vdots \\
&= (s-1) + \alpha_{2k}(\alpha_{2k-2}^{(s-1)}(n)) \\
&= s + \alpha_{2k}(\alpha_{2k-2}^{(s)}(n)).
\end{aligned}$$

Since $\alpha_{2k-2}^{(s)}(n) \in \{0, 1\}$, we have $\alpha_{2k}(\alpha_{2k-2}^{(s)}(n)) = 0$. Hence, $\alpha_{2k}(n) = s$, which is exactly what we wanted to show. ∎

We now define the Ackermann function A and its functional inverse α.

Definition 12.1.19 (Ackermann function). The *Ackermann function* $A : \mathbb{N} \longrightarrow \mathbb{N}$ is defined by

$$A(n) := A_n(n), \text{ for all } n \geq 0.$$

The reader can easily verify that $A(0) = 0$, $A(1) = 2$, $A(2) = 4$, $A(3) = 2^{16} = 65{,}536$. Moreover, we have

$$A(4) = A_3 \left(\underbrace{2^{2^{2^{\cdot^{\cdot^{2}}}}}}_{65,536} \right).$$

Definition 12.1.20 (inverse Ackermann function). The *inverse Ackermann function* $\alpha : \mathbb{N} \longrightarrow \mathbb{N}$ is defined by

$$\alpha(n) := \min\{s \geq 0 : A(s) \geq n\}, \text{ for all } n \geq 0.$$

By Lemma 12.1.10, we have $A(n) = A_n(n) \geq 2n \geq n$, for all $n \geq 0$. Therefore, the function α is well-defined. It is not difficult to verify that $\alpha(0) = 0$, $\alpha(1) = 1$, $\alpha(2) = 1$, $\alpha(3) = 2$, and $\alpha(65{,}536) = 3$. Although the function α is unbounded, it grows extremely slowly. In fact, for all practical applications, we have $\alpha(n) \leq 4$.

Lemma 12.1.21. *The function α is nondecreasing.*

PROOF   The proof is similar to that of Lemma 12.1.15.   ∎

We now consider the behavior of the function $\alpha_{2k}(n)$, for values of k that are close to $\alpha(n)$. Observe that for such k, the index of the function α_{2k} depends on n.

Lemma 12.1.22. *The following inequalities hold.*
1. $\alpha_{2\alpha(n)-2}(n) \geq \alpha(n)$, *for all $n \geq 1$,*
2. $\alpha_{2\alpha(n)}(n) \leq \alpha(n)$, *for all $n \geq 0$, and*
3. $\alpha_{2\alpha(n)+2}(n) \leq 4$, *for all $n \geq 0$.*

PROOF   Let $n \geq 1$. The definition of the function α implies that

$$A_{\alpha(n)-1}(\alpha(n) - 1) = A(\alpha(n) - 1) < n.$$

Combining this with the definition of the function $\alpha_{2\alpha(n)-2}(n)$, i.e.,

$$\alpha_{2\alpha(n)-2}(n) = \min\{s \geq 0 : A_{\alpha(n)-1}(s) \geq n\},$$

and the fact that the function $A_{\alpha(n)-1}$ is nondecreasing, we obtain that $\alpha_{2\alpha(n)-2}(n) > \alpha(n) - 1$. Since $\alpha_{2\alpha(n)-2}(n)$ and $\alpha(n)$ are integers, this proves the first inequality. To prove the second inequality, let $n \geq 0$. The definition of the function α implies that

$$A_{\alpha(n)}(\alpha(n)) = A(\alpha(n)) \geq n.$$

Since

$$\alpha_{2\alpha(n)}(n) = \min\{s \geq 0 : A_{\alpha(n)}(s) \geq n\},$$

it follows that $\alpha_{2\alpha(n)}(n) \leq \alpha(n)$.

It remains to prove the third inequality. Let $n \geq 0$. Lemma 12.1.13 implies that for all $k \geq 0$,

$$A_{k+1}(3) \geq A_k(4) \geq A_{k-1}(5) \geq \ldots \geq A_0(k + 4) = 2(k + 4) \geq k.$$

Combining this inequality with the fact that the function A_k is nondecreasing, we get

$$A_{k+1}(4) = A_k(A_{k+1}(3)) \geq A_k(k) = A(k),$$

for all $k \geq 0$. For $k := \alpha(n)$, this reads

$$A_{\alpha(n)+1}(4) \geq A(\alpha(n)).$$

By the definition of α, we have $A(\alpha(n)) \geq n$. Hence,

$$A_{\alpha(n)+1}(4) \geq n.$$

Then, the definition of the function value $\alpha_{2\alpha(n)+2}(n)$, that is,

$$\alpha_{2\alpha(n)+2}(n) = \min\{s \geq 0 : A_{\alpha(n)+1}(s) \geq n\},$$

immediately implies that $\alpha_{2\alpha(n)+2}(n) \leq 4$. ∎

12.1.5 Monotone diameter $2k$

In this section, we present the algorithm that solves Problem 12.1.2 (SHORTCUTTING TREE) for T-monotone diameters that are larger than 3. However, note that the achieved diameter of the resulting graph will be $2k$, rather than k.

Let T be a rooted tree with n vertices, let $k \geq 4$ be an integer, and let $\ell = \alpha_{k-2}(n)$. The algorithm will remove approximately n/ℓ cut vertices, together with their incident edges, such that each of the resulting components contains less than ℓ vertices. It constructs the set E'' as in algorithm TREEMONODIAM3 in Section 12.1.2, and calls itself recursively (with the same value of k) for each of the components. Next, the algorithm uses the structure of T to connect the cut vertices into a tree T', and calls itself recursively (with k replaced by $k - 2$) on this new tree. We will see that, in the final graph, any two vertices of T, such that one is an ancestor of the other, are connected by a T-monotone path, consisting of at most k edges. This will imply that the T-monotone diameter of this graph is less than or equal to $2k$. A formal description of the algorithm follows.

Algorithm TREEMONODIAM(T, n, r, x, k)

Comment: This algorithm takes as input a tree T having n vertices and that is rooted at r, the root x of the centroid tree $CT(T)$, and an integer $k \geq 1$. The algorithm returns a graph having T-monotone diameter less than or equal to $2k$.

If $k = 1$, then return the complete graph on the vertices of T. If $k = 2$, then call algorithm TREEMONODIAM2(T, n), and return the edge set that is returned by this algorithm. If $k = 3$, then call algorithm TREEMONODIAM3(T, n, x), and return the edge set that is returned by this algorithm.
Assume that $k \geq 4$. If $1 \leq n \leq k + 1$, then the algorithm returns the edge set E of T. Assume that $n \geq k + 2$.

Step 1: Let $\ell := \alpha_{k-2}(n)$. Use the centroid tree $CT(T)$ to compute the set CV_ℓ of cut vertices of T (see Lemma 12.1.5), and let $CV_\ell' := CV_\ell \cup \{r\}$.

Step 2: Construct a tree T' with vertex set CV_ℓ' and root r, by making each vertex u of CV_ℓ a child of the first vertex of CV_ℓ' on the path in T from u to r. Run algorithm CENTROIDDECOMP($T', |CV_\ell'|$), and let x' be the root of the centroid tree of T' that is returned by this algorithm.

Step 3: If $k = 4$, then run algorithm TREEMONODIAM2($T', |CV_\ell'|$) of Section 12.1.1. If $k = 5$, then run algorithm TREEMONODIAM3($T', |CV_\ell'|, x'$) of Section 12.1.2. If $k \geq 6$, then run algorithm TREEMONODIAM($T', |CV_\ell'|, r, x', k - 2$). Let E' be the edge set that is computed in this step.

Step 4: Compute the subtrees $T_1, T_2, \ldots, T_g$ obtained by removing the vertices of CV_ℓ from T, and compute the edge set

$$E'' := \{\{v, u\} : \ v \notin CV_\ell, u \in CV_\ell, \ u \text{ is a border vertex of the}$$
$$\text{subtree that has } v \text{ as a vertex}\}.$$

For each i with $1 \leq i \leq g$, compute the vertex r_i of T_i that is closest to the root of T, set x_i to the node of $CT(T)$ that represents T_i, run algorithm TREEMONODIAM($T_i, |T_i|, r_i, x_i, k$), and let E_i be the edge set returned by this algorithm.

Step 5: Return the edge set $E := E' \cup E'' \cup E_1 \cup E_2 \cup \ldots \cup E_g$.

Let us see why algorithm TREEMONODIAM(T, n, r, x, k) terminates. Assume that $k \geq 4$ and $n \geq k + 2$. Since $n \geq 6$, it follows from the definition of the function α_{k-2} that $\ell \geq 1$. Also, by inequality (12.2) in the proof of Lemma 12.1.17, we have $\ell = \alpha_{k-2}(n) \leq n - 1$, if k is even. It is easy to verify that this inequality also holds if k is odd. Hence, we have $\ell < n$, which implies that each tree T_i in the recursive call TREEMONODIAM($T_i, |T_i|, r_i, x_i, k$) has less than n vertices.

We now analyze the T-monotone diameter of the graph that is computed by algorithm TREEMONODIAM.

Lemma 12.1.23. *Let T be a rooted tree with vertex set V, let u and v be two distinct vertices of T such that u is an ancestor of v, let $k \geq 1$ be an integer, and let $G = (V, E)$ be the graph that is computed by algorithm* TREEMONODIAM(T, n, r, x, k). *There is a T-monotone path in G between u and v consisting of at most k edges.*

PROOF   The proof is by induction on k. If $k = 1$, then the claim clearly holds. If $k \in \{2, 3\}$, then the claim follows from Theorems 12.1.3 and 12.1.7.

Let $k \geq 4$, and assume the lemma holds for all trees and all values that are less than k. If the number of vertices of T is less than or equal to $k + 1$, then the lemma clearly holds. Let $n \geq k + 2$, and assume that the lemma holds for k, and for all trees having fewer than n vertices.

Consider the set CV'_ℓ of vertices in T that is computed in Step 1 of the algorithm. There are several different cases to consider.

First assume that u and v are both elements of CV'_ℓ. In the tree T' that is constructed in Step 2, u is an ancestor of v. Therefore, by the induction hypothesis, the graph (CV'_ℓ, E') that is computed in Step 3 contains a T'-monotone path between u and v, consisting of at most $k - 2$ edges. This path is a T-monotone path in the graph G.

Next assume that $u \in CV'_\ell$ and $v \notin CV'_\ell$. Let w be the first vertex of CV'_ℓ on the path in T from v to u. If $u = w$, then $\{v, u\}$ is an edge in G, which forms a T-monotone path between u and v. Assume that $u \neq w$. Since u is an ancestor of w in T', the graph G contains a T-monotone path between u and w consisting of at most $k - 2$ edges. Since $\{v, w\}$ is an edge in G, and since w is an ancestor of v, it follows that G contains a T-monotone path between u and v consisting of at most $k - 1$ edges. The case when $v \in CV'_\ell$ and $u \notin CV'_\ell$ is symmetric.

The next case is when neither u nor v is an element of CV'_ℓ, and these two vertices are in different subtrees (see Step 4 in the algorithm). Let w and w' be the first and last vertices of CV_ℓ on the path in T from u to v, respectively. If $w = w'$, then $\{u, w\}$ and $\{w, v\}$ are edges in G and form a T-monotone path between u and v. Assume that $w \neq w'$. Since w is an ancestor of w' in T', the graph G contains a T'-monotone path between w and w' consisting of at most $k - 2$ edges. Since $\{v, w\}$ and $\{w', v\}$ are edges in G, it follows that G contains a T-monotone path between u and v consisting of at most k edges.

The final case is when u and v are contained in the same subtree, say T_i. Observe that u is an ancestor of v in T_i. Therefore, by the induction hypothesis, the recursive call TREEMONODIAM($T_i, |T_i|, r_i, x_i, k$) in Step 4 computes a graph in which u and v are connected by a T_i-monotone path consisting of at most k edges. This path is also a path in G, and it is T-monotone. ∎

Lemma 12.1.24. *Let T be a rooted tree with n vertices, and let $k \geq 1$ be an integer. Algorithm* TREEMONODIAM(T, n, r, x, k) *computes a graph whose T-monotone diameter is less than or equal to $2k$.*

PROOF Let u and v be two distinct vertices of T and let w be their lowest common ancestor. The claim follows by applying Lemma 12.1.23 to w and u, and to w and v. ∎

Lemma 12.1.25. *Let $k \geq 2$ be an integer, and let $F_k(n)$ be the maximum number of edges in the graph computed by algorithm* TREEMONODIAM(T, n, r, x, k), *where T ranges over all trees having n vertices. Then,*

1. $F_k(n) \leq 2^k n \alpha_k(n)$, *if k is even, and*
2. $F_k(n) \leq 3 \cdot 2^{k-2} n \alpha_k(n) + 1$, *if k is odd.*

PROOF We give only the proof for even values of k. The case when k is odd can be analyzed in a similar way.

We will prove by induction on k that $F_k(n) \leq 2^k n \alpha_k(n)$, for all $n \geq 1$. We start the induction with $k = 2$. For this case, the claim follows from Theorem 12.1.3. Let $k \geq 4$, and assume that

$$F_{k-2}(s) \leq 2^{k-2} s \alpha_{k-2}(s), \tag{12.3}$$

for all $s \geq 1$. If $n = 1$, then $F_k(n) = 0 \leq 2^k n \alpha_k(n)$. If $2 \leq n \leq k + 1$, then $F_k(n) = n - 1 \leq 2^k n \alpha_k(n)$, because, by Lemma 12.1.16, $\alpha_k(n) \geq 1$. So let $n \geq k + 2$, and assume that

$$F_k(s) \leq 2^k s \alpha_k(s), \tag{12.4}$$

for all s with $1 \leq s < n$. Let T be a tree with n vertices for which the edge set E that is computed by algorithm TREEMONODIAM(T, n, r, x, k) has $F_k(n)$ edges.

The number of edges in the set E' that is computed in Step 3 of the algorithm is less than or equal to $F_{k-2}(|CV'_\ell|)$. By Lemma 12.1.5, we have $|CV'_\ell| = 1 + |CV_\ell| \leq 1 + 2n/\ell \leq 3n/\ell$. Therefore, by the induction hypothesis (12.3), and since the function α_{k-2} is nondecreasing, we have

$$|E'| \leq 2^{k-2}(3n/\ell)\alpha_{k-2}(n) = 3 \cdot 2^{k-2}n.$$

By Lemma 12.1.6, the number of edges in the set E'' that is computed in Step 4 of the algorithm is less than or equal to $3n$.

Let i be any integer with $1 \leq i \leq g$, and consider the edge set E_i that is computed in Step 4 of the algorithm. We have $|E_i| \leq F_k(|T_i|)$. Therefore, since $|T_i| < \ell < n$, and since the function α_k is nondecreasing, the induction hypothesis (12.4) implies that $|E_i| \leq 2^k |T_i| \alpha_k(\ell)$. By Lemma 12.1.16, we have

$$\alpha_k(n) = 1 + \alpha_k(\alpha_{k-2}(n)) = 1 + \alpha_k(\ell).$$

Hence,

$$\sum_{i=1}^{g} |E_i| \leq \sum_{i=1}^{g} 2^k |T_i|(\alpha_k(n) - 1) \leq 2^k n(\alpha_k(n) - 1).$$

We conclude that

$$
\begin{aligned}
F_k(n) &= |E| \\
&= |E'| + |E''| + \sum_{i=1}^{g} |E_i| \\
&\leq 3 \cdot 2^{k-2}n + 3n + 2^k n(\alpha_k(n) - 1) \\
&= 2^k n \alpha_k(n) + (3 \cdot 2^{k-2} + 3 - 2^k)n \\
&\leq 2^k n \alpha_k(n).
\end{aligned}
$$

This completes the proof. ∎

It remains to analyze the running time of algorithm TREEMONODIAM. For any integer $k \geq 2$, let $C_k(n)$ denote the worst-case running time of algorithm TREEMONODIAM(T, n, r, x, k), when given as input any tree T with n vertices that is rooted at r, and the root x of the centroid tree $CT(T)$.

By Theorems 12.1.3 and 12.1.7, $C_k(n) = O(n \log n)$ for $k \in \{2, 3\}$. Let $k \geq 4$. Step 1 of algorithm TREEMONODIAM(T, n, r, x, k) takes $O(n)$ time, whereas Step 2 takes $O(n \log n)$ time. The time for Step 3 is at most $C_{k-2}(3n/\alpha_{k-2}(n))$. Finally, Step 4 takes time $O(n) + \sum_{i=1}^{g} C_k(n_i)$, where n_i is the number of vertices of the tree T_i. Hence, we obtain the recurrence

$$C_k(n) = O(n \log n) + C_{k-2}(3n/\alpha_{k-2}(n)) + \sum_{i=1}^{g} C_k(n_i),$$

where $n_i < \alpha_{k-2}(n)$, for each i with $1 \le i \le g$, and $\sum_{i=1}^{g} n_i \le n$. As in the proof of Lemma 12.1.25, it can be shown that $C_k(n) = O(2^k n \alpha_k(n) \log n)$.

Since, by Lemma 12.1.4, the initial centroid tree $CT(T)$ of T can be computed in $O(n \log n)$ time, the entire algorithm for computing a graph whose T-monotone diameter is at most $2k$, when only given T as input, is $O(2^k n \alpha_k(n) \log n)$. We have proved the following result.

Theorem 12.1.26. *Let T be a tree with n vertices, and let $k \ge 4$ be an integer. In $O(2^k n \alpha_k(n) \log n)$ time, we can compute a graph on these vertices, having $O(2^k n \alpha_k(n))$ edges, and whose T-monotone diameter is less than or equal to $2k$.*

12.1.6 Shortcutting trees using $O(n)$ edges

Theorem 12.1.26 does not give us a shortcutting that uses $O(n)$ edges. In this section, we show that a simple variation of algorithm TREEMONODIAM, together with Exercise 2.8, leads to such a shortcutting.

We fix a constant c such that $2^{2\alpha(n)+2} \le n$, for all $n \ge c$.

Algorithm TREEMONODIAMLIN(T, n, r)

Comment: This algorithm takes as input a tree T having n vertices and that is rooted at r. It returns a graph with $O(n)$ edges, whose T-monotone diameter is $O(\alpha(n))$.

If $1 \le n < c$, then the algorithm returns the edge set E of T. Assume that $n \ge c$.

Step 1: Let $k := 2\alpha(n) + 2$ and $\ell := 2^k$. Use algorithm CENTROIDDECOMP(T, n) to compute a centroid tree $CT(T)$ of T. Use this centroid tree to compute the set CV_ℓ of cut vertices of T, see Lemma 12.1.5, and let $CV'_\ell := CV_\ell \cup \{r\}$.

Step 2: Construct a tree T' with vertex set CV'_ℓ and root r, by making each vertex u of CV_ℓ a child of the first vertex of CV'_ℓ on the path in T from u to r. Run algorithm CENTROIDDECOMP$(T', |CV'_\ell|)$, and let x' be the root of the centroid tree of T' that is returned by this algorithm.

Step 3: Run algorithm TREEMONODIAM$(T', |CV'_\ell|, r, x', k)$. Let E' be the edge set that is computed in this step.

Step 4: Compute the subtrees $T_1, T_2, \ldots, T_g$ obtained by removing the vertices of CV_ℓ from T, and compute the edge set

$$E'' := \{\{v, u\} : \ v \notin CV_\ell, u \in CV_\ell, \ u \text{ is a border vertex of the}$$
$$\text{subtree that has } v \text{ as a vertex}\}.$$

For each i with $1 \le i \le g$, let V_i be the vertex set of T_i, and compute a graph (V_i, E_i) having $O(|V_i|)$ edges, and whose T_i-monotone diameter is $O(\log |V_i|)$; see Exercise 2.8.

Step 5: Return the edge set $E := E' \cup E'' \cup E_1 \cup E_2 \cup \ldots \cup E_g$.

In exactly the same way as in Lemmas 12.1.23 and 12.1.24, it can be shown that the T-monotone diameter of the graph that is computed by this algorithm is

$$O(\max(c, k, \log \ell)) = O(\alpha(n)).$$

We estimate the number of edges in this graph. Assume that $n \geq c$. By Theorem 12.1.26 and Lemma 12.1.5, the size of the edge set E' that is computed in Step 3 satisfies

$$|E'| = O\left(2^k |CV'_\ell| \cdot \alpha_k(|CV'_\ell|)\right) = O\left(2^k (n/\ell)\alpha_k(n)\right) = O(n\alpha_k(n)).$$

Since, by Lemma 12.1.22, $\alpha_k(n) = \alpha_{2\alpha(n)+2}(n) \leq 4$, it follows that $|E'| = O(n)$. By Lemma 12.1.6, and since $n \geq \ell$, the size of the edge set E'' that is computed in Step 4 is less than or equal to $3n = O(n)$. Finally, we have

$$\sum_{i=1}^{g} |E_i| = O\left(\sum_{i=1}^{g} |V_i|\right) = O(n).$$

Hence, the total number of edges in the graph is $O(n)$. In a similar way, it can be shown that the algorithm takes $O(n \log n)$ time. We have proved the following result.

Theorem 12.1.27. *Let T be a tree with n vertices. In $O(n \log n)$ time, we can compute a graph on these vertices, having $O(n)$ edges, and whose T-monotone diameter is $O(\alpha(n))$.*

12.2 Spanners with low spanner diameter

We now show how the results of the previous section can be used to obtain spanners with low spanner diameter. The best results we have seen so far, are those of Theorems 4.3.10, 5.5.6, and 10.2.3, and Exercise 11.5, giving spanners with $O(n)$ edges and $O(\log n)$ spanner diameter.

Let S be a set of n points in $\mathbb{R}^d$, and let $t > 1$ be a real number. By the Dumbbell Theorem (Theorem 11.9.1), there exist $O((1/(t-1))^d \log(1/(t-1)))$ dumbbell trees having the following properties.

1. Each dumbbell tree has size $O(n)$ and stores the points of S at its leaves, and each internal node stores a representative point of S.
2. For any two leaves u and v of any dumbbell tree T, the geometric path corresponding to u and v is the path in $\mathbb{R}^d$ defined by the representatives of all nodes on the path in T between u and v.
3. For any two distinct points p and q of S, there is a dumbbell tree T such that the geometric path between p and q that corresponds to the leaves of T that store p and q, is a t-spanner path.

For each of these dumbbell trees T, let G_T be a shortcutting of T having T-monotone diameter k. Then for any two distinct points p and q of S, there is a dumbbell tree T such that

1. the geometric path P between p and q that corresponds to the leaves u and v of T that store p and q, is a t-spanner path, and
2. the graph G_T contains a T-monotone path Q between the leaves u and v in T consisting of at most k edges.

Since Q is a T-monotone path, and since the length of P is less than or equal to $t|pq|$, the triangle inequality implies that the geometric path corresponding to Q is a t-spanner path between p and q. Hence, the geometric graph implied by the collection of all graphs G_T constitutes a t-spanner for S, whose spanner diameter is less than or equal to k.

Therefore, by combining Theorems 11.9.1, 12.1.3, 12.1.7, 12.1.26, and 12.1.27, we obtain the main result of this chapter.

Theorem 12.2.1. *Let S be a set of n points in $\mathbb{R}^d$, and let $t > 1$ be a real number.*

1. *In time*

$$O\left(\frac{\log(1/(t-1))}{(t-1)^d} n \log n + n/(t-1)^{2d}\right),$$

a t-spanner for S can be computed, which has

$$O\left(\frac{\log(1/(t-1))}{(t-1)^d} n \log n\right)$$

edges, and whose spanner diameter is 2.

2. *In time*

$$O\left(\frac{\log(1/(t-1))}{(t-1)^d} n \log n + n/(t-1)^{2d}\right),$$

a t-spanner for S can be computed, which has

$$O\left(\frac{\log(1/(t-1))}{(t-1)^d} n \log \log n\right)$$

edges, and whose spanner diameter is 3.

3. *Let $k \geq 4$ be an integer. In time*

$$O\left(\frac{\log(1/(t-1))}{(t-1)^d} 2^k n \alpha_k(n) \log n + n/(t-1)^{2d}\right),$$

a t-spanner for S can be computed, which has

$$O\left(\frac{\log(1/(t-1))}{(t-1)^d} 2^k n \alpha_k(n)\right)$$

edges, and whose spanner diameter is 2k.

4. *In time*

$$O\left(\frac{\log(1/(t-1))}{(t-1)^d} n \log n + n/(t-1)^{2d}\right),$$

a t-spanner for S can be computed, which has

$$O\left(\frac{\log(1/(t-1))}{(t-1)^d} n\right)$$

edges, and whose spanner diameter is $O(\alpha(n))$.

In Theorem 12.2.1, we have seen that, for any constant $t > 1$ and any integer $k \geq 4$, a t-spanner with $O(2^k n \alpha_k(n))$ edges and spanner diameter $2k$ can be constructed. Using an improved solution for the shortcutting problem on trees, by Bodlaender, Tel, and Santoro [1994], we obtain a t-spanner with $O(k n \alpha_k(n))$ edges and spanner diameter k. It is not clear, however, if their construction can be implemented in subquadratic time. (For the case when the points are one-dimensional, this can be done; see Exercise 12.9.)

> **Open problem:** Let S be a set of n points in $\mathbb{R}^d$, let $t > 1$ be a real constant, and let $k \geq 4$ be an integer. Give a formal proof that there exists an algorithm that computes, in $O(n \log n + k n \alpha_k(n))$ time, a t-spanner for S, having $O(k n \alpha_k(n))$ edges, and whose spanner diameter is less than or equal to k.

Bodlaender, Tel, and Santoro [1994] prove lower bounds for the shortcutting problem on trees. It is possible that their proof technique can be used to solve the following two open problems.

> **Open problem:** Let $t > 1$ be a real constant, and let $k \geq 3$ be an integer. Prove that there exists a set S of n points in $\mathbb{R}^d$, such that every t-spanner for S, whose spanner diameter is less than or equal to k, contains $\Omega(kn\alpha_k(n))$ edges. (For $k = 2$, this is true, see Exercise 12.10.)

> **Open problem:** Let $t > 1$ be a real constant. Prove that there exists a set S of n points in $\mathbb{R}^d$, such that every t-spanner for S, that consists of $O(n)$ edges, has spanner diameter $\Omega(\alpha(n))$.

Exercises

12.1. Define the function $\text{Log}^* : \mathbb{N} \longrightarrow \mathbb{N}$ by

$$\text{Log}^*(n) := \min\{s \geq 0 : \underbrace{\lceil \log \lceil \log \ldots \lceil \log n \rceil \ldots \rceil \rceil}_{s} \leq 1\}.$$

Prove that $\text{Log}^*(n) = \log^*(n)$ for all $n \geq 0$.

12.2. Use Lemma 12.1.18 to verify the values of the functions α_k, for $k \leq 5$, that are given after Definition 12.1.14.

12.3. Prove that $\lim_{n \to \infty} \alpha(n) = \infty$.

12.4. Prove the second claim in Lemma 12.1.6.

12.5. Use Exercise 2.14 to give alternative proofs of Theorems 12.1.3 and 12.1.7, for trees whose degree is bounded from above by a constant.

12.6. In Section 12.1.6, we used a constant c, such that $2^{2\alpha(n)+2} \leq n$, for all $n \geq c$. Prove that such a constant c exists.

12.7. In this chapter, we have ignored the problem of computing the various values of the functions α_k and α that are used by the shortcutting algorithms. Give an algorithm that works in the algebraic computation-tree model and that computes these values such that the running times of the shortcutting algorithms do not increase asymptotically.

12.8. In the spanners of Theorem 12.2.1, any two points are connected by a spanner path having a small number edges. Give algorithms that actually compute such spanner paths.

12.9. Let S be a sorted set of n real numbers, let $t = 1$, and let $k \geq 2$ be an integer. Give an algorithm that computes, in $O(kn\alpha_k(n))$ time, a t-spanner for S, having $O(kn\alpha_k(n))$ edges, and whose spanner diameter is less than or equal to k.

12.10. Let $t \geq 1$ be a real number. Prove that there exists a set S of n real numbers, such that every t-spanner for S, whose spanner diameter is 2, contains $\Omega(n \log n)$ edges.

Bibliographic notes

The shortcutting problem of Section 12.1 is a natural one and, not surprisingly, has been discovered by several people. Yao [1982b] and Chandra, Fortune, and Lipton [1985] give solutions for lists (in the latter paper, the problem is studied in the context of computing semigroup products on unbounded fan-in circuits). Yao also proves lower bounds. Chazelle

[1987] and Alon and Schieber [1987] solve the shortcutting problem for trees. Alternative solutions are given by Bodlaender, Tel, and Santoro [1994] (who also prove lower bounds) and Thorup [1997].

The Ackermann function is due to Ackermann [1928]. It occurs in the theory of computation, as an example of a function that is recursive (i.e., computable by a Turing machine), but not primitive–recursive. The inverse Ackermann function $\alpha(n)$ appeared for the first time in the analysis of algorithms in Tarjan [1975], where he used it to analyze the well-known union-find algorithm. This function also appears in the analysis of many geometric algorithms, see the book by Sharir and Agarwal [1995].

The algorithms of Section 12.1 are based on Bodlaender, Tel, and Santoro [1994] and Alon and Schieber [1987]. A solution to Exercise 12.7 can be found in La Poutré [1990].

All results in Theorem 12.2.1 depend exponentially on the dimension d. Chan [1998] presents an algorithm that computes, in $O(d^2 n \log n)$ time, an $O(d^{3/2})$-spanner with $O(dn \log n)$ edges and spanner diameter 2.

13

Approximating the Stretch Factor of Euclidean Graphs

> Everything that exists exists in some degree, and if it exists in some degree it ought to be measured.
>
> —Mathematician's Bill of Rights

Let S be a set of n points in $\mathbb{R}^d$, and let $G = (S, E)$ be a connected Euclidean graph having the points of S as its vertices. (In this chapter, all graphs are undirected.) For any two points p and q of S, we denote by $\delta_G(p, q)$ the length of a shortest path in G between p and q. If there is no path in G between p and q, then $\delta_G(p, q) := \infty$. Recall that the stretch factor t^* of G is given by

$$t^* = \max\left\{\frac{\delta_G(p, q)}{|pq|} : p, q \in S, p \neq q\right\}.$$

We denote the number of vertices and edges of the graph G by n and k, respectively.

In this chapter, we consider the problem of computing the stretch factor t^* of G. Clearly, we can use any algorithm solving the *all-pairs-shortest-path* problem for G to compute t^*. Hence, running Dijkstra's algorithm – implemented using Fibonacci heaps (see Corollary 2.5.10) – from each vertex of G, gives the stretch factor of G, in $O(n^2 \log n + nk)$ time. For some classes of graphs, better running times can be obtained. For example, the lengths of the shortest paths between all pairs of vertices in a Euclidean planar graph can be computed in $O(n^2)$ total time. Therefore, the stretch factor of such a graph can be computed in $O(n^2)$ time. The stretch factor of a path, cycle, or tree can be computed in subquadratic time; see the references in the bibliographic notes at the end of this chapter. There are no known algorithm that computes the stretch factor in subquadratic time, for any other broad class of connected Euclidean graphs. A reasonable problem to consider is that of designing fast algorithms for computing *approximate* stretch factors.

Definition 13.0.1. Let G be a connected Euclidean graph, let t^* denote its stretch factor, and let $c_1 \geq 1$, $c_2 \geq 1$, and $t \geq 1$ be real numbers. We say that t is a (c_1, c_2)-*approximate stretch factor* of G if

$$t/c_1 \leq t^* \leq c_2 t.$$

We will show that the well-separated pair decomposition (WSPD) can be used to reduce the problem of approximating the stretch factor to that of computing (or approximating) the lengths of shortest paths between a "small" number of pairs of vertices. In Section 13.1, we present a first approximation algorithm, which gives good results only for simple classes of Euclidean graphs such as paths, cycles, and trees. In Section 13.2, we present a simpler algorithm: We show that in order to approximate the stretch factor of a Euclidean graph G with n vertices, it suffices to compute (or approximate) the lengths of shortest paths between $O(n)$ pairs of vertices. Surprisingly, these vertex-pairs depend only on the location in space of the vertex set of G; they do not depend on the edges of G.

13.1 The first approximation algorithm

Let S be a set of n points in $\mathbb{R}^d$, and let G be a connected Euclidean graph having the points of S as its vertices. Let $s > 0$ be a real number, and let

$$\{A_1, B_1\}, \{A_2, B_2\}, \ldots, \{A_m, B_m\}$$

denote an arbitrary WSPD for S with respect to the separation ratio s.

> **Approximating the stretch factor:** By Lemma 9.1.2, (i) all Euclidean distances between a point in A_i and a point in B_i are approximately equal, (ii) the distance between any two points in A_i is much smaller than any distance between a point in A_i and a point in B_i, and (iii) the distance between any two points in B_i is much smaller than any distance between a point in A_i and a point in B_i. Therefore, if we compute for each i with $1 \le i \le m$, a point $a_i \in A_i$ and a point $b_i \in B_i$ whose distance $\delta_G(a_i, b_i)$ in G is maximum, then the largest value of $\delta_G(a_i, b_i)/|a_i b_i|$ should be a good approximation to the stretch factor t^* of G.

This observation leads to our first approximation algorithm:

> **Algorithm** APPROXSF(G, ϵ)
>
> **Comment:** This algorithm takes as input a Euclidean graph G on a set S of points in $\mathbb{R}^d$ and a real number $\epsilon > 0$. Its output is a $(1, 1 + \epsilon)$-approximate stretch factor of G.
>
> **Step 1:** Using separation ratio $s = 4/\epsilon$, compute a WSPD $\{A_i, B_i\}$, $1 \le i \le m$, for the set S.
>
> **Step 2:** For each i with $1 \le i \le m$, compute two points a_i and b_i, with $a_i \in A_i$ and $b_i \in B_i$, such that
>
> $$\delta_G(a_i, b_i) = \max\{\delta_G(p, q) : p \in A_i, q \in B_i\},$$
>
> and compute $t_i := \delta_G(a_i, b_i)/|a_i b_i|$.
>
> **Step 3:** Report the value of t, defined as $t := \max(t_1, t_2, \ldots, t_m)$. Also report points a_i and b_i for which $t = t_i$.

The following lemma proves bounds on the approximation factor of this algorithm.

Lemma 13.1.1. *The value of t reported by algorithm* APPROXSF(G, ϵ) *is a $(1, 1 + \epsilon)$-approximate stretch factor of G. That is,*

$$t \le t^* \le (1 + \epsilon)t,$$

where t^* denotes the exact stretch factor of G.

PROOF   Since the output t of the algorithm can be written as $\delta_G(p, q)/|pq|$, for some points p and q in S with $p \ne q$, it is clear that $t \le t^*$. In the rest of this proof, we will show that $t^* \le (1 + \epsilon)t$.

Let p and q be two distinct points of S such that $t^* = \delta_G(p, q)/|pq|$. Let i be the index such that (i) $p \in A_i$ and $q \in B_i$, or (ii) $p \in B_i$ and $q \in A_i$. We may assume without loss of generality that (i) holds.

Consider the points $a_i \in A_i$ and $b_i \in B_i$ that were computed in Step 2 of the algorithm. We have $\delta_G(p, q) \leq \delta_G(a_i, b_i)$. By Lemma 9.1.2, we have $|a_i b_i| \leq (1 + 4/s)|pq| = (1 + \epsilon)|pq|$. It follows that

$$t^* = \frac{\delta_G(p, q)}{|pq|} \leq \frac{\delta_G(a_i, b_i)}{|pq|} \leq (1 + \epsilon)\frac{\delta_G(a_i, b_i)}{|a_i b_i|} = (1 + \epsilon)t_i \leq (1 + \epsilon)t.$$

This completes the proof. ∎

13.1.1 Applying algorithm APPROXSF

The main problem in efficiently implementing algorithm APPROXSF is the time complexity of Step 2. In this step, we are given a sequence $\{A_i, B_i\}$, $1 \leq i \leq m$, of pairs of sets, and for each such pair, we have to compute the maximum distance (in the graph G) between sets A_i and B_i. In general, this is a difficult problem. We will first show below that this can be done efficiently for the case when the graph G is a path or a tree. Our algorithm will take advantage of the fact that the well-separated point sets A_i and B_i are not arbitrary sets of points; rather, they are sets that are stored in subtrees of the split tree T.

Approximating the stretch factor of a path

Let G be a path on the points of S. We denote these points, in the order in which they appear along the path, by $p_1, p_2, \ldots, p_n$. Let ϵ be a positive real number.

Following algorithm APPROXSF, we start by computing a split tree T and a corresponding WSPD, $\{A_i, B_i\}$, $1 \leq i \leq m$, for S, with respect to the separation ratio $s = 4/\epsilon$. By Theorem 9.4.6, we can compute such a WSPD with $m = O(s^d n) = O(n/\epsilon^d)$, in $O(n \log n + n/\epsilon^d)$ time.

Recall that each pair $\{A_i, B_i\}$ is represented by two nodes u_i and v_i in T, whose subtrees contain exactly the points of A_i and B_i in their leaves, respectively.

Let us see how Step 2 of algorithm APPROXSF can be implemented. As preprocessing for this step, we traverse the split tree T in postorder, and store with each node u the smallest and largest indices of all points of S that are stored at the leaves of the subtree rooted at u. Also, we traverse the path G, and compute for each vertex $p_j, 2 \leq j \leq n$, the distance $\delta_G(p_1, p_j)$. Using this information, we can compute, for any two indices j and k with $0 \leq j < k < n$, the distance $\delta_G(p_j, p_k)$ as the difference between $\delta_G(p_1, p_k)$ and $\delta_G(p_1, p_j)$. Thus, this preprocessing can be done in time linear in the size of the split tree, that is, $O(n)$.

Consider any index i with $1 \leq i \leq m$. Step 2 requires us to compute points a_i and b_i, where $a_i \in A_i$ and $b_i \in B_i$, such that

$$\delta_G(a_i, b_i) = \max\{\delta_G(p, q) : p \in A_i, q \in B_i\}.$$

To find these points, consider the nodes u_i and v_i of the split tree T. Let j and j' be the smallest and largest indices that are stored with u_i, respectively. Similarly, let k and k' be the smallest and largest indices that are stored with v_i, respectively. Then it is clear that

$$\max\{\delta_G(p, q) : p \in A_i, q \in B_i\} = \max\left(\delta_G(p_j, p_{k'}), \delta_G(p_{j'}, p_k)\right).$$

Step 6: For each i with $1 \leq i \leq m$, do the following. Consider the pair $\{A_i, B_i\}$ in the WSPD, and the nodes u_i and v_i in the split tree such that $A_i = S_{u_i}$ and $B_i = S_{v_i}$, respectively.

If $dist_1(u_i) = -\infty$ or $dist_2(v_i) = -\infty$, then set $t_i' := -\infty$. Otherwise, consider the point $q_1 \in A_i \cap G_1$, $q_1 \neq v$, for which $dist_1(u_i) = \delta_G(q_1, v)$, and the point $q_2 \in B_i \cap G_2$, $q_2 \neq v$, for which $dist_2(v_i) = \delta_G(q_2, v)$. Set $t_i' := \delta_G(q_1, q_2)/|q_1 q_2|$.

Symmetrically, if $dist_2(u_i) = -\infty$ or $dist_1(v_i) = -\infty$, then set $t_i'' := -\infty$. Otherwise, consider the point $q_1 \in B_i \cap G_1$, $q_1 \neq v$, for which $dist_1(v_i) = \delta_G(q_1, v)$, and the point $q_2 \in A_i \cap G_2$, $q_2 \neq v$, for which $dist_2(u_i) = \delta_G(q_2, v)$. Set $t_i'' := \delta_G(q_1, q_2)/|q_1 q_2|$.

Observe that $\delta_G(q_1, q_2)$ can be easily computed as the sum of $\delta_G(q_1, v)$ and $\delta_G(q_2, v)$, both of which have been computed in Step 2.

Step 7: The last step is to compute

$$t := \max(t_1, t_2, t_1', t_2', \ldots, t_m', t_1'', t_2'', \ldots, t_m''),$$

and return the value of t.

The correctness of this algorithm is proved in the following lemma.

Lemma 13.1.4. *The given algorithm computes a $(1, 1 + \epsilon)$-approximate stretch factor of the tree G.*

PROOF   The proof is by induction on the number n of vertices of the tree G. The algorithm trivially computes the stretch factor (exactly) when $n \leq 2$. Let $n \geq 3$ and assume that the algorithm correctly computes a $(1, 1 + \epsilon)$-approximate stretch factor of any tree with less than n vertices.

Let t^* be the exact stretch factor of the tree G. Since each of the values t_1, t_2, $t_1', t_2', \ldots, t_m', t_1'', t_2'', \ldots, t_m''$ either is $-\infty$ or has the form $\delta_G(p, q)/|pq|$ for some distinct points p and q of S, we clearly have $t \leq t^*$. It remains to show that $t^* \leq (1 + \epsilon)t$.

Let p and q be two distinct points of S such that $t^* = \delta_G(p, q)/|pq|$. We distinguish two cases.

Case 1: p and q are both vertices in G_1 or both vertices in G_2.

We may assume without loss of generality that p and q are vertices in G_1. Let t_1^* be the exact stretch factor of the tree G_1. By the induction hypothesis, we have $t_1^* \leq (1 + \epsilon)t_1$. Since the path in G between p and q is completely contained in G_1, we have $t_1^* = t^*$. This implies that

$$t^* = t_1^* \leq (1 + \epsilon)t_1 \leq (1 + \epsilon)t.$$

Case 2: p and q are in different trees.

We may assume without loss of generality that p is a vertex in G_1 and q is a vertex in G_2. Let i be the index such that (i) $p \in A_i$ and $q \in B_i$, or (ii) $p \in B_i$ and $q \in A_i$. Assume without loss of generality that (i) holds. Consider the nodes u_i and v_i of the split tree such that $A_i = S_{u_i}$ and $B_i = S_{v_i}$.

Since $p \in A_i \cap G_1$, we know that $dist_1(u_i) \neq -\infty$. Let $q_1 \in A_i \cap G_1$ be such that $dist_1(u_i) = \delta_G(q_1, v)$. Then $\delta_G(p, v) \leq \delta_G(q_1, v)$. Similarly, since $q \in B_i \cap G_2$, $dist_2(v_i) \neq -\infty$. Let $q_2 \in B_i \cap G_2$ be such that $dist_2(v_i) = \delta_G(q_2, v)$. Then $\delta_G(q, v) \leq \delta_G(q_2, v)$. We have

$$t^* = \frac{\delta_G(p, q)}{|pq|} = \frac{\delta_G(p, v) + \delta_G(v, q)}{|pq|} \leq \frac{\delta_G(q_1, v) + \delta_G(v, q_2)}{|pq|} = \frac{\delta_G(q_1, q_2)}{|pq|}.$$

By Lemma 9.1.2, we have $|q_1q_2| \leq (1 + 4/s)|pq| = (1 + \epsilon)|pq|$. It follows that

$$t^* \leq (1 + \epsilon)\frac{\delta_G(q_1, q_2)}{|q_1q_2|} = (1 + \epsilon)t_i' \leq (1 + \epsilon)t.$$

This completes the proof.   ∎

Let $\mathcal{T}(n)$ denote the running time of the algorithm on any input tree having n vertices. It is easy to see that barring the two recursive calls in Step 3, the rest of the algorithm can be implemented in $O(n \log n + n/\epsilon^d)$ time. For n sufficiently large, there are positive integers n_1 and n_2, such that $n_1 \leq 2n/3, n_2 \leq 2n/3, n_1 + n_2 = n - 1$, and

$$\mathcal{T}(n) \leq c(n \log n + n/\epsilon^d) + \mathcal{T}(n_1 + 1) + \mathcal{T}(n_2 + 1),$$

where c is a positive constant that depends neither on n nor on ϵ. This recurrence solves to $\mathcal{T}(n) = O(n \log^2 n + (n/\epsilon^d) \log n)$. Hence, we have proved the following theorem.

Theorem 13.1.5. *Let S be a set of n points in $\mathbb{R}^d$, let G be a tree having the points of S as its vertices, and let $\epsilon > 0$ be a real number. In $O(n \log^2 n + (n/\epsilon^d) \log n)$ time, we can compute a $(1, 1 + \epsilon)$-approximate stretch factor of G.*

The following section shows how the above theorem can be improved.

13.2 A faster approximation algorithm

We have seen that even for simple classes of graphs, it is not obvious how to design an efficient implementation of algorithm APPROXSF. The main problem is the farthest pair computation in Step 2, in which we compute a point $a_i \in A_i$ and a point $b_i \in B_i$ for which the distance $\delta_G(a_i, b_i)$ between a_i and b_i in G is maximum. That is, we have to solve farthest pair queries between two sets of vertices. For paths, such queries are easy to solve. For trees, however, we already had to work harder.

In this section, we give a much simpler approximation algorithm. Recall that in Step 2 of algorithm APPROXSF, for every well-separated pair $\{A_i, B_i\}$, we use $\delta_G(a_i, b_i)/|a_ib_i|$ as a candidate for the approximate stretch factor of the graph G. Below, we prove that we can take *arbitrary* points $a_i \in A_i$ and $b_i \in B_i$, and use $\delta_G(a_i, b_i)/|a_ib_i|$, or an approximation to this quantity, as a candidate. This is surprising, because the distances in the graph G between points of A_i and points of B_i can vary greatly.

As a result, the problem of approximating the stretch factor of a Euclidean graph can be reduced to the problem of solving (approximate) shortest path queries for $O(n)$ pairs of points. Such queries can, in general, be solved more efficiently than farthest pair queries between sets of points that were required when implementing algorithm APPROXSF.

Our faster approximation algorithm will be based on a remarkable theorem. Before we state this theorem, we introduce some notation. Let S be a set of n points in $\mathbb{R}^d$, and let G be a connected Euclidean graph having the points of S as its vertices. Let t^* denote the exact stretch factor of G, and let p and q be two distinct points of S for which $t^* = \delta_G(p, q)/|pq|$. Let $\{A_i, B_i\}, 1 \leq i \leq m$, denote an arbitrary WSPD for S with respect to a separation ratio $s > 4$. Let i be the index such that (i) $p \in A_i$ and $q \in B_i$, or (ii) $p \in B_i$ and $q \in A_i$. Assume without loss of generality that (i) holds.

The theorem below states that all distances in the graph G between any point of A_i and any point of B_i are approximately equal. It is important to note that this theorem applies to the pair $\{A_i, B_i\}$ that contains p and q; it does not apply to all well-separated pairs in the decomposition.

Distances in G between A_i and B_i are approximately equal: Let $x \in A_i$ and $y \in B_i$. Since $|xy|$ and $|pq|$ are approximately equal, $\delta_G(x, y)$ cannot be much larger than $\delta_G(p, q)$. Assume that $\delta_G(x, y)$ is much smaller than $\delta_G(p, q)$. Since $\delta_G(p, q) \leq \delta_G(p, x) + \delta_G(x, y) + \delta_G(y, q)$, at least one of $\delta_G(p, x)$ and $\delta_G(y, q)$ is very large. Assume $\delta_G(p, x)$ is very large. Since $|px|$ is much smaller than $|pq|$, $\delta_G(p, x)/|px|$ must be larger than $\delta_G(p, q)/|pq|$, which is not possible.

Theorem 13.2.1. *Let S be a set of n points in $\mathbb{R}^d$, and let $s > 4$ be a real number. Let G be a connected Euclidean graph having the points of S as its vertices. Let t^* denote the exact stretch factor of G and let p and q be two distinct points of S for which $t^* = \delta_G(p, q)/|pq|$. Let $\{A_i, B_i\}$, $1 \leq i \leq m$, be an arbitrary WSPD for S, with respect to s. Let i be the index such that (i) $p \in A_i$ and $q \in B_i$, or (ii) $p \in B_i$ and $q \in A_i$. Let x be an arbitrary point of A_i and let y be an arbitrary point of B_i. Then*

$$\frac{s}{s+4} \leq \frac{\delta_G(p, q)}{\delta_G(x, y)} \leq \frac{(s+4)^2}{s(s-4)}.$$

PROOF We assume, without loss of generality, that $p \in A_i$ and $q \in B_i$. In this proof, we will repeatedly use Lemma 9.1.2, which relates Euclidean distances involving points in a well-separated pair. Since $\delta_G(x, y)/|xy| \leq \delta_G(p, q)/|pq|$, we have

$$\frac{\delta_G(x, y)}{\delta_G(p, q)} \leq \frac{|xy|}{|pq|} \leq 1 + \frac{4}{s} = \frac{s+4}{s},$$

proving the leftmost inequality. We claim that

$$\frac{\delta_G(p, q)}{|pq|} \leq \frac{s+4}{s-4} \frac{\delta_G(x, y)}{|xy|}. \tag{13.1}$$

From this, it will follow that

$$\frac{\delta_G(p, q)}{\delta_G(x, y)} = \frac{\delta_G(p, q)}{|pq|} \frac{|xy|}{\delta_G(x, y)} \frac{|pq|}{|xy|} \leq \frac{s+4}{s-4} \frac{|pq|}{|xy|} \leq \frac{s+4}{s-4} \left(1 + \frac{4}{s}\right) = \frac{(s+4)^2}{s(s-4)}.$$

So it remains to prove (13.1). By the triangle inequality, we have

$$\delta_G(p, q) \leq \delta_G(p, x) + \delta_G(x, y) + \delta_G(y, q).$$

Let us assume first that $x \neq p$ and $y \neq q$. By Lemma 9.1.2, we have $|px| \leq (2/s)|pq|$, $|yq| \leq (2/s)|pq|$, and $|xy| \leq (1 + 4/s)|pq|$. Using these inequalities, it follows that

$$
\begin{aligned}
t^* &= \frac{\delta_G(p, q)}{|pq|} \\
&\leq \frac{\delta_G(p, x)}{|pq|} + \frac{\delta_G(x, y)}{|pq|} + \frac{\delta_G(y, q)}{|pq|} \\
&\leq \frac{2}{s} \frac{\delta_G(p, x)}{|px|} + \left(1 + \frac{4}{s}\right) \frac{\delta_G(x, y)}{|xy|} + \frac{2}{s} \frac{\delta_G(y, q)}{|yq|} \\
&\leq \frac{2}{s} t^* + \left(1 + \frac{4}{s}\right) \frac{\delta_G(x, y)}{|xy|} + \frac{2}{s} t^* \\
&= \frac{4}{s} t^* + \left(1 + \frac{4}{s}\right) \frac{\delta_G(x, y)}{|xy|}.
\end{aligned}
$$

This inequality is equivalent to (13.1). If $x = p$ or $y = q$, then a similar calculation shows that (13.1) holds. ∎

13.2.1 The reduction

In this section, we give the faster approximation algorithm. First, we need a definition. Let p and q be two distinct vertices of a connected Euclidean graph G, and let $c \geq 1$ be a real number. We say that the real number $L(p, q)$ is a *c-approximation* to the length of a shortest path in G between p and q, if

$$L(p, q)/c \leq \delta_G(p, q) \leq L(p, q).$$

Let $\mathcal{G}$ be a class of connected Euclidean graphs, and let $c \geq 1$ be a real number. We assume that we have an algorithm ASP_c that takes as input (i) any graph G from the class $\mathcal{G}$, and (ii) any sequence of pairs of vertices of G. Algorithm ASP_c gives as output a c-approximation to $\delta_G(x, y)$ for every pair (x, y) in the sequence.

Algorithm FASTAPPROXSF(G, ϵ)

Comment: This algorithm takes as input a Euclidean graph G from the class $\mathcal{G}$ on a set S of points in $\mathbb{R}^d$, and a real number $\epsilon > 0$. Its output is a $(c, 1 + \epsilon)$-approximate stretch factor of G.

Step 1: Using a separation ratio of $s = 4(2 + \epsilon)/\epsilon$, compute a WSPD, $\{A_i, B_i\}$, $1 \leq i \leq m$, for S. For each i with $1 \leq i \leq m$, pick an arbitrary point $a_i \in A_i$ and an arbitrary point $b_i \in B_i$.

Step 2: Use algorithm ASP_c to compute, for each i with $1 \leq i \leq m$, a c-approximation $L(a_i, b_i)$ to the length $\delta_G(a_i, b_i)$ of a shortest path in G between a_i and b_i. For each i with $1 \leq i \leq m$, compute

$$t_i := L(a_i, b_i)/|a_i b_i|.$$

Step 3: Report the value of t, defined as $t := \max(t_1, t_2, \ldots, t_m)$. Also report points a_i and b_i for which $t = t_i$.

The following lemma bounds the approximation factor of the output of this algorithm.

Lemma 13.2.2. *The value of t reported by algorithm* FASTAPPROXSF(G, ϵ) *is a $(c, 1 + \epsilon)$-approximate stretch factor of G, that is,*

$$t/c \leq t^* \leq (1 + \epsilon)t,$$

where t^* denotes the exact stretch factor of G.

PROOF   Let j be the index such that $t = t_j = L(a_j, b_j)/|a_j b_j|$. Then

$$t \leq \frac{c \cdot \delta_G(a_j, b_j)}{|a_j b_j|} \leq c\, t^*.$$

In the rest of the proof, we will show that $t^* \leq (1 + \epsilon)t$.

Let p and q be two points of S that determine the stretch factor of G, that is, $t^* = \delta_G(p, q)/|pq|$. Let i be the index such that (i) $p \in A_i$ and $q \in B_i$, or (ii) $p \in B_i$ and $q \in A_i$. Assume without loss of generality that (i) holds.

Consider the points $a_i \in A_i$ and $b_i \in B_i$ that were chosen in Step 1 of the algorithm. We have seen in the proof of Theorem 13.2.1 – see (13.1) – that

$$t^* \leq \frac{s + 4}{s - 4} \frac{\delta_G(a_i, b_i)}{|a_i b_i|} = (1 + \epsilon) \frac{\delta_G(a_i, b_i)}{|a_i b_i|}.$$

It follows that

$$t^* \leq (1 + \epsilon)\frac{L(a_i, b_i)}{|a_i b_i|} = (1 + \epsilon)t_i \leq (1 + \epsilon)t.$$

This completes the proof. ∎

Remark 13.2.3. Even though the stretch factor t^* is defined by $\binom{n}{2}$ pairs of points, Lemma 13.2.2 shows that t^* can be approximated by solving approximate shortest path queries for only $O(n)$ pairs of points. Furthermore, the pairs of points on which these queries are solved depend *only* on the positions of the vertices, they do *not* depend on the edges of the graph G.

In the following theorem, we summarize the result of this section. We denote by $\mathcal{T}(n, k, \ell)$ the worst-case running time of algorithm ASP$_c$, when given (i) a graph $G \in \mathcal{G}$ having n vertices and k edges, and (ii) a sequence of c-approximate shortest path queries, consisting of ℓ pairs of vertices of G.

Theorem 13.2.4. *Let S be a set of n points in $\mathbb{R}^d$, let G be a Euclidean graph from the class $\mathcal{G}$ having the points of S as its vertices, and let ϵ be a positive real number. We can compute a $(c, 1 + \epsilon)$-approximate stretch factor of G, in*

$$O(n \log n + n/\epsilon^d) + \mathcal{T}(n, k, \beta_\epsilon n)$$

time, where β_ϵ is a real number that is proportional to $1/\epsilon^d$.

PROOF The proof follows from algorithm FASTAPPROXSF, Theorem 9.4.6, and Lemma 13.2.2. ∎

13.2.2 Applying algorithm FASTAPPROXSF

In order to implement algorithm FASTAPPROXSF for a specific class $\mathcal{G}$ of Euclidean graphs, we need an efficient algorithm that solves a batch of exact or approximate shortest pair queries. Clearly, the performance will depend on the class $\mathcal{G}$. We will indicate how such queries can be solved for several classes of graphs.

Paths, cycles, and trees

Let $\mathcal{G}$ be the class of Euclidean paths, cycles, or trees. For any graph G on n vertices in this class, we can, after an $O(n)$–time preprocessing, answer exact shortest path queries in $O(1)$ time if G is a path or cycle, and in $O(\log \log n)$ time if G is a tree. For paths and cycles, this is easy to prove, the claim for trees is left as an exercise; see Exercise 13.5. We observe that if we allow nonalgebraic operations, then we can even answer shortest path queries in a tree in $O(1)$ time.

Hence, we can apply Theorem 13.2.4 with $c = 1$ and $\mathcal{T}(n, k, \ell) = O(n + \ell)$ if G is a path or cycle, and $\mathcal{T}(n, k, \ell) = O(n + \ell \log \log n)$ if G is a tree, and get the following result.

Theorem 13.2.5. *Let S be a set of n points in $\mathbb{R}^d$, let G be a Euclidean path, cycle, or tree having the points of S as its vertices, and let ϵ be a positive real number. We can compute a $(1, 1 + \epsilon)$-approximate stretch factor of G in*

1. *$O(n \log n + n/\epsilon^d)$ time if G is a path or cycle, and*
2. *$O(n \log n + (n/\epsilon^d) \log \log n)$ time if G is a tree.*

It follows from Theorem 13.1.3 that the above result is optimal in the algebraic computation-tree model.

Planar graphs

For the next application, let $\mathcal{G}$ be the class of planar connected Euclidean graphs. Let G be a graph in this class on a set of n points in $\mathbb{R}^d$. Here is what is known. Any sequence of ℓ exact shortest path queries in G can be solved in

$$O\left(\ell^{2/3} n^{2/3} \log n + n^{4/3} \log^{1/3} n\right)$$

time. This is left as an exercise; see Exercise 13.8. Hence, we can apply Theorem 13.2.4 with $c = 1$ and

$$T(n, k, \ell) = O\left(\ell^{2/3} n^{2/3} \log n + n^{4/3} \log^{1/3} n\right).$$

This gives the following theorem.

Theorem 13.2.6. *Let S be a set of n points in $\mathbb{R}^d$, let G be a planar connected Euclidean graph having the points of S as its vertices, and let ϵ be a positive real number. In*

$$O\left(\frac{n^{4/3}}{\epsilon^{2d/3}} \log(n/\epsilon)\right)$$

time, we can compute a $(1, 1 + \epsilon)$-approximate stretch factor of G.

General Euclidean graphs

In our final application, we let $\mathcal{G}$ be the general class of connected Euclidean graphs. Let $G \in \mathcal{G}$ be any graph with n vertices and k edges. Observe that $k \geq n - 1$. Again, here is what is known. For any integer constant $\beta \geq 1$, and any real constant ϵ, such that $0 < \epsilon \leq 1/2$, any sequence of $(2\beta(1 + \epsilon))$-approximate shortest path queries can be solved in

$$O((k + \ell)n^{1/\beta} \log^2 n)$$

expected time, where ℓ is the number of queries. We leave this as an exercise; see Exercise 13.9. Applying Theorem 13.2.4 gives the following result.

Theorem 13.2.7. *Let S be a set of n points in $\mathbb{R}^d$, let G be a connected Euclidean graph having the points of S as its vertices and having k edges, let $\beta \geq 1$ be an integer constant, and let ϵ be a real constant such that $0 < \epsilon \leq 1/2$. In*

$$O(kn^{1/\beta} \log^2 n)$$

expected time, we can compute a $(2\beta(1 + \epsilon), 1 + \epsilon)$-approximate stretch factor of G.

By choosing different values for the integer constant β, Theorem 13.2.7 gives a trade-off between the running time and the approximation factor. For example, by choosing β large enough, the running time in Theorem 13.2.7 is almost linear in k, but then the approximation of the stretch factor is very weak (although it is still bounded by a constant).

Theorem 13.2.7 implies the following result for *sparse* graphs, that is, graphs having $O(n)$ edges.

Corollary 13.2.8. *Let S be a set of n points in $\mathbb{R}^d$, let G be a sparse connected Euclidean graph having the points of S as its vertices, let $\beta \geq 1$ be an integer constant, and let ϵ be a real constant such that $0 < \epsilon \leq 1/2$. In*

$$O(n^{1+1/\beta} \log^2 n)$$

expected time, we can compute a $(2\beta(1 + \epsilon), 1 + \epsilon)$-approximate stretch factor of G.

In Section 17.4, we will show that the results in Theorem 13.2.7 and Corollary 13.2.8 can be improved significantly if G is a Euclidean graph whose stretch factor t^* is known in advance to be bounded from above by a constant.

Exercises

13.1. Let S be a set of n points in $\mathbb{R}^d$, let G be a cycle on the points of S, and let ϵ be a positive constant. Show that algorithm APPROXSF(G, ϵ) can be implemented such that it runs in $O(n \log n)$ time. (*Hint:* Use the WSPD of Exercise 9.16 and a data structure that solves the *interval split-find problem* in $O(1)$ amortized time per operation. This data structure uses nonalgebraic operations.)

13.2. Prove Theorem 13.1.3 for the case when the graph G is a cycle.

13.3. Theorem 13.2.1 proved a result about the well-separated pair $\{A_i, B_i\}$, which contains the points p and q. Now prove the same result about the well-separated pair $\{A_j, B_j\}$, which is output by the algorithm FASTAPPROXSF. More formally, the problem is described as follows: Let S be a set of n points in $\mathbb{R}^d$ and let G be a connected Euclidean graph having the points of S as its vertices. Let t^* denote the exact stretch factor of G, and let p and q be two distinct points of S for which $t^* = \delta_G(p, q)/|pq|$. Consider an arbitrary WSPD, $\{A_i, B_i\}$, $1 \leq i \leq m$, for S, with separation ratio of $s > 4$. Let i be the index such that (i) $p \in A_i$ and $q \in B_i$, or (ii) $p \in B_1$ and $q \in A_i$. In Theorem 13.2.1, we have shown that all distances in the graph G between any point of A_i and any point of B_i are approximately equal. Run algorithm FASTAPPROXSF(G, ϵ), as given in Section 13.2.1, and let its output be t. Let j be the index such that $t = t_j$. Prove that all distances in G between any point of A_j and any point of B_j are approximately equal, and determine the approximation ratio.

13.4. Run algorithm FASTAPPROXSF(G, ϵ) using separation ratio $s = 4(1 + \epsilon)/\epsilon$. Prove that the output is a $(c, (1 + \epsilon)^2)$-approximate stretch factor of G.

13.5. Let G be a Euclidean tree having n nodes. Give an $O(n)$–time algorithm that preprocesses T in such a way that for any two nodes u and v, their distance $\delta_G(u, v)$ in G can be computed in $O(\log \log n)$ time.

13.6. Let G be a noncrossing path on a set of n vertices in the plane. If $x \in \mathbb{R}^2$, then we say that $x \in G$ if x is a vertex of G or x is in the interior of some edge of G. For any two points $x \in G$ and $y \in G$, let $\delta_G(x, y)$ denote the Euclidean distance traveled when walking along G from x to y. The *detour* $D(G)$ of G is defined as the maximum value of $\delta_G(x, y)/|xy|$ over all distinct points $x \in G$ and $y \in G$. Prove that there is a *vertex* of G and a point $y \in G$ for which $D(G) = \delta_G(x, y)/|xy|$.

13.7. Let G be a planar connected Euclidean graph with n vertices. Give an algorithm that preprocesses G in $O(n\sqrt{n})$ time into a data structure that allows exact shortest path queries to be solved in G in $O(\sqrt{n})$ time per query.

13.8. Let G be a planar connected Euclidean graph with n vertices. Give an algorithm that answers any sequence of ℓ exact shortest path queries in $O(\ell^{2/3} n^{2/3} \log n + n^{4/3} \log^{1/3} n)$ time.

13.9. Let G be a connected Euclidean graph with n vertices and k edges, let $\beta \geq 1$ be an integer constant, and let ϵ be a real constant, such that $0 < \epsilon \leq 1/2$. Give a randomized algorithm that answers any sequence of $(2\beta(1 + \epsilon))$-approximate shortest path queries in $O((k + \ell)n^{1/\beta} \log^2 n)$ expected time, where ℓ is the number of queries.

Bibliographic notes

This chapter is based on Narasimhan and Smid [1999] and Narasimhan and Smid [2000]. In Narasimhan and Smid [2000], algorithm FASTAPPROXSF is given using separation ratio $s = 4(1 + \epsilon)/\epsilon$, which results in a $(c, (1 + \epsilon)^2)$-approximate stretch factor (see Exercise 13.4). The coverage of Section 13.2 is new.

An algorithm that solves the all-pairs-shortest-path problem for planar graphs in $O(n^2)$ time is presented in Frederickson [1987].

The result on shortest path queries in planar graphs that was used to prove Theorem 13.2.6 (see also Exercise 13.8) is due to Cabello [2006]. A solution to Exercise 13.7 can be found in Arikati et al. [1996] and Djidjev [1997]; using this exercise, the running time in Theorem 13.2.6 becomes $O(n\sqrt{n}/\epsilon^d)$. The result on approximate shortest path queries in general graphs that was used to prove Theorem 13.2.7 (see also Exercise 13.9) is due to Cohen [1998].

A solution to Exercise 13.1 can be found in Narasimhan and Smid [1999]. The data structure for the interval split-find problem that is needed to solve this exercise is due to Imai and Asano [1987].

The notion of detour (see Exercise 13.6) appears in Ebbers-Baumann et al. [2004b]. Using an approach that is completely different from the one presented in this chapter, Agarwal et al. [2006] show that the exact stretch factor and the exact detour of a Euclidean path, tree, and cycle on n points in the plane can be computed in $O(n \log n)$, $O(n \log^2 n)$, and $O(n\sqrt{n} \log n)$ expected time, respectively. These authors also present algorithms for the three-dimensional versions of these problems. For more information about detour problems, see Section 20.9.

Klein et al. [2005] generalize the algorithms given in this chapter and those given in Agarwal et al. [2006], to compute (or approximate) the number of pairs of vertices whose stretch factor is larger than some given value k.

Narasimhan and Smid [2002] consider the following bottleneck stretch factor problem: Preprocess a set S of n points in $\mathbb{R}^d$ into a data structure that supports the queries of the following type: Given an arbitrary query value $b > 0$, compute an approximation to the stretch factor of the graph G_b, which is the graph on S containing all edges of length at most b.

PART IV

The Path-Greedy Algorithm and Its Analysis

14

Geometric Analysis: The Leapfrog Property

> 'No,' replied the Lord,'Your hands were made for blessing, not for striking.'
> Don Camillo sighed heavily. He genuflected and left the sanctuary. As he
> turned to make a final sign of the cross he found himself exactly behind
> Peppone who, on his knees, was apparently absorbed in prayer. 'Lord,'
> groaned Don Camillo, clasping his hands and gazing at the crucifix. 'My
> hands were made for blessing, but not my feet!' 'There is something in
> that,' replied the Lord from above the altar, 'but all the same, Don Camillo,
> bear it in mind: only one!' The kick landed like a thunderbolt and Peppone
> received it without so much as blinking an eye. Then he got to his feet
> and sighed with relief. 'I've been waiting for that for the last ten minutes,'
> he remarked. 'I feel better now.' 'So do I!' exclaimed Don Camillo, whose
> heart was now as light and serene as a May morning. The Lord said
> nothing at all, but it was easy enough to see that He too was pleased.
> —Giovanni Guareschi, *The Little World of Don Camillo*, 1951

14.1 Introduction and motivation

In Chapter 6, we introduced the w-gap property. We proved the Gap Theorem (Theorem 6.1.2), which states that any set of directed edges, whose endpoints are from a set S of n points in $\mathbb{R}^d$, and for which the w-gap property holds, for some constant $w > 0$, has a weight that is at most proportional to $\log n$ times the weight of a minimum spanning tree of S. We also showed in Theorem 6.2.1 that the weight of such a set of edges can be $\Omega(\log n)$ times the weight of a minimum spanning tree.

In this chapter, we introduce the *leapfrog property*. This property, like the gap property, restricts how a set of edges can be positioned in space. However, better bounds can be proved for it. As we will see, any set of edges satisfying the leapfrog property has small weight, that is, at most a constant times the weight of a minimum spanning tree of the endpoints.

To give the motivation for the leapfrog property, we briefly recall algorithm PATHGREEDY, which we have seen in Section 1.4, and which is considered in more detail in Chapter 15. Let S be a set of n points in $\mathbb{R}^d$, and let $t > 1$ be a real number. Algorithm PATHGREEDY(S, t) initializes a graph $G = (S, E)$, whose edge set E is empty. Then it goes through the $\binom{n}{2}$ pairs of distinct points of S, in nondecreasing order of their distances. The algorithm adds the pair $\{p, q\}$ to the edge set E, if and only if the length of a shortest path in the current graph G is larger than $t|pq|$. The final graph $G = (S, E)$ is a t-spanner for S.

Let p_1 and q_1 be two distinct points of S, and consider the moment when algorithm PATHGREEDY(S, t) tests the pair $\{p_1, q_1\}$. Assume that, at this moment, the edge set E

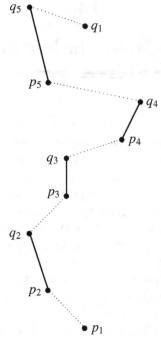

Figure 14.1: Algorithm PATHGREEDY(S, t) tests whether or not to include the pair $\{p_1, q_1\}$ as an edge in the path-greedy spanner.

contains edges $\{p_i, q_i\}$, $2 \leq i \leq k$, such that all distances

$$|p_1 p_2|, |q_2 p_3|, |q_3 p_4|, \ldots, |q_{k-1} p_k|, |q_k q_1| \tag{14.1}$$

are less than $|p_1 q_1|$. This situation is illustrated in Figure 14.1 for $k = 5$. The solid edges have already been picked by the algorithm. The pairs defining the distances in sequence (14.1) are shown as dotted edges in the figure. Each pair that defines a distance in this sequence either consists of two identical points or was already considered by the algorithm, and may or may not have been added as an edge to E. Therefore, each pair that defines a distance in sequence (14.1) is connected by a t-spanner path in the current graph G. We denote these t-spanner paths by $P_1, P_2, \ldots, P_k$. Obviously,

$$P_1, \{p_2, q_2\}, P_2, \{p_3, q_3\}, P_3, \ldots, P_{k-1}, \{p_k, q_k\}, P_k$$

is a (possibly nonsimple) path in the current graph G between the points p_1 and q_1, and its length is bounded from above by

$$\sum_{i=2}^{k} |p_i q_i| + t \left(|p_1 p_2| + \sum_{i=2}^{k-1} |q_i p_{i+1}| + |q_k q_1| \right). \tag{14.2}$$

If the quantity in (14.2) is less than or equal to $t|p_1 q_1|$, then the pair $\{p_1, q_1\}$ is not added to the edge set E, because a sufficiently short alternate path exists in the graph. In other words, if $\{p_1, q_1\}$ is an edge in the spanner that is computed by algorithm PATHGREEDY(S, t), then

$$t|p_1 q_1| < \sum_{i=2}^{k} |p_i q_i| + t \left(|p_1 p_2| + \sum_{i=2}^{k-1} |q_i p_{i+1}| + |q_k q_1| \right).$$

The leapfrog property defined below is a restatement of the above condition, regardless of whether or not all distances in (14.1) are less than $|p_1 q_1|$.

Definition 14.1.1 (Leapfrog Property). Let $t > 1$ be a real number. A set E of undirected edges in $\mathbb{R}^d$ is said to satisfy the t-*leapfrog property*, if for every $k \geq 2$, and for every sequence $\{p_1, q_1\}, \{p_2, q_2\}, \ldots, \{p_k, q_k\}$ of k pairwise distinct edges of E,

$$t|p_1 q_1| < \sum_{i=2}^{k} |p_i q_i| + t \left(|p_1 p_2| + \sum_{i=2}^{k-1} |q_i p_{i+1}| + |q_k q_1| \right).$$

Observe that this definition requires that the inequality holds for every permutation of the k edges, and for every labeling of their endpoints. In other words, for every set of k pairwise distinct edges, the leapfrog property gives $k! \, 2^k$ inequalities.

14.2 Relation to the gap property

How is the leapfrog property related to the gap property (see Definition 6.1.1)? While the gap property is defined on directed edges and is thus dependent on the chosen labeling for the endpoints of the segments, the leapfrog property is independent of how the endpoints are labeled. Also, the gap property is a local property, while the leapfrog property is of a more global nature. In this sense, the leapfrog property may be considered as an intrinsic property of a set of line segments. The leapfrog property generalizes the gap property in the sense described in Lemma 14.2.1 below.

Before we state the lemma, we recall the definition of the strong gap property. For a real number $w \geq 0$, a set of directed edges in $\mathbb{R}^d$ satisfies the strong w-gap property, if for any two distinct edges (p, q) and (r, s) in the set,

$$|pr| > w \cdot \min(|pq|, |rs|)$$

and

$$|qs| > w \cdot \min(|pq|, |rs|).$$

Recall our notation angle(pq, rs) for the angle between the directed edges (p, q) and $(r; s)$, which is defined to be the angle (in $[0, \pi]$) between the two vectors from the origin to the points $q - p$ and $s - r$, respectively.

Lemma 14.2.1. *Let $t > 1$ be a real number, and let E be a set of undirected edges in $\mathbb{R}^d$ satisfying the t-leapfrog property. Let θ be a real number, such that $0 < \theta < \pi/4$ and $\cos\theta - \sin\theta \geq 1/t$. Let $\{p, q\}$ and $\{r, s\}$ be two distinct edges in E with angle(pq, rs) $\leq \theta$. Then, the directed edges (p, q) and (r, s) satisfy the strong w-gap property, for*

$$w = \frac{1}{2} (\cos\theta - \sin\theta - 1/t).$$

PROOF We may assume without loss of generality that $|rs| \leq |pq|$. Thus, we have to show that $|pr| > w|rs|$ and $|qs| > w|rs|$.

Assume that $|pr| \leq w|rs|$. Then, all conditions in Lemma 6.4.1 are satisfied, and, therefore,

$$t|pr| + |rs| + t|sq| \leq t|pq|.$$

By taking $k = 2$, $p_1 = p$, $q_1 = q$, $p_2 = r$, and $q_2 = s$ in Definition 14.1.1, the above inequality contradicts the assumption that the edge set E satisfies the t-leapfrog property.

Hence, we have $|pr| > w|rs|$. In a symmetric way, the inequality $|qs| > w|rs|$ can be proven. ∎

By combining this lemma with the Gap Theorem (Theorem 6.1.2) and the technique of Theorem 5.3.3 for partitioning a set of edges into subsets of near-parallel edges, we obtain the following result:

Lemma 14.2.2. *Let $t > 1$ be a real number, let S be a set of n points in $\mathbb{R}^d$, and let $G = (S, E)$ be an undirected graph, such that E satisfies the t-leapfrog property.*

1. *The degree of every vertex of G is $O(1/(t - 1)^{d-1})$.*
2. *The weight $wt(E)$ of E satisfies*

$$wt(E) = O\left((1/(t - 1)^d) \cdot wt(MST(S)) \log n\right),$$

where $MST(S)$ denotes a minimum spanning tree of S.

PROOF We start by proving the first claim. Let p be a point of S, and let E_p be the set of all edges in E that are incident on p. We have to show that the size of E_p is $O(1/(t - 1)^{d-1})$.

Let $\vec{E}_p$ be the set of directed edges obtained by replacing each edge $\{p, q\}$ in E_p by the directed edge (p, q). We choose a real number θ, such that $0 < \theta < \pi/4$ and $\cos\theta - \sin\theta \geq 1/t$. By Theorem 5.3.3, we can partition $\vec{E}_p$ into $O(1/\theta^{d-1})$ subsets, such that angle$(pq, pr) \leq \theta$, for any two edges (p, q) and (p, r) that are in the same subset. By Lemma 14.2.1, each subset in this partition of $\vec{E}_p$ satisfies the strong w-gap property, for $w = (\cos\theta - \sin\theta - 1/t)/2$. Since $w \geq 0$, the Gap Theorem (Theorem 6.1.2) implies that each subset in this partition contains at most one element. It follows that $|E_p| = |\vec{E}_p| = O(1/\theta^{d-1})$. In order to obtain the best upper bound, we have to choose θ as large as possible. That is, we choose θ such that $0 < \theta < \pi/4$ and $\cos\theta - \sin\theta = 1/t$. Assuming that $t > 1$ and $t \to 1$, we have $\theta \sim t - 1$, and the first claim follows.

The second claim can be proved in a similar way, by again using the Gap Theorem, and using the analysis given after the proof of Lemma 7.2.2 for choosing the best value for θ. ∎

To further understand the relationship between the gap property and the leapfrog property, see Exercise 14.1.

14.3 A sufficient condition for the leapfrog property

Deciding whether or not a given set E of edges satisfies the leapfrog property does not appear to be easy, because the inequality in Definition 14.1.1 has to be verified for every $k \geq 2$, and for every sequence of k edges of E. In this section, we provide a simpler condition for the case when the edge set E forms a spanner of the endpoints. As we will see, this condition implies the leapfrog property.

We introduce the following notation. Let S be a set of n points in $\mathbb{R}^d$, let G be a connected Euclidean graph with vertex set S, and let p and q be two distinct points of S. We denote by $\delta_2(p, q)$ the length of a second shortest simple path in G between p and q. In order to define $\delta_2(p, q)$ more precisely, recall that a path is called simple if its vertices are pairwise distinct. Consider all distinct simple paths $P_1, P_2, \ldots, P_m$ between p and q, and let ℓ_i denote the length of P_i, $1 \leq i \leq m$. Note that the paths may have vertices or edges in common. We assume that these paths are numbered such that $\ell_1 \leq \ell_2 \leq \cdots \leq \ell_m$. If

$m \geq 2$, then we define $\delta_2(p, q) := \ell_2$, and we call P_2 a *second shortest path* between p and q. If $m = 1$, then there is only one simple path between p and q, and we define $\delta_2(p, q) := \infty$.

The following lemma gives a sufficient condition for the edge set of a spanner to satisfy the leapfrog property.

Lemma 14.3.1. *Let S be a set of n points in $\mathbb{R}^d$, let $t > 1$ be a real number, and let $G = (S, E)$ be an undirected t-spanner for S. Assume that $\delta_2(p, q) > t|pq|$, for every edge $\{p, q\}$ in E. Then, the edge set E satisfies the t-leapfrog property.*

PROOF Let $k \geq 2$, and let $\{p_i, q_i\}$, $1 \leq i \leq k$, be an arbitrary sequence of pairwise distinct edges in E. We have to show that the t-leapfrog property holds, that is,

$$t|p_1 q_1| < \sum_{i=2}^{k} |p_i q_i| + t \left(|p_1 p_2| + \sum_{i=2}^{k-1} |q_i p_{i+1}| + |q_k q_1| \right). \quad (14.3)$$

Let P_1 be a shortest path in G between p_1 and p_2. For each i with $2 \leq i \leq k - 1$, let P_i be a shortest path in G between q_i and p_{i+1}. Finally, let P_k be a shortest path in G between q_k and q_1. Since G is a t-spanner, the length $|P_i|$ of each path P_i is less than or equal to t times the distance between its endpoints. Let P be the (possibly nonsimple) path

$$P_1, \{p_2, q_2\}, P_2, \{p_3, q_3\}, P_3, \ldots, P_{k-1}, \{p_k, q_k\}, P_k$$

between p_1 and q_1, and let P' be a simple path between p_1 and q_1 obtained by removing all cycles from P. We distinguish two cases.

Case 1: The path P' consists of at least two edges.

In this case, we have

$$|P'| \leq |P|$$
$$= \sum_{i=1}^{k} |P_i| + \sum_{i=2}^{k} |p_i q_i|$$
$$\leq t \left(|p_1 p_2| + \sum_{i=2}^{k-1} |q_i p_{i+1}| + |q_k q_1| \right) + \sum_{i=2}^{k} |p_i q_i|.$$

Since $\{p_1, q_1\}$ is an edge of E, and since P' contains at least two edges, we have $\delta_2(p_1, q_1) \leq |P'|$. Then, the assumption of the lemma implies that

$$|P'| \geq \delta_2(p_1, q_1) > t|p_1 q_1|.$$

Hence, the required inequality (14.3) holds.

Case 2: The path P' consists of exactly one edge.

In this case, the nonsimple path P contains the edge $\{p_1, q_1\}$. In fact, there is an index j with $1 \leq j \leq k$, such that the path P_j contains this edge. Hence, we have

$$|p_1 q_1| \leq |P_j| \leq \sum_{i=1}^{k} |P_i|.$$

It follows that

$$t|p_1q_1| \le t \sum_{i=1}^{k} |P_i|$$

$$= t \left(|p_1p_2| + \sum_{i=2}^{k-1} |q_i\,p_{i+1}| + |q_kq_1| \right)$$

$$< \sum_{i=2}^{k} |p_iq_i| + t \left(|p_1p_2| + \sum_{i=2}^{k-1} |q_i\,p_{i+1}| + |q_kq_1| \right),$$

which proves that also in this case inequality (14.3) holds. ∎

14.4 The Leapfrog Theorem

The *Leapfrog Theorem* below bounds the total length of any set of edges that satisfies the leapfrog property.

Theorem 14.4.1 (Leapfrog Theorem). *Let $t > 1$ be a real number, let E be a set of undirected edges in $\mathbb{R}^d$ that satisfies the t-leapfrog property, and let S be the set of endpoints of the edges in E. Then,*

$$wt(E) \le c_{dt} \cdot wt(MST(S)),$$

where $MST(S)$ denotes a minimum spanning tree of S, and c_{dt} is a real number that depends only on d and t. If $t > 1$ and $t \to 1$, then

$$c_{dt} = O\left(1/(t-1)^{2d}\right).$$

The rest of this chapter gives the proof of this theorem.

14.4.1 Overview of the proof of the Leapfrog Theorem

Before starting the weight analysis, we perform a "cleanup phase," as described in Section 14.5. This is a conceptual step, in which we partition the edge set E into a "small" number of subsets, each one satisfying certain properties that help us analyzing the weight of the subset. One of the properties is that all edges in a subset are approximately parallel. Consider such a subset E', and assume that all edges in E' are approximately parallel to the d-th coordinate axis.

A key ingredient in our analysis of the weight of E' is the concept of a *dumbbell*. Each edge $e = \{p, q\}$ in E' defines a dumbbell, which consists of the line segment joining p and q, together with two *dumbbell heads* that are attached to p and q. These dumbbell heads are hypercylinders that are centered at p and q, respectively, their axes are parallel to the d-th coordinate axis, and their heights and radii are proportional to the length of the edge e; see Figure 14.2 in Section 14.5.3. Each hypercylinder is bounded by two *flat faces*, which are those parts that are extreme along the d-th coordinate axis, and a *side face*, which is the "cylindrical" part of the boundary.

Our partitioning of E is done in such a way that the edges of E' form a nested hierarchy (based on *pseudo-dumbbells*, which closely approximate the dumbbells), referred to as the *nesting tree*.

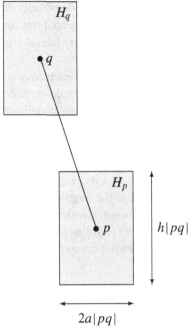

$$2a|pq|$$

Figure 14.2: The dumbbell D_e for the edge $e = (p, q)$ consists of the heads H_p and H_q, and the line segment joining p and q. Each head is a hypercylinder of height $h|pq|$ and radius $a|pq|$, that is centered at an endpoint of e, and whose axis is the line through the endpoint that is parallel to the d-th coordinate axis.

We remark that the dumbbells, as defined here, are different from those in Chapter 11, where the dumbbell heads were bounding boxes of point sets corresponding to nodes in the split tree. Moreover, the dumbbell hierarchy and the corresponding nesting tree is not to be confused with the dumbbell trees of Chapter 11 (even though they are based on the same principle).

Let $T := MST(S)$ be a minimum spanning tree of the set S of endpoints of the edges in E. The analysis that we present shows that the total weight of the edges in the subset E' is proportional to the weight of T.

Consider an edge e of E', and let p be any endpoint of e. Let $\mathcal{G}_p$ be the graph that is defined to be the connected portion of the union of (i) all edges of E' that are in p's head of the pseudo-dumbbell of e, and (ii) the portion of T that is inside this head and that is connected to p. Since T connects the points of S, it must pierce through each pseudo-dumbbell head in order to reach the corresponding endpoint. We partition the set E' of edges into two subsets, on the basis of the locations at which the graphs $\mathcal{G}_p$ intersect the boundaries of the pseudo-dumbbell heads of the edges in E'. For each edge $e = \{p, q\}$ of E', consider the graphs $\mathcal{G}_p$ and $\mathcal{G}_q$ that are inside the two heads of the pseudo-dumbbell of e. If none of these two graphs pierce any of the flat faces of the two pseudo-dumbbell heads, then we call e a *lateral* edge. All other edges of E' are termed as *non-lateral*. In other words, the pseudo-dumbbell heads of lateral edges are pierced only on their side faces by the graphs $\mathcal{G}_p$.

Our partitioning of the edge set E will be done in such a way that every subset E' contains only lateral edges or only non-lateral edges. We show separately that the weight of the edges in E' is $O(wt(T))$. This is tackled in Sections 14.6 and 14.7, respectively. The global techniques used in both cases are similar. In both, we perform a bottom-up analysis in the nesting tree that is defined by the pseudo-dumbbells of the edges in E'. However, the local techniques used are quite different. The analysis for the non-lateral edges uses the leapfrog property, whereas the analysis for the lateral edges uses only inherent local properties of Steiner minimum trees.

To achieve our analysis, we will show that for each edge e in E', there is a sufficiently large portion of T within the two heads of the pseudo-dumbbell of e, such that the length of e can be charged to this portion. Observe that the pseudo-dumbbell heads may contain other edges of E' that also need portions of T to be charged to. The charging will be done carefully enough so that there is always enough uncharged portion of the tree T to account for all these other edges.

For every edge e' of T, we assume that its length has two components: a "vertical" component denoted by $wt_V(e')$ (which is the length of e' along the d-th coordinate axis) and a "radial" component denoted by $wt_R(e')$ (which is the length of e' when ignoring the d-th coordinates). Our analysis employs a charging scheme, in such a way that each edge of E' is accounted for by the vertical and radial components of the lengths of the edges in T.

14.5 The cleanup phase

Let $t > 1$ be a real number, let E be a set of undirected edges in $\mathbb{R}^d$ that satisfies the t-leapfrog property, and let S be the set of endpoints of the edges in E.

Before we discuss the analysis of the weight of the edge set E, we show that this set can be partitioned into a "small" number of subsets, such that each subset contains edges that are *near-parallel*, *length-grouped*, and *base-separated*, and satisfy the *nested-dumbbells* property. Moreover, the edges in a subset are either all *lateral* or all *non-lateral*. All these terms are defined later. As will become clear in the analysis, this cleanup helps simplify the weight analyses of the edge set E.

The cleanup phase uses Lemma 14.2.1. Since a set of directed edges is needed to apply this lemma, we assume from now on that the edge set E is directed. In other words, we replace each undirected edge $\{p, q\}$ by either the directed edge (p, q) or the directed edge (q, p). For simplicity, we denote the resulting set of directed edges by E.

14.5.1 Near-parallel

> **Near-parallel:** The edge set E can be partitioned into subsets, such that the edges within each subset are near-parallel, that is, the angle between any two edges in the subset is bounded from above by some fixed value θ.

The following lemma makes this statement precise:

Lemma 14.5.1. *Let θ be a real number, such that $0 < \theta < \pi/4$ and $\cos\theta - \sin\theta > 1/t$. The set E of directed edges satisfying the t-leapfrog property can be partitioned into $O(1/\theta^{d-1})$ subsets, such that $\text{angle}(pq, rs) \leq \theta$, for any two edges (p, q) and (r, s) that are in the same subset. Every subset in this partition satisfies the strong w-gap property, for*

$$w = \frac{1}{2}(\cos\theta - \sin\theta - 1/t).$$

PROOF The lemma follows from Theorem 5.3.3 (which bounds the number of sets satisfying the required angle property) and Lemma 14.2.1 (which connects the leapfrog property and the gap property). ∎

14.5.2 Length-grouped and base-separated

Length-grouped and base-separated: Each subset in the partition of Lemma 14.5.1 can be further partitioned into subsets, such that in each subset, the following holds:

- *The edges are length-grouped*: Any two distinct edges have lengths that are either *nearly equal* (i.e., differ by at most a factor $1/\delta$) or *significantly* different (i.e., differ by at least a factor $1/\beta$), for some fixed values $0 < \beta < \delta < 1$.

- *The edges are base-separated*: Any two distinct edges that have nearly equal lengths satisfy the strong μ-gap property, for some fixed value $\mu \geq w$.

The following lemma gives a precise statement of these properties. We assume that θ and w are real numbers satisfying the conditions of Lemma 14.5.1.

Lemma 14.5.2. *Let β, δ, and μ be real numbers, such that $0 < \beta < \delta < 1$ and $\mu \geq w$, and let E' be any subset in the partition of Lemma 14.5.1. The set E' can be partitioned into*

$$O\left(\frac{\log(1/\beta)}{\log(1/\delta)} \left(1 + \frac{\mu}{w\delta}\right)^d\right)$$

subsets, such that for any two distinct edges (p, q) and (r, s) that are in the same subset and for which $|pq| \leq |rs|$, the following holds:

1. *$|rs| \leq |pq|/\delta$ or $|rs| \geq |pq|/\beta$.*
2. *If $|rs| \leq |pq|/\delta$, then $|pr| > \mu|pq|$ and $|qs| > \mu|pq|$ (in other words, (p, q) and (r, s) satisfy the strong μ-gap property).*

PROOF The lemma can be proved using the techniques of Sections 11.4 and 11.5, and the fact that the set E' satisfies the strong w-gap property. The details are left as an exercise; see Exercise 14.2. ∎

Remark 14.5.3. The proof of Lemma 14.5.2 uses the fact that the edge set E' satisfies the strong w-gap property. The lemma remains valid if we require only the strong w-gap property to hold for any two distinct edges (p, q) and (r, s) in E' for which $|pq| \leq |rs| \leq |pq|/\delta$. We will use this fact in Section 14.9.

14.5.3 Nested-dumbbells

Consider a subset of E in the partition of Lemma 14.5.2. We would like to store the edges in this subset in a nesting tree, such that the following holds, for any two distinct edges e and f in the same subset: f is stored in the subtree of e if and only if the dumbbell D_f is completely contained in one of the heads of the dumbbell D_e. This is possible if, for any two distinct edges e and f in the same subset, the dumbbells D_e and D_f are either disjoint or one dumbbell is completely contained in the head of the other dumbbell. Unfortunately, since the boundaries of some head of D_e and some head of D_f may overlap, the latter property does not necessarily hold. In this section, we will show, however, that by slightly modifying the dumbbells, we can achieve this property. The modified dumbbells will be called *pseudo-dumbbells*.

> **Nested-dumbbells:** Each subset of E in the partition of Lemma 14.5.2 can be stored in a nesting tree, such that the following holds, for any two distinct edges e and f in the same subset: f is stored in the subtree of e if and only if f's pseudo-dumbbell is completely contained in one of the heads of e's pseudo-dumbbell.

We assume that θ, w, β, δ, and μ are real numbers satisfying the conditions of Lemmas 14.5.1 and 14.5.2.

Let E'' be any subset of E in the partition of Lemma 14.5.2. Hence, any two edges in E'' are (i) near-parallel with parameter θ, (ii) length-grouped with parameters β and δ, and (iii) base-separated with parameter μ. We may assume without loss of generality that each edge (p, q) in E'' makes an angle of at most θ with the d-th coordinate axis, and that, along this axis, p is below q.

Before we can formalize the nested-dumbbells property for the edge set E'', we define the notion of a dumbbell. We assume from now on that $\beta < \cos \theta$. We choose real numbers a and h, such that

$$0 < a < h < \frac{\cos \theta - \beta}{1 + \beta}. \tag{14.4}$$

Let $e = (p, q)$ be an arbitrary edge in E''. We define the *dumbbell heads* (or, simply, the *heads*) of p and q to be the sets

$$H_p := \left\{ x \in \mathbb{R}^d : \sum_{i=1}^{d-1}(x_i - p_i)^2 \leq a^2 |pq|^2 \text{ and } |x_d - p_d| \leq h|pq|/2 \right\}$$

and

$$H_q := \left\{ x \in \mathbb{R}^d : \sum_{i=1}^{d-1}(x_i - q_i)^2 \leq a^2 |pq|^2 \text{ and } |x_d - q_d| \leq h|pq|/2 \right\},$$

respectively. In other words, the head H_p is the hypercylinder of height $h|pq|$ and radius $a|pq|$, that is centered at p, and whose axis is the line through p that is parallel to the d-th coordinate axis. We call the parts of the boundary of H_p that are extreme along the d-th coordinate axis the *flat* faces of H_p. Each of the two flat faces of H_p is contained in a hyperplane that is orthogonal to the d-th coordinate axis. The rest of the boundary of H_p will be called the *side face* of H_p. This side face is contained in the boundary of the hypercylinder of radius $a|pq|$, whose axis is the line through p that is parallel to the d-th coordinate axis.

The *dumbbell* D_e of the edge $e = (p, q)$ is defined to be the subset of $\mathbb{R}^d$ consisting of the two heads H_p and H_q, and the line segment joining p and q. See Figure 14.2 for an illustration.

Observe that, since the distance between p and q along the d-th coordinate axis is at least $|pq| \cos \theta$, and since $0 < h < \cos \theta$, the heads H_p and H_q of the dumbbell D_e are disjoint. The following lemma states that the dumbbell D_f of an edge f, which is significantly shorter than e, cannot intersect both heads of the dumbbell D_e.

Lemma 14.5.4. *Let $e = (p, q)$ and $f = (r, s)$ be two edges in E'', such that $|pq| \geq |rs|/\beta$. The dumbbell D_f cannot intersect both heads of the dumbbell D_e.*

PROOF   Along the d-th coordinate axis, the minimum distance between the two heads H_p and H_q is at least $(\cos\theta - h)|pq|$. On the other hand, along the same axis, the maximum distance between any two points of D_f is less than or equal to $(1 + h)|rs| \leq \beta(1 + h)|pq|$. By our choice of h, see (14.4); the latter quantity is less than $(\cos\theta - h)|pq|$.   ∎

Next, we prove that, for any two distinct edges e and f in E'' that have nearly equal lengths, the dumbbells D_e and D_f are far apart, provided the parameter β is sufficiently small and the parameter μ is sufficiently large.

Lemma 14.5.5. *Let $e = (p, q)$ and $f = (r, s)$ be two distinct edges in E'', where, along the d-th coordinate axis, p is below q, and r is below s, and assume that $|pq| \leq |rs| \leq |pq|/\delta$. Let C be the hypercylinder with center r, height $((2 + h)/(1 - 2\beta))|rs|$, and radius $((a + \sin\theta)/(1 - 2\beta))|rs|$, whose axis is the line through r that is parallel to the d-th coordinate axis. If $\beta < 1/2$ and*

$$\mu \geq (1 + a + h/2 + \sin\theta)\left(1 + \frac{1}{\delta(1 - 2\beta)}\right),\tag{14.5}$$

then D_e and C are disjoint. In particular, D_e and D_f are disjoint.

PROOF   Assume that D_e and C are not disjoint, and let z be a point in their intersection. (This point z may be on the edge e.) Then,

$$
\begin{aligned}
|pr| &\leq |pz| + |zr| \\
&\leq ((a + \sin\theta) + (1 + h/2))|pq| + \left(\frac{a + \sin\theta}{1 - 2\beta} + \frac{1 + h/2}{1 - 2\beta}\right)|rs|.
\end{aligned}
$$

Combining this with the assumption that $|rs| \leq |pq|/\delta$ and the inequality in (14.5), it follows that $|pr| \leq \mu|pq|$, contradicting the fact that e and f are base-separated with parameter μ. Hence, the dumbbell D_e and the hypercylinder C are disjoint. Since the dumbbell D_f is completely contained in C, D_e and D_f are disjoint as well.   ∎

As mentioned already, the boundaries of the heads of two different dumbbells may overlap so that a proper nesting of the dumbbells is, in general, not possible. To obtain a proper nesting, we will slightly deform the dumbbells. As we will see later, this yields pseudo-dumbbells that closely approximate the original dumbbells, a claim whose proof will require the following lemma. This lemma states that any set F of dumbbells that form a connected subset of $\mathbb{R}^d$ is contained in a hypercylinder whose size is proportional to the length of a longest dumbbell in F.

We define the *radial distance* between any two points x and y in $\mathbb{R}^d$ to be the Euclidean distance between the two points in $\mathbb{R}^{d-1}$ that are obtained by deleting the d-th coordinates from x and y. The *vertical distance* between x and y is defined as the absolute value of the difference between their d-th coordinates.

Lemma 14.5.6. *Let F be a subset of E'', and assume that the set*

$$\mathcal{D}_F := \bigcup_{f' \in F} D_{f'}$$

is a connected subset of $\mathbb{R}^d$. Let L be the length of a longest edge in F, and assume that $\beta < 1/2$ and

$$\mu \geq (1 + a + h/2 + \sin\theta)\left(1 + \frac{1}{\delta(1 - 2\beta)}\right).$$

Then, there exists a hypercylinder of height $((2 + h)/(1 - 2\beta))L$ and radius $((a + \sin\theta)/(1 - 2\beta))L$, whose axis is parallel to the d-th coordinate axis, that contains the set $\mathcal{D}_F$.

PROOF We first assume that the lengths of all edges in F are greater than or equal to δL. Let $f = (r, s)$ be an edge in F of length L, and let C be the hypercylinder in Lemma 14.5.5. We have seen in the proof of Lemma 14.5.5 that the dumbbell D_f is contained in C. Moreover, by Lemma 14.5.5, for each edge f' in $F \setminus \{f\}$, the dumbbell $D_{f'}$ has an empty intersection with C. Since the set $\mathcal{D}_F$ is connected, it follows that $F = \{f\}$ and, thus, the set $\mathcal{D}_F$ is contained in C.

We now consider the general case. Again, let $f = (r, s)$ be an edge in F of length L, and let C be the hypercylinder in Lemma 14.5.5. Recall that C is centered at r, has height $((2 + h)/(1 - 2\beta))|rs|$, radius $((a + \sin\theta)/(1 - 2\beta))|rs|$, and its axis is the line through r that is parallel to the d-th coordinate axis.

We first show that the length of each edge in $F \setminus \{f\}$ is less than or equal to βL. The proof is by contradiction. Thus, we assume that the set

$$F' := \{e' \in F \setminus \{f\} : |e'| > \beta L\}$$

is nonempty. Since the edge set E'' is length-grouped, each edge in F' has, in fact, length at least δL. Hence, by Lemma 14.5.5, we have $D_{e'} \cap C = \emptyset$ for each $e' \in F'$.

Since the set $\mathcal{D}_F$ is connected, there exists an edge e' in F', such that the dumbbells $D_{e'}$ and D_f are connected by dumbbells of edges that all have length at most βL. Consider such an edge e', and let F'' be a subset of F, such that

1. each edge in F'' has length at most βL,
2. the set $\mathcal{D}_{F''} := \bigcup_{e'' \in F''} D_{e''}$ is connected,
3. $\mathcal{D}_{F''}$ has a nonempty intersection with D_f, and
4. $\mathcal{D}_{F''}$ has a nonempty intersection with $D_{e'}$.

By an inductive argument, the set $\mathcal{D}_{F''}$ is contained in a hypercylinder C'' of height $\beta((2 + h)/(1 - 2\beta))L$ and radius $\beta((a + \sin\theta)/(1 - 2\beta))L$, whose axis is parallel to the d-th coordinate axis. In particular, C'' and D_f have a nonempty intersection. Therefore, the radial distance between r and any point of C'' is less than or equal to

$$(a + \sin\theta)L + \frac{2\beta(a + \sin\theta)}{1 - 2\beta}L = \frac{a + \sin\theta}{1 - 2\beta}L,$$

which is the radius of the hypercylinder C. Similarly, the vertical distance between r and any point of C'' is less than or equal to

$$(1 + h/2)L + \frac{\beta(2 + h)}{1 - 2\beta}L = \frac{1 + h/2}{1 - 2\beta}L,$$

which is half the height of the hypercylinder C. It follows that the set $\mathcal{D}_{F''}$ is completely contained in C. But then, since $\mathcal{D}_{F''} \cap D_{e'} \neq \emptyset$, the dumbbell $D_{e'}$ overlaps C, which is a contradiction. Thus, we have shown that the set F' is empty, that is, each edge in $F \setminus \{f\}$ has length at most βL.

Now we can complete the proof of the lemma. Consider the subset $\mathcal{D}_F \setminus D_f$ of $\mathbb{R}^d$. Each connected component of this subset touches D_f and is determined by edges of F of length at most βL. The arguments above show that each connected component is contained in the hypercylinder C. Thus, we have shown that the set $\mathcal{D}_F$ is contained in C. ∎

Now we are ready to define pseudo-dumbbells. Let $e = (p, q)$ be any edge in E'', and define

$$F_e := \{f \in E'' : |f| \le \beta|e|\}$$

and

$$\mathcal{D}_e := \bigcup_{f \in F_e} D_f.$$

Consider the connected components of $\mathcal{D}_e$, and let $\mathcal{C}_1, \mathcal{C}_2, \dots, \mathcal{C}_k$ be those connected components that intersect the boundary of the head H_p of the dumbbell D_e. We define the *pseudo-head* PH_p of p to be the connected component of the set $H_p \setminus \left(\bigcup_{i=1}^{k} \mathcal{C}_i \right)$ that contains p. Similarly, let $\mathcal{C}_1', \mathcal{C}_2', \dots, \mathcal{C}_\ell'$ be the connected components of $\mathcal{D}_e$ that intersect the boundary of the head H_q of D_e. The *pseudo-head* PH_q of q is defined to be the connected component of $H_q \setminus \left(\bigcup_{i=1}^{\ell} \mathcal{C}_i' \right)$ that contains q. We define the *pseudo-dumbbell* PD_e of e to be the subset of $\mathbb{R}^d$ consisting of the line segment joining p and q, and the two pseudo-heads PH_p and PH_q. We will refer to PH_p and PH_q as the heads of pseudo-dumbbell PD_e.

We now show that the pseudo-dumbbells approximate the original dumbbells. We assume that

$$\beta < \min \left(\frac{h}{4(1+h)}, \frac{a}{4a + 2\sin\theta} \right).$$

Let

$$h' := h - \frac{2\beta(2+h)}{1 - 2\beta}$$

and

$$a' := a - \frac{2\beta(a + \sin\theta)}{1 - 2\beta}.$$

Then $0 < h' < h$ and $0 < a' < a$. For each edge $e = (p, q)$ in E'', we define the *inner-dumbbell* ID_e to be the subset of $\mathbb{R}^d$ consisting of the line segment joining p and q, and the two *inner-heads*

$$IH_p := \left\{ x \in \mathbb{R}^d : \sum_{i=1}^{d-1} (x_i - p_i)^2 \le (a')^2 |pq|^2 \text{ and } |x_d - p_d| \le h'|pq|/2 \right\}$$

and

$$IH_q := \left\{ x \in \mathbb{R}^d : \sum_{i=1}^{d-1} (x_i - q_i)^2 \le (a')^2 |pq|^2 \text{ and } |x_d - q_d| \le h'|pq|/2 \right\}.$$

Thus, the inner-heads IH_p and IH_q are obtained by shrinking the heights and radii of the heads H_p and H_q to the values h' and a', respectively. We will refer to IH_p and IH_q as the heads of the inner-dumbbell ID_e.

Lemma 14.5.7. *Let e be an edge of E'', and let p be one of its endpoints. Then, the boundary of the pseudo-head PH_p is between the boundaries of the head H_p and the inner-head IH_p, that is,*

$$IH_p \subseteq PH_p \subseteq H_p.$$

PROOF It is clear that PH_p is contained in H_p. To prove that the inner-head IH_p and the boundary of the pseudo-head PH_p are disjoint, consider the connected components

$C_1, C_2, \ldots, C_k$ of the set $\mathcal{D}_e$ that intersect the boundary of the head H_p. By Lemma 14.5.6, each connected component C_i is contained in a hypercylinder of height $\beta((2+h)/(1-2\beta))|e|$ and radius $\beta((a+\sin\theta)/(1-2\beta))|e|$, whose axis is parallel to the d-th coordinate axis. Since C_i intersects the boundary of H_p, it follows from the definitions of h' and a' that C_i and the inner-head IH_p are disjoint.   ∎

The next lemma implies that the pseudo-dumbbells can be properly nested.

Lemma 14.5.8. *Let e and f be two distinct edges in E'', and assume that $|f| \leq |e|$. Then, either all the heads of the pseudo-dumbbells PD_e and PD_f are disjoint, or the pseudo-dumbbell PD_f is completely contained in one of the heads of the pseudo-dumbbell PD_e.*

PROOF   If any two heads of PD_e and PD_f are disjoint, then the lemma holds. Assume that some head of PD_e has a nonempty intersection with some head of PD_f. Then the dumbbells D_e and D_f are not disjoint and thus, by Lemma 14.5.5 and the length-grouping property, we have $|f| \leq \beta|e|$. If PD_f is not completely inside one of the heads of PD_e, then PD_f intersects the boundary of some head of PD_e, contradicting the definition of a pseudo-head.   ∎

Remark 14.5.9. It is possible that the edge set E'' contains two distinct edges e and f, such that $|f| \leq |e|$ and any two heads of the pseudo-dumbbells PD_e and PD_f are disjoint, but still, the pseudo-dumbbells PD_e and PD_f are not disjoint. If this is the case, then (i) the edge e (which is part of PD_e) intersects PD_f (which consists of the edge f and two pseudo-heads), or (ii) the edge f (which is part of PD_f) intersects PD_e (which consists of the edge e and two pseudo-heads). Also, by Lemma 14.5.5, this can be only the case if $|f| \leq \beta|e|$.

Let e_0 be a "dummy" edge, whose length is larger than $1/\beta$ times the length of a longest edge in E'', such that one of the heads of its "dummy" dumbbell D_0 contains the dumbbells of all edges in E''. We define the corresponding "dummy" pseudo-dumbbell PD_0 to be equal to D_0.

We now establish the nested-dumbbells property, by defining a tree $\mathcal{N}$, which will be referred to as the *nesting tree*. The rule used to construct this tree is encapsulated below.

Nesting Rule: The node set of the nesting tree $\mathcal{N}$ is the set $E'' \cup \{e_0\}$ of edges, where e_0 is the root. Let f be an arbitrary edge in E'', and let e be the shortest edge in $E'' \cup \{e_0\}$, such that $|f| < |e|$ and the pseudo-dumbbell PD_f is completely contained in one of the heads of the pseudo-dumbbell PD_e. Then, in the nesting tree $\mathcal{N}$, node e is the parent of node f.

Observe that, by Lemma 14.5.8, e is uniquely determined by f. Also, $\mathcal{N}$ is indeed a tree: If e is the parent of f, then, by definition, $|f| < |e|$, and, therefore, $\mathcal{N}$ does not contain any cycle.

Lemma 14.5.10. *Let e and f be two distinct edges in $E'' \cup \{e_0\}$. The following properties hold:*

1. *f is stored in the subtree of e (in the nesting tree $\mathcal{N}$), if and only if the pseudo-dumbbell PD_f is completely contained in one of the heads of the pseudo-dumbbell PD_e.*

2. *If f is stored in the subtree of e, then $|e| \geq |f|/\beta$.*

PROOF The first claim follows from the definition of the nesting tree and Lemma 14.5.8. The second claim follows from Lemmas 14.5.5 and 14.5.7, and the fact that the edges in $E'' \cup \{e_0\}$ are length-grouped with parameters β and δ.   ∎

We summarize the results of this section in the following lemma.

Lemma 14.5.11. *Let θ, β, δ, μ, a, and h be positive real numbers, such that $\theta < \pi/4$, $\cos\theta - \sin\theta > 1/t$, $\delta < 1$, $a < h < (\cos\theta - \beta)/(1 + \beta)$,*

$$\mu \geq \max\left(w, (1 + a + h/2 + \sin\theta)\left(1 + \frac{1}{\delta(1 - 2\beta)}\right)\right),$$

where $w = \frac{1}{2}(\cos\theta - \sin\theta - 1/t)$, and

$$\beta < \min\left(\delta, \cos\theta, \frac{h}{4(1 + h)}, \frac{a}{4a + 2\sin\theta}\right).$$

Let $h' = h - 2\beta(2 + h)/(1 - 2\beta)$ and $a' = a - 2\beta(a + \sin\theta)/(1 - 2\beta)$ be the height and radius parameters for the heads of the inner-dumbbells. Finally, let E'' be any subset in the partition of Lemma 14.5.2. Then, the edges of E'' can be stored in a nesting tree $\mathcal{N}$, such that the following holds, for any two distinct edges e and f in E'' with $|f| \leq |e|$: f is stored in the subtree of e if and only if the pseudo-dumbbell PD_f is completely contained in one of the heads of the pseudo-dumbbell PD_e.

14.5.4 Lateral and non-lateral edges

Let $\mathcal{T}$ be a minimum spanning tree of the set S of endpoints of the edges in E, and consider a subset E'' and its nesting tree $\mathcal{N}$, as in Lemma 14.5.11. For convenience, we introduce Steiner vertices at all locations where $\mathcal{T}$ pierces the boundaries of the heads of the pseudo-dumbbells of the edges in E''.

Let $e = (p, q)$ be an edge in E'', and consider one of the heads of the pseudo-dumbbell PD_e, say the head PH_p. We formalize the definition of the graph $\mathcal{G}_p$, that was introduced informally in Section 14.4.1: Consider the graph obtained by adding to $\mathcal{T}$ all edges of E'' that are completely contained in the pseudo-head PH_p. We define $\mathcal{G}_p$ to be the maximal connected subgraph of this graph that contains p and that is completely contained in the pseudo-head PH_p. We define the graph $\mathcal{G}_q$ similarly with respect to the point q. Since $\mathcal{T}$ connects all points of S, $\mathcal{G}_p$ contains at least one vertex that is on the boundary of PH_p and, similarly, $\mathcal{G}_q$ contains at least one vertex that is on the boundary of PH_q.

Consider the *flat faces* of the inner-head IH_p, that is, the parts of the boundary of IH_p that are extreme along the d-th coordinate axis. Let P^- and P^+ be the hyperplanes that are orthogonal to the d-th coordinate axis and that contain the lower and upper flat faces of IH_p, respectively. The pseudo-head PH_p contains two *flat faces*, where one flat face is defined to be the part of the boundary of PH_p that is below P^-, and the other flat face is defined to be the part of the boundary of PH_p that is above P^+. The remaining part of the boundary of PH_p is defined to be the *side face* of PH_p. The two flat faces and the side face of the pseudo-head PH_q are defined similarly with respect to q. Observe that a flat face or a side face need not be connected. Also, a flat face is, in general, not really flat.

We call the edge $e = (p, q)$ of E'' a *lateral* edge, if (i) no vertex of $\mathcal{G}_p$ is on any of the two flat faces of PH_p and (ii) no vertex of $\mathcal{G}_q$ is on any of the two flat faces of PH_q. Otherwise, e is called a *non-lateral* edge. Thus, if e is a non-lateral edge, then $\mathcal{G}_p$ touches one of the flat faces of PH_p or $\mathcal{G}_q$ touches one of the flat faces of PH_q.

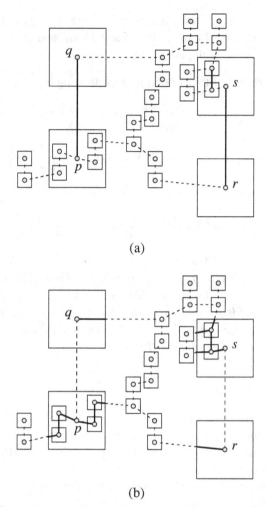

(a)

(b)

Figure 14.3: (a) The figure shows a collection of vertical edges, together with their pseudo-dumbbells. The dashed segments form the minimum spanning tree T of the endpoints. The three solid edges do not belong to T. (b) The figure shows the graphs $\mathcal{G}_p$, $\mathcal{G}_q$, $\mathcal{G}_r$, and $\mathcal{G}_s$, all drawn by solid segments. The edge (p, q) is lateral, whereas the edge (r, s) is non-lateral.

Figure 14.3 illustrates these notions. The top part (Figure 14.3(a)) shows a collection of vertical edges, together with their pseudo-dumbbells. (For convenience, the heads of these pseudo-dumbbells are drawn as squares.) The edges of the minimum spanning tree T are drawn as dashed segments. The three solid edges do not belong to T. The bottom part (Figure 14.3(b)) shows the same configuration of edges and pseudo-dumbbells. All the segments shown in the bottom part are either part of the minimum spanning tree T or the set E''. Among these, the edges that are part of the graphs $\mathcal{G}_p$, $\mathcal{G}_q$, $\mathcal{G}_r$, and $\mathcal{G}_s$ are drawn as solid segments. The rest are drawn as dashed segments. The edge (p, q) is lateral, because (i) the two leaves of $\mathcal{G}_p$ are on the side face of the pseudo-head PH_p and (ii) the leaf of $\mathcal{G}_q$ is on the side face of the pseudo-head PH_q. On the other hand, the edge (r, s) is non-lateral, because one leaf of $\mathcal{G}_s$ is on the flat face of the pseudo-head PH_s.

Consider the nesting tree $\mathcal{N}$ for the set E''. We "split" this tree into two nesting trees $\mathcal{N}^-$ and $\mathcal{N}^\perp$, where the former stores all lateral edges of E'', the latter stores all non-lateral edges of E'', both trees inherit the tree structure of $\mathcal{N}$, and both trees store the dummy edge e_0 in their roots. The following lemma follows from Lemma 14.5.11.

Lemma 14.5.12. *Let E'' be a subset of E, as in Lemma 14.5.11, and let $\mathcal{N}$ be the nesting tree for E''. We can transform $\mathcal{N}$ into nesting trees $\mathcal{N}^-$ and $\mathcal{N}^\perp$, such that $\mathcal{N}^-$ stores all lateral edges of E'', $\mathcal{N}^\perp$ stores all non-lateral edges of E'', and both $\mathcal{N}^-$ and $\mathcal{N}^\perp$ satisfy the properties of Lemma 14.5.11.*

14.5.5 Summarizing the cleanup phase

We started with a set E of edges that satisfy the t-leapfrog property, for some real number $t > 1$, chose real numbers $\theta, \beta, \delta, \mu, a$, and h, and defined

$$w := \frac{1}{2} \left(\cos \theta - \sin \theta - 1/t \right),$$

$$h' := h - \frac{2\beta(2 + h)}{1 - 2\beta},$$

and

$$a' := a - \frac{2\beta(a + \sin \theta)}{1 - 2\beta}.$$

These parameters were chosen such that $0 < \theta < \pi/4$, $\cos \theta - \sin \theta > 1/t$, $0 < \delta < 1$,

$$\mu \geq \max \left(w, (1 + a + h/2 + \sin \theta) \left(1 + \frac{1}{\delta(1 - 2\beta)} \right) \right),$$

$$0 < \beta < \min \left(\delta, \cos \theta, \frac{h}{4(1 + h)}, \frac{a}{4a + 2 \sin \theta} \right),$$

and

$$0 < a < h < \frac{\cos \theta - \beta}{1 + \beta}.$$

We have shown that the set E can be partitioned into

$$O \left(\frac{\log(1/\beta)}{\theta^{d-1} \log(1/\delta)} \left(1 + \frac{\mu}{w\delta} \right)^d \right)$$

subsets, such that the following properties hold for any two distinct edges that are in the same subset:

- near-parallel with parameter θ,
- length-grouped with parameters β and δ, and
- base-separated with parameter μ.

Furthermore,

- each subset in this partition contains either only lateral edges or only non-lateral edges, and
- each subset in this partition is represented by a nesting tree that satisfies the nested-dumbbells property.

14.6 Bounding the weight of non-lateral edges

Recall that E denotes the original set of edges that satisfy the t-leapfrog property, and that S denotes the set of endpoints of the edges in E. In this section, we consider a subset of E consisting only of non-lateral edges and satisfying the properties mentioned in Section 14.5.5. For ease of notation, we denote this subset by E. However, S will still denote the set of endpoints of the original edge set. The nesting tree for E is denoted by $\mathcal{N}$. Recall that the root of $\mathcal{N}$ stores the dummy edge e_0, which is not contained in E.

As in Section 14.5.3, we assume, without loss of generality, that each edge (p, q) in E makes an angle of at most θ with the d-th coordinate axis, and that, along this axis, p is below q. Moreover, we assume that the parameters θ, β, δ, μ, a, and h satisfy the inequalities given in Section 14.5.5.

Recall that a denotes the radius parameter of the dumbbell heads. The main goal of this section is to prove the following lemma.

Lemma 14.6.1. *Let E be a set of non-lateral edges satisfying the properties mentioned in Section 14.5.5, and let T be a minimum spanning tree of the point set S. Then, for an appropriate choice of the parameters, we have*

$$wt(E) \leq \frac{2}{a} \cdot wt(T).$$

Intuition: To prove Lemma 14.6.1, we will use the nesting tree $\mathcal{N}$ to "process" the edges of E in a bottom-up fashion. Consider any edge $e = (p, q)$ in E, and assume without loss of generality that the graph $\mathcal{G}_p$ touches one of the flat faces of the head PH_p of the pseudo-dumbbell PD_e. During the processing, we charge the length of e to the weight of a portion of a path in $\mathcal{G}_p$ that stretches from p to one of the flat faces of PH_p.

Recall that the *radial distance* between two points x and y in $\mathbb{R}^d$ is the Euclidean distance between the two points in $\mathbb{R}^{d-1}$ obtained by deleting the d-th coordinates from x and y, and that the *vertical distance* between x and y is the absolute value of the difference between their d-th coordinates. Also, recall that we have introduced Steiner vertices at all locations where T pierces the boundaries of the heads of the pseudo-dumbbells of the edges in E. (In order to obtain a rigorous analysis, more Steiner vertices have to be introduced. We leave the details as an exercise; see Exercise 14.8.)

For each edge e' of T, we define its *radial weight* $wt_R(e')$ to be the radial distance between the endpoints of e', and we define its *vertical weight* $wt_V(e')$ to be the vertical distance between the endpoints of e'. Without loss of generality, we assume that no edge of T is parallel to any of the d coordinate axes, so that the radial and vertical weights of all edges of T are strictly positive.

The analysis of the total weight of the edges in E uses a *potential function* Φ that contains the following components:

1. For every edge e' of T, $\Phi_R(e')$ and $\Phi_V(e')$ denote the *radial potential* and *vertical potential* of e', respectively.

2. For every edge e of E, $\Phi_D(e)$ denotes the *dumbbell potential* of e.

The potential function Φ is defined as

$$\Phi = \sum_{e' \in T} \left(\Phi_R(e') + \Phi_V(e') \right) + \sum_{e \in E} \Phi_D(e).$$

Observe that the edges of E as well as the edges of T have potentials associated with them. At the start of the analysis, we set the values of $\Phi_R(e')$ and $\Phi_V(e')$ to $wt_R(e')$ and

$wt_V(e')$, respectively, for every edge e' of $\mathcal{T}$, and we set the value of $\Phi_D(e)$ to zero, for every edge e in E.

Let Φ_0 be the initial value of Φ. Our goal is to prove the claim that

$$\Phi_0 \geq a \cdot wt(E). \tag{14.6}$$

From this, it would follow that

$$
\begin{aligned}
wt(E) &\leq \frac{1}{a} \cdot \Phi_0 \\
&= \frac{1}{a} \sum_{e' \in \mathcal{T}} \left(wt_R(e') + wt_V(e') \right) \\
&\leq \frac{2}{a} \sum_{e' \in \mathcal{T}} |e'| \\
&= \frac{2}{a} \cdot wt(\mathcal{T}).
\end{aligned}
$$

Thus, Lemma 14.6.1 follows from the inequality in (14.6).

As mentioned above, the analysis consists of processing the edges of E in a bottom-up fashion (with respect to the nesting tree $\mathcal{N}$). The processing of an edge e of E can be briefly described as follows.

> **Processing an edge e:** First, edges of $\mathcal{T}$ that lie within the heads of the pseudo-dumbbell PD_e of e may get *nulled out* by "transferring" their radial and vertical weights to the dumbbell potential of the edge e. Furthermore, the unused dumbbell potential of edges that are descendants of e in the nesting tree are also "transferred" to the dumbbell potential of the edge e. Finally, some of the dumbbell potential of edge e is used up to account for the weight of the edge e.

Later on, during the bottom-up processing, all the unused dumbbell potential of edge e is "transferred" to the dumbbell potential of an edge that is e's ancestor in the nesting tree, after which e is never considered again and its potential is set to zero for the rest of the analysis. In the next section, we will formally describe the main properties that are maintained during the processing.

14.6.1 The invariant $\mathcal{P}$

As before, let Φ_0 denote the initial value of the potential function. At any moment during the bottom-up processing of the edges of E, let Φ denote the current value of the potential function, and let W denote the total weight of all edges in E that have already been processed. During the processing, the following invariant $\mathcal{P}$ will be maintained:

$\mathcal{P}.1$: $\Phi_0 = \Phi + aW$.

$\mathcal{P}.2$: All current values of Φ_R, Φ_V, and Φ_D are nonnegative.

$\mathcal{P}.3$: For every edge e' of $\mathcal{T}$,

  (a) if e' has not been nulled out, then $\Phi_R(e') = wt_R(e')$ and $\Phi_V(e') = wt_V(e')$,
  (b) if e' has been nulled out, then $\Phi_R(e') = 0$ and $\Phi_V(e') = 0$.

$\mathcal{P}.4$: For every edge e of E that has been processed, but for which none of its proper ancestors in the current nesting tree $\mathcal{N}$ have been processed, we have $\Phi_D(e) \geq (2a + \sin\theta)|e|$.

After all edges of E have been processed, we have $W = wt(E)$. Hence, by the first and second properties in the invariant,

$$\Phi_0 = \Phi + aW \geq aW = a \cdot wt(E).$$

In other words, if we can show that the invariant is maintained during the processing of the edges, then the inequality in (14.6) holds and, therefore, Lemma 14.6.1 holds.

The main difficulty will be to prove that the dumbbell potentials Φ_D remain nonnegative during the processing. It is for this reason that we have included property $\mathcal{P}.4$. This property implies that there is sufficient unused dumbbell potential left in the edge for the accounting. We remark that the quantity $(2a + \sin\theta)|e|$ has been chosen because it is an upper bound on the radial distance between any two points that are in the same pseudo-dumbbell PD_e, a detail that will become important in Section 14.6.7.

Before we show how the edges of E are processed, let us verify that the invariant holds at the start of the process. At that moment, $\Phi_0 = \Phi$, no edge of E has been processed (thus, $W = 0$), and no edge of $\mathcal{T}$ has been nulled out. Clearly, the above properties $\mathcal{P}.1$ through $\mathcal{P}.4$ hold at this moment.

14.6.2 Processing one edge of E

Let $f = (x, y)$ be an arbitrary edge of E. Recall the definition of the graphs $\mathcal{G}_x$ and $\mathcal{G}_y$; see Section 14.5.4. Also, recall that $\mathcal{G}_x$ and $\mathcal{G}_y$ are completely contained in the heads PH_x and PH_y, respectively, of the pseudo-dumbbell PD_f. Since f is a non-lateral edge, either $\mathcal{G}_x$ or $\mathcal{G}_y$ (or both) touches one of the flat faces of a head of PD_f. We (arbitrarily) choose one of these two graphs that touches a flat face of a head of PD_f, and refer to this graph as the *non-lateral graph* of the edge f. The non-lateral graph will be used to account for the length of f and its ancestors, whereas the other graph is not used unless it is part of the non-lateral graph of some other ancestor edge.

As the processing proceeds in a bottom-up fashion, let $e = (p, q)$ be a shortest edge in E that has never been considered for processing, and assume that the invariant $\mathcal{P}$ holds at this moment. We assume without loss of generality that $\mathcal{G}_p$ is the non-lateral graph of e. Thus, $\mathcal{G}_p$ touches a flat face of the pseudo-head PH_p.

By Lemma 14.5.10, we have $|f| < |e|$, for every edge $f \neq e$ that is stored in the subtree of e (in the nesting tree $\mathcal{N}$). Therefore, all these edges f have already been processed.

The processing of edge e consists of performing the following four steps:

Step 1: For each edge f in E, such that

1. f is a child of e in the current nesting tree $\mathcal{N}$, and
2. the non-lateral graphs of f and e are disjoint,

make f a child of the parent of e.

Step 2: Set

$$\Phi_D(e) := \left\{ \sum_{e' \in \mathcal{G}_p \cap \mathcal{T}} \left(\Phi_R(e') + \Phi_V(e') \right) + \sum_{f: \text{child of } e} \Phi_D(f) \right\} - a|e|.$$

Step 3: For each child f of e, set $\Phi_D(f) := 0$.

Step 4: For each edge e' of $\mathcal{G}_p \cap \mathcal{T}$, set $\Phi_R(e') := 0$ and $\Phi_V(e') := 0$.

If e' is an edge of $\mathcal{G}_p \cap \mathcal{T}$, and $\Phi_R(e')$ and $\Phi_V(e')$ were positive prior to Step 4, then we say that e' is *nulled out* by the edge e.

> **Intuition:** In Step 1, the non-lateral graph of edge f is not needed to account for edge e, because it is disjoint from the non-lateral graph of e. However, since the unused dumbbell potential of f (which, by the invariant, is at least $(2a + \sin\theta)|f|$) may be useful later, f is moved up one level in the nesting tree $\mathcal{N}$. Observe that edge f continues to satisfy property $\mathcal{P}.4$. After Step 1, the non-lateral graph of e has a nonempty intersection with the non-lateral graphs of all its descendants.
>
> In Steps 2 and 3, each child f of e (in the modified nesting tree) "transfers" its dumbbell potential $\Phi_D(f)$ to the dumbbell potential $\Phi_D(e)$ of e. In Steps 2 and 4, each edge e' of $\mathcal{G}_p \cap \mathcal{T}$ that has not been nulled out yet, "transfers" its radial potential $\Phi_R(e')$ and vertical potential $\Phi_V(e')$ to the dumbbell potential $\Phi_D(e)$ of e.
>
> In Steps 2, 3, and 4, all the unused potential inside the pseudo-head PH_p is swept up, a quantity $a|e|$ is used to "pay" for the edge e, and the remaining amount is stored as unused dumbbell potential $\Phi_D(e)$.

Let Φ denote the value of the potential function just before edge e is processed. Let W denote the total weight of all edges in E that have been processed, again just before e is processed. Let Φ' and W' denote these quantities just after e has been processed.

Since the invariant holds before e is processed, we have $\Phi_0 = \Phi + aW$. Obviously, we have $W' = W + |e|$. Finally, it follows from Steps 2, 3, and 4 that $\Phi' - \Phi = -a|e|$. Therefore,

$$\Phi_0 = \Phi + aW = \Phi' + a|e| + aW = \Phi' + aW'$$

and, thus, property $\mathcal{P}.1$ in the invariant is maintained during the processing of e. It is clear that properties $\mathcal{P}.2$ and $\mathcal{P}.3$ are also maintained, except for the condition that the new value, $\Phi'_D(e)$, of $\Phi_D(e)$ is nonnegative. In fact, for property $\mathcal{P}.4$ to hold, $\Phi'_D(e)$ must be at least $(2a + \sin\theta)|e|$. In the following subsections, we will prove that $\Phi'_D(e) \geq (2a + \sin\theta)|e|$. From this, it will follow that all four parts of the invariant are maintained.

14.6.3 The charging path for edge e

Consider again the edge $e = (p, q)$ that was processed. Recall that we assume that $\mathcal{G}_p$ is the non-lateral graph of e. Our goal is to prove that, just after e has been processed, its dumbbell potential is greater than or equal to $(2a + \sin\theta)|e|$.

From now on, we consider the situation just after Step 1 in the processing of e. (In other words, just after the nesting tree $\mathcal{N}$ has been modified.) Let

$$\Phi'_D(e) := \left\{ \sum_{e' \in \mathcal{G}_p \cap \mathcal{T}} \left(\Phi_R(e') + \Phi_V(e') \right) + \sum_{f\,:\,\text{child of } e} \Phi_D(f) \right\} - a|e|.$$

Here, all potentials on the right-hand side are values just before edge e is processed, whereas $\Phi'_D(e)$ is the dumbbell potential of e, just after e has been processed. We have to show that $\Phi'_D(e) \geq (2a + \sin\theta)|e|$.

We consider a carefully chosen path P in $\mathcal{G}_p$ between p and some point on one of the flat faces of the pseudo-head PH_p (see Lemma 14.6.3). Observe that P consists of edges of $\mathcal{T}$ and edges of E and is completely contained in PH_p. After edge e has been processed, all edges of $P \cap \mathcal{T}$ have been nulled out.

We will show that at this moment (i.e., just after Step 1 in the processing of e), and for the specific path P that will be chosen later, the sum of

1.   the total radial and vertical potential of all edges of $P \cap \mathcal{T}$ and
2.   the total dumbbell potential of some appropriately chosen edges that are children of e

is "sufficiently large." In particular, we will show that $\Phi'_D(e) \geq (2a + \sin\theta)|e|$.

The sets P_N and P_{NN}: We define P_N to be the set consisting of

1.   all edges of $P \cap \mathcal{T}$ that have been nulled out (prior to the processing of edge e), and
2.   all edges of P that are not contained in $\mathcal{T}$.

We define P_{NN} to be the set of all edges of $P \setminus P_N$. Thus, P_{NN} consists of all edges of $P \cap \mathcal{T}$ that have not been nulled out.

The following lemma states some properties of the edges in P_N. We will use these properties at several places in our analysis.

Lemma 14.6.2. *Let e' be an edge of P_N. There exists an edge f in E, such that the following six properties hold:*

1.   *In the current nesting tree $\mathcal{N}$, f is a child of e.*
2.   *$|f| \leq \beta|e|$.*
3.   *$\Phi_D(f) \geq (2a + \sin\theta)|f|$.*
4.   *If e' is an edge of $\mathcal{T}$, then e' has been nulled out by some edge in the subtree of f.*
5.   *If e' is not an edge of $\mathcal{T}$, then e' is stored in the subtree of f.*
6.   *If $e' \neq f$, then e' is an edge of the non-lateral graph of f.*

PROOF   First assume that e' is not an edge of $\mathcal{T}$, that is, it is an edge of E. Since e' is contained in the pseudo-head PH_p, it follows from the nested-dumbbells property that, in the original nesting tree (i.e., before any edge of E has been processed), e' is in the subtree of e. During the processing of edges of E, e' may have moved up the tree. We claim, however, that at this moment (i.e., just after Step 1 in the processing of edge e), e' is still in the subtree of e. To prove this claim, assume that this is not the case. Then, during Step 1 of the processing of e, the child of e, say g, whose subtree contains e', was made a child of the parent of e. Thus, the non-lateral graphs of e and g are disjoint. Since e' is still in the subtree of g, the non-lateral graphs of e' and g are not disjoint. Since e' is an edge of P, it is an edge of the non-lateral graph of e. This implies that, since some endpoint of e' is a vertex of the non-lateral graph of e', the non-lateral graphs of e and e' are not disjoint. Thus, (i) the non-lateral graphs of e and g are disjoint, (ii) the non-lateral graphs of e' and g are not disjoint, and (iii) the non-lateral graphs of e and e' are not disjoint. Since e' is in the subtree of g, which is in the subtree of e, this is a contradiction because of the nested-dumbbells property. Hence, we have shown that at this moment, e' is indeed still in the subtree of e. Let f be the child of e, such that e' is in the subtree of f. Then obviously, the first claim in the lemma holds. The second claim follows from Lemma 14.5.10. Property $\mathcal{P}.4$ in the invariant implies that the third claim holds. The fourth claim does not apply, because e' is not an edge of $\mathcal{T}$. The fifth claim holds because of our choice of f. It remains to prove the sixth claim. Assume that $e' \neq f$. If e' is not contained in the head of PD_f that contains the non-lateral graph of f, then the non-lateral graphs of f and e' are disjoint, in which case e' is not in the subtree of f. Therefore, e' is contained in the head of PD_f that contains the non-lateral graph of f. Then it follows from the definition of the non-lateral graphs that e' is an edge of the non-lateral graph of f. Thus, the sixth claim holds.

Now assume that e' is an edge of $\mathcal{T}$. Then, since e' is an edge of P_N, this edge has been nulled out. Let g be the edge of E that has nulled out e'. Since the edges of E are processed in nondecreasing order of their lengths, we have $|g| \leq |e|$. Clearly, $g \neq e$. Since e' has been nulled out by g, e' is contained in one of the heads of PD_g. Since e' is also contained in the pseudo-head PH_p of PD_e, it follows that the pseudo-dumbbells PD_e and PD_g are not disjoint. Then, by the nested-dumbbells property, in the original nesting tree, g is in the subtree of e. As above, it can be shown that, at this moment (again, this is just after Step 1 in the processing of edge e), g is still in the subtree of e. Let f be the child of e, such that g is in the subtree of f. Obviously, the first and fourth claims hold, whereas the fifth claim does not apply to f. The second claim follows from Lemma 14.5.10. Property $\mathcal{P}.4$ in the invariant implies that the third claim holds. It remains to prove the sixth claim. Since e' has been nulled out by g, e' is an edge of the non-lateral graph of g. Hence, if $f = g$, the sixth claim holds. If $f \neq g$, then, by Lemma 14.5.10, PD_g is completely contained in one of the heads of PD_f. If PD_g is not in the head of PD_f containing the non-lateral graph of f, then g cannot be in the subtree of f. From this, it follows that also in this case, the sixth claim holds.   ■

The edge $\varphi(e')$: Let e' be an arbitrary edge in P_N, and consider the child f of e that has the properties stated in Lemma 14.6.2. We denote this edge f by $\varphi(e')$.

Let f be a child of e, and consider two distinct edges e' and e'' of P_N, such that $\varphi(e') = \varphi(e'') = f$. In general, it will not be the case that $e''' \in P_N$ and $\varphi(e''') = f$, for every edge e''' on the subpath of P joining e' and e''. We will show, however, that it is possible to choose the path P, such that this property does hold.

As before, we start with an arbitrary path P in $\mathcal{G}_p$ between p and some point on one of the flat faces of the pseudo-head PH_p. We will modify this path, such that the property mentioned above holds.

Starting at the endpoint p, we follow P until we reach the first edge e'_1, which is contained in P_N. Let $f = \varphi(e'_1)$, and let e'_2 be the last edge on P for which $e'_2 \in P_N$ and $\varphi(e'_2) = f$. By the sixth claim in Lemma 14.6.2, e'_1 and the non-lateral graph of f are not disjoint, as are e'_2 and the non-lateral graph of f. Let x be an endpoint of e'_1 that is a vertex of the non-lateral graph of f, and let y be an endpoint of e'_2 that is a vertex of the non-lateral graph of f. The non-lateral graph of f contains a path, say P_{xy}, between x and

y. In P, we replace the subpath between x and y by the path P_{xy}. We denote the resulting path by P again. Observe that this modifies the set P_N. The new path P has the following property: It consists of an initial portion, none of whose edges are in P_N. Then, it consists of a portion, all of whose edges e' are in P_N and satisfy $\varphi(e') = f$. The remaining portion of P has not been modified yet, but none of its edges e' satisfy $e' \in P_N$ and $\varphi(e') = f$. We now follow this remaining portion of P until we reach the first edge that is contained in P_N, and modify P as above. We continue making these modifications, until we obtain a path P, which satisfies the property in the following lemma.

Lemma 14.6.3. *There exists a path P in $\mathcal{G}_p$ between p and some point on one of the flat faces of the pseudo-head PH_p, for which the following property holds: Let f be a child of e, and let e' and e'' be two distinct edges of P_N, such that $\varphi(e') = \varphi(e'') = f$. Then, for every edge e''' on the subpath of P joining e' and e'', we have $e''' \in P_N$ and $\varphi(e''') = f$.*

The charging path P, the subset E_P of E, and the potential Φ_P of P: We choose a path P in $\mathcal{G}_p$ between p and some point on one of the flat faces of the pseudo-head PH_p, that satisfies the property in Lemma 14.6.3. We will refer to P as the *charging path* for edge e. We define

$$E_P := \{\varphi(e') : e' \in P_N\}.$$

In words, E_P is the set of children f of e, such that

1. some edge stored in the subtree of f has nulled out at least one edge of $P \cap T$
    or

2. some edge stored in the subtree of f is on the charging path P.

We define

$$\Phi_P := \sum_{e' \in P \cap T} \left(\Phi_R(e') + \Phi_V(e')\right) + \sum_{f \in E_P} \Phi_D(f).$$

In the following subsections, we will show that $\Phi_P \geq (3a + \sin\theta)|e|$. Since $\Phi_D'(e) \geq \Phi_P - a|e|$, this will imply that $\Phi_D'(e) \geq (2a + \sin\theta)|e|$.

Before we can prove that $\Phi_P \geq (3a + \sin\theta)|e|$, we need two preliminary results on sets of intervals.

14.6.4 A digression: two lemmas on intervals

Let $\mathcal{I}$ be a set of closed intervals on the real line. We define span($\mathcal{I}$) to be the union of all intervals in $\mathcal{I}$, that is,

$$\mathrm{span}(\mathcal{I}) := \bigcup_{I \in \mathcal{I}} I.$$

For any interval $I = [a, b]$, we denote the length of I by $|I|$. Thus, $|I| = b - a$. Observe that span($\mathcal{I}$) consists of a collection of pairwise disjoint intervals. The length $|\mathrm{span}(\mathcal{I})|$ is defined to be the sum of the lengths of these intervals.

In this section, we will present two lemmas that allow us to choose a subset $\mathcal{I}'$ of $\mathcal{I}$, such that the intervals in $\mathcal{I}'$ are pairwise disjoint, and $|\mathrm{span}(\mathcal{I}')|$ is proportional to $|\mathrm{span}(\mathcal{I})|$. Both these lemmas will be used in later subsections.

Lemma 14.6.4. *Let $\mathcal{I}$ be a set of closed intervals on the real line. There exists a subset $\mathcal{I}'$ of $\mathcal{I}$, such that the intervals in $\mathcal{I}'$ are pairwise disjoint and $|\mathrm{span}(\mathcal{I}')| \geq |\mathrm{span}(\mathcal{I})|/3$.*

PROOF   The proof is left as an exercise (see Exercise 14.4).   ∎

We define the *gap* between two disjoint intervals $I = [a_1, b_1]$ and $J = [a_2, b_2]$, where $b_1 < a_2$, to be the real number $a_2 - b_1$.

For real numbers β' and δ', we say that the intervals in the set $\mathcal{I}$ are *length-grouped with parameters β' and δ'*, if for any two intervals I and J in $\mathcal{I}$, with $|I| \leq |J|$, we have $|J| \leq |I|/\delta'$ or $|J| \geq |I|/\beta'$.

Lemma 14.6.5. *Let β' and δ' be real numbers, such that $0 < \beta' < \delta' < 1$, and let $\mathcal{I}$ be a set of closed intervals on the real line that are length-grouped with parameters β' and δ'. There exists a subset $\mathcal{I}'$ of $\mathcal{I}$, such that the following holds:*

1. $|\mathrm{span}(\mathcal{I}')| \geq \dfrac{\delta'(1-\beta')}{2(1-\beta')+\delta'(3-\beta')} |\mathrm{span}(\mathcal{I})|$.

2. *Any two distinct intervals I and J in $\mathcal{I}'$ are disjoint, and the gap between them is larger than $|I|/\delta'$.*

3. *Any two intervals $I \in \mathcal{I}'$ and $J \in \mathcal{I}$, for which $|J| \geq |I|/\beta'$, are disjoint.*

PROOF   Obviously, we may assume that the set $\mathcal{I}$ is nonempty. We present a greedy algorithm whose output is a set $\mathcal{I}'$ of intervals satisfying the three requirements.

Step 1: Initialize $\mathcal{I}_0 := \mathcal{I}$; $\mathcal{I}' := \emptyset$, and $k := 0$.

Step 2: If $\mathcal{I}_0 = \emptyset$, then the algorithm terminates. Assume that $\mathcal{I}_0 \neq \emptyset$. Let I_k be a longest interval in $\mathcal{I}_0$, and let a_k and b_k be the real numbers such that $I_k = [a_k, b_k]$. Let $\mathcal{I}'_k$ be the set of all intervals J in $\mathcal{I}_0$ for which

$$J \cap \left[a_k - (b_k - a_k)/\delta', b_k + (b_k - a_k)/\delta'\right] \neq \emptyset.$$

Step 3: For every interval J in $\mathcal{I}'_k$, add to $\mathcal{I}'_k$ all intervals $I \in \mathcal{I}_0$ for which $|J| \geq |I|/\beta'$ and $I \cap J \neq \emptyset$. Repeat this step until no more such intervals I can be added to $\mathcal{I}'_k$.

Step 4: Set $\mathcal{I}' := \mathcal{I}' \cup \{I_k\}$, $\mathcal{I}_0 := \mathcal{I}_0 \setminus \mathcal{I}'_k$, $k := k + 1$, and go to Step 2.

We now show that the set $\mathcal{I}' = \{I_0, I_1, \ldots, I_{k-1}\}$ satisfies the three claims in the lemma. It follows from the algorithm that the second claim holds. The proof of this fact is left as an exercise; see Exercise 14.5.

To prove the first claim, we first observe that the sets $\mathcal{I}'_0, \mathcal{I}'_1, \ldots, \mathcal{I}'_{k-1}$ form a partition of $\mathcal{I}$. Let j be an integer with $0 \leq j \leq k - 1$, and consider the j-th iteration of the algorithm. Since I_j is a longest interval in $\mathcal{I}_0$, we have, after Step 2,

$$|\mathrm{span}(\mathcal{I}'_j)| \leq (3 + 2/\delta')|I_j|.$$

In Step 3, intervals are added to $\mathcal{I}'_j$, whose span has length at most

$$2|I_j|\left(\beta' + (\beta')^2 + (\beta')^3 + \cdots\right) = \frac{2\beta'}{1-\beta'}|I_j|.$$

It follows that after Step 3,

$$|\mathrm{span}(\mathcal{I}'_j)| \leq (3 + 2/\delta')|I_j| + \frac{2\beta'}{1-\beta'}|I_j| = \frac{2(1-\beta')+\delta'(3-\beta')}{\delta'(1-\beta')}|I_j|.$$

Therefore,

$$|\mathrm{span}(\mathcal{I}')| = \sum_{j=0}^{k-1} |I_j|$$

$$\geq \frac{\delta'(1-\beta')}{2(1-\beta') + \delta'(3-\beta')} \sum_{j=0}^{k-1} |\mathrm{span}(\mathcal{I}'_j)|$$

$$\geq \frac{\delta'(1-\beta')}{2(1-\beta') + \delta'(3-\beta')} |\mathrm{span}(\mathcal{I})|,$$

which proves that the first claim holds.

Finally, we prove that the third claim holds. Let j be an integer with $0 \leq j \leq k-1$, and let J be an interval in $\mathcal{I}$ such that $|J| \geq |I_j|/\beta'$. We have to show that I_j and J are disjoint. Assume that $I_j \cap J \neq \emptyset$. In the j-th iteration of the algorithm, I_j is a longest interval in $\mathcal{I}_0$ and, therefore, J is not in $\mathcal{I}_0$ at that moment. Let m be the integer such that J is deleted from $\mathcal{I}_0$ during iteration m. Then $m < j$ and $J \in \mathcal{I}'_m$. But then, in Step 2 or 3 of iteration m, the interval I_j is added to $\mathcal{I}'_m$, which implies that I_j cannot be chosen in iteration j. This is a contradiction.   ∎

14.6.5 Choosing a subset E'_P of E_P

We continue the analysis that will lead to the proof of our claim at the end of Section 14.6.3 that $\Phi_P \geq (3a + \sin\theta)|e|$. Recall from Section 14.6.3 that E_P is the set of all children f of e, such that (i) some edge stored in the subtree of f has nulled out at least one edge of $P \cap T$, or (ii) some edge stored in the subtree of f is on the charging path P. In this section, we show how to pick a subset E'_P of E_P that will be used in the proof of the claim that $\Phi_P \geq (3a + \sin\theta)|e|$.

For any closed and bounded subset X of $\mathbb{R}^d$, we define the *vertical* span of X, denoted by $\mathrm{span}_V(X)$, to be the closed interval that is obtained by projecting X orthogonally onto the d-th coordinate axis.

Recall from Section 14.6.3 that P_N is the set consisting of (i) all edges of $P \cap T$ that have been nulled out (as before, this is prior to the processing of edge e), and (ii) all edges of $P \setminus T$. Also, P_{NN} is the set of all edges of $P \cap T$ that have not been nulled out. By property $\mathcal{P}.3$ in the invariant, we have $\Phi_V(e') = wt_V(e')$ for every edge e' in P_{NN}, and $\Phi_V(e') = 0$ for every edge e' in $P_N \cap T$. First assume that

$$\left| \bigcup_{e' \in P_{NN}} \mathrm{span}_V(e') \right| \geq (3a + \sin\theta)|e|.$$

Then it follows from the definition of Φ_P, that

$$\Phi_P \geq \sum_{e' \in P \cap T} \Phi_V(e')$$

$$= \sum_{e' \in P_{NN}} wt_V(e')$$

$$= \sum_{e' \in P_{NN}} |\mathrm{span}_V(e')|$$

$$\geq \left| \bigcup_{e' \in P_{NN}} \mathrm{span}_V(e') \right|$$

$$\geq (3a + \sin\theta)|e|,$$

which is exactly what we want to show. Hence, from now on, we assume that

$$\left| \bigcup_{e' \in P_{NN}} \mathrm{span}_V(e') \right| < (3a + \sin\theta)|e|.$$

Recall that P is a path between p and some point on one of the flat faces of the pseudo-head PH_p. Using Lemma 14.5.7, it follows that

$$\left| \bigcup_{e' \in P} \mathrm{span}_V(e') \right| \geq h'|e|/2,$$

where h' is the height parameter of the inner-dumbbells. Hence,

$$h'|e|/2 \leq \left| \left(\bigcup_{e' \in P_N} \mathrm{span}_V(e') \right) \cup \left(\bigcup_{e' \in P_{NN}} \mathrm{span}_V(e') \right) \right|$$

$$\leq \left| \bigcup_{e' \in P_N} \mathrm{span}_V(e') \right| + \left| \bigcup_{e' \in P_{NN}} \mathrm{span}_V(e') \right|.$$

It follows that

$$\left| \bigcup_{e' \in P_N} \mathrm{span}_V(e') \right| > (h'/2 - 3a - \sin\theta)|e|.$$

In the rest of the analysis of the non-lateral edges, we do not need the pseudo-dumbbells any more. All arguments that follow will be based on the (regular) dumbbells only.

Let e' be an arbitrary edge in P_N, and consider the child $\varphi(e')$ of e that has the properties stated in Lemma 14.6.2. It follows from the sixth claim in Lemma 14.6.2 that $\mathrm{span}_V(e') \subseteq \mathrm{span}_V(D_{\varphi(e')})$. Therefore, we have

$$\bigcup_{e' \in P_N} \mathrm{span}_V(e') \subseteq \bigcup_{e' \in P_N} \mathrm{span}_V(D_{\varphi(e')}),$$

which implies that

$$\left| \bigcup_{e' \in P_N} \mathrm{span}_V(D_{\varphi(e')}) \right| \geq \left| \bigcup_{e' \in P_N} \mathrm{span}_V(e') \right| > (h'/2 - 3a - \sin\theta)|e|.$$

The sets of intervals, Y and Y_{span}: We define

$$Y := \{\mathrm{span}_V(D_{\varphi(e')}) : e' \in P_N\}$$

and

$$Y_{\mathrm{span}} := \{I \in Y : I \subseteq \mathrm{span}_V(P)\}.$$

In plain terms, Y contains intervals corresponding to the vertical spans of the dumbbells of all edges of E that are children of e and that have (i) nulled out some edge of $P \cap T$ or (ii) whose subtree contains an edge of $P \setminus T$. The set Y_{span} contains only those intervals of Y that do not extend beyond the vertical span of P.

Hence, we have

$$\left| \bigcup_{I \in Y} I \right| > (h'/2 - 3a - \sin\theta)|e|.$$

If e' is an edge in P_N, then, by Lemma 14.6.2, $|\varphi(e')| \le \beta|e|$ and, therefore,

$$|\mathrm{span}_V(D_{\varphi(e')})| = wt_V(\varphi(e')) + h|\varphi(e')| \le (1+h)|\varphi(e')| \le \beta(1+h)|e|.$$

Since e' is an edge of P, and e' has a nonempty intersection with the dumbbell $D_{\varphi(e')}$, $\mathrm{span}_V(D_{\varphi(e')})$ has a nonempty intersection with $\mathrm{span}_V(P)$. Therefore, we have

$$\left| \bigcup_{I \in Y_{\mathrm{span}}} I \right| \ge \left| \bigcup_{I \in Y} I \right| - 4\beta(1+h)|e| > (h'/2 - 3a - \sin\theta - 4\beta(1+h))|e|. \qquad (14.7)$$

From now on, we assume that

$$h' > 6a + 2\sin\theta + 8\beta(1+h), \qquad (14.8)$$

implying that the right-hand side in (14.7) is positive. We also assume that

$$\beta(1+h)^2 < \delta(h + \cos\theta)^2. \qquad (14.9)$$

The following lemma implies that we can apply Lemma 14.6.5 to the set Y_{span}.

Lemma 14.6.6. *The intervals in Y_{span} are length-grouped with parameters*

$$\beta' := \frac{\beta(1+h)}{h + \cos\theta}$$

and

$$\delta' := \frac{\delta(h + \cos\theta)}{1 + h}.$$

PROOF First observe that, because of (14.9), $0 < \beta' < \delta' < 1$. Let I_1 and I_2 be two distinct intervals in Y_{span}, and assume that $|I_1| \le |I_2|$. We have to prove that $|I_2| \le |I_1|/\delta'$ or $|I_2| \ge |I_1|/\beta'$.

Let e_1' and e_2' be edges in P_N, such that $I_1 = \mathrm{span}_V(D_{\varphi(e_1')})$ and $I_2 = \mathrm{span}_V(D_{\varphi(e_2')})$. Since

$$|I_1| = wt_V(\varphi(e_1')) + h|\varphi(e_1')|,$$

we have

$$(h + \cos\theta)|\varphi(e_1')| \leq |I_1| \leq (1 + h)|\varphi(e_1')|.$$

In a symmetric way, we obtain the inequalities

$$(h + \cos\theta)|\varphi(e_2')| \leq |I_2| \leq (1 + h)|\varphi(e_2')|.$$

Using these inequalities, together with the fact that $\varphi(e_1')$ and $\varphi(e_2')$ are length-grouped with parameters β and δ, the lemma follows. ∎

From now on, we assume that the parameters β' and δ' satisfy the following inequality:

$$\frac{\delta'(1 - \beta')}{2(1 - \beta') + \delta'(3 - \beta')} \geq 1/6. \tag{14.10}$$

Lemma 14.6.7. *There exists a subset Y' of Y_{span}, such that the following properties hold:*

1. $\sum_{I \in Y'} |I| \geq (h' - 6a - 2\sin\theta - 8\beta(1 + h))|e|/12.$
2. *Each interval in Y' is contained in $\text{span}_V(P)$.*
3. *Any two distinct intervals I and J in Y' are disjoint, and the gap between them is larger than $|I|/\delta'$.*
4. *Any two intervals $I \in Y'$ and $J \in Y_{\text{span}}$, for which $|J| \geq |I|/\beta'$, are disjoint.*

PROOF The lemma follows by applying Lemma 14.6.5 and the inequalities in (14.7) and (14.10) to the set Y_{span}. ∎

Now, given E_P, which was defined to be the set $\{\varphi(e') : e' \in P_N\}$, we are ready to define a subset E_P' as follows:

The subset Y' of Y_{span} and the subset E_P' of E_P: Y' is the subset of Y_{span}, as given by Lemma 14.6.7. We define

$$E_P' := \{\varphi(e') \in E_P : e' \in P_N \text{ and } \text{span}_V(D_{\varphi(e')}) \in Y'\}.$$

Intuitively, Y' is a subset of disjoint vertical intervals from Y_{span} that together cover a "sufficiently large" fraction of the vertical span of P, while leaving "sufficiently large" gaps between the intervals. The set E_P' is simply the set of edges whose dumbbells have vertical spans represented in Y'.

For any edge $\varphi(e')$ in E_P', we have

$$|\text{span}_V(D_{\varphi(e')})| = wt_V(\varphi(e')) + h|\varphi(e')| \leq (1 + h)|\varphi(e')|.$$

Therefore,

$$\sum_{f \in E_P'} |f| \geq \frac{1}{1 + h} \sum_{f \in E_P'} |\text{span}_V(D_f)|$$

$$= \frac{1}{1 + h} \sum_{I \in Y'} |I|$$

$$\geq \frac{h' - 6a - 2\sin\theta - 8\beta(1 + h)}{12(1 + h)} |e|. \tag{14.11}$$

If f is an edge in E'_P, then $f \in E_P$ and, by Lemma 14.6.2, $\Phi_D(f) \geq (2a + \sin\theta)|f|$. Hence, it follows from the definition of Φ_P that

$$\Phi_P \geq \sum_{f \in E'_P} \Phi_D(f)$$

$$\geq (2a + \sin\theta) \sum_{f \in E'_P} |f|$$

$$\geq \frac{(2a + \sin\theta)\left(h' - 6a - 2\sin\theta - 8\beta(1+h)\right)}{12(1+h)} |e|.$$

At this point, it is tempting to choose the parameters in such a way that the quantity on the right-hand side is at least $(3a + \sin\theta)|e|$. For this to be possible, however, h' has to be at least 12. This obviously contradicts the requirement that the two heads of any inner-dumbbell are disjoint. As a result, a more refined analysis is needed to complete the proof of the claim that $\Phi_P \geq (3a + \sin\theta)|e|$.

14.6.6 Decomposing the charging path P

If f is an edge of E'_P, then, by the definition of E'_P, we have $\mathrm{span}_V(D_f) \in Y'$, and there is at least one edge e' in P_N, such that $f = \varphi(e')$. Also, by the sixth claim in Lemma 14.6.2, e' is contained in the dumbbell D_f.

The edge e'_f in P_N, the subpath P_f of P, and the subset E_f of E_P: For each edge f of E'_P, we define the following:

1. e'_f is a fixed edge of P_N, such that $f = \varphi(e'_f)$.

2. P_f is the subpath of the charging path P that contains e'_f and whose vertical span is equal to $\mathrm{span}_V(D_f)$.

3. E_f is the set of children g of e, such that

   (a) $\mathrm{span}_V(D_g) \in Y_{\mathrm{span}}$ (i.e., the dumbbell D_g does not extend beyond the vertical span of P) and

   (b) $g = \varphi(e')$ for some edge e' of P_f that is contained in P_N.

The subpath P_f is illustrated in Figure 14.4 for the case when $f \neq e'_f$. Observe that, by the second claim in Lemma 14.6.7, $\mathrm{span}_V(D_f) \subseteq \mathrm{span}_V(P)$ and, thus, P_f exists.

If $g \in E_f$, then (i) some edge in the subtree of g has nulled out at least one edge e' of $P_f \cap T$, or (ii) some edge e' in the subtree of g is an edge of P_f. Observe that $f \in E_f$, because e'_f is an edge of P_f. Also, $E_f \subseteq E_P$.

Lemma 14.6.8. *Let f_1 and f_2 be two distinct edges in E'_P. Then, the paths P_{f_1} and P_{f_2} are disjoint, and the sets E_{f_1} and E_{f_2} are disjoint.*

PROOF Since $\mathrm{span}_V(P_{f_1}) = \mathrm{span}_V(D_{f_1}) \in Y'$ and $\mathrm{span}_V(P_{f_2}) = \mathrm{span}_V(D_{f_2}) \in Y'$, it follows from Lemma 14.6.7 that the vertical spans of P_{f_1} and P_{f_2} are disjoint. Therefore, the paths P_{f_1} and P_{f_2} are disjoint as well.

To prove the second claim, assume that $E_{f_1} \cap E_{f_2} \neq \emptyset$. Let g be an edge in the intersection of E_{f_1} and E_{f_2}. Since f_1 and f_2 are distinct, we have $g \neq f_1$ or $g \neq f_2$. We assume without loss of generality that $g \neq f_1$.

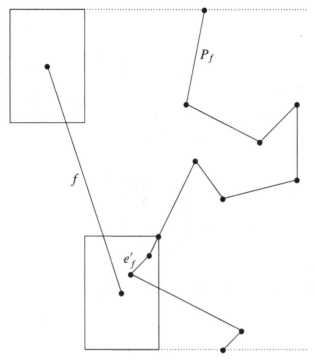

Figure 14.4: The subpath P_f of the charging path P, for the case when $f \neq e'_f$. The vertical span of P_f is equal to the vertical span of the dumbbell D_f.

Since $g \in E_{f_1}$, there exists an edge e' on P_{f_1}, such that $e' \in P_N$ and $g = \varphi(e')$. By the sixth claim in Lemma 14.6.2, we have $\mathrm{span}_V(e') \subseteq \mathrm{span}_V(D_g)$. Since e' is an edge on the path P_{f_1}, we have

$$\mathrm{span}_V(e') \subseteq \mathrm{span}_V(P_{f_1}) = \mathrm{span}_V(D_{f_1}).$$

Hence,

$$\mathrm{span}_V(D_{f_1}) \cap \mathrm{span}_V(D_g) \neq \emptyset. \tag{14.12}$$

In particular, it follows that $g \neq f_2$. In a symmetric way, we can prove that

$$\mathrm{span}_V(D_{f_2}) \cap \mathrm{span}_V(D_g) \neq \emptyset. \tag{14.13}$$

Since the edges f_1 and g are distinct and length-grouped with parameters β and δ, there are three possible cases.

Case 1: $|g| \geq |f_1|/\beta$.

First observe that $\mathrm{span}_V(D_{f_1}) \in Y'$ and $\mathrm{span}_V(D_g) \in Y_{\mathrm{span}}$. Since

$$|\mathrm{span}_V(D_g)| = wt_V(g) + h|g| \geq (h + \cos\theta)|g| \geq \frac{h + \cos\theta}{\beta}|f_1|$$

and

$$|\mathrm{span}_V(D_{f_1})| = wt_V(f_1) + h|f_1| \leq (1 + h)|f_1|,$$

we have

$$|\mathrm{span}_V(D_g)| \geq |\mathrm{span}_V(D_{f_1})|/\beta',$$

where β' is as in Lemma 14.6.6. This, together with (14.12), contradicts the fourth property in Lemma 14.6.7.

Case 2: $\delta \leq |f_1|/|g| \leq 1/\delta$.

It follows from (14.12) and (14.13) that the gap between the intervals $\text{span}_V(D_{f_1})$ and $\text{span}_V(D_{f_2})$ is less than or equal to

$$|\text{span}_V(D_g)| \leq (1+h)|g|$$
$$\leq \frac{1+h}{\delta}|f_1|$$
$$\leq \frac{1+h}{\delta(h+\cos\theta)}|\text{span}_V(D_{f_1})|$$
$$= |\text{span}_V(D_{f_1})|/\delta',$$

where δ' is as in Lemma 14.6.6. Since both $\text{span}_V(D_{f_1})$ and $\text{span}_V(D_{f_2})$ are contained in Y', this contradicts the third property in Lemma 14.6.7.

Case 3: $|f_1| \geq |g|/\beta$.

In this case, the gap between the intervals $\text{span}_V(D_{f_1})$ and $\text{span}_V(D_{f_2})$ is less than or equal to

$$|\text{span}_V(D_g)| \leq (1+h)|g|$$
$$\leq \beta(1+h)|f_1|$$
$$\leq \frac{\beta(1+h)}{h+\cos\theta}|\text{span}_V(D_{f_1})|$$
$$\leq |\text{span}_V(D_{f_1})|/\delta'.$$

As in Case 2, this contradicts the third property in Lemma 14.6.7.   ∎

The potential of P_f: For each edge f in E'_P, we define

$$\Phi_f := \sum_{e' \in P_f \cap T} \left(\Phi_R(e') + \Phi_V(e')\right) + \sum_{g \in E_f} \Phi_D(g).$$

It follows from Lemma 14.6.8 and the definition of Φ_P given at the end of Section 14.6.3 that

$$\Phi_P \geq \sum_{f \in E'_P} \Phi_f. \tag{14.14}$$

Let A and B be the real numbers such that $\text{span}_V(P) = [A, B]$, and define the interval I_P by

$$I_P := [A + \beta(1+h)|e|, B - \beta(1+h)|e|].$$

The subset E''_P of E'_P: We define

$$E''_P := \{f \in E'_P : \text{span}_V(D_f) \subseteq I_P\}.$$

For any edge f in E'_P, we have, by the definition of E'_P, $\text{span}_V(D_f) \in Y'$. Since Y' is a subset of Y_{span}, it follows from the definition of Y_{span} that

$$\text{span}_V(D_f) \subseteq \text{span}_V(P) = [A, B].$$

Also, by Lemma 14.6.2, we have $|f| \leq \beta |e|$. Finally, we observe that

$$|\text{span}_V(D_f)| \leq (1 + h)|f| \leq \beta(1 + h)|e|.$$

Therefore, since the vertical spans of the edges in E'_P are pairwise disjoint, we have

$$\sum_{f \in E''_P} |f| \geq \sum_{f \in E'_P} |f| - 4\beta(1 + h)|e|. \tag{14.15}$$

We assume from now on that

$$h' > 6a + 2\sin\theta + 8\beta(1 + h) + 48\beta(1 + h)^2, \tag{14.16}$$

and define the positive real number ξ by

$$\xi := \frac{12(1 + h)(3a + \sin\theta)}{h' - 6a - 2\sin\theta - 8\beta(1 + h) - 48\beta(1 + h)^2}. \tag{14.17}$$

In the next section, we will show that $\Phi_f \geq \xi |f|$, for each $f \in E''_P$. Combining this with (14.11), (14.14), and (14.15), and the fact that $E''_P \subseteq E'_P$ will imply that

$$\Phi_P \geq \sum_{f \in E'_P} \Phi_f$$

$$\geq \sum_{f \in E''_P} \Phi_f$$

$$\geq \xi \sum_{f \in E''_P} |f|$$

$$\geq \xi \left(\sum_{f \in E'_P} |f| - 4\beta(1 + h)|e| \right)$$

$$\geq \xi \left(\frac{h' - 6a - 2\sin\theta - 8\beta(1 + h)}{12(1 + h)} - 4\beta(1 + h) \right) |e|$$

$$= (3a + \sin\theta)|e|.$$

14.6.7 The analysis of Φ_f

In this section, we fix an edge f in E''_P. Thus, $f \in E'_P$ and $\text{span}_V(D_f) \subseteq I_P$. We will prove that $\Phi_f \geq \xi |f|$. Recall from the previous subsection that this suffices to complete the proof of Lemma 14.6.1.

Recall the set E_f that was defined in the beginning of Section 14.6.6. Also, recall that, for any edge e' of P_N, $\varphi(e')$ denotes the edge of E (which is a child of e in the nesting tree) that has the properties stated in Lemma 14.6.2.

Lemma 14.6.9. *Let g be a child of e, let e' be an edge on the path P_f, and assume that $e' \in P_N$ and $\varphi(e') = g$. Then, $g \in E_f$.*

PROOF We have to show that $\text{span}_V(D_g) \in Y_{\text{span}}$. It follows from Lemma 14.6.2 that $\text{span}_V(e') \subseteq \text{span}_V(D_g)$ and $|g| \leq \beta |e|$. Since

$$\text{span}_V(e') \subseteq \text{span}_V(P_f) = \text{span}_V(D_f),$$

we have $\text{span}_V(D_f) \cap \text{span}_V(D_g) \neq \emptyset$. Observe that

$$|\text{span}_V(D_g)| \leq (1 + h)|g| \leq \beta(1 + h)|e|.$$

This, together with the fact that $\mathrm{span}_V(D_f) \subseteq I_P$, implies that $\mathrm{span}_V(D_g) \subseteq \mathrm{span}_V(P)$. Since $\mathrm{span}_V(D_g) \in Y$ (which holds because $e' \in P_N$), it follows that $\mathrm{span}_V(D_g) \in Y_{\mathrm{Span}}$. ∎

Our proof of the claim that $\Phi_f \geq \xi|f|$ is by contradiction. Hence, from now on, we assume that $\Phi_f < \xi|f|$.

> **Intuition:** We assume that $\Phi_f < \xi|f|$. Then, the path P_f must pass through dumbbells that have nulled out large portions of it. Since P_f is sufficiently close to the edge f, the edges corresponding to these very same dumbbells contradict the leapfrog property.

Let x and y be arbitrary vertices of the path P_f, and let Q be the subpath of P_f between x and y. We partition Q into subpaths in the following way. Follow the path Q from x to y, and let e'_1 be the first edge that is in P_N. Let g_1 be the child of e such that $\varphi(e'_1) = g_1$. In other words, g_1 is the child of e such that (i) e'_1 has been nulled out by some edge in the subtree of g_1 (this is the case if e'_1 is an edge of T) or (ii) e'_1 is stored in the subtree of g_1 (this is the case if e'_1 is an edge of $Q \setminus T$; in this case, e'_1 may be equal to g_1). Let x_1 be the first vertex of e'_1, which is reached when following Q from x to y, and let R_1 be the (possibly empty) subpath of Q between x and x_1. Let Q_1 be the maximal subpath of Q, having the property that for each edge e' of Q_1, $e' \in P_N$ and $\varphi(e') = g_1$. Observe that, by Lemma 14.6.3, Q_1 is well-defined. The vertex x_1 is an endpoint of Q_1; let y_1 be the other endpoint of this subpath. By Lemma 14.6.2, Q_1 is completely contained in the dumbbell D_{g_1}. Also, by Lemma 14.6.3, no edge e' on the subpath of Q between y_1 and y satisfies $e' \in P_N$ and $\varphi(e') = g_1$.

Next, follow the path Q from y_1 to y, and let e'_2 be the first edge that is in P_N. Let g_2 be the child of e, such that $\varphi(e'_2) = g_2$. Observe that $g_2 \neq g_1$. Let x_2 be the first vertex of e'_2 that is reached when following Q from y_1 to y, and let R_2 be the (possibly empty) subpath of Q between y_1 and x_2. Let Q_2 be the maximal subpath of Q, having the property that for each edge e' of Q_2, $e' \in P_N$ and $\varphi(e') = g_2$. This subpath Q_2 has x_2 as an endpoint; let y_2 be the other endpoint. Continuing in this way, we obtain a partition

$$Q = R_1 Q_1 R_2 Q_2 \ldots R_{m-1} Q_{m-1} R_m$$

of Q into subpaths, and sequences $x_1, \ldots, x_m$, $y_0, \ldots, y_{m-1}$, $e'_1, \ldots, e'_{m-1}$, and $g_1, \ldots, g_{m-1}$, where $y_0 = x$ and $x_m = y$, such that the following properties hold:

1. For each i with $1 \leq i \leq m$, R_i is a (possibly empty) subpath between y_{i-1} and x_i, and no edge on this subpath is in P_N.

2. For each i with $1 \leq i \leq m - 1$, g_i is a child of e, and Q_i is a subpath between x_i and y_i. This subpath contains the edge e'_i, and for each edge e' on Q_i, $e' \in P_N$ and $\varphi(e') = g_i$. By Lemma 14.6.3, Q_i is well-defined and, by Lemma 14.6.2, Q_i is completely contained in the dumbbell D_{g_i}.

3. The edges $g_1, \ldots, g_{m-1}$ are pairwise distinct and, by Lemma 14.6.9, are all contained in E_f.

Denoting the radial distance between any two points p and q in $\mathbb{R}^d$ by $|pq|_R$, we apply the triangle inequality and obtain

$$|xy|_R \le \sum_{i=1}^{m} |y_{i-1}x_i|_R + \sum_{i=1}^{m-1} |x_i y_i|_R$$
$$\le \sum_{i=1}^{m} \sum_{e' \in R_i} wt_R(e') + \sum_{i=1}^{m-1} |x_i y_i|_R.$$

Consider any index i with $1 \le i \le m - 1$. Since x_i and y_i are both in the dumbbell D_{g_i}, we have $|x_i y_i|_R \le (2a + \sin\theta)|g_i|$. Moreover, since g_i is a child of e, we have $\Phi_D(g_i) \ge (2a + \sin\theta)|g_i|$. We next observe that for each i with $1 \le i \le m$, and for each edge e' on R_i, we have $wt_R(e') = \Phi_R(e')$, because e' is not contained in P_N. It follows that

$$|xy|_R \le \sum_{e' \in Q \cap T} \Phi_R(e') + \sum_{i=1}^{m-1} \Phi_D(g_i) \le \Phi_f < \xi|f|. \tag{14.18}$$

Let p_f and q_f be the endpoints of the edge f, where p_f is below q_f along the d-th coordinate axis. Recall that e'_f is a representative edge on the path P_f, such that $e'_f \in P_N$ and $f = \varphi(e'_f)$. Moreover, e'_f is contained in the dumbbell D_f. We may assume without loss of generality that the head H_{p_f} of D_f contains an endpoint of e'_f.

We choose vertices x and y on the path P_f, such that $|p_f x|_R$ and $|p_f y|_R$ are minimum and maximum, respectively. Since H_{p_f} contains an endpoint of e'_f, we have $|p_f x|_R \le a|f|$. Therefore,

$$|p_f y|_R \le |p_f x|_R + |xy|_R < (a + \xi)|f|. \tag{14.19}$$

Let C_f be the hypercylinder with radius $(a + \xi)|f|$, whose axis is the line through p_f that is parallel to the d-th coordinate axis, and whose vertical span is equal to the vertical span of D_f. Then the path P_f is completely contained in C_f. The following lemma states that every edge in $E_f \setminus \{f\}$ is significantly shorter than f, provided that the parameter μ is chosen sufficiently large.

Lemma 14.6.10. *Let g be an edge in $E_f \setminus \{f\}$. If*

$$\mu \ge (a + 1 + h/2)(1 + 1/\delta) + (\xi + \sin\theta)/\delta, \tag{14.20}$$

then $|g| \le \beta|f|$.

PROOF Since the edges of E are length-grouped with parameters β and δ, we have (i) $|g| \ge |f|/\beta$, (ii) $\delta \le |f|/|g| \le 1/\delta$, or (iii) $|f| \ge |g|/\beta$.

Since $f \in E''_P$, which is a subset of E'_P, the definition of E'_P implies that $\mathrm{span}_V(D_f) \in Y'$. Also, by the definition of the set E_f, we have $\mathrm{span}_V(D_g) \in Y_{\mathrm{span}}$ (i.e., the dumbbell's vertical span does not extend beyond that of P), and $g = \varphi(e'_g)$ for some edge e'_g of P_f that is contained in the set P_N. By Lemma 14.6.2, we have

$$\mathrm{span}_V(e'_g) \subseteq \mathrm{span}_V(D_g).$$

Since e'_g is an edge on P_f, we have

$$\text{span}_V(e'_g) \subseteq \text{span}_V(P_f) = \text{span}_V(D_f).$$

It follows that the intersection of the vertical spans of D_f and D_g is nonempty. Therefore, by the fourth property in Lemma 14.6.7, we have

$$|\text{span}_V(D_g)| < |\text{span}_V(D_f)|/\beta'.$$

A simple calculation shows that $|g| < |f|/\beta$. Hence, (i) above does not hold.

Assume that (ii) holds. Let z be one of the endpoints of e'_g, and let p_g be the lower (along the d-th coordinate axis) endpoint of g. Since z is a vertex of P_f (which is contained in the hypercylinder C_f), we have

$$|p_f z| < (a + \xi + 1 + h/2)|f|.$$

Since z is in one of the heads of D_g, we have

$$|p_g z| \leq (a + \sin\theta + 1 + h/2)|g|.$$

If $|f| \leq |g|$, then, since $|g| \leq |f|/\delta$,

$$\begin{aligned}
|p_f p_g| &\leq |p_f z| + |z p_g| \\
&< ((a + 1 + h/2)(1 + 1/\delta) + \xi + (\sin\theta)/\delta)|f| \\
&\leq \mu|f|,
\end{aligned}$$

contradicting the fact that f and g are base-separated with parameter μ. Therefore, (ii) does not hold. If $|g| \leq |f|$, then in a similar way, using the fact that $|f| \leq |g|/\delta$, we obtain the inequality $|p_f p_g| < \mu|g|$, which again contradicts the fact that f and g are base-separated with parameter μ. Thus, also in this case, (ii) does not hold, implying that (iii) must hold. ∎

Let A_f and B_f be the real numbers such that $\text{span}_V(D_f) = [A_f, B_f]$, and define the interval I_f by

$$I_f := [A_f + h|f|, B_f - h|f|]. \tag{14.21}$$

Thus, I_f is the vertical gap between the two heads of the dumbbell D_f.

The subpath Q_f of P_f: We choose a subpath Q_f of P_f such that $\text{span}_V(Q_f) = I_f$.

The subpath Q_f is illustrated in Figure 14.5. After adding the appropriate Steiner points to Q_f, we choose subpaths $Q_f^1, Q_f^2, \ldots, Q_f^\ell$ of Q_f, having the following four properties:

1. The interiors of the vertical spans of these subpaths are pairwise disjoint.
2. $\bigcup_{j=1}^\ell \text{span}_V(Q_f^j) = \text{span}_V(Q_f)$.
3. For each j with $1 \leq j \leq \ell$, the subpath Q_f^j is monotone along the d-th coordinate axis.
4. For each j with $1 \leq j < \ell$, when following Q_f (starting at the endpoint whose d-th coordinate is minimum), the subpath Q_f^j is encountered before Q_f^{j+1}.

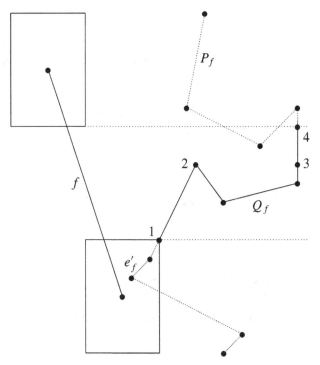

Figure 14.5: The subpath Q_f of the path P_f of Figure 14.4. The vertical span of Q_f is equal to the vertical gap between the heads of the dumbbell D_f. The subpath Q_f^1 has vertices 1 and 2 as its endpoints, whereas vertices 3 and 4 are the endpoints of the subpath Q_f^2.

In plain terms, the collection of subpaths are fragments of Q_f that are monotone along the d-th coordinate axis and monotone along Q_f, have disjoint vertical spans, and together cover the same vertical span as Q_f. For the example in Figure 14.5, one Steiner point (labeled 3) has to be added to Q_f, and there are two subpaths that satisfy these properties: The subpath Q_f^1 has as endpoints the two vertices labeled 1 and 2, whereas the subpath Q_f^2 has as endpoints the two vertices labeled 3 and 4. The points labeled 2 and 3 have equal d-th coordinates.

First observe that

$$\sum_{j=1}^{\ell} |\mathrm{span}_V(Q_f^j)| = |\mathrm{span}_V(Q_f)| \geq (\cos\theta - h)|f|.$$

It follows from the definition of Φ_f and our assumption that

$$\sum_{j=1}^{\ell} \sum_{e' \in Q_f^j \cap T} \Phi_V(e') \leq \sum_{e' \in Q_f \cap T} \Phi_V(e') \leq \Phi_f < \xi|f|.$$

Recall that, for each edge e' of $Q_f \cap T$, $\Phi_V(e')$ is equal to $wt_V(e')$ if e' is not an element of P_N, and zero otherwise. Let $Q_{f,N}$ be the set of all edges of $\bigcup_{j=1}^{\ell} Q_f^j$ that are contained in P_N, and let $Q_{f,NN}$ be the set of all remaining edges of $\bigcup_{j=1}^{\ell} Q_f^j$. Then,

$$\left| \bigcup_{e' \in Q_{f,NN}} \mathrm{span}_V(e') \right| \leq \sum_{e' \in Q_{f,NN}} wt_V(e') = \sum_{j=1}^{\ell} \sum_{e' \in Q_f^j \cap T} \Phi_V(e') < \xi|f|$$

and

$$\left| \bigcup_{j=1}^{\ell} \bigcup_{e' \in Q_f^j} \text{span}_V(e') \right| \leq \left| \bigcup_{e' \in Q_{f,N}} \text{span}_V(e') \right| + \left| \bigcup_{e' \in Q_{f,NN}} \text{span}_V(e') \right|$$

$$< \left| \bigcup_{e' \in Q_{f,N}} \text{span}_V(e') \right| + \xi |f|.$$

Since

$$\left| \bigcup_{j=1}^{\ell} \bigcup_{e' \in Q_f^j} \text{span}_V(e') \right| = \sum_{j=1}^{\ell} |\text{span}_V(Q_f^j)| \geq (\cos \theta - h)|f|,$$

it follows that

$$\left| \bigcup_{e' \in Q_{f,N}} \text{span}_V(e') \right| > (\cos \theta - h - \xi)|f|.$$

The right-hand side in this inequality is positive, if we assume that

$$\xi < \cos \theta - h. \tag{14.22}$$

Let e' be an arbitrary edge of $Q_{f,N}$, and consider the edge $\varphi(e')$. Observe that, by Lemma 14.6.9, $\varphi(e') \in E_f$. Moreover, by Lemma 14.6.2, $\text{span}_V(e') \subseteq \text{span}_V(D_{\varphi(e')})$. Hence,

$$\bigcup_{e' \in Q_{f,N}} \text{span}_V(e') \subseteq \bigcup_{e' \in Q_{f,N}} \text{span}_V(D_{\varphi(e')}),$$

which implies that

$$\left| \bigcup_{e' \in Q_{f,N}} \text{span}_V(D_{\varphi(e')}) \right| \geq \left| \bigcup_{e' \in Q_{f,N}} \text{span}_V(e') \right| > (\cos \theta - h - \xi)|f|.$$

Hence, if we define

$$Z := \{\text{span}_V(D_{\varphi(e')}) : e' \in Q_{f,N}\},$$

then we have

$$\left| \bigcup_{I \in Z} I \right| > (\cos \theta - h - \xi)|f|.$$

By Lemma 14.6.4, there exists a subset Z' of Z, such that the intervals in Z' are pairwise disjoint and

$$\sum_{I \in Z'} |I| \geq \frac{\cos \theta - h - \xi}{3} |f|.$$

The subset E_f' of E_f: We define

$$E_f' := \{\varphi(e') : e' \in Q_{f,N} \text{ and } \text{span}_V(D_{\varphi(e')}) \in Z'\}.$$

It follows from Lemma 14.6.9 that $E'_f \subseteq E_f$. Moreover, the vertical spans of the edges in E'_f are pairwise disjoint, and

$$\sum_{g \in E'_f} |g| \geq \sum_{g \in E'_f} \frac{|\text{span}_V(D_g)|}{1+h} = \frac{1}{1+h} \sum_{I \in Z'} |I| \geq \frac{\cos\theta - h - \xi}{3(1+h)} |f|. \tag{14.23}$$

Observe that, by the inequality in (14.22), the set E'_f is nonempty.

Lemma 14.6.11. *The edge f is not contained in E'_f.*

PROOF Assume that $f \in E'_f$. Let e' be an edge of $Q_{f,N}$, such that $f = \varphi(e')$. Since e' overlaps at least one of the heads of D_f, the vertical span of Q_f is not equal to the interval I_f. This is a contradiction. ∎

We write $E'_f = \{g_1, g_2, \ldots, g_k\}$. Since $E'_f \neq \emptyset$, we have $k \geq 1$. In the next section, we will prove that the sequence $f, g_1, g_2, \ldots, g_k$ of edges does not satisfy the t-leapfrog property. This will contradict our assumption that $\Phi_f < \xi|f|$ and, thus, will imply that $\Phi_f \geq \xi|f|$.

14.6.8 Contradicting the leapfrog property

For each i with $1 \leq i \leq k$, let p_i and q_i be the endpoints of the edge g_i, where, along the d-th coordinate axis, p_i is below q_i. We may assume without loss of generality that, again along the d-th coordinate axis, g_i is below g_{i+1}, for each i with $1 \leq i < k$. Recall that p_f and $\dot{q}_f$ are the endpoints of f, and that, along the d-th coordinate axis, p_f is below q_f.

To prove that the edges $f, g_1, g_2, \ldots, g_k$ do not satisfy the t-leapfrog property, we will show that

$$\sum_{i=1}^{k} |g_i| + t \left(|p_f p_1| + \sum_{i=1}^{k-1} |q_i p_{i+1}| + |q_k q_f| \right) \leq t|f|. \tag{14.24}$$

We denote the vertical distance between any two points p and q in $\mathbb{R}^d$ by $|pq|_V$. Recall that $|pq|_V$ is the absolute value of the difference between the d-th coordinates of p and q.

For each i with $1 \leq i \leq k$, let e'_i be an edge of $Q_{f,N}$ such that $g_i = \varphi(e'_i)$. Since $E'_f \subseteq E_f$, it follows from Lemmas 14.6.10 and 14.6.11 that $|g_i| \leq \beta|f|$ for each i with $1 \leq i \leq k$. Recall from Lemma 14.6.2 that e'_i overlaps at least one of the heads of D_{g_i}. Moreover, since e'_i is an edge on the path Q_f, we have $\text{span}_V(e'_i) \subseteq I_f$, where I_f is defined in (14.21).

We start by analyzing the vertical distances between the pairs of points appearing on the left-hand side of (14.24). We claim that, along the d-th coordinate axis, p_1 is above p_f. To prove this claim, let x be a point in $\mathbb{R}^d$ that is on the top flat face of the (lower) head H_{p_f} of D_f. Thus, the d-th coordinate of x is equal to the left endpoint of the interval I_f. If p_1 is above x, then p_1 is obviously above p_f. Assume that p_1 is below x. Then, since $\text{span}_V(D_{g_1}) \cap I_f \neq \emptyset$,

$$|p_1 x|_V \leq (1 + h/2)|g_1| \leq \beta(1 + h/2)|f|.$$

Since we assume that $\beta < h/(4(1+h))$ (see Section 14.5.5), it follows that

$$|p_1 x|_V < (h/2)|f| = |p_f x|_V,$$

proving that also in this case, p_1 is above p_f. In a symmetric way, it can be shown that q_k is below q_f. Combining this with the fact that the vertical spans of $g_1, g_2, \ldots, g_k$ are pairwise disjoint and sorted along the d-th coordinate axis, it follows that

$$|p_f p_1|_v + \sum_{i=1}^{k-1} |q_i p_{i+1}|_v + |q_k q_f|_v$$

$$= |p_f p_1|_v + |p_1 q_k|_v - \sum_{i=1}^{k} |p_i q_i|_v + |q_k q_f|_v$$

$$= |p_f q_f|_v - \sum_{i=1}^{k} |p_i q_i|_v$$

$$\leq |f| - \sum_{i=1}^{k} |g_i| \cos \theta. \tag{14.25}$$

Next, we analyze the radial distances between the pairs of points appearing on the left-hand side of (14.24). Let z be one of the endpoints of e_1'. Since z is a vertex of the path P_f, it follows from (14.19) that $|p_f z|_R < (a + \xi)|f|$. Since z is in one of the heads of D_{g_1}, we have

$$|p_1 z|_R \leq (a + \sin \theta)|g_1| \leq \beta(a + \sin \theta)|f|.$$

Thus,

$$|p_f p_1|_R \leq |p_f z|_R + |z p_1|_R < (a + \xi + \beta(a + \sin \theta))|f|. \tag{14.26}$$

An upper bound on $|q_k q_f|_R$ is obtained in a similar way: Let z' be one of the endpoints of e_k'. Then

$$|q_k z'|_R \leq (a + \sin \theta)|g_k| \leq \beta(a + \sin \theta)|f|$$

and

$$|q_f z'|_R \leq |q_f p_f|_R + |p_f z'|_R < |f| \sin \theta + (a + \xi)|f| = (a + \xi + \sin \theta)|f|.$$

Thus,

$$|q_k q_f|_R \leq |q_k z'|_R + |z' q_f|_R < (a + \xi + \sin \theta + \beta(a + \sin \theta))|f|. \tag{14.27}$$

Finally, we consider the sum $\sum_{i=1}^{k-1} |q_i p_{i+1}|_R$. For each i with $1 \leq i \leq k$, consider the maximal subpath of Q_f having the property that $e' \in P_N$ and $\varphi(e') = g_i$ for all edges e' on this subpath. (By Lemma 14.6.3, this subpath is well-defined.) Let x_i and y_i be the endpoints of this subpath of Q_f. Since y_i is in one of the heads of the dumbbell D_{g_i}, we have

$$\sum_{i=1}^{k-1} |q_i y_i|_R \leq (a + \sin \theta) \sum_{i=1}^{k-1} |g_i|.$$

Similarly, since x_{i+1} is in one of the heads of $D_{g_{i+1}}$, we have

$$\sum_{i=1}^{k-1} |x_{i+1} p_{i+1}|_R \leq (a + \sin \theta) \sum_{i=1}^{k-1} |g_{i+1}|.$$

We next claim that

$$\sum_{i=1}^{k-1} |y_i x_{i+1}|_R < \xi |f|, \tag{14.28}$$

which can be proved using an analysis that is similar to the one that we used to prove (14.18). The proof of (14.28) uses the fact that $E'_f \subseteq E_f$, and is left as an exercise; see Exercise 14.6. Thus,

$$\sum_{i=1}^{k-1} |q_i p_{i+1}|_R \leq \sum_{i=1}^{k-1} (|q_i y_i|_R + |y_i x_{i+1}|_R + |x_{i+1} p_{i+1}|_R)$$

$$< 2(a + \sin \theta) \sum_{i=1}^{k} |g_i| + \xi |f|. \tag{14.29}$$

The inequalities (14.25), (14.26), (14.27), and (14.29) imply that the left-hand side in (14.24) is less than or equal to

$$(1 - t \cos \theta + 2t(a + \sin \theta)) \sum_{i=1}^{k} |g_i| + t (1 + 2a + 3\xi + \sin \theta + 2\beta(a + \sin \theta)) |f|.$$

We assume that

$$\cos \theta > 2(a + \sin \theta) + 1/t, \tag{14.30}$$

which is equivalent to $1 - t \cos \theta + 2t(a + \sin \theta) < 0$. This, together with (14.23), implies that the left-hand side in (14.24) is less than or equal to

$$\frac{(1 - t \cos \theta + 2t(a + \sin \theta))(\cos \theta - h - \xi)}{3(1 + h)} |f|$$
$$+ t (1 + 2a + 3\xi + \sin \theta + 2\beta(a + \sin \theta)) |f|,$$

which is less than or equal to $t|p_f q_f| = t|f|$, if

$$\xi \leq \frac{(t \cos \theta - 1 - 2t(a + \sin \theta))(\cos \theta - h)}{t \cos \theta - 1 - 2t(a + \sin \theta) + 9t(1 + h)}$$
$$- \frac{3t(1 + h)(2a + \sin \theta + 2\beta(a + \sin \theta))}{t \cos \theta - 1 - 2t(a + \sin \theta) + 9t(1 + h)}. \tag{14.31}$$

Recall that ξ is defined in (14.17). Assuming that the parameters $\theta, \beta, \delta, \mu, a,$ and h can be chosen such that the inequalities in (14.8), (14.9), (14.10), (14.16), (14.20), (14.22), (14.30), and (14.31), and those given in Section 14.5.5, are satisfied, we have completed the analysis of the non-lateral edge set E, and, therefore, the proof of Lemma 14.6.1. We will consider the choice of these parameters in Section 14.8.

14.7 Bounding the weight of lateral edges

In this section, we consider a subset of E (which is the original set of edges that satisfy the t-leapfrog property) that consists of lateral edges only and that satisfies the properties mentioned in Section 14.5.5. For ease of notation, we denote this subset by E. We will denote the set of endpoints of the original edge set by S. We assume without loss of generality that each edge (p, q) in E makes an angle of at most θ with the d-th coordinate axis. We also assume that the parameters $\theta, \beta, \delta, \mu, a,$ and h satisfy the inequalities given in Section 14.5.5. Recall that a denotes the radius parameter of the dumbbell heads. In this section we prove the following lemma:

Lemma 14.7.1. *Let E be a set of lateral edges satisfying the properties mentioned in Section 14.5.5, and let T be a minimum spanning tree of the point set S. Then, for an appropriate choice of the parameters, we have*

$$wt(E) = O\left(\frac{1}{a} \cdot wt(T)\right).$$

> **Intuition:** Lemma 14.7.1 will be proved by "processing" the edges of E in a bottom-up fashion. We will show that the length of every edge $e = (p, q)$ of the lateral set E can be charged to the *radial* components of the weights of the portion of T that is in the head PH_p of the pseudo-dumbbell PD_e.

Surprisingly, the analysis of the lateral set E does not use the fact that the edges satisfy the leapfrog property. Instead, the entire analysis is based on the so-called *Sparse Ball Theorem* (Theorem 14.10.3), which states a basic local property of Steiner minimum trees. A precise statement and proof of this theorem will be given in Section 14.10.

In the next section, we will describe the main properties that are maintained during the processing of the edges of E.

14.7.1 The invariant $\mathcal{Q}$

During the processing of the edges of the lateral edge set E, the minimum spanning tree T will be modified. From now on, T will always refer to the minimum spanning tree of the point set S, whereas T' will denote the current tree. Thus, before any edges of E have been processed, T and T' are equal. Recall that we have introduced Steiner vertices at all locations where T pierces the boundaries of the heads of the pseudo-dumbbells of the edges in E. During the processing, some points of S will not be vertices of T'. Also, T' will contain Steiner vertices.

We denote by W the total weight of all edges in E that have been processed. As before, we use $|pq|_R$ and $|pq|_V$ to denote the radial and vertical distances, respectively, between any two points p and q in $\mathbb{R}^d$. Also, $wt_R(T)$ and $wt_R(T')$ denote the sum of the radial weights of all edges in T and T', respectively.

During the processing of the edges in E, the following invariant $\mathcal{Q}$ will be maintained:

$\mathcal{Q}.1$: T' is a tree.

$\mathcal{Q}.2$: There exists a real constant α (that depends only on the dimension d) with $0 < \alpha < 1$, such that

$$wt_R(T) \geq wt_R(T') + \left(\alpha a' - \sin\theta - \frac{6a\beta}{1-\beta}\right) W.$$

Note that the parameters a, a', β, and θ are as described in Section 14.5.5.

$\mathcal{Q}.3$: For every edge f in E that has not been processed and for each endpoint x of f, there exists a point $\upsilon(x)$ in S, such that the following three properties hold:

$\mathcal{Q}.3.1$: $\upsilon(x)$ is a vertex of T'.

$\mathcal{Q}.3.2$: $\upsilon(x)$ is in the head PH_x of the pseudo-dumbbell PD_f.

$\mathcal{Q}.3.3$: If $\upsilon(x) \neq x$, then there exists an edge g in E, such that

$Q.3.3.1$: g has been processed,

$Q.3.3.2$: $\upsilon(x)$ is in one of the heads of the pseudo-dumbbell PD_g,

$Q.3.3.3$: $|x\upsilon(x)|_R \leq (2a/(1 - \beta))|g|$, and

$Q.3.3.4$: $|x\upsilon(x)|_V \leq (h/(1 - \beta))|g|$.

Assume that $\upsilon(x) \neq x$. Since the edges of E will be processed in nondecreasing order of their lengths, we have $|g| \leq |f|$. Properties $Q.3.2$ and $Q.3.3.2$ imply that some head of PD_f has a nonempty intersection with some head of PD_g. Thus, by the length-grouping and nested-dumbbells properties, we have $|g| \leq \beta|f|$, implying that the vertex $\upsilon(x)$ is close to x.

Before we can state property $Q.4$ of the invariant, we introduce some notation. Recall the graphs $\mathcal{G}_x$ (for each endpoint x of each edge of E) that were defined in Section 14.5.4. We define a generalization of these graphs, which, for convenience, we denote by $\mathcal{G}_x$ again. These graphs are based on

1. the tree T',
2. the edges of E that have not been processed, and
3. the vertices $\upsilon(x)$ of T',

and are defined in the following way: Let $f = (x, y)$ be any edge in E that has not been processed, and consider one of the heads of the pseudo-dumbbell PD_f, say the head PH_x. Consider the graph obtained by adding to T' the edges $(\upsilon(p), \upsilon(q))$, for all edges (p, q) in E that have not been processed and that are contained in the pseudo-head PH_x. We define $\mathcal{G}_x$ to be the maximal connected subgraph of this graph that contains the vertex $\upsilon(x)$ and that is completely contained in the pseudo-head PH_x. We define the graph $\mathcal{G}_y$ similarly with respect to the other endpoint y of f. (Thus, $\mathcal{G}_y$ is connected to the vertex $\upsilon(y)$.)

Thus the main difference between the earlier definition of $\mathcal{G}_x$ from Section 14.5.4 and the definition above is the fact that the graph $\mathcal{G}_x$ is defined with respect to the current tree T', and with respect to vertices $\upsilon(p)$ instead of p. Furthermore, the graph $\mathcal{G}_x$ includes only edges $(\upsilon(p), \upsilon(q))$, which are close approximations of unprocessed edges (p, q) from E.

We can now state the fourth property of the invariant:

$Q.4$: For every edge f in E that has not been processed and for each endpoint x of f, no vertex of the graph $\mathcal{G}_x$ is on any of the flat faces of the head PH_x of the pseudo-dumbbell PD_f.

Property $Q.3$ states that the endpoint x of the edge f (that has not been processed) is either a vertex of the current tree T', or there exists a vertex $\upsilon(x)$ of T' that is sufficiently close to x. Property $Q.4$ states that all unprocessed edges f remain as lateral edges, even after the processing of an edge e, and hence will eventually be processed in a manner similar to edge e. Observe that the notion of being lateral is based on the current graph $\mathcal{G}_x$.

After all edges of E have been processed, we have $W = wt(E)$. Then, it follows from property $Q.2$ that

$$wt_R(T) \geq wt_R(T') + \left(\alpha a' - \sin\theta - \frac{6a\beta}{1 - \beta}\right)W$$

$$\geq \left(\alpha a' - \sin\theta - \frac{6a\beta}{1 - \beta}\right)W$$

$$= \left(\alpha a' - \sin\theta - \frac{6a\beta}{1 - \beta}\right) \cdot wt(E).$$

We assume from now on that

$$\alpha a' - \sin\theta - \frac{6\alpha\beta}{1-\beta} \geq \frac{1}{2}\alpha a. \tag{14.32}$$

This implies that

$$wt(E) \leq \frac{2}{\alpha a} \cdot wt_R(T) \leq \frac{2}{\alpha a} \cdot wt(T).$$

Thus, if we can show how to maintain the invariant during the processing of the edges of E, then we will have proved Lemma 14.7.1.

Let us verify that the invariant holds before any edge of E has been processed. At that moment, we have $W = 0$ and $T' = T$. We define $\upsilon(x) := x$ for each endpoint x of each edge of E. Since $\mathcal{G}_x$ is exactly the graph as defined in Section 14.5.4, the invariant holds at this moment.

In the next sections, we will show how the invariant can be maintained during the processing of an edge of E.

14.7.2 Processing one edge of E

Let $e = (p, q)$ be a shortest edge in E that has not been processed, and assume that the invariant holds at this moment. Observe that, by Lemma 14.5.10, each edge f that is contained in one of the heads of the pseudo-dumbbell PD_e has already been processed.

We fix one endpoint of e, say p, and define T_p' to be the maximal portion of the tree T' that contains the vertex $\upsilon(p)$ and that is completely contained in the head PH_p of the pseudo-dumbbell PD_e. By property $\mathcal{Q}.3.2$, $\upsilon(p)$ is in PH_p and, therefore, T_p' is well-defined. In what follows, we show that T_p' can be modified so that it accounts for the weight of edge e while maintaining the invariant.

Let $u_1, u_2, \ldots, u_k$ be the intersections of T_p' with the boundary of the pseudo-head PH_p. Since T_p' is a subgraph of $\mathcal{G}_p$, it follows from property $\mathcal{Q}.4$, that all these intersection points are on the side face of PH_p. Since T' is a tree (by property $\mathcal{Q}.1$), and $\upsilon(p)$ and $\upsilon(q)$ are in different heads of PD_e (by property $\mathcal{Q}.3.2$), we have $k \geq 1$.

We follow the path in the tree T' from $\upsilon(q)$ to $\upsilon(p)$, and consider the first element of $\{u_1, u_2, \ldots, u_k\}$ that is encountered. We assume without loss of generality that this first element is u_1.

Let $\upsilon(p)^\perp$ be the orthogonal projection of $\upsilon(p)$ onto the hyperplane $x_d = 0$, and for each i with $1 \leq i \leq k$, let $u_i^\perp$ be the orthogonal projection of u_i onto this hyperplane. Let $T_p''^\perp$ be a Steiner minimum tree of the points $\upsilon(p)^\perp, u_1^\perp, u_2^\perp, \ldots, u_k^\perp$. Observe that $T_p''^\perp$ is contained in $\mathbb{R}^{d-1}$. Let $e''^\perp$ be a longest edge on the path in $T_p''^\perp$ between $\upsilon(p)^\perp$ and $u_1^\perp$. We apply the inverse of the projection to the tree $T_p''^\perp$ to obtain a Steiner tree T_p''. Formally, T_p'' is a Steiner tree of the points $\upsilon(p), u_1, u_2, \ldots, u_k$, such that

1. the orthogonal projection of T_p'' onto the hyperplane $x_d = 0$ is equal to $T_p''^\perp$, and

2. T_p'' is completely contained in the head PH_p of the pseudo-dumbbell PD_e.

Finally, we denote by e'' the edge of T_p'', whose orthogonal projection onto the hyperplane $x_d = 0$ is equal to $e''^\perp$.

The processing of edge e consists of performing the following three steps:

Step 1: In the tree T', replace the portion T'_p by the tree T''_p.

Step 2: Add the edge $(\upsilon(p), \upsilon(q))$ to the tree resulting from Step 1.

Step 3: Delete the edge e'' from the graph resulting from Step 2.

> **Intuition:** Recall that we compare the total weight of the edges in E to the radial weight of the edges of the minimum spanning tree T; see property $\mathcal{Q}.2$ in the invariant. In other words, the vertical components of the weights of the edges of T are ignored. Since $wt_R(T''_p) \leq wt_R(T'_p)$, the tree resulting from Step 1 has a smaller radial weight than the tree T'. The edge $(\upsilon(p), \upsilon(q))$ that is added in Step 2 is almost vertical and, thus, its radial weight is small. It follows from our choice of the vertex u_1 that the graph resulting from Step 2 contains a cycle that contains the path in T''_p between $\upsilon(p)$ and u_1. Therefore, by deleting the edge e'' in Step 3, we obtain a tree again. It follows from the Sparse Ball Theorem in Section 14.10 that the radial weight of e'' (which is equal to the weight of $e''^{\perp}$) is proportional to the length of the edge e of E being processed. In other words, the radial weight of e'' is used to "pay" for the edge e.

After e has been processed as described above, there may be an edge f in E that has not been processed yet, such that for one of its endpoints x, the point $\upsilon(x)$ is a vertex of the tree T'_p that is replaced in Step 1. In this case, $\upsilon(x)$ will not be a vertex of the tree that results from Step 3. As we will see later, however, if we redefine $\upsilon(x)$ to be the point $\upsilon(p)$, then property $\mathcal{Q}.3$ will hold again.

Remark 14.7.2. The point $\upsilon(x)$ only has to be redefined if the old vertex $\upsilon(x)$ is in the pseudo-head PH_p and, thus, x is close to p (as compared to the length of the edge e). Using the fact that the edges of E satisfy the strong gap property (see Section 14.5.1), and by choosing the parameters appropriately, we can guarantee that $|xp|$ is large compared to the length of e. In this way, $\upsilon(x)$ will be equal to x during the entire processing of the edges of E. We do not consider this, however, because in Section 14.9, we generalize the proof of the Leapfrog Theorem to the case when the strong gap property holds only for edges that have approximately the same length. In that case, the vertex $\upsilon(x)$ may change during the processing of the edges.

We denote by T'', the graph that results after applying Steps 1, 2, and 3. As we have seen above, T'' is a tree and, thus, property $\mathcal{Q}.1$ in the invariant holds after e has been processed. In the following subsections, we will show that properties $\mathcal{Q}.2$, $\mathcal{Q}.3$, and $\mathcal{Q}.4$ also hold at this moment.

14.7.3 Analyzing the radial weight of T''

In this section, we will prove that, after edge $e = (p, q)$ has been processed, property $\mathcal{Q}.2$ in the invariant still holds.

We consider the situation just before e is processed. Consider again the intersections $u_1, u_2, \ldots, u_k$ of the portion T'_p of T' with the side face of the head PH_p of the pseudo-dumbbell PD_e. Recall that $\upsilon(p)^{\perp}, u_1^{\perp}, u_2^{\perp}, \ldots, u_k^{\perp}$ denote the orthogonal projections of the points $v(p), u_1, u_2, \ldots, u_k$ onto the hyperplane $x_d = 0$. We define $p^\perp$ to be the orthogonal projection of p onto the hyperplane $x_d = 0$.

The following lemma states that the points $u_1^\perp, u_2^\perp, \ldots, u_k^\perp$ are outside of a ball centered at $v(p)^\perp$, whose radius is at least proportional to the length of the edge e. From now on, we assume that

$$\beta < \frac{a'}{2a + a'}. \tag{14.33}$$

Lemma 14.7.3. *Let* $B^\perp$ *be the ball in the hyperplane* $x_d = 0$, *with center* $v(p)^\perp$ *and radius*

$$\left(a' - \frac{2a\beta}{1 - \beta}\right) |pq|.$$

Then, none of the points $u_1^\perp, u_2^\perp, \ldots, u_k^\perp$ *are in the interior of* $B^\perp$.

PROOF First observe that, because of (14.33), the radius of $B^\perp$ is positive. Let i be an index with $1 \leq i \leq k$. We have to show that

$$|v(p)^\perp u_i^\perp| \geq \left(a' - \frac{2a\beta}{1 - \beta}\right) |pq|. \tag{14.34}$$

By Lemma 14.5.7, the pseudo-head PH_p contains the inner-head IH_p. The boundary of this inner-head is contained in a hypercylinder centered at p, having radius $a'|pq|$, and whose axis is parallel to the d-th coordinate axis. Since u_i is on the side face of PH_p, it follows that $|pu_i|_R \geq a'|pq|$. Therefore, we have

$$a'|pq| \leq |pu_i|_R = |p^\perp u_i^\perp| \leq |p^\perp v(p)^\perp| + |v(p)^\perp u_i^\perp| = |pv(p)|_R + |v(p)^\perp u_i^\perp|.$$

Hence, if $v(p) = p$, then $a'|pq| \leq |v(p)^\perp u_i^\perp|$, from which (14.34) follows. Assume that $v(p) \neq p$. By property $Q.3.3$ in the invariant, there exists an edge g in E, such that (i) g has been processed, (ii) $v(p)$ is in one of the heads of the pseudo-dumbbell PD_g, and (iii) $|pv(p)|_R \leq (2a/(1 - \beta))|g|$. Since, by property $Q.3.2$, $v(p)$ is in the head PH_p of PD_e, it follows that the pseudo-dumbbells PD_e and PD_g are not disjoint. Since g has been processed and e has not been processed, we have $|g| \leq |e|$. Then, it follows from the length-grouping property and Lemma 14.5.5 that $|g| \leq \beta|e| = \beta|pq|$. Hence,

$$\begin{aligned} a'|pq| &\leq |pv(p)|_R + |v(p)^\perp u_i^\perp| \\ &\leq \frac{2a}{1 - \beta} |g| + |v(p)^\perp u_i^\perp| \\ &\leq \frac{2a\beta}{1 - \beta} |pq| + |v(p)^\perp u_i^\perp|, \end{aligned}$$

which is equivalent to (14.34).   ■

In the following lemma, we prove that the edge e'' in Step 3 of the processing of the edge e has a radial weight that is at least proportional to the length of e.

Lemma 14.7.4. *Consider the edge* e'' *that is deleted in Step 3 of the processing of the edge* $e = (p, q)$. *There exists a real constant* α *(that depends only on the dimension* d*), such that* $0 < \alpha < 1$ *and*

$$wt_R(e'') \geq \alpha \left(a' - \frac{2a\beta}{1 - \beta}\right) |pq|.$$

PROOF   Recall from Section 14.7.2, that $e''^{\perp}$ is a longest edge on the path in the tree $T_p''^{\perp}$ between $\upsilon(p)^{\perp}$ and $u_1^{\perp}$, and that $e''^{\perp}$ is the orthogonal projection of e'' onto the hyperplane $x_d = 0$. In other words, $wt_R(e'')$ is equal to the length of $e''^{\perp}$.

The tree $T_p''^{\perp}$ is a Steiner minimum tree of the points $\upsilon(p)^{\perp}, u_1^{\perp}, u_2^{\perp}, \ldots, u_k^{\perp}$. All points $u_i^{\perp}$ are on the boundary of or outside the ball $B^{\perp}$ in Lemma 14.7.3; recall that $B^{\perp}$ is centered at $\upsilon(p)^{\perp}$. Then, the Sparse Ball Theorem in Section 14.10 (applied in the $(d-1)$-dimensional space $x_d = 0$) implies that there exists a constant α with $0 < \alpha < 1$, such that the length of $e''^{\perp}$ is at least α times the radius of $B^{\perp}$. This completes the proof.   ∎

We are now ready to prove that property $Q.2$ in the invariant is maintained during the processing of the edge e. Recall that T' denotes the tree in property $Q.1$, just before e is processed, whereas T'' denotes this tree, just after e has been processed. It follows from Steps 1, 2, and 3 in Section 14.7.2 that

$$wt_R(T'') = wt_R(T') - wt_R(T_p') + wt_R(T_p'') + |\upsilon(p)\upsilon(q)|_R - wt_R(e'').$$

Since the orthogonal projection of T_p' onto the hyperplane $x_d = 0$ is a Steiner tree of the points $\upsilon(p)^{\perp}, u_1^{\perp}, u_2^{\perp}, \ldots, u_k^{\perp}$, and since $T_p''^{\perp}$ is a Steiner minimum tree of these points, we have

$$wt_R(T_p'') = wt(T_p''^{\perp}) \leq wt_R(T_p').$$

Next we observe that

$$|\upsilon(p)\upsilon(q)|_R \leq |\upsilon(p)p|_R + |pq|_R + |q\upsilon(q)|_R$$
$$\leq |\upsilon(p)p|_R + |pq|\sin\theta + |q\upsilon(q)|_R.$$

An analysis that is similar to the one in the proof of Lemma 14.7.3 shows that

$$|\upsilon(p)p|_R \leq \frac{2\alpha\beta}{1-\beta}|pq|$$

and

$$|q\upsilon(q)|_R \leq \frac{2\alpha\beta}{1-\beta}|pq|.$$

By combining these inequalities with the lower bound on $wt_R(e'')$ in Lemma 14.7.4 and the fact that $0 < \alpha < 1$, we obtain

$$wt_R(T'') \leq wt_R(T') + \left(\frac{4\alpha\beta}{1-\beta} + \sin\theta\right)|pq| - \alpha\left(a' - \frac{2\alpha\beta}{1-\beta}\right)|pq|$$
$$\leq wt_R(T') - \left(\alpha a' - \sin\theta - \frac{6\alpha\beta}{1-\beta}\right)|pq|. \tag{14.35}$$

Let W denote the total weight of the edges of E that have been processed, just before e is processed. Let W' denote this quantity just after e has been processed. Thus, $W' = W + |pq|$. By property $Q.2$ in the invariant, we have

$$wt_R(T) \geq wt_R(T') + \left(\alpha a' - \sin\theta - \frac{6\alpha\beta}{1-\beta}\right)W.$$

By combining this with the inequality in (14.35), it follows that

$$wt_R(T) \geq wt_R(T'') + \left(\alpha a' - \sin\theta - \frac{6a\beta}{1-\beta} \right) W'.$$

Thus, property $Q.2$ in the invariant is maintained during the processing of the edge e.

14.7.4 Property $Q.3$ is maintained

To prove that property $Q.3$ in the invariant is maintained, we choose an edge f in E that has not been processed (just after $e = (p, q)$ has been processed). Let x be one of the endpoints of f.

Recall that T' denotes the tree in property $Q.1$, prior to the processing of e, whereas T'' denotes this tree, just after e has been processed. Consider the point $\upsilon(x)$ of S, just before edge e is processed. If $\upsilon(x)$ is a vertex of the tree T'', then obviously, property $Q.3$ still holds after e has been processed. Assume that $\upsilon(x)$ is not a vertex of T''. Define

$$\upsilon_{new}(x) := \upsilon(p)$$

and

$$g_{new} := e.$$

We will show that, after e has been processed, property $Q.3$ holds for T'', $\upsilon_{new}(x)$, and g_{new}.

Obviously, $\upsilon_{new}(x)$ is a point of S that is a vertex of T'', that is, $Q.3.1$ holds. To prove that $Q.3.2$ holds, we have to show that $\upsilon_{new}(x)$ is in the head PH_x of the pseudo-dumbbell PD_f. That is, we have to show that $\upsilon(p)$ is contained in PH_x. Since the invariant holds before e is processed, $\upsilon(x)$ is contained in PH_x. Recall from the way we process the edge e that each vertex of T' that is not a vertex of T'' is contained in the head PH_p of the pseudo-dumbbell PD_e. Therefore, since $\upsilon(x)$ is a vertex of T', but not of T'', $\upsilon(x)$ is contained in PH_p. Hence, the pseudo-dumbbells PD_f and PD_e have a nonempty intersection. Since f has not been processed, we have $|e| \leq |f|$. Then, it follows from the nested-dumbbells property that PD_e is completely contained in the pseudo-head PH_x. Since, by $Q.3.2$, $\upsilon(p)$ is contained in one of the heads of PD_e, it follows that $\upsilon(p)$ is contained in PH_x. Thus, $Q.3.2$ holds.

It remains to show that property $Q.3.3$ holds for $\upsilon_{new}(x)$ and g_{new}. We assume that $\upsilon_{new}(x) \neq x$. Obviously, g_{new} has been processed and, thus, $Q.3.3.1$ holds. Property $Q.3.3.2$ follows from the fact that $\upsilon(p)$ is contained in the head PH_p of the pseudo-dumbbell PD_e. To prove $Q.3.3.3$ and $Q.3.3.4$, there are two cases, depending on whether or not $\upsilon(x)$ and x are equal. We consider only the case when $\upsilon(x) \neq x$. (The easier case when $\upsilon(x) = x$ is left as an exercise; see Exercise 14.9.) Since $Q.3$ holds just before e is processed, there exists an edge g in E, such that

1. g has been processed (before e is processed),
2. $\upsilon(x)$ is in one of the heads of the pseudo-dumbbell PD_g,
3. $|x\upsilon(x)|_R \leq (2a/(1-\beta))|g|$, and
4. $|x\upsilon(x)|_V \leq (h/(1-\beta))|g|$.

We have seen above that $\upsilon(x)$ is contained in the head PH_p of the pseudo-dumbbell PD_e. We also know from the invariant that $\upsilon(p)$ is contained in PH_p. Therefore, using the fact that the pseudo-head PH_p is contained in the head H_p of the dumbbell D_e, we have

$$|\upsilon(x)\upsilon_{\text{new}}(x)|_R = |\upsilon(x)\upsilon(p)|_R \le 2a|e|$$

and

$$|\upsilon(x)\upsilon_{\text{new}}(x)|_V = |\upsilon(x)\upsilon(p)|_V \le h|e|.$$

Since $\upsilon(x)$ is in the head PH_p of PD_e and in one of the heads of PD_g, the pseudo-dumbbells PD_e and PD_g have a nonempty intersection. Since g was processed before e, we have $|g| \le |e|$. Thus, it follows from the length-grouping property and Lemma 14.5.5, that $|g| \le \beta|e|$. By combining the above inequalities, we obtain

$$|x\upsilon_{\text{new}}(x)|_R \le |x\upsilon(x)|_R + |\upsilon(x)\upsilon_{\text{new}}(x)|_R$$
$$\le \frac{2a}{1-\beta}|g| + 2a|e|$$
$$\le \frac{2a\beta}{1-\beta}|e| + 2a|e|$$
$$= \frac{2a}{1-\beta}|e|$$
$$= \frac{2a}{1-\beta}|g_{\text{new}}|.$$

In a similar way, we obtain

$$|x\upsilon_{\text{new}}(x)|_V \le \frac{h}{1-\beta}|g_{\text{new}}|.$$

Thus, properties $\mathcal{Q}.3.3.3$ and $\mathcal{Q}.3.3.4$ hold. This completes the proof of our claim that property $\mathcal{Q}.3$ is maintained during the processing of the edge e.

14.7.5 Property $\mathcal{Q}.4$ is maintained

In this section, we will show that property $\mathcal{Q}.4$ in the invariant is maintained during the processing of the edge $e = (p, q)$. For any edge that has not been processed, and for any of its endpoints x, we denote by $\upsilon(x)$ the point of S in property $\mathcal{Q}.3$ of the invariant, prior to the processing of e. Let $\upsilon'(x)$ denote this point just after e has been processed. We have seen in Section 14.7.4 that, if $\upsilon'(x) \ne \upsilon(x)$, then $\upsilon'(x) = \upsilon(p)$.

Let f be an edge in E that has not been processed (just after e has been processed), and let x be one of the endpoints of f. We denote the graph in property $\mathcal{Q}.4$ for the point x, just before e is processed, by $\mathcal{G}_x$. Let $\mathcal{G}'_x$ denote this graph just after e has been processed.

Let P be an arbitrary path in $\mathcal{G}'_x$ between $\upsilon'(x)$ and some point, say u, on the boundary of the head PH_x of the pseudo-dumbbell PD_f. To prove that property $\mathcal{Q}.4$ holds, we have to show that u is on the side face of PH_x. We will show that P can be converted to a path in $\mathcal{G}_x$ between $\upsilon(x)$ and u. This will imply that u is on the side face of PH_x, because property $\mathcal{Q}.4$ holds before e is processed.

Clearly, if P is a path in $\mathcal{G}_x$, we are done. Thus, we assume that P is not a path in $\mathcal{G}_x$. Then, some portion of P must have a nonempty intersection with the head PH_p of the pseudo-dumbbell PD_e. Since $|e| \le |f|$, the nested-dumbbells property implies that PD_e is completely contained in PH_x.

We consider three types of subpaths of P. The first type is a subpath P' that is contained in the head PH_p of the pseudo-dumbbell PD_e, and whose endpoints v and w are vertices of the tree T_p'' that are on the boundary of PH_p. Observe that v and w are on the side face of PH_p. It follows from Step 1 in the processing of e, that the tree T_p' contains a path between v and w that is completely contained in PH_p.

The second type is a subpath P', such that (i) one of its endpoints v is a vertex of T_p'' that is on the boundary of PH_p, (ii) the last edge on P' is $(v'(y), v'(z))$, for some edge (y, z) that is either equal to e or has not been processed, and (iii) the path P' minus the last edge is completely contained in the head PH_p of the pseudo-dumbbell PD_e. In this case, we have $v'(y) = v(p)$, $v'(z) = v(z)$, and $v'(z)$ is not contained in PH_p. It follows from Steps 1 and 2 in the processing of e that the tree T_p' contains a path between $v(y)$ and $v(p)$, and a path between v and $v(p)$. Hence, we can convert P' to the concatenation of (i) the path in T_p' between v and $v(y)$, and (ii) the edge $(v(y), v(z))$.

The third type is a subpath P' that consists of two edges $(v'(y_1), v'(z_1))$ and $(v'(y_2), v'(z_2))$, for some distinct edges (y_1, z_1) and (y_2, z_2), each of which is either equal to e or has not been processed, such that $v'(z_1) = v'(y_2)$ is contained in PH_p. In this case, we have $v'(z_1) = v'(y_2) = v(p)$, $v'(y_1) = v(y_1)$, and $v'(z_2) = v(z_2)$, and $v'(y_1)$ and $v'(z_2)$ are not contained in PH_p. It follows from Steps 1 and 2 in the processing of e that the tree T_p' contains a path between $v(z_1)$ and $v(p)$, and a path between $v(y_2)$ and $v(p)$. Hence, we can convert P' to the concatenation of (i) the edge $(v(y_1), v(z_1))$, (ii) the path in T_p' between $v(z_1)$ and $v(y_2)$, and (iii) the edge $(v(y_2), v(z_2))$.

Starting with the path P, we convert each subpath that is of one of the three types, as described above. Each subpath that is not of one any these types remains unchanged. This results in a path between the points $v(x)$ and u. This path is, in fact, a path in the graph $\mathcal{G}_x$. This completes the proof of the claim that property $\mathcal{Q}.4$ is maintained during the processing of the edge e.

Assuming that the parameters $\theta, \beta, \delta, \mu, a$, and h can be chosen such that the inequalities in (14.32) and (14.33), and those given in Section 14.5.5, are satisfied, we have completed the analysis of the lateral edge set E, and, therefore, the proof of Lemma 14.7.1. We will consider the choice of these parameters in the next section.

14.8 Completing the proof of the Leapfrog Theorem

Let $t > 1$ be a real number, let E be a set of undirected edges in $\mathbb{R}^d$ that satisfies the t-leapfrog property, and let S be the set of endpoints of the edges in E. Let $\theta, \beta, \delta, \mu, a$, and h be real numbers, and let $w := (\cos\theta - \sin\theta - 1/t)/2$. Assume that these parameters are chosen, such that all inequalities in Section 14.5.5, as well as those in (14.8), (14.9), (14.10), (14.16), (14.20), (14.22), (14.30), (14.31), (14.32), and (14.33) are satisfied. (Recall that ξ is defined in (14.17) and α is a constant that is given by Lemma 14.7.4.) Then it follows from the results in Section 14.5.5, Lemmas 14.6.1 and 14.7.1, that

$$wt(E) = O\left(\frac{\log(1/\beta)}{a\theta^{d-1}\log(1/\delta)}\left(1 + \frac{\mu}{w\delta}\right)^d\right) \cdot wt(MST(S)). \tag{14.36}$$

To complete the proof of the Leapfrog Theorem (Theorem 14.4.1), it remains to choose the parameters, such that all requirements are satisfied. We claim that this is the case, if we take $\beta = \min(10^{-4}, \alpha/49)$, $\delta = 99/100$, $h = 1/100$, $\mu = 5$, $a = (t-1)/(10^6 t)$, and θ such that $0 < \theta < \pi/4$,

$$\sin \theta \le \min\left(\alpha a/8, \frac{t-1}{200t}\right),$$

and

$$\cos \theta \ge \max\left(91/100, 1 + \frac{1375a}{9/1000 - 18a} - \frac{7}{9}\frac{t-1}{t}\right).$$

We leave the (tedious) verification of this claim as an exercise (see Exercise 14.11).

If $t > 1$ and $t \to 1$, then the parameters a, θ, and w are proportional to $t - 1$. In this case, since the other parameters β, δ, and μ are constants, the quantity in (14.36) is proportional to $1/(t-1)^{2d}$. This completes the proof of the Leapfrog Theorem.

14.9 A variant of the leapfrog property

The analysis of algorithm PATHGREEDY (see Section 1.4) utilizes the Leapfrog Theorem to show that the weight of the edges produced is proportional to the weight of a minimum spanning tree of the points. However, the cluster-based implementation of this algorithm, presented in Chapter 15, throws in another complication. Although the output of algorithm PATHGREEDY satisfies the leapfrog property, the output of the cluster-based implementation satisfies the following weaker version of the leapfrog property.

Definition 14.9.1 (Generalized Leapfrog Property). Let t_1 and t_2 be real numbers, such that $1 < t_1 < t_2$. A set E of undirected edges in $\mathbb{R}^d$ is said to satisfy the (t_1, t_2)-*leapfrog property*, if for every $k \ge 2$, and for every sequence $\{p_1, q_1\}, \{p_2, q_2\}, \ldots, \{p_k, q_k\}$ of k pairwise distinct edges of E,

$$t_1 |p_1 q_1| < \sum_{i=2}^{k} |p_i q_i| + t_2 \left(|p_1 p_2| + \sum_{i=2}^{k-1} |q_i p_{i+1}| + |q_k q_1| \right).$$

What can we say about the total weight of a set of edges satisfying the generalized leapfrog property? We claim that the analysis given for the leapfrog property can be used for this case as well.

Recall that in the first step of our previous analysis, we partitioned the edge set into near-parallel subsets, see Section 14.5.1. By Lemma 14.2.1, each subset satisfies the strong w-gap property, for some parameter w that only depends on t and the angle parameter θ. For the generalized leapfrog property, this does not hold; see Exercise 14.13. Fortunately, as pointed out in Remark 14.5.3 (see also Remark 14.7.2), it is sufficient to have the following weaker version of this property:

Lemma 14.9.2. *Let t_1 and t_2 be real numbers, such that $1 < t_1 < t_2$, and let E be a set of undirected edges that satisfies the (t_1, t_2)-leapfrog property. Let δ and θ be real numbers, such that $(t_2 - t_1)/(t_2 - 1) < \delta < 1$, $0 < \theta < \pi/4$, and $\cos\theta - \sin\theta > (t_2 - t_1 + \delta)/(\delta t_2)$, and define*

$$w := \frac{1}{2}(\cos\theta - \sin\theta) - \frac{t_2 - t_1 + \delta}{2\delta t_2}.$$

Let $\{p, q\}$ and $\{r, s\}$ be two distinct edges in E, such that $\mathrm{angle}(pq, rs) \le \theta$ and $|rs| \le |pq| \le |rs|/\delta$. Then, the directed edges (p, q) and (r, s) satisfy the strong w-gap property, that is, $|pr| > w|rs|$ and $|qs| > w|rs|$.

PROOF Observe that the parameters δ and θ can be chosen such that the requirements in the statement of the lemma hold, and that $w > 0$. The proof follows from an analysis that is similar to the one in the proofs of Lemmas 6.4.1 and 14.2.1. The details are left as an exercise; see Exercise 14.14. ∎

Theorem 14.9.3 (Generalized Leapfrog Theorem). *There exists an absolute constant ϕ with $0 < \phi < 1$, such that the following holds. Let t_1 and t_2 be real numbers, such that $1 < 1 - \phi + \phi t_2 < t_1 < t_2$, let S be a set of points in $\mathbb{R}^d$, and let E be a set of edges, whose endpoints are from S, and that satisfies the (t_1, t_2)-leapfrog property. Then,*

$$wt(E) \leq c_{dt_1 t_2} \cdot wt(MST(S)),$$

where $MST(S)$ denotes a minimum spanning tree of S, and $c_{dt_1 t_2}$ is a real number that depends only on d, t_1, and t_2. If $t_2 > 1$ and $t_2 \to 1$, then

$$c_{dt_1 t_2} = O\left(1/(t_2 - 1)^{2d}\right).$$

PROOF A close inspection of the proof of the Leapfrog Theorem reveals that the proof remains valid, provided that the parameters, θ, β, δ, μ, a, and h are chosen in the following way: First, all restrictions in Section 14.5.5 are satisfied, except that the inequality $\cos\theta - \sin\theta > 1/t$ is replaced by the inequalities in Lemma 14.9.2; this lemma also gives the new value for w. Second, all inequalities in (14.8), (14.9), (14.10), (14.16), (14.20), (14.22), (14.32), and (14.33) are satisfied. Third, the inequality in (14.30) is replaced by

$$\cos\theta > 2(a + \sin\theta) + 1/t_2.$$

Finally, in order to contradict the (t_1, t_2)-leapfrog property, as we did in Section 14.6.8, we obtain

$$\sum_{i=1}^{k} |g_i| + t_2 \left(|p_f p_1| + \sum_{i=1}^{k-1} |q_i p_{i+1}| + |q_k q_f| \right)$$
$$\leq \frac{(1 - t_2 \cos\theta + 2t_2(a + \sin\theta))(\cos\theta - h - \xi)}{3(1 + h)} |f|$$
$$+ t_2 (1 + 2a + 3\xi + \sin\theta + 2\beta(a + \sin\theta)) |f|,$$

which is less than or equal to $t_1 |f|$, if

$$\xi \leq \frac{3t_1(1 + h) + (t_2 \cos\theta - 1 - 2t_2(a + \sin\theta))(\cos\theta - h)}{9t_2(1 + h) + t_2 \cos\theta - 1 - 2t_2(a + \sin\theta)}$$
$$- \frac{3t_2(1 + h)(1 + 2a + \sin\theta + 2\beta(a + \sin\theta))}{9t_2(1 + h) + t_2 \cos\theta - 1 - 2t_2(a + \sin\theta)}.$$

This inequality for ξ replaces the one in (14.31). Observe that the definition of ξ in (14.17) remains the same.

All these requirements are satisfied, if we take $\phi = 233/303$, $\beta = \min(10^{-4}, \alpha/49)$, $\delta = 99/100$, $h = 1/100$, $\mu = 5$,

$$a = \min\left(\frac{t_2 - 1}{10^6 t_2}, \frac{t_1 - (1 - \phi) - \phi t_2}{10^5 t_2}\right),$$

and θ such that $0 < \theta < \pi/4$, $\cos\theta > 91/100$,

$$\sin\theta \leq \min\left(\alpha a/8, \frac{t_2 - 1}{200 t_2}\right),$$

$$\cos\theta - \sin\theta > \frac{t_2 - t_1 + \delta}{\delta t_2},$$

$$\cos\theta > 1/100 + 2/10^6 + \left(1 - 1/100 - 2/10^6\right)/t_2,$$

and

$$\cos\theta \geq 1 + \frac{1375a}{9/1000 - 18a} - \frac{7}{9}\frac{t_2 - 1}{t_2} + \frac{101}{30}\frac{t_2 - t_1}{t_2}.$$

If $t_2 > 1$ and $t_2 \to 1$, then the parameters a, θ, and w are proportional to $t_2 - 1$. Details are left as an exercise; see Exercise 14.15. ∎

14.10 The Sparse Ball Theorem

A crucial ingredient in Section 14.7.3 is the following capsuled property of a Steiner minimum tree T of a set S of $n \geq 2$ points:

> **Basic Idea:** Let p be an element of S, and let B be a ball centered at p, such that B does not contain any other point of S. Consider the portion of T that is inside B and that is connected to p. Then, every path in this portion that starts at p and ends at some point on the boundary of B must necessarily contain an edge whose length is at least proportional to the radius of B.

In this section, we will prove this result, where we assume, without loss of generality, that p is the origin. Before we give a precise statement of this result, we mention some basic properties of Steiner minimum trees.

Lemma 14.10.1. *Let S be a set of n points in $\mathbb{R}^d$, and let T be a Steiner minimum tree of S. The following properties hold:*

1. The degree in T of every Steiner point is equal to 3.

2. The degree in T of every point of S is less than or equal to 3.

3. T contains at most $n - 2$ Steiner points.

Lemma 14.10.2. *Let $R > 0$ be a real number, and let S be a set of n points in $\mathbb{R}^d$ that are contained in a ball of radius R. If $n \geq 2^d$, then the weight of a Steiner minimum tree of S is less than or equal to*

$$8Rn^{1-1/d}.$$

PROOF The proof is left as an exercise; see Exercise 14.17. Observe that the lemma, with a larger constant, also follows from Exercise 6.3. ∎

We introduce the following notation, where R is an arbitrary positive real number:

- S denotes a set of n points in $\mathbb{R}^d$ that contains the origin,
- T denotes a Steiner minimum tree of S,
- $B(R)$ denotes the ball with radius R that is centered at the origin,

- $T(R)$ denotes the portion of T within $B(R)$ that is connected to the origin (observe that, since T is clipped at the boundary of $B(R)$, $T(R)$ is not exactly a subtree of T),
- $s(R)$ denotes the number of Steiner points of $T(R)$, and
- $b(R)$ denotes the number of intersections of $T(R)$ with the boundary of $B(R)$.

Theorem 14.10.3 (Sparse Ball Theorem). *Let S be a set of n points in $\mathbb{R}^d$, such that the origin is an element of S. Let R and r be real numbers, such that $R > r > 0$. Assume that the origin is the only point of S that is contained in $B(R)$. Let*

$$\kappa := \max\left(2^{2^{2^{3d}}}, 2^{2^{\frac{2R}{(R-r)\log\frac{d}{d-1}}}}\right).$$

Then, the following are true:

1. *$s(r) \le \kappa$.*
2. *Every path in $T(r)$ between the origin and some point on the boundary of $B(r)$ contains an edge of length at least $r/(\kappa + 1)$.*

If r is a constant fraction of R, then κ is bounded by a constant that depends only on the dimension d. In this case, the theorem implies that every path in $T(R)$ between the origin and some point on the boundary of $B(R)$ contains an edge whose length is $\Omega(R)$.

We first show that the second claim in this theorem follows from the first claim. Indeed, consider any path P in $T(r)$ between the origin and some point on the boundary of $B(r)$. Then the length of P is greater than or equal to r. On the other hand, the number of edges on P is less than or equal to $\kappa + 1$. Therefore, P must contain an edge whose length is greater than or equal to $r/(\kappa + 1)$.

It remains to prove the first claim in the Sparse Ball Theorem. In Section 14.10.1, we prove a recurrence relation for the function s. In Section 14.10.2, we apply this recurrence relation to obtain estimates for the number of Steiner points in progressively smaller balls. In Section 14.10.3, we combine these estimates, which will result in a proof of the first claim in the Sparse Ball Theorem. In the rest of this section, we assume that the premises of this theorem are satisfied.

14.10.1 A recurrence relation for the number of Steiner points

In this section, we prove the basic recurrence relation for the function s. This recurrence states that by shrinking a ball centered at the origin, the number of Steiner points inside the ball is reduced by a "large" factor.

Lemma 14.10.4. *Let x and y be real numbers, such that $0 < x < y \le R$ and $s(y) \ge 2^d$. Assume that the boundaries of the balls $B(x)$ and $B(y)$ do not contain any Steiner points of T. Then,*

$$s(x) \le \frac{8y}{y - x}(s(y) + 4)^{1 - 1/d}.$$

PROOF   Let k be the degree (in T) of the origin. By Lemma 14.10.1, we have $1 \le k \le 3$. Since the ball $B(x)$ contains only one point of S, and since, again by Lemma 14.10.1, the degree of every Steiner point is equal to 3, we have $b(x) = s(x) + k$. Thus,

$$s(x) < b(x) \le s(x) + 3.$$

In a symmetric way, we obtain the inequality

$$s(y) < b(y) \leq s(y) + 3.$$

We number the intersections of $T(x)$ with the boundary of $B(x)$ arbitrarily from one to $b(x)$. For each i with $1 \leq i \leq b(x)$, let T_i denote the portion of $T(y) \setminus T(x)$ that is connected to the i-th intersection of $T(x)$ with the boundary of $B(x)$. Since the origin is the only point of S that is in the ball $B(y)$, and since the portion T_i is not connected to the origin, T_i must intersect the boundary of $B(y)$. It follows that

$$\sum_{i=1}^{b(x)} wt(T_i) \geq b(x)(y - x).$$

For each j with $1 \leq j \leq b(y)$, let z_j be a point of $T(y)$ that is on the boundary of $B(y)$, and let $T'(y)$ be a Steiner minimum tree of the origin and the points $z_1, z_2, \ldots, z_{b(y)}$. By Lemma 14.10.2, we have

$$wt(T'(y)) \leq 8y \, (b(y) + 1)^{1-1/d} \, .$$

We claim that

$$wt(T'(y)) \geq b(x)(y - x).$$

Assume this is not the case. Then, by replacing, in T, the portions T_i, $1 \leq i \leq b(x)$, by $T'(y)$, we obtain a Steiner tree for the point set S, whose weight is less than that of T. This is obviously a contradiction.

By combining the above inequalities, we get

$$\begin{aligned}
s(x) &\leq b(x) \\
&\leq \frac{1}{y - x} \cdot wt(T'(y)) \\
&\leq \frac{8y}{y - x} \, (b(y) + 1)^{1-1/d} \\
&\leq \frac{8y}{y - x} \, (s(y) + 4)^{1-1/d} \, .
\end{aligned}$$

This completes the proof of the lemma. ∎

Recall the parameters R and r in the Sparse Ball Theorem. If we apply Lemma 14.10.4 with $y = R$, then we get

$$s(x) = O\left(\frac{1}{1 - x/R} \, n^{1-1/d} \right),$$

because, by Lemma 14.10.1, $s(R) \leq n$. In words, by shrinking the radius of the ball centered at the origin, from R to x, the number of Steiner points inside this ball decreases from n to the product of $n^{1-1/d}$ and a factor that is proportional to $1/(1 - x/R)$. In the next section, we define a specific sequence $R = X_0 > X_1 > X_2 > \ldots$ of real numbers, having the property that the values $s(X_i)$ decrease rapidly. As a result, we will have $s(X_\ell) \leq \kappa$, for some index ℓ. In fact, the sequence has the property that such an index ℓ exists, for which $X_\ell \geq r$. From this, the first claim in the Sparse Ball Theorem will follow, because $s(r) \leq s(X_\ell) \leq \kappa$.

14.10.2 Applying the recurrence relation

We start by defining the sequence $X_0, X_1, X_2, \ldots$ of real numbers, having the properties mentioned above. Let $X_0 := R$ and, for each $i \geq 0$ and $j \geq 0$, let

$$
n_i := \begin{cases} s(X_i) & \text{if } X_i > 0, \\ 0 & \text{if } X_i \leq 0, \end{cases}
$$

$$
x_{ij} := X_i - \frac{jR}{(\log \log n_i)^2},
$$

$$
k_i := \left\lfloor \frac{\log \log n_i}{\log \frac{d}{d-1}} \right\rfloor,
$$

and

$$
X_{i+1} := x_{ik_i}.
$$

Observe that these values are defined only if $n_i \geq 3$, because only then $\log \log n_i$ is nonzero. We assume that, for each $i \geq 0$ and $j \geq 0$, the boundary of the ball $B(x_{ij})$ does not contain any Steiner point of $\mathcal{T}$. If this is not the case, then we perturb x_{ij} by an infinitesimal amount. Thus, we can apply Lemma 14.10.4 to the values x_{ij}. The following lemma follows immediately from the definitions above.

Lemma 14.10.5. *Let $i \geq 0$ and assume that $n_i \geq 3$. Then, $n_{i+1} \leq n_i$ and*

$$
X_i - \frac{R}{\log \frac{d}{d-1} \log \log n_i} \leq X_{i+1} < X_i \leq R.
$$

By applying Lemma 14.10.4, with $x = x_{i,j+1}$ and $y = x_{ij}$, we obtain the following result:

Lemma 14.10.6. *Let $i \geq 0$ and $j \geq 0$ be integers, and assume that $n_i \geq 3$, $X_{i+1} > 0$, $j < k_i$, and $s(x_{ij}) \geq 2^d$. Then,*

$$
s(x_{i,j+1}) \leq 2^{4-1/d} (\log \log n_i)^2 \left(s(x_{ij}) \right)^{1-1/d}.
$$

PROOF We first observe that $0 < x_{i,j+1} < x_{ij} \leq R$. Hence, we can apply Lemma 14.10.4 with $x = x_{i,j+1}$ and $y = x_{ij}$. Using the facts that $X_i \leq R$ and $s(x_{ij}) \geq 2^d \geq 4$, we obtain

$$
\begin{aligned}
s(x_{i,j+1}) &\leq \frac{8x_{ij}}{x_{ij} - x_{i,j+1}} \left(s(x_{ij}) + 4 \right)^{1-1/d} \\
&= 8 \left(\frac{X_i}{R} (\log \log n_i)^2 - j \right) \left(s(x_{ij}) + 4 \right)^{1-1/d} \\
&\leq 8(\log \log n_i)^2 \left(2 \cdot s(x_{ij}) \right)^{1-1/d} \\
&= 2^{4-1/d} (\log \log n_i)^2 \left(s(x_{ij}) \right)^{1-1/d},
\end{aligned}
$$

proving the lemma.   ∎

The next lemma states that the values n_i decrease very rapidly.

Lemma 14.10.7. *Let $i \geq 0$ be an integer, and assume that $n_{i+1} \geq 2^d$. Then,*

$$
n_{i+1} \leq 2^{4d+1} (\log \log n_i)^{2d}.
$$

PROOF Let $k = k_i$. We first observe that $n_i \geq n_{i+1} \geq 3$. Moreover, we have $X_{i+1} > 0$, because otherwise, n_{i+1} would be zero. Finally, we have $s(x_{ij}) \geq s(x_{ik}) = n_{i+1} \geq 2^d$ for each j with $0 \leq j < k$. Therefore, we can apply Lemma 14.10.6 repeatedly for $j = 0, 1, \ldots, k - 1$, yielding

$$n_{i+1} = s(x_{ik}) \leq \left(2^{4-1/d}(\log \log n_i)^2\right)^{\sum_{j=0}^{k-1}(1-1/d)^j} (s(x_{i0}))^{(1-1/d)^k}.$$

Since

$$k = \left\lfloor \frac{\log \log n_i}{\log \frac{d}{d-1}} \right\rfloor > \frac{\log \log n_i}{\log \frac{d}{d-1}} - 1,$$

we have

$$(1 - 1/d)^k = 2^{-k \log \frac{d}{d-1}} \leq 2^{-\log \log n_i + \log \frac{d}{d-1}} = \frac{d}{d-1} \cdot \frac{1}{\log n_i}.$$

Hence, since $s(x_{i0}) = n_i$, we have

$$(s(x_{i0}))^{(1-1/d)^k} = 2^{(1-1/d)^k \log n_i} \leq 2^{\frac{d}{d-1}} \leq 4.$$

The proof is completed by using the fact that $\sum_{j=0}^{k-1}(1 - 1/d)^j \leq d$. ∎

Next, we apply Lemma 14.10.7 to obtain an upper bound on n_i in terms of n. For any integer $k \geq 0$, we use $\log^{(k)} n$ to denote the k-fold iteration of the logarithm function. (For $k = 0$, $\log^{(k)} n = n$.) Recall that

$$\log^* n = \min\{k \geq 0 : \log^{(k)} n \leq 1\}.$$

Lemma 14.10.8. *Let $\ell \geq 0$ be an integer, such that $2\ell \leq \log^* n - \log^*(4d)$ and $n_\ell \geq 2^d$. Then, for all i with $0 \leq i \leq \ell$,*

$$n_i \leq 2^{6d+1} \left(\log^{(2i)} n\right)^{2d}.$$

PROOF The proof is by induction on i. If $i = 0$, then $\log^{(2i)} n = n$ and, by Lemma 14.10.1, $n_i \leq n$. Hence, in this case, the claim obviously holds. Let $0 \leq i \leq \ell - 1$, and assume that

$$n_i \leq 2^{6d+1} \left(\log^{(2i)} n\right)^{2d}.$$

Since $n_{i+1} \geq n_\ell \geq 2^d$, we can apply Lemma 14.10.7, and obtain

$$
\begin{aligned}
n_{i+1} &\leq 2^{4d+1}(\log \log n_i)^{2d} \\
&\leq 2^{4d+1} \left(\log \log \left(2^{6d+1} \left(\log^{(2i)} n\right)^{2d}\right)\right)^{2d} \\
&= 2^{4d+1} \left(\log \left(6d + 1 + 2d \log^{(2i+1)} n\right)\right)^{2d}.
\end{aligned}
$$

Since $2\ell \leq \log^* n - \log^*(4d)$, we have

$$\log^{(2i+1)} n \geq \log^{(2\ell-1)} n \geq 4d \geq 6 + 1/d.$$

It follows that

$$
\begin{aligned}
n_{i+1} &\leq 2^{4d+1} \left(\log \left(3d \log^{(2i+1)} n\right)\right)^{2d} \\
&= 2^{4d+1} \left(\log(3d) + \log^{(2i+2)} n\right)^{2d}.
\end{aligned}
$$

Since $2\ell \leq \log^* n - \log^*(4d)$, we have

$$\log^{(2i+2)} n \geq \log^{(2\ell)} n \geq \log(4d) \geq \log(3d).$$

Thus,

$$n_{i+1} \leq 2^{4d+1} \left(2 \log^{(2i+2)} n \right)^{2d}$$
$$= 2^{6d+1} \left(\log^{(2i+2)} n \right)^{2d}.$$

This completes the proof. ∎

The next lemma states that n_i is bounded from above by a constant if i is approximately equal to $\frac{1}{2} \log^* n$.

Lemma 14.10.9. *Let* $L := \frac{1}{2} \log^* n - \frac{1}{2} \log^*(4d)$. *Assume that* $L \geq 0$ *and* $n_L \geq 2^d$. *Then,*

$$n_L \leq 2^{8d^2+6d+1}.$$

PROOF By Lemma 14.10.8, we have

$$n_L \leq 2^{6d+1} \left(\log^{(2L)} n \right)^{2d} = 2^{6d+1} \left(\log^{(\log^* n - \log^*(4d))} n \right)^{2d}.$$

Since

$$\log^{(\log^* n - \log^*(4d))} n \leq \underbrace{2^{2^{\cdot^{\cdot^2}}}}_{\log^*(4d)} < 2^{4d},$$

the lemma follows. ∎

The next lemma gives a sufficient condition for X_ℓ to be "large."

Lemma 14.10.10. *Let* $\ell \geq 2$ *be an integer, and assume that* $n_{\ell-1} \geq 2^d$ *and* $\log \log \log n_{\ell-2} \geq 3d$. *Then,*

$$X_\ell \geq R \left(1 - \frac{2}{\log \frac{d}{d-1} \log \log n_{\ell-1}} \right).$$

PROOF Let i be an integer with $0 \leq i \leq \ell - 2$. It follows from Lemma 14.10.5 and the assumption that $n_{i+1} \geq n_{\ell-1} \geq 2^d$. Therefore, we can apply Lemma 14.10.7, and obtain

$$\log \log n_{i+1} \leq \log \log \left(2^{4d+1} (\log \log n_i)^{2d} \right)$$
$$= \log (4d + 1 + 2d \log \log \log n_i)$$
$$\leq \log (3d \log \log \log n_i)$$
$$= \log(3d) + \log \log \log \log n_i$$
$$\leq 2 \log \log \log \log n_i$$
$$\leq \frac{1}{2} \log \log n_i.$$

This inequality implies that, for each i with $0 \leq i \leq \ell - 2$,

$$\log \log n_i \geq 2^{\ell-1-i} \log \log n_{\ell-1}.$$

Observe that the latter inequality also holds if $i = \ell - 1$. Therefore,

$$\sum_{i=0}^{\ell-1} \frac{1}{\log \log n_i} \leq \frac{1}{\log \log n_{\ell-1}} \sum_{i=0}^{\ell-1} \left(\frac{1}{2} \right)^{\ell-1-i} \leq \frac{2}{\log \log n_{\ell-1}}.$$

By combining this inequality with Lemma 14.10.5, we obtain

$$X_\ell \geq X_0 - \sum_{i=0}^{\ell-1} \frac{R}{\log \frac{d}{d-1} \log \log n_i}$$

$$= R \left(1 - \sum_{i=0}^{\ell-1} \frac{1}{\log \frac{d}{d-1} \log \log n_i} \right)$$

$$\geq R \left(1 - \frac{2}{\log \frac{d}{d-1} \log \log n_{\ell-1}} \right).$$

This completes the proof. ∎

14.10.3 Completing the proof of the Sparse Ball Theorem

We are now ready to prove the first claim in the Sparse Ball Theorem (Theorem 14.10.3). Recall that

$$\kappa = \max \left(2^{2^{2^{3d}}}, 2^{2^{\frac{2R}{(R-r)\log \frac{d}{d-1}}}} \right).$$

We have to prove that $s(r) \leq \kappa$. Define $L := \frac{1}{2} \log^* n - \frac{1}{2} \log^*(4d)$. If $L \leq 0$, then $s(r) \leq s(R) = n_0 \leq n \leq 2^{4d} \leq \kappa$. Hence, we may assume that $L \geq 1$. There are three possible cases.

Case 1: $n_0 \leq \kappa$.
   In this case, we have $s(r) \leq s(R) = n_0 \leq n \leq \kappa$.

Case 2: There exists an integer ℓ with $1 \leq \ell \leq L - 1$, such that $n_{\ell-1} \geq \kappa$ and $n_\ell < \kappa$.
   If $\ell \geq 2$, then it follows from Lemma 14.10.10 that $X_\ell \geq r$. In fact, it is easy to verify that this inequality also holds if $\ell = 1$. Therefore, $s(r) \leq s(X_\ell) = n_\ell \leq \kappa$.

Case 3: $n_{L-1} \geq \kappa$.
   It follows from Lemma 14.10.10 that $X_L \geq r$. (This is also true if $L = 1$.) Therefore, by applying Lemma 14.10.9, it follows that

$$s(r) \leq s(X_L) = n_L \leq 2^{8d^2+6d+1} \leq \kappa.$$

In conclusion, we have completed all the pieces of the proof of the Leapfrog Theorem. The proof contains a number of useful ideas. First, it includes ideas to break down the geometric proof into one set of arguments that apply in the vertical direction and a completely different set of arguments that apply in the radial direction. This turned out to be useful, even though there was nothing in the problem or the solution that suggested such a dichotomy. Second, many of the charging arguments used in the proof borrow ideas from amortized analysis. Finally, the proof of the Sparse Ball Theorem contains arguments that are of an asymptotic flavor.

Exercises

14.1. Prove the following two claims:

   1. The converse of Lemma 14.2.1 is not true: Let $w \geq 0$ and $t > 1$ be real numbers. Give an example of a set $\vec{E}$ of directed edges that are all vertical and satisfy the strong w-gap property, but for which the corresponding set E of undirected edges does not satisfy the t-leapfrog property.

2. Let $w > 0$ and δ be real numbers, such that $0 < \delta < \min(1, 1/(2w))$, and let (p, q) and (r, s) be two distinct directed edges, such that $\delta \le |pq|/|rs| \le 1/\delta$. Assume that the set $\vec{E} = \{(p, q), (r, s)\}$ satisfies the strong w-gap property. Prove that the set $E = \{\{p, q\}, \{r, s\}\}$ of undirected edges satisfies the t-leapfrog property, for $t = \delta/(1 - 2w\delta)$.

14.2. Prove Lemma 14.5.2 and the claim made in Remark 14.5.3.

14.3. In Section 14.6.3, we defined the charging path P to be a path in the graph $\mathcal{G}_p$ between p and some point on one of the flat faces of the pseudo-head PH_p, that satisfies the conditions in Lemma 14.6.3. Prove that $\mathcal{G}_p$ may contain such a path P that does not satisfy the conditions in Lemma 14.6.3.

14.4. Prove Lemma 14.6.4.

14.5. Prove the second claim in Lemma 14.6.5.

14.6. Prove inequality (14.28) in Section 14.6.8.

14.7. In Sections 14.6.2–14.6.8, we have proved that the invariant $\mathcal{P}$ is maintained during the processing of any edge e of the non-lateral edge set E. Verify this proof for an edge e that is a leaf in the original nesting tree for E.

14.8. In Section 14.5.4, we introduced Steiner vertices at all locations where the minimum spanning tree $\mathcal{T}$ pierces the boundaries of the heads of the pseudo-dumbbells. In order to obtain a rigorous analysis in Section 14.6, more Steiner vertices have to be introduced. Explain which Steiner vertices have to be introduced, and show that these can be introduced *before* the processing of the edges (as explained in Section 14.6.2) starts.

14.9. In Section 14.7.4, we proved properties $\mathcal{Q}.3.3.3$ and $\mathcal{Q}.3.3.4$ for the case when $\upsilon(x) \neq x$. Prove that these two properties also hold if $\upsilon(x) = x$.

14.10. In Section 14.5.4, we use the graphs $\mathcal{G}_p$ and $\mathcal{G}_q$ to define the notion of the edge $e = (p, q)$ being lateral or non-lateral. Let $\mathcal{T}_p$ be the maximum portion of the minimum spanning tree of S that contains p as a vertex and that is contained in the head PH_p of the pseudo-dumbbell PD_e. Define $\mathcal{T}_q$ similarly with respect to q. Assume that we define the notion of e being lateral or non-lateral using the trees $\mathcal{T}_p$ and $\mathcal{T}_q$, instead of the graphs $\mathcal{G}_p$ and $\mathcal{G}_q$. Prove that (i) the analysis of the non-lateral edges, as given in Section 14.6, remains valid, but (ii) the analysis of the lateral edges, as given in Section 14.7, does not remain valid.

14.11. Consider the choice for the parameters θ, β, δ, μ, a, and h, as given in Section 14.8. Prove that these parameters satisfy all requirements that are needed to complete the proof of the Leapfrog Theorem.

Hint: The assumption that $\cos\theta \ge 91/100$ implies that $9\delta/10 \le \delta' \le \delta$ and $9\beta'/10 \le \beta \le \beta'$, from which the inequality in (14.10) follows. Prove that

$$\xi \le \frac{25a}{\frac{2}{1000} - 4a}.$$

The inequality in (14.31) is satisfied if

$$\xi \le \frac{9}{110}(\cos\theta - 1/t) - \frac{t - 1}{55t}.$$

14.12. Prove that the Leapfrog Theorem (Theorem 14.4.1) remains valid if we only require that the inequality

$$t|p_1 q_1| < \sum_{i=2}^{k} |p_i q_i| + t\left(|p_1 p_2| + \sum_{i=2}^{k-1} |q_i p_{i+1}| + |q_k q_1|\right)$$

holds for every $k \ge 2$, and for every sequence $\{p_1, q_1\}, \{p_2, q_2\}, \dots, \{p_k, q_k\}$ of k pairwise distinct edges, such that $|p_1 q_1| \ge |p_i q_i|$ for all i with $2 \le i \le k$.

14.13. Let t_1, t_2, and w be real numbers, such that $t_2 > t_1 > 1$ and $w > 0$. Give an example of four pairwise distinct points p, q, r, and s in $\mathbb{R}^2$, such that the vectors $\vec{pq}$ and $\vec{rs}$ are parallel, the set

$E = \{\{p, q\}, \{r, s\}\}$ satisfies the (t_1, t_2)-leapfrog property, and the set $\vec{E} = \{(p, q), (r, s)\}$ does not satisfy the w-gap property.

14.14. Prove Lemma 14.9.2.

14.15. Prove the Generalized Leapfrog Theorem (Theorem 14.9.3).

14.16. Prove that the weight of a Steiner minimum tree for n points in the unit hypercube in $\mathbb{R}^d$ is at most

$$\frac{d^{3/2}}{d - 1} \cdot \frac{n^{1-1/d}}{1 - n^{-1/d}}.$$

14.17. Prove that the weight of a Steiner minimum tree for n points in the unit ball in $\mathbb{R}^d$ is at most

$$\frac{2d}{d - 1} \cdot \frac{n^{1-1/d}}{1 - n^{-1/d}}.$$

Furthermore, if $n \geq 2^d$ and $d \geq 2$, the weight is at most

$$8n^{1-1/d}.$$

Bibliographic notes

This chapter is largely based on results that appeared in Das, Heffernan, and Narasimhan [1993] and Das, Narasimhan, and Salowe [1995]. The leapfrog property was introduced by Das, Heffernan, and Narasimhan [1993]. The Leapfrog Theorem (Theorem 14.4.1) was also given in the same paper. However, the proof was confined to edges in three-dimensional space, and only a sketch of the proof was given. The proof provided here is a modified version of that sketch and includes all the details. The proof for the lateral edges was modified to use the Sparse Ball Theorem (Theorem 14.10.3, due to Rao and Smith [1998].

A number of results on Steiner minimum trees were used in this chapter. A proof of Lemma 14.10.1 can be found in Gilbert and Pollak [1968] and Hwang, Richards, and Winter [1992]. Bounds on the weights of Steiner minimum trees and minimum spanning trees in unit hypercubes and unit balls were computed by Few [1955] (see also Hwang, Richards, and Winter [1992]). The improved versions (see Lemma 14.10.2, and Exercises 14.16 and 14.17) appeared in Smith [1988] and Rao and Smith [1998].

15

The Path-Greedy Algorithm

> Do not go where the path may lead, go instead where there is no path and leave a trail.
>
> —Ralph Waldo Emerson

So far, in this book, we have presented two different greedy algorithms to compute a sparse spanner. In Section 1.4, we presented algorithm PATHGREEDY, while in Chapter 7, we presented algorithm GAPGREEDY.

Algorithm GAPGREEDY was designed such that its output satisfied the strong gap property. As a result, the Gap Theorem (Theorem 6.1.2) immediately implied that the weight of the graph computed by this algorithm was $O(\log n)$ times the weight of a minimum spanning tree of the points. The fact that the graph computed by the gap-greedy algorithm had a small stretch factor, however, was not obvious.

Algorithm PATHGREEDY, as presented in Section 1.4, was a simple greedy algorithm that generalized Kruskal's minimum spanning tree. After sorting all the pairs of points based on their distance, the pairs were considered in sorted order. In each iteration, the decision whether or not to add an edge was made by checking whether there was a "short" path connecting the endpoints. Because of the condition that was tested, it was obvious that the output of algorithm PATHGREEDY had a small stretch factor (see Lemma 1.4.1). We will often refer to its output as the *path-greedy spanner*.

No further analysis of algorithm PATHGREEDY was presented in Section 1.4. It was not clear whether the algorithm outputs a sparse graph, whether its degree was small, or whether there were nontrivial bounds on its weight. In this chapter, we address these questions regarding the analysis of algorithm PATHGREEDY.

In Section 15.1.1, we show a simple proof that the spanner computed by algorithm PATHGREEDY satisfies the strong gap property of Section 6.1. Hence, the degree of each point is bounded by a constant (and, thus, the spanner only has a linear number of edges), and the weight of the spanner is $O(\log n)$ times the weight of a minimum spanning tree of the points.

In Section 15.1.2, we prove that for random points in the unit hypercube, the weight of this spanner is proportional to the weight of a minimum spanning tree of the points, with high probability, thus providing some evidence that the weight of the spanner output by algorithm PATHGREEDY may, in fact, have weight $O(1)$ times the weight of a minimum spanning tree of the points.

The above results are improved in Section 15.1.3, where we prove that, in fact, for any point set, the edge set of the spanner output by algorithm PATHGREEDY satisfies the leapfrog property of Chapter 14, implying immediately that its weight is proportional to the weight of a minimum spanning tree of the points.

Finally, we tackle the problem of an efficient implementation of algorithm PATHGREEDY. The improvements lead us to variants, which we refer to as the FASTPATHGREEDY and RAMPATHGREEDY algorithms. The basic version of the path-greedy algorithm has a high running time, because it explicitly considers each pair of points. It turns out to be sufficient, however, to consider pairs of points that are connected by an edge in an initial spanner G'. The improved algorithm computes a path-greedy spanner G of G'. Hence, by "transitivity," G is a spanner of the given set of points. In Section 15.2, we use graph clustering techniques to design a variant of the path-greedy algorithm called FASTPATHGREEDY with a running time of $O(n \log^2 n / \log \log n)$.

The clustering-based algorithm of Section 15.2 works in the algebraic computation-tree model. In Section 15.3, we give an $O(n \log n)$–time implementation of an improved path-greedy algorithm (called RAMPATHGREEDY) that uses indirect addressing as an additional operation.

All spanners in this chapter are undirected.

15.1 Analysis of the simple greedy algorithm PATHGREEDY

Let S be a set of n points in $\mathbb{R}^d$ and let $t > 1$ be a real number. Algorithm PATHGREEDY(S, t) (see Section 1.4) starts with a graph G on vertex set S and no edges. It considers all pairs of distinct points of S in nondecreasing order of their distances. If $\{p, q\}$ is the current pair of points being considered, then the algorithm adds the edge $\{p, q\}$ to G if the distance between p and q in the current graph G is larger than $t|pq|$.

15.1.1 Preliminary analysis of the path-greedy spanner

Consider the t-spanner $G = (S, E)$ computed by algorithm PATHGREEDY(S, t). There are three questions that come to mind. First, how many edges does the graph G have? Second, can we prove a nontrivial upper bound on the maximum degree of any vertex of G? Finally, can we prove a nontrivial upper bound on the total weight of the edges of G? We will show that we can apply the Gap Theorem (Theorem 6.1.2) to answer these questions. In order to apply this theorem, we need a set of directed edges. We obtain such a set by giving each edge of E an arbitrary direction. We denote the resulting set of directed edges by $\vec{E}$.

Lemma 15.1.1. *Let $G = (S, E)$ be the t-spanner computed by algorithm* PATHGREEDY(S, t). *Let θ and w be real numbers, such that $0 < \theta < \pi/4$, $0 \le w < (\cos\theta - \sin\theta)/2$, and $t \ge 1/(\cos\theta - \sin\theta - 2w)$. Let (p, q) and (r, s) be two distinct edges in the set $\vec{E}$, and assume that* angle$(pq, rs) \le \theta$. *Then, the edges (p, q) and (r, s) satisfy the strong w-gap property.*

PROOF We will first show that $|pr| > w \cdot \min(|pq|, |rs|)$. (In particular, this will imply that $p \ne r$.) The proof is by contradiction. So assume that $|pr| \le w \cdot \min(|pq|, |rs|)$. We may assume without loss of generality that algorithm PATHGREEDY(S, t) examines the pair $\{r, s\}$ before it examines $\{p, q\}$. Hence, $|rs| \le |pq|$. By Lemma 6.4.1, we have $|pr| < |pq|$, $|sq| < |pq|$, and

$$t|pr| + |rs| + t|sq| \le t|pq|. \tag{15.1}$$

Consider the moment when algorithm PATHGREEDY(S, t) examines the pair $\{p, q\}$. At this moment, edge $\{r, s\}$ has already been added to E. Also, in case $p \ne r$, the algorithm has already examined the pair $\{p, r\}$, and if $s \neq q$, the pair $\{s, q\}$ has already been examined. Hence, at this moment, the graph G contains (i) a t-spanner path between p and r, (ii) the edge $\{r, s\}$, and (iii) a t-spanner path between s and q. The concatenation of these is a path between p and q, and by (15.1), the length of this path is less than, or equal to, $t|pq|$. This is a contradiction to the fact that edge $\{p, q\}$ is added to E.

Since angle$(pq, rs) = $ angle(qp, sr), it follows in a completely symmetric way that $|qs| > w \cdot \min(|pq|, |rs|)$. Hence, we have shown that any two distinct edges in $\vec{E}$ satisfy the strong w-gap property of Definition 6.1.1, provided their angle is at most θ. ∎

We partition the edges of $\vec{E}$ into subsets such that any two edges within the same subset make an angle of at most θ. By Theorem 5.3.3, such a partition exists consisting of $O(1/\theta^{d-1})$ subsets. By Lemma 15.1.1, each subset in this partition satisfies the strong w-gap property. Observe that this result holds for any choice of θ and w in the given range, whereas the spanner G depends only on the value of t. Recall that the Gap Theorem (Theorem 6.1.2) proved a bound on the degree and weight of a set of directed edges satisfying the w-gap property. Applying this theorem, we obtain the following result:

Theorem 15.1.2. *Let S be a set of n points in $\mathbb{R}^d$, let $t > 1$ be a real number, and let $G = (S, E)$ be the t-spanner that is computed by algorithm PATHGREEDY(S, t). For any two real numbers θ and w with $0 < \theta < \pi/4$, $0 \leq w < (\cos\theta - \sin\theta)/2$, and $t \geq 1/(\cos\theta - \sin\theta - 2w)$,*

1. *the degree in G of each point of S is $O(1/\theta^{d-1})$, and*
2. *if $w > 0$, the weight of G is*

$$O\left(\frac{1}{w\theta^{d-1}} \log n\right)$$

times the weight of a minimum spanning tree of S.

As mentioned already, Theorem 15.1.2 holds for any choice of θ and w in the given range. To obtain the smallest upper bound on the degree of the spanner, we must choose θ as large as possible, such that $\cos\theta - \sin\theta \geq 2w + 1/t$. Let $w = 0$, and write $t = 1 + \epsilon$, where ϵ is positive and close to zero. Then we want to choose θ such that $0 < \theta < \pi/4$ and

$$\cos\theta - \sin\theta = 1/t \sim 1 - \epsilon.$$

Since ϵ is small, θ is small as well, and we have

$$\cos\theta - \sin\theta \sim 1 - \theta.$$

It follows that we can take θ to be proportional to $\epsilon = t - 1$, and obtain the following result:

Corollary 15.1.3. *Let S be a set of n points in $\mathbb{R}^d$, let $t > 1$ be a real number, and let G be the t-spanner that is computed by algorithm PATHGREEDY(S, t). The degree in G of each point of S is*

$$O\left(\left(\frac{1}{t-1}\right)^{d-1}\right).$$

In Section 6.3, we showed that the maximum weight of a set of directed edges that satisfy the w-gap property and whose endpoints are in the unit hypercube is given by $c_{dw}n^{1-1/d}$ (for an appropriate constant c_{dw}, which depends only on d and w). Applying

Theorem 6.3.1 to each of the subsets in the partition of $\vec{E}$ defined above, we obtain the following result:

Theorem 15.1.4. *Let S be a set of n points in the d-dimensional unit hypercube $[0, 1]^d$, where $d \geq 2$, and let $t > 1$ be a real number. Let $G = (S, E)$ be the t-spanner that is computed by algorithm* PATHGREEDY(S, t). *Let θ and w be arbitrary real numbers such that $0 < w \leq 2/\sqrt{d}, 0 < \theta < \pi/4, 0 < w < (\cos\theta - \sin\theta)/2$, and $t \geq 1/(\cos\theta - \sin\theta - 2w)$. Then*

$$wt(E) = O\left(\frac{c_{dw}}{\theta^{d-1}} \cdot n^{1-1/d}\right),$$

where c_{dw} is given in Theorem 6.3.1.

15.1.2 Probabilistic analysis of the path-greedy spanner

At this moment, we know that the weight of the path-greedy spanner is $O(\log n)$ times the weight of a minimum spanning tree of the point set. In this section, we prove a probabilistic upper bound for the weight of the path-greedy spanner for the case when the points are randomly chosen in the unit hypercube $[0, 1]^d$.

For any set S of n points, we denote its minimum spanning tree by $MST(S)$. We know from Exercise 6.3 that the weight of $MST(S)$ is $O(n^{1-1/d})$, if all points of S are in the unit hypercube. In Lemma 15.1.6 below, we prove that this upper bound is tight with high probability, if the points are chosen independently and uniformly at random from $[0, 1]^d$. Before we can prove this lemma, we need an estimate for a sum of binomial coefficients. The *binary entropy* function $H : [0, 1] \to \mathbb{R}$ is defined by

$$H(x) := \begin{cases} -x \log x - (1 - x) \log(1 - x) & \text{if } 0 < x < 1, \\ 0 & \text{if } x = 0 \text{ or } x = 1. \end{cases}$$

Observe that H is a continuous function. It is also easy to see that $2^{-H(x)} = x^x(1 - x)^{(1-x)}$.

Lemma 15.1.5. *For any positive integer n and any real number α with $0 \leq \alpha \leq 1/2$, we have*

$$\sum_{k=0}^{\lfloor \alpha n \rfloor} \binom{n}{k} \leq 2^{n \cdot H(\alpha)}.$$

PROOF   The inequality holds if $\alpha = 0$, because both sides of the inequality evaluate to 1. So assume that $0 < \alpha \leq 1/2$. Using Newton's binomial theorem, we get

$$1 = (\alpha + (1 - \alpha))^n$$

$$= \sum_{k=0}^{n} \binom{n}{k} \alpha^k (1 - \alpha)^{n-k}$$

$$\geq \sum_{k=0}^{\lfloor \alpha n \rfloor} \binom{n}{k} \alpha^k (1 - \alpha)^{n-k}$$

$$= \sum_{k=0}^{\lfloor \alpha n \rfloor} \binom{n}{k} (1 - \alpha)^n \left(\frac{\alpha}{1 - \alpha}\right)^k.$$

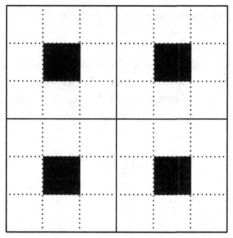

Figure 15.1: Partitioning the unit hypercube into n large hypercubes for the case when $d = 2$ and $n = 4$. Each large hypercube is partitioned into 3^d cells. The cells in the centers of the large hypercubes are black, and all other cells are white.

Since $0 < \alpha \le 1/2$, we have $0 < \alpha/(1 - \alpha) \le 1$. Therefore,

$$1 \ge \sum_{k=0}^{\lfloor \alpha n \rfloor} \binom{n}{k}(1 - \alpha)^n \left(\frac{\alpha}{1 - \alpha}\right)^{\alpha n}$$

$$= 2^{-n \cdot H(\alpha)} \sum_{k=0}^{\lfloor \alpha n \rfloor} \binom{n}{k},$$

which is exactly the claim in the lemma.   ■

Lemma 15.1.6. *Let n be such that $n^{1/d}$ is an integer, let S be a set of n points that are chosen independently and uniformly at random from $[0, 1]^d$. There are constants $c > 0$ and ρ with $0 < \rho < 1$, such that*

$$\Pr\left(wt(MST(S)) < c \cdot n^{1-1/d}\right) \le \rho^n.$$

PROOF   We start by partitioning the unit hypercube $[0, 1]^d$ into n hypercubes having sides of length $(1/n)^{1/d}$. Each of these hypercubes is called a *large* hypercube. We further partition each large hypercube into 3^d *small* hypercubes having sides of length $(1/3)(1/n)^{1/d}$. We call each of these $3^d n$ small hypercubes a *cell*. For each large hypercube, we color the cell that is in its center *black*. All other cells are colored *white*. (See Figure 15.1 for an illustration.) Observe that there are exactly n black cells. Also, the distance between any two points that are in different black cells is at least $(2/3)(1/n)^{1/d}$. We say that a cell is *empty* if it does not contain any point of S; otherwise, the cell is said to be *nonempty*.

Let α with $0 < \alpha < 1/2$ be a constant, whose value will be determined later. Assume that at least αn black cells are nonempty. Let S' be the set of all points of S that are contained in the black cells. Consider a shortest traveling salesperson tour $TSP(S')$ of S'. It is clear that

$$wt(TSP(S')) \ge \frac{2}{3}\left(\frac{1}{n}\right)^{1/d} \alpha n = \frac{2}{3}\alpha \cdot n^{1-1/d}.$$

Then it follows from Exercises 1.6 and 1.7 that

$$wt(MST(S)) \geq \frac{1}{3}\alpha \cdot n^{1-1/d}.$$

Hence we have shown that

$$\text{Pr(at least } \alpha n \text{ black cells are nonempty)}$$
$$\leq \Pr\left(wt(MST(S)) \geq \frac{1}{3}\alpha \cdot n^{1-1/d}\right),$$

which implies that

$$\Pr\left(wt(MST(S)) < \frac{1}{3}\alpha \cdot n^{1-1/d}\right)$$
$$= 1 - \Pr\left(wt(MST(S)) \geq \frac{1}{3}\alpha \cdot n^{1-1/d}\right)$$
$$\leq 1 - \text{Pr(at least } \alpha n \text{ black cells are nonempty)}$$
$$= 1 - \text{Pr(at most } (1-\alpha)n \text{ black cells are empty)}$$
$$= \text{Pr(more than } (1-\alpha)n \text{ black cells are empty)}.$$

Let k be any integer such that $(1-\alpha)n \leq k \leq n$. We estimate the probability that k black cells are empty. Since there are $\binom{n}{k}$ possible ways to choose k black cells, and the total volume of k black cells is equal to $k(1/3)^d(1/n)$, we have

$$\text{Pr(}k \text{ black cells are empty)} \leq \binom{n}{k}\left(1 - k\left(\frac{1}{3}\right)^d\frac{1}{n}\right)^n$$
$$\leq \binom{n}{k}\left(1 - (1-\alpha)\left(\frac{1}{3}\right)^d\right)^n.$$

This implies that

$$\Pr\left(wt(MST(S)) < \frac{1}{3}\alpha \cdot n^{1-1/d}\right)$$
$$\leq \sum_{k=\lceil(1-\alpha)n\rceil}^{n} \text{Pr(}k \text{ black cells are empty)}$$
$$\leq \sum_{k=\lceil(1-\alpha)n\rceil}^{n} \binom{n}{k}\left(1 - (1-\alpha)\left(\frac{1}{3}\right)^d\right)^n$$
$$= \left(1 - (1-\alpha)\left(\frac{1}{3}\right)^d\right)^n \sum_{k=0}^{\lfloor\alpha n\rfloor}\binom{n}{k}$$
$$\leq \left(1 - (1-\alpha)\left(\frac{1}{3}\right)^d\right)^n 2^{n\cdot H(\alpha)}$$
$$= \left(\left(1 - (1-\alpha)\left(\frac{1}{3}\right)^d\right)2^{H(\alpha)}\right)^n,$$

where the last inequality follows from Lemma 15.1.5.

We claim that there is a choice for α, such that $0 < \alpha < 1/2$ and

$$\left(1 - (1 - \alpha)\left(\frac{1}{3}\right)^d\right) 2^{H(\alpha)} < 1. \tag{15.2}$$

This follows from the observations that (i) the expression on the left-hand side is a continuous function of α, $0 \leq \alpha \leq 1/2$, and (ii) for $\alpha = 0$, this function has value $1 - (1/3)^d$, which is strictly less than 1.

Given an α for which (15.2) holds, we complete the proof by defining

$$\rho := \left(1 - (1 - \alpha)\left(\frac{1}{3}\right)^d\right) 2^{H(\alpha)},$$

and $c := \alpha/3$.   ∎

Now we can prove the main result of this section. It states that if the set S is chosen randomly in the unit hypercube, then with high probability, the weight of the path-greedy spanner for S is proportional to the weight of $MST(S)$.

Theorem 15.1.7. *Let n be such that $n^{1/d}$ is an integer, let S be a set of n points that are chosen independently and uniformly at random from $[0, 1]^d$, where $d \geq 2$, and let $t > 1$ be a real constant. Let $G = (S, E)$ be the t-spanner that is computed by algorithm* PATHGREEDY(S, t). *There are constants $c' > 0$ and ρ with $0 < \rho < 1$, such that*

$$\Pr\left(wt(E) \geq c' \cdot wt(MST(S))\right) \leq \rho^n.$$

PROOF Since the points of S are contained in the unit hypercube, we know from Theorem 15.1.4 that

$$wt(E) \leq c_0 \cdot n^{1-1/d},$$

for some constant c_0. Therefore, if $wt(E) \geq c' \cdot wt(MST(S))$, then we have $wt(MST(S)) \leq (c_0/c') \cdot n^{1-1/d}$. Let c and ρ be the constants in Lemma 15.1.6. Then by taking $c' := c_0/c$, the claim follows from Lemma 15.1.6.   ∎

As a corollary to this theorem, we show that for point sets S that are randomly chosen in the unit hypercube, the expected weight of the path-greedy spanner for S is proportional to the weight of $MST(S)$.

Corollary 15.1.8. *Let n be such that $n^{1/d}$ is an integer, let S be a set of n points that are chosen independently and uniformly at random from $[0, 1]^d$, where $d \geq 2$, and let $t > 1$ be a real constant. Let $G = (S, E)$ be the t-spanner that is computed by algorithm* PATHGREEDY(S, t). *There is a constant $c'' > 0$, such that*

$$\mathbb{E}\left(\frac{wt(E)}{wt(MST(S))}\right) \leq c'',$$

if n is sufficiently large.

PROOF We start by observing that for any set V of n points in $\mathbb{R}^d$, the weight of the path-greedy spanner for V is at most equal to n^2 times $wt(MST(V))$. To prove this, let D denote the diameter of the set V. It is clear that $wt(MST(V)) \geq D$. Also, each edge of the path-greedy spanner has length at most D. Since the spanner has at most n^2 edges, the claim follows.

Let c' and ρ be the constants in Theorem 15.1.7. Let X denote the event "$wt(E) < c' \cdot wt(MST(S))$," and let $\overline{X}$ denote the complement of X. Then, using conditional expectations, we get

$$
\mathbb{E}\left(\frac{wt(E)}{wt(MST(S))}\right) = \Pr(X) \cdot \mathbb{E}\left(\frac{wt(E)}{wt(MST(S))}\,\middle|\, X\right)
$$
$$
+ \Pr\left(\overline{X}\right) \cdot \mathbb{E}\left(\frac{wt(E)}{wt(MST(S))}\,\middle|\, \overline{X}\right)
$$
$$
\leq 1 \cdot c' + \rho^n \cdot n^2.
$$

Hence, if n is large enough so that $\rho^n \cdot n^2 \leq 1$, then we have

$$
\mathbb{E}\left(\frac{wt(E)}{wt(MST(S))}\right) \leq c' + 1,
$$

that is, we can take $c'' := c' + 1$.   ■

15.1.3 Improved weight analysis of the path-greedy spanner

In the previous section, we proved that, with high probability, the weight of the path-greedy spanner is $O(wt(MST(S)))$, for point sets S that are randomly chosen in the unit hypercube. In this section, we will prove that this upper bound in fact holds for any point set.

We start by recalling the leapfrog property of Chapter 14 (see Definition 14.1.1). For any real number $t > 1$, a set E of undirected edges in $\mathbb{R}^d$ satisfies the t-leapfrog property, if for every $k \geq 2$, and for every sequence $\{p_i, q_i\}$, $1 \leq i \leq k$, of pairwise distinct edges in E, we have

$$
t|p_1 q_1| < \sum_{i=2}^{k} |p_i q_i| + t\left(|p_1 p_2| + \sum_{i=2}^{k-1} |q_i p_{i+1}| + |q_k q_1|\right). \tag{15.3}
$$

In Section 14.1, we used the path-greedy algorithm to motivate the definition of the leapfrog property. We showed that (15.3) holds for certain sequences of edges. In this section, we show that (15.3) in fact holds for *any* sequence of edges of the path-greedy spanner.

We recall the following notation. Let G be a connected Euclidean graph, and let p and q be two distinct vertices of G. We denote by $\delta_2(p, q)$ the length of a second shortest simple path in G between p and q. (For a formal definition, refer to Section 14.3.)

In a t-spanner, any two points p and q are connected by a path of length at most $t|pq|$. The following lemma states that for every edge $\{p, q\}$ of the path-greedy spanner, the length of a second shortest path between p and q, if it exists, is larger than $t|pq|$.

Lemma 15.1.9. *Let S be a set of n points in $\mathbb{R}^d$, let $t > 1$ be a real number, and let $G = (S, E)$ be the t-spanner that is computed by algorithm PathGreedy(S, t). For every edge $\{p, q\}$ in E, we have*

$$
\delta_2(p, q) > t|pq|.
$$

PROOF If $\delta_2(p, q) = \infty$, then the claim clearly holds. Hence, we may assume that $\delta_2(p, q)$ is finite. Let $P = (p = p_0, p_1, p_2, \ldots, p_k = q)$ be a path in G between p and q consisting of at least two edges and having length $\delta_2(p, q)$. Observe that $k \geq 2$. We have to show that the length $|P|$ of P is larger than $t|pq|$. Consider the cycle

$$C := (p_0, p_1, p_2, \ldots, p_k, p_0)$$

in the graph G. Let $\{x, y\}$ be the edge of C that was added last by the path-greedy algorithm. Then $\{x, y\}$ is a longest edge of C. We denote by C_{xy} the path in G between x and y that is obtained by deleting the edge $\{x, y\}$ from C.

Consider the moment when the path-greedy algorithm examines the pair $\{x, y\}$. At that moment, the algorithm has already added all edges of C_{xy} to the graph G. Since the algorithm adds the edge $\{x, y\}$ to G, the length $|C_{xy}|$ of the path C_{xy} is larger than $t|xy|$. Also, since $|pq| \leq |xy|$, we have $|P| \geq |C_{xy}|$. It follows that

$$\delta_2(p, q) = |P| \geq |C_{xy}| > t|xy| \geq t|pq|,$$

proving the claim.   ∎

Lemmas 15.1.9 and 14.3.1 immediately imply the following result:

Lemma 15.1.10. *Let S be a set of n points in $\mathbb{R}^d$, let $t > 1$ be a real number, and let $G = (S, E)$ be the t-spanner that is computed by algorithm* PATHGREEDY(S, t). *The edge set E satisfies the t-leapfrog property.*

> **The path-greedy algorithm operates economically:** Any two points p and q are connected by a path of length at most $t|pq|$. On the other hand, for every edge $\{p, q\}$ of the path-greedy spanner, the length of a second shortest path between p and q is larger than $t|pq|$. This implies that the edge set of this spanner satisfies the leapfrog property.

The Leapfrog Theorem (Theorem 14.4.1) states that the weight of any set of edges that satisfy the leapfrog property is proportional to the weight of a minimum spanning tree of the endpoints. Thus, by combining the Leapfrog Theorem, Corollary 15.1.3, and Lemma 15.1.10, we get the main result of this section.

Theorem 15.1.11. *Let S be a set of n points in $\mathbb{R}^d$, let $t > 1$ be a real number, and let $G = (S, E)$ be the t-spanner that is computed by algorithm* PATHGREEDY(S, t).

1. *The degree in G of each point of S is*

$$O\left(\left(\frac{1}{t-1}\right)^{d-1}\right).$$

2. *The weight of G is*

$$O\left(\left(\frac{1}{t-1}\right)^{2d} \cdot wt(MST(S))\right),$$

where $MST(S)$ denotes a minimum spanning tree of S.

15.2 An efficient implementation of algorithm PATHGREEDY

Let us consider the time complexity of algorithm PATHGREEDY(S, t), assuming that t is a constant. The algorithm examines $\binom{n}{2}$ pairs of points. For each pair $\{p, q\}$, it computes the distance between p and q in the current graph G. Using Dijkstra's algorithm (see Section 2.5 and Corollary 2.5.10), one such distance computation can be done in $O(n \log n)$ time. (Here we use the fact that the graph G contains $O(n)$ edges.) Hence, the overall running time of algorithm PATHGREEDY(S, t) is $O(n^3 \log n)$.

In this section, we present a series of improvements, ending up with a new algorithm (referred to later as algorithm FASTPATHGREEDY), which is quite close to algorithm PATHGREEDY in spirit. We will show that algorithm FASTPATHGREEDY computes a spanner of bounded degree and having weight proportional to the weight of a minimum spanning tree of the point set, in $O(n \log^2 n / \log \log n)$ time. In Section 15.2.1, we give a high-level description of the algorithm. The details are worked out in subsequent subsections.

15.2.1 Overview of an improved path-greedy algorithm

On the basis of the observations above on how algorithm PATHGREEDY works, we present a first improvement to the algorithm.

Speeding up the path-greedy algorithm – Idea #1: The algorithm sorts the $\binom{n}{2}$ interpoint distances and inspects each pair for inclusion in the spanner. This is expensive, because it effectively starts with a complete graph. Instead, we could start with a $\sqrt{t/t'}$-spanner G' with $O(n)$ edges obtained using any "quick-and-dirty" spanner algorithm and then compute a $\sqrt{tt'}$-spanner of G', using a variant of algorithm PATHGREEDY that inspects only the edges of G'.

Thus, we can improve the running time by using the fact that the notion of being a spanner is "transitive." To be more precise, we do the following. Given a set S of n points in $\mathbb{R}^d$ and a real number $t > 1$, we first compute an arbitrary $\sqrt{t/t'}$-spanner G' for S, for some real number t' with $1 < t' < t$. Then we run the path-greedy algorithm, with parameter $\sqrt{tt'}$, on the edges of G'. This results in a $\sqrt{tt'}$-spanner G of G'. Since G' is a $\sqrt{t/t'}$-spanner for S, it is not difficult to see that G is a t-spanner for S.

How does **Idea #1** affect the analysis of the previous section (Section 15.1.3) and the time complexity of PATHGREEDY? First, since we start with a $\sqrt{t/t'}$-spanner G' with $O(n)$ edges, the output G will also have $O(n)$ edges. Second, if we start with a bounded-degree spanner G', then the output G will be of bounded degree as well. Third, a generalization of Lemma 15.1.9 shows that, for every edge $\{p, q\}$ of G, we have $\delta_2(p, q) > \sqrt{tt'}|pq|$, where $\delta_2(p, q)$ denotes the length of a second shortest path in G between p and q. Then, a generalization of Lemma 14.3.1 shows that the edge set of the computed spanner G satisfies the $(\sqrt{tt'}, t)$-leapfrog property of Section 14.9. Hence, if t is a constant and t' is chosen appropriately, then the Generalized Leapfrog Theorem (Theorem 14.9.3) implies that the weight of the spanner G is proportional to the weight of a minimum spanning tree of S. To analyze the time complexity, we first note that a $\sqrt{t/t'}$-spanner of bounded degree and with $O(n)$ edges can be computed in $O(n \log n)$ time (see Theorem 10.1.3 in Section 10.1). Therefore, the time complexity of the improved algorithm is

$O(n \log n)$ times the number of edges of the $\sqrt{t/t'}$-spanner, giving us an $O(n^2 \log n)$–time algorithm.

For the following discussion, we assume that we have four real numbers $t > 1, t' > 1$, $\mu > 1$, and α, such that $t > t'$ and $0 < \alpha < 1/2$. As explained above, first we compute a bounded degree $\sqrt{t/t'}$-spanner $G' = (S, E')$. Thus, G' has $O(n)$ edges. Let D denote the maximum length of any edge of E', and let E_0 be the set of all edges of E' whose lengths are less than, or equal to, D/n. Since the number of edges of E_0 is $O(n)$, it is clear that $wt(E_0) = O(D) = O(wt(MST(S)))$. Therefore, it does no harm for us to make all the edges in E_0 a part of the final t-spanner G computed by our algorithm. In the rest of the algorithm, a subset of $E' \setminus E_0$ will be selected using the path-greedy strategy. In order to select this subset efficiently, we need a fast method to answer shortest-path queries in the partially constructed spanner. That brings us to **Idea #2**.

> **Speeding up the path-greedy algorithm – Idea #2:** The basic test for deciding whether or not to add an edge $\{p, q\}$ to the spanner relies on a shortest path computation. However, it suffices to have *approximate* shortest path information for this test. This is achieved by maintaining a simpler graph, referred to as the *cluster graph*, in which distances between vertices approximate corresponding distances in the partially constructed spanner.

Note that the resulting spanner may not be identical to the one obtained with exact shortest path queries, although it will be shown to retain all the properties that are critical to the analyses and the proofs.

The algorithm partitions the edge set $E' \setminus E_0$ into $\lceil \log_\mu n \rceil$ groups, such that edges within each group differ in length by at most μ. Then it examines the edges of $E' \setminus E_0$, going from one group to the next one, in nondecreasing order of their lengths. While examining these edges, the final t-spanner $G = (S, E)$ for S is computed.

> **Speeding up the path-greedy algorithm – Idea #3:** As mentioned before, the shortest path computations are made on a cluster graph. An edge is added to the spanner whenever the shortest path test in the cluster graph determines that the shortest path in the partially constructed spanner is too long. As edges are added to the spanner, the corresponding cluster graph must also be updated. In fact, as more edges are added to the spanner, longer edges are examined and added to it. The idea is to periodically make the cluster graph simpler and coarser. To prevent the cost of updating and simplifying the cluster graph from becoming too high, edges are processed in $O(\log_\mu n)$ batches or "groups."

We give a brief description of how the algorithm processes one group of edges. Let the lengths of all edges in this group be between W and μW. First, the algorithm computes a *cluster graph H* for the partially constructed spanner G in the following way. The vertices of G are covered by subsets, called *clusters*, such that

1. each cluster has a representative vertex, called its *center*;
2. each vertex in a cluster is within distance αW, in G, from the cluster center; and
3. any two distinct cluster centers have distance more than αW in G.

The cluster graph H has the cluster centers as its vertices. Any two vertices u and v of H are connected by an edge (i) if the distance in G between the cluster centers u and v is at most W or (ii) if there is an edge in G joining two vertices, one of which is in the cluster of u and the other of which is in the cluster of v. The weight of any edge of H is (approximately) equal to the distance in G between the corresponding cluster centers. We remark that the actual cluster graph is slightly different. Details are presented in Section 15.2.2. The essential ideas, however, are captured by the description given here.

The cluster graph H has the following important properties:

1. For any two vertices u and v of H, the distance in H between u and v is approximately equal to the distance in G between u and v;

2. the degree of each vertex of H is $O(\mu^d)$;

3. the weight of each edge of H is larger than αW; and

4. each point of S is contained in $O(1)$ clusters.

Any edge $\{p, q\}$ in the current group of edges is processed as follows. For each cluster containing p, and each cluster containing q, the algorithm computes the distance $\delta_H(u, v)$ between the two corresponding cluster centers u and v. Since the smallest value $\delta_H(u, v)$ obtained approximates the distance in G between p and q, the algorithm uses $\delta_H(u, v)$ to decide whether or not edge $\{p, q\}$ is to be added to the graph G. If $\{p, q\}$ is added to G, then the graph H is modified locally in order to represent a valid cluster graph for the new graph G.

Speeding up distance computations

The main reason to maintain a cluster graph is to speed up distance computations. Why are distance computations likely to be faster in the cluster graph than in the partially constructed spanner? For one, the cluster graph is likely to be sparser. But that is not so critical, since both graphs can be shown to contain only $O(n)$ edges. Note that in order to check whether the distance between a pair of points p and q is at most $\sqrt{tt'}|pq|$, one needs to run Dijkstra's shortest path algorithm from one of the points, say p, and check whether q is reached within the required distance. The time complexity is related to the number of points within distance $\sqrt{tt'}|pq|$ and the number of edges on the path between p and q.

In order to understand this, we make a short digression. Suppose that you have an *unweighted* graph, that is, all edges have the same weight. Now, suppose that you want to test whether the distance between two given vertices is at most c, where c is a constant. If n_c is an upper bound on the number of vertices within distance c, then the time complexity of running Dijkstra's single-source algorithm from a query point is $O(n_c \log n_c)$. Furthermore, if the graph has bounded degree Δ, then $n_c = \Delta^c$; if Δ is a constant, then the distance test can be done in $O(1)$ time. Now, let us go through the same argument, but with a *weighted* graph in which all vertices have degree bounded by Δ, and all the edges have approximately the same weight (i.e., they are all within a small factor μ of each other, say between W and μW). Then it is easy to see that the number of vertices within distance $\mu c W$ is given by $n_c = O(\Delta^{\mu c})$. If Δ and μ are bounded by constants, then the time it takes to test whether the distance between two given vertices is at most cW remains $O(1)$.

In fact, we will show in our discussions below that we exploit these observations, by maintaining the cluster graphs in such a way that $n_t = O(\log n)$, thereby making the cost of a distance test to be $O(\log n \log \log n)$. We encapsulate the above idea as follows.

> **Speeding up the path-greedy algorithm: Distance computations – Idea #4:**
> The cluster graph is maintained in such a way that when performing a distance test for a pair of points $\{p, q\}$, with $|pq|$ in the range $(W, \mu W]$, the cluster graph is a bounded degree graph with edges of lengths in the range $(\alpha W, \mu W + 2\alpha W]$.

Going back to our discussion of the cluster graph, to estimate the time needed to process $\{p, q\}$, we observe that (i) each edge of H has weight more than αW, (ii) H has degree $O(\mu^d)$, (iii) $|pq| \le \mu W$, and (iv) G is a partial spanner in the sense that any pair of points having Euclidean distance less than W is connected by a t-spanner path. Therefore, we can use a packing argument to show that, when computing $\delta_H(u, v)$, only $O(\mu^{2d})$ vertices of H have to be explored, starting in u, before vertex v is reached. In fact, using Dijkstra's algorithm, $\delta_H(u, v)$ can be computed in $O(\mu^{2d})$ time.

After all edges of the current group have been processed, the algorithm sets $W := \mu W$, computes – from scratch – a new "coarser" cluster graph H, and processes the next group of edges.

We will prove that the graph $G = (S, E)$ computed by the algorithm is a t-spanner for S and, for an appropriate choice of α, the edge set $E \setminus E_0$ satisfies the (t', t)-leapfrog property of Section 14.9. Hence, G has bounded degree (because it is a subgraph of the initial spanner G') and, if t' is chosen appropriately, its weight is proportional to the weight of a minimum spanning tree of S.

Let us finally consider the total running time of the algorithm. Computing the cluster graph H can be done in $O(n \log n + \mu^d n)$ time. Recall that this has to be done for each of the $\lceil \log_\mu n \rceil$ groups. For each of the $O(n)$ edges of $E' \setminus E_0$, the algorithm spends $O(\mu^{2d})$ time. Hence, the total running time is

$$O\left(n \log n \log_\mu n + \mu^d n \log_\mu n + n\mu^{2d}\right).$$

By choosing $\mu = (\log n)^{1/(2d)}$, we obtain a running time of $O(n \log^2 n / \log \log n)$.

This concludes the informal description of the algorithm. As mentioned already, we will work out the details in the following subsections.

> **The main ingredients:** Partition the edge set of the initial spanner G' into $\log_\mu n$ groups such that within each group, edges differ in length by at most μ. Run the path-greedy algorithm on the edges of G' by processing all the groups one after another. Approximate the partially constructed spanner G by a cluster graph H in which shortest path queries for pairs of points that are "close" together can be solved fast.

Now we move on to the details.

15.2.2 Clustering weighted graphs

We start by defining the notions of a cluster cover and a cluster graph. Since these concepts are not limited to Euclidean graphs, we define them for general weighted graphs.

Let $G = (V, E)$ be an arbitrary undirected weighted graph. We denote the weight of any edge $\{u, v\}$ of E by $wt_G(u, v)$. We assume that these weights are strictly positive and satisfy the triangle inequality (see Section 2.2.1). For any two vertices u and v of V, we denote by $\delta_G(u, v)$ the minimum weight of any path in G between u and v. If there is no path between u and v, then $\delta_G(u, v) = \infty$. Observe that, because of the triangle inequality, we have $\delta_G(u, v) = wt_G(u, v)$ for any edge $\{u, v\}$ of E.

The notions of a cluster and a cluster cover of G are defined in a natural way, as follows:

Definition 15.2.1. Let $R > 0$ be a real number and let v be a vertex of V. The *R-cluster* with *center* v is the set

$$\{u \in V : \delta_G(v, u) \leq R\}.$$

We call R the *radius* of the cluster.

Definition 15.2.2. Let $R > 0$ be a real number, let $m \geq 1$ be an integer, and let $v_1, v_2, \ldots, v_m$ be m pairwise distinct vertices of V. For any i with $1 \leq i \leq m$, let C_i be the R-cluster with center v_i. We say that the set $C = \{C_1, C_2, \ldots, C_m\}$ is a *R-cluster cover* of the graph G, if

1. $C_1 \cup C_2 \cup \cdots \cup C_m = V$, and
2. $\delta_G(v_i, v_j) > R$, for all distinct indices i and j with $1 \leq i \leq m$ and $1 \leq j \leq m$.

Observe that two R-clusters C_i and C_j of a R-cluster cover may have vertices in common. However, since we require that $\delta_G(v_i, v_j) > R$, each cluster center belongs to a unique R-cluster. We are now ready to define the cluster graph.

Definition 15.2.3. Let W and α be real numbers, such that $W > 0$ and $0 < \alpha < 1/2$. Let $C = \{C_1, C_2, \ldots, C_m\}$ be an (αW)-cluster cover of the graph G, and, for each i with $1 \leq i \leq m$, let v_i be the center of C_i. The *cluster graph H* is the weighted graph defined as follows.

1. H has V as its vertex set.
2. Edges of H are denoted as $[u, v]$. These edges are undirected.
3. The edge set of H consists of the following edges.
   (a) For each i with $1 \leq i \leq m$ and each $u \in C_i$, $[u, v_i]$ is an edge of H. These edges are called *intra-cluster edges*.
   (b) For each i and j with $1 \leq i \leq m$, $1 \leq j \leq m$, and $i \neq j$, $[v_i, v_j]$ is an edge of H, if
       (i) $\delta_G(v_i, v_j) \leq W$, or
       (ii) $\delta_G(v_i, v_j) > W$ and there is an edge $\{u, v\} \in E$ such that $u \in C_i$ and $v \in C_j$.
       These edges are called *inter-cluster edges*. If the first condition holds, then we refer to the edge as a *short* inter-cluster edge; else we refer to it as a *long* inter-cluster edge.
4. The weight $wt_H(u, v)$ of an intra-cluster edge $[u, v]$ and a short inter-cluster edge $[u, v]$ is defined as $wt_H(u, v) := \delta_G(u, v)$.
5. The weight $wt_H(v_i, v_j)$ of a long inter-cluster edge $[v_i, v_j]$ is defined as

$$\min\{\delta_G(v_i, u) + wt_G(u, v) + \delta_G(v, v_j) : u \in C_i, v \in C_j, \{u, v\} \in E\}.$$

Observe that for each i with $1 \leq i \leq m$, $[v_i, v_i]$ is an intra-cluster edge of H, having weight zero.

If $[u, v]$ is an intra-cluster edge or a short inter-cluster edge, then we defined its weight $wt_H(u, v)$ to be the weight of a shortest path in G between u and v. The weight $wt_H(v_i, v_j)$ of a long inter-cluster edge $[v_i, v_j]$ is defined differently. We could have defined $wt_H(v_i, v_j)$ to be equal to $\delta_G(v_i, v_j)$. Since the latter quantity can be much larger than W, however, we would need too much time to compute it. The above definition is designed to "estimate" $wt_H(v_i, v_j)$ as efficiently as possible. Moreover, we will see that it is a close approximation to $\delta_G(v_i, v_j)$, which suffices for our purposes.

For any two vertices u and v of V, we denote by $\delta_H(u, v)$ the minimum weight of any path in H between u and v. If such a path does not exist, then $\delta_H(u, v) = \infty$. The basic idea behind a cluster graph is summarized in the capsule below.

Cluster graph – basic idea: Given parameters α and W, constructing the cluster graph involves first constructing clusters of radius αW. These clusters may overlap, but each cluster center belongs to only one cluster, thus ensuring that cluster centers are not too close to each other. All vertices in a cluster are joined by an intra-cluster edge to their cluster centers. This guarantees that in the cluster graph, the shortest path between points does not contain a large number of short edges. The cluster graph also contains two types of inter-cluster edges, which are "local," in the following sense. Two cluster centers are joined by a *short* inter-cluster edge if they are within distance W from each other in the original graph; they are connected by a *long* inter-cluster edge if there is an edge connecting some vertex in one cluster with that in the other cluster.

15.2.3 The cluster graph H approximates G

Having defined the cluster graph H above, we will now argue that the construction was meaningful and that H is a good approximation of the original graph G.

Throughout this section, $G = (V, E)$ is a graph as in Section 15.2.2. Furthermore, W and α are real numbers such that $W > 0$ and $0 < \alpha < 1/2$, $\mathcal{C} = \{C_1, C_2, \ldots, C_m\}$ is a (αW)-cluster cover of the graph G, and H is the corresponding cluster graph. Let v_i be the center of cluster C_i, for $1 \le i \le m$.

We prove in Lemmas 15.2.5 and 15.2.6 that for any two vertices u and v that are "far" apart in G, the values $\delta_G(u, v)$ and $\delta_H(u, v)$ are approximately equal. We start with some simple, but useful properties of the weights of the edges in the cluster graph.

Lemma 15.2.4. *Let $[u, v]$ be any edge of the cluster graph H, and let L be the maximum weight of any edge of G.*

1. *In the graph G, u and v are connected by a path.*
2. $\delta_G(u, v) \le wt_H(u, v)$.
3. *If $[u, v]$ is an intra-cluster edge, then $wt_H(u, v) \le \alpha W$.*
4. *If $[u, v]$ is an inter-cluster edge, then*

$$\alpha W < wt_H(u, v) \le \max(W, L + 2\alpha W).$$

5. *If $[u, v]$ is an inter-cluster edge, then $wt_H(u, v) \le 4\alpha W + \delta_G(u, v)$.*

PROOF We prove only the last claim, because the other ones are obvious. So assume that $[u, v]$ is an inter-cluster edge. If it is a short inter-cluster edge, then, by definition, $wt_H(u, v) = \delta_G(u, v)$, which is clearly less than, or equal to, $4\alpha W + \delta_G(u, v)$. Assume that $[u, v]$ is a long inter-cluster edge. Let x and y be vertices of V such that x is a vertex of the (αW)-cluster having center u, y is a vertex of the (αW)-cluster having center v, $\{x, y\}$ is an edge of E, and

$$wt_H(u, v) = \delta_G(u, x) + wt_G(x, y) + \delta_G(y, v).$$

By the triangle inequality, we have

$$
\begin{aligned}
wt_G(x, y) &= \delta_G(x, y) \\
&\leq \delta_G(x, u) + \delta_G(u, v) + \delta_G(v, y) \\
&\leq \alpha W + \delta_G(u, v) + \alpha W.
\end{aligned}
$$

Hence,

$$
\begin{aligned}
wt_H(u, v) &= \delta_G(u, x) + wt_G(x, y) + \delta_G(y, v) \\
&\leq \alpha W + wt_G(x, y) + \alpha W \\
&\leq 4\alpha W + \delta_G(u, v),
\end{aligned}
$$

proving the last claim of the lemma. ∎

Next, we prove that distances in G are bounded from above by distances in H.

Lemma 15.2.5. *For any two vertices u and v of V, we have*

$$\delta_G(u, v) \leq \delta_H(u, v).$$

PROOF If $u = v$ or $\delta_H(u, v) = \infty$, then the claim clearly holds. So assume that $u \neq v$, and that $\delta_H(u, v)$ is finite. Let $u = u_0, u_1, \ldots, u_k = v$ be a path in H between u and v having weight $\delta_H(u, v)$. By Lemma 15.2.4, any two vertices u_i and u_{i+1} are connected by a path in G, $0 \leq i < k$. The triangle inequality and Lemma 15.2.4 imply that

$$\delta_G(u, v) \leq \sum_{i=0}^{k-1} \delta_G(u_i, u_{i+1}) \leq \sum_{i=0}^{k-1} wt_H(u_i, u_{i+1}) = \delta_H(u, v),$$

proving the claim. ∎

The next lemma is a sort of converse to Lemma 15.2.5. It states that distances in H are "not much" larger than distances in G, for any two vertices that are "far" apart. It should be noted that the lemma need not be true for vertices that are "close" to each other.

Lemma 15.2.6. *Let u and v be any two vertices of V such that $\delta_G(u, v) > (1 - 2\alpha)W$. Let C be a (αW)-cluster cover of G. Furthermore, assume that no cluster in C contains both u and v. Then,*

$$\delta_H(u, v) \leq \frac{1 + 18\alpha}{1 - 2\alpha} \cdot \delta_G(u, v).$$

PROOF We write the (αW)-cluster cover as $C = \{C_1, C_2, \ldots, C_m\}$. Let v_i be the center of cluster C_i, for $1 \leq i \leq m$. First observe that u and v are distinct vertices. If $\delta_G(u, v) = \infty$, then the claim clearly holds. Hence, we may assume that $\delta_G(u, v) < \infty$. Let P be a

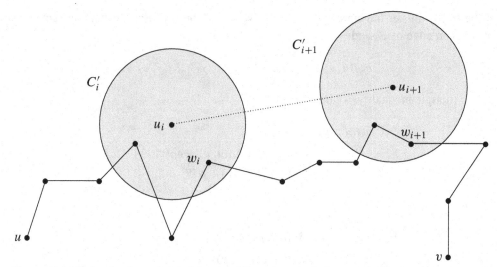

Figure 15.2: Converting the path P in the graph G between u and v into a path Q in the cluster graph H. The solid edges represent the path P, whereas the dotted line represents the inter-cluster edge $[u_i, u_{i+1}]$ of H. Note that C'_i and C'_{i+1} represent (αW)-clusters in G, they do not represent Euclidean balls.

path in G between u and v having minimum weight. We will construct a path Q in the cluster graph H between u and v having weight at most $(1 + 18\alpha)/(1 - 2\alpha)$ times the weight of P. This will prove the lemma.

In the rest of the proof, we will use the following terminology. For any vertex w of the path P, we denote by $P(w)$ the subpath of P consisting of all vertices that are between w and v, not including w, but including v. If x and y are vertices of P, and if x is a vertex of $P(y)$, then we say that (i) x is *closer* to v than y, and (ii) y is *farther* from v than x. Finally, for any index i with $1 \le i \le m$, such that $P(w) \cap C_i \ne \emptyset$, the *last vertex* of $P(w)$ in the (αW)-cluster C_i is the vertex of $P(w) \cap C_i$ that is closest to v. Similarly, the *first vertex* of $P(w)$ in C_i is the vertex of $P(w) \cap C_i$ that is farthest from v.

The path Q is constructed as follows. We start by taking an arbitrary (αW)-cluster from $\mathcal{C}$ that contains u. Denote this cluster and its center by C'_1 and u_1, respectively. Then we initialize Q as the path containing the single intra-cluster edge $[u, u_1]$. By the assumption of the lemma, v is not contained in C'_1. We consider all (αW)-clusters $C_i \in \mathcal{C}$ such that (i) $[u_1, v_i]$ is an inter-cluster edge of H, and (ii) the subpath $P(u)$ and C_i have a nonempty intersection. (Recall that v_i is the center of the cluster C_i.) It follows from the definition of the cluster graph H that there is at least one such cluster C_i. Among these clusters, let C_i be one for which the last vertex of $P(u)$ in C_i is closest to v. Then we define $C'_2 := C_i$, u_2 as the center of C'_2, and w_2 as the last vertex of $P(u)$ in C'_2. We add the inter-cluster edge $[u_1, u_2]$ to the path Q.

If v is not contained in C'_2, then we extend the path Q in a similar way. That is, we consider all (αW)-clusters $C_i \in \mathcal{C}$ such that (i) $[u_2, v_i]$ is an inter-cluster edge of H, and (ii) $P(w_2) \cap C_i \ne \emptyset$. Among all these, let C_i be one for which the last vertex of $P(w_2)$ in C_i is closest to v. Then we define $C'_3 := C_i$, u_3 as the center of C'_3, w_3 as the last vertex of $P(u)$ in C'_3, and add the inter-cluster edge $[u_2, u_3]$ to the path Q (see Figure 15.2).

We keep on extending the path $Q = (u, u_1, u_2, \dots, u_k)$, until the vertex v is contained in the (αW)-cluster C'_k. Then we complete Q, by adding the intra-cluster edge $[u_k, v]$. Algorithm CONVERTTOCLUSTERPATH provides a formal description of the construction of the path Q.

Algorithm CONVERTTOCLUSTERPATH($G, H, \mathcal{C}, P$)

Comment: This algorithm converts the path P in G between u and v into a path Q in the cluster graph H.

$C_1' :=$ any (αW)-cluster that contains u;
$u_1 :=$ center of C_1';
$Q :=$ path in H consisting of the intra-cluster edge $[u, u_1]$;
$w_1 := u$;
$k := 1$;
while $v \notin C_k'$
do ($* u_k$ is the center of C_k', w_k is a vertex of P, $w_k \in C_k' \; *$)
    among all (αW)-clusters C_i such that
    (i) $[u_k, v_i]$ is an inter-cluster edge of H, and
    (ii) $P(w_k)$ and C_i have a nonempty intersection,
    let C_i be one such that the last vertex of $P(w_k)$ in C_i is
    closest to v;
    $u_{k+1} := v_i$;
    $C_{k+1}' := C_i$;
    $w_{k+1} :=$ last vertex of $P(w_k)$ in C_{k+1}';
    add the inter-cluster edge $[u_k, u_{k+1}]$ to Q;
    $k := k + 1$
endwhile;
add the intra-cluster edge $[u_k, v]$ to Q;
report the path $Q = (u, u_1, u_2, \ldots, u_k, v)$

Consider the resulting path

$$Q = (u, u_1, u_2, \ldots, u_k, v)$$

in H between u and v. Since no single (αW)-cluster from $\mathcal{C}$ contains both u and v, we have $k \geq 2$. Observe that for each i with $1 \leq i \leq k$, u_i is the center of the cluster C_i'. Also, it follows from our construction that the clusters C_i', $1 \leq i \leq k$, are pairwise distinct.

In the rest of the proof, we will show that the weight (in H) of the path Q is less than, or equal to, $(1 + 18\alpha)/(1 - 2\alpha)$ times the weight (in G) of the path P. From this, it will follow that

$$\delta_H(u, v) \leq \frac{1 + 18\alpha}{1 - 2\alpha} \cdot \delta_G(u, v).$$

We will denote the weights of P and Q by $wt_G(P)$ and $wt_H(Q)$, respectively.

We distinguish three cases, depending on whether $k = 2$, k is odd, or k is even and greater than or equal to 4.

Case 1: $k = 2$.

In this case, the path Q consists of the intra-cluster edge $[u, u_1]$, the inter-cluster edge $[u_1, u_2]$, and the intra-cluster edge $[u_2, v]$. Since u is a vertex of the (αW)-cluster C_1', we have $\delta_G(u, u_1) \leq \alpha W$. Similarly, we have $\delta_G(u_2, v) \leq \alpha W$. By Lemma 15.2.4, we

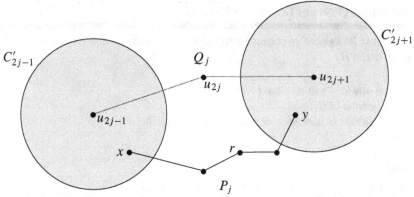

Figure 15.3: Illustrating Case 2 in the proof of Lemma 15.2.6. Note that C'_{2j-1} and C'_{2j+1} represent (αW)-clusters in G, they do not represent Euclidean balls. The subpath P_j of P is shown, as is the corresponding (dotted) subpath Q_j of Q.

have $wt_H(u_1, u_2) \le 4\alpha W + \delta_G(u_1, u_2)$. Combining these inequalities with the triangle inequality, we obtain

$$
\begin{aligned}
wt_H(Q) &= wt_H(u, u_1) + wt_H(u_1, u_2) + wt_H(u_2, v) \\
&= \delta_G(u, u_1) + wt_H(u_1, u_2) + \delta_G(u_2, v) \\
&\le 6\alpha W + \delta_G(u_1, u_2) \\
&\le 6\alpha W + \delta_G(u_1, u) + \delta_G(u, v) + \delta_G(v, u_2) \\
&\le 8\alpha W + \delta_G(u, v).
\end{aligned}
$$

By the assumption of the lemma, we have $\delta_G(u, v) > (1 - 2\alpha)W$. It follows that

$$
wt_H(Q) \le \left(\frac{8\alpha}{1 - 2\alpha} + 1 \right) \cdot \delta_G(u, v) \le \frac{1 + 18\alpha}{1 - 2\alpha} \cdot \delta_G(u, v).
$$

Case 2: $k \ge 3$ and k is odd.

Recall that $w_1 = u$, and w_j is the last vertex on $P(w_{j-1})$ that is in C'_j, $2 \le j \le k$. For each j with $1 \le j \le (k-1)/2$,

1. let P_j be the subpath of P between the vertex w_{2j-1} and the first vertex on $P(w_{2j})$ that is in C'_{2j+1}, including both end-vertices, and
2. let Q_j be the subpath of Q containing the two inter-cluster edges $[u_{2j-1}, u_{2j}]$ and $[u_{2j}, u_{2j+1}]$.

Observe that any two subpaths P_j and $P_{j'}$, with $j \ne j'$, are disjoint, except possibly for their end-vertices.

We first show that the weight $wt_H(Q_j)$ of any subpath Q_j is bounded from above by a constant (depending on α only) times the weight $wt_G(P_j)$ of the subpath P_j.

So let us fix j with $1 \le j \le (k-1)/2$. Let x be the end-vertex of P_j that is in C'_{2j-1}, and let y be the end-vertex of P_j that is in C'_{2j+1} (see Figure 15.3). We claim that

$$
wt_G(P_j) > (1 - 2\alpha)W. \tag{15.4}
$$

Assume that this is not the case. Then,

$$
\begin{aligned}
\delta_G(u_{2j-1}, u_{2j+1}) &\leq \delta_G(u_{2j-1}, x) + \delta_G(x, y) + \delta_G(y, u_{2j+1}) \\
&\leq 2\alpha W + \delta_G(x, y) \\
&\leq 2\alpha W + wt_G(P_j) \\
&\leq W.
\end{aligned}
$$

Hence, since the (αW)-clusters C'_{2j-1} and C'_{2j+1} are distinct, $[u_{2j-1}, u_{2j+1}]$ is an inter-cluster edge of H. This is a contradiction to the choice of the vertex u_{2j}. Hence, we have proved (15.4).

Let r be any vertex on the subpath P_j that is in the (αW)-cluster C'_{2j}. We have

$$
\begin{aligned}
wt_H(u_{2j-1}, u_{2j}) &\leq 4\alpha W + \delta_G(u_{2j-1}, u_{2j}) \\
&\leq 4\alpha W + \delta_G(u_{2j-1}, x) + \delta_G(x, r) + \delta_G(r, u_{2j}) \\
&\leq 6\alpha W + \delta_G(x, r),
\end{aligned}
$$

and, similarly,

$$
wt_H(u_{2j}, u_{2j+1}) \leq 6\alpha W + \delta_G(r, y).
$$

This implies that

$$
\begin{aligned}
wt_H(Q_j) &= wt_H(u_{2j-1}, u_{2j}) + wt_H(u_{2j}, u_{2j+1}) \\
&\leq 12\alpha W + \delta_G(x, r) + \delta_G(r, y) \\
&= 12\alpha W + \delta_G(x, y) \\
&= 12\alpha W + wt_G(P_j) \\
&< \left(\frac{12\alpha}{1 - 2\alpha} + 1\right) \cdot wt_G(P_j) \\
&= \frac{1 + 10\alpha}{1 - 2\alpha} \cdot wt_G(P_j).
\end{aligned}
$$

Since the latter inequality holds for any j, it follows that

$$
\begin{aligned}
wt_H(Q) &= wt_H(u, u_1) + \sum_{j=1}^{(k-1)/2} wt_H(Q_j) + wt_H(u_k, v) \\
&\leq \alpha W + \sum_{j=1}^{(k-1)/2} \frac{1 + 10\alpha}{1 - 2\alpha} \cdot wt_G(P_j) + \alpha W \\
&\leq 2\alpha W + \frac{1 + 10\alpha}{1 - 2\alpha} \cdot wt_G(P) \\
&= 2\alpha W + \frac{1 + 10\alpha}{1 - 2\alpha} \cdot \delta_G(u, v).
\end{aligned}
$$

By the assumption of the lemma, we have $\delta_G(u, v) > (1 - 2\alpha)W$. Therefore,

$$
wt_H(Q) \leq \left(\frac{2\alpha}{1 - 2\alpha} + \frac{1 + 10\alpha}{1 - 2\alpha}\right) \cdot \delta_G(u, v) \leq \frac{1 + 18\alpha}{1 - 2\alpha} \cdot \delta_G(u, v).
$$

Case 3: $k \geq 4$ and k is even.

For each j with $1 \leq j \leq (k-2)/2$, define the subpaths P_j and Q_j as in Case 2. Then it can be proved in exactly the same way as in Case 2 that

$$wt_H(Q_j) < \frac{1+10\alpha}{1-2\alpha} \cdot wt_G(P_j),$$

$1 \leq j \leq (k-2)/2$.

We have not considered yet the last inter-cluster edge $[u_{k-1}, u_k]$ of Q. Let $P_{k/2}$ be the subpath of P between the vertices w_{k-1} and v, including both end-vertices. Then

$$wt_H(u_{k-1}, u_k) \leq 4\alpha W + \delta_G(u_{k-1}, u_k)$$
$$\leq 4\alpha W + \delta_G(u_{k-1}, w_{k-1}) + \delta_G(w_{k-1}, v) + \delta_G(v, u_k)$$
$$\leq 6\alpha W + wt_G(P_{k/2}).$$

Since $0 < \alpha < 1/2$, it follows that

$$wt_H(u_{k-1}, u_k) \leq 6\alpha W + \frac{1+10\alpha}{1-2\alpha} \cdot wt_G(P_{k/2}).$$

Therefore, we get

$$wt_H(Q) = wt_H(u, u_1) + \sum_{j=1}^{(k-2)/2} wt_H(Q_j) + wt_H(u_{k-1}, u_k) + wt_H(u_k, v)$$
$$\leq 8\alpha W + \frac{1+10\alpha}{1-2\alpha} \cdot \delta_G(u, v)$$
$$\leq \left(\frac{8\alpha}{1-2\alpha} + \frac{1+10\alpha}{1-2\alpha} \right) \cdot \delta_G(u, v)$$
$$= \frac{1+18\alpha}{1-2\alpha} \cdot \delta_G(u, v).$$

This completes the proof.   ∎

15.2.4 Cluster graphs of partial spanners

We have defined the cluster graph H for an arbitrary weighted graph $G = (V, E)$ satisfying the triangle inequality. We now consider the special case when the graph G is a "partial" spanner. As we will see, for this case, we can apply a packing argument to prove a nontrivial upper bound on the number of clusters that contain any given point. Also, we can prove a nontrivial upper bound on the degree of the subgraph of the cluster graph H induced by the inter-cluster edges. In Section 15.2.5, we will use these facts to give efficient algorithms for constructing the cluster graph H and for answering shortest path queries in H.

Let S be a set of n points in $\mathbb{R}^d$ and let $G = (S, E)$ be an undirected graph. In this section, the weight (or length) $wt_G(p, q)$ of any edge $\{p, q\} \in E$ is defined as the Euclidean distance between p and q, i.e., $wt_G(p, q) = |pq|$. As before, we denote by $\delta_G(p, q)$ the length of a shortest path in G between any two points p and q of S. If such a path does not exist, then $\delta_G(p, q) = \infty$.

Let $t > 1$ and $X > 0$ be real numbers. We say that the graph G is an X-*partial t-spanner* for S, if for any two points p and q of S with $|pq| \leq X$, we have $\delta_G(p, q) \leq t|pq|$.

Why is the concept of a partial spanner useful? For example, after algorithm PATHGREEDY(S, t) (see Section 1.4) has examined all pairs of points whose Euclidean distance is X, the graph G constructed so far by this algorithm is an X-partial t-spanner for S. Note that the characteristics of algorithm FastPathGreedy are slightly different (see Exercise 15.4).

The following capsule describes the basic idea of a packing argument.

Packing argument: Let $K \subseteq \mathbb{R}^d$ and let $q \in \mathbb{R}^d$, such that all points of K are "close" to q, and any two distinct points in K are "far" apart. Then a packing argument gives an upper bound on the size of K. In our case, we let K be a subset of the set of cluster centers. The points in K were chosen so that they were far from each other in G. But, the fact that G is a partial spanner implies that any two distinct points in K also have a "large" Euclidean distance. The argument would thus show that not many cluster centers are "close" to an arbitrary point q.

In the rest of this section, we will use several parameters, whose values will be carefully chosen in subsequent sections. A summary of these parameters is given below.

The parameters $[n, d, t, W, \alpha, \beta, \gamma, \mu]$ associated with clustering: We have a set S of n points in $\mathbb{R}^d$ and a Euclidean graph $G = (S, E)$. The other parameters are real numbers with the following constraints: $t > 1$, $W > 0$, $0 < \alpha < 1/2$, $\beta > 0$, $\gamma > 0$, and $\mu > 1$. The parameters are used in the following contexts:

- G is a (βW)-partial t-spanner for S.
- The length of each edge of G is less than or equal to μW.
- $C = \{C_1, C_2, \ldots, C_m\}$ is an (αW)-cluster cover of G, v_i is the center of C_i, $1 \leq i \leq m$, and H is the corresponding cluster graph.
- We use the cluster graph H to answer queries of the following form: Given any two points p and q of S and any real number L such that $0 < L \leq \gamma W$, is there a path in H between p and q whose weight is less than or equal to L?

The two main results in this section follow from the following lemma, which gives an upper bound on the number of cluster centers that are contained in any ball of radius $O(W)$.

Lemma 15.2.7. *Let $\lambda > 0$ be a real number and let B be a ball in $\mathbb{R}^d$ having radius λW. The number of (αW)-cluster centers that are in or on the boundary of B is less than or equal to*

$$\left(1 + \frac{2\lambda}{\min(\beta, \alpha/t)}\right)^d.$$

PROOF Let v_i and v_j be two distinct cluster centers and assume that $|v_i v_j| \leq \beta W$. Since the graph G is a (βW)-partial t-spanner for S, we have $\delta_G(v_i, v_j) \leq t|v_i v_j|$. On the other hand, the definition of (αW)-cluster cover implies that $\delta_G(v_i, v_j) > \alpha W$. Combining these two inequalities gives $|v_i v_j| > (\alpha/t) \cdot W$. Hence, we have shown that

$$|v_i v_j| > \min(\beta, \alpha/t) \cdot W \tag{15.5}$$

for any two distinct cluster centers v_i and v_j.

Let $\rho := \min(\beta, \alpha/t) \cdot W/2$. Furthermore, let ℓ be the number of cluster centers that are in or on the boundary of the ball B. We may assume without loss of generality that these cluster centers are $v_1, v_2, \ldots, v_\ell$. For any i with $1 \leq i \leq \ell$, let B_i be the ball centered at v_i and having radius ρ. Also, let B' be the ball of radius $\rho' := \lambda W + \rho$ having the same center as B. Then it follows from (15.5) that the balls B_i, $1 \leq i \leq \ell$, are pairwise disjoint. Also, all these balls are contained in B'.

Any ball in $\mathbb{R}^d$ of radius r has volume $c_d r^d$, where $c_d = \pi^{d/2}/\Gamma(d/2+1)$ (see (6.2) in Section 6.3). It follows that

$$\ell \leq \frac{c_d (\rho')^d}{c_d \rho^d} = \left(1 + \frac{2\lambda}{\min(\beta, \alpha/t)}\right)^d,$$

which is exactly the claim of the lemma.   ∎

Lemma 15.2.8. *Let p be any point of S. The number of (αW)-clusters that contain p is less than or equal to*

$$\left(1 + \frac{2\alpha}{\min(\beta, \alpha/t)}\right)^d.$$

PROOF Let B be the ball in $\mathbb{R}^d$ with center p and radius αW. Let i be any index such that p is contained in the (αW)-cluster C_i. Recall that v_i denotes the center of this cluster. We have $|v_i p| \leq \delta_G(v_i, p) \leq \alpha W$, i.e., v_i is in or on the boundary of B. The claim follows by applying Lemma 15.2.7 with $\lambda = \alpha$.   ∎

Lemma 15.2.9. *Let i be any index such that $1 \leq i \leq m$. The number of inter-cluster edges in the cluster graph H that are incident to the cluster center v_i is less than or equal to*

$$\left(1 + \frac{2\mu + 4\alpha}{\min(\beta, \alpha/t)}\right)^d.$$

PROOF Let B be the ball in $\mathbb{R}^d$ with center v_i and radius $(\mu + 2\alpha)W$. Consider any inter-cluster edge $[v_i, v_j]$. By Lemma 15.2.4, we have

$$\delta_G(v_i, v_j) \leq wt_H(v_i, v_j) \leq \max(W, \mu W + 2\alpha W) = (\mu + 2\alpha)W,$$

where the last equality follows from the fact that $\mu > 1$. Hence, we have $|v_i v_j| \leq (\mu + 2\alpha)W$, i.e., v_j is in or on the boundary of B. Applying Lemma 15.2.7 with $\lambda = \mu + 2\alpha$ proves the claim.   ∎

15.2.5 Clustering algorithms for partial spanners

In this section, we present a collection of algorithms that are needed in the fast spanner algorithm, which is described in the following section (Section 15.2.6), where all these pieces will be tied together.

Throughout this section, we assume that S is a set of n points in $\mathbb{R}^d$ and $t > 1$, $W > 0$, $0 < \alpha < 1/2$, $\beta > 0$, $\gamma > 0$, and $\mu > 1$ are real numbers. Furthermore, we assume that $G = (S, E)$ is a (βW)-partial t-spanner for S and that the length of each edge of G is less than or equal to μW.

We will give efficient algorithms that (i) perform limited-radius single-source computations, (ii) compute an (αW)-cluster cover of G, (iii) compute the corresponding cluster graph H, and (iv) decide if $\delta_H(p, q) \leq L$, when given any two points p and q of S, and any real number L, such that $0 < L \leq \gamma W$.

Algorithm SINGLESOURCE(G', p, R)

Recall that this algorithm was described earlier in Section 2.5. It takes as input any undirected graph G' whose edges have positive weights, any vertex p of G', and any positive real number R. The output consists of the following:

- The set A of all vertices q of G' for which $\delta_{G'}(p, q) \leq R$.

- For each vertex $q \in A$, the value of $\delta_{G'}(p, q)$.

It was shown (see Section 2.5) that this algorithm can be implemented as a variant of Dijkstra's algorithm that terminates as soon as it reaches a vertex q for which $\delta_{G'}(p, q) > R$.

By Theorem 2.5.9, the running time of algorithm SINGLESOURCE(G', p, R) is

$$O\left(|A| \log |A| + \sum_{q \in A} \deg_{G'}(q)\right). \tag{15.6}$$

If we denote the number of vertices of the graph G' by n, then the expression in (15.6) is clearly

$$O\left(|A| \log n + \sum_{q \in A} \deg_{G'}(q)\right). \tag{15.7}$$

In the algorithms that follow, we will use algorithm SINGLESOURCE as a subroutine, with G' being either the partial spanner G or the subgraph of the cluster graph H induced by the inter-cluster edges.

Algorithm CLUSTERCOVER(G, R)

Comment: The input for this algorithm consists of the (βW)-partial t-spanner G for S and any positive real number R. The algorithm computes the following:

- An R-cluster cover $\mathcal{C} = \{C_1, C_2, \ldots, C_m\}$ of G, for some m with $1 \leq m \leq n$, and for each i with $1 \leq i \leq m$, the center v_i of C_i.

- For each point q of S, a list containing the indices of all R-clusters that contain q.

Algorithm CLUSTERCOVER(G, R) uses a simple greedy strategy. It takes an arbitrary point v_1 of S and runs algorithm SINGLESOURCE(G, v_1, R). This gives the first R-cluster C_1 with center v_1. Then the algorithm marks all points of C_1, takes an arbitrary point $v_2 \in S$ that is not marked, and runs algorithm SINGLESOURCE(G, v_2, R). This results in the second R-cluster C_2 having v_2 as its center. The algorithm marks all points of C_2, and proceeds in the same way with an arbitrary point $v_3 \in S$ that is not marked. The algorithm terminates as soon as all points are marked. At that moment, it has computed a valid R-cluster cover of G. The algorithm can easily be extended such that it computes for each point q of S, a list containing all indices i for which $q \in C_i$.

By (15.7), the running time of algorithm CLUSTERCOVER(G, R) is

$$O\left(n + \sum_{i=1}^{m}\left(|C_i| \log n + \sum_{q \in C_i} \deg_G(q)\right)\right).$$

We analyze this summation for the case when $R = \alpha W$. It follows from Lemma 15.2.8 that

$$\sum_{i=1}^{m} |C_i| = \sum_{q \in S} |\{i : q \in C_i\}| \leq \left(1 + \frac{2\alpha}{\min(\beta, \alpha/t)}\right)^d n.$$

Similarly, we have

$$\sum_{i=1}^{m} \sum_{q \in C_i} \deg_G(q) = \sum_{q \in S} \sum_{i : q \in C_i} \deg_G(q) \leq \left(1 + \frac{2\alpha}{\min(\beta, \alpha/t)}\right)^d \sum_{q \in S} \deg_G(q)$$

$$= 2 \left(1 + \frac{2\alpha}{\min(\beta, \alpha/t)}\right)^d |E|.$$

(Recall that E denotes the edge set of the graph G.) Hence, the running time of algorithm CLUSTERCOVER$(G, \alpha W)$ is

$$O\left(\left(1 + \frac{\alpha}{\min(\beta, \alpha/t)}\right)^d (n \log n + |E|)\right). \tag{15.8}$$

Algorithm CLUSTERGRAPH(G, α, W)

Comment: This algorithm takes as input the (βW)-partial t-spanner $G = (S, E)$ and the real numbers α and W such that $0 < \alpha < 1/2$ and $W > 0$. Its output consists of the following:

- The output of algorithm CLUSTERCOVER$(G, \alpha W)$.

- The cluster graph H for G.

- For each edge $[p, q]$ of H, its weight $wt_H(p, q)$.

It consists of the following three steps:

Step 1: Run algorithm CLUSTERCOVER$(G, \alpha W)$.

Let $\mathcal{C} = \{C_1, C_2, \ldots, C_m\}$ be the (αW)-cluster cover that is computed in this first step, and let v_i be the center of C_i, $1 \leq i \leq m$.
We can easily extend Step 1 such that it computes all intra-cluster edges $[v_i, q]$ of H, where $1 \leq i \leq m$ and $q \in C_i$, together with their weights $wt_H(v_i, q)$. (Recall that, by definition, $wt_H(v_i, q) = \delta_G(v_i, q)$, which is computed when running algorithm SINGLESOURCE$(G, v_i, \alpha W)$.) In Steps 2 and 3 below, the inter-cluster edges and their weights will be computed.

Step 2: For each i with $1 \leq i \leq m$, do the following:

2.1: Run algorithm SINGLESOURCE(G, v_i, W).

2.2: For each cluster center v_j that is reported in Step 2.1, and for which $j \neq i$, add $[v_i, v_j]$ to H as a short inter-cluster edge. Observe that the weight $wt_H(v_i, v_j)$ of this edge, which is equal to $\delta_G(v_i, v_j)$, is computed when running algorithm SINGLESOURCE(G, v_i, W).

Step 3: For each edge $\{p, q\}$ of the edge set E of G, do the following. Consider all indices i and j such that $i \neq j$, $p \in C_i$, and $q \in C_j$. For all such i and j,

3.1: if $[v_i, v_j]$ is not an edge of H yet, add it as a long inter-cluster edge, and set $wt_H(v_i, v_j) := \delta_G(v_i, p) + |pq| + \delta_G(q, v_j)$.

3.2: Otherwise, set $wt_H(v_i, v_j) := \min(wt_H(v_i, v_j), \delta_G(v_i, p) + |pq| + \delta_G(q, v_j))$.

Observe that the values of $\delta_G(v_i, p)$ and $\delta_G(q, v_j)$ that are needed in Step 3 have been computed already in Step 1. If, in Step 3.2, $[v_i, v_j]$ is a short inter-cluster edge, then $wt_H(v_i, v_j)$ is left unchanged, because $\delta_G(u, v) = wt_G(u, v)$ for any edge $\{u, v\}$ of E. Using this, the correctness of the algorithm is clear.

Now for the time complexity analysis. Recall that the time for Step 1 is given by (15.8). To analyze Step 2, let A_i be the set of all points $q \in S$ such that $\delta_G(v_i, q) \leq W$. By (15.7), the total time for Step 2 is

$$O\left(\sum_{i=1}^{m}\left(|A_i|\log n + \sum_{q \in A_i} \deg_G(q)\right)\right).$$

We further analyze this summation. First observe that

$$\sum_{i=1}^{m}|A_i| = \sum_{q \in S}|\{i : \delta_G(q, v_i) \leq W\}|.$$

Since $|qv_i| \leq \delta_G(q, v_i)$, we have

$$|\{i : \delta_G(q, v_i) \leq W\}| \leq |\{i : |qv_i| \leq W\}|.$$

Therefore, if we apply Lemma 15.2.7 with $\lambda = 1$, then we get

$$\sum_{i=1}^{m}|A_i| \leq \left(1 + \frac{2}{\min(\beta, \alpha/t)}\right)^d n.$$

Similarly, we obtain the bound

$$\sum_{i=1}^{m}\sum_{q \in A_i} \deg_G(q) \leq 2\left(1 + \frac{2}{\min(\beta, \alpha/t)}\right)^d |E|.$$

Hence, the total time for Step 2 is

$$O\left(\left(1 + \frac{1}{\min(\beta, \alpha/t)}\right)^d (n \log n + |E|)\right).$$

Finally, we analyze the time for Step 3. Consider any edge $\{p, q\}$ of E. By Lemma 15.2.8, there are at most

$$\left(1 + \frac{2\alpha}{\min(\beta, \alpha/t)}\right)^{2d}$$

pairs (i, j) of indices such that $p \in C_i$ and $q \in C_j$. For each such pair for which $i \neq j$, we have to check whether $[v_i, v_j]$ already exists as an inter-cluster edge. If we store the inter-cluster edges using adjacency lists, then this checking can be done in time proportional to the degree of v_i (or v_j) in the subgraph of H induced by the inter-cluster edges. By Lemma 15.2.9, this degree is at most

$$\left(1 + \frac{2\mu + 4\alpha}{\min(\beta, \alpha/t)}\right)^d.$$

If $[v_i, v_j]$ does not exist yet, we can insert it in $O(1)$ time into the adjacency lists of v_i and v_j. Finally, given the positions of $[v_i, v_j]$ in the adjacency lists of v_i and v_j, the value of $wt_H(v_i, v_j)$ can be initialized or recomputed in $O(1)$ time. Hence, the total time for Step 3 is

$$O\left(\left(1 + \frac{\alpha}{\min(\beta, \alpha/t)}\right)^{2d}\left(1 + \frac{\mu + \alpha}{\min(\beta, \alpha/t)}\right)^d |E|\right).$$

Since $\alpha < 1/2$, by adding the time bounds for all three steps, it follows that the overall running time of algorithm CLUSTERGRAPH(G, α, W) is

$$O\left(\left(1 + \frac{1}{\min(\beta, \alpha/t)}\right)^d (n \log n + |E|)\right.$$

$$\left. + \left(1 + \frac{\alpha}{\min(\beta, \alpha/t)}\right)^{2d}\left(1 + \frac{\mu + \alpha}{\min(\beta, \alpha/t)}\right)^d |E|\right). \qquad (15.9)$$

Algorithm SHORTPATH(H, p, q, L)

Comment: This algorithm takes as input any two distinct points p and q of S and any positive real number L. Its output is *true* if there is a path in H between p and q whose weight is less than, or equal to, L. If such a path does not exist, the algorithm returns *false*. Algorithm SHORTPATH(H, p, q, L) makes the following three steps.

Step 1: Mark all cluster centers v_j such that q is contained in the (αW)-cluster C_j. Initialize a Boolean variable *bool* to *false*.

Step 2: For each index i such that p is contained in the (αW)-cluster C_i, do the following:

Step 2.1: Run algorithm SINGLESOURCE(H', v_i, L), where H' is the subgraph of H induced by the inter-cluster edges.

Step 2.2: Consider all cluster centers v_j that are reported in Step 2.1. For each such v_j, check if (i) v_j is marked, and (ii) $wt_H(p, v_i) + \delta_{H'}(v_i, v_j) + wt_H(v_j, q) \leq L$. If (i) and (ii) hold, then set *bool* to *true*.

Step 3: Unmark all cluster centers that were marked in Step 1, and return the variable *bool*.

The correctness proof of this algorithm is left as an exercise; see Exercise 15.5. We analyze its running time for the case when $L \leq \gamma W$. It follows from Lemma 15.2.8 that the time for Steps 1 and 3 is

$$O\left(\left(1 + \frac{\alpha}{\min(\beta, \alpha/t)}\right)^d\right).$$

To analyze Step 2, consider any index i such that $p \in C_i$. Let A_i be the set of cluster centers v_j for which $\delta_{H'}(v_i, v_j) \leq L$. By (15.6), Step 2.1 takes

$$O\left(|A_i| \log |A_i| + \sum_{v_j \in A_i} \deg_{H'}(v_j)\right)$$

time, where $\deg_{H'}(v_j)$ denotes the degree of v_j in the graph H'.

We first prove an upper bound on the size of A_i. Let v_j be any point of A_i. Then $\delta_{H'}(v_i, v_j) \leq L \leq \gamma W$. Hence, $|v_i v_j|$ is also less than, or equal to, γW. That is, all elements of A_i are cluster centers that are in or on the boundary of the ball with center v_i and radius γW. Therefore, by Lemma 15.2.7, we have

$$|A_i| \leq \left(1 + \frac{2\gamma}{\min(\beta, \alpha/t)}\right)^d.$$

By Lemma 15.2.9, the degree in H' of any cluster center v_j is less than, or equal to,

$$\left(1 + \frac{2\mu + 4\alpha}{\min(\beta, \alpha/t)}\right)^d.$$

Therefore, for any fixed i, Step 2.1 takes time proportional to

$$\left(1 + \frac{\gamma}{\min(\beta, \alpha/t)}\right)^d \left(\log\left(1 + \frac{\gamma}{\min(\beta, \alpha/t)}\right) + \left(1 + \frac{\mu + \alpha}{\min(\beta, \alpha/t)}\right)^d\right).$$

Next, we consider Step 2.2. If the cluster center v_j is reported in Step 2.1, then we know the value of $\delta_{H'}(v_i, v_j)$. Since this value is equal to $\delta_H(v_i, v_j)$, we spend $O(|A_i|)$ time in Step 2.2, for any fixed i.

Finally, Lemma 15.2.8 gives an upper bound on the number of indices i that are considered in Step 2.

Hence, we have shown that for any L with $0 < L \leq \gamma W$, the total running time of algorithm SHORTPATH(H, p, q, L) is proportional to

$$\left(1 + \frac{\alpha}{\min(\beta, \alpha/t)}\right)^d \left(1 + \frac{\gamma}{\min(\beta, \alpha/t)}\right)^d$$
$$\times \left(\log\left(1 + \frac{\gamma}{\min(\beta, \alpha/t)}\right) + \left(1 + \frac{\mu + \alpha}{\min(\beta, \alpha/t)}\right)^d\right). \tag{15.10}$$

15.2.6 The fast spanner algorithm

Having described all the pieces, we are now ready to present our fast implementation of the path-greedy algorithm. The algorithm takes as input a set S of n points in $\mathbb{R}^d$, two real numbers $t > 1$ and $t' > 1$ such that $t > t'$, and two real numbers $\mu > 1$ and α such that $0 < \alpha < 1/2$. A formal description of this algorithm, which we denote by FASTPATHGREEDY(S, t, t', α, μ), is given below.

Algorithm FASTPATHGREEDY(S, t, t', α, μ)

Comment: This is the cluster-based path-greedy algorithm that improves upon algorithm
PATHGREEDY. Here, S is a set of n points in $\mathbb{R}^d$, $t > 1$, $t' > 1$, $t > t'$, $0 < \alpha < 1/2$, and
$\mu > 1$.

Compute a bounded-degree $\sqrt{t/t'}$-spanner $G' = (S, E')$ for S,
using the algorithm of Section 10.1.1;
Sort the edges of E' in nondecreasing order of their lengths
(ties are broken arbitrarily);
$D :=$ maximum length of any edge of E';
$I_0 := (0, D/n]$;
$E_0 :=$ sorted sequence of edges of E' having lengths in I_0;
for $k := 1$ **to** $\lceil \log_\mu n \rceil$
do $I_k := (\mu^{k-1}D/n, \mu^k D/n]$;
$\quad E_k :=$ sorted sequence of edges of E' having lengths in I_k;
endfor;
$E := E_0$; $G := (S, E)$; $W := D/n$;
for $k := 1$ **to** $\lceil \log_\mu n \rceil$
do $H :=$ CLUSTERGRAPH(G, α, W);
$\quad$ **for each** edge $\{p, q\}$ of E_k (* considered in sorted order *)
$\quad$ **do if** SHORTPATH$(H, p, q, \sqrt{tt'}|pq|) = $ *false*
$\quad\quad$ **then** $E := E \cup \{\{p, q\}\}$;
$\quad\quad\quad G := (S, E)$;
$\quad\quad\quad$ **for all** cluster centers v_i and v_j, $i \neq j$, such that p is in
$\quad\quad\quad\quad\quad v_i$'s cluster and q is in v_j's cluster
$\quad\quad\quad$ **do if** $[v_i, v_j]$ is an inter-cluster edge in H
$\quad\quad\quad\quad$ **then** $wt_H(v_i, v_j) :=$
$\quad\quad\quad\quad\quad\quad \min(wt_H(v_i, v_j), wt_H(v_i, p) + |pq| + wt_H(q, v_j))$
$\quad\quad\quad\quad$ **else** add $[v_i, v_j]$ as an inter-cluster edge to H;
$\quad\quad\quad\quad\quad wt_H(v_i, v_j) := wt_H(v_i, p) + |pq| + wt_H(q, v_j)$
$\quad\quad\quad\quad$ **endif**
$\quad\quad\quad$ **endfor**
$\quad\quad$ **endif**
$\quad$ **endfor**;
$\quad W := \mu W$
endfor;
return the graph $G = (S, E)$

Before we turn to the correctness proof of this algorithm, let us consider the other three
parameters, viz. W, β, and γ, that we used in the previous subsections. As can be seen in
algorithm FASTPATHGREEDY, the parameter W has different values during the algorithm.
During the phase in which the edges of E_k are examined, we have $W = \mu^{k-1}D/n$.
Furthermore, each edge of E_k has length larger than W, but less than, or equal to, μW.
Hence if the algorithm answers a query SHORTPATH(H, p, q, L) with $L = \sqrt{tt'}|pq|$,
then $0 < L \leq \sqrt{tt'} \cdot \mu W$. That is, we can take the parameter γ to be equal to $\mu\sqrt{tt'}$.
The parameter β should have a value such that G is a (βW)-partial t-spanner for S.
In Lemma 15.2.12 below, we will prove that we can take $\beta = \sqrt{t'/t}$. Observe that the

algorithm does not need to "know" the parameters β and γ; they are used only in the correctness proof and in the analysis of the running time.

The parameter t' will be needed in the weight analysis of the graph $G = (S, E)$ that is computed by the algorithm. In Section 15.2.8, we will show that, for an appropriate choice of α, the edge set $E \setminus E_0$ satisfies the (t', t)-leapfrog property. Hence, by choosing t' appropriately, we can apply the Generalized Leapfrog Theorem (Theorem 14.9.3) for the analysis. Finally, the parameter μ will be chosen in such a way that we obtain the best time bound.

15.2.7 The correctness proof of algorithm FASTPATHGREEDY

The main result of this section will be a proof that algorithm FASTPATHGREEDY computes a t-spanner for S. We define *phase k* to be the iteration of algorithm FASTPATHGREEDY(S, t, t', α, μ) in which the edges of E_k are processed.

Lemma 15.2.10. *Let k be an integer, such that $1 \leq k \leq \lceil \log_\mu n \rceil$. Consider phase k of algorithm FASTPATHGREEDY(S, t, t', α, μ). Then,*

1. *the (αW)-cluster cover that is computed at the beginning of phase k remains a valid cluster cover for G throughout this phase, and*

2. *the graph H is a valid cluster graph for G throughout phase k.*

PROOF The proof is by induction. At the beginning of phase k, algorithm CLUSTERGRAPH(G, α, W) computes a valid (αW)-cluster cover, say, $\{C_1, C_2, \ldots, C_m\}$ of G, and a valid cluster graph H for G.

Consider any edge $\{p, q\}$ of E_k, and assume that immediately before this edge is examined, $\{C_1, C_2, \ldots, C_m\}$ is a valid (αW)-cluster cover and H is a valid cluster graph for the current graph G. We may assume that $\{p, q\}$ is added to E, because otherwise the graphs G and H do not change.

Since the length of the edge $\{p, q\}$ is larger than W, and since $0 < \alpha < 1/2$, the following four claims are easy to verify. First, when adding $\{p, q\}$ to E, $\{C_1, C_2, \ldots, C_m\}$ remains a valid (αW)-cluster cover of the new graph G. Second, when adding $\{p, q\}$ to E, no new intra-cluster edge arises in H and the weights of all existing intra-cluster edges do not change. Third, when adding $\{p, q\}$ to E, no new short inter-cluster edge arises in H and the weights of all existing short inter-cluster edges do not change. Finally, when $\{p, q\}$ is added to E, the algorithm correctly adds new long inter-cluster edges to H, gives them the correct weights, and correctly updates the weights of existing long inter-cluster edges.

Hence, we have shown that immediately after $\{p, q\}$ has been examined, $\{C_1, C_2, \ldots, C_m\}$ is a valid (αW)-cluster cover and H is a valid cluster graph for the new graph G. ∎

Remark 15.2.11. We have not yet proved that, at any moment during algorithm FASTPATHGREEDY, the graph G is a (βW)-partial t-spanner for S, for some appropriate value of β. Algorithms CLUSTERGRAPH and SHORTPATH were described assuming that G is a (βW)-partial t-spanner for S. This fact is, however, not used in the correctness proofs of these two algorithms; it is used only in the analysis of their running times. Therefore, the above proof is a correct proof of Lemma 15.2.10.

Lemma 15.2.12. *During algorithm* FASTPATHGREEDY(S, t, t', α, μ), *the graph G is a* $(\sqrt{t'/t} \cdot W)$-*partial t-spanner for S.*

PROOF Let k be any integer such that $1 \leq k \leq \lceil \log_\mu n \rceil$. During phase k, the value of W is equal to $\mu^{k-1} D / n$ and the edges considered in this phase have weights in the range $(W, \mu W]$. Consider the graph $G = (S, E)$ at the beginning of phase k. (Hence, if $k = 1$, then $E = E_0$.)

Let $\{x, y\}$ be any edge of the $\sqrt{t/t'}$-spanner G', such that $|xy| \leq W$. We will show that $\delta_G(x, y) \leq \sqrt{tt'}|xy|$. If edge $\{x, y\}$ has been added to E, then $\delta_G(x, y) = |xy| \leq t|xy|$. Assume that this edge was not added to E. Then clearly, edge $\{x, y\}$ is not in E_0, and $\{x, y\}$ was examined in phase i, for some integer i with $1 \leq i < k$. Then $\delta_{\widehat{H}}(x, y) \leq \sqrt{tt'}|xy|$, where $\widehat{H}$ is the cluster graph at the moment when $\{x, y\}$ was examined. Hence, by Lemma 15.2.5, we have $\delta_{\widehat{G}}(x, y) \leq \sqrt{tt'}|xy|$, where $\widehat{G}$ is the graph G at the moment when the algorithm examined $\{x, y\}$. Since $\widehat{G}$ is a subgraph of G, we have $\delta_G(x, y) \leq \sqrt{tt'}|xy|$.

Hence, we have shown the following. Let G be the graph at the beginning of phase k. For any edge $\{x, y\}$ of G' such that $|xy| \leq W$, we have $\delta_G(x, y) \leq \sqrt{tt'}|xy|$. In the rest of the proof, we will use this fact to show that G is a $(\sqrt{t'/t} \cdot W)$-partial t-spanner for S.

Let a and b be any two points of S such that $|ab| \leq \sqrt{t'/t} \cdot W$. Let $a = a_0, a_1, \ldots, a_\ell = b$ be a shortest path in G' between a and b. Since the length of this path is less than, or equal to, $\sqrt{t/t'}|ab|$, each of its edges has length at most $\sqrt{t/t'}|ab|$, which is less than, or equal to, W. Therefore, we have

$$\delta_G(a, b) \leq \sum_{i=0}^{\ell-1} \delta_G(a_i, a_{i+1})$$
$$\leq \sqrt{tt'} \sum_{i=0}^{\ell-1} |a_i a_{i+1}|$$
$$= \sqrt{tt'} \cdot \delta_{G'}(a, b)$$
$$\leq \sqrt{tt'} \cdot \sqrt{t/t'} \cdot |ab|$$
$$= t|ab|.$$

This proves that, at the beginning of phase k, the graph G is a $(\sqrt{t'/t} \cdot W)$-partial t-spanner for S. Since W does not change during this phase, and since G is modified only by edge insertions, the proof is complete. ∎

The above proof can easily be extended to a proof of the following result.

Lemma 15.2.13. *Algorithm* FASTPATHGREEDY(S, t, t', α, μ) *computes a t-spanner for S.*

15.2.8 The weight analysis of the spanner

We now show that the weight of the spanner computed by the improved algorithm FASTPATHGREEDY(S, t, t', α, μ) is proportional to the weight of a minimum spanning tree of the point set S, provided the parameters t' and α are carefully chosen. The proof is a simple extension of the proof given in Section 15.1.3 for the weight analysis of the basic version PATHGREEDY.

We denote by $\delta_{G,2}(p,q)$ the Euclidean length of a second shortest path in the graph G between the points p and q. (In Section 14.3, the notion of a second shortest path was formally defined.)

We start by generalizing Lemma 15.1.9. In the lemmas below, we use the edge set E_0 as defined in algorithm FASTPATHGREEDY.

Lemma 15.2.14. *Let S be a set of n points in $\mathbb{R}^d$ and let $t > 1, t' > 1, \alpha > 0,$ and $\mu > 1$ be real numbers, such that $t > t'$ and*

$$\alpha \le \frac{\sqrt{t} - \sqrt{t'}}{2\sqrt{t} + 18\sqrt{t'}}.$$

Let $G = (S, E)$ be the output of algorithm FASTPATHGREEDY(S, t, t', α, μ). For any edge $\{p, q\}$ in $E \setminus E_0$, we have

$$\delta_{G,2}(p, q) > t'|pq|.$$

PROOF If $\delta_{G,2}(p, q) = \infty$, then the claim obviously holds. Thus, we may assume that $\delta_{G,2}(p, q)$ is finite. Let $P = (p = p_0, p_1, p_2, \ldots, p_\ell = q)$ be a second shortest path in G between p and q, consisting of at least two edges. (Hence, $\ell \ge 2$.) We have to show that the length of this path is larger than $t'|pq|$. Consider the cycle

$$C := (p_0, p_1, p_2, \ldots, p_\ell, p_0),$$

which is a cycle in the graph G. Let $\{x, y\}$ be the edge of C that was added last by the algorithm. Then, $\{x, y\}$ is a longest edge of C, and $\{x, y\} \notin E_0$. Let C_{xy} denote the path in G between x and y that is obtained by deleting the edge $\{x, y\}$ from C.

Consider the moment when algorithm FASTPATHGREEDY examines the edge $\{x, y\}$. At that moment, the algorithm has already added all edges of C_{xy} to the graph G. Let $\widehat{G}$ be the graph G immediately before $\{x, y\}$ is examined, and let $\widehat{H}$ be the corresponding cluster graph (for cluster radius αW). Since the algorithm adds the edge $\{x, y\}$ to $\widehat{G}$, we have $\delta_{\widehat{H}}(x, y) > \sqrt{tt'}|xy|$.

Since $0 < \alpha < 1/2$ and $|xy| > W$, no (αW)-cluster in the cluster cover of $\widehat{G}$ contains both x and y. Also, we have $\delta_{\widehat{G}}(x, y) \ge |xy| > W > (1 - 2\alpha)W$. Then, Lemma 15.2.6 implies that

$$\delta_{\widehat{G}}(x, y) \ge \frac{1 - 2\alpha}{1 + 18\alpha} \cdot \delta_{\widehat{H}}(x, y) > \frac{1 - 2\alpha}{1 + 18\alpha} \sqrt{tt'}|xy| \ge \frac{1 - 2\alpha}{1 + 18\alpha} \sqrt{tt'}|pq|.$$

Since $|pq| \le |xy|$, we have $|P| \ge |C_{xy}|$. It follows that

$$\delta_{G,2}(p, q) = |P| \ge |C_{xy}| \ge \delta_{\widehat{G}}(x, y) > \frac{1 - 2\alpha}{1 + 18\alpha} \sqrt{tt'}|pq|.$$

Our assumption on α implies that the quantity on the right-hand side is greater than, or equal to, $t'|pq|$. ∎

Lemma 15.2.14 can be used to prove that the subset $E \setminus E_0$ of the edge set E of the spanner computed by algorithm FASTPATHGREEDY satisfies the (t', t)-leapfrog property. Recall that this property states that for every $\ell \ge 2$, and for every sequence $\{p_i, q_i\}$, $1 \le i \le \ell$, of pairwise distinct edges in $E \setminus E_0$, we have

$$t'|p_1q_1| < \sum_{i=2}^{\ell} |p_iq_i| + t\left(|p_1p_2| + \sum_{i=2}^{\ell-1} |q_i p_{i+1}| + |q_\ell q_1|\right).$$

We state this result in the following lemma. The proof is left to the reader, because it is almost identical to the proof of Lemma 14.3.1.

Lemma 15.2.15. *Let S be a set of n points in $\mathbb{R}^d$ and let $t > 1, t' > 1, \alpha > 0$, and $\mu > 1$ be real numbers, such that $t > t'$ and*

$$\alpha \leq \frac{\sqrt{t} - \sqrt{t'}}{2\sqrt{t} + 18\sqrt{t'}}.$$

Let $G = (S, E)$ be the output of algorithm FASTPATHGREEDY(S, t, t', α, μ). *The edge set $E \setminus E_0$ satisfies the (t', t)-leapfrog property.*

According to the Generalized Leapfrog Theorem (Theorem 14.9.3 in Section 14.9), there exists an absolute constant ϕ with $0 < \phi < 1$, such that the following holds: For all real numbers t and t' with $1 < 1 - \phi + \phi t < t' < t$, the weight of any set of edges satisfying the (t', t)-leapfrog property is proportional to the weight of a minimum spanning tree of the endpoints of the edges. This implies the following result.

Theorem 15.2.16. *Let S be a set of n points in $\mathbb{R}^d$, and let t, t', α, and μ be real numbers, such that $1 < 1 - \phi + \phi t < t' < t, \mu > 1$, and*

$$0 < \alpha \leq \frac{\sqrt{t} - \sqrt{t'}}{2\sqrt{t} + 18\sqrt{t'}}.$$

1. Algorithm FASTPATHGREEDY(S, t, t', α, μ) *computes a t-spanner $G = (S, E)$ for S.*

2. The degree in G of each point of S is

$$O\left(\left(\frac{1}{\sqrt{t/t'} - 1}\right)^{2d-1}\right).$$

3. The weight of G is

$$O\left(\left(\left(\frac{1}{\sqrt{t/t'} - 1}\right)^{2d-1} + \left(\frac{1}{t - 1}\right)^{2d}\right) \cdot wt(MST(S))\right),$$

where $MST(S)$ denotes a minimum spanning tree of S.

PROOF The first claim follows from Lemma 15.2.13. Consider the initial bounded-degree $\sqrt{t/t'}$-spanner $G' = (S, E')$ that is computed by the algorithm. Since G is a subgraph of G', the second claim follows from Theorem 10.1.3. Let D be the maximum length of any edge of E', and consider the set E_0 of all edges of E' having length at most D/n. Since $wt(MST(S)) \geq D$, we have

$$wt(E_0) \leq (D/n)|E_0| = O\left(\left(\frac{1}{\sqrt{t/t'} - 1}\right)^{2d-1} \cdot wt(MST(S))\right).$$

The upper bound on $wt(E \setminus E_0)$ follows from Lemma 15.2.15 and the Generalized Leapfrog Theorem (Theorem 14.9.3). ∎

15.2.9 The running time of algorithm FASTPATHGREEDY

Finally, we analyze the running time of algorithm FASTPATHGREEDY. Let S be a set of n points in $\mathbb{R}^d$ and let $t > 1, t' > 1, \mu > 1$, and α be real numbers such that $t > t'$ and $0 < \alpha < 1/2$.

Algorithm FastPathGreedy(S, t, t', α, μ) starts by computing a bounded-degree $\sqrt{t/t'}$-spanner $G' = (S, E')$ for S. By Theorem 10.1.3, this spanner can be computed in time

$$O\left(\frac{\log(1/(\sqrt{t/t'} - 1))}{(\sqrt{t/t'} - 1)^d} n \log n\right). \tag{15.11}$$

Again by Theorem 10.1.3, we have

$$|E'| = O\left(\left(\frac{1}{\sqrt{t/t'} - 1}\right)^{2d-1} n\right).$$

Next, algorithm FastPathGreedy sorts the edges of E' in nondecreasing order of their lengths, partitions E' into pairwise disjoint subsets E_k, $0 \le k \le \lceil \log_\mu n \rceil$, and initializes G to the graph (S, E_0). The time for this part of the algorithm is

$$O\left(|E'| \log n\right). \tag{15.12}$$

Consider the main loop of the algorithm in which the edges of $E' \setminus E_0$ are processed. Let k be any integer such that $1 \le k \le \lceil \log_\mu n \rceil$, and consider phase k, that is, the iteration in which the edges of E_k are processed.

First, a cluster graph H for the current graph G is computed. The time to compute H is given by (15.9). Since $0 < \alpha < 1/2$ and, by Lemma 15.2.12, $\beta = \sqrt{t'/t}$, we have $\min(\beta, \alpha/t) = \alpha/t$. Also, it is clear that at any moment, the graph G is a subgraph of the initial $\sqrt{t/t'}$-spanner G'. Hence, the number of edges of G is always bounded from above by $|E'|$. Therefore, the time for computing the cluster graph H is

$$O\left(\left(1 + \frac{t}{\alpha}\right)^d (n \log n + |E'|) + t^{2d}\left(\left(1 + \frac{\mu}{\alpha}\right)t\right)^d |E'|\right)$$

$$= O\left((t/\alpha)^d n \log n + t^{3d}(\mu/\alpha)^d |E'|\right). \tag{15.13}$$

After computing H, the algorithm examines all edges of E_k. For any such edge $\{p, q\}$, the time for answering the query ShortPath$(H, p, q, \sqrt{tt'}|pq|)$ is given by (15.10). We have seen in Section 15.2.6 that $\gamma = \mu\sqrt{tt'}$. Therefore, we get an upper bound of

$$O\left(t^{7d/2} \left(t'\right)^{d/2} (\mu/\alpha)^{2d}\right) \tag{15.14}$$

on the time for one such query. If $\{p, q\}$ is added as an edge to G, then the algorithm updates the cluster graph, by considering all (αW)-clusters that contain p and all (αW)-clusters that contain q. By Lemma 15.2.8, the number of pairs of clusters considered is less than, or equal to, $(1 + 2t)^{2d} = O(t^{2d})$. For each such pair of clusters, the algorithm checks whether the corresponding inter-cluster edge $[v_i, v_j]$ already exists. If it does, its weight is updated. Otherwise, $[v_i, v_j]$ is added to H and its weight is computed. If we store the inter-cluster edges using adjacency lists, then, by Lemma 15.2.9, the algorithm spends

$$O\left(\left(1 + \frac{\mu + \alpha}{\min(\beta, \alpha/t)}\right)^d\right) = O\left(t^d(\mu/\alpha)^d\right)$$

time for each pair of clusters. Hence, after adding the edge $\{p, q\}$ to G, the algorithm spends

$$O\left(t^{3d}(\mu/\alpha)^d\right) \tag{15.15}$$

time to update the cluster graph.

Thus, the total running time of algorithm FastPathGreedy(S, t, t', α, μ) is the sum of

1. the quantities in (15.11) and (15.12),

2. $O(\log_\mu n)$ times the quantity in (15.13), and

3. $|E'|$ times the sum of the quantities in (15.14) and (15.15).

Let us see how to choose the parameters so as to get the best result. We assume that we are given the point set S and the real number $t > 1$, and want to compute, as fast as possible, a bounded-degree t-spanner of low weight. We obtain the best time bound by choosing t' as small as possible, and α as large as possible. Hence, to satisfy the conditions of Theorem 15.2.16, we take t' slightly larger than $1 - \phi + \phi t$ and $\alpha = (\sqrt{t} - \sqrt{t'})/(2\sqrt{t} + 18\sqrt{t'})$.

Let us write $t = 1 + \epsilon$, where ϵ is a small positive real number. Then $\sqrt{t} \sim 1 + \epsilon/2$, $t' \sim 1 + \phi\epsilon$, $\sqrt{t'} \sim 1 + \phi\epsilon/2$, $\sqrt{t/t'} \sim 1 + (1 - \phi)\epsilon/2$, and $\alpha \sim \epsilon(1 - \phi)/40$. Hence, the total running time of algorithm FastPathGreedy(S, t, t', α, μ) is

$$O\left(\frac{1}{\epsilon^d \log \mu} n \log^2 n + \frac{\mu^d}{\epsilon^{3d-1} \log \mu} n \log n + \frac{\mu^{2d}}{\epsilon^{4d-1}} n\right). \qquad (15.16)$$

If we choose $\mu = 2$, then we get a running time of $O(n \log^2 n)$. The best time bound is obtained by taking

$$\mu = (\log n)^{1/(2d)}.$$

For this value of μ, the quantity in (15.16) is $O(n \log^2 n / \log \log n)$. Hence, we have proved the following result:

Theorem 15.2.17. *Let S be a set of n points in $\mathbb{R}^d$ and let $t > 1$ be a real number. In*

$$O\left(\frac{1}{(t-1)^d} \frac{n \log^2 n}{\log \log n} + \frac{1}{(t-1)^{3d-1}} \frac{n \log^{3/2} n}{\log \log n} + \frac{1}{(t-1)^{4d-1}} n \log n\right)$$

time, a t-spanner for S can be computed,

1. *in which each point has degree $O(1/(t-1)^{2d-1})$, and*

2. *whose weight is*

$$O\left(\frac{1}{(t-1)^{2d}} \cdot wt(MST(S))\right),$$

where $MST(S)$ denotes a minimum spanning tree of S.

Remark 15.2.18. Algorithm FastPathGreedy starts with the $\sqrt{t/t'}$-spanner G' of Theorem 10.1.3. Consider the modification of this algorithm that (i) starts with an *arbitrary* $\sqrt{t/t'}$-spanner G' and (ii) takes for E_0 the set consisting of all edges of G' whose lengths are at most D/n^2. This modified algorithm computes a t-spanner G for S, whose weight is $O(1/(t-1)^2)$ times the weight of a minimum spanning tree of S.

1. Is there a nontrivial bound on the degree of G? The answer is "no": Let $x = (\sqrt{t} + \sqrt{t'})/(\sqrt{t} - \sqrt{t'})$, let S be the one-dimensional point set defined as $S = \{0, x, x^2, x^3, \ldots, x^{n-1}\}$, and let G' be the graph with vertex set S and edge set $\{\{0, x^i\} : 1 \le i \le n - 1\}$. Then, G' is a $\sqrt{t/t'}$-spanner for S. The t-spanner G that is computed by the modified algorithm FastPathGreedy is equal to G' and, therefore, G contains a vertex of degree $n - 1$.

2. Is there a nontrivial bound on the number of edges of G? Again, the answer is "no": Let S' be a set of $n - 1$ points in $\mathbb{R}^d$ that are very close to the origin, let p be a point in $\mathbb{R}^d$ that is very far away from the origin, and let $S := S' \cup \{p\}$. Let G' be the graph that consists of an arbitrary spanner G'' for S', and one edge between p and one of the points of S'. Then, G' is a $\sqrt{t/t'}$-spanner for S, and the t-spanner G that is computed by the modified algorithm FASTPATHGREEDY is equal to G'. Hence, if we take for G'' the complete graph on S', then the t-spanner G consists of $\Theta(n^2)$ edges.

Algorithm FASTPATHGREEDY can be implemented in the algebraic computation-tree model that was introduced in Section 3.1. Theorem 15.2.17 gives the fastest known algorithm for computing a t-spanner of low weight in this model.

> **Open problem:** Is there an algebraic computation-tree algorithm that, when given a set S of n points in $\mathbb{R}^d$ and a real constant $t > 1$, computes, in $O(n \log n)$ time, a t-spanner for S, whose weight is proportional to the weight of a minimum spanning tree of S? Can such a spanner of bounded degree be computed in $O(n \log n)$ time?

In the next section, we will show that, in a more powerful model of computation, a variant of algorithm FASTPATHGREEDY can be implemented, such that its running time is $O(n \log n)$.

15.3 A faster algorithm that uses indirect addressing

The algorithm that will be presented in this section works in the algebraic computation-tree model in which additionally any indirect addressing operation takes unit time. We do not assume that the floor-function can be computed in unit time. (See also Exercises 3.11 and 3.13.) This algorithm is again based on the path-greedy strategy and is designed along the same lines as the algorithm of Section 15.2. In Section 15.3.1, we give an overview of the algorithm and describe the main differences with algorithm FASTPATHGREEDY.

15.3.1 Overview of the algorithm

The main structure of the algorithm is the same as that of algorithm FASTPATHGREEDY, described in Section 15.2. The input consists of a set S of n points in $\mathbb{R}^d$ and three real numbers $t > 1$, $t' > 1$, and α, such that $t > t' > 1$ and $0 < \alpha < 1/2$.

As in algorithm FASTPATHGREEDY, a bounded-degree $\sqrt{t/t'}$-spanner $G' = (S, E')$ is computed first. Let E_0 be the set of all edges of E' whose lengths are less than, or equal to, D/n, where D is the maximum length of any edge of E', and let $G = (S, E_0)$.

The algorithm partitions the edge set $E' \setminus E_0$ into $\lceil \log n \rceil$ groups $E_1, E_2, \ldots$, such that edges within each group differ in length by at most 2. (Hence, the parameter μ of Section 15.2 is equal to 2.) Then, the algorithm processes the edges of $E' \setminus E_0$, processing one group after another in nondecreasing order of their lengths.

At the beginning of phase k, that is, the iteration in which group E_k is processed, a cluster cover and the corresponding cluster graph H are computed. The new ingredient is that these are not computed on the basis of the Euclidean lengths of the edges of the partially constructed spanner G, but rather on "simpler" weights that approximate the Euclidean lengths. These edge weights are integers in the range $1, 2, \ldots, O(n)$, and how closely they approximate the Euclidean lengths depends on the index k. (In particular, there is a separate integer weight function for each phase; the approximation gets coarser as k increases.)

The advantage of these integer edge weights is that a cluster cover and the corresponding cluster graph can be computed in $O(n)$ time, provided the cluster centers are known in advance. The main tool used is a multiple-sources shortest paths algorithm that basically runs Dijkstra's single-source algorithm "in parallel," using the cluster centers as sources. Recall that in Dijkstra's algorithm (see Section 2.5), we used a Fibonacci heap to maintain the lengths of the shortest paths computed so far. Since the edge weights are "small" integers, we can use one single array to maintain these lengths for all sources. It is in this part of the algorithm that the power of indirect addressing is used; the indices of the array are used to represent the lengths of the shortest paths computed so far.

One problem that is left is how to choose the cluster centers. If $k = 1$, that is, in the first phase, we use the same greedy approach as in algorithm CLUSTERCOVER of Section 15.2.5, to compute the cluster centers in $O(n \log n)$ time. We show that for each $k \geq 1$, we can use the cluster centers of phase k to compute, in $O(n)$ time, cluster centers for phase $k + 1$.

Recall that all results on cluster covers and cluster graphs of Sections 15.2.2 and 15.2.3 were presented for arbitrary undirected weighted graphs that satisfy the triangle inequality. Therefore, these results are valid if we use our integer edge weights. (These integer weights satisfy the triangle inequality.)

Given the cluster graph H, any edge $\{p, q\}$ in E_k is processed as in algorithm FASTPATHGREEDY, except that now the integer edge weights of phase k are used to decide if $\{p, q\}$ is added to G.

The overall running time of the algorithm will be $O(n \log n)$. We will use an analysis similar to those in Sections 15.2.7 and 15.2.8 to prove that the final graph $G = (S, E)$ is a t-spanner for S and, for an appropriate choice of α, the edge set $E \setminus E_0$ satisfies the (t', t)-leapfrog property. Hence, the algorithm computes a t-spanner of bounded degree and, if t' is chosen appropriately, its weight is proportional to the weight of a minimum spanning tree of S.

This concludes the informal description of the main ingredients of the algorithm. In the following subsections, we will fill in the details. Since some of these details are quite subtle, we have decided to present them in a "modular" form. This means that the algorithm computes some of the information more than once. We believe, however, that in this way, it is easier to follow the presentation.

The main ingredients: Partition the edge set of the initial spanner G' into $\log n$ groups such that within each group, edges differ in length by at most a factor of 2. Run the path-greedy algorithm on the edges of G' by processing the groups one after another. During phase k, that is, when processing the k-th group, approximate the partially constructed spanner G by a cluster graph H. Furthermore, scale all the edge weights so that they are integers in the range $[0, cn]$, and such that they approximate their true lengths. Compute the cluster centers in $O(n)$ time using the cluster centers of the previous phase. Given these cluster centers for phase k, run Dijkstra's algorithm "in parallel" from all these cluster centers, and compute H in $O(n)$ time. Use H to answer shortest path queries for pairs of points that are "close" together, in $O(1)$ time.

15.3.2 The integer weight functions

In this section, we define the integer weights that will be used by our algorithm to approximate Euclidean distances. We start by giving the motivation of how these integer weights are defined. Let k be an integer such that $0 \leq k \leq \lceil \log n \rceil$, and let

$$W_k := 2^{k-1} D/n,$$

where D is the maximum Euclidean length of any edge in the initial spanner G'. In phase k, our algorithm processes all edges of G' whose Euclidean lengths are in the interval $(W_k, 2W_k]$. For each such edge $\{p, q\}$, the algorithm decides if the cluster graph H contains a path between p and q, having length at most $c|pq|$, for some constant c. Hence, all paths that need to be dealt with have lengths at most $2cW_k$. The idea is to make this maximum possible length correspond to the integer $c'n$, for some constant c'.

We now formally define the integer edge weights. Let ϵ be a real number such that $0 < \epsilon < 1/2$. For any integer k with $0 \leq k \leq \lceil \log n \rceil$, we define

$$U_k := \epsilon W_k/n = \epsilon \, 2^{k-1} D/n^2,$$

and for any two points p and q in $\mathbb{R}^d$, we define

$$wt^k(p, q) := \lceil |pq|/U_k \rceil.$$

Let $G = (S, E)$ be an arbitrary graph whose vertex set S is a set of points in $\mathbb{R}^d$. If p and q are two points of S, then we denote by $\delta_G(p, q)$ the length of a shortest path in G between p and q, with respect to the Euclidean metric. Furthermore, $\delta_G^k(p, q)$ will denote the length of a shortest path in G between p and q, with respect to the weight function wt^k. As before, if p and q are not connected by a path, then $\delta_G(p, q)$ and $\delta_G^k(p, q)$ are both infinity.

We prove some simple lemmas, showing the relationships between the different weight functions.

Lemma 15.3.1. *For any two points p and q in S and any integer k with $0 \leq k \leq \lceil \log n \rceil$, we have*

$$\delta_G(p, q) \leq \delta_G^k(p, q) \cdot U_k < \delta_G(p, q) + \epsilon W_k.$$

PROOF The first inequality follows from the fact that $|xy| \leq wt^k(x, y) \cdot U_k$ for any two points x and y. The second inequality follows from the facts that $wt^k(x, y) < 1 + |xy|/U_k$ for any two points x and y, and the shortest path between p and q contains less than n edges. ∎

The next lemma follows immediately from Lemma 15.3.1. It states that $\delta_G^k(p, q) \cdot U_k$ and $\delta_G(p, q)$ are approximately equal, provided that p and q are "far" apart.

Lemma 15.3.2. *Let k be an integer with $0 \leq k \leq \lceil \log n \rceil$, and let p and q be two points of S, such that $\delta_G(p, q) \geq W_k$. Then,*

$$\delta_G(p, q) \leq \delta_G^k(p, q) \cdot U_k < (1 + \epsilon) \cdot \delta_G(p, q).$$

The following lemma states that the weights wt^k come from an integral universe of size $O(n)$. The proof follows immediately from the definitions of W_k, U_k, and wt^k.

Lemma 15.3.3. *Let k be an integer with $0 \leq k \leq \lceil \log n \rceil$, and let p and q be any two distinct points in $\mathbb{R}^d$, such that $|pq| \leq 2W_k$. Then,*

$$1 \leq wt^k(p, q) < 3n/\epsilon.$$

The final lemma of this subsection states the relation between δ_G^k and δ_G^{k+1}.

Lemma 15.3.4. *Let k be an integer with $0 \leq k < \lceil \log n \rceil$, and let p and q be two points of S. Then,*

1. $\delta_G^{k+1}(p, q) \leq \delta_G^k(p, q) \leq 2 \cdot \delta_G^{k+1}(p, q)$ *and*
2. $\delta_G^k(p, q) > 2 \cdot \delta_G^{k+1}(p, q) - n.$

PROOF   The first inequality in 1. follows from the fact that

$$wt^{k+1}(x, y) = \left\lceil \frac{|xy|}{2U_k} \right\rceil \leq \left\lceil \frac{|xy|}{U_k} \right\rceil = wt^k(x, y)$$

for any two points x and y. To prove the second inequality in 1., first observe that for any two points x and y, we have

$$wt^k(x, y) = 2 \cdot \frac{1}{2} \left\lceil \frac{|xy|}{U_k} \right\rceil \leq 2 \left\lceil \frac{1}{2} \left\lceil \frac{|xy|}{U_k} \right\rceil \right\rceil.$$

Using the fact that $\lceil z/2 \rceil = \lceil \lceil z \rceil / 2 \rceil$ for any $z \in \mathbb{R}$, it follows that

$$wt^k(x, y) \leq 2 \left\lceil \frac{|xy|}{2U_k} \right\rceil = 2 \cdot wt^{k+1}(x, y).$$

This implies the second inequality in 1.

The inequality in 2. follows from the fact that for any two points x and y, we have

$$wt^{k+1}(x, y) = \left\lceil \frac{|xy|}{2U_k} \right\rceil = \left\lceil \frac{1}{2} \left\lceil \frac{|xy|}{U_k} \right\rceil \right\rceil \leq \frac{1}{2} \left\lceil \frac{|xy|}{U_k} \right\rceil + \frac{1}{2} = \frac{1}{2} \cdot wt^k(x, y) + \frac{1}{2}. \qquad \blacksquare$$

We mentioned already that our algorithm will use the integer weight function wt^k during phase k. Since the value of k increases during the algorithm, the weights of the partially constructed spanner have to be recomputed at the beginning of each phase. If we keep track of the values U_k and use the ceiling-function $\lceil x \rceil$, then the integer weight $wt^k(p, q)$ can be easily computed. In the rest of this section, we show how these weights can be computed within the algebraic computation-tree model.

Recall that in phase k, all edges of the partially constructed spanner and all edges that are considered in this phase have Euclidean lengths at most $2W_k$. Hence, by Lemma 15.3.3, all relevant weights wt^k are integers in the range from 1 to $\lfloor 3n/\epsilon \rfloor$.

Let T be a balanced binary search tree, whose nodes store the integers $1, 2, \ldots, \lfloor 3n/\epsilon \rfloor$. Each node storing, say, the integer ℓ, stores pointers to its two children, and a pointer to the node storing the integer $\lceil \ell/2 \rceil$. This tree can be constructed in the algebraic computation-tree model, in $O((n/\epsilon) \log(n/\epsilon))$ time. (The proof of this claim is left as an exercise; see Exercise 15.10.) Below, we define two operations on the tree T.

Algorithm INTEGRALIZE(p, q, k)

Comment: This algorithm takes as input two distinct points p and q of the set S and an integer k, such that $0 \leq k \leq \lceil \log n \rceil$ and $|pq| \leq 2W_k$. The algorithm returns the value of $wt^k(p, q)$ and a pointer to the node of T that stores this value.

Step 1: Compute $x := |pq|/U_k$.

Step 2: Search in T for the smallest element greater than, or equal to, x.

Step 3: Return a pointer to the node found in Step 2 and the integer stored therein.

Observe that $\lceil x \rceil = wt^k(p, q)$. It is clear that the running time of this algorithm is $O(\log(n/\epsilon))$. As will be shown later, the value U_k needed in the above algorithm is precomputed. Also, this algorithm is run exactly once for each edge in E_k.

Algorithm REINTEGRALIZE(p, q, k, u)

Comment: This algorithm takes as input two distinct points p and q of S, an integer k such that $1 \leq k \leq \lceil \log n \rceil$ and $|pq| \leq 2W_k$, and the node u of T that stores the value of $wt^{k-1}(p, q)$. The algorithm returns the value of $wt^k(p, q)$ and a pointer to the node of T that stores this value.

Step 1: Follow the pointer that is stored in node u to the node, say v, that stores the integer $\lceil wt^{k-1}(p, q)/2 \rceil$.

Step 2: Return a pointer to v and the integer stored therein.

The value $\lceil wt^{k-1}(p, q)/2 \rceil$ is indeed equal to $wt^k(p, q)$, because

$$\left\lceil \frac{wt^{k-1}(p, q)}{2} \right\rceil = \left\lceil \frac{1}{2} \left\lceil \frac{|pq|}{U_{k-1}} \right\rceil \right\rceil = \left\lceil \frac{|pq|}{2U_{k-1}} \right\rceil = wt^k(p, q).$$

The running time of algorithm REINTEGRALIZE(p, q, k, u) is $O(1)$. As shown later, this algorithm is run at most $O(\log n)$ times for each edge in E.

15.3.3 Some packing results

We now generalize the results of Section 15.2.4. Throughout this section, we will use the following parameters. We have a set S of n points in $\mathbb{R}^d$, an integer k with $0 \leq k \leq \lceil \log n \rceil$, and real numbers $t > 1$, $0 < \epsilon < \alpha < 1/2$, $\chi \geq \alpha$, and $\beta > 0$. Furthermore, $G = (S, E)$ is a graph with vertex set S. We make the following assumptions.

- G is a Euclidean (βW_k)-partial t-spanner for S, that is, $\delta_G(p, q) \leq t|pq|$ for any two points p and q in S for which $|pq| \leq \beta W_k$.
- The Euclidean length of each edge of E is less than, or equal to, $2W_k$.
- $v_1, v_2, \ldots, v_m$ are pairwise distinct points of S such that $\delta_G^k(v_i, v_j) > \alpha n/\epsilon$ for all $i \neq j$.
- For any i with $1 \leq i \leq m$, C_i denotes the set

$$C_i = \{p \in S : \delta_G^k(v_i, p) \leq \chi n/\epsilon\}.$$

Lemma 15.3.5. *Let* $\lambda > 0$ *be a real number and let* B *be a ball in* $\mathbb{R}^d$ *having Euclidean radius* λW_k. *The number of indices* i *for which* v_i *is in or on the boundary of* B *is less than or equal to*

$$\left(1 + \frac{2\lambda}{\min(\beta, (\alpha - \epsilon)/t)}\right)^d.$$

PROOF Consider any two distinct indices i and j, and assume that $|v_i v_j| \leq \beta W_k$. Since G is a (βW_k)-partial t-spanner for S, we have $\delta_G(v_i, v_j) \leq t|v_i v_j|$. On the other hand, by our third assumption, we have $\delta_G^k(v_i, v_j) \cdot U_k > (\alpha n/\epsilon)U_k = \alpha W_k$. Hence, by applying Lemma 15.3.1, we obtain

$$\delta_G(v_i, v_j) > \delta_G^k(v_i, v_j) \cdot U_k - \epsilon W_k > (\alpha - \epsilon)W_k.$$

It follows that $|v_i v_j| \geq (1/t) \cdot \delta_G(v_i, v_j) > ((\alpha - \epsilon)/t)W_k$. Hence, we have shown that

$$|v_i v_j| > \min(\beta, (\alpha - \epsilon)/t) \cdot W_k$$

for any two distinct indices i and j. The rest of the proof involves the same packing arguments as in the proof of Lemma 15.2.7. ∎

Lemma 15.3.6. *Let* p *be any point of* S. *The number of indices* i *for which* $p \in C_i$ *is less than, or equal to,*

$$\left(1 + \frac{2\chi}{\min(\beta, (\alpha - \epsilon)/t)}\right)^d.$$

PROOF Let B be the ball in $\mathbb{R}^d$ with center p and Euclidean radius χW_k. Let i be any index such that $p \in C_i$. Then $\delta_G^k(v_i, p) \cdot U_k \leq (\chi n/\epsilon)U_k = \chi W_k$. By Lemma 15.3.1, we have $\delta_G(v_i, p) \leq \delta_G^k(v_i, p) \cdot U_k$. Hence, $|v_i p| \leq \delta_G(v_i, p) \leq \chi W_k$, that is, v_i is in or on the boundary of B. The claim follows by applying Lemma 15.3.5 with $\lambda = \chi$. ∎

In Section 15.2.2, we have defined the notions of a cluster, a cluster cover, and a cluster graph for general weighted graphs. These notions apply to the graph G using the weight function wt^k; see also Exercise 15.11. We denote the integer weights of the cluster graph H by wt_H^k. (Hence, wt_H^k is defined in terms of wt^k and δ_G^k.) The results of Section 15.2.3 are valid for these integer weights.

Lemma 15.3.7. *Let* $\chi = \alpha$, *and let* $\{C_1, C_2, \ldots, C_m\}$ *be a* $(\alpha n/\epsilon)$-*cluster cover of* G *with respect to the weight function* wt^k. *Let* H *be the corresponding cluster graph. Let* i *be any index such that* $1 \leq i \leq m$. *The number of inter-cluster edges in* H *that are incident to* v_i *is at most*

$$\left(1 + \frac{4 + 4\alpha + 2\epsilon}{\min(\beta, (\alpha - \epsilon)/t)}\right)^d.$$

PROOF   Let B be the ball in $\mathbb{R}^d$ with center v_i and Euclidean radius $(2 + 2\alpha + \epsilon)W_k$. Consider any inter-cluster edge $[v_i, v_j]$ of H. By Lemma 15.2.4, we have

$$\delta_G^k(v_i, v_j) \le wt_H^k(v_i, v_j) \le \max(n/\epsilon, L + 2\alpha n/\epsilon),$$

where L is the largest weight (with respect to wt^k) of any edge of E. Let $\{p, q\}$ be an edge of E such that $wt^k(p, q) = L$. Then,

$$L = \lceil |pq|/U_k \rceil < 1 + |pq|/U_k \le 1 + 2W_k/U_k = 1 + 2n/\epsilon,$$

and, hence, $\delta_G^k(v_i, v_j) \le 1 + 2n/\epsilon + 2\alpha n/\epsilon$. It follows that

$$\begin{aligned}
\delta_G^k(v_i, v_j) \cdot U_k &\le ((2 + 2\alpha)n/\epsilon + 1)U_k \\
&= (2 + 2\alpha)W_k + U_k \\
&\le (2 + 2\alpha + \epsilon)W_k.
\end{aligned}$$

Since $|v_i v_j| \le \delta_G(v_i, v_j)$, Lemma 15.3.1 implies that

$$|v_i v_j| \le \delta_G^k(v_i, v_j) \cdot U_k \le (2 + 2\alpha + \epsilon)W_k,$$

that is, v_j is in or on the boundary of B. Applying Lemma 15.3.5 with $\lambda = 2 + 2\alpha + \epsilon$ proves the claim. ■

15.3.4 A multiple-sources shortest paths algorithm

In Section 15.2.5, we used algorithm SINGLESOURCE to compute a cluster cover of the partially constructed spanner G. The centers of the clusters were determined one after another, using a simple greedy strategy. In Section 15.3.5, we will show how a cluster cover can be computed if the cluster centers are known in advance; the main tool used is a multiple-sources shortest paths algorithm, which we present in the current section. In Sections 15.3.6 and 15.3.7, we will see how the cluster centers themselves can be computed.

We assume that the reader is familiar with algorithm SINGLESOURCE of Section 2.5.

> **The basic approach:** Algorithm MULTIPLESOURCES(G, K, L, wt) takes as input a graph G whose edge weights are given by the integer function wt, a set $K = \{v_1, v_2, \ldots, v_m\}$ of source vertices, and a real number L. It returns, for each $v_i \in K$, the set of all vertices u such that $\delta_G(v_i, u) \le L$.
>
> The algorithm does the following: It runs m single-source algorithms "in parallel," using the vertices $v_i, 1 \le i \le m$, as sources. Since all edge weights are positive integers, and since we are interested only in shortest path distances that are less than, or equal to, L, we can use one single array $A[0 .. L]$ to represent all the m priority queues, one for each source vertex v_i. Each array entry $A[j]$ is a list storing all pairs (v_i, u) of vertices having the property that the length of the shortest path in G between v_i and u found so far is equal to j. Hence, addresses in A are used to represent shortest path lengths.

We give a formal specification of the algorithm that accomplishes this task.

Algorithm MULTIPLESOURCES(G, K, L, wt)

Input

- An undirected graph $G = (V, E)$ with positive-integer edge weights given by the function wt. These weights define a shortest path distance function on G, which we denote by δ_G.
- A set $K = \{v_1, v_2, \ldots, v_m\}$ of m pairwise distinct vertices of V.
- A real number $L > 0$.

Output

- For each i with $1 \le i \le m$, a list containing the set C_i of all vertices u of V for which $\delta_G(v_i, u) \le L$. For simplicity, we denote this list by C_i.
- For each i with $1 \le i \le m$ and for each $u \in C_i$, the value of $\delta_G(v_i, u)$.
- For each $u \in V$, a list F_u containing all indices i for which $u \in C_i$.

The algorithm that meets this specification will maintain the following invariants.

Invariants:

1. $A[0 .. L]$ is an array, where, for each j with $0 \le j \le L$, $A[j]$ is a list of ordered pairs (v_i, u) of vertices. If (v_i, u) is in the list $A[j]$, then the shortest path in G between v_i and u found so far has length j.

2. For each $u \in V$, P_u is a list containing pointers to all nodes of the lists $A[0], A[1], \ldots, A[L]$ that contain the pair (v_i, u) for some i with $1 \le i \le m$.

3. For each i with $1 \le i \le m$, C_i is a list containing all vertices u for which the value of $\delta_G(v_i, u)$ has been computed already and for which this value is at most L.

4. For each $u \in V$, F_u is a list containing all indices i for which u is contained C_i.

We first describe the steps that are needed to initialize the algorithm.

Algorithm MULTIPLESOURCES(G, K, L, wt)   **(Continued)**

Initialization steps

1. Delete all edges $\{u, v\}$ from E with $wt(u, v) > L$. For simplicity, denote the resulting edge set by E again.

2. For each j with $0 \le j \le L$, initialize an empty list $A[j]$.

3. For each $u \in V$, initialize empty lists P_u and F_u.

4. For each i with $1 \le i \le m$, do the following: Add the pair (v_i, v_i) to the list $A[0]$; add to P_{v_i} a pointer to the occurrence of (v_i, v_i) in $A[0]$; and initialize an empty list C_i.

Next, we show how one step of the iteration is performed.

Algorithm MULTIPLESOURCES(G, K, L, wt)   **(Continued)**

Iteration ℓ, $\ell = 0, 1, \ldots L$:   For each pair (v_i, u) in $A[\ell]$, do the following:

1. Add vertex u to list C_i, and add index i to list F_u.

2. For each vertex $u' \in V$ for which $\{u, u'\} \in E$, $i \notin F_{u'}$, and $\ell + wt(u, u') \leq L$, do the following:

   2.1. If list $P_{u'}$ contains a pointer to the pair (v_i, u'), then proceed to Step 2.2. Otherwise, add pair (v_i, u') to list $A[\ell + wt(u, u')]$, and add to $P_{u'}$ a pointer to the occurrence of (v_i, u') in list $A[\ell + wt(u, u')]$.

   2.2. Follow the pointer in $P_{u'}$ to the occurrence of (v_i, u') in list, say, $A[\ell']$. If $\ell + wt(u, u') < \ell'$, then
   - add (v_i, u') to list $A[\ell + wt(u, u')]$,
   - delete (v_i, u') from list $A[\ell']$,
   - replace the pointer in $P_{u'}$ to the occurrence of (v_i, u') in $A[\ell']$ by a pointer to the occurrence of (v_i, u') in $A[\ell + wt(u, u')]$.

3. Delete from P_u the pointer to the occurrence of (v_i, u) in $A[\ell]$.

4. Delete the pair (v_i, u) from $A[\ell]$.

This concludes the description of algorithm MULTIPLESOURCES(G, K, L, wt). We leave the correctness proof of this algorithm as an exercise; see Exercise 15.12.

Remark 15.3.8. Steps 2.1 and 2.2 are the only places in the entire algorithm of Section 15.3 in which indirect addressing is used.

In the rest of this section, we analyze the running time of algorithm MULTIPLESOURCES(G, K, L, wt). We denote the number of vertices of G by n, and define

$$M := \max_{u \in V} |\{i : 1 \leq i \leq m, u \in C_i\}|, \tag{15.17}$$

where C_i denotes this list at the end of the algorithm. In other words, M is the largest m_u, $u \in V$, where m_u is the number of clusters that u belongs to. Furthermore, we denote by $\deg_G(u)$ the degree of the vertex u in the graph G.

It is clear that the initialization steps take $O(n + L + |E|)$ time. To bound the time for the rest of the algorithm, first observe that, at any time, each of the lists P_u and F_u, for $u \in V$, has size at most M.

First consider a pair (v_i, u) from list $A[\ell]$, examined in iteration ℓ. Steps 1, 3, and 4 take $O(1)$, $O(M)$, and $O(1)$ time, respectively. In Step 2, $\deg_G(u)$ vertices u' are considered. For each such vertex u', the algorithm spends (i) $O(M)$ time to check whether i is in $F_{u'}$, (ii) $O(M)$ time to check whether $P_{u'}$ contains a pointer to the pair (v_i, u'), whereas (iii) the rest takes $O(1)$ time. At the end of Step 1, u has been added to C_i and the pair (v_i, u) has been deleted from the "priority queue." During the rest of the algorithm, the pair (v_i, u) is never considered again. This implies that, over all iterations, the time complexity is

$$O\left(L + \sum_{i=1}^{m}\left(|C_i| + M\sum_{u \in C_i}\deg_G(u)\right)\right).$$

Simple algebraic manipulations show that $\sum_{i=1}^{m}|C_i| \leq Mn$ and

$$\sum_{i=1}^{m}\sum_{u \in C_i}\deg_G(u) \leq 2M|E|.$$

Hence, we have proved the following result:

Theorem 15.3.9. *Algorithm* MULTIPLESOURCES(G, K, L, wt) *takes*

$$O\left(L + Mn + M^2|E|\right)$$

time, where M is defined in (15.17).

15.3.5 Computing a cluster cover and the cluster graph

In this section we describe algorithm RAMCLUSTERGRAPH, which is the equivalent of algorithm CLUSTERGRAPH (described in Section 15.2.5) for the faster spanner construction algorithm. (Here RAM indicates that the algorithm uses indirect addressing.) Algorithm RAMCLUSTERGRAPH will meet the following specification.

Algorithm RAMCLUSTERGRAPH(G, α, K, k)

Input

- A set S of n points in $\mathbb{R}^d$.
- An integer k with $1 \leq k \leq \lceil \log n \rceil$.
- Real numbers $t > 1$, $0 < \epsilon < \alpha < 1/2$, and $\beta > 0$.
- A graph $G = (S, E)$, which is a Euclidean (βW_k)-partial t-spanner for S, with edges of Euclidean length at most $2W_k$.
- A set $K = \{v_1, v_2, \ldots, v_m\}$ of pairwise distinct points of S, such that $\delta_G^k(v_i, v_j) > \alpha n/\epsilon$ for all $i \neq j$. Furthermore, a $(\alpha n/\epsilon)$-cluster cover of G (with respect to the weights wt^k) with cluster centers $v_1, v_2, \ldots, v_m$ exists, that is, for each $p \in S$, there is an index i such that $\delta_G^k(v_i, p) \leq \alpha n/\epsilon$.

Output

- For each i with $1 \leq i \leq m$, a list C_i containing all points $p \in S$ for which $\delta_G^k(v_i, p) \leq \alpha n/\epsilon$. Hence, $\{C_1, C_2, \ldots, C_m\}$ is a $(\alpha n/\epsilon)$-cluster cover of G with respect to the weights wt^k. Also, for each i with $1 \leq i \leq m$ and for each $p \in C_i$, the value of $\delta_G^k(v_i, p)$.
- For each $p \in S$, a list F_p storing all i for which $p \in C_i$.
- The cluster graph H corresponding to the $(\alpha n/\epsilon)$-cluster cover, with weight $wt_H^k(p, q)$ for each edge $[p, q]$ of H.

Before we give a formal description of algorithm RAMCLUSTERGRAPH, observe that, by Lemma 15.3.3, $1 \leq wt^k(p, q) \leq \lfloor 3n/\epsilon \rfloor$, for each edge $\{p, q\} \in E$.

Algorithm RAMCLUSTERGRAPH(G, α, K, k) **(Continued)**

Step 1: Run algorithm MULTIPLESOURCES$(G, K, \alpha n/\epsilon, wt^k)$. We have seen in Section 15.3.4 that this yields

- lists C_i, $1 \leq i \leq m$, where C_i stores all points $p \in S$ for which $\delta_G^k(v_i, p) \leq \alpha n/\epsilon$,
- the values $\delta_G^k(v_i, p)$ for all $1 \leq i \leq m$ and $p \in C_i$, and
- lists F_p, $p \in S$, where F_p stores all indices i for which $p \in C_i$.

Step 2: Compute all intra-cluster edges $[v_i, p]$, where $1 \leq i \leq m$ and $p \in C_i$, and set $wt_H^k(v_i, p) := \delta_G^k(v_i, p)$.

Step 3: Run algorithm MULTIPLESOURCES$(G, K, n/\epsilon, wt^k)$. This gives

- lists C_i', $1 \leq i \leq m$, where C_i' stores all points $p \in S$ for which $\delta_G^k(v_i, p) \leq n/\epsilon$,
- the values $\delta_G^k(v_i, p)$ for all $1 \leq i \leq m$ and $p \in C_i'$, and
- lists F_p', $p \in S$, where F_p' stores all indices i for which $p \in C_i'$.

Step 4: For each j with $1 \leq j \leq m$, consider all elements i in the list F_{v_j}'. For each such i with $i \neq j$, add $[v_i, v_j]$ to the edge set of H as a short inter-cluster edge, and set $wt_H^k(v_i, v_j) := \delta_G^k(v_i, v_j)$.

Step 5: In this step, the long inter-cluster edges are computed. For each edge $\{p, q\}$ of E, for each index $i \in F_p$, and for each index $j \in F_q$ with $i \neq j$, do the following:

5.1: If $[v_i, v_j]$ is not an edge of H yet, add it as a long inter-cluster edge, and set $wt_H^k(v_i, v_j) := \delta_G^k(v_i, p) + wt^k(p, q) + \delta_G^k(q, v_j)$.

5.2: Otherwise, set $wt_H^k(v_i, v_j) := \min(wt_H^k(v_i, v_j), \delta_G^k(v_i, p) + wt^k(p, q) + \delta_G^k(q, v_j))$.

This concludes the description of algorithm RAMCLUSTERGRAPH. We leave the correctness proof to the reader. To bound the running time of the algorithm, we define

$$M_1 := \max_{p \in S} |\{i : 1 \leq i \leq m, p \in C_i\}|, \tag{15.18}$$

$$M_2 := \max_{p \in S} |\{i : 1 \leq i \leq m, p \in C_i'\}|,$$

and M_3 as the maximum number of inter-cluster edges that are incident on any point v_i, $1 \leq i \leq m$.

By Theorem 15.3.9, Steps 1 and 3 take time $O(\alpha n/\epsilon + M_1 n + M_1^2|E|)$ and $O(n/\epsilon + M_2 n + M_2^2|E|)$, respectively. The time for Step 2 is proportional to $\sum_{i=1}^m |C_i| \leq M_1 n$, whereas the time for Step 4 is proportional to

$$\sum_{j=1}^m |F_{v_j}'| = \sum_{j=1}^m |\{i : 1 \leq i \leq m, v_j \in C_i'\}| \leq M_2 m \leq M_2 n.$$

Finally, the time for Step 5 is proportional to

$$\sum_{\{p,q\}\in E} |F_p| \cdot |F_q| \cdot M_3 \le M_1^2 M_3 |E|.$$

Since $M_1 \le M_2$, it follows that algorithm RAMCLUSTERGRAPH(G, α, K, k) takes

$$O\left(n/\epsilon + M_2 n + (M_2^2 + M_1^2 M_3)|E|\right) \tag{15.19}$$

total time. It remains to prove upper bounds on $M_1, M_2,$ and M_3. These follow immediately from our packing results of Section 15.3.3. Applying Lemma 15.3.6 with $\chi = \alpha$ shows that

$$M_1 \le \left(1 + \frac{2\alpha}{\min(\beta, (\alpha - \epsilon)/t)}\right)^d. \tag{15.20}$$

Lemma 15.3.6, applied with $\chi = 1$, implies that

$$M_2 \le \left(1 + \frac{2}{\min(\beta, (\alpha - \epsilon)/t)}\right)^d.$$

Finally, by Lemma 15.3.7, we have

$$M_3 \le \left(1 + \frac{4 + 4\alpha + 2\epsilon}{\min(\beta, (\alpha - \epsilon)/t)}\right)^d.$$

15.3.6 Computing the cluster centers

Algorithm RAMCLUSTERGRAPH(G, α, K, k) presented in the previous section takes the set K of cluster centers as part of its input. We showed that the cluster graph can be computed efficiently in $O(n)$ time. This implies that as the $O(\log n)$ groups of edges are processed, the total time to compute the cluster graph is $O(n \log n)$. Next, our goal is to show that computing the cluster centers for the $O(\log n)$ iterations can also be done in $O(n \log n)$ time. Here we show how this can be achieved.

The algorithm uses GREEDYCENTERS to compute the centers only for $k = 1$, that is, before the first group of edges is processed, and will be shown to run in $O(n \log n)$ time. However, for later iterations ($k > 1$), algorithm RECOMPUTECENTERS is used. In contrast to GREEDYCENTERS, algorithm RECOMPUTECENTERS will be shown to run in $O(n)$ time. Thus, the idea is to use a brute force algorithm for the first iteration and more efficient schemes for later iterations.

Algorithm GREEDYCENTERS(G, α)

Input: A set S of n points in $\mathbb{R}^d$, and real numbers $t > 1$, $0 < \epsilon < \alpha < 1/2$, and $\beta > 0$. Furthermore, $G = (S, E)$ is a Euclidean (βW_1)-partial t-spanner for S, and each edge of E has Euclidean length at most $2W_1$.

Output: A subset $\{v_1, v_2, \dots, v_m\}$ of S, for some m, such that there exists an $(\alpha n/\epsilon)$-cluster cover of G, with respect to the weights wt^1.

Algorithm: The algorithm follows a greedy approach. It chooses an arbitrary point v_1 of S and runs algorithm SINGLESOURCE($G, v_1, \alpha n/\epsilon$) of Section 2.5, using the weight function wt^1. This gives the set $C_1 := \{p \in S : \delta_G^1(v_1, p) \leq \alpha n/\epsilon\}$. The algorithm marks all points of C_1, chooses an arbitrary point v_2 that is not marked, and runs algorithm SINGLESOURCE($G, v_2, \alpha n/\epsilon$), again using the weight function wt^1. Then the algorithm marks all points of the set $C_2 := \{p \in S : \delta_G^1(v_2, p) \leq \alpha n/\epsilon\}$, chooses an arbitrary point v_3 that is not marked, and proceeds in the same way, until all points of S are marked.

Let $v_1, v_2, \dots, v_m$ be the points that are computed by this algorithm, and let $C_i := \{p \in S : \delta_G^1(v_i, p) \leq \alpha n/\epsilon\}$, for $1 \leq i \leq m$. It follows from Theorem 2.5.9, that algorithm GREEDYCENTERS(G, α) takes

$$O\left(\sum_{i=1}^{m}\left(|C_i| \log n + \sum_{p \in C_i} \deg_G(p)\right)\right)$$

time, see also (15.7) in Section 15.2.5. This quantity is bounded by

$$O(M_1 n \log n + M_1 |E|), \tag{15.21}$$

where M_1 is defined in (15.18). An upper bound on M_1 is given in (15.20).

15.3.7 Recomputing the cluster centers

Algorithm GREEDYCENTERS(G, α) of the previous section will be used only in the first phase of our spanner algorithm, that is, when $k = 1$. In all later phases, the algorithm will use the cluster centers of the previous phase to compute the cluster centers for the current phase. Given these cluster centers, the corresponding cluster cover and cluster graph will be computed using algorithm RAMCLUSTERGRAPH of Section 15.3.5.

We start by introducing the situation at the end of phase k or, equivalently, at the beginning of phase $k + 1$. We have a set S of n points in $\mathbb{R}^d$, a graph $G = (S, E)$ with vertex set S, an integer k with $1 \leq k < \lceil \log n \rceil$, and real numbers $t > 1$, $0 < \alpha < 1/2$, $0 < \epsilon < \alpha/2$, and $\beta > 0$. To set up the stage, we observe that the following conditions are satisfied.

- G is a Euclidean (βW_{k+1})-partial t-spanner for S.
- The Euclidean length of each edge of E is less than, or equal to, $2W_k$.
- $v_1, v_2, \dots, v_m$ is a sequence of pairwise distinct points of S such that $\delta_G^k(v_i, v_j) > \alpha n/\epsilon$ for all $i \neq j$.
- For $1 \leq i \leq m$, $C_i := \{p \in S : \delta_G^k(v_i, p) \leq \alpha n/\epsilon\}$ is the $(\alpha n/\epsilon)$-cluster, with respect to the weights wt^k, centered at v_i.

- $\{C_1, C_2, \ldots, C_m\}$ is an $(\alpha n/\epsilon)$-cluster cover of G, with respect to the weights wt^k. Hence, for each $p \in S$, there is an index i such that $\delta_G^k(v_i, p) \le \alpha n/\epsilon$.

> **Goal:** Use $v_1, v_2, \ldots, v_m$ to compute a subset V' of S, whose elements can be used as cluster centers with respect to the weights wt^{k+1}. Hence, V' must have the following properties:
>
> - $\delta_G^{k+1}(u, v) > \alpha n/\epsilon$, for all u and v in V' with $u \ne v$.
> - For each $p \in S$, there is a $u \in V'$, such that $\delta_G^{k+1}(u, p) \le \alpha n/\epsilon$.

Algorithm RECOMPUTECENTERS, which achieves this goal in three stages, is now described in detail.

Algorithm RECOMPUTECENTERS$(G, \alpha, \{v_1, v_2, \ldots, v_m\}, k)$

Input: A set S of n points in $\mathbb{R}^d$, an integer k with $1 \le k < \lceil \log n \rceil$, real numbers $t > 1$, $0 < \alpha < 1/2$, $0 < \epsilon < \alpha/2$, and $\beta > 0$, and a subset $\{v_1, v_2, \ldots, v_m\}$ of S, for some m, such that there exists an $(\alpha n/\epsilon)$-cluster cover of G, with respect to the weights wt^k. Furthermore, $G = (S, E)$ is a Euclidean (βW_{k+1})-partial t-spanner for S, and each edge of E has Euclidean length at most $2W_k$.

Output: A subset $V' = \{v_1', v_2', \ldots, v_{m'}'\}$ of S, for some m', such that there exists an $(\alpha n/\epsilon)$-cluster cover of G, with respect to the weights wt^{k+1}.

Algorithm: The algorithm works in three stages, each of which is described separately below.

We start with the first stage of RECOMPUTECENTERS.

First stage of RECOMPUTECENTERS$(G, \alpha, \{v_1, v_2, \ldots, v_m\}, k)$

Run algorithm MULTIPLESOURCES$(G, \{v_1, v_2, \ldots, v_m\}, \alpha n/\epsilon, wt^{k+1})$ of Section 15.3.4. This gives $(\alpha n/\epsilon)$-clusters $C_1', C_2', \ldots, C_m'$ centered at the points $v_1, v_2, \ldots, v_m$, with respect to the weights wt^{k+1}. Thus,

$$C_i' = \{p \in S : \delta_G^{k+1}(v_i, p) \le \alpha n/\epsilon\},$$

for each i with $1 \le i \le m$.

By Theorem 15.3.9, this first stage takes

$$O(\alpha n/\epsilon + M_4 n + M_4^2 |E|) \tag{15.22}$$

time, where

$$M_4 := \max_{p \in S} |\{i : 1 \le i \le m, p \in C_i'\}|. \tag{15.23}$$

To prove an upper bound on M_4, we define $C_i'' := \{p \in S : \delta^k(v_i, p) \le 2\alpha n/\epsilon\}$ for $1 \le i \le m$, and $M'' := \max_{p \in S} |\{i : 1 \le i \le m, p \in C_i''\}|$. Applying Lemma 15.3.6, with $\chi = 2\alpha$, shows that

$$M'' \le \left(1 + \frac{4\alpha}{\min(\beta, (\alpha - \epsilon)/t)}\right)^d.$$

By Lemma 15.3.4, we have $\delta_G^k(v_i, p) \leq 2 \cdot \delta_G^{k+1}(v_i, p)$. This implies that $C_i' \subseteq C_i''$, for $1 \leq i \leq m$, and, hence, $M_4 \leq M''$. Therefore, we have

$$M_4 \leq \left(1 + \frac{4\alpha}{\min(\beta, (\alpha - \epsilon)/t)}\right)^d. \tag{15.24}$$

The fact that $\delta_G^{k+1}(v_i, p) \leq \delta_G^k(v_i, p)$ (see Lemma 15.3.4) implies that $C_i \subseteq C_i'$ for $1 \leq i \leq m$. Hence, the sets C_i', $1 \leq i \leq m$, cover the set S. It may happen, however, that some of the centers are "too close" together. That is, there may be indices i and j with $i \neq j$, such that $\delta_G^{k+1}(v_i, v_j) \leq \alpha n/\epsilon$.

Observe that, by our assumption, we have $\delta_G^k(v_i, v_j) > \alpha n/\epsilon$ for all $i \neq j$. Also by Lemma 15.3.4, we have $\delta_G^{k+1}(v_i, v_j) \geq \delta_G^k(v_i, v_j)/2$. It follows that for all $i \neq j$,

$$\delta_G^{k+1}(v_i, v_j) > \alpha n/(2\epsilon). \tag{15.25}$$

The clusters $C_1', C_2', \ldots, C_m'$ have the desired radius of $\alpha n/\epsilon$ under the coarser weight function wt^{k+1}. These clusters have roughly twice the radius as that of the clusters $C_1, C_2, \ldots, C_m$, which have radius of $\alpha n/\epsilon$ under the weight function wt^k.

The first stage: The clusters $C_1', C_2', \ldots, C_m'$ cover the sets S. For any two distinct cluster centers v_i and v_j, we have $\delta_G^{k+1}(v_i, v_j) > \alpha n/(2\epsilon)$. Since our goal is to choose cluster centers that are at least $\alpha n/\epsilon$ apart from each other, we may have to discard some of these cluster centers in the second stage.

The second stage uses a greedy approach to select a subset K_0 of $\{v_1, v_2, \ldots, v_m\}$, such that $\delta_G^{k+1}(u, v) > \alpha n/\epsilon$ for any two distinct points u and v of K_0. The algorithm is as follows, where we assume that initially, all points of S are unmarked.

Second stage of RECOMPUTECENTERS$(G, \alpha, \{v_1, v_2, \ldots, v_m\}, k)$

$K_0 := \emptyset$;
for $i := 1$ **to** m
do if v_i is not marked
    then $K_0 := K_0 \cup \{v_i\}$;
        for each j such that $v_j \in C_i'$
        do mark point v_j
        endfor
    endif
endfor;
unmark all points of S

Lemma 15.3.10. *Consider the set K_0 at the end of the second stage, and let u and v be two distinct points of K_0. We have $\delta_G^{k+1}(u, v) > \alpha n/\epsilon$.*

PROOF Assume that $\delta_G^{k+1}(u, v) \leq \alpha n/\epsilon$. We may assume without loss of generality that u was inserted into K_0 before v. Let i be the index such that $u = v_i$. At the moment when the algorithm inserts u into K_0, all points v_j that are contained in C_i' are marked. Since $\delta_G^{k+1}(u, v) \leq \alpha n/\epsilon$, point v is one of these points v_j. Hence, when u is inserted into K_0, point v is marked. This implies that v is never inserted into K_0, which is a contradiction. ∎

The running time of the second stage is

$$O\left(n + \sum_{i=1}^{m} |C_i'|\right) = O(n + M_4 n) = O(M_4 n), \tag{15.26}$$

where M_4 is defined in (15.23). An upper bound on M_4 is given in (15.24).

> **The second stage:** We have discarded a set of cluster centers from the set $\{v_1, v_2, \ldots, v_m\}$ to obtain a subset K_0, whose elements are sufficiently far apart from each other to serve as cluster centers for phase $k + 1$ (see Lemma 15.3.10). However, we may have discarded too many. It may happen that the $(\alpha n/\epsilon)$-clusters, with respect to the weights wt^{k+1}, centered at the points of K_0, do not cover the set S. If this is the case, then we have to compute more cluster centers. This will be done by repeatedly performing the third stage.

The third stage

Let K be the set of cluster centers computed so far. We assume that $\delta_G^{k+1}(u, v) > \alpha n/\epsilon$ for all u and v in K with $u \neq v$. Initially, $K = K_0$.

We start by running a greedy algorithm that selects a subset K' of S such that (i) $\delta_G^{k+1}(p, u) > \alpha n/\epsilon$ for all $p \in K'$ and $u \in K$, and (ii) $|C_i' \cap K'| \leq 1$ for all i with $1 \leq i \leq m$. Here, C_i' is the $(\alpha n/\epsilon)$-cluster, with respect to the weights wt^{k+1}, centered at v_i, that was computed in the first stage. We denote this algorithm by GREEDYSELECT. It uses a Boolean variable $Choose(p)$ for each $p \in S$. If $Choose(p) = false$, then point p either has been added to K' already or cannot be added to K' without violating (i) or (ii) above.

Algorithm GREEDYSELECT(G, K, α, k)

Comment: This algorithm greedily augments the set of cluster centers K to include at most one point from each C_i' with at least one uncovered point.

```
MULTIPLESOURCES(G, K, αn/ε, wt^{k+1});
for each p ∈ S do Choose(p) := true endfor;
for each u ∈ K
do for each p with δ_G^{k+1}(u, p) ≤ αn/ε
    do Choose(p) := false
    endfor
endfor;
K' := ∅;
for i := 1 to m
do if C_i' contains a point p such that Choose(p) = true
    then let p ∈ C_i' such that Choose(p) = true;
        K' := K' ∪ {p};
        for each q ∈ C_i'
        do Choose(q) := false
        endfor
    endif
endfor
return K';
```

If the set K' returned by algorithm GREEDYSELECT is empty, then the set K is a valid set of cluster centers for phase $k+1$, and we are done with the third stage; otherwise, we proceed to GREEDYREFINE.

Before we analyze algorithm GREEDYSELECT, we claim that after its completion, $Choose(p) = false$ for all $p \in S$. We leave the proof as an exercise; see Exercise 15.13.

Lemma 15.3.11. *Consider the set K' that is returned by algorithm GREEDYSELECT. The following two properties hold:*

1. $\delta_G^{k+1}(p, u) > \alpha n / \epsilon$ *for each $p \in K'$ and each $u \in K$.*
2. $|C_i' \cap K'| \leq 1$ *for each i with $1 \leq i \leq m$.*

PROOF Let $p \in K'$ and $u \in K$. Immediately before K' is initialized to the empty set, we have $Choose(p) = true$, because otherwise p would not have been inserted into K'. This implies that $\delta_G^{k+1}(p, u) > \alpha n / \epsilon$.

To prove the second claim, assume that $C_i' \cap K' \neq \emptyset$. Let p be the point of $C_i' \cap K'$ that was inserted first into K'. At the moment when p is inserted into K', the algorithm sets $Choose(q)$ to *false* for all $q \in C_i'$. Hence, at the end of the algorithm, $C_i' \cap K'$ contains only the point p. ∎

To estimate the running time of algorithm GREEDYSELECT, we define

$$M_5 := \max_{p \in S} |\{u \in K : \delta_G^{k+1}(u, p) \leq \alpha n / \epsilon\}|. \tag{15.27}$$

By Theorem 15.3.9, algorithm MULTIPLESOURCES$(G, K, \alpha n / \epsilon, wt^{k+1})$ takes $O(\alpha n / \epsilon + M_5 n + M_5^2 |E|)$ time. The rest of the algorithm takes

$$O\left(n + \sum_{u \in K} |\{p \in S : \delta_G^{k+1}(u, p) \leq \alpha n / \epsilon\}| + \sum_{i=1}^{m} |C_i'|\right)$$

time, which is $O(M_5 n + M_4 n)$, where M_4 is defined in (15.23). An upper bound on M_4 is given in (15.24). By Lemma 15.3.6, applied with $\chi = \alpha$ and k replaced by $k + 1$, we have

$$M_5 \leq \left(1 + \frac{2\alpha}{\min(\beta, (\alpha - \epsilon)/t)}\right)^d. \tag{15.28}$$

Since $M_5 \leq M_4$, the running time of algorithm GREEDYSELECT is

$$O(\alpha n / \epsilon + M_4 n + M_5^2 |E|). \tag{15.29}$$

After algorithm GREEDYSELECT: Assume that K' is nonempty. It may happen that K' contains points p and q such that $\delta_G^{k+1}(p, q) \leq \alpha n / \epsilon$. Therefore, we now run the following greedy algorithm GREEDYREFINE that selects a subset K'' of K', whose elements are "sufficiently far" apart from each other.

Algorithm GREEDYREFINE(G, K', α, k)

Comment: This algorithm greedily discards all cluster centers from K' that are not sufficiently far from the other centers. It assumes that initially, all points of S are unmarked.

MULTIPLESOURCES(G, K', $\alpha n/\epsilon$, wt^{k+1});
$K'' := \emptyset$;
for each $u \in K'$
do if u is not marked
    then $K'' := K'' \cup \{u\}$;
        for each $p \in S$ with $\delta_G^{k+1}(u, p) \leq \alpha n/\epsilon$
        do mark point p
        endfor
    endif
endfor;
unmark all points of S;
return K'';

Lemma 15.3.12. *Consider the set K'' that is returned by algorithm* GREEDYREFINE, *and let u and v be two distinct points of $K \cup K''$. Then $\delta_G^{k+1}(u, v) > \alpha n/\epsilon$.*

PROOF If u and v are both elements of K, then the claim holds by the assumption made on K. If u and v are both elements of K'', then the claim follows from algorithm GREEDYREFINE (see also the proof of Lemma 15.3.10). If $u \in K$ and $v \in K''$, then the claim follows from Lemma 15.3.11 and the fact that $K'' \subseteq K'$. ∎

Let us analyze the running time of algorithm GREEDYREFINE. We define

$$M_6 := \max_{p \in S} |\{u \in K' : \delta_G^{k+1}(u, p) \leq \alpha n/\epsilon\}|.$$

By Theorem 15.3.9, the call to MULTIPLESOURCES(G, K', $\alpha n/\epsilon$, wt^{k+1}) takes $O(\alpha n/\epsilon + M_6 n + M_6^2|E|)$ time. The time for the rest of the algorithm is proportional to

$$\sum_{u \in K'} |\{p \in S : \delta_G^{k+1}(u, p) \leq \alpha n/\epsilon\}|,$$

which is less than or equal to $M_6 n$. Hence, the running time of algorithm GREEDYREFINE is

$$O(\alpha n/\epsilon + M_6 n + M_6^2|E|). \tag{15.30}$$

We will prove below that

$$M_6 \leq \left(1 + \frac{4\alpha}{\min(\beta, (\alpha/2 - \epsilon)/t)}\right)^d. \tag{15.31}$$

Let p be an arbitrary point of S, and let $u_1, u_2, \ldots, u_\ell$ be all points of K' such that $\delta_G^{k+1}(u_i, p) \leq \alpha n/\epsilon$, $1 \leq i \leq \ell$.

Consider how the set K' was constructed: For each i with $1 \leq i \leq \ell$, let v_i' be the point of $\{v_1, v_2, \ldots, v_m\}$ that "gave rise to" u_i. That is, when algorithm GREEDYSELECT considered v_i', it chose u_i as a point for which $Choose(u_i) = true$, and this point u_i was inserted into K'. Observe that $\delta_G^{k+1}(v_i', u_i) \leq \alpha n/\epsilon$. Also, the points v_i', $1 \leq i \leq \ell$, are pairwise distinct.

We fix i and j such that $1 \leq i \leq \ell$, $1 \leq j \leq \ell$, and $i \neq j$. By (15.25), we have $\delta_G^{k+1}(v_i', v_j') > \alpha n/(2\epsilon)$. Assume that $|v_i' v_j'| \leq \beta W_{k+1}$. Since G is a Euclidean (βW_{k+1})-partial t-spanner, we have $\delta_G(v_i', v_j') \leq t|v_i' v_j'|$. Applying Lemma 15.3.1, we obtain

$$
\begin{aligned}
\delta_G(v_i', v_j') &> \delta_G^{k+1}(v_i', v_j') \cdot U_{k+1} - \epsilon W_{k+1} \\
&> (\alpha n/(2\epsilon)) U_{k+1} - \epsilon W_{k+1} \\
&= (\alpha/2 - \epsilon) W_{k+1}.
\end{aligned}
$$

It follows that $|v_i' v_j'| > (\alpha/2 - \epsilon) W_{k+1}/t$. Hence, we always have

$$
|v_i' v_j'| > \min(\beta, (\alpha/2 - \epsilon)/t) \cdot W_{k+1} \tag{15.32}
$$

for all $i \neq j$.

Next consider an arbitrary index i with $1 \leq i \leq \ell$. We observe that

$$
|pv_i'| \leq |pu_i| + |u_i v_i'| \leq \delta_G(p, u_i) + \delta_G(u_i, v_i'),
$$

which, by Lemma 15.3.1, is less than or equal to

$$
\delta_G^{k+1}(p, u_i) \cdot U_{k+1} + \delta_G^{k+1}(u_i, v_i') \cdot U_{k+1}.
$$

The latter expression is bounded from above by $2(\alpha n/\epsilon) U_{k+1} = 2\alpha W_{k+1}$. Hence, we have shown that

$$
|pv_i'| \leq 2\alpha W_{k+1} \tag{15.33}
$$

for all i with $1 \leq i \leq \ell$.

The inequalities (15.32) and (15.33) imply that we can apply a packing argument to prove an upper bound on ℓ. A straightforward analysis shows that

$$
\ell \leq \left(1 + \frac{4\alpha}{\min(\beta, (\alpha/2 - \epsilon)/t)} \right)^d.
$$

This proves (15.31).

Overview of the third stage

Let us summarize what we have done during one iteration of the third stage.

Enlargening K to $K \cup K''$: We start with a set K of points that are "sufficiently" far apart from each other, that is, $\delta_G^{k+1}(u, v) > \alpha n/\epsilon$ for all u and v in K with $u \neq v$. First, algorithm GREEDYSELECT uses $C_1', C_2', \ldots, C_m'$ to compute a set K' of points, such that the points in K' are sufficiently far apart from the points in K, and $|C_i' \cap K'| \leq 1$ for each i. Then, algorithm GREEDYREFINE selects a subset K'' of K', whose elements are sufficiently far apart from each other. As a result, all points in the union $K \cup K''$ are sufficiently far apart from each other.

Initially, $K = K_0$, which is computed in the second stage. In each iteration of the third stage, K is enlarged, until this set is large enough so that it contains the centers of a valid cluster cover of the graph G for phase $k + 1$. In other words, the third stage can be terminated as soon as the set K'' returned by a call to GREEDYREFINE is empty. Note that it can actually be terminated as soon as the set K' returned by a call to GREEDYSELECT is empty. However, it is convenient to describe it as shown below.

The third stage can thus be summarized as follows.

Third stage of RECOMPUTECENTERS$(G, \alpha, \{v_1, v_2, \ldots, v_m\}, k)$

Comment: We assume that K_0 is the set of cluster centers at the end of the second stage. This stage comprises of a repeated sequence of steps involving augmenting the set of cluster centers and then pruning them down.

$K := K_0$;
repeat
$\qquad K' := $ GREEDYSELECT(G, K, α, k);
$\qquad K'' := $ GREEDYREFINE(G, K', α, k);
$\qquad K := K \cup K''$;
until $K'' = \emptyset$;
return K;

The values of K at the end of each iteration of the repeat-loop of the third stage can be written down as a nested sequence

$$K_0 \subset K_1 \subset K_2 \subset \cdots \subset K_L$$

of subsets of S, where, for $0 \leq \ell < L$, $K_{\ell+1}$ is the set $K_\ell \cup K''$ that is obtained by applying the third stage to the set $K := K_\ell$. The index L is the smallest integer such that the sets $\{p \in S : \delta_G^{k+1}(u, p) \leq \alpha n/\epsilon\}$, $u \in K_L$, form an $(\alpha n/\epsilon)$-cluster cover of G, with respect to the weights wt^{k+1}. Recall that $\delta_G^{k+1}(u, v) > \alpha n/\epsilon$ for any two distinct points u and v in K_L.

In the rest of this section, we prove an upper bound on L, that is, on the number of times that we perform the third stage. The basis for this proof is the following lemma, which states the following. Consider any point q of S, and assume that q is not covered by the clusters centered at the points of K_ℓ. When we enlarge K_ℓ to $K_{\ell+1}$, a cluster center is added that is "close" to q.

Lemma 15.3.13. *Let* $0 \leq \ell < L$ *and let* q *be a point of* S. *Assume that* $\delta_G^{k+1}(v, q) > \alpha n/\epsilon$ *for all* $v \in K_\ell$. *Then the set* $K_{\ell+1} \setminus K_\ell$ *contains a point* u *such that* $|qu| \leq 3\alpha W_{k+1}$.

PROOF Let $K := K_\ell$. Recall how we compute the set $K_{\ell+1}$: We use algorithm GREEDYSELECT to compute a subset K' of S, use algorithm GREEDYREFINE to compute a subset K'' of K', and set $K_{\ell+1} := K \cup K''$.

Consider the algorithm that computes K'. Immediately before K' is initialized to the empty set, the value of $Choose(q)$ is *true*. Let i be the integer, $1 \leq i \leq m$, such that $Choose(q)$ is set to *false* during the iteration in which C_i' is considered. (The index i exists, see Exercise 15.13.) Observe that $q \in C_i'$. Let p be the point of C_i' that is inserted into K' during this iteration. Observe that p is not contained in K. Applying the triangle inequality and Lemma 15.3.1 shows that

$$|qp| \leq |qv_i| + |v_i p| \leq \delta_G(q, v_i) + \delta_G(v_i, p) \leq \delta_G^{k+1}(q, v_i) \cdot U_{k+1} + \delta_G^{k+1}(v_i, p) \cdot U_{k+1}.$$

Since p and q are both contained in C_i', it follows that

$$|qp| \leq 2(\alpha n/\epsilon)U_{k+1} = 2\alpha W_{k+1}.$$

First assume that $p \in K''$. Then $p \in K_{\ell+1} \setminus K_\ell$ and $|qp| \leq 3\alpha W_{k+1}$. Hence, the claim of the lemma holds with $u := p$.

It remains to consider the case when $p \notin K''$. In this case, it follows from algorithm GREEDYREFINE that there is point $u \in K''$ such that $\delta_G^{k+1}(u, p) \leq \alpha n/\epsilon$. Hence, $u \in K_{\ell+1} \setminus K_\ell$, and

$$|qu| \leq |qp| + |pu| \leq 2\alpha W_{k+1} + \delta_G(p, u).$$

Since $\delta_G(p, u) \leq \alpha W_{k+1}$, it follows that $|qu| \leq 3\alpha W_{k+1}$. ∎

Lemma 15.3.14. *Let L be as defined above. We have*

$$L \leq \left(1 + \frac{6\alpha}{\min(\beta, (\alpha - \epsilon)/t)}\right)^d.$$

PROOF Let q be a point of S such that $\delta_G^{k+1}(v, q) > \alpha n/\epsilon$ for all $v \in K_{L-1}$. By Lemma 15.3.13, the set K_L contains L pairwise distinct points $u_1, u_2, \ldots, u_L$ such that $|qu_\ell| \leq 3\alpha W_{k+1}$ for all $1 \leq \ell \leq L$. Furthermore, we know that $\delta_G^{k+1}(u_i, u_j) > \alpha n/\epsilon$ for all $i \neq j$. From this, it easily follows that

$$|u_i u_j| > \min(\beta, (\alpha - \epsilon)/t) \cdot W_{k+1}$$

for all $i \neq j$. The proof can be completed by applying a, by now familiar, packing argument. ∎

We have now completed the description and analysis of the three stages of algorithm RECOMPUTECENTERS(G, α, V, k) that uses the centers $V = \{v_1, v_2, \ldots, v_m\}$ of an $(\alpha n/\epsilon)$-cluster cover of G, with respect to the weights wt^k, to compute centers of an $(\alpha n/\epsilon)$-cluster cover of G, with respect to the weights wt^{k+1}. (The conditions on the parameters in this algorithm are given at the beginning of Section 15.3.7.) The running time of this algorithm is the sum of the quantities in (15.22) and (15.26), plus L times the sum of the quantities in (15.29) and (15.30). This gives an overall time bound of

$$O\left((\alpha n/\epsilon)L + M_6 Ln + M_6^2 L |E|\right). \tag{15.34}$$

Upper bounds on M_6 and L are given in (15.31) and Lemma 15.3.14, respectively.

15.3.8 Answering short-path queries

As usual, we start by introducing the parameters. We have a set S of n points in $\mathbb{R}^d$, an integer k with $1 \leq k \leq \lceil \log n \rceil$, and real numbers $t > 1$, $0 < \epsilon < \alpha < 1/2$, and $\beta > 0$. Furthermore, $G = (S, E)$ is a Euclidean (βW_k)-partial t-spanner for S, each edge of E has Euclidean length at most $2W_k$, $\{C_1, C_2, \ldots, C_m\}$ is an $(\alpha n/\epsilon)$-cluster cover of G, with respect to the weights wt^k, v_i is the center of C_i for $1 \leq i \leq m$, and H is the corresponding cluster graph.

Given two distinct points p and q of S, and a positive real number R, we want to decide if $\delta_H^k(p, q) \leq R$. This query can be answered using algorithm SHORTPATH(H, p, q, R) of Section 15.2.5, of course using the weights wt^k. Recall that the output of this algorithm is *true*, if there is a path in H between p and q whose weight (with respect to wt^k) is less than, or equal to, R. If such a path does not exist, then the algorithm returns *false*.

Let $\gamma > 0$. We analyze the running time of algorithm SHORTPATH(H, p, q, R) for the case when $R \leq \gamma n/\epsilon$.

Applying Lemma 15.3.6 with $\chi = \alpha$ shows that Steps 1 and 3 take

$$O\left(\left(1 + \frac{\alpha}{\min(\beta, (\alpha - \epsilon)/t)}\right)^d\right)$$

time. Steps 2.1 and 2.2 are executed for at most

$$\left(1 + \frac{2\alpha}{\min(\beta, (\alpha - \epsilon)/t)}\right)^d$$

indices i. Consider one such index i. Let $A_i := \{v_j : \delta^k_{H'}(v_i, v_j) \le R\}$, where H' is the subgraph of H induced by the inter-cluster edges. For this i, Step 2.1 takes

$$O\left(|A_i| \log |A_i| + \sum_{v_j \in A_i} \deg_{H'}(v_j)\right)$$

time, whereas Step 2.2 takes $O(|A_i|)$ time.

We first prove an upper bound on the size of A_i. Let v_j be any point of A_i. Then, $\delta^k_{H'}(v_i, v_j) \le R \le \gamma n/\epsilon$. By Lemma 15.3.1, we have

$$|v_i v_j| \le \delta_G(v_i, v_j) \le \delta^k_G(v_i, v_j) \cdot U_k,$$

whereas by Lemma 15.2.5, we have $\delta^k_G(v_i, v_j) \le \delta^k_H(v_i, v_j) \le \delta^k_{H'}(v_i, v_j)$. It follows that

$$|v_i v_j| \le \delta^k_{H'}(v_i, v_j) \cdot U_k \le (\gamma n/\epsilon) U_k = \gamma W_k.$$

We have shown that all elements of A_i are cluster centers that are in or on the boundary of the ball with center v_i and Euclidean radius γW_k. Then, Lemma 15.3.5 implies that

$$|A_i| \le \left(1 + \frac{2\gamma}{\min(\beta, (\alpha - \epsilon)/t)}\right)^d.$$

An upper bound on the degree in H' of any cluster center v_j is given by Lemma 15.3.7:

$$\deg_{H'}(v_j) \le \left(1 + \frac{4 + 4\alpha + 2\epsilon}{\min(\beta, (\alpha - \epsilon)/t)}\right)^d.$$

If we combine all these bounds, then we have shown that for any R with $0 < R \le \gamma n/\epsilon$, algorithm SHORTPATH$(H, p, q, R)$ takes time proportional to

$$\left(1 + \frac{\alpha}{\min(\beta, (\alpha - \epsilon)/t)}\right)^d \left(1 + \frac{\gamma}{\min(\beta, (\alpha - \epsilon)/t)}\right)^d$$

$$\times \left(\log\left(1 + \frac{\gamma}{\min(\beta, (\alpha - \epsilon)/t)}\right) + \left(1 + \frac{1 + \alpha + \epsilon}{\min(\beta, (\alpha - \epsilon)/t)}\right)^d\right). \quad (15.35)$$

15.3.9 The fast spanner algorithm

Having described all necessary subroutines, we are now ready to present the complete spanner algorithm.

Algorithm RAMPATHGREEDY(S, t, t', α)

Input: A set S of n points in $\mathbb{R}^d$, two real numbers $t > 1$ and $t' > 1$ such that $t > t'$, and a real number α such that $0 < \alpha < 1/2$. The value of ϵ that we used before will be equal to $\alpha/4$.

Output: A t-spanner $G = (S, E)$ for S that, for an appropriate choice of α, satisfies the (t', t)-leapfrog property.

Details of algorithm RAMPATHGREEDY(S, t, t', α) follow.

Algorithm RAMPATHGREEDY(S, t, t', α)

Step 1: Compute a bounded-degree $\sqrt{t/t'}$-spanner $G' = (S, E')$ for S, using the algorithm of Section 10.1.1.

Step 2: Sort the edges of E' by nondecreasing Euclidean lengths (where ties are broken arbitrarily).

Step 3: Compute the maximum Euclidean length D of any edge of E', set $I_0 := (0, D/n]$ and $W_0 := D/(2n)$, and compute E_0 as the sorted sequence of all edges of E' whose Euclidean lengths are in I_0.

For $k = 1, 2, \ldots, \lceil \log n \rceil$, set $W_k := 2W_{k-1}$, $U_k := (\alpha W_k)/(4n)$ and $I_k := (W_k, 2W_k]$, and compute E_k as the sorted sequence of all edges of E' whose Euclidean lengths are in I_k.

Step 4: Construct the balanced binary search tree T, storing the integers $1, 2, \ldots, \lfloor 12n/\alpha \rfloor$, that was defined in Section 15.3.2.

Step 5: For each edge $\{p, q\} \in E_0$, perform $u_{pq} := $ INTEGRALIZE($p, q, 0$); see Section 15.3.2. (Recall that this function returns the node u_{pq} of T that stores $wt^0(p, q)$. Also, it stores with edge $\{p, q\}$, the value of $wt^0(p, q)$.)

Step 6: Set $E := E_0$ and $G := (S, E)$.

Step 7: Do the following for $k = 1, 2, \ldots, \lceil \log n \rceil$:

7.1: For each edge $\{p, q\} \in E_k$, perform $u_{pq} := $ INTEGRALIZE(p, q, k).

7.2: For each edge $\{p, q\} \in E$, perform $u_{pq} := $ REINTEGRALIZE(p, q, k, u_{pq}); see Section 15.3.2.

7.3: If $k = 1$, then set $K := $ GREEDYCENTERS(G, α) (see Section 15.3.6); else, set $K := $ RECOMPUTECENTERS($G, \alpha, K, k - 1$) (see Section 15.3.7).

7.4: Perform $H := $ RAMCLUSTERGRAPH(G, α, K, k); see Section 15.3.5.

7.5: Do the following:

for each edge $\{p, q\}$ of E_k (∗ consider the edges in sorted order ∗)
do if SHORTPATH($H, p, q, \sqrt{tt'}|pq|/U_k$) = *false*
   then $E := E \cup \{\{p, q\}\}$;
      $G := (S, E)$;
      for all cluster centers $v_i \in K$ and $v_j \in K$ such that
         p is in v_i's cluster and q is in v_j's cluster and $v_i \neq v_j$
      do if $[v_i, v_j]$ is an inter-cluster edge in H
        then $wt_H^k(v_i, v_j) :=$
           $\min(wt_H^k(v_i, v_j), wt_H^k(v_i, p) + wt^k(p, q) + wt_H^k(q, v_j))$
        else add $[v_i, v_j]$ as an inter-cluster edge to H;
           $wt_H^k(v_i, v_j) := wt_H^k(v_i, p) + wt^k(p, q) + wt_H^k(q, v_j)$
        endif
      endfor
   endif
endfor

Step 8: Return the graph G.

In Sections 15.3.2–15.3.8, we used three parameters, viz. ϵ, β, and γ. As mentioned already, we take $\epsilon = \alpha/4$. If in Step 7.5, the algorithm answers a query

SHORTPATH(H, p, q, R) with $R = \sqrt{tt'}|pq|/U_k$, then

$$0 < R \le 2\sqrt{tt'}W_k/U_k = 2\sqrt{tt'}n/\epsilon.$$

Hence, we can take the parameter γ to be equal to $2\sqrt{tt'}$. The parameter β should be chosen such that, at any moment, G is a (βW_k)-partial t-spanner for S. In Lemma 15.3.16, we will prove that we can take $\beta = \sqrt{t'/t}$. Observe that the algorithm does not have to "know" the parameters β and γ.

15.3.10 The correctness proof

In this section, we will prove that algorithm RAMPATHGREEDY computes a t-spanner for the point set S. The proof is a direct generalization of the results of Section 15.2.7. We define *phase k* to be the iteration of algorithm RAMPATHGREEDY in which the edges of E_k are processed.

Lemma 15.3.15. *Let k be any integer such that $1 \le k \le \lceil \log n \rceil$ and consider phase k of algorithm* RAMPATHGREEDY(S, t, t', α).

1. *The $(\alpha n/\epsilon)$-cluster cover that is computed at the beginning of phase k remains a valid cluster cover for G throughout this phase.*

2. *The graph H is a valid cluster graph for G throughout phase k.*

PROOF In Step 7.4 of phase k, algorithm RAMCLUSTERGRAPH(G, α, K, k) computes a valid $(\alpha n/\epsilon)$-cluster cover of G and a valid cluster graph H, with respect to the weight function wt^k. Denote the clusters by $C_1, C_2, \ldots, C_m$, and let v_i be the center of C_i, $1 \le i \le m$. Hence, $K = \{v_1, v_2, \ldots, v_m\}$.

Let $\{p, q\}$ be an arbitrary edge of E_k, and assume that immediately before this edge is examined in Step 7.5, $\{C_1, C_2, \ldots, C_m\}$ is a valid $(\alpha n/\epsilon)$-cluster cover, and H is a valid cluster graph for the current graph G. We may assume that $\{p, q\}$ is added to the edge set E of G, because otherwise the graphs G and H do not change. The four claims below imply that the claims of the lemma hold immediately after $\{p, q\}$ has been added to E.

First, after $\{p, q\}$ has been added to E, $\{C_1, C_2, \ldots, C_m\}$ is a valid $(\alpha n/\epsilon)$-cluster cover of the new graph G. This claim follows from the fact that $|pq| > W_k$ and, therefore,

$$wt^k(p, q) = \lceil |pq|/U_k \rceil \ge |pq|/U_k > W_k/U_k = n/\epsilon > \alpha n/\epsilon.$$

This inequality also implies the second claim: When $\{p, q\}$ is added to E, no new intra-cluster edge arises in H, and the weights (with respect to wt^k) of all existing intra-cluster edges do not change.

Third, when $\{p, q\}$ is added to E, no new short inter-cluster edge arises in H, and the weights (with respect to wt^k) of all existing short inter-cluster edges do not change. This claim follows from the fact that $\delta_G^k(v_i, v_j) \le n/\epsilon$ for any short inter-cluster edge $[v_i, v_j]$. On the other hand, we have seen above that $wt^k(p, q) > n/\epsilon$.

Fourth, when $\{p, q\}$ is added to E in Step 7.5, the algorithm correctly adds new long inter-cluster edges to H, gives them the correct weights (with respect to wt^k), and correctly updates the weights of existing long inter-cluster edges. ∎

Observe that the proof above is correct, even though we did not prove yet that, at any moment during phase k, the graph G is a (βW_k)-partial t-spanner for S. See also Remark 15.2.11.

Lemma 15.3.16. *Let k be any integer such that $1 \leq k \leq \lceil \log n \rceil$. During phase k of algorithm* RAMPATHGREEDY(S, t, t', α), *the graph G is a $(\sqrt{t'/t} \cdot W_k)$-partial t-spanner for S.*

PROOF   Consider the graph $G = (S, E)$ at the beginning of phase k, and let $\{x, y\}$ be any edge of the $\sqrt{t/t'}$-spanner G', such that $|xy| \leq W_k$. We will prove that $\delta_G(x, y) \leq \sqrt{tt'}|xy|$.

If $\{x, y\}$ is an edge of E, then $\delta_G(x, y) = |xy|$ and the claim clearly holds. Thus, we may assume that $\{x, y\} \notin E$. Then, $\{x, y\} \notin E_0$ and, hence, this edge was examined in phase i, for some integer i with $1 \leq i < k$. Hence, $\delta^i_{\widehat{H}}(x, y) \leq \sqrt{tt'}|xy|/U_i$, where $\widehat{H}$ is the cluster graph at the moment when $\{x, y\}$ was examined in Step 7.5. Hence, by Lemma 15.2.5, we have $\delta^i_{\widehat{G}}(x, y) \leq \sqrt{tt'}|xy|/U_i$, where $\widehat{G}$ is the graph G at the moment when the algorithm examined $\{x, y\}$. Since $\widehat{G}$ is a subgraph of G, we also have $\delta^i_G(x, y) \leq \sqrt{tt'}|xy|/U_i$. Then, by Lemma 15.3.1, we have

$$\delta_G(x, y) \leq \delta^i_G(x, y) \cdot U_i \leq \sqrt{tt'}|xy|.$$

The proof of the lemma can now be completed in exactly the same way as in the proof of Lemma 15.2.12. ∎

As in Section 15.2.7, the above proof can easily be extended to a proof of the following result.

Lemma 15.3.17. *Algorithm* RAMPATHGREEDY(S, t, t', α) *computes a t-spanner for S.*

15.3.11 The weight analysis

In this section, we generalize the results of Section 15.2.8 to prove that the weight of the t-spanner computed by algorithm RAMPATHGREEDY(S, t, t', α) is proportional to the weight of a minimum spanning tree of S, provided that the parameters t' and α are chosen appropriately.

For any two distinct points p and q of S, we denote by $\delta_{G,2}(p, q)$ the Euclidean length of a second shortest path in the graph G between p and q. (See Section 14.3 for a formal definition.)

Lemma 15.3.18. *Let S be a set of n points in $\mathbb{R}^d$ and let $t > 1$, $t' > 1$, and $\alpha > 0$ be real numbers, such that $t > t'$ and*

$$\alpha \leq \frac{\sqrt{t} - \sqrt{t'}}{2\sqrt{t} + 21\sqrt{t'}}.$$

Let $G = (S, E)$ be the output of algorithm RAMPATHGREEDY(S, t, t', α). *For any edge $\{p, q\}$ in $E \setminus E_0$, we have*

$$\delta_{G,2}(p, q) > t'|pq|.$$

PROOF   We may assume that $\delta_{G,2}(p, q)$ is finite. Let $P = (p = p_0, p_1, p_2, \ldots, p_\ell = q)$ be a second shortest path in G between p and q, with respect to the Euclidean metric. (Hence, $\ell \geq 2$.) We have to show that the Euclidean length $|P|$ of P is larger than $t'|pq|$. Consider the cycle

$$C := (p_0, p_1, p_2, \ldots, p_\ell, p_0),$$

which is a cycle in G. Let $\{x, y\}$ be the edge of C that was added last to G by the algorithm. Then, $\{x, y\}$ is a longest edge of C, and $\{x, y\} \notin E_0$. Let C_{xy} denote the path in G between x and y that is obtained by deleting the edge $\{x, y\}$ from C.

Consider the moment when algorithm RAMPATHGREEDY examines the edge $\{x, y\}$, and let k be the number of the phase in which this happens. At that moment, all edges of C_{xy} appear already in G. Let $\widehat{G}$ be the graph G immediately before $\{x, y\}$ is examined, and let $\widehat{H}$ be the corresponding cluster graph. Since $\{x, y\}$ is added to $\widehat{G}$, we have $\delta_{\widehat{H}}^k(x, y) > \sqrt{tt'}|xy|/U_k$.

Assume that there is an $(\alpha n/\epsilon)$-cluster in the cluster cover of $\widehat{G}$ that contains both x and y. Then $\delta_{\widehat{G}}^k(x, y) \leq 2\alpha n/\epsilon$ and, hence,

$$|xy| \leq \delta_{\widehat{G}}^k(x, y) \leq \delta_{\widehat{G}}^k(x, y) \cdot U_k \leq (2\alpha n/\epsilon)U_k = 2\alpha W_k < W_k.$$

On the other hand, we know that $|xy| > W_k$, which is a contradiction. Hence, no cluster in the cluster cover of $\widehat{G}$ contains both x and y. Furthermore, we have

$$\delta_{\widehat{G}}^k(x, y) \geq \delta_{\widehat{G}}(x, y)/U_k \geq |xy|/U_k > W_k/U_k > (1 - 2\alpha)n/\epsilon.$$

Hence, by Lemma 15.2.6, we have

$$\begin{aligned}
\delta_{\widehat{G}}^k(x, y) &\geq \frac{1 - 2\alpha}{1 + 18\alpha} \cdot \delta_{\widehat{H}}^k(x, y) \\
&> \frac{1 - 2\alpha}{1 + 18\alpha} \sqrt{tt'}|xy|/U_k \\
&\geq \frac{1 - 2\alpha}{1 + 18\alpha} \sqrt{tt'}|pq|/U_k.
\end{aligned}$$

Since $\delta_{\widehat{G}}(x, y) \geq |xy| > W_k$, Lemma 15.3.2 implies that

$$\delta_{\widehat{G}}(x, y) > \frac{1}{1 + \epsilon} \cdot \delta_{\widehat{G}}^k(x, y) \cdot U_k.$$

Hence,

$$\delta_{G,2}(p, q) = |P| \geq |C_{xy}| \geq \delta_{\widehat{G}}(x, y) > \frac{1}{1 + \epsilon} \frac{1 - 2\alpha}{1 + 18\alpha} \sqrt{tt'}|pq|.$$

Our assumption on α implies that $(1 - 2\alpha)\sqrt{tt'} \geq (1 + 21\alpha)t'$. Finally, since $\epsilon = \alpha/4$ and $0 < \alpha < 1/2$, we have $(1 + \epsilon)(1 + 18\alpha) \leq 1 + 21\alpha$. It follows that $\delta_{G,2}(p, q) > t'|pq|$. ∎

If α satisfies the condition of Lemma 15.3.18, then a proof similar to the one of Lemma 14.3.1 shows that the subset $E \setminus E_0$ of the edge set E of the spanner computed by algorithm RAMPATHGREEDY satisfies the (t', t)-leapfrog property.

According to the Generalized Leapfrog Theorem (Theorem 14.9.3 in Section 14.9), there exists an absolute constant ϕ with $0 < \phi < 1$, such that the following holds: For all real numbers t and t' with $1 < 1 - \phi + \phi t < t' < t$, the weight of any set of edges satisfying the (t', t)-leapfrog property is proportional to the weight of a minimum spanning tree of the endpoints of the edges. Hence, we have proved the following result.

Theorem 15.3.19. *Let S be a set of n points in $\mathbb{R}^d$, and let t, t', and α be real numbers, such that $1 < 1 - \phi + \phi t < t' < t$ and*

$$0 < \alpha \leq \frac{\sqrt{t} - \sqrt{t'}}{2\sqrt{t} + 21\sqrt{t'}}.$$

1. Algorithm RAMPATHGREEDY(S, t, t', α) *computes a t-spanner* $G = (S, E)$ *for* S.

2. The degree in G *of each point of* S *is*

$$O\left(\left(\frac{1}{\sqrt{t/t'} - 1}\right)^{2d-1}\right).$$

3. The weight of G *is*

$$O\left(\left(\left(\frac{1}{\sqrt{t/t'} - 1}\right)^{2d-1} + \left(\frac{1}{t - 1}\right)^{2d}\right) \cdot wt(MST(S))\right),$$

where $MST(S)$ *denotes a minimum spanning tree of* S.

15.3.12 The running time

In this final section, we analyze the running time of algorithm RAMPATHGREEDY. Let S be a set of n points in $\mathbb{R}^d$, and let $t > 1, t' > 1$, and $\alpha > 0$ be real numbers, such that $t > t'$ and $\alpha < 1/2$. Recall that we take ϵ to be equal to $\alpha/4$. Furthermore, we have $\beta = \sqrt{t'/t}$ and $\gamma = 2\sqrt{tt'}$. Therefore,

$$\min(\beta, (\alpha - \epsilon)/t) = (\alpha - \epsilon)/t = 3\alpha/(4t)$$

and

$$\min(\beta, (\alpha/2 - \epsilon)/t) = (\alpha/2 - \epsilon)/t = \alpha/(4t).$$

We consider each step of the algorithm separately (see Section 15.3.9), and for each one, give an upper bound on its running time.

Step 1: By Theorem 10.1.3, the time to compute the initial bounded-degree $\sqrt{t/t'}$-spanner $G' = (S, E')$ is

$$O\left(\frac{\log(1/(\sqrt{t/t'} - 1))}{(\sqrt{t/t'} - 1)^d} n \log n\right).$$

Again by Theorem 10.1.3, we have

$$|E'| = O\left(\left(\frac{1}{\sqrt{t/t'} - 1}\right)^{2d-1} n\right).$$

Observe that, at any time during algorithm RAMPATHGREEDY, the partially constructed spanner $G = (S, E)$ has at most $|E'|$ edges.

Steps 2 and 3: These two steps take $O(|E'| \log n)$ and $O(|E'|)$ time, respectively.

Step 4: The binary tree T can be constructed in $O((n/\alpha) \log(n/\alpha))$ time, see Section 15.3.2 and Exercise 15.10.

The total time for INTEGRALIZE**:** During the entire algorithm, the function INTEGRALIZE is called exactly once for each edge of G' (see Steps 5 and 7.1). Since one such call takes $O(\log(n/\alpha))$ time (see Section 15.3.2), the total time for this part of the algorithm is $O(|E'| \log(n/\alpha))$.

The total time for REINTEGRALIZE**:** During the entire algorithm, the function REINTEGRALIZE is called at most $\lceil \log n \rceil$ times for each edge of G' (see Step 7.2). Since one call takes $O(1)$ time (see Section 15.3.2), the total time for this part of the algorithm is $O(|E'| \log n)$.

Step 7.3: In this step, algorithm GREEDYCENTERS(G, α) is called once, and algorithm RECOMPUTECENTERS$(G, \alpha, K, k - 1)$ is called $\lceil \log n \rceil - 1$ times. The total time for Step 7.3 is given by (15.21) plus $O(\log n)$ times the expression in (15.34), which gives an upper bound of $O(t^{3d}|E'| \log n)$.

Step 7.4: In this step, algorithm RAMCLUSTERGRAPH(G, α, K, k) is called $\lceil \log n \rceil$ times. Using (15.19), this gives a total time bound of

$$O\left(\left(\left(\frac{t}{\alpha}\right)^{2d} + \frac{t^{3d}}{\alpha^d}\right)|E'| \log n\right).$$

Step 7.5: In this part of the algorithm, each edge $\{p, q\}$ of $E' \setminus E_0$ is considered once. By (15.35), the time for answering one query SHORTPATH is

$$O\left(\frac{t^{3d}}{\alpha^{2d}}\left(\sqrt{tt'}\right)^d\right). \tag{15.36}$$

If $\{p, q\}$ is added as an edge to G, then the algorithm updates the cluster graph by considering all $(\alpha n/\epsilon)$-clusters that contain p, and all $(\alpha n/\epsilon)$-clusters that contain q. By Lemma 15.3.6, applied with $\chi = \alpha$, the number of pairs of clusters considered is less than or equal to $(1 + 8t/3)^{2d} = O(t^{2d})$. For each such pair of clusters, the algorithm checks whether the corresponding inter-cluster edge $[v_i, v_j]$ exists in H. If it does, its weight is updated. Otherwise, $[v_i, v_j]$ is added to H and its weight is computed. By storing the inter-cluster edges using adjacency lists, the algorithm spends

$$O\left(\left(\frac{t}{\alpha}\right)^d\right) \tag{15.37}$$

time for each pair of clusters (see Lemma 15.3.7). This proves that the total time for Step 7.5 is bounded by $|E'|$ times the quantity in (15.36) plus $O(t^{2d}|E'|)$ times the quantity in (15.37), which is

$$O\left(\frac{t^{3d}}{\alpha^{2d}}\left(\sqrt{tt'}\right)^d |E'|\right).$$

Steps 6 and 8: These two steps clearly take $O(|E'|)$ time.

By taking the sum of all these bounds, it follows that the total running time of algorithm RAMPATHGREEDY(S, t, t', α) is proportional to

$$\frac{\log(1/(\sqrt{t/t'} - 1))}{(\sqrt{t/t'} - 1)^d} n \log n + \left(|E'| + n/\alpha\right) \log(n/\alpha)$$

$$+ \left(\left(\frac{t}{\alpha}\right)^{2d} + \frac{t^{3d}}{\alpha^d}\right)|E'| \log n + \frac{t^{3d}}{\alpha^{2d}}\left(\sqrt{tt'}\right)^d |E'|. \tag{15.38}$$

It remains to choose the parameters t' and α so as to get the best result. As in Section 15.2.9, we should choose t' as small as possible, and α as large as possible. If we take t' slightly larger than $1 - \phi + \phi t$ and $\alpha = (\sqrt{t} - \sqrt{t'})/(2\sqrt{t} + 21\sqrt{t'})$, then the conditions of Theorem 15.3.19 are satisfied.

We write $t = 1 + \epsilon'$, where ϵ' is a small positive real number. Then $\sqrt{t} \sim 1 + \epsilon'/2, t' \sim 1 + \phi\epsilon', \sqrt{t'} \sim 1 + \phi\epsilon'/2, \sqrt{t/t'} \sim 1 + (1 - \phi)\epsilon'/2$, and $\alpha \sim \epsilon'(1 - \phi)/46$. Hence, the time bound in (15.38) becomes

$$O\left(\frac{1}{(t - 1)^{4d-1}} n \log n\right).$$

This proves the final result of this chapter.

Theorem 15.3.20. *Let S be a set of n points in $\mathbb{R}^d$ and let $t > 1$ be a real number. In*

$$O\left(\frac{1}{(t-1)^{4d-1}}\, n\log n\right)$$

time, a t-spanner for S can be computed,

1. *in which each point has degree $O(1/(t-1)^{2d-1})$, and*

2. *whose weight is*

$$O\left(\frac{1}{(t-1)^{2d}}\cdot wt(MST(S))\right),$$

where $MST(S)$ denotes a minimum spanning tree of S.

Remark 15.3.21. All claims in Remark 15.2.18 are also valid for algorithm RAMPATHGREEDY.

Exercises

15.1. Show how to choose the values of θ and w in Theorem 15.1.4 so as to obtain the best possible upper bound on the weight of the edge set E.

15.2. Give an example of a point set S that contains two distinct points p and q, such that the spanner computed by algorithm PATHGREEDY(S, t) contains only one simple path between p and q.

15.3. Given an example of an undirected weighted graph $G = (V, E)$ that satisfies the triangle inequality, and an R-cluster cover of G, such that

1. G has a vertex that is contained in $|V| - 1$ clusters, and

2. the maximum degree of the subgraph of the cluster graph H induced by the inter-cluster edges is $|V| - 1$.

15.4. Show that after algorithm FASTPATHGREEDY(S, t, t', α, μ) has examined all pairs of points whose Euclidean distance is X, the spanner graph G constructed so far by it is an $(X/\sqrt{t/t'})$-partial t-spanner for S.

15.5. Prove the correctness of algorithm SHORTPATH given in Section 15.2.5.

15.6. Prove Lemma 15.2.13.

15.7. Let S be a set of n points in $\mathbb{R}^d$, and let t, t', α, and μ be real numbers such that $t > t' > 1, 0 < \alpha < \min(1/2, (\sqrt{tt'} - 1)/8)$, and $\mu > 1$. Consider algorithm FASTPATHGREEDY(S, t, t', α, μ). Consider the moment when this algorithm adds an edge $\{p, q\}$ to the edge set E. Let i and j be indices such that, at that moment, p is in the (αW)-cluster C_i, and q is in the (αW)-cluster C_j. Prove that immediately before $\{p, q\}$ is added to the edge set E, this set does not contain any edge $\{x, y\}$ such that $x \in C_i$ and $y \in C_j$. Hence, at this moment, the cluster graph H does not contain the inter-cluster edge $[v_i, v_j]$, where v_i and v_j are the centers of C_i and C_j, respectively.

15.8. We obtained the $O(n\log^2 n/\log\log n)$–time bound in Theorem 15.2.17 by choosing $\mu = (\log n)^{1/(2d)}$. Prove that there is no choice for μ that gives an asymptotically better time bound.

15.9. Verify the claims in Remark 15.2.18.

15.10. Prove that the binary search tree T, which was defined in Section 15.3.2, can be constructed, in the algebraic computation-tree model, in $O((n/\epsilon)\log(n/\epsilon))$ time.

15.11. In Section 15.3, we used clusters, cluster covers, and cluster graphs for the partially constructed spanner G, on the basis of the integer weight function wt^k. The results of Sections 15.2.2 and 15.2.3 require that wt^k satisfies the triangle inequality. Prove that this is the case, that is, $wt^k(p, q) \leq wt^k(p, r) + wt^k(r, q)$ for any three edges $\{p, q\}$, $\{p, r\}$, and $\{r, q\}$ of G.

15.12. Prove the correctness of algorithm MULTIPLESOURCES(G, K, L, wt) that was presented in Section 15.3.4. In particular, prove that $\delta(v_i, u) = \ell$ immediately after vertex u has been added to the list C_i in Step 1.

15.13. Prove that at the end of algorithm GREEDYSELECT of Section 15.3.7, $Choose(p) = false$ for all $p \in S$.

Bibliographic notes

The path-greedy algorithm first appeared in Althöfer et al. [1993]. According to them, it was discovered independently by Bern in 1989. The algorithm also appears in Soares [1994], who proves that the path-greedy spanner has bounded degree. Theorem 15.1.2 is due to Chandra et al. [1995]. Theorem 15.1.4 and Section 15.1.2 are based on Chandra [1994]. See also Karp and Steele [1985] for related probabilistic results. Das et al. [1993] mention that the path-greedy spanner satisfies the leapfrog property. The proof we gave in Section 15.1.3 is due to Das and Narasimhan [1997].

Section 15.2 follows Das and Narasimhan [1997] and Gudmundsson, Levcopoulos, and Narasimhan [2002a]. Das and Narasimhan use the value $\mu = 2$. Consequently, they obtain a time bound of $O(n \log^2 n)$. Gudmundsson et al. give a more refined analysis of the algorithm, leading to the value $\mu = (\log n)^{1/(2d)}$ that we used in Section 15.2.9.

The results of Section 15.3 are based on Gudmundsson, Levcopoulos, and Narasimhan [2002a].

PART V

Further Results on Spanners and Applications

16

The Distance Range Hierarchy

> It was a perfect title, in that it crystallized the article's niggling mind-lessness, its funereal parade of yawn-enforcing facts, the pseudo-light it threw upon non-problems.
>
> —Kingsley Amis, *Lucky Jim*, 1954

In Chapter 9, we introduced the well-separated pair decomposition (WSPD) of a set S of n points in $\mathbb{R}^d$. This decomposition consists of a sequence of pairs of subsets of S that are well-separated with respect to a given separation ratio. Assume that we take for each pair $\{A, B\}$ in this sequence an arbitrary representative point x_A in A and an arbitrary representative point y_B in B. By the definition of the WSPD, for any two distinct points p and q in S, there is a pair $\{A, B\}$ in the WSPD such that (i) $p \in A$ and $q \in B$ or (ii) $p \in B$ and $q \in A$. Assume without loss of generality that (i) holds. Then, by Lemma 9.1.2, both $|px_A|$ and $|qy_B|$ are small compared to $|pq|$ and, hence, $|pq|$ and $|x_A y_B|$ are approximately equal. In this way, we can approximate all the $\binom{n}{2}$ distances determined by the points of S using only m distances of the form $|x_A y_B|$, where m is the number of pairs in the WSPD. Since there exists a WSPD with $m = O(n)$ pairs (see Chapter 9), the $\Theta(n^2)$ distances can be approximated by $O(n)$ distances. The drawback of the WSPD is that finding the pair $\{A, B\}$ for which (i) or (ii) holds takes $O(\log n)$ time (see Theorems 9.5.2 and 9.5.6).

In this chapter, we introduce a hierarchical decomposition that has properties similar to those of the WSPD, but will allow finding the pairs more efficiently. What is this new decomposition? Given a set S of n points in $\mathbb{R}^d$, we will show how to compute a sequence $L_1, L_2, \ldots, L_\ell$ of real numbers and a sequence $S_1, S_2, \ldots, S_\ell$ of subsets of S, where $\ell = O(n)$ and $\sum_{i=1}^{\ell} |S_i| = O(n)$, such that the following holds. For any two distinct points p and q of S, there exists an index i (which is not necessarily unique) and two points x and y in S_i such that

1. both $|px|$ and $|qy|$ are small compared to $|pq|$ and, therefore, $|pq|$ is approximately equal to $|xy|$, and

2. $|xy|$ is within a factor of $n^{O(1)}$ of L_i.

Given the points p and q, we obtain this index i and these points x and y by performing a lowest common ancestor computation in a tree having size $O(n)$. Hence, i, x, and y can be computed in $O(\log \log n)$ time in the algebraic computation-tree model (see Theorem 2.3.6) and in $O(1)$ time if we add indirect addressing to this model (see Theorem 2.3.5).

Assume that we want to solve some problem that involves distances between pairs of points of S. Then using this decomposition, we obtain an approximate solution by solving the problem for each subset S_i, $1 \leq i \leq \ell$, separately. The advantage is that for each set S_i, we have to consider only distances that are within a factor of $n^{O(1)}$ of the fixed real number

L_i. Because of this property, we call this decomposition the *distance range hierarchy* for the point set S.

This chapter is organized as follows. In Section 16.1, we define the hierarchical decomposition based on an arbitrary spanner G for the point set S and prove its main properties. Besides the sequences L_i and S_i, $1 \leq i \leq \ell$, mentioned above, we construct a sequence $G_i = (S_i, F_i)$, $1 \leq i \leq \ell$, of graphs that approximate the spanner G in the following sense. For any two distinct points p and q of S, consider the index i and the points x and y in S_i as above. Then the shortest-path distance between p and q in G is approximately equal to the shortest-path distance between x and y in G_i.

In Section 16.2, we apply the results of Section 16.1 to an arbitrary spanner for the point set S and obtain the distance range hierarchy for S.

In Section 16.3, we combine the distance hierarchy with well-separated pairs to design an efficient algorithm for *pruning* any given spanner G. That is, we show how to compute a $(1 + \epsilon)$-spanner of G having $O(n)$ edges.

For any graph G, we will denote by $\delta_G(x, y)$ the length of a shortest path in G between the vertices x and y. If $t > 1$ and $L > 0$ are real numbers, then we say that G is an L-*partial t-spanner* if for any two vertices x and y with $|xy| < L$, we have $\delta_G(x, y) \leq t|xy|$.

The graphs G_i mentioned above have the property that $\delta_{G_i}(x, y) \leq t|xy|$, provided that $|xy|$ is within a factor of $n^{O(1)}$ of L_i. In Section 16.4, we extend each graph G_i to a graph G'_i that is an L_i-partial spanner for the point set S_i. In this way, we obtain the distance range hierarchy for an arbitrary spanner G for the point set S.

Throughout this chapter, we consider undirected t-spanners, where the value of t may be large. We will present all algorithms in this chapter in the algebraic computation-tree model. If we add indirect addressing to this model, then the running times can be improved.

16.1 The basic hierarchical decomposition

Let S be a set of n points in $\mathbb{R}^d$, let $t \geq 1$ be a real number, and let $G = (S, E)$ be a t-spanner for S. We assume that $n \geq 2t$. We also fix a real constant $c \geq 7$.

> **Outline:** We partition the edge set E of the spanner G into subsets $E_1, E_2, \ldots, E_\ell$, where $\ell = O(|E|)$, such that within each subset, edge lengths are within a factor of $n^{O(1)}$ of each other. By considering, for any index i, each connected component of the graph $(S, E_1 \cup \cdots \cup E_{i-2})$ as a super-vertex, we obtain a sequence $G_i = (S_i, F_i)$, $1 \leq i \leq \ell$, of Euclidean graphs, whose total size is $O(|E|)$. Each of these graphs G_i has the property that for vertices x and y such that $|xy|$ is within a factor of $n^{O(1)}$ of the edge lenghts in E_i, the values of $\delta_G(x, y)$ and $\delta_{G_i}(x, y)$ are approximately equal. The sequence G_i, $1 \leq i \leq \ell$, of graphs defines a natural hierarchical representation of the points of S. This hierarchy has the property that for any two points p and q of S, a lowest common ancestor computation gives an index i and two vertices x and y of G_i such that (i) both $|px|$ and $|qy|$ are small compared to $|pq|$, and (ii) $|xy|$ is within a factor of $n^{O(1)}$ of the edge lenghts in E_i. As a result, $\delta_{G_i}(x, y)$ is approximately equal to $\delta_G(p, q)$.

16.1.1 Partitioning the edge set E

We start by partitioning the edge set of the t-spanner $G = (S, E)$ into subsets. For a reason that will become clear in the proofs of Lemmas 16.1.11, 16.1.12, and 16.1.13, some of these subsets are empty. The algorithm is denoted by EDGEPARTITION and described below.

Algorithm EDGEPARTITION(G)

Comment: This algorithm takes as input a t-spanner $G = (S, E)$. It returns a sequence $\mathcal{L} = (L_1, L_2, \ldots, L_\ell)$ of real numbers, and a sequence $\mathcal{E} = (E_1, E_2, \ldots, E_\ell)$ of edge sets that form a partition of E.

Step 1: Initialize $E' := E$.

Step 2: Compute the length L of a shortest edge in E' and set $L_1 := n^c L$, $L_2 := n^c L_1$, and $L_3 := n^c L_2$.

    Step 2.1: Compute the set E_1 consisting of all edges in E' whose lengths are less than L_1 and compute the set $E' := E' \setminus E_1$.

    Step 2.2: Compute the set E_2 consisting of all edges in E' whose lengths are less than L_2 and compute the set $E' := E' \setminus E_2$.

    Step 2.3: Compute the set E_3 consisting of all edges in E' whose lengths are less than L_3 and compute the set $E' := E' \setminus E_3$.

    Step 2.4: Initialize $i := 3$.

Step 3: If $E_i = \emptyset$ and $E' = \emptyset$, then go to Step 4. Otherwise, do the following.

    Step 3.1: If $E_i \neq \emptyset$, then set $L_{i+1} := n^c L_i$, else let L be the length of a shortest edge in E' and set $L_{i+1} := n^c L$.

    Step 3.2: Compute the set E_{i+1} consisting of all edges in E' whose lengths are less than L_{i+1}, compute the set $E' := E' \setminus E_{i+1}$, set $i := i + 1$, and go to Step 3.

Step 4: Set $\ell := i$. Output the sequence $\mathcal{L} = (L_1, L_2, \ldots, L_\ell)$ of real numbers and the sequence $\mathcal{E} = (E_1, E_2, \ldots, E_\ell)$ of edge sets.

Lemma 16.1.1. *Given the t-spanner $G = (S, E)$, algorithm* EDGEPARTITION(G) *takes* $O(|E| \log n)$ *time.*

PROOF If the edges of E are sorted in nondecreasing order of their lengths, then the algorithm can be implemented such that its running time is $O(|E|)$. Clearly, sorting the edges can be done in $O(|E| \log n)$ time.

For each i with $1 \leq i \leq \ell$, we define the interval I_i by

$$I_i := (L_i / n^c, L_i).$$

The following lemma states some properties of the sequences L_i, E_i, and I_i, $1 \leq i \leq \ell$, that will be used throughout the rest of this chapter. The proof follows from algorithm EDGEPARTITION(G). In the proofs of Lemmas 16.1.11, 16.1.12, and 16.1.13, it will become clear why we need the fifth and sixth properties. ∎

Lemma 16.1.2. *The following properties hold:*

1. *For each i with $1 \leq i \leq \ell - 1$, for each $L \in I_i$, and for each $L' \in I_{i+1}$, we have $L < L'$.*

2. *For each i with $1 \leq i \leq \ell$ and for each edge $\{p, q\}$ in E_i, we have $|pq| \in I_i$, i.e., $L_i / n^c \leq |pq| < L_i$.*

3. *For each edge $\{p, q\} \in E$, there is a unique index i with $1 \leq i \leq \ell$ such that $\{p, q\} \in E_i$ and, hence, $|pq| \in I_i$.*

4. *For each i with $1 \leq i \leq \ell - 1$, we have $L_{i+1} \geq n^c L_i$.*

5. $L_2 = n^c L_1$ *and* $L_3 = n^c L_2$.

6. *For each i with $1 \leq i \leq \ell - 1$ and for which $E_i \neq \emptyset$, we have $L_{i+1} = n^c L_i$.*

7. $E_\ell = \emptyset$.

8. $3 \leq \ell \leq 2|E| + 1$.

16.1.2 A hierarchy of Euclidean graphs

Consider the sequence L_i, $1 \leq i \leq \ell$, of real numbers and the sequence E_i, $1 \leq i \leq \ell$, of edge sets that are returned by algorithm EDGEPARTITION(G) in Section 16.1.1. We will give an algorithm that uses these sequences to define a sequence $G_i = (S_i, F_i)$, $1 \leq i \leq \ell$, of Euclidean graphs. As we will see, this sequence defines a natural hierarchical representation of the points of S, in terms of a sequence U_i, $1 \leq i \leq \ell$, of forests. The algorithm is denoted by HIERARCHICALDECOMPOSITION and described below.

Algorithm HIERARCHICALDECOMPOSITION($G, \mathcal{L}, \mathcal{E}$)

Comment: This algorithm takes as input a t-spanner $G = (S, E)$, and the sequences $\mathcal{L}$ and $\mathcal{E}$ that are returned by algorithm EDGEPARTITION(G).

Define $S_1 := S$, $F_1 := E_1$, $G_1 := (S_1, F_1)$, $S_2 := S$, $F_2 := E_1 \cup E_2$, and $G_2 := (S_2, F_2)$.

For each connected component C of G_1, let T_C be the tree whose root stores the index 1 (to indicate that it is a tree in the forest U_1) and an arbitrary point of C. This root has $|C|$ children (which are leaves), each one storing a unique point of C. Hence, T_C consists of $|C| + 1$ nodes. The forest U_1 is the collection of the trees T_C, where C ranges over all connected components of G_1. We define the forest U_2 in the same way with respect to the graph G_2. The root of each tree in this forest stores the index 2 (to indicate that it is a tree in the forest U_2).

For $i = 3, 4, \ldots, \ell$, do the following:

Step 1: Initialize both F_i and S_i as the empty set.

Step 2: For each edge $\{p, q\}$ in $E_{i-1} \cup E_i$, do the following (refer to Figure 16.1): let x be the point stored at the root of the tree in U_{i-2} in which p is stored at a leaf. Let y be the point stored at the root of the tree in U_{i-2} in which q is stored at a leaf. If $x \neq y$, then insert x and y into S_i (if they are not already inserted), and then insert the edge $\{x, y\}$ into F_i.

Having done this for all edges $\{p, q\}$ in $E_{i-1} \cup E_i$, we have obtained the graph $G_i = (S_i, F_i)$.

Step 3: For each connected component C of G_i, do the following. Choose an arbitrary point z in C. Consider all trees T in U_{i-2} such that the points stored in their roots form the set C. Construct a tree whose root stores the index i and the point z, and that has the roots of all these trees T as its children.

Step 4: The forest U_i consists of all trees that are obtained from Step 3 and all trees in U_{i-2} whose roots store a point that is not in S_i.

Step 5: Output the trees $U_{\ell-1}$ and U_ℓ, the sequence $\mathcal{S} = (S_1, \ldots, S_\ell)$ of point sets, and the sequence $\mathcal{G} = (G_1, \ldots, G_\ell)$ of graphs, where $G_i = (S_i, F_i)$, for $1 \leq i \leq \ell$.

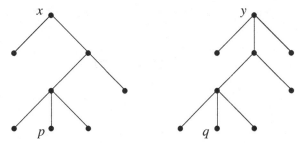

Figure 16.1: The point p is stored in the tree of the forest U_{i-2} whose root stores the point x. The point q is stored in the tree of the forest U_{i-2} whose root stores the point y. Since $x \neq y$, the edge $\{p, q\}$ of $E_{i-1} \cup E_i$ is represented by the edge $\{x, y\}$ in the graph G_i. Since x and y belong to the same connected component of G_i, the two trees (possibly with some other trees) are merged in Step 3 of the algorithm.

Remark 16.1.3. The edges of F_i may not be edges in G. It is convenient to think of the nodes x and y in Step 2 as "supernodes" from level $i - 2$ of the hierarchy; these supernodes represent connected components of G_{i-2}. Edges in F_i connect supernodes from level $i - 2$.

The following lemma follows from the way the forest U_i is defined and the facts that $E_\ell = \emptyset$ (see Lemma 16.1.2) and the spanner G is connected.

Lemma 16.1.4. *The following properties hold:*

1. *For each i with $1 \leq i \leq \ell$, the trees in the forest U_i are in one-to-one correspondence with the connected components of the graph with vertex set S and edge set $E_1 \cup E_2 \cup \cdots \cup E_i$.*

2. *Each of U_ℓ and $U_{\ell-1}$ consists of one single tree whose leaves are in one-to-one correspondence with the points of S.*

Remark 16.1.5. Intuitively, G_i contains edges of a certain length group (see Lemma 16.1.8). Observe that if $\{x, y\} \in F_i$, then x and y are contained in S_i. The connected components of G_i are represented by trees in the forest U_i. But U_i may have more. In Step 4, we add to U_i all trees of U_{i-2} that involve points not incident to edges in G_i. So the roots of trees in U_i may involve points not in S_i. Consequently, S_i may have points not in S_{i-1} or S_{i-2}. Thus the sets $S_1, \ldots, S_\ell$ do not necessarily form a "containment" hierarchy.

Next, we prove upper bounds on the total size of the graphs G_i, $1 \leq i \leq \ell$, and the trees $U_{\ell-1}$ and U_ℓ, and on the time needed to construct them.

Lemma 16.1.6. *The following properties hold:*

1. $\sum_{i=1}^{\ell} |S_i| \leq 2n + 4|E| = O(|E|)$.

2. $\sum_{i=1}^{\ell} |F_i| \leq 2|E|$.

3. *Both $U_{\ell-1}$ and U_ℓ have size $O(n)$.*

4. *Given the sequences L_i and E_i, $1 \leq i \leq \ell$, we can compute the sequence G_i, $1 \leq i \leq \ell$, of graphs and the trees $U_{\ell-1}$ and U_ℓ in $O(|E| \log n)$ time.*

PROOF First observe that $|S_1| = |S_2| = n$, $|F_1| = |E_1|$, and $|F_2| = |E_1| + |E_2|$. Let i be any index with $3 \leq i \leq \ell$. Since G_i does not contain vertices of degree 0, we have $|S_i| \leq 2|F_i|$. It is clear from algorithm HIERARCHICALDECOMPOSITION$(G, \mathcal{L}, \mathcal{E})$ that $|F_i| \leq |E_{i-1}| + |E_i|$. It follows that

$$\sum_{i=1}^{\ell} |F_i| \leq 2 \sum_{i=1}^{\ell} |E_i| = 2|E|$$

and

$$\sum_{i=1}^{\ell} |S_i| \leq 2n + 2 \sum_{i=3}^{\ell} |F_i| \leq 2n + 4|E|.$$

Since the spanner G is a connected graph, E contains at least $n - 1$ edges. Therefore, $2n + 4|E| = O(|E|)$.

By Lemma 16.1.4, each of U_ℓ and $U_{\ell-1}$ consists of a tree with n leaves. Each internal node in these trees has at least two children. Therefore, both trees have size $O(n)$.

It remains to prove the claim on the running time. To obtain a fast implementation of Steps 2 and 3, we use a union-find data structure that supports union-operations in $O(1)$ time and find-operations in $O(\log n)$ time; see Exercise 2.20. Observe that the connected components of a graph can be computed in time that is proportional to the number of its vertices and edges. Using these results, the sequence $G_i = (S_i, F_i)$, $1 \leq i \leq \ell$, of graphs and the sequence U_i, $1 \leq i \leq \ell$, of forests can be computed in time

$$O\left(\sum_{i=1}^{\ell} (|S_i| + |F_i|) + \sum_{i=3}^{\ell} (|E_{i-1}| + |E_i|) \log n \right) = O(|E| \log n).$$

This completes the proof. ∎

Remark 16.1.7. We have seen that both trees $U_{\ell-1}$ and U_ℓ have size $O(n)$. It follows from Step 3 of the algorithm that the index i is stored with some node in one of these trees if and only if the set S_i is nonempty. Therefore, even though ℓ can be proportional to $|E|$, the number of nonempty graphs G_i in the sequence is only $O(n)$.

16.1.3 Properties of the hierarchical decomposition

In this section, we will prove several properties of the hierarchical decomposition. As we will see in Section 16.1.4, these properties allow us to obtain, for any two given distinct points p and q of S, an index i with $1 \leq i \leq \ell$, and two points x and y in S_i, such that both $|px|$ and $|qy|$ are small as compared to $|pq|$, and $|xy|$ is within a factor of $n^{O(1)}$ of L_i.

We start by proving that points stored in the same tree of the forest U_i are within a distance of $O(nL_i)$ from each other, and that edge lengths in G_i are $O(L_i)$.

Lemma 16.1.8. *The following properties hold:*

1. *For any i with $1 \leq i \leq \ell$, let p and x be two points that are stored in the same tree of the forest U_i. Then $|px| < nL_i$.*

2. *For each i with $1 \leq i \leq \ell$, every edge in G_i has length less than $2L_i$.*

PROOF If p and x are in the same tree of the forest U_i, then, by Lemma 16.1.4, they are in the same connected component of the graph G^i with vertex set S and edge set $E_1 \cup E_2 \cup \cdots \cup E_i$. Since the length of each edge in G^i is less than L_i, and since any path between p and x in G^i contains less than n edges, it follows that $|px| \leq \delta_{G^i}(p, x) < nL_i$. This proves the first claim.

The second claim clearly holds if $i \in \{1, 2\}$. Assume that $3 \le i \le \ell$, and let $\{a, b\}$ be an arbitrary edge of G_i. Then $a \ne b$ and there is an edge $\{p, q\}$ in $E_{i-1} \cup E_i$ such that the forest U_{i-2} contains two distinct trees T' and T'' such that (i) the root of T' stores a, (ii) p is stored in T', (iii) the root of T'' stores b, and (iv) q is stored in T''. By the first claim, we have $|ap| < nL_{i-2}$ and $|qb| < nL_{i-2}$. Therefore,

$$|ab| \le |ap| + |pq| + |qb| < 2nL_{i-2} + |pq|.$$

Since $\{p, q\} \in E_{i-1} \cup E_i$, we have $|pq| < L_i$. Moreover, by Lemma 16.1.2, $L_{i-2} \le L_i/n^{2c}$. It follows that

$$|ab| < 2nL_{i-2} + |pq| < 2L_i/n^{2c-1} + L_i \le 2L_i,$$

where the last inequality follows from the fact that $n^{2c-1} \ge 2$. Hence, we have shown that the length of every edge in G_i is less than $2L_i$. ∎

Recall from Lemma 16.1.4 that both $U_{\ell-1}$ and U_ℓ consist of a single tree storing all the points of S in its leaves. Therefore, for any two points p and q in S, the lowest common ancestor of the leaves of $U_{\ell-1}$ or U_ℓ storing p and q is well-defined.

Lemma 16.1.9. *Let p and q be distinct points of S, let U be the tree $U_{\ell-1}$ or U_ℓ, let u be the lowest common ancestor of the leaves in U that store p and q, and let v and w be the children of u that contain p and q in their subtrees, respectively. Let x and y be the points of S that are stored in v and w, respectively, and let i be the index that is stored with u. If $i \ge 3$, then the following inequalities hold:*

1. $|px| < nL_{i-2}$,
2. $|qy| < nL_{i-2}$,
3. $|xy| < 2nL_{i-2} + |pq|$,
4. $|pq| < 2nL_{i-2} + |xy|$,
5. $|pq| \ge L_{i-2}/t$,
6. $|xy| \ge L_{i-2}/t$.

PROOF Let j be the index stored with v. Then $1 \le j \le i - 2$ and v is the root of a tree in the forest U_j. Hence, by Lemma 16.1.8, $|px| < nL_j \le nL_{i-2}$, proving the first claim. The second claim follows in a symmetric way. From these first two claims, we obtain

$$|xy| \le |xp| + |pq| + |qy| < 2nL_{i-2} + |pq|,$$

proving the third claim. The fourth claim can be proved in a symmetric way.

To prove the fifth claim, assume that $|pq| < L_{i-2}/t$. Since G is a t-spanner, we have $\delta_G(p, q) \le t|pq| < L_{i-2}$. Hence, p and q are connected by a path in the graph with vertex set S and edge set $E_1 \cup E_2 \cup \cdots \cup E_{i-2}$. But then, by Lemma 16.1.4, p and q are stored in the same tree in the forest U_{i-2}, which is a contradiction to the assumption that their lowest common ancestor u stores the index i. The sixth claim follows by a similar argument. ∎

For the next four lemmas, we fix two distinct points p and q of S. Moreover, we will use the following notation.

- Let u be the lowest common ancestor of the leaves in $U_{\ell-1}$ that store p and q. Let v and w be the children of u that contain p and q in their subtrees, respectively. Let x and y be the points of S that are stored at v and w, respectively, and let i be the index that is stored with u.

- Let u' be the lowest common ancestor of the leaves in U_ℓ that store p and q. Let v' and w' be the children of u' that contain p and q in their subtrees, respectively. Let x' and y' be the points of S that are stored at v' and w', respectively, and let i' be the index that is stored with u'.

The next lemma shows that $i' = i \pm 1$. In Lemmas 16.1.11, 16.1.12, and 16.1.13, we will prove that $|xy|$ is within a factor of $n^{O(1)}$ of L_i or $|x'y'|$ is within a factor of $n^{O(1)}$ of $L_{i'}$.

Lemma 16.1.10. *We have $i' = i - 1$ or $i' = i + 1$.*

PROOF Observe that $U_{\ell-1}$ stores only odd indices and U_ℓ stores only even indices, or vice versa. We may assume without loss of generality that $i' \geq i + 1$. Hence, we have to prove that $i' = i + 1$.

Assume that $i' \geq i + 3$. Then $i' \geq 4$ and, by Lemma 16.1.2, $L_i \leq L_{i'-3} \leq L_{i'-2}/n^c$. Moreover, by Lemma 16.1.9, $L_{i'-2} \leq t|pq|$. It follows that

$$L_i \leq t|pq|/n^c.$$

First assume that $i = 1$. Then p and q are connected by a path in the graph G_1 with vertex set S and edge set E_1. Let L be the length of a longest edge on a shortest path between p and q in this graph. Then $|pq| \leq \delta_{G_1}(p, q) < nL < nL_1$. Since $n^{c-1} \geq t$, it follows that

$$L_1 \leq t|pq|/n^c < tL_1/n^{c-1} \leq L_1,$$

which is a contradiction. If $i = 2$, then a similar argument shows that $L_2 < L_2$, which is again a contradiction. Hence, we know that $i \geq 3$. By Lemma 16.1.9, $L_{i-2} \leq t|xy|$ and $|pq| < 2nL_{i-2} + |xy|$. Therefore,

$$
\begin{aligned}
L_i &\leq t|pq|/n^c \\
&< t\left(2nL_{i-2} + |xy|\right)/n^c \\
&\leq t\left(2tn|xy| + |xy|\right)/n^c \\
&= \left(2t^2n + t\right)|xy|/n^c.
\end{aligned}
$$

Since, by our assumptions, $c \geq 7$ and $n \geq 2t$, we have $2t^2n + t \leq n^{c-1}$. It follows that $L_i < |xy|/n$, contradicting the first claim in Lemma 16.1.8. Hence, we have proved that $i' = i + 1$. ∎

Lemma 16.1.11. *If $\{i, i'\} = \{1, 2\}$, then $L_i/n^{c+1} \leq |xy| < L_i/t$ or $L_{i'}/n^{c+1} \leq |x'y'| < L_{i'}/t$.*

PROOF We may assume without loss of generality that $i = 1$ and $i' = 2$. First observe that $x = x' = p$ and $y = y' = q$. Hence, we have to prove that $L_1/n^{c+1} \leq |pq| < L_1/t$ or $L_2/n^{c+1} \leq |pq| < L_2/t$.

Let L be the length of a longest edge on a shortest path between p and q in the graph G. Then $L \leq \delta_G(p, q)$. Since G is a t-spanner, we have $\delta_G(p, q) \leq t|pq|$. It follows that $|pq| \geq L/t$. Since the length of a shortest edge in G is equal to L_1/n^c, we have $L \geq L_1/n^c$ and, therefore,

$$|pq| \geq L/t \geq L_1/(tn^c) \geq L_1/n^{c+1},$$

where the last inequality follows from the fact that $n \geq t$. If $|pq| < L_1/t$, then the claim in the lemma holds. So assume that $|pq| \geq L_1/t$. By Lemma 16.1.2, we have $L_2 = n^c L_1$. It follows that

$$|pq| \geq L_1/t = L_2/(tn^c) \geq L_2/n^{c+1}.$$

It remains to show that $|pq| < L_2/t$. Since $i = 1$, p and q are connected by a path in the graph G_1 with vertex set S and edge set E_1. Let L' be the length of a longest edge on a shortest path between p and q in G_1. Then $L' < L_1$ and

$$|pq| \leq \delta_{G_1}(p, q) < nL' < nL_1 = L_2/n^{c-1} \leq L_2/t,$$

completing the proof. ∎

Lemma 16.1.12. *If $\{i, i'\} = \{2, 3\}$, then $L_i/n^{c+1} \leq |xy| < L_i/t$ or $L_{i'}/n^{c+1} \leq |x'y'| < L_{i'}/t$.*

PROOF We may assume without loss of generality that $i = 3$ and $i' = 2$. Since $i' = 2$, we have $x' = p$ and $y' = q$. Hence, we have to prove that $L_3/n^{c+1} \leq |xy| < L_3/t$ or $L_2/n^{c+1} \leq |pq| < L_2/t$.

By Lemmas 16.1.2 and 16.1.9, we have $L_2 = n^c L_1$ and $|pq| \geq L_1/t$. Therefore,

$$|pq| \geq L_1/t = L_2/(tn^c) \geq L_2/n^{c+1}.$$

If $|pq| < L_2/t$, then the claim in the lemma holds. So assume that $|pq| \geq L_2/t$.

By Lemma 16.1.2, we have $L_3 = n^c L_2$. Let L be the length of a longest edge on a shortest path between p and q in the graph G_2 with vertex set S and edge set $E_1 \cup E_2$. (Since $i' = 2$, such a path exists.) Then $L < L_2$ and

$$|pq| \leq \delta_{G_2}(p, q) < nL < nL_2 = L_3/n^{c-1}.$$

By Lemma 16.1.9, we have $|xy| < 2nL_1 + |pq|$. Hence,

$$|xy| < 2nL_1 + L_3/n^{c-1} = 2L_3/n^{2c-1} + L_3/n^{c-1} \leq L_3/t,$$

where the last inequality follows from the fact that

$$2/n^{2c-1} + 1/n^{c-1} \leq 2/n^{c-1} \leq 1/t,$$

which, in turn, follows from the facts that $n^c \geq 2$ and $n^{c-1} \geq 2t$. It remains to prove that $|xy| \geq L_3/n^{c+1}$. Using Lemma 16.1.9, we get

$$|xy| > |pq| - 2nL_1 \geq L_2/t - 2nL_1 = L_3/(tn^c) - 2L_3/n^{2c-1}.$$

Since $n^{c-2} \geq 2$ and $n \geq 2t$, we have

$$1/n^{c+1} + 2/n^{2c-1} \leq 2/n^{c+1} \leq 1/(tn^c).$$

It follows that

$$|xy| > \left(1/(tn^c) - 2/n^{2c-1}\right) L_3 \geq L_3/n^{c+1}.$$

This completes the proof. ∎

In the previous two lemmas, we have considered the case when either i or i' is equal to 2. By Lemma 16.1.10, the remaining case is when i and i' are both greater than or equal to 3.

Lemma 16.1.13. *If* $i \geq 3$ *and* $i' \geq 3$, *then* $L_i/n^{c+1} \leq |xy| < L_i/t$ *or* $L_{i'}/n^{c+1} \leq |x'y'| < L_{i'}/t$.

PROOF By Lemma 16.1.10, we may assume without loss of generality that $i' = i + 1$. Since, by Lemma 16.1.9, $|xy| < 2nL_{i-2} + |pq|$ and $|pq| < 2nL_{i'-2} + |x'y'| = 2nL_{i-1} + |x'y'|$, we have

$$|xy| < 2nL_{i-2} + 2nL_{i-1} + |x'y'|$$
$$\leq 2L_{i-1}/n^{c-1} + 2nL_{i-1} + |x'y'|$$
$$\leq 3nL_{i-1} + |x'y'|.$$

Hence,

$$|xy| < 3L_i/n^{c-1} + |x'y'|. \tag{16.1}$$

In a symmetric way, we obtain the inequality

$$|x'y'| < 3L_i/n^{c-1} + |xy|. \tag{16.2}$$

By Lemma 16.1.8, we have $|xy| < nL_i$. This, together with (16.2), implies that

$$|x'y'| < \left(3/n^{c-1} + n\right)L_i \leq \left(3/n^{2c-1} + 1/n^{c-1}\right)L_{i+1} \leq L_{i+1}/t,$$

where the last inequality follows from the fact that $n \geq 2t$. If $|x'y'| \geq L_{i+1}/n^{c+1}$, then the lemma holds. So from now on, we assume that

$$|x'y'| < L_{i+1}/n^{c+1}. \tag{16.3}$$

Let L' be the length of a longest edge on a shortest path between x' and y' in the graph G. Since $L' \leq \delta_G(x', y') \leq t|x'y'|$, it follows that $L'/t \leq |x'y'|$. Let j' be the index such that L' is contained in the interval $I_{j'}$. Then $L_{j'}/n^c \leq L'$ and, therefore,

$$L_{j'}/n^{c+1} \leq L_{j'}/(tn^c) \leq L'/t \leq |x'y'|. \tag{16.4}$$

By combining (16.3) and (16.4), it follows that $L_{j'} < L_{i+1}$, which implies that $j' \leq i$. We claim that $j' = i$. To prove this, assume that $j' \leq i - 1$. Then x' and y' are connected by a path in the graph with vertex set S and edge set $E_1 \cup E_2 \cup \cdots \cup E_{i-1}$. Hence, by Lemma 16.1.4, x' and y' are stored in the same tree in the forest U_{i-1}, which is a contradiction.

Since $L' \in I_{j'} = I_i$, the edge set E_i is nonempty. Therefore, by Lemma 16.1.2, we have $L_{i+1} = n^c L_i$. Then it follows from (16.1) and (16.3) that

$$|xy| < 3L_i/n^{c-1} + L_{i+1}/n^{c+1} = 3L_i/n^{c-1} + L_i/n \leq L_i/t.$$

It remains to prove that $|xy| \geq L_i/n^{c+1}$. We will prove this inequality by contradiction. So we assume that $|xy| < L_i/n^{c+1}$. Let L be the length of a longest edge on a shortest path between x and y in the graph G and let j be the index such that $L \in I_j$. An argument similar to the one that was used to obtain (16.4) shows that $L_j/n^{c+1} \leq |xy|$ and, hence, $L_j \leq n^{c+1}|xy| < L_i$. Therefore, $j \leq i - 1$. If $j \leq i - 2$, then x and y are contained in the same tree in the forest U_{i-2}, which we know is not the case. Therefore, $j = i - 1$ and, hence, the points x and y are stored in the same tree in the forest U_{i-1}. Let T be the tree in U_{i-1} that stores x and y. By Lemma 16.1.4, the subset of S stored in T is the union of one or more subsets of S that are stored in trees in U_{i-2}. We also know that p and x are stored in the same tree in U_{i-2}, and q and y are stored in the same tree in U_{i-2}. Therefore, p and q are both stored in T. But then, the lowest common ancestor of the leaves in U_ℓ storing p and q stores an index that is less than or equal to $i - 1$. This is a contradiction.   ∎

16.1.4 Querying the hierarchical decomposition

The reason why the hierarchical decomposition of Section 16.1.2 is interesting is that the properties detailed in Section 16.1.3 imply an algorithm that efficiently does the following: Given any two distinct query points p and q of S, it is possible to compute an index i with $1 \le i \le \ell$, and two points x and y in S_i such that both $|px|$ and $|qy|$ are small compared to $|pq|$, and $|xy|$ is within a factor of $n^{O(1)}$ of L_i. The data structure for answering this type of queries consists of the following.

1. The sequence $\mathcal{L} = (L_1, L_2, \ldots, L_\ell)$ of real numbers that was defined in Section 16.1.1.
2. The sequence $\mathcal{S} = (S_1, S_2, \ldots, S_\ell)$ of subsets of S that was defined in Section 16.1.2.
3. The two trees $U_{\ell-1}$ and U_ℓ that were defined in Section 16.1.2. We assume that both trees have been preprocessed such that lowest common ancestor queries can be answered efficiently (see Sections 2.3.2 and 2.3.3, and Exercise 2.10).

The query algorithm is described below.

Algorithm QUERYHD($\mathcal{L}, \mathcal{S}, U_{\ell-1}, U_\ell, p, q$)

Comment: This algorithm takes as input two distinct points p and q of S. It returns an index i with $1 \le i \le \ell$, and two points x and y in S_i.

Step 1: Compute the lowest common ancestor u of the leaves in $U_{\ell-1}$ storing p and q, and compute the children v and w of u that contain p and q in their subtrees, respectively. Let x and y be the points of S that are stored at v and w, respectively. Finally, let i be the index that is stored with u.

Step 2: Compute the lowest common ancestor u' of the leaves in U_ℓ storing p and q, and compute the children v' and w' of u' that contain p and q in their subtrees, respectively. Let x' and y' be the points of S that are stored at v' and w', respectively. Finally, let i' be the index that is stored with u'.

Step 3: If $L_i/n^{c+1} \le |xy| < L_i/t$, then return the index i and the points x and y of S_i. Otherwise, return the index i' and the points x' and y' of $S_{i'}$.

It follows from Lemmas 16.1.10, 16.1.11, 16.1.12, and 16.1.13 that (i) $L_i/n^{c+1} \le |xy| < L_i/t$ or (ii) $L_{i'}/n^{c+1} \le |x'y'| < L_{i'}/t$. Assume, for ease of notation, that (i) holds.

Lemma 16.1.14. *The following properties hold:*
1. *Both $|px|$ and $|qy|$ are less than $|xy|/n^{c-2}$.*
2. *Both $|px|$ and $|qy|$ are less than $2|pq|/n^{c-2}$.*
3. *$1 - 2/n^{c-2} < |pq|/|xy| < 1 + 2/n^{c-2}$.*

PROOF   If $i \in \{1, 2\}$, then $x = p$ and $y = q$, and the claims clearly hold. Assume that $i \ge 3$. By Lemmas 16.1.2 and 16.1.9, we have

$$|px| < nL_{i-2} \le L_i/n^{2c-1} \le |xy|/n^{c-2}.$$

In a symmetric way, we obtain the inequality $|qy| < |xy|/n^{c-2}$, proving the first claim. The triangle inequality gives

$$|pq| \leq |px| + |xy| + |yq| < |xy| + 2|xy|/n^{c-2} = \left(1 + 2/n^{c-2}\right)|xy|$$

and

$$|xy| \leq |xp| + |pq| + |qy| < |pq| + 2|xy|/n^{c-2}.$$

The latter inequality can be rewritten as

$$\left(1 - 2/n^{c-2}\right)|xy| < |pq|,$$

proving the third claim. Using the inequality $1/(1 - \alpha) \leq 1 + 2\alpha$ for $0 \leq \alpha \leq 1/2$, it follows that

$$
\begin{aligned}
|px| &< |xy|/n^{c-2} \\
&< \left(1/n^{c-2}\right)\frac{|pq|}{1 - 2/n^{c-2}} \\
&\leq \left(1/n^{c-2}\right)\left(1 + 4/n^{c-2}\right)|pq| \\
&\leq 2|pq|/n^{c-2}.
\end{aligned}
$$

In a symmetric way, we obtain the inequality $|qy| < 2|pq|/n^{c-2}$, proving the second claim. ∎

16.1.5 The graphs G_i approximate the spanner G

Until now, we have considered only properties of the Euclidean distances implied by the hierarchical decomposition. In this section, we compare shortest-path distances in the spanner G with shortest-path distances in the sequence G_i, $1 \leq i \leq \ell$, of graphs. More specifically, we will prove the following. Let p and q be two distinct points of S. Let i be the index and let x and y be the points of S_i that are returned by algorithm QUERYHD($\mathcal{L}, \mathcal{S}, U_{\ell-1}, U_\ell, p, q$) of Section 16.1.4. Then $\delta_G(p, q)$ and $\delta_{G_i}(x, y)$ are approximately equal. We will prove this claim in Lemma 16.1.17.

We will need the following two lemmas, which state that for pairs x and y of points in S_i with $L_i/n^{c+4} \leq |xy| < L_i/t$, the values of $\delta_G(x, y)$ and $\delta_{G_i}(x, y)$ are approximately equal. Although for the proof of Lemma 16.1.17, we need only this result for the case when $L_i/n^{c+1} \leq |xy| < L_i/t$, later in Section 16.4, we use this result for the larger range of $|xy|$.

Lemma 16.1.15. *Let i be an index such that $1 \leq i \leq \ell$, and let x and y be vertices of G_i such that $L_i/n^{c+4} \leq |xy| < L_i/t$. Then,*

$$\delta_{G_i}(x, y) \leq \left(1 + 2/n^{c-6}\right) \cdot \delta_G(x, y).$$

PROOF   We have $\delta_{G_i}(x, y) = \delta_G(x, y)$ for $i \in \{1, 2\}$; see Exercise 16.1. Hence, we may assume that $i \geq 3$. Let $P = (x = x_0, x_1, \ldots, x_k = y)$ be a shortest path between x and y in the graph G. Since G is a t-spanner, the length of P is less than or equal to $t|xy|$, which is less than L_i. Therefore, $|x_j x_{j+1}| < L_i$ for each j with $0 \leq j \leq k - 1$.

We first show how to convert P to a path Q between x and y in the graph G_i. Then, we prove that the length of Q is less than or equal to $1 + 2/n^{c-6}$ times the length of P. The following invariant will be maintained during the conversion of P to Q.

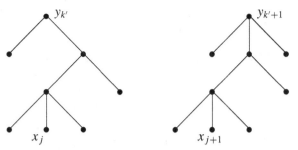

Figure 16.2: The points x_j and x_{j+1} are stored in different trees of the forest U_{i-2}. Since $\{x_j, x_{j+1}\}$ is an edge in $E_{i-1} \cup E_i$, $\{y_{k'}, y_{k'+1}\}$ is an edge of G_i. We convert the edge $\{x_j, x_{j+1}\}$ of the path P in G to the edge $\{y_{k'}, y_{k'+1}\}$ of the path Q in G_i.

Invariant: The subpath $x = x_0, x_1, \ldots, x_j$ of P has been converted to a path $Q = (y_0, y_1, \ldots, y_{k'})$ in G_i, where $y_0 = x_0$. The point $y_{k'}$ is stored at the root of the tree in the forest U_{i-2} that stores x_j.

We start the conversion by setting $j := 0$, $k' := 0$, and $y_0 := x_0$. Since x_0 is a vertex of G_i, the invariant holds at this moment.

We now assume that $0 \leq j < k$. There are two possible cases.

Case 1: x_j and x_{j+1} are stored in the same tree of the forest U_{i-2}. In this case, we set $j := j + 1$, and leave k' unchanged. Observe that the invariant is maintained in this case.

Case 2: x_j and x_{j+1} are stored in different trees of the forest U_{i-2}, as shown in Figure 16.2. Since $|x_j x_{j+1}| < L_i$, the edge $\{x_j, x_{j+1}\}$ is contained in $E_1 \cup E_2 \cup \cdots \cup E_i$. Since x_j and x_{j+1} are in different trees of U_{i-2}, however, this edge cannot be contained in $E_1 \cup E_2 \cup \cdots \cup E_{i-2}$; see Lemma 16.1.4. Hence, $\{x_j, x_{j+1}\}$ is an edge in $E_{i-1} \cup E_i$. Let $y_{k'+1}$ be the point stored at the root of the tree in U_{i-2} that contains x_{j+1}. Then $\{y_{k'}, y_{k'+1}\}$ is an edge of G_i. Therefore, if we set $j := j + 1$ and $k' := k' + 1$, the invariant still holds.

We continue extending the path Q until $j = k$. Observe that, since y is a vertex of G_i, the last vertex of Q is equal to $x_k = y$. Therefore, the final path Q is indeed a path between x and y in the graph G_i.

It remains to estimate the length of Q. Consider the edge $\{y_{k'}, y_{k'+1}\}$ obtained in the second case above. By Lemma 16.1.8, both $|y_{k'} x_j|$ and $|x_{j+1} y_{k'+1}|$ are less than

$$nL_{i-2} \leq L_i / n^{2c-1} \leq |xy| / n^{c-5}.$$

It follows that

$$|y_{k'} y_{k'+1}| \leq |y_{k'} x_j| + |x_j x_{j+1}| + |x_{j+1} y_{k'+1}| < |x_j x_{j+1}| + 2|xy|/n^{c-5}.$$

Since the path Q contains less than n edges, it follows that the length of Q is less than the length of P plus $2|xy|/n^{c-6}$. That is,

$$\delta_{G_i}(x, y) < \delta_G(x, y) + 2|xy|/n^{c-6}.$$

Since $|xy| \leq \delta_G(x, y)$, the proof is complete.   ∎

Lemma 16.1.16. *Let i be an index such that $1 \leq i \leq \ell$ and let x and y be vertices of G_i such that $L_i/n^{c+4} \leq |xy| < L_i/t$. Then*

$$\delta_G(x, y) \leq \left(1 + 2(t+1)/n^{c-6}\right) \cdot \delta_{G_i}(x, y).$$

PROOF   It follows from Exercise 16.1 that $\delta_G(x, y) = \delta_{G_i}(x, y)$ for $i \in \{1, 2\}$. Hence, we may assume that $i \geq 3$. Let $\{a, b\}$ be an arbitrary edge in G_i. We will prove an upper bound on $\delta_G(a, b)$. It follows from the definition of G_i that there is an edge $\{p, q\}$ in G such that (i) $\{p, q\} \in E_{i-1} \cup E_i$, (ii) a is stored at the root of the tree in the forest U_{i-2} that contains p, and (iii) b is stored at the root of the tree in the forest U_{i-2} that contains q. By Lemma 16.1.8, both $|pa|$ and $|bq|$ are less than $nL_{i-2} \leq L_i/n^{2c-1}$. Therefore,

$$|pq| \leq |pa| + |ab| + |bq| < |ab| + 2L_i/n^{2c-1}.$$

Since G is a t-spanner, we have

$$\delta_G(a, p) \leq t|ap| < tL_i/n^{2c-1}$$

and

$$\delta_G(q, b) \leq t|qb| < tL_i/n^{2c-1}.$$

By combining these inequalities and using the triangle inequality for δ_G, it follows that

$$\delta_G(a, b) \leq \delta_G(a, p) + |pq| + \delta_G(q, b) < |ab| + 2(t+1)L_i/n^{2c-1}. \qquad (16.5)$$

Now consider the points x and y. Since $\delta_G(x, y) < \infty$, it follows from Lemma 16.1.15 that x and y are connected by a path in the graph G_i. Let k be the number of edges on a shortest path between x and y in G_i. By applying (16.5) to each edge on this path, we obtain

$$\begin{aligned}
\delta_G(x, y) &< \delta_{G_i}(x, y) + k \cdot 2(t+1)L_i/n^{2c-1} \\
&< \delta_{G_i}(x, y) + 2(t+1)L_i/n^{2c-2} \\
&\leq \delta_{G_i}(x, y) + 2(t+1)|xy|/n^{c-6}.
\end{aligned}$$

Since $|xy| \leq \delta_{G_i}(x, y)$, the proof is complete.   ∎

Lemma 16.1.17. *Let p and q be two distinct points of S. Let i be the index and let x and y be the points of S_i that are returned by algorithm QUERYHD of Section 16.1.4. Then,*
1. *$\delta_G(p, q) \leq \left(1 + 3(t+1)/n^{c-6}\right) \cdot \delta_{G_i}(x, y)$ and*
2. *$\delta_{G_i}(x, y) \leq \left(1 + 3/n^{c-6}\right) \cdot \delta_G(p, q)$.*

PROOF   First, by Step 3 of algorithm QUERYHD, we know that $L_i/n^{c+1} \leq |xy| < L_i/t$ (see Section 16.1.4). By Lemma 16.1.14, each of $|px|$ and $|qy|$ is less than both $|xy|/n^{c-2}$ and $2|pq|/n^{c-2}$. By Lemmas 16.1.15 and 16.1.16, we have

$$\delta_{G_i}(x, y) \leq \left(1 + 2/n^{c-6}\right) \cdot \delta_G(x, y)$$

and

$$\delta_G(x, y) \leq \left(1 + 2(t+1)/n^{c-6}\right) \cdot \delta_{G_i}(x, y).$$

By combining these inequalities, we obtain

$$\delta_G(p, q) \leq \delta_G(p, x) + \delta_G(x, y) + \delta_G(y, q)$$
$$\leq t|px| + \left(1 + 2(t + 1)/n^{c-6}\right) \cdot \delta_{G_i}(x, y) + t|yq|$$
$$< 2t|xy|/n^{c-2} + \left(1 + 2(t + 1)/n^{c-6}\right) \cdot \delta_{G_i}(x, y)$$
$$\leq \left(2t/n^{c-2} + 1 + 2(t + 1)/n^{c-6}\right) \cdot \delta_{G_i}(x, y)$$
$$\leq \left(1 + 3(t + 1)/n^{c-6}\right) \cdot \delta_{G_i}(x, y).$$

In a similar way, we obtain

$$\delta_{G_i}(x, y) \leq \left(1 + 2/n^{c-6}\right) \cdot \delta_G(x, y)$$
$$\leq \left(1 + 2/n^{c-6}\right) (\delta_G(x, p) + \delta_G(p, q) + \delta_G(q, y))$$
$$\leq \left(1 + 2/n^{c-6}\right) (t|xp| + \delta_G(p, q) + t|qy|)$$
$$< \left(1 + 2/n^{c-6}\right) \left(4t|pq|/n^{c-2} + \delta_G(p, q)\right)$$
$$\leq \left(1 + 2/n^{c-6}\right) \left(4t/n^{c-2} + 1\right) \cdot \delta_G(p, q)$$
$$\leq \left(1 + 3/n^{c-6}\right) \cdot \delta_G(p, q),$$

where the last inequality follows from the fact that $4t/n^4 + 8t/n^{c-2} \leq 1$ (which can be shown using our assumptions that $n \geq 2t$ and $c \geq 7$).   ∎

16.1.6 Summarizing the hierarchical decomposition

In this section, we summarize the main properties of the hierarchical decomposition. Recall that we are given a set S of n points in $\mathbb{R}^d$, a real number $t \geq 1$, a t-spanner $G = (S, E)$ for S, and a real constant $c \geq 7$. We assume that $n \geq 2t$. We have shown that we can compute, in $O(|E| \log n)$ time,

1. a sequence $L_1, L_2, \ldots, L_\ell$ of real numbers, where $\ell = O(|E|)$,
2. a sequence $S_1, S_2, \ldots, S_\ell$ of subsets of S such that $\sum_{i=1}^{\ell} |S_i| = O(|E|)$,
3. a sequence $G_i = (S_i, F_i)$, $1 \leq i \leq \ell$, of graphs such that $\sum_{i=1}^{\ell} |F_i| = O(|E|)$, and
4. two rooted trees $U_{\ell-1}$ and U_ℓ, each storing the points of S at its leaves and having size $O(n)$,

such that the following holds. For any two distinct points p and q of S, there exist an index i with $1 \leq i \leq \ell$, and two points x and y in S_i, such that

1. $L_i/n^{c+1} \leq |xy| < L_i/t$,
2. both $|px|$ and $|qy|$ are less than $|xy|/n^{c-2}$,
3. both $|px|$ and $|qy|$ are less than $2|pq|/n^{c-2}$,
4. $1 - 2/n^{c-2} < |pq|/|xy| < 1 + 2/n^{c-2}$,
5. $\delta_G(p, q) \leq \left(1 + 3(t + 1)/n^{c-6}\right) \cdot \delta_{G_i}(x, y)$, and
6. $\delta_{G_i}(x, y) \leq \left(1 + 3/n^{c-6}\right) \cdot \delta_G(p, q)$.

Given p and q, the values of i, x, and y can be computed by answering two lowest common ancestor queries, one in the tree $U_{\ell-1}$ and the other in the tree U_ℓ. Hence, in the algebraic computation-tree model, i, x, and y can be computed in $O(\log \log n)$ time (see Theorem 2.3.6), whereas $O(1)$ time suffices if we add indirect addressing to this model (see Theorem 2.3.5).

Remark 16.1.18. If we define $L'_i := L_i/t$ for $1 \leq i \leq \ell$, then the inequality in 1. above can be replaced by

$$L'_i/n^{c+1} \leq |xy| < L'_i.$$

If we assume that $n \geq 3(t+1)$ and $c > 7$, then the inequality in 5. above can be replaced by

$$\delta_G(p,q) \leq \left(1 + 1/n^{c-7}\right) \cdot \delta_{G_i}(x,y).$$

In this way, the main properties of the hierarchical decomposition do not depend on the value of t, except that we need that $t = O(n)$. In fact, by using a larger value of c, properties similar to those above still hold if t is at most polynomial in n.

In Section 16.2, we will use the hierarchical decomposition to obtain the distance range hierarchy for a set of points. In Section 16.4, we will extend the sequence G_i of graphs to a sequence G'_i of partial spanners. By combining these graphs G'_i with the hierarchical decomposition, we will obtain the distance range hierarchy for an arbitrary spanner.

16.2 The distance range hierarchy for point sets

The results of Section 16.1 immediately give us the distance range hierarchy for a set S of n points in $\mathbb{R}^d$: First, use Corollary 9.4.7 to compute the WSPD-spanner $G = (S, E)$, with stretch factor $t = 2$ and $|E| = O(n)$. (In fact, any constant value can be used for t.) Then apply the results of the previous section to this spanner G. In this way, we obtain the following theorem (see also Remark 16.1.18).

Theorem 16.2.1 (DRH Theorem). *Let S be a set of n points in $\mathbb{R}^d$, and let $c \geq 7$ be a real constant. In $O(n \log n)$ time, we can compute*

1. *a sequence $L_1, L_2, \ldots, L_\ell$ of real numbers, where $\ell = O(n)$,*
2. *a sequence $S_1, S_2, \ldots, S_\ell$ of subsets of S such that $\sum_{i=1}^{\ell} |S_i| = O(n)$, and*
3. *two rooted trees $U_{\ell-1}$ and U_ℓ, each storing the points of S at its leaves and having size $O(n)$,*

such that the following holds. For any two distinct points p and q of S, there exist an index i with $1 \leq i \leq \ell$ and two points x and y in S_i such that

1. *$L_i/n^{c+1} \leq |xy| < L_i$,*
2. *both $|px|$ and $|qy|$ are less than $|xy|/n^{c-2}$,*
3. *both $|px|$ and $|qy|$ are less than $2|pq|/n^{c-2}$, and*
4. *$1 - 2/n^{c-2} < |pq|/|xy| < 1 + 2/n^{c-2}$.*

Given p and q, the trees $U_{\ell-1}$ and U_ℓ can be used to compute the values of i, x, and y, in $O(\log \log n)$ time in the algebraic computation-tree model, and in $O(1)$ time if we add indirect addressing to this model.

> **Distance range hierarchy:** Suppose we are given an arbitrary point set S and want to solve some problem that involves distances between pairs of points of S. Using Theorem 16.2.1, we obtain an approximate solution by solving the problem for each subset S_i, $1 \le i \le \ell$. Observe that for the set S_i, we have to consider only distances that are within a factor of $n^{O(1)}$ of the fixed real number L_i.

Therefore, this decomposition for point set S has applications in problems that become "easier" if the distances are within a polynomial factor of each other. In Section 16.3, we will present an application for which the latter property is crucial.

16.3 An application: Pruning spanners

Let S be a set of n points in $\mathbb{R}^d$, let $t \ge 1$ be a real number, and let $G = (S, E)$ be a t-spanner for S. We consider the problem of approximating G by a sparse graph. To be more precise, given a real number $\epsilon > 0$, we want to compute a linear-sized (i.e., the number of edges is $O(n)$) subgraph G' of G, such that G' is a $(1 + \epsilon)$-spanner for G, that is, $\delta_{G'}(p, q) \le (1 + \epsilon) \cdot \delta_G(p, q)$ for all points p and q in S. We refer to this process as *pruning* the t-spanner G.

In Section 16.3.1, we present a general framework for solving this pruning problem. In Section 16.3.2, we show that the well-separated pair decomposition of Chapter 9 can be used to obtain an algorithm that fits in this framework and that solves the pruning problem in $O(|E| \log n)$ time. In Sections 16.3.3 and 16.3.4, we show how the distance range hierarchy of Section 16.2 can be used to improve the running time, in the algebraic computation-tree model, to $O(n \log n + |E| \log \log n)$.

Algorithms FASTPATHGREEDY of Section 15.2.6 and RAMPATHGREEDY of Section 15.3.9 can be used to compute a $(1 + \epsilon)$-spanner G' of G. The output G', however, does not necessarily have $O(n)$ edges; see Remarks 15.2.18 and 15.3.21. Moreover, these algorithms start by sorting the edges of G and, therefore, the running time is $\Omega(|E| \log n)$. As we will show, the pruning algorithm of Sections 16.3.3 and 16.3.4 does produce a $(1 + \epsilon)$-spanner of G with $O(n)$ edges, without sorting the edges of G.

16.3.1 A general framework for pruning spanners

Let $a_1, a_2, \ldots, a_m$ and $b_1, b_2, \ldots, b_m$ be points of S, where $a_i \ne b_i$ for all i. Now consider the set

$$P = \{\{a_1, b_1\}, \{a_2, b_2\}, \ldots, \{a_m, b_m\}\}.$$

Let $s := ((1 + \epsilon)(8t + 4) + 4)/\epsilon$. Assume that for each edge $\{p, q\}$ in E, there is an index i such that

1. $|pa_i| \le (2/s)|a_i b_i|$ and $|q b_i| \le (2/s)|a_i b_i|$, or
2. $|pb_i| \le (2/s)|a_i b_i|$ and $|q a_i| \le (2/s)|a_i b_i|$.

In other words, for each edge $\{p, q\}$ in E, the set P contains a "close approximation." Algorithm GREEDYPRUNE(G, P) below uses this set P to compute a $(1 + \epsilon)$-spanner G' for G having at most m edges. We say that this algorithm prunes the graph G *with respect to* the set P of pairs.

Algorithm GREEDYPRUNE(G, P)

Comment: This algorithm takes as input a t-spanner $G = (S, E)$ and a set P of pairs of points satisfying the properties mentioned above. It returns a $(1 + \epsilon)$-spanner G' of G.

Construct a sequence C_i, $1 \leq i \leq m$, of lists, in the following way. Initially, all these lists are empty. For each edge $\{p, q\}$ in E, let i be an (arbitrary) index i such that 1. or 2. above is satisfied. Then we add the edge $\{p, q\}$ to the list C_i.
    We define G' to be the graph with vertex set S and whose edge set E' contains exactly one (arbitrary) edge from each nonempty list C_i, $1 \leq i \leq m$. Output G'.

The lemma below shows that algorithm GREEDYPRUNE is correct.

Lemma 16.3.1. *The graph $G' = (S, E')$ that is returned by algorithm* GREEDYPRUNE *(G, P) is a $(1 + \epsilon)$-spanner of $G = (S, E)$.*

PROOF   It suffices to prove that $\delta_{G'}(p, q) \leq (1 + \epsilon)|pq|$ for each edge $\{p, q\}$ of E. We will prove this by induction on the length of the edge $\{p, q\}$.

To start the induction, let $\{p, q\}$ be a shortest edge in E. Let i be the index such that $\{p, q\} \in C_i$. Then (i) $|pa_i| \leq (2/s)|a_ib_i|$ and $|qb_i| \leq (2/s)|a_ib_i|$, or (ii) $|pb_i| \leq (2/s)|a_ib_i|$ and $|qa_i| \leq (2/s)|a_ib_i|$. We may assume without loss of generality that (i) holds. Let $\{x, y\}$ be the edge of C_i that is contained in E'. Observe that (i) $|xa_i| \leq (2/s)|a_ib_i|$ and $|yb_i| \leq (2/s)|a_ib_i|$, or (ii) $|xb_i| \leq (2/s)|a_ib_i|$ and $|ya_i| \leq (2/s)|a_ib_i|$. Again, we may assume without loss of generality that (i) holds. If not, we reverse the roles of x and y.

Since G is a t-spanner for S, we have

$$\delta_G(p, x) \leq t|px| \leq t(|pa_i| + |a_ix|) \leq (4t/s)|a_ib_i|.$$

Using the triangle inequality, we obtain

$$|a_ib_i| \leq |a_ip| + |pq| + |qb_i| \leq (4/s)|a_ib_i| + |pq|,$$

which can be rewritten as

$$|a_ib_i| \leq \frac{s}{s - 4}|pq|.$$

Since $s > 4(t + 1)$, it follows that

$$\delta_G(p, x) \leq \frac{4t}{s} \frac{s}{s - 4}|pq| = \frac{4t}{s - 4}|pq| < |pq|.$$

Hence, if $p \neq x$, then the length of each edge on a shortest path in G between p and x is less than $|pq|$. Since $\{p, q\}$ is a shortest edge in E, it follows that $p = x$.

In a symmetric way, we have $q = y$. Hence, $\{p, q\}$ is an edge of E', which implies that $\delta_{G'}(p, q) = |pq| \leq (1 + \epsilon)|pq|$. This completes the basis of the induction.

Now assume that $\{p, q\}$ is not a shortest edge in E. Furthermore, assume that $\delta_{G'}(u, v) \leq (1 + \epsilon)|uv|$ for all edges $\{u, v\}$ in E with $|uv| < |pq|$. Let i be the index and let $\{x, y\}$ be the edge of E' as above. Hence, we have $|pa_i| \leq (2/s)|a_ib_i|$, $|qb_i| \leq (2/s)|a_ib_i|$, $|xa_i| \leq (2/s)|a_ib_i|$, and $|yb_i| \leq (2/s)|a_ib_i|$.

Exactly as before, we have

$$\delta_G(p, x) \leq \frac{4t}{s - 4}|pq| < |pq|;$$

therefore, each edge on the shortest path in G between p and x has length less than $|pq|$. By induction, it follows that

$$\delta_{G'}(p, x) \le (1 + \epsilon) \cdot \delta_G(p, x) \le (1 + \epsilon)\frac{4t}{s - 4}|pq|.$$

In a completely symmetric way, we get

$$\delta_{G'}(y, q) \le (1 + \epsilon)\frac{4t}{s - 4}|pq|.$$

Hence,

$$\delta_{G'}(p, q) \le \delta_{G'}(p, x) + |xy| + \delta_{G'}(y, q) \le (1 + \epsilon)\frac{8t}{s - 4}|pq| + |xy|.$$

Since

$$
\begin{aligned}
|xy| &\le |xa_i| + |a_i b_i| + |b_i y| \\
&\le (1 + 4/s)|a_i b_i| \\
&\le (1 + 4/s)\frac{s}{s - 4}|pq| \\
&= \frac{s + 4}{s - 4}|pq|,
\end{aligned}
$$

and using our choice of s, it follows that

$$\delta_{G'}(p, q) \le (1 + \epsilon)\frac{8t}{s - 4}|pq| + \frac{s + 4}{s - 4}|pq| = (1 + \epsilon)|pq|.$$

∎

The above process is summarized as follows.

Summary: Assume that we are given a spanner $G = (S, E)$ and a set P of pairs $\{a_i, b_i\}$, $1 \le i \le m$, of points in S such that for each edge $\{p, q\}$ in E, there exists a pair $\{a_i, b_i\}$ in P that is "close" to $\{p, q\}$, i.e., both $|pa_i|$ and $|qb_i|$ are small compared to $|a_i b_i|$. Under these conditions, algorithm GREEDYPRUNE essentially prunes G using set P as a "guide." Each edge of G is "mapped" to a pair in P, and in the pruned subgraph, for each pair in P we retain one edge that is mapped to it (if there are any). This results in a spanner G' for G having at most m edges. In order to apply this general framework, we need

- an algorithm that computes such a set P, preferably of size $m = O(n)$, and
- an algorithm that computes, for each edge $\{p, q\}$ in E, a pair in P that is close to it.

16.3.2 A pruning algorithm based on well-separated pairs

We obtain our first pruning algorithm by a straightforward application of the well-separated pair decomposition (WSPD) of Chapter 9.

Let $s := ((1 + \epsilon)(8t + 4) + 4)/\epsilon$. By Theorems 9.4.6 and 9.5.6, we can compute, in $O(n \log n + s^d n)$ time, a representation of a WSPD $\{A_i, B_i\}$, $1 \le i \le m$, of S with separation ratio s and $m = O(s^d n)$, such that for any two distinct points p and q in S, the index i with $p \in A_i$ and $q \in B_i$ or $p \in B_i$ and $q \in A_i$ can be computed in $O(\log n + 1/s) = O(\log n)$ time. Observe that $s^d = O((1 + 1/\epsilon)^d t^d)$.

If we define P as the set of all pairs $\{a_i, b_i\}$, $1 \leq i \leq m$, where a_i and b_i are arbitrary points in A_i and B_i, respectively, then we can apply the construction of Section 16.3.1 and obtain the following result.

Theorem 16.3.2. *Let S be a set of n points in $\mathbb{R}^d$, let $t \geq 1$ and $\epsilon > 0$ be real numbers, and let $G = (S, E)$ be a t-spanner for S. A $(1 + \epsilon)$-spanner for G having $O((1 + 1/\epsilon)^d t^d n)$ edges can be computed in $O((1 + 1/\epsilon)^d t^d n + |E| \log n)$ time.*

Remark 16.3.3. As t becomes larger, t-spanners become sparser. While it is not surprising that the time complexity has a factor of $(1 + 1/\epsilon)^d$, it is interesting to note that the time complexity of this pruning algorithm also has a factor of t^d, implying that it increases with t.

16.3.3 Setting the stage for the distance range hierarchy

The pruning algorithm of Section 16.3.2 spends $O(\log n)$ time for each edge of the spanner G. In this section and Section 16.3.4, we will show how the distance range hierarchy can be used to improve this to $O(\log \log n)$.

> **Outline:** Using the distance range hierarchy of Section 16.2, we can approximate each edge $\{p, q\}$ of the spanner G by a pair $\{x, y\}$ such that x and y are points of some set S_i in the hierarchy and $|xy|$ is within a factor of $n^{O(1)}$ of the real number L_i associated with S_i. By using a WSPD for S_i, we can approximate the pair $\{x, y\}$ by a pair $\{a, b\}$, as we did in Section 16.3.2. Hence, $\{a, b\}$ approximates the edge $\{p, q\}$. By Theorem 16.2.1, we can obtain the pair $\{x, y\}$ in $O(\log \log n)$ time. In this section, we show how the fact that $|xy|$ and L_i are within a factor of $n^{O(1)}$ of each other can be used to obtain the pair $\{a, b\}$ in $O(\log \log n)$ time.

Let s be a real number, and consider the split tree T and the corresponding WSPD $\{A_i, B_i\}$, $1 \leq i \leq m$, of S with separation ratio s and $m = O(s^d n)$; see Chapter 9. We assume for convenience that $s \geq 1$. (In fact, it suffices for s to be bounded from below by a positive constant.)

Let $k > 0$ be a constant, let $L > 0$ be a real number, and let Q be a set of pairs of points in S such that $L/n^k \leq |xy| \leq L$ for each pair $\{x, y\} \in Q$. In this section, we show how to efficiently compute, for each element $\{x, y\}$ of Q, the index i for which $x \in A_i$ and $y \in B_i$ or $x \in B_i$ and $y \in A_i$.

The algorithm that we will present generalizes the results of Section 9.5.2. As in Section 9.5.2, it is based on several properties of the split tree and well-separated pairs.

Recall that the *bounding box* of a bounded subset A of $\mathbb{R}^d$ is the smallest axes-parallel d-dimensional hyperrectangle that contains A. Let

$$\alpha := \frac{2}{(s + 4)\sqrt{d}}.$$

Let A and B be two bounded subsets of $\mathbb{R}^d$, let x be a point in A, and let y be a point in B. Recall Lemma 9.5.4, which states the following:

- If A and B are well-separated with respect to s, then the lengths of all sides of the bounding boxes of A and B are less than or equal to $(2/s)|xy|$.

- If the lengths of all sides of the bounding boxes of A and B are less than or equal to $\alpha|xy|$, then A and B are well-separated with respect to s.

Recall from Section 9.3 that every node u of the split tree T stores the bounding box $R(u)$ of the set of all points that are stored in the subtree rooted at u. For each point $x \in S$, we define the following two nodes of the split tree T.

1. u_x is the highest node u on the path from the leaf storing x to the root, such that the lengths of all sides of $R(u)$ are less than or equal to $(2/s)L$.

2. u'_x is the highest node u on the path from the leaf storing x to the root, such that the lengths of all sides of $R(u)$ are less than or equal to $\alpha L/n^k$.

The proof of the following lemma is left as an exercise; see Exercise 16.3.

Lemma 16.3.4. *By traversing the split tree T, all nodes u_x and u'_x, with $x \in S$, can be computed in $O(n)$ time.*

Next, we define for each element $e = \{x, y\}$ in Q, the following four nodes in T.

1. u_{ex} is the highest node u on the path from the leaf storing x to the root, such that the lengths of all sides of $R(u)$ are less than or equal to $(2/s)|xy|$.

2. u'_{ex} is the highest node u on the path from the leaf storing x to the root, such that the lengths of all sides of $R(u)$ are less than or equal to $\alpha|xy|$.

3. The nodes u_{ey} and u'_{ey} are defined similarly with respect to point y.

Recall that for each pair $\{A_i, B_i\}$ in the WSPD, there are two nodes v_i and w_i in T such that A_i is the set of points of S stored in the subtree rooted at v_i, and B_i is the set of points of S stored in the subtree rooted at w_i. The following lemma is a direct generalization of Lemma 9.5.5. Its proof uses our assumption that $s \geq 1$.

Lemma 16.3.5. *Let $e = \{x, y\}$ be an element of Q and let i be the index such that $x \in A_i$ and $y \in B_i$ or $x \in B_i$ and $y \in A_i$.*

1. *If we follow the path in T from the leaf storing x to the root, then we encounter, in this order, the nodes u'_x, u'_{ex}, v_i, u_{ex}, and u_x.*

2. *The path in T between u'_x and u_x contains $O(\log n)$ nodes.*

3. *The path in T between u'_{ex} and u_{ex} contains $O(1)$ nodes.*

4. *Given pointers to the nodes u_{ex} and u_{ey}, we can compute the nodes v_i and w_i in $O(1)$ time.*

For each point x in S, let T_x be a balanced binary search tree storing the $O(\log n)$ nodes on the path in T between u'_x and u_x. The search information stored with each node u is the length of a longest side of the bounding box $R(u)$. All trees T_x with $x \in S$ can be computed in $O(n \log n)$ time.

Lemma 16.3.6. *Let $e = \{x, y\}$ be an element of Q. Using the trees T_x and T_y, we can compute the two nodes u_{ex} and u_{ey} in $O(\log \log n)$ time.*

The proof is left as an exercise; see Exercise 16.3. The previous two lemmas imply an algorithm for computing, for each of the elements $\{x, y\}$ in Q, the index i for which $x \in A_i$ and $y \in B_i$, or $x \in B_i$ and $y \in A_i$. The total running time, when given the split tree and the WSPD, is $O(n \log n + |Q| \log \log n)$. Since each tree T_x has size $O(\log n)$, the amount of space used is $O(n \log n)$. Since all elements in Q are given in advance, however, the space requirement can be reduced to $O(n)$. We summarize the results of this section.

Lemma 16.3.7. *Let S be a set of n points in $\mathbb{R}^d$, and let $s \geq 1$ be a real number. Assume we are given the split tree T and the corresponding WSPD $\{A_i, B_i\}$, $1 \leq i \leq m$, of S with separation ratio s and $m = O(s^d n)$. Let $k > 0$ be a constant, let $L > 0$ be a real number, and let Q be a set of pairs of points in S such that $L/n^k \leq |xy| \leq L$ for each element $\{x, y\} \in Q$. In $O(n \log n + |Q| \log \log n)$ time, we can compute, for each element $\{x, y\}$ in Q, the index i for which $x \in A_i$ and $y \in B_i$, or $x \in B_i$ and $y \in A_i$.*

16.3.4 A pruning algorithm based on the distance range hierarchy

Let S be a set of n points in $\mathbb{R}^d$, let $t \geq 1$ be a real number, let $G = (S, E)$ be a t-spanner for S, let $\epsilon > 0$ be a real number, and let $s = ((1 + \epsilon)(8t + 4) + 4)/\epsilon$. We assume that $n \geq 2t$ and $n^5 \geq s + 2$.

Using Theorem 16.2.1 (applied with $c = 7$), we compute in $O(n \log n)$ time the distance range hierarchy for S. Hence, we have a sequence $L_1, L_2, \ldots, L_\ell$ of real numbers such that $\ell = O(n)$ and a sequence $S_1, S_2, \ldots, S_\ell$ of subsets of S such that $\sum_{i=1}^{\ell} |S_i| = O(n)$. For any two distinct points p and q of S, we can compute in $O(\log \log n)$ time, an index i and two points x and y in S_i such that $L_i/n^8 \leq |xy| < L_i$ and both $|px|$ and $|qy|$ are less than $|xy|/n^5$.

For each i with $1 \leq i \leq \ell$ and $S_i \neq \emptyset$, we use Theorem 9.4.6 to compute a split tree T_i and a corresponding WSPD $\{A_j^i, B_j^i\}$, $1 \leq j \leq m_i$, of S_i with separation ratio $2s$ and $m_i = O(s^d|S_i|)$. The total time needed for this is proportional to

$$\sum_{i=1}^{\ell} \left(|S_i| \log |S_i| + s^d|S_i| \right) = O\left(n \log n + s^d n\right),$$

where we use the convention that $\log 0 = 0$.

For each i and j with $1 \leq i \leq \ell$, $1 \leq j \leq m_i$, and $S_i \neq \emptyset$, let a_j^i and b_j^i be arbitrary points in A_j^i and B_j^i, respectively, and define

$$P := \{\{a_j^i, b_j^i\} : 1 \leq i \leq \ell, 1 \leq j \leq m_i, S_i \neq \emptyset\}.$$

Observe that

$$|P| = \sum_{1 \leq i \leq \ell, S_i \neq \emptyset} m_i = O\left(s^d \sum_{i=1}^{\ell} |S_i|\right) = O(s^d n).$$

The next lemma shows that the set P satisfies the premises of the general framework of Section 16.3.1.

Lemma 16.3.8. *For each edge $\{p, q\}$ in E, there are indices i and j with $1 \leq i \leq \ell$ and $1 \leq j \leq m_i$, such that*

1. $|pa_j^i| \leq (2/s)|a_j^i b_j^i|$ *and* $|qb_j^i| \leq (2/s)|a_j^i b_j^i|$, *or*
2. $|pb_j^i| \leq (2/s)|a_j^i b_j^i|$ *and* $|qa_j^i| \leq (2/s)|a_j^i b_j^i|$.

PROOF Let $\{p, q\}$ be an arbitrary edge of E. By the properties of the distance range hierarchy, there exist an index i and two points x and y in S_i such that $|px| < |xy|/n^5$ and $|qy| < |xy|/n^5$. By the definition of the WSPD, there exists an index j such that (i) $x \in A_j^i$ and $y \in B_j^i$ or (ii) $x \in B_j^i$ and $y \in A_j^i$. We may assume without loss of generality that (i) holds.

Consider the point a^i_j in the set A^i_j and the point b^i_j in the set B^i_j. Since we chose the separation ratio for the WSPD to be $2s$, we know from Lemma 9.1.2 that $|xa^i_j| \le |a^i_j b^i_j|/s$ and $|xy| \le (1 + 2/s)|a^i_j b^i_j|$. It follows that

$$\begin{aligned}|pa^i_j| &\le |px| + |xa^i_j| \\ &\le |xy|/n^5 + |a^i_j b^i_j|/s \\ &\le \left((1 + 2/s)/n^5 + 1/s\right)|a^i_j b^i_j| \\ &\le (2/s)|a^i_j b^i_j|,\end{aligned}$$

where the last inequality follows from our assumption that $n^5 \ge s + 2$. By a symmetric argument, it can be shown that $|qb^i_j| \le (2/s)|a^i_j b^i_j|$. ∎

We proceed as follows. Initialize empty lists Q_i, $1 \le i \le \ell$. For each edge $\{p, q\}$ in E, use Theorem 16.2.1 to compute the corresponding index i and the two points x and y in S_i, and add $\{x, y\}$ to the list Q_i. The total time for this is $O(|E| \log \log n)$. Observe that $\sum_{i=1}^{\ell} |Q_i| \le |E|$ and each set Q_i satisfies the premises of Lemma 16.3.7 (for $k = 8$). Therefore, in $O(|S_i| \log |S_i| + |Q_i| \log \log n)$ time, we can compute for each element $\{x, y\}$ in Q_i, the index j for which $x \in A^i_j$ and $y \in B^i_j$ or $x \in B^i_j$ and $y \in A^i_j$. Having done this for all i with $1 \le i \le \ell$, we can apply the general construction of Section 16.3.1. The details of algorithm PRUNESPANNER are provided below.

Algorithm PRUNESPANNER(G, t, ϵ)

Comment: This algorithm takes as input a t-spanner $G = (S, E)$ and a real number $\epsilon > 0$. It returns a $(1 + \epsilon)$-spanner G' of G having $O(n)$ edges.

Step 1: Compute the distance range hierarchy with $c = 7$, according to Theorem 16.2.1. Let $S_1, S_2, \ldots, S_\ell$ be the subsets of S in the hierarchy.

Step 2: For every i with $1 \le i \le \ell$, set $Q_i := \emptyset$.

Step 3: For each edge $\{p, q\} \in E$, compute the index i and the two points x and y, according to Theorem 16.2.1, and add $\{x, y\}$ to Q_i.

Step 4: For each i with $1 \le i \le \ell$ and for which $S_i \ne \emptyset$, do the following:

Step 4.1: Compute the split tree T_i for S_i.

Step 4.2: Compute the well-separated pair decomposition of S_i, $\{\{A^i_1, B^i_1\}, \ldots, \{A^i_{m_i}, B^i_{m_i}\}\}$, using separation ratio $2s$, where $s = ((1 + \epsilon)(8t + 4) + 4)/\epsilon$. Pick arbitrary points $a^i_j \in A^i_j$ and $b^i_j \in B^i_j$ from each well-separated pair to define the set $P_i := \{\{a^i_j, b^i_j\} : 1 \le j \le m_i\}$.

Step 4.3: Combine Lemma 16.3.7 (applied to the sets $Q_1, Q_2, \ldots, Q_\ell$) with algorithm GREEDYPRUNE$(G, P_1 \cup P_2 \cup \cdots \cup P_\ell)$ to prune G. Let the pruned graph be $G' = (S, E')$.

Step 5: Return the graph $G' = (S, E')$.

Hence, we have proved the following result.

Theorem 16.3.9. *Let S be a set of n points in $\mathbb{R}^d$, let $t \ge 1$ and $\epsilon > 0$ be real numbers such that $n \ge 2t$ and $n^5 = \Omega((1 + 1/\epsilon)t)$, and let $G = (S, E)$ be a t-spanner for S. A*

$(1 + \epsilon)$-*spanner for G having* $O((1 + 1/\epsilon)^d t^d n)$ *edges can be computed in time*

$$O\left(n \log n + (1 + 1/\epsilon)^d t^d n + |E| \log \log n\right).$$

Remark 16.3.10. Algorithm PRUNESPANNER presented in this section works in the algebraic computation-tree model. If we add indirect addressing to this model, then the $\log \log n$ term can be eliminated from the running time; see the bibliographic notes at the end of this chapter.

> **Open problem:** Given a set S of n points in $\mathbb{R}^d$, real numbers $t > 1$ and $\epsilon > 0$, and a t-spanner $G = (S, E)$ for S, is there an algorithm that computes, in $O(|E|)$ time, a $(1 + \epsilon)$-spanner G' of G with $O(n)$ edges? Of course, the constants in the Big-Oh bounds may depend on t and ϵ. Can such a spanner G' be computed without accessing every edge of G? In other words, can it be modified to run in $o(|E|)$ time?

We have shown that every t-spanner $G = (S, E)$ contains a subgraph $G' = (S, E')$, such that $|E'| = O(n)$ and G' is a $(1 + \epsilon)$-spanner of G (and, hence, G' is a $((1 + \epsilon)t)$-spanner of S). This leads to the question of whether such a spanner G' exists in which the degree of each point is bounded by a constant. It turns out that this is not the case; see Exercise 16.7.

16.4 The distance range hierarchy for spanners

Let S be a set of n points in $\mathbb{R}^d$, let $t \geq 1$ be a real number, and let $G = (S, E)$ be a t-spanner for S. We fix a real number $\epsilon > 0$ and assume that

$$n \geq \max((1 + \epsilon)t, 2(t + 1)/\epsilon).$$

Observe that this implies that $n \geq 2t$, a fact that we need to apply the hierarchical decomposition of Section 16.1.6.

Assume that we have computed a hierarchical decomposition of G with $c = 7$. According to Section 16.1.6, we get the sequences L_i, S_i, and $G_i = (S_i, F_i)$, $1 \leq i \leq \ell$. Recall that $\ell = O(|E|)$, $\sum_{i=1}^{\ell} |S_i| = O(|E|)$, and $\sum_{i=1}^{\ell} |F_i| = O(|E|)$.

Let i be an index with $1 \leq i \leq \ell$ and let x and y be two points of S_i such that $L_i/n^{11} \leq |xy| < L_i/t$. It follows from Lemmas 16.1.15 and 16.1.16, and our assumption on n, that

$$\delta_G(x, y)/(1 + \epsilon) \leq \delta_{G_i}(x, y) \leq (1 + \epsilon) \cdot \delta_G(x, y). \tag{16.6}$$

Therefore, since G is a t-spanner, we have

$$\delta_{G_i}(x, y) \leq (1 + \epsilon)t|xy|. \tag{16.7}$$

In other words, any two points x and y in S_i with $L_i/n^{11} \leq |xy| < L_i/t$ are connected by a $((1 + \epsilon)t)$-spanner path in the graph G_i. In Section 17.3, we will need a graph for which (16.7) holds for *each* pair x and y of points for which $|xy| < L_i/t$. That is, we need an (L_i/t)-partial $((1 + \epsilon)t)$-spanner for the point set S_i.

In this section, we extend each graph G_i to a graph G_i' that is an (L_i/t)-partial $((1 + \epsilon)t)$-spanner for S_i. Using these new graphs, we will obtain the distance range hierarchy for the t-spanner G.

16.4.1 The partial spanners G'_i

We define $G'_1 := G_1$ and $G'_2 := G_2$. For each i with $3 \leq i \leq \ell$ and $S_i \neq \emptyset$, let G^0_i be the WSPD-spanner, with stretch factor $((1 + \epsilon)t)$, for the vertex set S_i of G_i; see Corollary 9.4.7. (In fact, we can take any $((1 + \epsilon)t)$-spanner for S_i. Taking the WSPD-spanner, however, gives good bounds on the number of edges of G^0_i and the time needed to compute it.) For each nonempty set S_i, we define G'_i to be the graph with vertex set S_i and whose edge set is the union of

1. the edge set of G_i and
2. the set of all edges of G^0_i whose lengths are less than or equal to L_i/n^{10}.

If S_i is the empty set, we define G'_i to be the empty graph, that is, $G'_i = (\emptyset, \emptyset)$.

Lemma 16.4.1. *Given the graphs $G_i = (S_i, F_i)$, $1 \leq i \leq \ell$, the sequence G'_i, $1 \leq i \leq \ell$, can be computed in $O(|E| \log n + s^d |E|)$ time, where*

$$s = O\left(\frac{(1+\epsilon)t}{(1+\epsilon)t - 1}\right).$$

The total number of edges in the graphs G'_i, $1 \leq i \leq \ell$, is $O(s^d |E|)$.

PROOF According to Theorem 9.2.1, for each i with $3 \leq i \leq \ell$ and $S_i \neq \emptyset$, the $((1 + \epsilon)t)$-spanner G^0_i is obtained from a WSPD with separation ratio

$$s = 4\frac{(1+\epsilon)t + 1}{(1+\epsilon)t - 1} = O\left(\frac{(1+\epsilon)t}{(1+\epsilon)t - 1}\right).$$

Hence, by Theorem 9.4.6, the total time for computing all graphs G^0_i is proportional to (we use the convention that $\log 0 = 0$)

$$\sum_{i=3}^{\ell} \left(|S_i| \log |S_i| + s^d |S_i|\right) = O\left(|E| \log n + s^d |E|\right),$$

and their total number of edges is proportional to $\sum_{i=3}^{\ell} s^d |S_i| = O(s^d |E|)$. Therefore, the sequence of graphs G'_i, $1 \leq i \leq \ell$, can be computed in time

$$O\left(|E| \log n + s^d |E| + \sum_{i=1}^{\ell} |F_i|\right) = O\left(|E| \log n + s^d |E|\right).$$

The total number of edges in these graphs is

$$O\left(s^d |E| + \sum_{i=1}^{\ell} |F_i|\right) = O\left(s^d |E|\right). \qquad \blacksquare$$

The following lemma states that G'_i is an (L_i/t)-partial $((1 + \epsilon)t)$-spanner for S_i. Moreover, it states that for each pair of points in S_i whose Euclidean distance is within a factor of $n^{O(1)}$ of L_i, the shortest-path distances in the graphs G and G'_i are approximately equal.

Lemma 16.4.2. *Let i be an index with $1 \leq i \leq \ell$ and let x and y be two vertices of G_i' such that $|xy| < L_i/t$.*

1. *We have $\delta_{G_i'}(x, y) \leq (1 + \epsilon)t|xy|$.*

2. *If $|xy| \geq L_i/n^8$, then*

$$\delta_G(x, y)/(1 + \epsilon) \leq \delta_{G_i'}(x, y) \leq (1 + \epsilon) \cdot \delta_G(x, y).$$

PROOF Using Exercise 16.1, it can be shown that both claims are true if $i \in \{1, 2\}$. Hence, we may assume that $i \geq 3$. If $|xy| \geq L_i/n^{11}$, then the first claim follows from (16.7) and the fact that G_i is a subgraph of G_i'. Assume that $|xy| < L_i/n^{11}$. Since G_i^0 is a $((1 + \epsilon)t)$-spanner for S_i, we have

$$\delta_{G_i^0}(x, y) \leq (1 + \epsilon)t|xy| < (1 + \epsilon)tL_i/n^{11} \leq L_i/n^{10},$$

where the last inequality follows from our assumption that $n \geq (1 + \epsilon)t$. Hence, any shortest path in G_i^0 between x and y is completely contained in G_i'. Therefore, we have

$$\delta_{G_i'}(x, y) \leq \delta_{G_i^0}(x, y) \leq (1 + \epsilon)t|xy|,$$

proving the first claim.

To prove the second claim, assume that $|xy| \geq L_i/n^8$. Since G_i is a subgraph of G_i', we have $\delta_{G_i'}(x, y) \leq \delta_{G_i}(x, y)$, whereas by (16.6), $\delta_{G_i}(x, y) \leq (1 + \epsilon) \cdot \delta_G(x, y)$. It remains to prove that $\delta_G(x, y) \leq (1 + \epsilon) \cdot \delta_{G_i'}(x, y)$.

Let $x = x_0, x_1, \ldots, x_k = y$ be a shortest path between x and y in G_i'. (Since $\delta_G(x, y) < \infty$, the rightmost inequality in the second claim implies that this path exists.) Let j be any index with $0 \leq j \leq k - 1$ and consider the edge $\{x_j, x_{j+1}\}$ in G_i'. First, assume that $\{x_j, x_{j+1}\}$ is an edge in G_i. Then it follows from the proof of Lemma 16.1.16 (see (16.5)) that

$$\delta_G(x_j, x_{j+1}) \leq |x_j x_{j+1}| + 2(t + 1)L_i/n^{13}.$$

If $\{x_j, x_{j+1}\}$ is not an edge in G_i, then it must be an edge in G_i^0 and $|x_j x_{j+1}| \leq L_i/n^{10}$. In this case, we have

$$\delta_G(x_j, x_{j+1}) \leq t|x_j x_{j+1}| \leq tL_i/n^{10}.$$

Hence, in either case, we get the upper bound

$$\delta_G(x_j, x_{j+1}) \leq |x_j x_{j+1}| + 2(t + 1)L_i/n^{13} + tL_i/n^{10}$$
$$\leq |x_j x_{j+1}| + 2tL_i/n^{10}$$
$$\leq |x_j x_{j+1}| + 2t|xy|/n^2.$$

It follows that

$$\delta_G(x, y) \leq \sum_{j=0}^{k-1} \delta_G(x_j, x_{j+1}) \leq \delta_{G_i'}(x, y) + k \cdot 2t|xy|/n^2.$$

Since $k < n$ and $n \geq 2t/\epsilon$, we obtain

$$\delta_G(x, y) \leq \delta_{G_i'}(x, y) + 2t|xy|/n \leq \delta_{G_i'}(x, y) + \epsilon|xy|.$$

The proof is completed by observing that $|xy| \leq \delta_{G_i'}(x, y)$. ∎

16.4.2 The partial spanners G'_i approximate the spanner G

We now prove the generalization of Lemma 16.1.17 to the graphs G'_i.

Lemma 16.4.3. *Let p and q be two distinct points of S. Let i be the index and let x and y be the points of S_i that are returned by algorithm* QUERYHD *of Section 16.1.4. Then,*

1. $\delta_G(p, q) \leq (1 + 2\epsilon) \cdot \delta_{G'_i}(x, y)$, *and*
2. $\delta_{G'_i}(x, y) \leq (1 + 2\epsilon) \cdot \delta_G(p, q)$.

PROOF   First observe that $L_i/n^8 \leq |xy| < L_i/t$ (see Section 16.1.4). Moreover, x and y are vertices of the graph G'_i. By Lemma 16.4.2, we have $\delta_G(x, y) \leq (1 + \epsilon) \cdot \delta_{G'_i}(x, y)$. We know from Section 16.1.6 that both $|px|$ and $|qy|$ are less than $|xy|/n^5$. By using these inequalities and the fact that G is a t-spanner, we obtain

$$
\begin{aligned}
\delta_G(p, q) &\leq \delta_G(p, x) + \delta_G(x, y) + \delta_G(y, q) \\
&\leq t|px| + (1 + \epsilon) \cdot \delta_{G'_i}(x, y) + t|yq| \\
&\leq 2t|xy|/n^5 + (1 + \epsilon) \cdot \delta_{G'_i}(x, y) \\
&\leq \epsilon|xy| + (1 + \epsilon) \cdot \delta_{G'_i}(x, y) \\
&\leq (1 + 2\epsilon) \cdot \delta_{G'_i}(x, y).
\end{aligned}
$$

The proof of the second claim is similar:

$$
\begin{aligned}
\delta_{G'_i}(x, y) &\leq (1 + \epsilon) \cdot \delta_G(x, y) \\
&\leq (1 + \epsilon)(\delta_G(x, p) + \delta_G(p, q) + \delta_G(q, y)) \\
&\leq (1 + \epsilon)(t|xp| + \delta_G(p, q) + t|qy|) \\
&\leq (1 + \epsilon)\left(4t|pq|/n^5 + \delta_G(p, q)\right) \\
&\leq (1 + \epsilon)\left(4t/n^5 + 1\right) \cdot \delta_G(p, q) \\
&\leq (1 + 2\epsilon) \cdot \delta_G(p, q),
\end{aligned}
$$

where the last inequality follows from the fact that $n^5 \geq 4t(1 + 1/\epsilon)$. ∎

16.4.3 The main result

By combining the results of Sections 16.4.1 and 16.4.2 with those of Sections 16.1.6 and 16.3.4, we obtain the distance range hierarchy for any spanner.

Theorem 16.4.4 (DRH Theorem for Spanners). *Let S be a set of n points in $\mathbb{R}^d$, let $t \geq 1$ be a real number, let $G = (S, E)$ be a t-spanner for S, and let ϵ be a real number such that $0 < \epsilon \leq 2$. Assume that $n \geq \max((1 + \epsilon/4)^2 t, ((8 + 2\epsilon)t + 8)/\epsilon)$. In*

$$
O\left(|E| \log \log n + (t/\epsilon)^d n \log n + \frac{t^{2d}}{(t - 1)^d \epsilon^d} n\right)
$$

time, we can compute

1. *a sequence $L_1, L_2, \ldots, L_\ell$ of real numbers, where $\ell = O((t/\epsilon)^d n)$,*
2. *a sequence $S_1, S_2, \ldots, S_\ell$ of subsets of S, such that $\sum_{i=1}^\ell |S_i| = O((t/\epsilon)^d n)$,*
3. *two rooted trees $U_{\ell-1}$ and U_ℓ, each storing the points of S at its leaves and having size $O(n)$, and*

4. *a sequence $G'_1, G'_2, \ldots, G'_\ell$ of graphs, such that the total of the number of edges in these graphs is*

$$O\left(\frac{t^{2d}}{(t-1)^d \epsilon^d} n\right),$$

and for each i with $1 \le i \le \ell$, G'_i is an L_i-partial $((1+\epsilon)t)$-spanner for S_i.

This decomposition satisfies the following additional properties. For any two distinct points p and q of S, the trees $U_{\ell-1}$ and U_ℓ can be used to compute, in $O(\log \log n)$ time, an index i with $1 \le i \le \ell$ and two points x and y in S_i such that

1. $L_i/n^8 \le |xy| < L_i$,
2. *both $|px|$ and $|qy|$ are less than $|xy|/n^5$,*
3. *both $|px|$ and $|qy|$ are less than $2|pq|/n^5$,*
4. $1 - 2/n^5 < |pq|/|xy| < 1 + 2/n^5$,
5. $\delta_G(p, q) \le (1+\epsilon) \cdot \delta_{G'_i}(x, y)$, *and*
6. $\delta_{G'_i}(x, y) \le (1+\epsilon) \cdot \delta_G(p, q)$.

PROOF We start by using Theorem 16.3.9 to compute a $(1 + \epsilon/4)$-spanner $G' = (S, E')$ for G with $|E'| = O((t/\epsilon)^d n)$. Thus, we first obtain a pruned graph with only a linear number of edges. Observe that G' is a $((1 + \epsilon/4)t)$-spanner for the point set S and that it can be computed in time

$$O\left(n \log n + (t/\epsilon)^d n + |E| \log \log n\right).$$

Since the number of edges in G' is only linear, we can afford to build the required distance range hierarchy. Therefore, we apply the results of Sections 16.1.6, 16.4.1, and 16.4.2 to the spanner G', where we replace $G = (S, E)$ by $G' = (S, E')$, replace ϵ by $\epsilon/4$, and replace t by $(1 + \epsilon/4)t$. Hence, by the results in Section 16.1.6 and Lemmas 16.4.1 and 16.4.2, we obtain in $O(|E'| \log n + (t/(t-1))^d |E'|)$ time, two trees U_ℓ and $U_{\ell-1}$, sequences L_i, S_i, and G'_i, $1 \le i \le \ell$, such that $\ell = O(|E'|)$, $\sum_{i=1}^\ell |S_i| = O(|E'|)$, the total number of edges of the graphs G'_i is $O((t/(t-1))^d |E'|)$, and for each i with $1 \le i \le \ell$, G'_i is an $(L_i/((1 + \epsilon/4)t))$-partial $((1 + \epsilon/4)^2 t)$-spanner for S_i. Since $(1 + \epsilon/4)^2 t \le (1 + \epsilon)t$, each graph G'_i is an $(L_i/((1 + \epsilon/4)t))$-partial $((1 + \epsilon)t)$-spanner for S_i.

Given any two distinct points p and q in S, we can compute, in $O(\log \log n)$ time, an index i and two points x and y in S_i, such that (i) $L_i/n^8 \le |xy| < L_i/((1 + \epsilon/4)t)$, (ii) both $|px|$ and $|qy|$ are less than $|xy|/n^5$, (iii) both $|px|$ and $|qy|$ are less than $2|pq|/n^5$, (iv) $1 - 2/n^5 < |pq|/|xy| < 1 + 2/n^5$, (v) $\delta_{G'}(p, q) \le (1 + \epsilon/2) \cdot \delta_{G'_i}(x, y)$, and (vi) $\delta_{G'_i}(x, y) \le (1 + \epsilon/2) \cdot \delta_{G'}(p, q)$.

Since G' is a subgraph of G, we have $\delta_G(p, q) \le \delta_{G'}(p, q)$. Moreover, since G' is a $(1 + \epsilon/4)$-spanner for G, we have $\delta_{G'}(p, q) \le (1 + \epsilon/4) \cdot \delta_G(p, q)$. Hence, (v) and (vi), together with our assumption that $0 < \epsilon \le 2$, imply that $\delta_G(p, q) \le (1 + \epsilon) \cdot \delta_{G'_i}(x, y)$ and $\delta_{G'_i}(x, y) \le (1 + \epsilon) \cdot \delta_G(p, q)$. The proof of the theorem is completed by renaming $L_i/((1 + \epsilon/4)t)$ as L_i. ∎

In Chapter 17, we will use Theorem 16.4.4 to give an efficient algorithm for approximating shortest paths in an arbitrary spanner.

Exercises

16.1. Let G be a t-spanner for a point set S, let L be a real number, let G' be the subgraph of G consisting of all edges of G whose lengths are less than L, and let p and q be two points of S such that $|pq| < L/t$. Prove that $\delta_{G'}(p, q) = \delta_G(p, q)$.

16.2. Prove that the result in Section 16.3.2 can also be obtained if we let s take the value $4(1 + (1 + \epsilon)t)/\epsilon$.

16.3. Work out the details for Section 16.3.3. In particular, the following problems are nontrivial: (a) How can all nodes u_x and u'_x be computed for all points in S in $O(n)$ time? (b) How can all trees T_x be computed for all points in S in $O(n \log n)$ time? (c) How can the space requirement for computing all trees T_x be reduced to $O(n)$?

16.4. In Section 16.3.4, we computed, for each i with $1 \le i \le \ell$ and $S_i \ne \emptyset$, a well-separated pair decomposition $\{A^i_j, B^i_j\}$, $1 \le j \le m_i$, of the set S_i. Is the union of all these sequences a well-separated pair decomposition for the point set S?

16.5. Let S be a set of n points in $\mathbb{R}^d$, let $t \ge 1$ be a real constant, let $G = (S, E)$ be a t-spanner for S, and let $\theta > 0$ be a real constant. Consider a collection $C_1, C_2, \ldots, C_h$ of simplicial cones of angular diameter θ, all having their apex at the origin, and that cover $\mathbb{R}^d$, where h is a constant that depends only on θ.

Let $G' = (S, E')$ be the subgraph of G that is obtained by taking, for each $p \in S$ and each i with $1 \le i \le h$, a shortest edge $\{p, q\}$ in E for which $q - p \in C_i$.

Does there exist a constant t' such that the graph G' is a t'-spanner of G?

16.6. Let S be a set of n points in $\mathbb{R}^d$, let $t \ge 1$ be a real constant, let $G = (S, E)$ be a t-spanner for S, and let $\epsilon > 0$ be a real constant. Let $k > 0$ be a real constant, and assume that the distance between any two distinct points of S is in the interval $[1, n^k]$. For any $p \in S$, denote by $E(p)$ the set of all edges in E that are incident on p.

Let $\epsilon_0 := \epsilon/(2(1 + t(1 + \epsilon)))$. For each $p \in S$, partition $E(p)$ into subsets

$$E_i(p) := \{\{p, q\} \in E(p) : (1 + \epsilon_0)^i \le |pq| < (1 + \epsilon_0)^{i+1}\}.$$

Let θ be a positive real constant such that $0 < \theta < \pi/4$ and $\cos\theta - \sin\theta \ge 1 - \epsilon/(2t(1 + \epsilon))$. Consider a collection $C_1, C_2, \ldots, C_h$ of simplicial cones of angular diameter θ, all having their apex at the origin, and that cover $\mathbb{R}^d$, where h is a constant that depends only on t and ϵ. Further partition each subset $E_i(p)$ into h subsets

$$E_{ij}(p) := \{\{p, q\} \in E_i(p) : q - p \in C_j\}.$$

Let $G' = (S, E')$ be the subgraph of G that is obtained by taking exactly one (arbitrary) edge from each nonempty set $E_{ij}(p)$.

Prove that (i) G' has $O(\min(|E|, n \log n))$ edges, (ii) G' can be computed in $O(|E| \log \log n)$ time, and (iii) G' is a $(1 + \epsilon)$-spanner of G. (*Hint:* Use Lemma 4.1.4.)

16.7. A tree T is called a *star* if all edges of T have one vertex in common. Let $t > 1$ be a real number. Give an example of a set S of n points in $\mathbb{R}^d$ and a star $T = (S, E)$, such that T is a t-spanner of S. Conclude that there exist spanners that cannot be pruned to a spanner of bounded degree.

Bibliographic notes

The distance range hierarchy appeared (implicitly) in Gudmundsson et al. [2002c] and Gudmundsson et al. [2004]. The problem of pruning spanners (see Section 16.3) first appeared in Gudmundsson et al. [2002b]. These authors present the pruning algorithm of Section 16.3.2, a solution for Exercise 16.6 and an algorithm for pruning the spanner G'

in this exercise. The pruning algorithms in Sections 16.3.1, 16.3.3, and 16.3.4 are due to Gudmundsson, Narasimhan, and Smid [2005].

All algorithms presented in this chapter work in the algebraic computation-tree model. Using Section 15.3 and a nontrivial extension of Section 17.1, the results can be improved in the model that additionally uses indirect addressing. The details can be found in Gudmundsson et al. [2004] and Gudmundsson, Narasimhan, and Smid [2005].

17

Approximating Shortest Paths in Spanners

We have seen many algorithms for computing t-spanners. For some of them, it is clear from the construction how to compute t-spanner paths. For example, this is true for the Θ-graph of Chapter 4 and the spanner obtained from the well-separated pair decomposition (see Section 9.2 and Theorem 9.5.2). If the value of t is large, however, the t-spanner path computed may be much longer than the actual shortest path. On the other hand, for some of the spanners that we have seen in previous chapters, it is not clear how a t-spanner path can be computed efficiently. In this chapter, we consider the problem of approximating the lengths of shortest paths in arbitrary spanners.

Let $G = (S, E)$ be a t-spanner for a set S of n points in $\mathbb{R}^d$. For any two points p and q of S, we denote by $\delta_G(p, q)$ the length of a shortest path between p and q in G. If $\epsilon > 0$ and Δ are real numbers, then we say that Δ is a $(1 + \epsilon)$-*approximation* to the shortest-path distance between p and q in G if

$$\delta_G(p, q) \leq \Delta \leq (1 + \epsilon) \cdot \delta_G(p, q).$$

In Section 17.2, we present a data structure that can be used to compute $(1 + \epsilon)$-approximate shortest-path distances for points p and q in S that are "far" apart. That is, if D is the length of a longest edge in G, then the Euclidean distance between p and q must be larger than D/C, where $C > 2$ is a real number that may depend on n. The main idea is to store a sequence of cluster graphs that were used in the cluster-based path-greedy algorithm of Section 15.2. That is, the data structure consists of a sequence of cluster graphs of increasing coarseness, each of which helps answer approximate shortest path queries for pairs of points whose Euclidean distance belong to a specific interval. We start this chapter in Section 17.1 with presenting a "bucketing" tool that allows us to find the "correct" cluster graph for any given pair of points in S.

In Section 17.3, we show how arbitrary $(1 + \epsilon)$-approximate shortest path queries in G can be answered. Our approach is as follows. Using the distance range hierarchy for the spanner G (see Section 16.4), we approximate G by a sequence $G'_1, G'_2, \ldots, G'_\ell$ of partial spanners. As we have seen in Theorem 16.4.4, this sequence has the property that for any two distinct points p and q in S, there exists an index i and two vertices x and y of G'_i such that $\delta_{G'_i}(x, y)$ is a $(1 + \epsilon)$-approximation to $\delta_G(p, q)$. Moreover, x and y are sufficiently far apart so that the algorithm of Section 17.2 can be applied to G'_i to compute an approximation to $\delta_{G'_i}(x, y)$.

Throughout this chapter, we consider undirected t-spanners, where the value of t may be large. The algorithms to be presented work in the algebraic computation-tree model. Using the results of Section 15.3, the results in this chapter can be improved in the algebraic computation-tree model extended with indirect addressing; see the references in the bibliographic notes at the end of this chapter.

17.1 Bucketing distances

Let $\epsilon > 0$ be a real number. For any two distinct points p and q in $\mathbb{R}^d$ and for any real number $\lambda \geq 1$, we define the *bucket index* $\text{BINDEX}_\epsilon(\lambda, p, q)$ to be the integer i such that $(1 + \epsilon)^{i-1} < |pq|/\lambda \leq (1 + \epsilon)^i$, that is,

$$\text{BINDEX}_\epsilon(\lambda, p, q) = \left\lceil \log_{1+\epsilon} \left(\frac{|pq|}{\lambda} \right) \right\rceil = \left\lceil \frac{\log |pq| - \log \lambda}{\log(1 + \epsilon)} \right\rceil.$$

Let K be a positive integer. We consider the problem of constructing a data structure, such that for any real number $\lambda \geq 1$ and for any two points p and q in $\mathbb{R}^d$ with $\lambda < |pq| \leq K$, the value of $\text{BINDEX}_\epsilon(\lambda, p, q)$ can be computed efficiently. Observe that, since $\lambda \geq 1$,

$$1 \leq \text{BINDEX}_\epsilon(\lambda, p, q) \leq \lceil \log_{1+\epsilon} K \rceil = O((\log K)/\epsilon).$$

If the ceiling and logarithm functions are available as unit-time operations, then a bucket index query can clearly be answered in $O(1)$ time. To get an algorithm that works in the algebraic computation-tree model, we store the sorted sequence $(1 + \epsilon)^i$, $0 \leq i \leq \lceil \log_{1+\epsilon} K \rceil$, in a balanced binary search tree. With each value $(1 + \epsilon)^i$ in this tree, we also store the integer i. This tree can clearly be built in $O((\log K)/\epsilon)$ time and can be used to answer bucket index queries in $O(\log((\log K)/\epsilon)) = O(\log \log K + \log(1/\epsilon))$ time. This gives the following result:

Lemma 17.1.1. *Let K be a positive integer, and let $\epsilon > 0$ be a real number. In $O((\log K)/\epsilon)$ time, we can build a data structure of size $O((\log K)/\epsilon)$, such that for any real number $\lambda \geq 1$ and for any two points p and q in $\mathbb{R}^d$ with $\lambda < |pq| \leq K$, the value of $\text{BINDEX}_\epsilon(\lambda, p, q)$ can be computed in $O(\log \log K + \log(1/\epsilon))$ time.*

17.2 Approximate shortest path queries for points that are separated

Let S be a set of n points in $\mathbb{R}^d$, let $t > 1$ be a real number, and let $G = (S, E)$ be a t-spanner for S. In this section, we show how approximate shortest path queries in G can be answered for pairs of points that are "far" apart. To be more precise, let D be the length of a longest edge in G, let $\epsilon > 0$ be a real number, and let $C > 2$ be a real number that may depend on n. We will show how to preprocess G into a data structure, such that for any two points p and q of S with $|pq| > D/C$, a $(1 + \epsilon)$-approximation to the shortest-path distance between p and q in G; that is, a real number Δ such that

$$\delta_G(p, q) \leq \Delta \leq (1 + \epsilon) \cdot \delta_G(p, q),$$

can be computed. We may assume without loss of generality that $D = C$. (If this is not the case, then we scale the coordinates of the points of S.) Hence, the length of each edge of G is less than or equal to C, and we want to answer approximate shortest path queries for pairs p and q of points in S for which $|pq| > 1$.

17.2.1 The general approach

Our data structure will be based on the cluster-based implementation of the path-greedy spanner algorithm (see Section 15.2). We will apply the results of that section with

- t replaced by $(1 + \epsilon)t$,
- t' replaced by $(1 + \epsilon)/t$,
- the roles of G and G' interchanged, and
- the roles of E and E' interchanged.

> **Outline:** The cluster-based path-greedy algorithm computes a spanner of the spanner G, by processing the edges of G in a sequence of phases and maintaining a cluster graph H. During each phase, this graph H has the following properties. First, $\delta_H(p, q)$ approximates $\delta_G(p, q)$, provided the Euclidean distance between p and q is approximately equal to the lengths of the edges that are processed in this phase. Second, the value of $\delta_H(p, q)$ can easily be computed for such points p and q. This suggests to store one cluster graph H for each phase. Given any two query points p and q with $|pq| > 1$, we can use Lemma 17.1.1 to find a cluster graph H for which $\delta_H(p, q)$ approximates $\delta_G(p, q)$.

Remark 17.2.1. In Section 15.2, we assume that the parameter t' is larger than 1. As mentioned above, we replace t' by $(1 + \epsilon)/t$, which may be less than 1. Fortunately, all results in Section 15.2, except those that analyze the weight of the spanner produced by algorithm FASTPATHGREEDY, remain valid for parameters $t > 1$ and $t' > 0$ with $tt' > 1$. In our case, these conditions are satisfied, because we replace t by $(1 + \epsilon)t$ and t' by $(1 + \epsilon)/t$. Also, we do not use the weight of the spanner produced by algorithm FASTPATHGREEDY.

We briefly recall those parts of algorithm FASTPATHGREEDY of Section 15.2 that are relevant for our approximate shortest-path data structure. The input to the cluster-based path-greedy algorithm consists of

1. real numbers $t > 1$, $\epsilon > 0$, $\mu > 1$, $\lambda \geq 1$, and $0 < \alpha < 1/4$, and
2. the t-spanner $G = (S, E)$ for S.

We define

$$E_0 := \{\{p, q\} \in E : |pq| \leq \lambda\}$$

and, for $i \geq 1$,

$$E_i := \{\{p, q\} \in E : \mu^{i-1}\lambda < |pq| \leq \mu^i\lambda\}.$$

The sets E_i, $0 \leq i \leq \lceil \log_\mu(C/\lambda) \rceil$, partition the edge set E of G. (Strictly speaking, they do not form a partition, because some of the sets E_i may be empty.) For each i with $1 + \lceil \log_\mu(C/\lambda) \rceil \leq i \leq 2 + \lfloor \log_\mu(nC/\lambda) \rfloor$, we define $E_i := \emptyset$.

The algorithm initializes $E' := E_0$ and $G' := (S, E')$. Then it processes the edge sets E_i, for $i = 1, 2, \ldots, 2 + \lfloor \log_\mu(nC/\lambda) \rfloor$, one after another.

Consider *phase i*, that is, the iteration in which the edges of E_i are processed. (In algorithm FASTPATHGREEDY, the value of W is equal to $\mu^{i-1}\lambda$ during this phase.) At the start of phase i, the algorithm computes the cluster graph H of the current graph G', by calling algorithm CLUSTERGRAPH(G', α, $\mu^{i-1}\lambda$) (see Section 15.2.5). Then, all edges of E_i are considered in sorted order of their lengths. If $\{p, q\}$ is the current edge of E_i, then the algorithm decides if $\delta_H(p, q) > (1 + \epsilon)|pq|$ and, if so, adds $\{p, q\}$ to the edge set E' of G' and updates the cluster graph H.

We now state the main properties that are maintained during this algorithm.

Property 17.2.2. *At any moment during the algorithm, we have $\delta_{G'}(p, q) \leq \delta_H(p, q)$ for all points p and q in S.*

PROOF   See Lemma 15.2.5.   ∎

Property 17.2.3. *Let i be an integer with $1 \leq i \leq 2 + \lfloor \log_\mu(nC/\lambda) \rfloor$. At any moment during phase i, we have*

$$\delta_H(p, q) \leq \frac{1 + 18\alpha}{1 - 2\alpha} \cdot \delta_{G'}(p, q)$$

for all points p and q in S with $\delta_{G'}(p, q) > (1 - 2\alpha)\mu^{i-1}\lambda$.

PROOF   See Lemma 15.2.6. This lemma requires that no cluster in the $(\alpha\mu^{i-1}\lambda)$-cluster cover of G' contains both p and q. This condition is satisfied because we assume that $0 < \alpha < 1/4$.   ∎

Property 17.2.4. *Let i be an integer with $1 \leq i \leq 2 + \lfloor \log_\mu(nC/\lambda) \rfloor$ and consider the graph G' at the start of phase i. For each edge $\{p, q\}$ of G for which $|pq| \leq \mu^{i-1}\lambda$, we have $\delta_{G'}(p, q) \leq (1 + \epsilon)|pq|$.*

PROOF   The claim follows from the proof of Lemma 15.2.12.   ∎

Property 17.2.5. *Let i be an integer with $1 \leq i \leq 2 + \lfloor \log_\mu(nC/\lambda) \rfloor$. At any moment during phase i and for any two points p and q of S, it takes*

$$O\left(\frac{(1 + \epsilon)^{5d} \mu^{2d} t^{3d}}{\alpha^{2d}} \right)$$

time to decide if $\delta_H(p, q) \leq (1 + \epsilon)^2 \mu^i \lambda$. If this is the case, then the value of $\delta_H(p, q)$ can be computed within this time bound.

PROOF   The decision can be made by running algorithm SHORTPATH(H, p, q, $(1 + \epsilon)^2 \mu^i \lambda$) (see Section 15.2.5). For the claim on the running time, see (15.10); in this equation, replace t by $(1 + \epsilon)t$, replace t' by $(1 + \epsilon)/t$, and take $\gamma = (1 + \epsilon)^2 \mu$ and $\beta = 1/t$.   ∎

Let p and q be two points of S such that $|pq| > \lambda$. We will show how the sequence of cluster graphs that is computed during the path-greedy algorithm can be used to approximate the length of a shortest path between p and q in G. Let $i \geq 1$ be the integer such that $\mu^{i-1}\lambda < |pq| \leq \mu^i \lambda$. Then

$$\mu^{i-1} < |pq|/\lambda \leq \delta_G(p, q)/\lambda \leq nD/\lambda = nC/\lambda$$

(since we assume that $D = C$) and, therefore, $i \leq 1 + \lfloor \log_\mu(nC/\lambda) \rfloor$. Consider the graph G' and the corresponding cluster graph H at the end of phase i, that is, when the algorithm has just processed all edges of E_i. Assume that we have chosen μ such that $\mu > t$. Furthermore, assume that $|pq| \leq \mu^i \lambda/t$. Since G' is a subgraph of G, we have

$$\delta_G(p, q) \leq \delta_{G'}(p, q).$$

By Property 17.2.2, we have

$$\delta_{G'}(p, q) \leq \delta_H(p, q).$$

Since $\delta_{G'}(p, q) \geq |pq| > \mu^{i-1}\lambda > (1 - 2\alpha)\mu^{i-1}\lambda$, we have, by Property 17.2.3,

$$\delta_H(p, q) \leq \frac{1 + 18\alpha}{1 - 2\alpha} \cdot \delta_{G'}(p, q).$$

Since G is a t-spanner for S, we have $\delta_G(p, q) \leq t|pq| \leq \mu^i\lambda$. Hence, the length of each edge on a shortest path between p and q in G is less than or equal to $\mu^i\lambda$. Since G' is the graph at the start of phase $i + 1$, it follows from Property 17.2.4 that

$$\delta_{G'}(p, q) \leq (1 + \epsilon) \cdot \delta_G(p, q).$$

Combining these inequalities yields

$$\delta_G(p, q) \leq \delta_H(p, q) \leq \frac{1 + 18\alpha}{1 - 2\alpha} \cdot (1 + \epsilon) \cdot \delta_G(p, q).$$

Hence, by choosing $\alpha = \epsilon/(2\epsilon + 20)$, we have

$$\delta_G(p, q) \leq \delta_H(p, q) \leq (1 + \epsilon)^2 \cdot \delta_G(p, q), \tag{17.1}$$

that is, $\delta_H(p, q)$ is a $(1 + \epsilon)^2$-approximation to $\delta_G(p, q)$. (Recall that we need $0 < \alpha < 1/4$. This is true if $0 < \epsilon < 10$.)

Since $\delta_H(p, q) \leq (1 + \epsilon)^2 \cdot \delta_G(p, q) \leq (1 + \epsilon)^2\mu^i\lambda$, Property 17.2.5 gives an upper bound on the time needed to compute $\delta_H(p, q)$.

If we replace ϵ by $\epsilon/3$ in the entire construction, and assume that $0 < \epsilon \leq 3$, then (17.1) implies that

$$\delta_G(p, q) \leq \delta_H(p, q) \leq (1 + \epsilon) \cdot \delta_G(p, q).$$

We have obtained the following result:

Lemma 17.2.6. *Let $0 < \epsilon \leq 3$ and $\lambda \geq 1$ be real numbers, let μ be a real number with $\mu > t$, and let $\alpha = \epsilon/(2\epsilon + 60)$. Assume that we run the cluster-based path-greedy algorithm on the t-spanner G as described above. Let p and q be two points of S such that $|pq| > \lambda$, let $i \geq 1$ be the integer such that $\mu^{i-1}\lambda < |pq| \leq \mu^i\lambda$, and let H be the cluster graph at the end of phase i. If $|pq| \leq \mu^i\lambda/t$, then $\delta_H(p, q)$ is a $(1 + \epsilon)$-approximation to the shortest-path distance between p and q in G. Moreover, given the value of i and the cluster graph H, the value of $\delta_H(p, q)$ can be computed in $O(\mu^{2d}t^{3d}/\epsilon^{2d})$ time.*

> **Summary:** We can compute an approximation to $\delta_G(p, q)$, provided that $|pq| \leq \mu^i\lambda/t$, i.e., the distance $|pq|$ is contained in the initial part of the interval $(\mu^{i-1}\lambda, \mu^i\lambda)$. This condition can be satisfied by running the path-greedy algorithm for different values for λ. The details will be given in Section 17.2.2.

17.2.2 The data structure

Let $t > 1$, $0 < \epsilon \leq 3$, and μ be real numbers such that $\mu > t$, let $\alpha = \epsilon/(2\epsilon + 60)$, and let $G = (S, E)$ be a t-spanner for the point set S. For any j with $0 \leq j \leq \lfloor \log_{\mu/t} \mu \rfloor$, let $\lambda_j := (\mu/t)^j$. Observe that $1 \leq \lambda_j \leq \mu$. For each such j, we run the path-greedy algorithm on the t-spanner G, as described in Section 17.2.1, using the following partition of E:

$$E_0^j := \{\{p, q\} \in E : |pq| \leq \lambda_j\}$$

and, for $1 \leq i \leq 2 + \lfloor \log_\mu (nC/\lambda_j) \rfloor$,

$$E_i^j := \{\{p, q\} \in E : \mu^{i-1}\lambda_j < |pq| \leq \mu^i \lambda_j\}.$$

For each such i and j, let H_i^j be the cluster graph at the end of phase i of the j-th run of the path-greedy algorithm. The data structure consists of the following:

1. The collection of cluster graphs H_i^j, where $0 \leq j \leq \lfloor \log_{\mu/t} \mu \rfloor$ and $1 \leq i \leq 2 + \lfloor \log_\mu (nC/\lambda_j) \rfloor$.

2. The data structure of Lemma 17.1.1 for answering queries $\text{BINDEX}_{\mu-1}(1, p, q)$ for points p and q of S with $1 < |pq| \leq nC$.

3. The data structure of Lemma 17.1.1 for answering queries $\text{BINDEX}_{\mu/t-1}(\lambda, p, q)$ for real numbers $\lambda \geq 1$ and points p and q of S with $\lambda < |pq| \leq \mu nC$.

We now show how this data structure can be used to answer approximate shortest path queries in G.

Algorithm RESTRICTEDAPPROXSHORTESTPATH(p, q)

Comment: This algorithm takes as input two points p and q of S, such that $|pq| > 1$. It returns a $(1 + \epsilon)$-approximation to the length of a shortest path between p and q in G.

Step 1: Compute $i := \text{BINDEX}_{\mu-1}(1, p, q)$.

Step 2: Compute $j := \text{BINDEX}_{\mu/t-1}(\mu^{i-1}, p, q) - 1$.

Step 3: Use Lemma 17.2.6 to compute and return the value of $\delta_{H_i^j}(p, q)$.

To prove the correctness of this algorithm, we first observe that the index i that is computed in Step 1 has the property that $\mu^{i-1} < |pq| \leq \mu^i$. Next, the index j that is computed in Step 2 has the properties that

$$\lambda_j = (\mu/t)^j < |pq|/\mu^{i-1} \leq (\mu/t)^{j+1} = (\mu/t)\lambda_j,$$

$|pq| > \lambda_j$, and $0 \leq j \leq \lfloor \log_{\mu/t} \mu \rfloor$. It follows that

$$\mu^{i-1}\lambda_j < |pq| \leq \mu^i \lambda_j/t.$$

Hence, by Lemma 17.2.6, the value of $\delta_{H_i^j}(p, q)$ is a $(1 + \epsilon)$-approximation to the length of a shortest path between p and q in G.

We next analyze the running time of the query algorithm. By Lemma 17.1.1, the time to compute i and j is

$$O(\log \log(nC) + \log(1/(\mu - 1)) + \log \log(\mu nC) + \log(1/(\mu/t - 1))),$$

which is

$$O(\log \log(\mu nC) + \log(t/(\mu - t))).$$

Combining this with Lemma 17.2.6, it follows that the total time to answer the $(1 + \epsilon)$-approximate shortest path query for p and q is

$$O\left(\log \log(\mu nC) + \log(t/(\mu - t)) + \mu^{2d} t^{3d}/\epsilon^{2d}\right).$$

We next analyze the amount of space needed to store the data structure. By Lemma 17.1.1, the size of the two data structures for answering BINDEX-queries is

$$O((\log(nC))/(\mu - 1) + (\log(\mu nC))/(\mu/t - 1)) = O((t/(\mu - t))\log(\mu nC)).$$

It follows from the definition of the cluster graph (see Section 15.2.2) and Lemmas 15.2.8 and 15.2.9 that the size of one cluster graph is $O((\mu t/\epsilon)^d n)$. (In these two lemmas, replace t by $(1 + \epsilon)t$, take $\beta = 1/t$, and use the facts that α is proportional to ϵ, and ϵ is bounded from above by a constant.) Since the number of cluster graphs that we store is less than or equal to

$$(1 + \log_{\mu/t} \mu)(2 + \log_\mu(nC)) = O(1 + \log_{\mu/t}(\mu nC)),$$

the total size of the approximate shortest path data structure is

$$O\left(\frac{\mu^d t^d}{\epsilon^d}(1 + \log_{\mu/t}(\mu nC))n\right).$$

Finally, we estimate the time needed to build the data structure. We leave it to the reader to verify that the time to build the BINDEX-structures is less than the time for the different runs of the path-greedy algorithm. Let j be an integer with $0 \leq j \leq \lfloor \log_{\mu/t} \mu \rfloor$ and consider the j-th run of the path-greedy algorithm.

The algorithm starts by sorting the edges of E by their lengths and partitioning them into subsets E_i^j. This can clearly be done in $O(|E| \log n)$ time. Let i be an integer with $1 \leq i \leq 2 + \lfloor \log_\mu(nC/\lambda_j) \rfloor$ and consider phase i of the algorithm. First, the cluster graph H for the current graph G' is computed. By (15.9), this takes time

$$O((t/\epsilon)^d n \log n + (\mu^d t^{3d}/\epsilon^d)|E|).$$

(In (15.9), replace t by $(1 + \epsilon)t$, take $\beta = 1/t$, and use the facts that α is proportional to ϵ, and ϵ is bounded from above by a constant.) After H has been computed, the algorithm processes the edges of E_i^j. Consider one such edge $\{p, q\}$. The algorithm decides if $\delta_H(p, q) > (1 + \epsilon)|pq|$, which, by (15.14), takes $O(\mu^{2d} t^{3d}/\epsilon^{2d})$ time. If this is the case, then the algorithm updates the graph H, which, by (15.15), takes $O(\mu^d t^{3d}/\epsilon^d)$ time. Hence, the total time for phase i is

$$O\left((t/\epsilon)^d n \log n + (\mu^d t^{3d}/\epsilon^d)|E| + (\mu^{2d} t^{3d}/\epsilon^{2d})|E_i^j|\right).$$

Since the algorithm makes $O(1 + \log_\mu(nC))$ phases, a straightforward calculation shows that the total time for the j-th run is

$$O\left(\frac{t^d}{\epsilon^d \log \mu} n(\log n) \log(nC) + \frac{\mu^d t^{3d}}{\epsilon^d \log \mu}|E| \log(nC) + \frac{\mu^{2d} t^{3d}}{\epsilon^{2d}}|E|\right).$$

Since we run this algorithm for $O(\log_{\mu/t} \mu)$ values of j, we have proved the following result:

Theorem 17.2.7. *Let S be a set of n points in $\mathbb{R}^d$, let $t > 1$, $0 < \epsilon \leq 3$, and $\mu > t$ be real numbers, and let $G = (S, E)$ be a t-spanner for S. Let D be the length of a longest edge in G, and let $C > 2$ be a real number. In*

$$O\left(\frac{t^d}{\epsilon^d \log(\mu/t)} n(\log n) \log(nC) + \frac{\mu^d t^{3d}}{\epsilon^d \log(\mu/t)}|E| \log(nC) + \frac{\mu^{2d} t^{3d} \log \mu}{\epsilon^{2d} \log(\mu/t)}|E|\right)$$

time, we can preprocess G into a data structure of size

$$O\left(\frac{\mu^d t^d}{\epsilon^d}(1 + \log_{\mu/t}(\mu nC))n\right),$$

*such that for any two points p and q in S with $|pq| > D/C$, a $(1 + \epsilon)$-approximation to
the shortest-path distance between p and q in G can be computed in time*

$$O\left(\log\log(\mu nC) + \log(t/(\mu - t)) + \frac{\mu^{2d}t^{3d}}{\epsilon^{2d}}\right).$$

Remark 17.2.8. The size of the data structure does not depend on the number of edges
of the given t-spanner $G = (S, E)$. If we are required to store G, then we have to add the
size of E to the space bound.

In the next section, we will need a generalization of Theorem 17.2.7. Recall that, for
real numbers $t > 1$ and $L > 0$, the graph $G = (S, E)$ is an L-*partial t-spanner* for the
point set S, if for any two points p and q of S with $|pq| < L$, we have $\delta_G(p, q) \le t|pq|$.
The following theorem states that Theorem 17.2.7 remains true even for partial spanners.
The proof is left as an exercise; see Exercise 17.2.

Theorem 17.2.9. *Let S be a set of n points in $\mathbb{R}^d$, let $t > 1$, $L > 0$, $0 < \epsilon \le 3$, and $\mu > t$
be real numbers, let $G = (S, E)$ be an L-partial t-spanner for S, and let $C > 2$ be a real
number. In*

$$O\left(\frac{t^d}{\epsilon^d \log(\mu/t)} n(\log n)\log(nC) + \frac{\mu^d t^{3d}}{\epsilon^d \log(\mu/t)}|E|\log(nC) + \frac{\mu^{2d}t^{3d}\log\mu}{\epsilon^{2d}\log(\mu/t)}|E|\right)$$

time, we can preprocess G into a data structure of size

$$O\left(\frac{\mu^d t^d}{\epsilon^d}\left(1 + \log_{\mu/t}(\mu nC)\right)n\right),$$

*such that for any two points p and q in S with $L/C \le |pq| < L$, a $(1 + \epsilon)$-approximation
to the shortest-path distance between p and q in G can be computed in time*

$$O\left(\log\log(\mu nC) + \log(t/(\mu - t)) + \frac{\mu^{2d}t^{3d}}{\epsilon^{2d}}\right).$$

17.3 Arbitrary approximate shortest path queries

The data structure of Theorem 17.2.9 can be used to answer only approximate shortest
path queries for pairs of points whose Euclidean distance is within a factor of C of some
fixed real number L. In this section, we will combine this result with the distance range
hierarchy of Theorem 16.4.4 to answer arbitrary approximate shortest path queries.

We are given a set S of n points in $\mathbb{R}^d$, real numbers $t > 1$, $0 < \epsilon \le 1$ and $\mu >
(1 + \epsilon/4)t$, and a t-spanner $G = (S, E)$. We assume that $n \ge \max((1 + \epsilon/16)^2 t, ((32 +
2\epsilon)t + 32)/\epsilon)$.

17.3.1 Computing the distance range hierarchy for G

We apply Theorem 16.4.4 (see also Section 16.1.6) to the t-spanner G, with ϵ replaced
by $\epsilon/4$. This gives, in time

$$O\left(|E|\log\log n + (t/\epsilon)^d n\log n + \frac{t^{2d}}{(t-1)^d\epsilon^d}n\right),$$

1. a sequence $L_1, L_2, \ldots, L_\ell$ of real numbers, where $\ell = O((t/\epsilon)^d n)$,
2. a sequence $S_1, S_2, \ldots, S_\ell$ of subsets of S, such that $\sum_{i=1}^{\ell}|S_i| = O((t/\epsilon)^d n)$,

3. a sequence $G_i' = (S_i, F_i')$, $1 \leq i \leq \ell$, of graphs, such that each G_i' is an L_i-partial $((1 + \epsilon/4)t)$-spanner for S_i, and

$$\sum_{i=1}^{\ell} |F_i'| = O\left(\frac{t^{2d}}{(t-1)^d \epsilon^d} n\right),$$

and

4. two rooted trees $U_{\ell-1}$ and U_ℓ, each storing the points of S at its leaves and having size $O(n)$.

By Theorem 16.4.4, these sequences have the following property. For any two distinct points p and q of S, we can use the trees $U_{\ell-1}$ and U_ℓ to compute, in $O(\log \log n)$ time, an index i with $1 \leq i \leq \ell$ and two points x and y in S_i, such that

$$L_i/n^8 \leq |xy| < L_i, \tag{17.2}$$

$$\delta_G(p, q) \leq (1 + \epsilon/4) \cdot \delta_{G_i'}(x, y), \tag{17.3}$$

and

$$\delta_{G_i'}(x, y) \leq (1 + \epsilon/4) \cdot \delta_G(p, q). \tag{17.4}$$

17.3.2 Preprocessing the distance range hierarchy

For each i with $1 \leq i \leq \ell$ and $S_i \neq \emptyset$, we apply Theorem 17.2.9 to the graph $G_i' = (S_i, F_i')$, with ϵ replaced by $\epsilon/4$, t replaced by $(1 + \epsilon/4)t$, L replaced by L_i, and $C = n^8$. Hence, we preprocess G_i' in

$$O\left(\frac{t^d}{\epsilon^d \log(\mu/t)} |S_i| \log^2 n + \frac{\mu^d t^{3d}}{\epsilon^d \log(\mu/t)} |F_i'| \log n + \frac{\mu^{2d} t^{3d} \log \mu}{\epsilon^{2d} \log(\mu/t)} |F_i'|\right)$$

time into a data structure of size

$$O\left(\frac{\mu^d t^d}{\epsilon^d} \left(1 + \log_{\mu/t}(\mu n)\right) |S_i|\right),$$

such that the following holds. For any two points x and y in S_i with $L_i/n^8 \leq |xy| < L_i$, we can compute in

$$O\left(\log \log(\mu n) + \log(t/(\mu - t)) + \frac{\mu^{2d} t^{3d}}{\epsilon^{2d}}\right)$$

time a value Δ such that

$$\delta_{G_i'}(x, y) \leq \Delta \leq (1 + \epsilon/4) \cdot \delta_{G_i'}(x, y). \tag{17.5}$$

17.3.3 Answering approximate shortest path queries in G

We now present the algorithm that approximates the length of a shortest path in the t-spanner G, between any two points of S.

Algorithm APPROXSHORTESTPATH(p, q)

Comment: This algorithm takes as input two distinct points p and q of S. It returns a $(1 + \epsilon)$-approximation to the length of a shortest path between p and q in G.

Step 1: Use the distance range hierarchy of Section 17.3.1 to compute an index i and two vertices x and y in S_i for which (17.2), (17.3), and (17.4) hold.

Step 2: Use the data structure of Section 17.3.2 for G'_i to compute a value Δ for which (17.5) holds.

Step 3: Return the value $\Delta' := (1 + \epsilon/4)\Delta$.

To prove the correctness of this query algorithm, observe that

$$\delta_G(p, q) \leq (1 + \epsilon/4) \cdot \delta_{G'_i}(x, y) \leq (1 + \epsilon/4)\Delta = \Delta'$$

and

$$\Delta' = (1 + \epsilon/4)\Delta \leq (1 + \epsilon/4)^2 \cdot \delta_{G'_i}(x, y) \leq (1 + \epsilon/4)^3 \cdot \delta_G(p, q).$$

Since we assume that $0 < \epsilon \leq 1$, we have $(1 + \epsilon/4)^3 \leq 1 + \epsilon$ and, hence, Δ' is a $(1 + \epsilon)$-approximation to the shortest-path distance between p and q in the spanner G.

Observe that the only information that is needed to answer $(1 + \epsilon)$-approximate shortest path queries are the trees $U_{\ell-1}$ and U_ℓ, and the data structures of Section 17.3.2 for the graphs G'_i, $1 \leq i \leq \ell$. Therefore, we have proved the following result:

Theorem 17.3.1. *Let S be a set of n points in $\mathbb{R}^d$, let $t > 1$, $0 < \epsilon \leq 1$, and $\mu > (1 + \epsilon/4)t$ be real numbers such that*

$$n \geq \max\left((1 + \epsilon/16)^2 t, ((32 + 2\epsilon)t + 32)/\epsilon\right)$$

and let $G = (S, E)$ be a t-spanner for S. In

$$O\left(|E| \log \log n + \frac{t^{2d}}{\epsilon^{2d} \log(\mu/t)} n \log^2 n + \frac{\mu^d t^{5d}}{\epsilon^{2d}(t - 1)^d \log(\mu/t)} n \log n\right.$$

$$\left. + \frac{\mu^{2d} t^{5d} \log \mu}{\epsilon^{3d}(t - 1)^d \log(\mu/t)} n\right)$$

time, we can preprocess G into a data structure of size

$$O\left(\frac{\mu^d t^{2d}}{\epsilon^{2d}} \left(1 + \log_{\mu/t}(\mu n)\right) n\right),$$

such that for any two distinct points p and q in S, a $(1 + \epsilon)$-approximation to the shortest-path distance between p and q in G can be computed in time

$$O\left(\log \log(\mu n) + \log(t/(\mu - t)) + \frac{\mu^{2d} t^{3d}}{\epsilon^{2d}}\right).$$

Remark 17.3.2. Observe that the size of the data structure does not depend on the number of edges of G. If we are required to store this graph, then we have to add the size of its edge set E to the space bound.

The bounds in Theorem 17.3.1 depend on the value of μ. Let us assume that t and ϵ are constants and that we want a query time of $O(\log \log n)$. Then we obtain the best preprocessing time by taking $\mu = (\log \log n)^{1/(2d)}$.

Theorem 17.3.3. *Let S be a set of n points in $\mathbb{R}^d$, let $t > 1$ and $0 < \epsilon \leq 1$ be real constants, and let $G = (S, E)$ be a t-spanner for S. In*

$$O\left(|E| \log \log n + n \log^2 n / \log \log \log n\right)$$

time, we can preprocess G into a data structure of size

$$O\left(n \log n \sqrt{\log \log n} / \log \log \log n\right),$$

such that for any two points p and q in S, a $(1 + \epsilon)$-approximation to the shortest-path distance in G between p and q can be computed in $O(\log \log n)$ time.

The algorithms presented so far work in the algebraic computation-tree model. Using Section 15.3, Remark 16.3.10, and a nontrivial extension of Section 17.1, the results can be improved in the model that additionally uses indirect addressing. We state this result without proof and, for ease of notation, for the case when t and ϵ are constants.

Theorem 17.3.4. *Let S be a set of n points in $\mathbb{R}^d$, let $t > 1$ and $0 < \epsilon \leq 1$ be real constants, and let $G = (S, E)$ be a t-spanner for S. In the algebraic computation-tree model extended with indirect addressing, we can preprocess G in $O(|E| + n \log n)$ time into a data structure of size $O(n \log n)$, such that for any two points p and q in S, a $(1 + \epsilon)$-approximation to the shortest-path distance in G between p and q can be computed in $O(1)$ time.*

This leads us to the following two open problems.

Open problem: Improve the preprocessing time, space requirement, and/or query time in Theorems 17.3.1, 17.3.3, and 17.3.4.

Open problem: The results in this chapter give only an approximation to the length of a shortest path between two query points p and q in the t-spanner G, not the approximate shortest path itself. Let k be the minimum number of edges on any $(1 + \epsilon)$-approximate shortest path between p and q. Is there an algorithm that computes a $(1 + \epsilon)$-approximate shortest path with $O(k)$ edges in $O(f(n) + k)$ time, where $f(n) = o(n)$?

17.4 An application: Approximating the stretch factor of Euclidean graphs

Let S be a set of n points in $\mathbb{R}^d$, let $G = (S, E)$ be a connected Euclidean graph, and let t^* be the stretch factor of G. In Chapter 13, we have considered the problem of approximating the value of t^*. In Section 13.2, we presented algorithm FASTAPPROXSF, which does the following: First, it computes a well-separated pair decomposition $\{A_i, B_i\}$, $1 \leq i \leq m$, for S, where $m = O(n)$. Then, for each i with $1 \leq i \leq m$, the algorithm picks an arbitrary point a_i in A_i, and an arbitrary point b_i in B_i, and an approximation $L(a_i, b_i)$ to the shortest-path distance in G between a_i and b_i is computed. The algorithm returns the value t', which is defined to be $t' := \max_{1 \leq i \leq m} L(a_i, b_i) / |a_i b_i|$. The approximation factor of this algorithm, that is, the relation between t' and the exact stretch factor t^*, is given by Lemma 13.2.2. In Section 13.2.2, we applied algorithm FASTAPPROXSF to several classes of graphs. The most general result is given in Theorem 13.2.7.

Assume that we know, in advance, an upper bound t on the stretch factor t^* of the graph G. In other words, we know that G is a t-spanner for S, and want to approximate the smallest real number t^* for which G is a t^*-spanner. Then we can combine algorithm FASTAPPROXSF with the results in Section 17.3.3, and obtain a fast algorithm for approximating t^*. In particular, if t is a constant, then by combining Theorem 13.2.4 with Theorems 17.3.3 and 17.3.4, we obtain the following result. (For ease of notation, we state the result for the case only when ϵ is a constant.)

Theorem 17.4.1. *Let S be a set of n points in $\mathbb{R}^d$, let $G = (S, E)$ be a Euclidean graph, and let $t > 1$ and $\epsilon > 0$ be real constants, such that the stretch factor of G is less than or equal to t. We can compute a real number t', such that*

$$t'/(1 + \epsilon) \leq t^* \leq (1 + \epsilon)t',$$

where t^* is the exact stretch factor of G,

1. *in $O(|E| \log \log n + n \log^2 n / \log \log n)$ time in the algebraic computation-tree model, and*

2. *in $O(|E| + n \log n)$ time, if we add indirect addressing to this model.*

Exercises

17.1. We have used Lemma 17.1.1 in Section 17.2.2. Explain why this lemma can be applied.

17.2. Prove Theorem 17.2.9.

17.3. The result of Theorem 17.3.1 depends on the value of μ. Assume that t and ϵ are constants and we want a query time of $O(\log \log n)$. How should we choose μ if we want to minimize the space bound?

17.4. Let $t > 1$ and $\epsilon > 0$ be real constants and let $G = (S, E)$ be a t-spanner whose vertex set S consists of n points in $\mathbb{R}^d$. Consider queries of the following two types:

(1) Given a subset X of S, compute a $(1 + \epsilon)$-approximation to

$$\min\{\delta_G(p, q) : p, q \in X, p \neq q\}.$$

(2) Given subsets X and Y of S, compute a $(1 + \epsilon)$-approximation to

$$\min\{\delta_G(p, q) : p \in X, q \in Y\}.$$

Design a data structure that can be used to answer these types of queries in $O(|X|(q(n) + \log |X|))$ and $O((|X| + |Y|)(q(n) + \log(|X| + |Y|)))$ time, respectively, where $q(n)$ is the time needed to compute a $(1 + \epsilon)$-approximation to the shortest-path distance in G between any two query points.

Bibliographic notes

This chapter is based on Gudmundsson et al. [2002b] and Gudmundsson et al. [2004]. These authors present the improvement when indirect addressing is added to the algebraic computation-tree model. They also present a solution to Exercise 17.4.

18

Fault-Tolerant Spanners

> Don't find fault, find a remedy.
>
> —Henry Ford

This chapter considers the problem of incorporating *fault-tolerance* into spanner networks. Fault tolerance is intimately related to the graph-theoretic concept of *connectivity*. The vertex (resp. edge) connectivity of a graph is defined to be the minimum number of vertices (resp. edges) that need to be removed in order to disconnect it. Fault-tolerant networks are usually designed by making them highly connected.

In this chapter, we show how to construct geometric networks that are more than just resilient to vertex or edge faults; they also have good spanner properties. Thus, our goal is to construct graphs having the property that when a small number of vertices and/or edges fail, the remaining graph still contains "short" paths between each pair of points. In Section 18.1, we will give a formal definition of this notion of a fault-tolerant spanner. In Section 18.2, we prove that any fault-tolerant spanner that is resilient to vertex faults, is also resilient to edge faults. As a result, when analyzing the spanner properties of fault-tolerant networks, it suffices to consider vertex faults, thereby simplifying the analysis. In Section 18.3, we present a simple algorithm that converts any spanner G into a fault-tolerant spanner G'. If D is the maximum degree of G, and if k is the number of vertex faults that G' is resilient to, then G' has degree $O(D^{k+1})$ and weight $O(kD^k)$ times the weight of G. In the remaining sections, we show that several spanner constructions that have been presented in this book can be generalized to obtain fault-tolerant spanners. In Section 18.4, we show that the well-separated pair decomposition of Chapter 9 leads to a k-fault-tolerant spanner with $O(k^2n)$ edges. In Section 18.5, we show that the Θ-graph of Section 4.1 can be generalized to obtain a k-fault-tolerant spanner with $O(kn)$ edges. A generalization of the transformation of Section 4.2, which combines sink spanners with the Θ-graph, leads to a k-fault-tolerant spanner of degree $O(k^2)$. In Section 18.6, we show that the path-greedy algorithm of Section 1.4 can be generalized to obtain a k-fault-tolerant spanner of degree $O(k)$, whose weight is $O(k^2)$ times the weight of a minimum spanning tree of the points. Unfortunately, it is not clear whether there exists an efficient implementation of this algorithm. It turns out, however, that the gap-greedy algorithm of Chapter 7 can be generalized to an efficient algorithm that computes a k-fault-tolerant spanner of degree $O(k)$, whose weight is $O(k^2 \log n)$ times the weight of a minimum spanning tree of the points.

In this chapter, we consider undirected graphs.

18.1 Definition of a fault-tolerant spanner

Let S be a set of n points in $\mathbb{R}^d$, let $t > 1$ be a real number, let $k \geq 0$ be an integer, and let $G = (S, E)$ be an undirected Euclidean graph with vertex set S.

The notion of G being a t-spanner that is resilient to k or less vertex faults is easy to define:

Vertex fault-tolerant spanner: We require that for any subset S' of S having size at most k, the graph obtained from $G = (S, E)$ by removing all vertices of S', together with their incident edges, is a t-spanner for the points of $S \setminus S'$.

To define the notion of G being a t-spanner that is resilient to k or less edge faults, we have to be more careful. A first idea is to require that for any subset $E' \subseteq E$ of size at most k, the graph obtained from G by removing all edges of E', that is, the graph $(S, E \setminus E')$, is a t-spanner for the points of S. It is not difficult to see, however, that such a graph does not exist for all sets S of points: Let S be the set containing two distinct points p and q that are close together, and whose other points are far away from these two points. Since the graph G is a t-spanner for S, it contains the edge $\{p, q\}$. If this edge, however, is contained in E', then the length of any path in $(S, E \setminus E')$ between p and q is much larger than the Euclidean distance $|pq|$.

This example leads us to the second idea: We require that for any subset $E' \subseteq E$ of size at most k, any two points p and q are connected, in the graph $(S, E \setminus E')$, by a path whose length is at most t times the length of a k-th shortest path between p and q in the complete graph on S. Again, such a graph does not exist for all sets S: Let A be a "small" set of points that are close to the origin, and let B be a set of points that are far away from the origin, whose minimum distance is large, and that contains a point p on the negative x_1-axis, and a point q on the positive x_1-axis. Let $S := A \cup B$, and $k := \binom{|A|+2}{2}$. Observe that the graph G contains at most k edges connecting points in the set $A \cup \{p, q\}$. Moreover, the complete graph on S contains

$$\sum_{i=0}^{|A|} \binom{|A|}{i} i! \geq |A|!$$

paths between p and q, whose lengths are close to the Euclidean distance $|pq|$. Hence, if $k \leq |A|!$, then the length of a k-th shortest path between p and q in the complete graph on S is roughly equal to $|pq|$. Let E' be the set of all edges in G between points of $A \cup \{p, q\}$. Then $|E'| \leq k$. Moreover, the length of any path between p and q in the graph $(S, E \setminus E')$ is much larger than the length of a k-th shortest path between p and q in the complete graph on S.

This discussion leads us to the appropriate definition of a t-spanner that is resilient to k or less edge faults:

Edge fault-tolerant spanner: For any subset $E' \subseteq E$ of size at most k, and for any two points p and q of S, there is a path between p and q in the graph $(S, E \setminus E')$, whose length is at most t times the length of a shortest path between p and q in the graph obtained by deleting E' from the complete graph on S. Observe that this is the best possible path "under the circumstances."

We now define these notions formally. We need the following notation. For a given set S of points, let K_S denote the complete Euclidean graph on S. Let $G = (S, E)$ be an undirected Euclidean graph, let E' be a subset of E, and let S' be a subset of S.

1. $G \setminus S'$ denotes the graph with vertex set $S \setminus S'$, and edge set consisting of all edges of E that have both endpoints in $S \setminus S'$. $G \setminus S'$ is therefore the induced subgraph of G on the vertex set $S \setminus S'$.

2. $G \setminus E'$ denotes the graph $(S, E \setminus E')$.

3. $G \setminus (S', E')$ denotes the graph with vertex set $S \setminus S'$, and edge set the set of all edges of $E \setminus E'$ that have both endpoints in $S \setminus S'$.

Definition 18.1.1. Let S be a set of n points in $\mathbb{R}^d$, let $t > 1$ be a real number, let $k \geq 0$ be an integer, and let $G = (S, E)$ be an undirected Euclidean graph.

1. G is called a *k-vertex fault-tolerant t-spanner* for S, or (k, t)-*VFTS*, if for any subset S' of S with size at most k, the graph $G \setminus S'$ is a t-spanner for the points of $S \setminus S'$.

2. G is called a *k-edge fault-tolerant t-spanner* for S, or (k, t)-*EFTS*, if the following holds for any subset E' of E with size at most k:

   - For any two points p and q in S, the graph $G \setminus E'$ contains a path between p and q, whose length is at most t times the length of a shortest path between p and q in the graph $K_S \setminus E'$.

3. G is called a *k-fault-tolerant t-spanner* for S, or (k, t)-*FTS*, if the following holds for any subset S' of S, and any subset E' of E such that $|S'| + |E'| \leq k$:

   - For any two points p and q in $S \setminus S'$, the graph $G \setminus (S', E')$ contains a path between p and q, whose length is at most t times the length of a shortest path between p and q in the graph $K_S \setminus (S', E')$.

18.2 Vertex fault-tolerance is equivalent to fault-tolerance

We have defined spanners that are resilient to vertex faults, edge faults, or both. But how are these concepts related? It follows immediately from Definition 18.1.1 that any (k, t)-FTS is also a (k, t)-VFTS and a (k, t)-EFTS. In this section, we will prove that the converse is also true: Any (k, t)-VFTS is a (k, t)-FTS and, hence, also a (k, t)-EFTS. This result implies that in the rest of this chapter, we can concentrate on constructing spanners that are resilient to vertex faults.

More formally, let S be a set of n points in $\mathbb{R}^d$, let $k \geq 0$ be an integer, let $t > 1$ be a real number, and let $G = (S, E)$ be a (k, t)-VFTS for S. We will prove that G is a (k, t)-FTS for S.

Let S' be any subset of S of size k', and let E' be any subset of E of size k'', such that $k' + k'' \leq k$. We may assume without loss of generality that no edge of E' is incident to any point of S'; otherwise, we can decrease k'' accordingly.

Let p and q be two arbitrary points of $S \setminus S'$. To prove that G is a (k, t)-FTS, we have to show that the graph $G \setminus (S', E')$ contains a path between p and q, whose length is at most t times the length of a shortest path between p and q in the graph $K_S \setminus (S', E')$.

We may assume that $p \neq q$. The following lemma considers the case when $\{p, q\}$ is an edge of the graph $K_S \setminus (S', E')$.

Lemma 18.2.1. *Assume that $\{p, q\}$ is an edge of $K_S \setminus (S', E')$. Then the graph $G \setminus (S', E')$ contains a path between p and q, whose length is at most $t|pq|$.*

PROOF Let S'' be a subset of $S \setminus \{p, q\}$ that is obtained by taking for each edge of E', an arbitrary endpoint that is not equal to p or q. Since $\{p, q\}$ is not an edge of E', it is possible to choose such a subset S''. (For example, if $\{a, b\}$ and $\{b, c\}$ are edges of E', then S'' can contain the endpoints a and b; or a and c; or b and c; or only b.) Observe that this set S'' contains at most k'' points.

Let G' be the graph $G \setminus (S' \cup S'')$. Observe that

$$|S' \cup S''| = |S'| + |S''| \leq k' + k'' \leq k.$$

Since the graph G is a (k, t)-VFTS for S, it follows from Definition 18.1.1 that G' is a t-spanner for the set $S \setminus (S' \cup S'')$. By our construction, p and q are vertices of G'. Therefore, G' contains a path P between p and q, whose length is at most $t|pq|$. This path neither contains any vertices of S' nor any edges of E'. Hence, P is a path in the graph $G \setminus (S', E')$. ∎

Now we can consider the general case. That is, we are ready to show that the graph $G \setminus (S', E')$ contains a path between p and q, whose length is at most t times the length of a shortest path between p and q in the graph $K_S \setminus (S', E')$.

Let P be a shortest path between p and q in the graph $K_S \setminus (S', E')$. Write the vertices on this path as $p = p_0, p_1, p_2, \ldots, p_\ell = q$. For each i with $0 \leq i < \ell$, $\{p_i, p_{i+1}\}$ is an edge of $K_S \setminus (S', E')$. By Lemma 18.2.1, the graph $G \setminus (S', E')$ contains a path Q_i between p_i and p_{i+1}, whose length is at most $t|p_i p_{i+1}|$. Let Q be the concatenation of $Q_0, Q_1, \ldots, Q_{\ell-1}$. Then, Q is a path in $G \setminus (S', E')$ between p and q, whose length is bounded from above by

$$\sum_{i=0}^{\ell-1} |Q_i| \leq \sum_{i=0}^{\ell-1} t|p_i p_{i+1}| = t|P|.$$

We have thus proved the following theorem:

Theorem 18.2.2. *Let S be a set of n points in $\mathbb{R}^d$, let $k \geq 0$ be an integer, let $t > 1$ be a real number, and let $G = (S, E)$ be an undirected Euclidean graph. Then G is a (k, t)-VFTS for S if and only if G is a (k, t)-FTS for S.*

18.3 A simple transformation

In order to address the issue of constructing fault-tolerant spanners, we give a simple construction that transforms any spanner into a k-fault-tolerant spanner.

Let S be a set of n points in $\mathbb{R}^d$, let $t > 1$ be a real number, and let $k \geq 0$ be an integer. Let G be an arbitrary t-spanner for S. The transformed graph G' is obtained by connecting each point p of S to all points that are reachable in G, from p, by a path having at most $k + 1$ edges. Algorithm SIMPLEFTS describes precisely how this is achieved.

Algorithm SIMPLEFTS(G, k)

Comment: This algorithm takes as input a t-spanner $G = (S, E)$ and an integer $k \geq 0$.
It returns a (k, t)-FTS G'.

Step 1: For every point $p \in S$,

- compute the set $N(p)$, consisting of all points of $S \setminus \{p\}$ that are connected to p by a path in G having at most $k + 1$ edges, and
- compute the set E_p of edges, defined as

$$E_p := \{\{p, q\} : q \in N(p)\}.$$

Step 2: Return the transformed graph $G' = (S, E')$, where

$$E' := \bigcup_{p \in S} E_p.$$

Observe that G is a subgraph of G'. Intuitively, it is clear that G' is a k-fault-tolerant t-spanner for S. In the following lemma, we give a formal proof of this fact.

Lemma 18.3.1. *The graph G' that is returned by algorithm* SIMPLEFTS(G, k) *is a (k, t)-FTS for S.*

PROOF By Theorem 18.2.2, it suffices to show that G' is a (k, t)-VFTS for S. Let S' be any subset of S with size at most k, and let p and q be two points of $S \setminus S'$. We have to show that the graph $G' \setminus S'$ contains a path between p and q, whose length is at most $t|pq|$. We may assume that $p \neq q$.

Since G is a t-spanner for S, this graph contains a path P between p and q, whose length is at most $t|pq|$. Write the vertices of this path P as

$$p = q_0, q_1, q_2, \ldots, q_\ell = q.$$

We will construct a path Q between p and q in the graph $G' \setminus S'$, which is a subpath of P. Then, the triangle inequality implies that the length of Q is at most that of P. This will prove the lemma.

First assume that $\ell \leq k + 1$. Then, $q \in N(p)$ and, hence, $\{p, q\}$ is an edge of G'. Since p and q are both contained in $S \setminus S'$, $\{p, q\}$ is an edge of $G' \setminus S'$, and we can take for Q the path consisting of this single edge.

Assume from now on that $k + 2 \leq \ell$. The following algorithm constructs the path $Q = (p_0, p_1, \ldots)$ incrementally.

Step 1: Define $p_0 := p$, $i := 0$, and $j := 0$. Go to Step 2.

Step 2: At this moment, $Q = (p_0, p_1, \ldots, p_i)$ is a path in $G' \setminus S'$, j is the index such that $p_i = q_j$, and $j + k + 2 \leq \ell$. In particular, $p_i \neq q$ and $q_j \in S \setminus S'$.
If there is an index m with $j + 1 \leq m \leq j + k + 1$, such that

1. $m + k + 2 \leq \ell$, and
2. q_m is a vertex of $S \setminus S'$,

then go to Step 3. Otherwise, go to Step 4.

Step 3: Since q_j and q_m are both vertices of $S \setminus S'$, and $q_m \in N(q_j)$, we know that $\{q_j, q_m\}$ is an edge of $G' \setminus S'$. Therefore, we define $p_{i+1} := q_m$, set $i := i + 1$ and $j := m$, and go to Step 2.

Step 4: We know that $p_i = q_j$ and $j + k + 2 \leq \ell$. Moreover, for all m with $j + 1 \leq m \leq j + k + 1$, such that q_m is a vertex of $S \setminus S'$, we have $m + k + 1 \geq \ell$.

We claim that there is an index m with $j + 1 \leq m \leq j + k + 1$, such that $\{q_j, q_m\}$ and $\{q_m, q\}$ are both edges of $G' \setminus S'$.

Assume this claim is true. Then we define $p_{i+1} := q_m$ and $p_{i+2} := q$, and the construction of the path Q between p and q is complete.

It remains to prove the claim. Since S' has size at most k, there is an index m with $j + 1 \leq m \leq j + k + 1$, such that $q_m \in S \setminus S'$. Hence, $q_m \in N(q_j)$ and $\{q_j, q_m\}$ is an edge of $G' \setminus S'$. Our assumption implies that $m + k + 1 \geq \ell$. Therefore, $q = q_\ell \in N(q_m)$ and $\{q_m, q\}$ is an edge of G'. Since q_m and q are both contained in $S \setminus S'$, edge $\{q_m, q\}$ is contained in $G' \setminus S'$. This proves the claim.

To complete the proof of the lemma, we have to show that the algorithm terminates. Each time Step 3 is executed, the path Q is extended by a new point. Therefore, at some moment, Step 4 must be executed. At that moment, Q reaches q, and the algorithm terminates. ∎

The following lemma gives some additional properties of the graph G', in case we start with a t-spanner G of bounded degree.

Lemma 18.3.2. *Let D be the maximum degree of any vertex of the t-spanner G, and let $G' = (S, E')$ be the graph that is returned by algorithm SIMPLEFTS(G, k).*

1. *In the transformed graph G', the degree of each point of S is at most $2D^{k+1}$.*
2. *Given the t-spanner G, the transformed graph G' can be computed in $O(D^{k+1}n)$ time.*

PROOF Let p be any point of S. Since G is connected, $D \geq 2$. Thus, we have

$$|N(p)| \leq D + D^2 + D^3 + \cdots + D^{k+1} \leq 2D^{k+1}.$$

For any point q, we have $\{p, q\} \in E'$ if and only if $q \in N(p)$ or $p \in N(q)$. Since $q \in N(p)$ if and only if $p \in N(q)$, it follows that the degree, in G', of point p is bounded from above by $2D^{k+1}$.

The transformed graph G' can easily be constructed in $O(D^{k+1}n)$ time, by computing $N(p)$ for each point p. ∎

If we apply Lemmas 18.3.1 and 18.3.2 to the t-spanner of Theorem 10.1.3, then we get the following result:

Theorem 18.3.3. *Let S be a set of n points in $\mathbb{R}^d$, let $k \geq 0$ be an integer, and let $t > 1$ be a real number. In*

$$O\left(\frac{\log(1/(t-1))}{(t-1)^d} n \log n + \frac{1}{(t-1)^{(2d-1)(k+1)}} n\right)$$

time, a (k, t)-FTS for S can be computed, in which each point has degree $O(1/(t-1)^{(2d-1)(k+1)})$.

The next lemma gives an upper bound on the weight of the transformed graph G', for the case when the t-spanner G has bounded degree.

Lemma 18.3.4. *Let D be the maximum degree of any vertex of the t-spanner G, and let $G' = (S, E')$ be the graph that is returned by algorithm* SIMPLEFTS(G, k). *The weight of G' is bounded from above by $8(k + 1)D^k$ times the weight of G.*

PROOF   We use the following charging scheme to prove an upper bound on the total edge length of the graph G'. Let $\{p, q\}$ be any edge of the transformed graph G', and consider any path P in the original graph G between p and q, containing at most $k + 1$ edges. (Observe that such a path exists.) We write the vertices of P as

$$p_0 = p, p_1, p_2, \ldots, p_\ell = q.$$

Hence, $\ell \leq k + 1$. We charge the length $|pq|$ of edge $\{p, q\}$ to the edges of the path P, in such a way that no edge $\{p_i, p_{i+1}\}$, $0 \leq i < \ell$, is charged by more than $|p_i p_{i+1}|$. Since by the triangle inequality, the Euclidean distance $|pq|$ is at most the total length of P, this is possible.

For each edge e of G, let n_e be the number of times this edge is charged. Then the total edge length of G' is at most $\sum_{e \in G} n_e |e|$, where $|e|$ denotes the length of edge e. We will show that $n_e \leq 8(k + 1)D^k$. This will imply that the total edge length of G' is at most $8(k + 1)D^k \sum_{e \in G} |e|$, which is equal to $8(k + 1)D^k$ times the total edge length of G. Hence, this will prove the lemma.

Let e be any edge of G, and let it have endpoints a and b. Every time e is charged, there are two points p and q, such that there is a path between p and q in G, containing at most $k + 1$ edges, e being one of them. Assume without loss of generality that, on this path, a is between p and b. Let i be the number of edges on the subpath between p and a. Then $0 \leq i \leq k$. If j denotes the number of edges on the subpath between b and q, then $0 \leq j \leq k - i$.

If we fix i and j, then the number of possibilities for p is at most

$$1 + D + D^2 + D^3 + \cdots + D^i \leq 2D^i,$$

where the inequality follows from the fact that $D \geq 2$. Similarly, the number of possibilities for q is at most

$$1 + D + D^2 + D^3 + \cdots + D^j \leq 2D^j.$$

It follows that

$$n_e \leq \sum_{i=0}^{k} 2D^i \sum_{j=0}^{k-i} 2D^j$$

$$= 4 \sum_{i=0}^{k} D^i \left(1 + D + D^2 + \cdots + D^{k-i}\right)$$

$$\leq 8 \sum_{i=0}^{k} D^i D^{k-i}$$

$$= 8(k + 1)D^k.$$

This completes the proof.   ∎

If we apply Lemmas 18.3.1, 18.3.2, and 18.3.4 to the t-spanner of Theorem 15.2.17, then we obtain an algorithm that constructs, in the algebraic computation-tree model, a (k, t)-FTS for S that has nontrivial bounds on its degree and weight. By using Theorem 15.3.20 (instead of Theorem 15.2.17), we obtain an algorithm that works in the algebraic computation-tree model in which additionally any indirect addressing operation takes unit time. For simplicity, we state only the latter result in the following theorem:

Theorem 18.3.5. *Let S be a set of n points in $\mathbb{R}^d$, let $k \geq 0$ be an integer, and let $t > 1$ be a real number. In*

$$O\left(\frac{1}{(t-1)^{4d-1}}\, n \log n + \frac{1}{(t-1)^{(2d-1)(k+1)}}\, n\right)$$

time, a (k, t)-FTS for S can be computed, in which each point has degree

$$O\left(\frac{1}{(t-1)^{(2d-1)(k+1)}}\right),$$

and whose weight is

$$O\left(\frac{k}{(t-1)^{(2d-1)k+2d}} \cdot wt(MST(S))\right),$$

where $MST(S)$ denotes a minimum spanning tree of S.

18.4 Fault-tolerant spanners based on well-separated pairs

The number of edges in the k-fault-tolerant t-spanners of Theorems 18.3.3 and 18.3.5 is exponential in k. In this section, we give an algorithm for constructing such spanners that use only a polynomial number of edges. The construction uses the well-separated pair decomposition (WSPD) of Chapter 9.

Let S be a set of n points in $\mathbb{R}^d$, let $t > 1$ be a real number, and let $k \geq 0$ be an integer. Consider an arbitrary WSPD

$$\{A_1, B_1\}, \{A_2, B_2\}, \ldots, \{A_m, B_m\}$$

for S, with separation ratio $s = 4(t+1)/(t-1)$. In Section 9.2, we saw that we obtain a t-spanner for S by adding an edge between an arbitrary point of A_i and an arbitrary point of B_i, for each well-separated pair $\{A_i, B_i\}$. We generalize this spanner to obtain a k-fault-tolerant t-spanner by adding more than one edge (in fact, we add $O(k^2)$ edges) for each well-separated pair.

18.4.1 Definition of the graph G

We define a graph G with vertex set S. In Section 18.4.2, we will show that G is a k-fault-tolerant t-spanner for S.

For each i with $1 \leq i \leq m$, we define a set E_i of edges. The edge set E of the graph G is then defined as $E := \bigcup_{i=1}^{m} E_i$.

Let i be any index such that $1 \leq i \leq m$, and consider the well-separated pair $\{A_i, B_i\}$. We may assume without loss of generality that $|A_i| \geq |B_i|$. To define the edge set E_i, we distinguish three cases. The most general case is dealt with in Case 1, which corresponds to the case when both A_i and B_i have at least $k + 1$ points.

Case 1: $|B_i| \geq k + 1$.

Choose $k + 1$ points a_j, $1 \leq j \leq k + 1$, in A_i, and $k + 1$ points b_j, $1 \leq j \leq k + 1$, in B_i. Observe that these points need to be pairwise distinct. Let E_i be the set of $k + 1$ edges, defined as

$$E_i := \{\{a_j, b_j\} : 1 \leq j \leq k + 1\}.$$

Case 2: $|B_i| \leq k$ and $|A_i| \geq k + 1$.

Choose $k + 1$ pairwise distinct points a_j, $1 \leq j \leq k+1$, in A_i. Let $B_i = \{b_1, b_2, \ldots, b_x\}$, where $x := |B_i| \leq k$. The edge set E_i is defined as

$$E_i := \{\{a_j, b_\ell\} : 1 \leq j \leq k + 1, 1 \leq \ell \leq x\}.$$

Observe that $|E_i| = x(k + 1) \leq k(k + 1)$.

Case 3: $|A_i| \leq k$.

In this case, the set E_i is defined as the edge set of the complete bipartite graph on the points of $A_i \cup B_i$, that is,

$$E_i := \{\{a, b\} : a \in A_i, b \in B_i\}.$$

Hence, we have $|E_i| = |A_i| \cdot |B_i| \leq k^2$.

This concludes the definition of our graph G. Observe that E, the edge set of G, has size $O(kn + k^2 m) = O(k^2 m)$.

18.4.2 The graph G is a (k, t)-FTS

We now prove that our graph G is indeed a k-fault-tolerant t-spanner for the set S. By Theorem 18.2.2, it suffices to show that G is a (k, t)-VFTS. To prove this, let S' be an arbitrary subset of S of size at most k. We have to show that for any two points p and q of $S \setminus S'$, the graph $G \setminus S'$ contains a path between p and q, whose length is at most $t|pq|$.

We will prove this by induction on the rank of the distance $|pq|$ in the sorted sequence of distances in $S \setminus S'$. To start the induction, the claim clearly holds if $p = q$. Assume from now on that p and q are two distinct points of $S \setminus S'$. Moreover, assume that for any two points a and b in $S \setminus S'$, with $|ab| < |pq|$, the graph $G \setminus S'$ contains a path between a and b, whose length is at most $t|ab|$.

Let i be the index such that (i) $p \in A_i$ and $q \in B_i$, or (ii) $p \in B_i$ and $q \in A_i$. We assume without loss of generality that (i) holds, and that $|A_i| \geq |B_i|$. We distinguish three cases.

Case 1: $|B_i| \geq k + 1$.

Consider the $k + 1$ points a_j, $1 \leq j \leq k + 1$, in A_i, and the $k + 1$ points b_j, $1 \leq j \leq k + 1$, in B_i, that were chosen in the construction of G.

Lemma 18.4.1. *There is an index j with $1 \leq j \leq k + 1$, such that the graph $G \setminus S'$ contains*

1. *the edge $\{a_j, b_j\}$;*
2. *a path P between p and a_j, whose length is at most $t|pa_j|$; and*
3. *a path Q between q and b_j, whose length is at most $t|b_j q|$.*

PROOF   Since S' has size at most k, there is an index j with $1 \leq j \leq k + 1$, such that a_j and b_j are both contained in $S \setminus S'$. Let j be an arbitrary index having this property. Then $\{a_j, b_j\}$ is an edge of $G \setminus S'$.

By Lemma 9.1.2, we have $|pa_j| \leq (2/s)|pq|$, which is less than $|pq|$, because $s > 2$. Therefore, by the induction hypothesis, the graph $G \setminus S'$ contains a path P between p and a_j, whose length is at most $t|pa_j|$. By a symmetric argument, the graph $G \setminus S'$ contains a path Q between q and b_j, whose length is at most $t|b_j q|$.   ■

We can now complete the proof for Case 1. Consider the index j, and the paths P and Q of Lemma 18.4.1. Let R be the path in $G \setminus S'$ between p and q, that is obtained by concatenating path P, edge $\{a_j, b_j\}$, and path Q. By the properties of well-separated pairs proved in Chapter 9, we know that $|pa_j|$ and $|b_j q|$ are much smaller than $|a_i b_j|$. Then it follows in exactly the same way as in Section 9.2 that the length of this path R is at most $t|pq|$.

Case 2: $|B_i| \leq k$ and $|A_i| \geq k + 1$.

Consider the $k + 1$ points a_j, $1 \leq j \leq k + 1$, in A_i that were chosen in the construction of G. Let b_j, $1 \leq j \leq x := |B_i|$, be the points of B_i. Observe that q is one of the b_j's. Also, in G, point q is connected by an edge to each point a_j, $1 \leq j \leq k + 1$.

Let j be an index such that a_j is a vertex of $G \setminus S'$. Then $\{a_j, q\}$ is an edge of $G \setminus S'$. It follows in the same way as in the proof of Lemma 18.4.1 that $G \setminus S'$ contains a path P between p and a_j, whose length is at most $t|pa_j|$. Then, just as in Case 1, it follows that the path consisting of P, followed by edge $\{a_j, q\}$, is a path in the graph $G \setminus S'$ between p and q, whose length is at most $t|pq|$.

Case 3: $|A_i| \leq k$.

In this case, G contains the complete bipartite graph on $A_i \cup B_i$ as a subgraph. Since p and q are both points of $S \setminus S'$, we know that $\{p, q\}$ is an edge of $G \setminus S'$. That is, $G \setminus S'$ contains a path between p and q, having length $|pq|$, which is at most $t|pq|$.

We have thus proved the following result:

Theorem 18.4.2. *Let S be a set of n points in $\mathbb{R}^d$, let $k \geq 0$ be an integer, and let $t > 1$ be a real number. Let*

$$\{A_1, B_1\}, \{A_2, B_2\}, \ldots, \{A_m, B_m\}$$

be an arbitrary WSPD for S, with separation ratio $s = 4(t + 1)/(t - 1)$. The graph $G = (S, E)$ defined in Section 18.4.1 is a (k, t)-FTS for S. This graph contains $O(k^2 m)$ edges.

18.4.3 Constructing the graph G

The algorithm for constructing the graph G follows immediately from the previous results. Given the set S, the integer $k \geq 0$, and the real number $t > 1$, we use the algorithm given in Chapter 9 (see Theorem 9.4.6), to compute a WSPD for S of size $m = O(n)$, in $O(n \log n)$ time. For each pair $\{A_i, B_i\}$ in this WSPD, we construct the corresponding edge set E_i. If Case 1 applies, then we construct E_i in $O(k)$ time. If Case 2 or 3 applies, then we need $O(k^2)$ time to construct E_i.

Theorem 18.4.3. *Let S be a set of n points in $\mathbb{R}^d$, let $k \geq 0$ be an integer, and let $t > 1$ be a real number. In $O(n \log n + k^2 n/(t - 1)^d)$ time, a (k, t)-FTS for S can be computed that contains $O(k^2 n/(t - 1)^d)$ edges.*

PROOF Let $s = 4(t + 1)/(t - 1)$. It follows from Theorem 9.4.6 and the discussion above that the graph G can be constructed in $O(n \log n + k^2 n/(t - 1)^d)$ time and contains $O(k^2 n/(t - 1)^d)$ edges. By Theorem 18.4.2, G is a (k, t)-FTS for S. ∎

By using the result in Exercise 9.16, Theorem 18.4.3 can be improved for values of k that are larger than $\log n$:

Theorem 18.4.4. *Let S be a set of n points in $\mathbb{R}^d$, let $k \geq 0$ be an integer, and let $t > 1$ be a real number. In $O((kn \log n)/(t - 1)^d)$ time, a (k, t)-FTS for S can be computed that contains $O((kn \log n)/(t - 1)^d)$ edges.*

The proof of this theorem is left as an exercise; see Exercise 18.1.

18.5 Fault-tolerant spanners with $O(kn)$ edges

Theorems 18.4.3 and 18.4.4 give algorithms for constructing k-fault-tolerant spanners with $O(k^2n)$ and $O(kn \log n)$ edges, respectively. Can we do better? The answer is "yes": By generalizing the Θ-graph of Section 4.1, we obtain the following result:

Theorem 18.5.1. *Let S be a set of n points in $\mathbb{R}^d$, let $k \geq 0$ be an integer, and let $t > 1$ be a real number. In*

$$O\left(\frac{1}{(t-1)^{d-1}} \left(n \log^{d-1} n \log k + kn \log \log n\right)\right)$$

time, a (k, t)-FTS for S can be computed that contains $O(kn/(t - 1)^{d-1})$ edges.

We claim that this result is optimal in terms of the number of edges. Indeed, let G be an arbitrary (k, t)-FTS for a set S of n points in $\mathbb{R}^d$. If we remove any k edges from G, then the resulting graph is connected. Therefore, the degree of each vertex in G must be at least $k + 1$ and, thus, G must have at least $(k + 1)n/2 = \Omega(kn)$ edges.

Open problem: Is there an algorithm that constructs a k-fault-tolerant t-spanner with $O(kn)$ edges in $O(n \log n + kn)$ time?

In Sections 4.2 and 5.5.3, we showed that a spanner of bounded degree can be obtained, by combining sink spanners with a spanner whose edges can be directed such that each vertex has bounded outdegree. This construction can be generalized to obtain k-fault-tolerant spanners. If we apply this generalized construction to the (k, t)-FTS of Theorem 18.5.1, then we obtain a (k, t)-FTS, in which the degree of each vertex is $O(k^2)$. In the next section, we will show how to obtain a (k, t)-FTS of degree $O(k)$.

18.6 Fault-tolerant spanners of low degree and low weight

As we have seen in Section 18.5, every k-fault-tolerant spanner has degree at least $k + 1$. What can we say about the weight of such spanners? Let k be an even integer, and consider a set A of $1 + k/2$ points that are all close to the origin. Let B be a set of $n - 1 - k/2$ points that are all close together, but at distance roughly one from the origin. Let G be an arbitrary (k, t)-FTS for the set $S := A \cup B$, where t is a constant close to one. Since the degree of each vertex of G is at least $k + 1$, every point of A has to be connected by an edge to at least $1 + k/2$ points of B. Therefore, G contains $\Omega(k^2)$ edges, all having length roughly equal to 1. On the other hand, the weight of a minimum spanning tree of S is roughly equal to 1.

Thus, there exist point sets S, such that the weight of every (k, t)-FTS for S is $\Omega(k^2) \cdot wt(MST(S))$, where $MST(S)$ denotes a minimum spanning tree of S. In this section, we show how to obtain, for any point set S, a (k, t)-FTS of weight $O(k^2) \cdot wt(MST(S))$, in which every vertex has degree $O(k)$.

18.6.1 A generalization of the path-greedy algorithm

The algorithm below is a generalization of algorithm PATHGREEDY of Section 1.4. This algorithm uses the concept of vertex-disjoint paths: For any two distinct vertices p and q of a graph, two paths between p and q are said to be *vertex-disjoint*, if p and q are the only common vertices of these paths.

Algorithm FTPATHGREEDY(S, k, t)

Comment: This algorithm takes as input a set S of n points in $\mathbb{R}^d$, an integer $k \geq 0$, and a real number $t > 1$. It returns a (k, t)-FTS for S.

> sort the $\binom{n}{2}$ pairs of distinct points in nondecreasing order of their
> distances (break ties arbitrarily), and store them in list L;
> $E := \emptyset$;
> $G := (S, E)$;
> **for each** $\{p, q\} \in L$ (∗ consider pairs in sorted order ∗)
> **do if** G does not contain $k + 1$ vertex-disjoint t-spanner paths
>   between p and q
>   **then** $E := E \cup \{\{p, q\}\}$;
> $G := (S, E)$
>   **endif**
> **endfor**;
> output the graph G

Observe that for $k = 0$, algorithm FTPATHGREEDY(S, k, t) is identical to algorithm PATHGREEDY(S, t). The proof of the following lemma is left as an exercise, see Exercise 18.3.

Lemma 18.6.1. *The output of algorithm* FTPATHGREEDY(S, k, t) *is a* (k, t)-*FTS for* S.

In Sections 18.6.2 and 18.6.3, we will analyze the degree and the weight of the fault-tolerant path-greedy spanner.

We fix a set S of n points in $\mathbb{R}^d$, an integer $k \geq 0$, and a real number $t > 1$. Let $G = (S, E)$ be the (k, t)-FTS that is returned by algorithm FTPATHGREEDY(S, k, t). For our analysis, we need a real number θ, such that $0 < \theta < \pi/4$ and $t \geq 1/(\cos \theta - \sin \theta)$. Moreover, our analysis uses (a variant of) the following theorem from graph theory:

Theorem 18.6.2 (Menger). *Let H be an undirected graph with vertex set V, let $k \geq 0$ be an integer, and let u and v be two distinct vertices of H. Then, H contains $k + 1$ vertex-disjoint paths between u and v, if and only if for every subset V' of $V \setminus \{u, v\}$ with $|V'| \leq k$, u and v are connected by a path in the graph $H \setminus V'$.*

18.6.2 Bounding the degree of the fault-tolerant path-greedy spanner

In this section, we will prove that the degree of every vertex of G is $O(k)$. We start with the following lemma, which follows from Lemma 4.1.4.

Lemma 18.6.3. *Let p, q, and r be three pairwise distinct points of S, such that $\{p, r\}$ is an edge of G, $|pr| \leq |pq|$ and* angle$(pq, pr) \leq \theta$. *Let Q be an arbitrary t-spanner path in G between r and q, and let P be the path obtained by concatenating $\{p, r\}$ and Q. Then, Q is a t-spanner path in G between p and q.*

The next lemma is the basis for our claim that the graph G has degree $O(k)$. The lemma can be proved using Lemma 18.6.3.

Lemma 18.6.4. *Let p be a point of S, and let C be a cone with apex p and angular diameter θ. Then, the graph G contains at most $k + 1$ edges $\{p, q\}$ for which $q \in C$.*

By combining Lemma 18.6.4 with Theorem 5.3.3, we obtain the following result:

Lemma 18.6.5. *The degree of every vertex of G is $O(k/(t - 1)^{d-1})$.*

18.6.3 Bounding the weight of the fault-tolerant path-greedy spanner

In this section, we prove that the edge set E of the (k, t)-FTS $G = (S, E)$ can be partitioned into $O(k^2)$ subsets, each of which satisfies the t-leapfrog property of Chapter 14; see Definition 14.1.1. (In fact, each subset satisfies the version of the leapfrog property given in Exercise 14.12.) Thus, the Leapfrog Theorem (Theorem 14.4.1) implies that the weight of G is $O(k^2)$ times the weight of a minimum spanning tree of S.

Throughout this section, we assume for simplicity that the Euclidean distances between all $\binom{n}{2}$ pairs of points in S are distinct.

Lemma 18.6.6. *Let $e = \{p, q\}$ be an edge in E. There exists a subset S_e of $S \setminus \{p, q\}$, such that $|S_e| \leq k$, and for which the following property holds: Let G_e be the graph consisting of all edges of $G \setminus S_e$ having length less than $|pq|$. Then, the length of every path in G_e between p and q is larger than $t|pq|$.*

PROOF Since the edge e is included in the edge set E, it follows from algorithm FTPATHGREEDY that G contains at most k vertex-disjoint t-spanner paths between p and q, all of whose edges have length less than $|pq|$. The claim follows from a variant of Theorem 18.6.2. ∎

We start by partitioning the edge set E into subsets, such that any two edges in the same subset make an angle of at most θ. By Theorem 5.3.3, such a partition exists, consisting of $O(1/\theta^{d-1})$ subsets. Below, every subset E' in this partition will be further subdivided.

We fix a subset E' in the partition of E. For any edge e in E, we define

$$F'_e := \{f \in E' : |f| < |e| \text{ and } f \cap S_e \neq \emptyset\},$$

where S_e is the set in Lemma 18.6.6. In words, F'_e is the set of all edges in E' that are shorter than $|e|$, and that are incident to at least one vertex of S_e. Observe that, by Lemma 18.6.4, every point of S_e is incident to at most $k + 1$ edges in E'. Combining this with Lemma 18.6.6, it follows that

$$|F'_e| \leq (k + 1)|S_e| \leq k(k + 1).$$

We use the following procedure to partition the edge set E' into subsets $E'_0, E'_1, \ldots, E'_{k(k+1)}$:

1. Initially, $E'_i = \emptyset$ for all i with $0 \le i \le k(k+1)$.

2. Consider all edges of E', in increasing order of their lengths. If e is the current edge, then e is added to a set E'_i that does not contain any element of F'_e.

Observe that this partition exists, because $|F'_e| \le k(k+1)$.

Lemma 18.6.7. *Each of the sets $E'_0, E'_1, \ldots, E'_{k(k+1)}$ satisfies the version of the t-leapfrog property given in Exercise 14.12.*

PROOF We fix one of the subsets in the partition of E'. For ease of notation, we assume that this subset is E'_0. Let $\ell \ge 2$ and let $\{p_1, q_1\}, \{p_2, q_2\}, \ldots, \{p_\ell, q_\ell\}$ be an arbitrary sequence of pairwise distinct edges of E'_0, such that $|p_1 q_1| > |p_i q_i|$ for all i with $2 \le i \le \ell$. We have to show that

$$t|p_1 q_1| < \sum_{i=2}^{\ell} |p_i q_i| + t \left(|p_1 p_2| + \sum_{i=2}^{\ell-1} |q_i p_{i+1}| + |q_\ell q_1| \right). \tag{18.1}$$

If $|p_1 q_1| < |p_1 p_2|$, $|p_1 q_1| < |q_\ell q_1|$, or $|p_1 q_1| < |q_i p_{i+1}|$ for some i with $2 \le i \le \ell - 1$, then the inequality in (18.1) obviously holds. Hence, we may assume that $|p_1 q_1| > |p_1 p_2|$, $|p_1 q_1| > |q_\ell q_1|$, and $|p_1 q_1| > |q_i p_{i+1}|$ for all i with $2 \le i \le \ell - 1$.

Denote the edge $\{p_1, q_1\}$ by e, and consider the subset S_e of $S \setminus \{p_1, q_1\}$ and the graph G_e, as given in Lemma 18.6.6. Recall that the length of every path in G_e between p_1 and q_1 is larger than $t|p_1 q_1|$. We will construct a path Q in G_e between p_1 and q_1, such that

$$|Q| \le \sum_{i=2}^{\ell} |p_i q_i| + t \left(|p_1 p_2| + \sum_{i=2}^{\ell-1} |q_i p_{i+1}| + |q_\ell q_1| \right), \tag{18.2}$$

where $|Q|$ denotes the length of Q. From this, the inequality in (18.1) will follow.

The construction of the path Q will use the fact that

$$S_e \cap \{p_1, p_2, \ldots, p_\ell, q_1, q_2, \ldots, q_\ell\} = \emptyset.$$

The proof of this claim is by contradiction: If $p_i \in S_e$, for some i with $2 \le i \le \ell$, then $\{p_i, q_i\} \cap S_e \ne \emptyset$. Since $|p_i q_i| < |p_1 q_1| = |e|$, it follows that $\{p_i, q_i\}$ is contained in the set F'_e. But then, since $\{p_i, q_i\} \in E'_0$, our procedure for partitioning E' did not add the edge e to the set E'_0, which is a contradiction. Thus, none of the points p_i, $2 \le i \le \ell$, are contained in S_e. Since $S_e \subseteq S \setminus \{p_1, q_1\}$, it is clear that p_1 is not contained in S_e. A similar argument shows that none of the points q_i, $1 \le i \le \ell$, are contained in S_e. Let $\{x, y\}$ be an arbitrary pair in the set

$$\{\{p_1, p_2\}, \{q_2, p_3\}, \{q_3, p_4\}, \ldots, \{q_{\ell-1}, p_\ell\}, \{q_\ell, q_1\}\}.$$

Recall that $|xy| < |p_1 q_1| = |e|$. It follows from algorithm FTPATHGREEDY that either $\{x, y\}$ is an edge in E or the graph G contains $k+1$ vertex-disjoint t-spanner paths between x and y, all of whose edges have length less than $|xy| < |e|$. Thus, since $x \notin S_e$, $y \notin S_e$, and $|S_e| \le k$, the graph G_e contains a t-spanner path Q_{xy} between x and y.

Let Q be the concatenation of path $Q_{p_1 p_2}$, edge $\{p_2, q_2\}$, path $Q_{q_2 p_3}$, edge $\{p_3, q_3\}$, \ldots, path $Q_{q_{\ell-1} p_\ell}$, edge $\{p_\ell, q_\ell\}$, and path $Q_{q_\ell q_1}$. Then, Q is a path in G_e between p_1 and q_1, for which the inequality in (18.2) holds. This completes the proof. ∎

In summary, we have partitioned the edge set E into $O(k^2/\theta^{d-1})$ subsets, each of which satisfies the version of the t-leapfrog property given in Exercise 14.12. Then, the Leapfrog Theorem (Theorem 14.4.1) implies that

$$wt(E) = O\left(k^2/(t-1)^{3d-1}\right) \cdot wt(MST(S)).$$

By combining this with Lemmas 18.6.1 and 18.6.5, we obtain the following result:

Theorem 18.6.8. *Let S be a set of n points in $\mathbb{R}^d$, let $k \geq 0$ be an integer, and let $t > 1$ be a real number. Algorithm* FTPATHGREEDY(S, k, t) *computes a (k, t)-FTS for S, in which every vertex has degree $O(k/(t-1)^{d-1})$, and whose weight is*

$$O\left(\frac{k^2}{(t-1)^{3d-1}}\right) \cdot wt(MST(S)).$$

Unfortunately, it is not clear how an efficient implementation of algorithm FTPATHGREEDY, or a variant of it, can be obtained.

How about generalizing the gap-greedy algorithm of Chapter 7? We claim that this does lead to an efficient algorithm, at the cost of an $O(\log n)$ increase in the weight bound:

Theorem 18.6.9. *Let S be a set of n points in $\mathbb{R}^d$, let $k \geq 0$ be an integer, and let $t > 1$ be a real number. In*

$$O\left(\frac{1}{(t-1)^{d-1}}\left(kn\log^d n + nk^2\log k\right)\right)$$

time, a (k, t)-FTS for S can be computed in which every vertex has degree $O(k/(t-1)^{d-1})$, and whose weight is

$$O\left(\frac{k^2\log n}{(t-1)^d}\right) \cdot wt(MST(S)).$$

The following two open problems arise from the discussion above.

> **Open problem:** Is there an algorithm that constructs a k-fault-tolerant t-spanner of degree $O(k)$ in $O(n\log n + kn)$ time?

> **Open problem:** Is there an algorithm that constructs, in $O(n\log n + kn)$ time, a k-fault-tolerant t-spanner, whose weight is bounded by $O(k^2)$ times the weight of a minimum spanning tree of S?

Exercises

18.1. Use Exercise 9.16 to prove Theorem 18.4.4.

18.2. Prove Theorem 18.5.1. Also, prove the claim made at the end of Section 18.5 about constructing a k-fault-tolerant spanner of degree $O(k^2)$.

18.3. Prove Lemma 18.6.1.

18.4. Work out the details in Section 18.6.2.

18.5. Complete the proof of Lemma 18.6.6.

18.6. In the analysis in Section 18.6.3, we assumed that the Euclidean distances between all $\binom{n}{2}$ pairs of points in S are distinct. Prove that the analysis is still valid for point sets S that do not satisfy this assumption.

18.7. Prove Theorem 18.6.9.

Bibliographic notes

Fault-tolerant spanners were introduced in Levcopoulos, Narasimhan, and Smid [1998]. Sections 18.1–18.4 are based on their paper, and on the follow-up paper Levcopoulos, Narasimhan, and Smid [2002]. The result of Section 18.2 that every spanner that is resilient to vertex faults is also resilient to edge faults also appears in Lukovszki [1999a]. Section 18.5 is based on Lukovszki [1999a]. The generalizations of the path- and gap-greedy algorithms in Section 18.6 are due to Czumaj and Zhao [2004].

Theorem 18.6.2 is due to Menger [1927]. A proof can be found, for example, in the books by Harary [1972] and Bollobás [1998].

19

Designing Approximation Algorithms
with Spanners

> The difference between expected and achieved results could, in fact, be expressed in an exact relation, called the *Snafu equation*, involving the Finagle constants.
> — Francis P. Chisholm, *The Chisholm Effect: Basic Laws of Frustration, Mishap and Delay*, 1963

In this chapter we consider approximation algorithms for geometric optimization problems that use geometric networks of low weight satisfying specific properties. Given an input of size n (usually a set of n points in $\mathbb{R}^d$) and a real number $\epsilon > 0$, a *polynomial-time approximation scheme (PTAS)* is an algorithm that computes a solution that is within a factor of $1 + \epsilon$ of the optimal solution, in time that is polynomial in n, assuming that ϵ is a constant.

In Section 19.1, we present a generic PTAS that can be used for geometric optimization problems having the property that it is possible to quickly compute a sparse graph that contains an approximately optimal solution. In the remaining sections, we illustrate how to use the generic PTAS to obtain an $O(n \log n)$–time algorithm that computes, for any given set S of n points in $\mathbb{R}^d$, a tour of S whose weight is at most $1 + \epsilon$ times the weight of an optimal traveling salesperson tour of S. For this problem, it is essential that there is a fast algorithm that computes a $(1 + \epsilon)$-spanner for S with $O(n)$ edges and whose weight is within a (possibly large) constant factor of the weight of a minimum spanning tree of S. In Chapter 15, we have seen that such a spanner can be computed in $O(n \log n)$ time; see Theorem 15.3.20.

The generic PTAS uses dynamic programming. Therefore, throughout this chapter, the model of computation will be the algebraic computation-tree, in which additionally any indirect addressing operation takes unit time.

19.1 The generic polynomial-time approximation scheme

In this section, we present the PTAS in general terms. We assume that the optimization problem to be approximately solved takes as input a set S of n points in $\mathbb{R}^d$. The generic PTAS makes the following steps:

1. **The perturbation step:** The input is made *well-rounded*; that is, the points of S are perturbed so that they all occupy grid positions on a uniform grid. The grid size is chosen in such a way that the optimal solutions for S and the perturbed point set are approximately equal.

2. **The sparse graph computation step:** A sparse graph on the perturbed point set is computed, which contains an optimal or near-optimal solution to the problem.

3. **The quadtree construction step:** A hypercube containing the perturbed point set is shifted by a random vector, and a quadtree is computed using a recursive geometric partitioning of the shifted hypercube.

4. **The patching step:** The amount of "interaction" in an optimal or near-optimal solution between adjacent hypercubes in the quadtree is reduced, by using a series of "patching" steps. The result is a graph that contains an optimal or near-optimal solution and that is "r-light" (meaning that the "interaction" between adjacent hypercubes is of "size" at most r).

5. **The dynamic programming step:** Because of Step 4, each hypercube in the quadtree generates only a small number of subproblems. Dynamic programming is applied to solve all these subproblems, by traversing the quadtree in postorder.

Step 2 involves computing a sparse graph and is specific to the application. For the case of the traveling salesperson problem, a $(1 + \epsilon)$-spanner of low weight suffices. Steps 4 and 5 are also specific to the application, whereas Steps 1 and 3 are more or less generic.

In the rest of this chapter, we show how the generic PTAS can be used to design an $O(n \log n)$–time algorithm that computes a $(1 + \epsilon)$-approximation to the traveling salesperson problem.

Throughout the rest of this chapter, we fix a set S of n points in $\mathbb{R}^d$. A *tour* of S is defined to be a cycle $T = (p_1, p_2, \ldots, p_n, p_1)$ with vertex set S, which visits each point of S exactly once and returns to its starting point. The weight $wt(T)$ of T is defined to be $\sum_{i=1}^{n} |p_i p_{i+1}|$, where $p_{n+1} := p_1$. The *traveling salesperson problem* is to compute a tour of S of minimum weight. We call such a tour a *traveling salesperson tour of S*, and denote it by $TSP(S)$.

We will apply the generic approximation scheme to the problem of finding a tour of S, whose weight is at most $(1 + \epsilon) \cdot wt(TSP(S))$. Throughout the rest of this chapter, ϵ is a real number with $0 < \epsilon < 1$.

19.2 The perturbation step

This step perturbs the set of points, as described below.

> **Basic idea:** The input is made *well-rounded*; that is, the input points are perturbed so that they occupy grid positions on a uniform grid. The net effect is that all points can be thought of as having integer coordinates in the range $[0, O(n)]$. The grid granularity is chosen such that the error caused by the perturbation is small.

Since we are looking only for approximate solutions, it is clear that there should be no harm in "snapping" each input point to a nearby grid point. Points that occupy the same grid position are replaced by one single point. As we will see, if the grid is defined appropriately, the resulting increase in the weight of the solution is bounded. The main purpose of the perturbation step is to ensure that the quadtree that is computed in a later step has only $O(\log n)$ levels. In the process, it also helps simplify the descriptions of the quadtree decomposition.

Let B be the side length of a smallest axes-parallel hypercube that contains all points of S. We may assume without loss of generality that $S \subseteq [0, B]^d$. (If this is not the case, then we can translate S.) Let $MST(S)$ denote a minimum spanning tree of S, and let M be the weight of a 2-approximate minimum spanning tree of S. Thus,

$$wt(MST(S)) \leq M \leq 2 \cdot wt(MST(S)). \tag{19.1}$$

We define

$$L := 2^{\lfloor \log(4Bn\sqrt{d}/(\epsilon M)) \rfloor}.$$

By Exercise 6.3, we have $M = O(B \cdot n^{1-1/d})$ and, therefore, L is a positive integer. Since $B \leq wt(MST(S)) \leq M$, we have

$$L \leq 4Bn\sqrt{d}/(\epsilon M) \leq 4n\sqrt{d}/\epsilon = O(n/\epsilon). \tag{19.2}$$

Moreover, we have

$$L \geq 2^{\log(4Bn\sqrt{d}/(\epsilon M))-1} = 2Bn\sqrt{d}/(\epsilon M). \tag{19.3}$$

We place a uniform grid on the hypercube $[0, B]^d$, consisting of L^d cells, where each cell is a hypercube with sides of length B/L. For each point p in S, let p' be a grid point that is nearest to p, and define

$$S' := \{p' : p \in S\}.$$

We remark that we consider S' to be a set; that is, multiple points at the same grid point are replaced by one single point. We state the following lemma without proof.

Lemma 19.2.1. *Let p and q be two points of S, and consider the corresponding points p' and q' in S'. Then, the following inequalities hold:*

1. $|pp'| \leq \sqrt{d}B/(2L)$.
2. $|p'q'| \leq |pq| + \sqrt{d}B/L$.
3. $|pq| \leq |p'q'| + \sqrt{d}B/L$.

The next lemma states that the traveling salesperson tours (and the minimum spanning trees) of S and S' have approximately the same weight.

Lemma 19.2.2. *The following inequalities are true:*

1. $wt(TSP(S')) \leq (1 + \epsilon) \cdot wt(TSP(S))$.
2. $wt(TSP(S)) \leq (1 + \epsilon) \cdot wt(TSP(S'))$.
3. $wt(MST(S')) \leq (1 + \epsilon) \cdot wt(MST(S))$.
4. $wt(MST(S)) \leq (1 + \epsilon) \cdot wt(MST(S'))$.

PROOF We prove only the first claim. Let $T = (S, E)$ be a tour of S with weight $wt(TSP(S))$. Define T' to be the graph with vertex set S' and edge set

$$E' = \{\{p', q'\} : \{p, q\} \in E, p' \neq q'\}.$$

Then, T' is a (possibly nonsimple) cycle that visits each point of S'. Using Lemma 19.2.1 and the inequality in (19.3), we obtain

$$wt(T') \leq wt(T) + n\sqrt{d}B/L$$
$$\leq wt(T) + \epsilon M/2.$$

By the inequality in (19.1) and Exercise 1.6, we have

$$M \leq 2 \cdot wt(MST(S)) \leq 2 \cdot wt(T).$$

Therefore, we have

$$wt(T') \leq (1 + \epsilon) \cdot wt(T).$$

The first claim follows by observing that $wt(TSP(S'))$ is less than or equal to $wt(T')$. ∎

Each point p' of S' can be written as $p' = (i_1 B/L, i_2 B/L, \ldots, i_d B/L)$, for some integers $i_1, i_2, \ldots, i_d$ in $[0, L]$. It turns out to be convenient to scale the coordinates of these points. That is, we define $p'' := (i_1, i_2, \ldots, i_d)$ and

$$P := \{p'' : p' \in S'\}.$$

Then, by (19.2),

$$P \subseteq [0, L]^d = [0, O(n/\epsilon)]^d.$$

Later, we will need the following upper bound on the weight of a minimum spanning tree of P:

Lemma 19.2.3. *We have* $wt(MST(P)) = O(n/\epsilon)$.

PROOF Since P is obtained by scaling S', we have $wt(MST(P)) = (L/B) \cdot wt(MST(S'))$. Then, using Lemma 19.2.2 and the definition of L in Section 19.2, it follows that

$$
\begin{aligned}
wt(MST(P)) &\leq \frac{(1+\epsilon)L}{B} \cdot wt(MST(S)) \\
&\leq \frac{(1+\epsilon)LM}{B} \\
&\leq \frac{4(1+\epsilon)n\sqrt{d}}{\epsilon} \\
&= O(n/\epsilon),
\end{aligned}
$$

where we have used our assumption that $\epsilon < 1$. ∎

We finish this section by analyzing the amount of time needed for the perturbation step.

Lemma 19.2.4. *Given the set S and the real number ϵ with $0 < \epsilon < 1$, the perturbed and scaled point set P can be computed in $O(n \log(n/\epsilon))$ time.*

PROOF The side length B of a smallest axes-parallel hypercube that contains S can clearly be computed in $O(n)$ time. By Theorem 10.3.11, the weight M of a 2-approximate minimum spanning tree of S can be computed in $O(n \log n)$ time. Using d binary searches in a set consisting of $L + 1$ integers (one search for each dimension), the sets S' and P can be computed in $O(n \log L) = O(n \log(n/\epsilon))$ time. Observe that the floor function is not used. ∎

19.3 The sparse graph computation step

Recall that our goal is to compute an approximation to the optimal traveling salesperson tour of the original set S. By Lemma 19.2.2, it is sufficient to compute an approximation to the optimal traveling salesperson tour of the perturbed and scaled set P.

> **Basic idea:** Every spanner contains an approximation to the optimal traveling salesperson tour of the points. A$(1 + \epsilon)$-spanner G for the perturbed and scaled point set P is computed. After G has been appropriately modified in the patching step, it still contains an approximation to the optimal traveling salesperson tour. In order to obtain an efficient algorithm, it is essential that the spanner G contains $O(n)$ edges and that its weight is $O(wt(MST(P)))$.

Until now, we have considered only tours of point sets. If G is a graph with vertex set P, then a *tour of P in G* is a (possibly nonsimple) cycle in G that visits each point of P at least once. The next lemma states that every spanner for P contains a tour whose weight is proportional to the weight of an optimal traveling salesperson tour of P.

Lemma 19.3.1. *Let $t > 1$ be a real number, and let G be an arbitrary t-spanner for P. Then, there is a tour of P in G, whose weight is at most $t \cdot wt(TSP(P))$.*

PROOF The lemma follows by replacing every edge of an optimal traveling salesperson tour of P by a t-spanner path in G. ∎

Thus, we can use any spanner to obtain an approximation to the optimal traveling salesperson tour of P. As we will see later, in order to obtain a fast approximation algorithm, we need to choose a spanner G for P with $O(n)$ edges and whose weight is $O(wt(MST(P)))$. By Theorem 15.3.20, there exists an efficient algorithm that computes such a spanner G:

Lemma 19.3.2. *In*

$$O\left(\frac{1}{\epsilon^{4d-1}} n \log n\right)$$

time, a $(1 + \epsilon)$-spanner G for P can be computed, such that
1. *the number of edges of G is $O(n/\epsilon^{2d-1})$ and*
2. *the weight of G is*

$$O\left(\frac{1}{\epsilon^{2d}} \cdot wt(MST(P))\right).$$

From now on, G will denote the $(1 + \epsilon)$-spanner for P as given by Lemma 19.3.2. Observe that, by Lemma 19.2.3,

$$wt(G) = O\left(n/\epsilon^{2d+1}\right). \tag{19.4}$$

By Lemma 19.3.1, it suffices to compute a tour of P in G, whose weight is approximately minimum. The next two steps in Sections 19.4 and 19.6 will approximate G by a graph G' that is more amenable to search for such a tour.

19.4 The quadtree construction step

A quadtree structure is needed for later steps. Its construction is described below.

> **Basic idea:** A hypercube containing the perturbed and scaled point set P is expanded and shifted by a random amount. Then, a quadtree is computed using the shifted hypercube. This step is required to identify a hierarchy of subproblems for the dynamic programming step. In the patching step in Section 19.6, this hierarchy will be used to bound the amount of interaction between neighboring hypercubes in the quadtree. A random shift allows us to bound the expected increase in weight when the spanner G is patched.

Recall that $P \subseteq [0, L]^d$. We pick integers $a_1, a_2, \ldots, a_d$ in $[1, L]$, and define $\mathbf{a} := (a_1, a_2, \ldots, a_d)$. For each i with $1 \le i \le d$, we extend the unit grid on the hypercube $[0, L]^d$ along dimension i, by adding

1. a_i grid planes before the first grid plane, and
2. $L - a_i$ grid planes after the last grid plane.

Then we translate the enlarged hypercube by the vector $(1/2, 1/2, \ldots, 1/2)$. We denote the resulting hypercube by $C(\mathbf{a})$. Thus,

$$C(\mathbf{a}) = \prod_{i=1}^{d} [-a_i + 1/2, 2L - a_i + 1/2].$$

This hypercube has sides of length $2L$, and each point of P is at the center of a unit hypercube.

We define the *dissection* of $C(\mathbf{a})$ to be the following recursive partition into smaller hypercubes. The root of the dissection stores $C(\mathbf{a})$. Consider any node u storing a hypercube C'. We partition C' into 2^d hypercubes of equal size. Then, node u gets 2^d children, one child for each of these smaller hypercubes. If u stores a hypercube with sides of length one, then the process stops (for u), and u is a leaf in the dissection. Thus, this dissection process defines a *dissection tree* of height $1 + \log L = O(\log(n/\epsilon))$, which consists of

$$\sum_{i=0}^{1+\log L} (2L/2^i)^d = O(L^d) = O((n/\epsilon)^d)$$

nodes. Observe that each nonleaf node in the dissection tree has $2^d - 1$ siblings and shares a $((d-1)$-dimensional) hyperplanar boundary with at most d of them.

A hyperplane is called a *grid hyperplane* with respect to $C(\mathbf{a})$, if it is orthogonal to one of the coordinate axes and has an integer distance from a face of $C(\mathbf{a})$ along this axis. Thus, any grid hyperplane is of the form $x_i = j + 1/2$, for some integers i and j with $1 \le i \le d$.

For any graph G' with vertex set P, and for any grid hyperplane h, we define $I(G', h)$ to be the number of edges of G' that cross h. (Since no point of P is on any grid hyperplane, the notion of an edge crossing h is well-defined.) Furthermore, we define

$$I(G') := \sum_{h:\text{grid hyperplane}} I(G', h).$$

The following lemma relates the value of $I(G')$ to the weight of the graph G'.

Lemma 19.4.1. *Let G' be a graph with vertex set P. Then,*

$$I(G') \leq \sqrt{d} \cdot wt(G').$$

PROOF Let $x = (x_1, x_2, \ldots, x_d)$ and $y = (y_1, y_2, \ldots, y_d)$ be two distinct points of P, and assume that $\{x, y\}$ is an edge of G'. The straight-line edge $\{x, y\}$ crosses the same grid hyperplanes as any shortest Manhattan path between x and y. Recall that x and y are not contained in any grid hyperplane. Also, for each i with $1 \leq i \leq d$, $|x_i - y_i|$ is a nonnegative integer. It follows that the contribution of the edge $\{x, y\}$ to the summation $I(G')$ is equal to $\sum_{i=1}^{d} |x_i - y_i|$, which is less than or equal to $\sqrt{d}|xy|$. ∎

Lemma 19.4.2. *For the spanner G of Lemma 19.3.2, we have*

$$I(G) = O\left(n/\epsilon^{2d+1}\right).$$

PROOF The claim follows from Lemma 19.4.1 and the bound in (19.4). ∎

Let h be a grid hyperplane. We define the *level* of h to be the smallest integer i, such that the dissection of $C(\mathbf{a})$ contains a hypercube with sides of length $2L/2^i$, one of whose faces is contained in h. If such an i does not exist (i.e., if h does not intersect the hypercube $C(\mathbf{a})$), then we define the level of h to be ∞. Thus, if the level of h is finite, then it is an integer in $\{0, 1, \ldots, 1 + \log L\}$.

In Section 19.6, the shift vector $\mathbf{a}$ will be chosen randomly in $\{1, 2, \ldots, L\}^d$. As a result, the level of a grid hyperplane will be a random variable. The following lemma gives the probability distribution of this random variable.

Lemma 19.4.3. *Let h be a grid hyperplane, and let i be an integer with $0 \leq i \leq 1 + \log L$. Assume that the values of $a_1, a_2, \ldots, a_d$ that define the shift vector $\mathbf{a}$ are chosen independently and uniformly at random from the set $\{1, 2, \ldots, L\}$. Then, the probability that the level of h is equal to i is at most $2^{i-1}/L$.*

PROOF We may assume without loss of generality that h is given by the equation $x_1 = j + 1/2$, for some integer j. Assume that the level of h is equal to i. Then the dissection tree contains a hypercube with sides of length $2L/2^i = L/2^{i-1}$, and h contains one of the two faces of this hypercube that are extreme along the first coordinate axes. This is possible only if a_1 is a multiple of $L/2^{i-1}$, i.e., $a_1 \in \{k \cdot L/2^{i-1} : 1 \leq k \leq 2^{i-1}\}$. The lemma follows from the fact that a_1 is randomly chosen in $\{1, 2, \ldots, L\}$. ∎

Until now, we have proved several properties about the dissection tree. We emphasize that we do *not* compute this tree, because it contains $O((n/\epsilon)^d)$ nodes. For our application, it suffices to compute a subtree of the dissection tree, which we call the *quadtree $QT(P, \mathbf{a})$* of P with respect to the shift vector $\mathbf{a}$. This quadtree consists of all nodes u in the dissection tree, such that at least one of the 2^d hypercubes stored at u and its siblings contains at least one point of P.

Given the point set P and the shift vector $\mathbf{a}$, the quadtree $QT(P, \mathbf{a})$ can be constructed recursively, where the recursion terminates at a node u as soon as the hypercube stored at u contains at most one point of P. Thus, this tree has height $O(\log L) = O(\log(n/\epsilon))$, at most $2^d n = O(n)$ leaves, $O(n \log(n/\epsilon))$ nodes, and can be constructed in a top-down manner in $O(n \log(n/\epsilon))$ time. The proof of this claim is left as an exercise; see Exercise 19.1.

Lemma 19.4.4. *For any shift vector* $\mathbf{a}$*, the quadtree* $QT(P, \mathbf{a})$ *has the following properties:*

1. *It has height* $O(\log(n/\epsilon))$.
2. *It has* $O(n \log(n/\epsilon))$ *nodes.*
3. *It can be constructed in* $O(n \log(n/\epsilon))$ *time.*

19.5 A digression: Constructing a light graph of low weight

In the patching step that will be presented in Section 19.6, we need a special type of graph that connects a given set of points that is contained in some face of a hypercube in the quadtree $QT(P, \mathbf{a})$. In this section, we will specify the requirements for this graph, and we give an efficient algorithm that computes such a graph. Observe that a face of a hypercube in $QT(P, \mathbf{a})$ is a hypercube in $\mathbb{R}^{d-1}$. For ease of notation, we will present our algorithm for a hypercube in $\mathbb{R}^d$. In other words, in Section 19.6, we will apply the algorithm with d replaced by $d - 1$.

If C is a hypercube in $\mathbb{R}^d$ with sides of length ℓ, where $\ell > 1$, then we define the *reduced hypercube* of C to be the hypercube C_0 obtained by shrinking C by an additive factor of $1/2$. Thus, if $C = \prod_{i=1}^{d}[a_i, a_i + \ell]$, then the reduced hypercube of C is $\prod_{i=1}^{d}[a_i + 1/2, a_i + \ell - 1/2]$. We define the *graph* of C_0 to be the graph whose vertex set consists of the 2^d corners of C_0 and whose edge set consists of the $d2^{d-1}$ edges of C_0.

Let ℓ be a positive integer that is a power of 2, and let C be a hypercube in $\mathbb{R}^d$ with sides of length ℓ. Recall that a grid hyperplane with respect to C is a hyperplane that is orthogonal to one of the coordinate axes and that has an integer distance from a face of C along this axis. Let V be a set of m points in C, and assume that no point of V is contained in any grid hyperplane. We say that a spanning graph H of V is *light with respect to* C if it satisfies the following properties:

1. H is completely contained in the hypercube C.
2. The vertex set of H contains V.
3. No vertex of H is contained in any grid hyperplane.
4. For every hypercube C' in the dissection of C, with $C' \neq C$, and for every face f of C', there is at most one edge in H that crosses f; if such an edge exists, then it is contained in an edge of the graph of the reduced hypercube of the parent of C'.

Our goal is to compute a light spanning graph H, whose weight is "small." Observe that an exact or approximate minimum spanning tree of V has weight $O(\ell \cdot m^{1-1/d})$; see Exercise 6.3. However, this graph may not satisfy the fourth requirement. The following algorithm computes a graph that does satisfy all four requirements and whose weight is $O(\ell \cdot m^{1-1/d})$.

Algorithm LIGHTGRAPH(V, C, ℓ, d)

Comment: This algorithm takes as input a hypercube C in $\mathbb{R}^d$ with sides of length ℓ (which is a power of 2), and a set V of m points in C, such that no point of V is contained in any grid hyperplane. The algorithm returns a spanning graph H of V, which is light with respect to C, and whose weight is $O(\ell \cdot m^{1-1/d})$.

    if $d = 1$
    then $H :=$ path consisting of the points of V in sorted order along
              the interval C
    else if $\ell = 1$
        then $c :=$ center of C;
             $H :=$ 2-approximate minimum spanning tree of $V \cup \{c\}$
        else $H :=$ graph of the reduced hypercube of C;
             partition C into hypercubes $C_1, C_2, \ldots, C_{2^d}$ of equal size;
             for $j := 1$ **to** 2^d
             do $V_j := V \cap C_j$;
                if $V_j \neq \emptyset$
                  then $H_j :=$ LIGHTGRAPH($V_j, C_j, \ell/2, d$);
                      $H := H \cup H_j$
                endif
             endfor
        endif
    endif;
    modify H such that no two edges overlap;
    return H

The second last line in this algorithm needs some explanation. Before this line is executed, the graph H may contain edges $\{a, b\}$ and $\{a', b'\}$, such that the line segment ab is contained in the line segment $a'b'$. In the second last line, these two edges are replaced by the three pairwise nonoverlapping edges $\{a', a\}$, $\{a, b\}$, and $\{b, b'\}$. (If $a = a'$ or $b = b'$, then the two edges are replaced by two nonoverlapping edges.)

In Figure 19.1, an example is given for a set V of nine points in a two-dimensional hypercube C (i.e., a square) with sides of length $\ell = 16$. The grid hyperplanes (which are lines) are indicated by dashed lines, whereas the graph H, which is returned by algorithm LIGHTGRAPH($V, C, \ell, 2$), is indicated by solid lines. The points of V that are in a unit square of the dissection of C, together with the center of this unit square, are connected by an approximate minimum spanning tree.

The algorithm as presented above uses the graph of the reduced hypercube of C. We remark that it is in fact sufficient for our purposes to use a spanning tree of this graph.

The following lemma proves the correctness of algorithm LIGHTGRAPH.

Lemma 19.5.1. *Let H be the graph that is returned by algorithm LIGHTGRAPH(V, C, ℓ, d). Then, the following properties hold:*

1. *H is a spanning graph of V, which is light with respect to C.*
2. *If $d = 1$, then $wt(H) \leq \ell$.*
3. *If $d \geq 2$, then $wt(H) = O(\ell \cdot m^{1-1/d})$.*

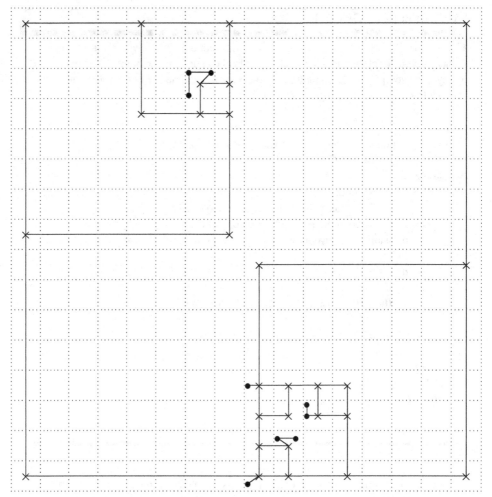

Figure 19.1: Illustrating algorithm LIGHTGRAPH(V, C, ℓ, d), where V is the set of nine points indicated by •, C is a square in $\mathbb{R}^2$, $\ell = 16$, and $d = 2$. The grid hyperplanes are indicated by the dashed lines. The graph H, which is returned by the algorithm, is indicated by the solid lines. The vertices of the graphs of the reduced hypercubes are indicated by ×.

PROOF The first claim is left as an exercise; see Exercise 19.2. If $d = 1$, then the weight of H is less than the length ℓ of the interval C, proving the second claim. To prove the third claim, assume that $d \geq 2$. If $\ell = 1$, then, by Exercise 6.3,

$$wt(H) = O\big((m+1)^{1-1/d}\big) = O\big(\ell \cdot m^{1-1/d}\big).$$

In the rest of this proof, we assume that $\ell \geq 2$. We say that a call to algorithm LIGHTGRAPH is at level i, if the hypercube in this call has sides of length $\ell/2^i$. Consider one call to algorithm LIGHTGRAPH at level i, where $0 \leq i < \log \ell$. In this call, the graph of a reduced hypercube is added to H; this graph has weight $O(\ell/2^i)$. Since the number of calls at level i is at most 2^{id}, the total amount of weight that is added to H at level i is

$$O\big(2^{id} \cdot \ell/2^i\big) = O\big(2^{(d-1)i}\ell\big).$$

Thus, if k is the integer such that

$$2^k \le m^{1/d} < 2^{k+1},$$

then the total amount of weight that is added to H at levels $0, 1, \ldots, k$ is proportional to

$$
\begin{aligned}
\sum_{i=0}^{k} 2^{(d-1)i} \ell &= \frac{2^{(d-1)(k+1)} - 1}{2^{d-1} - 1} \ell \\
&\le 2\ell \cdot 2^{(d-1)k} \\
&\le 2\ell \cdot m^{(d-1)/d} \\
&= O\!\left(\ell \cdot m^{1-1/d}\right).
\end{aligned}
\tag{19.5}
$$

We next estimate the total amount of weight that is added to H at levels $k+1$, $k+2, \ldots, \log \ell - 1$. Consider a point p of V. The total weight of the graphs of the reduced hypercubes that are constructed in the calls involving p at these levels is proportional to

$$\sum_{i \ge k+1} \ell/2^i = O\!\left(\ell/2^{k+1}\right) = O\!\left(\ell/m^{1/d}\right).$$

Thus, since $|V| = m$, the total amount of weight that is added to H at levels $k+1$, $k+2, \ldots, \log \ell - 1$ is

$$O\!\left(\ell \cdot m^{1-1/d}\right).
\tag{19.6}$$

Finally, we estimate the total weight that is added to H at level $\log L$. Let h be the number of unit hypercubes in the dissection of C that contain at least one point of V. For each j with $1 \le j \le h$, let m_j be the number of points of V that are contained in the j-th nonempty unit hypercube. Observe that $\sum_{j=1}^{h} m_j = m$. By Exercise 6.3, the total weight that is added to H at level $\log L$ is

$$O\!\left(\sum_{j=1}^{h} (m_j + 1)^{1-1/d}\right) = O\!\left(\sum_{j=1}^{h} m_j^{1-1/d}\right).
\tag{19.7}$$

Let the function f be defined by $f(x) := -x^{1-1/d}$ for $x > 0$. Since $f''(x) > 0$ for all $x > 0$, the function f is convex. Therefore,

$$f\!\left(\sum_{j=1}^{h} m_j/h\right) \le \sum_{j=1}^{h} f(m_j)/h,$$

which rewrites to

$$\sum_{j=1}^{h} m_j^{1-1/d} \le h \left(\sum_{j=1}^{h} m_j/h\right)^{1-1/d} = h(m/h)^{1-1/d} = h^{1/d} m^{1-1/d}.$$

Since the dissection of C consists of ℓ^d unit hypercubes, we have $h \le \ell^d$. Therefore, we have

$$\sum_{j=1}^{h} m_j^{1-1/d} \le \ell \cdot m^{1-1/d}.
\tag{19.8}$$

By combining (19.5)–(19.8), it follows that the weight of the graph H is $O(\ell \cdot m^{1-1/d})$. ■

We next analyze the running time of algorithm LIGHTGRAPH.

Lemma 19.5.2. *The running time of algorithm* LIGHTGRAPH(V, C, ℓ, d) *is*

$$O(m \log m + m \log \ell).$$

PROOF If $d = 1$, then the claim obviously holds. Assume that $d \geq 2$. We have seen in Lemma 10.3.11 that a 2-approximate minimum spanning tree of a set of k points in $\mathbb{R}^d$ can be computed in $O(k \log k)$ time; in other words, each of these k points "contributes" $O(\log k)$ to this time bound. The lemma follows from the facts that the recursion depth of algorithm LIGHTGRAPH(V, C, ℓ, d) is $O(\log \ell)$, and each point of V "contributes" $O(\log m + \log \ell)$ to the total running time. ■

19.6 The patching step

Recall that G denotes the $(1 + \epsilon)$-spanner for P as given by Lemma 19.3.2. In order to make the dynamic programming step efficient, we need to limit the amount of "interaction" between sibling hypercubes of the quadtree $QT(P, \mathbf{a})$. This will be done by modifying the spanner G, such that the edges of the modified graph cross hypercube boundaries at only a small number of positions.

> **Basic idea:** The amount of "interaction" between sibling hypercubes of the quadtree $QT(P, \mathbf{a})$ is reduced by using a series of "patching" steps. These steps ensure that the number of times the edges cross the boundary between any two sibling hypercubes is bounded by a small quantity. The result is an "r-light graph" (which may not be a spanner). If the shift vector $\mathbf{a}$ is randomly chosen then, with probability at least $1/2$, this graph contains a tour of P, whose weight is approximately equal to $wt(TSP(P))$.

Let G' be a graph that is contained in the shifted hypercube $C(\mathbf{a})$, and whose vertex set contains P. Assume that no vertex of G' is contained in any grid hyperplane. For a positive integer r, we say that G' is r-*light with respect to* the quadtree $QT(P, \mathbf{a})$, if the following holds: Consider any two sibling hypercubes in $QT(P, \mathbf{a})$ that share a face f (which is a $(d - 1)$-dimensional hypercube). Then, G' contains at most r edges that cross f.

Thus, the property of being r-light implies that the amount of interaction between sibling quadtree boxes is bounded by the parameter r. It will become clear later how this property is used in the dynamic programming step.

In the rest of this section, we show how the spanner G can be transformed into an r-light graph G'. As we will see, the additive increase in weight of the graph G' (as compared to the weight of G) is proportional to the weight of G divided by r. Thus, by choosing the parameter r sufficiently large, the weight of G' is only slightly larger than that of G. This, combined with the fact that the weight of G is proportional to the weight of a minimum spanning tree of P, will imply that G' contains a "short" tour of P.

The algorithm that transforms the spanner G into an r-light graph G' is denoted by PATCH(G, r) and will be presented later. The heart of this algorithm is the BOUNDARYPATCH procedure, which patches the spanner with respect to a face f of a

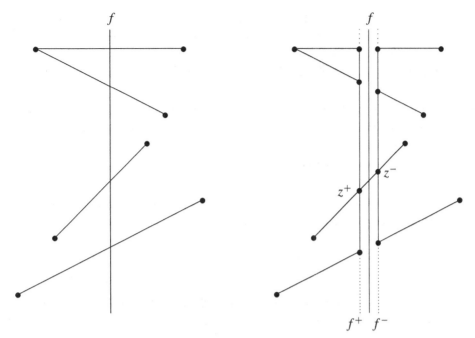

Figure 19.2: Illustration of algorithm BOUNDARYPATCH for $d = 2$.

hypercube in the dissection of $C(\mathbf{a})$. Observe that f is a $(d-1)$-dimensional hypercube that is contained in a grid hyperplane. Also, the intersection between the dissection of $C(\mathbf{a})$ and the face f is a $(d-1)$-dimensional dissection. Because of this, we can use algorithm LIGHTGRAPH of Section 19.5. Algorithm BOUNDARYPATCH is described below. The situation is illustrated for $d = 2$ in Figure 19.2.

Algorithm BOUNDARYPATCH(G', f, V)

Comment: This algorithm takes as input a graph G' that is contained in the shifted hypercube $C(\mathbf{a})$, whose vertex set contains P, such that no vertex is contained in any grid hyperplane. The input parameter f is the face of some hypercube in the dissection of $C(\mathbf{a})$, whereas V is the set of all intersection points between f and the edges of G'. The algorithm returns a graph that contains at most one edge that crosses f.

If $V = \emptyset$, then return the graph G' and terminate. Assume that $V \neq \emptyset$. Run algorithm LIGHTGRAPH(V, f, ℓ, $d-1$) of Section 19.5, where ℓ is the side length of f, and let H_f be the graph that is returned by this algorithm.

    Draw two "shadow" faces f^+ and f^- parallel to f, one on either side of f and infinitesimally away from f. Let H_f^+ and H_f^- be copies of H_f translated to the faces f^+ and f^-, respectively. Finally, let z be an arbitrary element of V, and let z^+ and z^- be the corresponding points in f^+ and f^-, respectively.

    Modify the graph G' as follows. First, add the graphs H_f^+ and H_f^-, and add a *patching bridge* $\{z^+, z^-\}$. Next, for each edge $\{x, y\}$ of G' that crosses f, do the following: Let x^+ be the intersection between $\{x, y\}$ and f^+, and let x^- be the intersection between $\{x, y\}$ and f^-. Replace the edge $\{x, y\}$ by the two edges $\{x, x^+\}$ and $\{x^-, y\}$. Return the resulting graph.

Observe that the patching bridge is the only edge that crosses the face f after algorithm BOUNDARYPATCH(G', f, V) is applied. The following lemma bounds the weight of the output of algorithm BOUNDARYPATCH(G', f, V) in terms of the weight of the input graph G'. Recall that $I(G', f)$ denotes the number of edges of G' that cross f.

Lemma 19.6.1. *Let G'' be the output of algorithm* BOUNDARYPATCH(G', f, V), *and let ℓ be the side length of f.*

1. *If $d = 2$, then $wt(G'') \leq wt(G') + 2\ell$.*
2. *If $d > 2$, then $wt(G'') = wt(G') + O(\ell \cdot (I(G', f))^{1-1/(d-1)})$.*

PROOF First observe that $|V| = I(G', f)$. If $V = \emptyset$, then $G'' = G'$, and the claim obviously holds. Assume that $V \neq \emptyset$. It follows from the algorithm that

$$wt(G'') = wt(G') + 2 \cdot wt(H_f),$$

where H_f is the graph returned by algorithm LIGHTGRAPH(V, f, ℓ, $d - 1$). In this case, the claim follows from Lemma 19.5.1. ∎

The following lemma states the running time of algorithm BOUNDARYPATCH(G', f, V). Recall that this algorithm gets the set V of intersections between f and the edges of G' as part of its input.

Lemma 19.6.2. *The running time of algorithm* BOUNDARYPATCH(G', f, V) *is*

$$O\big(I(G', f)\big(\log I(G', f) + \log(n/\epsilon)\big)\big).$$

PROOF Let ℓ be the side length of f. It follows from Lemma 19.5.2 that the running time of algorithm BOUNDARYPATCH(G', f, V) is

$$O(|V| \log |V| + |V| \log \ell).$$

Since $|V| = I(G', f)$ and $\ell \leq 2L = O(n/\epsilon)$, the lemma follows. ∎

In the rest of this section, we will use the following terminology. A *hypercube* will always be a d-dimensional hypercube in the dissection of $C(\mathbf{a})$. A *face* will always be a face of some hypercube. Thus, a face is a $(d - 1)$-dimensional hypercube.

Algorithm PATCH is given below. It starts with the spanner G for P as given by Lemma 19.3.2, and calls algorithm BOUNDARYPATCH for every face f, such that (i) f is contained in some face of some hypercube in the quadtree $QT(P, \mathbf{a})$, and (ii) f is crossed by more than r edges of the current graph. The algorithm considers these faces in order of their side lengths from the smallest to the largest possible side length.

Recall that the level of a grid hyperplane h is the smallest integer j, such that the dissection of $C(\mathbf{a})$ contains a hypercube with sides of length $2L/2^j$, one of whose faces is contained in h.

Algorithm PATCH(G, r)

Comment: This algorithm takes as input the $(1 + \epsilon)$-spanner G for the set P, and a positive integer r. It returns a graph G' that is $(r + d - 1)$-light with respect to the quadtree $QT(P, \mathbf{a})$.

$G' := G$
for $j := 1 + \log L$ **down to** 0
do for each grid hyperplane h whose level is at most j
    do partition $h \cap C(\mathbf{a})$ into $2^{j(d-1)}$ faces, each having sides of
        length $2L/2^j$;
        for each face f in this partition that is contained in some
                face of some hypercube that is stored in $QT(P, \mathbf{a})$
        do $V :=$ set of intersections between f and the edges of G';
          if $|V| > r$
          then $G' :=$ BOUNDARYPATCH(G', f, V)
          endif
        endfor
    endfor
endfor;
modify G' such that no two edges overlap;
return G'

Observe that algorithm BOUNDARYPATCH(G', f, V) is called on the *current* graph G'. Having eliminated all crossings between f and the edges of G', this algorithm adds a patching bridge. This patching bridge crosses f and is an edge of the new graph G'. Therefore, the crossing due to the patching bridge may be eliminated in later calls to algorithm BOUNDARYPATCH.

Lemma 19.6.3. *Let f be a face and assume that* BOUNDARYPATCH(G', f, V) *is called during algorithm* PATCH(G, r). *At the moment when* BOUNDARYPATCH(G', f, V) *is called, we have $I(G', f) \leq I(G, f)$.*

PROOF Let h be the grid hyperplane that contains f, and let j be the integer, such that f has sides of length $2L/2^j$. Assume that, at the moment when algorithm BOUNDARYPATCH(G', f, V) is called, we have $I(G', f) > I(G, f)$. Then, before this call, crossings have been introduced on f. Thus, there exists an integer j', a grid hyperplane h', and a face f' in h', such that (i) $j' \geq j$, (ii) h' is orthogonal to h, (iii) f' properly intersects f, and (iv) during iteration j' of the outer for-loop, algorithm BOUNDARYPATCH(G', f', V') is called. Observe that f' has sides of length $2L/2^{j'}$. Since f' properly intersects f, it follows from properties of the dissection that $2L/2^{j'} > 2L/2^j$, that is, $j' < j$, which contradicts (i). ∎

Consider the graph G' that is returned by algorithm PATCH(G, r). In the next lemma, we prove that G' is s-light with respect to the quadtree $QT(P, \mathbf{a})$, where $s = r + d - 1$. Recall the definition of G' being s-light with respect to $QT(P, \mathbf{a})$: For every face f that is common to two sibling hypercubes in $QT(P, \mathbf{a})$, the graph G' contains at most s edges that cross f.

Lemma 19.6.4. *For every integer $r \geq 1$, the graph G' that is returned by algorithm* PATCH(G, r) *is $(r + d - 1)$-light with respect to $QT(P, \mathbf{a})$.*

PROOF   Let f be a face that is common to two sibling hypercubes in $QT(P, \mathbf{a})$, let j be the integer such that f has sides of length $2L/2^j$, and let h be the grid hyperplane that contains f. Then, the level of h is equal to j.

Consider iteration j of the outer for-loop. This is the last iteration in which h is considered. In iteration j, f is one of the faces that is considered. Thus, immediately after h has been considered for the last time, the graph G' contains at most r edges that cross f. Later during the algorithm, however, new crossings may arise on f. This can happen only because of grid hyperplanes h', such that (i) h' is orthogonal to h, (ii) h' touches f, and (iii) the level of h' is less than the level of h. There are $2(d - 1)$ grid hyperplanes h' for which conditions (i) and (ii) hold, but only $d - 1$ of these have a level that is less than the level of h; the level of the other $d - 1$ grid hyperplanes is equal to the level of h. In other words, there are $d - 1$ grid hyperplanes h' that satisfy all three conditions. Let h' be one of these grid hyperplanes, and let j' be its level. Thus, $j' \leq j - 1$.

Let j'' be any integer with $j' \leq j'' \leq j - 1$, and let f'' be the face in h', such that f'' has sides of length $2L/2^{j''}$ and f'' touches f. We may assume without loss of generality that the shadow face $(f'')^+$ of f'' intersects f. Consider iteration j'' of the outer for-loop, and assume that algorithm BOUNDARYPATCH(G', f'', V'') is called, where V'' is the set of all intersections between f'' and the edges of the graph G' at that moment. In this call, a graph is constructed that is contained in the shadow face $(f'')^+$; thus, some edges of this graph may cross f. Consider the intersection between $(f'')^+$ and the hypercubes in the quadtree $QT(P, \mathbf{a})$. This intersection is contained in the $((d - 1)$-dimensional) dissection of $(f'')^+$. Therefore, it follows from Lemma 19.5.1 that the call BOUNDARYPATCH(G', f'', V'') gives rise to at most one crossing on the face f. In fact, this crossing is the same for each j'' with $j' \leq j'' \leq j - 1$.

Hence, we have shown that after iteration j of the outer for-loop, at most $d - 1$ new crossings appear on the face f. It follows that after algorithm PATCH(G, r) has terminated, the graph G' contains at most $r + d - 1$ edges that cross f. ∎

We next consider the running time of algorithm PATCH(G, r).

Lemma 19.6.5. *For every integer $r \geq 1$, algorithm* PATCH(G, r) *takes $O((n/\epsilon^{2d+1})$ $\log(n/\epsilon))$ time.*

PROOF   Using Lemmas 19.6.2 and 19.6.3, it can be shown that the total running time of algorithm PATCH(G, r) is $O(I(G)(\log I(G) + \log(n/\epsilon)))$ plus the total amount of time needed to compute the sets V for all calls to algorithm BOUNDARYPATCH. Using the quadtree $QT(P, \mathbf{a})$, all these sets V can be computed in $O(I(G) \log L) = O(I(G) \log(n/\epsilon))$ time. Since $I(G) = O(n/\epsilon^{2d+1})$ (see Lemma 19.4.2), the claim in the lemma follows. ∎

We now analyze the weight of the graph G' that is returned by algorithm PATCH(G, r). Lemma 19.6.1 guarantees an upper bound on the increase in the weight of G' in one single call to algorithm BOUNDARYPATCH. We would like to show that after all calls to BOUNDARYPATCH have been completed, the total increase in weight is small. Below, we show that this is the case for the *expected* total increase in weight, assuming that the shift vector $\mathbf{a}$ is randomly chosen. It turns out to be convenient to treat the cases when $d = 2$ and $d > 2$ separately.

Lemma 19.6.6 (Patching Lemma, $d = 2$). *Assume that the values of a_1 and a_2 that define the shift vector **a** are chosen independently and uniformly at random in $\{1, 2, \ldots, L\}$. Let G' be the output of algorithm* PATCH(G, r). *Then,*

$$\mathbb{E}(wt(G') - wt(G)) \leq \frac{4\sqrt{2}}{r} \cdot wt(G).$$

PROOF Let h be a grid hyperplane. We analyze the expected contribution to $wt(G') - wt(G)$ that is due to h. For any integer j with $0 \leq j \leq 1 + \log L$, we define c_j to be the number of times that algorithm BOUNDARYPATCH is called when h is processed during iteration j of the outer for-loop. Let i be the level of h. Then, i is a random variable, and for all $j \geq i$, c_j does not depend on i. We first claim that

$$\sum_{j=0}^{1+\log L} c_j \leq I(G, h)/r.$$

To prove this claim, observe that prior to a call of BOUNDARYPATCH(G', f, V), the graph G' has at least $r + 1$ edges that cross f. Immediately after this call, G' contains only one edge that crosses f. Thus, each call to BOUNDARYPATCH that is due to h reduces the number of edges that cross h by at least r. The claim then follows from Lemma 19.6.3 and the fact that at the start of algorithm PATCH(G, r), the graph G' contains $I(G, h)$ edges that cross h.

The faces f that are considered in iteration j have length $2L/2^j$. (Since $d = 2$, these faces are line segments.) Therefore, by Lemma 19.6.1, the total contribution to $wt(G') - wt(G)$ due to h is less than or equal to

$$\sum_{j=i}^{1+\log L} \frac{4L}{2^j} \cdot c_j.$$

Using Lemma 19.4.3, it follows that the total expected contribution to $wt(G') - wt(G)$ due to h is less than or equal to

$$\sum_{i=0}^{1+\log L} \frac{2^{i-1}}{L} \sum_{j=i}^{1+\log L} \frac{4L}{2^j} \cdot c_j = 2 \sum_{j=0}^{1+\log L} c_j \sum_{i=0}^{j} 2^{i-j}$$

$$\leq 4 \sum_{j=0}^{1+\log L} c_j$$

$$\leq \frac{4}{r} \cdot I(G, h).$$

If we apply this upper bound to all grid hyperplanes h and use the linearity of expectation, then we obtain

$$\mathbb{E}(wt(G') - wt(G)) \leq \sum_{h:\text{grid hyperplane}} \frac{4}{r} \cdot I(G, h) = \frac{4}{r} \cdot I(G).$$

Since, by Lemma 19.4.1, $I(G) \leq \sqrt{2} \cdot wt(G)$, the proof is complete. ∎

Lemma 19.6.7 (Patching Lemma, $d > 2$). *Assume that the values of $a_1, a_2, \ldots, a_d$ that define the shift vector **a** are chosen independently and uniformly at random in $\{1, 2, \ldots, L\}$. Let G' be the output of algorithm* PATCH(G, r). *Then,*

$$\mathbb{E}(wt(G') - wt(G)) = O\left(\frac{1}{r^{1/(d-1)}} \cdot wt(G)\right).$$

PROOF Let h be a grid hyperplane. As in the proof of Lemma 19.6.6, we analyze the expected contribution to $wt(G') - wt(G)$ that is due to h. For any integer j with $0 \le j \le 1 + \log L$, let c_j be the number of times that algorithm BOUNDARYPATCH is called when h is processed during iteration j of the outer for-loop. For each k with $1 \le k \le c_j$, we define m_{jk} to be the decrease in the number of edges of the graph G' that cross h during the k-th call to algorithm BOUNDARYPATCH in iteration j of the outer for-loop.

In one execution of algorithm BOUNDARYPATCH, at least $r + 1$ crossings are replaced by one crossing. Therefore, we have $m_{jk} \ge r$. Also,

$$\sum_{j=0}^{1+\log L} \sum_{k=1}^{c_j} m_{jk} \le I(G, h).$$

Let i be the level of h. The faces f that are considered in iteration j have length $2L/2^j$. Therefore, by Lemma 19.6.1, the total contribution to $wt(G') - wt(G)$ due to h is

$$O\left(\sum_{j=i}^{1+\log L} \sum_{k=1}^{c_j} \frac{L}{2^j} \left(m_{jk} + 1\right)^{1-1/(d-1)} \right).$$

Using Lemma 19.4.3, it follows that the total expected contribution to $wt(G') - wt(G)$ due to h is

$$O\left(\sum_{i=0}^{1+\log L} \frac{2^i - 1}{L} \sum_{j=i}^{1+\log L} \sum_{k=1}^{c_j} \frac{L}{2^j} \left(m_{jk} + 1\right)^{1-1/(d-1)} \right)$$

$$= O\left(\sum_{j=0}^{1+\log L} \sum_{k=1}^{c_j} \left(m_{jk} + 1\right)^{1-1/(d-1)} \sum_{i=0}^{j} 2^{i-j} \right)$$

$$= O\left(\sum_{j=0}^{1+\log L} \sum_{k=1}^{c_j} \left(m_{jk} + 1\right)^{1-1/(d-1)} \right)$$

$$= O\left(\sum_{j=0}^{1+\log L} \sum_{k=1}^{c_j} \left(m_{jk} + 1\right) \frac{1}{(m_{jk} + 1)^{1/(d-1)}} \right).$$

Since $m_{jk} \ge r$, the latter quantity is

$$O\left(\frac{1}{r^{1/(d-1)}} \sum_{j=0}^{1+\log L} \sum_{k=1}^{c_j} \left(m_{jk} + 1\right) \right).$$

Again using the fact that $m_{jk} \ge r$, we have

$$m_{jk} + 1 \le m_{jk} + m_{jk}/r \le 2m_{jk}.$$

Therefore, the total expected contribution to $wt(G') - wt(G)$ due to h is

$$O\left(\frac{1}{r^{1/(d-1)}} \sum_{j=0}^{1+\log L} \sum_{k=1}^{c_j} m_{jk} \right) = O\left(\frac{1}{r^{1/(d-1)}} \cdot I(G, h) \right).$$

By applying this upper bound to all grid hyperplanes h, and using the linearity of expectation, it follows that

$$\mathbb{E}(wt(G') - wt(G)) = O\left(\sum_{h:\text{grid hyperplane}} \frac{1}{r^{1/(d-1)}} \cdot I(G,h)\right)$$

$$= O\left(\frac{1}{r^{1/(d-1)}} \cdot I(G)\right).$$

Since, by Lemma 19.4.1, $I(G) \leq \sqrt{d} \cdot wt(G)$, the proof is complete. ∎

It is interesting to note that although, by Lemma 19.6.1, the increase in weight due to a single application of algorithm BOUNDARYPATCH is proportional to the side length of the face with respect to which the algorithm is applied, the Patching Lemma (Lemmas 19.6.6 and 19.6.7) shows that the overall expected increase in weight is independent of the total side lengths of the faces of the grid hyperplane.

Consider again the graph G' that is computed by algorithm PATCH(G, r). Observe that the vertex set of G' contains P. We define a *tour of P in G'* to be a (possibly nonsimple) cycle in G' that visits each point of P at least once.

We now use the Patching Lemma to obtain an efficient randomized algorithm that computes a shift vector $\mathbf{a}$ for which the graph G' that is computed by algorithm PATCH(G, r) contains a tour of P, whose weight is approiximately equal to $wt(TSP(P))$.

Algorithm GOODSHIFTVECTOR(P, r)

Comment: This algorithm takes as input the set P that was defined in Section 19.2, and an integer $r \geq d$. It returns a shift vector $\mathbf{a}$, the corresponding quadtree $QT(P, \mathbf{a})$, and the graph G' that is computed by algorithm PATCH(G, r).

Step 1: Compute the $(1 + \epsilon)$-spanner G of Lemma 19.3.2.

Step 2: Choose $a_1, a_2, \ldots, a_d$ independently and uniformly at random in $\{1, 2, \ldots, L\}$, construct the quadtree $QT(P, \mathbf{a})$, where $\mathbf{a} = (a_1, a_2, \ldots, a_d)$, and run algorithm PATCH$(G, r - d + 1)$. Let G' be the output of this patching algorithm.

Step 3: Compute the weights of G and G'. If

$$wt(G') - wt(G) \leq 2 \cdot \frac{\alpha}{r^{1/(d-1)}} \cdot wt(G),$$

where α is the constant in the Big-Oh bound in the Patching Lemma (Lemmas 19.6.6 and 19.6.7), then return $\mathbf{a}$, $QT(P, \mathbf{a})$, and G'. Otherwise, go back to Step 2.

The following lemma states the main properties of the output of algorithm GOODSHIFTVECTOR. The third claim in this lemma states that the graph G' that is returned by this algorithm contains a tour C' of P, whose length is at most $(1 + \delta) \cdot wt(TSP(P))$, for some real number $\delta > 0$, provided that r is chosen such that $\epsilon^{2d} r^{1/(d-1)} \gg 1$.

Lemma 19.6.8. *Consider the set P that was defined in Section 19.2, and let r be an integer with $r \geq d$. In $O((n/\epsilon^{4d-1}) \log n)$ expected time, algorithm* GOODSHIFTVECTOR(P, r)

computes a shift vector **a**, *the corresponding quadtree* $QT(P, \mathbf{a})$, *and a graph* G', *such that the following properties hold:*

1. *P is contained in the vertex set of* G'.

2. G' *is* r-*light with respect to* $QT(P, \mathbf{a})$.

3. *There exists a tour* C' *of* P *in* G' *that has the following properties:*

    (a) C' *traverses each edge of* G' *at most once in each direction.*

    (b) *The weight of* C' *is at most*

$$\left(1 + \epsilon + O\left(\frac{1}{\epsilon^{2d} r^{1/(d-1)}}\right)\right) \cdot wt(TSP(P)).$$

PROOF   Recall Markov's inequality, which states that, with probability at least $1/2$, the value of a nonnegative random variable X is at most twice the expected value of X. As a result, the expected number of times that Steps 2 and 3 are carried out is at most 2. The claim on the expected running time in the lemma thus follows from Lemmas 19.3.2, 19.4.4, and 19.6.5. The first two claims in the lemma follow from Lemma 19.6.4.

It remains to prove the third claim. Consider the $(1 + \epsilon)$-spanner G for P. Let C be a tour of P in G, whose weight is minimum. The graph G' is obtained by running algorithm PATCH$(G, r - d + 1)$. This algorithm transforms C into a tour C' of P in G': Initially, C' is equal to C. Consider the current tour C' and assume that algorithm BOUNDARYPATCH(G', f, V) is called for some face f. Let $\{x, y\}$ be an edge of C' that crosses f. Using the notation of algorithm BOUNDARYPATCH, we obtain a new tour of P, by replacing $\{x, y\}$ by the concatenation of (i) the edge $\{x, x^+\}$, (ii) the path in T_f^+ between x^+ and z^+, (iii) the patching bridge $\{z^+, z^-\}$, (iv) the path in T_f^- between z^- and x^-, and (v) the edge $\{x^-, y\}$.

Consider the tour C' of P that is obtained after all calls to BOUNDARYPATCH have been completed. Assume that there is an edge $\{x, y\}$ of G', such that C' traverses this edge twice in the direction from x to y. Then, we can write C' as $R_1, x, y, R_2, x, y, R_3$, where R_1, R_2, and R_3 are (possibly nonsimple) paths in G'. Consider the tour that is the concatenation of R_1, the reverse of R_2, and R_3. This tour still visits all points of P. By repeatedly applying these short-cutting steps, we obtain a tour C' of P in G', which traverses each edge of G' at most once in each direction. Observe that this tour C' is basically the union of C and a collection of paths in the graphs in shadow faces that are added during algorithm PATCH$(G, r - d + 1)$. Since each edge in any of these graphs is traversed at most twice, it follows that

$$wt(C') \leq wt(C) + 2\left(wt(G') - wt(G)\right)$$

and, therefore, by the condition in Step 3 of algorithm GOODSHIFTVECTOR,

$$wt(C') \leq wt(C) + O\left(\frac{1}{r^{1/(d-1)}} \cdot wt(G)\right).$$

By Lemma 19.3.1, we have $wt(C) \leq (1 + \epsilon) \cdot wt(TSP(P))$, whereas by Lemma 19.3.2 and Exercise 1.6, $wt(G) = O(1/\epsilon^{2d}) \cdot wt(TSP(P))$. It follows that

$$wt(C') \leq (1 + \epsilon) \cdot wt(TSP(P)) + O\left(\frac{1}{\epsilon^{2d} r^{1/(d-1)}} \cdot wt(TSP(P))\right),$$

completing the proof of the third claim.   ∎

Consider the output **a**, $QT(P, \mathbf{a})$, and G' of algorithm GOODSHIFTVECTOR(P, r). Lemma 19.6.8 implies that we can use dynamic programming to compute a minimum-weight tour of P in the r-light graph G'. The following *Structure Theorem* allows us to simplify the dynamic programming algorithm.

For every face f that is common to two sibling hypercubes in $QT(P, \mathbf{a})$, we define the *portals* of f to be the intersections between f and the edges of G'. Observe that each such face contains at most r portals. Let P' be the union of P and the set of all portals. We define a *tour of P in P'* to be a (possibly nonsimple) cycle C whose vertex set is contained in P' and that visits each point of P exactly once. The Structure Theorem states that we can ignore the graph G', and compute a minimum-weight tour of P in P' that visits each portal at most twice. This tour crosses any face that is common to two sibling hypercubes only at portals, and its weight is approximately equal to $wt(TSP(P))$, provided that the value of r is sufficiently large.

Theorem 19.6.9 (Structure Theorem). *Consider the set P that was defined in Section 19.2, and let r be an integer with $r \geq d$. In $O((n/\epsilon^{4d-1}) \log n)$ expected time, we can compute a shift vector $\mathbf{a}$, the corresponding quadtree $QT(P, \mathbf{a})$, and a set P' of points, such that the following properties hold:*

1. *$P \subseteq P'$.*

2. *Each point of $P' \setminus P$ is contained in a face that is common to some pair of sibling hypercubes in $QT(P, \mathbf{a})$.*

3. *For every face f that is common to two sibling hypercubes in $QT(P, \mathbf{a})$, P' contains at most r points that are in f.*

4. *There exists a tour C of P in P' that has the following properties:*

   (a) *C visits each point of $P' \setminus P$ at most twice.*

   (b) *C is $(2r)$-light with respect to $QT(P, \mathbf{a})$. That is, for every face f that is common to two sibling hypercubes in $QT(P, \mathbf{a})$, every crossing of C with f is at a vertex of $P' \setminus P$.*

   (c) *The weight of C is at most*

   $$\left(1 + \epsilon + O\left(\frac{1}{\epsilon^{2d} r^{1/(d-1)}}\right)\right) \cdot wt(TSP(P)).$$

PROOF   Consider the shift vector $\mathbf{a}$, the corresponding quadtree $QT(P, \mathbf{a})$, and the graph G', as given by Lemma 19.6.8. We define P' to be the union of P and the set of all crossings between edges of G' and faces that are common to two sibling hypercubes in $QT(P, \mathbf{a})$.

The first and second claims in the theorem obviously hold. The third claim follows from the fact that the graph G' is r-light with respect to $QT(P, \mathbf{a})$. To prove the fourth claim, consider the tour C' of P in G', as given in Lemma 19.6.8. Observe that each point of $P' \setminus P$ is in the interior of some edge of G'. Since G' is r-light with respect to $QT(P, \mathbf{a})$, and since C' traverses each edge of G' at most once in each direction, it follows that C' is $(2r)$-light with respect to $QT(P, \mathbf{a})$, and C' visits each point of $P' \setminus P$ at most twice. Consider a portion of C' whose endpoints are on the boundary of some hypercube that is stored in $QT(P, \mathbf{a})$, and that is completely contained in this hypercube. Let x and y be the endpoints of this portion. Observe that x and y are elements of $P' \setminus P$. By shortcutting, we replace this portion (which is a path in G') by a path that visits only points of P'. This new path is still contained in the same hypercube. Having done this for all hypercubes in $QT(P, \mathbf{a})$, we have obtained a tour C of P in P' that satisfies the requirements in the fourth claim in the theorem. (We may have to perform more shortcutting steps to guarantee that each point of P is traversed exactly once.)   ∎

In the next section, we will show how dynamic programming can be used to compute a minimum-weight tour of P in P' that satisfies conditions 4.(a)–(c) in the Structure Theorem. The next lemma states that such a tour leads to a tour of the original point set S, whose weight is approximately equal to $wt(TSP(S))$, assuming that the parameter r is chosen sufficiently large.

Lemma 19.6.10. *Let C be a minimum-weight tour of P in P' that satisfies conditions 4.(a)–(c) in the Structure Theorem. In $O(rn \log(n/\epsilon))$ time, we can convert C to a tour T of the original point set S, such that*

$$wt(T) \leq \left((1+\epsilon) \left(1 + \epsilon + O\left(\frac{1}{\epsilon^{2d} r^{1/(d-1)}} \right) \right) + \epsilon \right) \cdot wt(TSP(S)).$$

PROOF Recall from Section 19.2 that the set P is a scaled copy of the set S', where S' is obtained by moving each point of S to the nearest grid point in the uniform grid with sides of length B/L. We convert C to a tour T of S through the following sequence of steps:

1. By shortcutting, convert C to a tour C' of P. Thus, C' visits each point of P exactly once and returns to the starting point.
2. By scaling, convert C' to a tour C'' of S'.
3. By applying a transformation similar to the one in the proof of Lemma 19.2.2, convert C'' to a tour T of S.

It follows from Lemma 19.4.4 and the Structure Theorem (Theorem 19.6.9) that the number of edges of C is $O(rn \log(n/\epsilon))$. This implies that the entire conversion from C to T can be done in $O(rn \log(n/\epsilon))$ time.

To estimate the weight of the tour T, we make the following observations: By the Structure Theorem, we have

$$wt(C) \leq \left(1 + \epsilon + O\left(\frac{1}{\epsilon^{2d} r^{1/(d-1)}} \right) \right) \cdot wt(TSP(P)).$$

By scaling and Lemma 19.2.2, we have

$$wt(TSP(P)) = \frac{L}{B} \cdot wt(TSP(S')) \leq \frac{(1+\epsilon)L}{B} \cdot wt(TSP(S)).$$

By scaling and the triangle inequality, we have

$$wt(C'') = \frac{B}{L} \cdot wt(C') \leq \frac{B}{L} \cdot wt(C).$$

Finally, an argument that is similar to the one in the proof of Lemma 19.2.2 shows that

$$wt(T) \leq wt(C'') + \epsilon \cdot wt(TSP(S)).$$

By combining these bounds, it follows that the weight of T is bounded from above by the quantity that is stated in the lemma. ∎

19.7 The dynamic programming step

Let r be an integer with $r \geq d$. We assume that we have already computed a shift vector $\mathbf{a}$, the corresponding quadtree $QT(P, \mathbf{a})$, and the set P', as given by the Structure Theorem (Theorem 19.6.9). Recall that each point of $P' \setminus P$ is called a portal, and that it is in a face that is common to some pair of sibling hypercubes in $QT(P, \mathbf{a})$. Moreover, each such face contains at most r portals.

In this section, we give an algorithm that computes a minimum-weight tour of P in P' that satisfies conditions 4.(a)–(c) in the Structure Theorem. The strategy is to find portions of this tour in each of the hypercubes in $QT(P, \mathbf{a})$, and then "stitch" them together.

> **Basic idea:** Dynamic programming is applied to solve a hierarchy of subproblems that are generated from the quadtree. Three things need to be specified for this step to work: The subproblems to be solved, a procedure for solving the "basis" subproblems (for leaves of the quadtree), and a procedure for combining optimal solutions to subproblems to optimally solve larger subproblems. The basis subproblems can be solved efficiently, because they involve only $O(r)$ portals and at most one point of P. Combining subproblems can be done efficiently: The interactions between subproblems is bounded, because we want an optimal tour that is $(2r)$-light with respect to the quadtree.

Consider a minimum-weight tour C of P in P' that satisfies conditions 4.(a)–(c) in the Structure Theorem, and let H be any hypercube in the quadtree $QT(P, \mathbf{a})$. The part of C that is inside H consists of a collection of paths, such that (i) each endpoint of each path is a portal on the boundary of H, (ii) each point of $P \cap H$ is on exactly one of these paths, and (iii) each portal on the boundary of H occurs at most twice as an endpoint of these paths. (The endpoints of one path may be the same.) Let A denote the set of all portals on the faces of H, and let m be the size of A. Then, $m \le 2dr$, and the subproblems for the hypercube H are specified by the following inputs:

1. An integer k with $1 \le k \le m$.
2. A sequence $b_1, b'_1, b_2, b'_2, \ldots, b_k, b'_k$ of points in A, such that each element of A appears at most twice in this sequence.

The solution to this subproblem consists of a collection of k paths, such that

1. for each i with $1 \le i \le k$, the i-th path is between b_i and b'_i,
2. each point of $P \cap H$ is on exactly one of these paths, and
3. the total weight of these paths is minimum.

Observe that the optimal tour C of P in P' "contains" the solution to one of these subproblems for H.

We first estimate the number of subproblems that are generated by H. For any k with $1 \le k \le m$, there are $\binom{2m}{2k}$ ways to choose $2k$ elements in A, such that each element of A is chosen at most twice. Given $2k$ such elements, there are $(2k)!$ ways to label them $b_1, b'_1, b_2, b'_2, \ldots, b_k, b'_k$. Since b_i and b'_i can be considered to be an unordered pair, it follows that the number of subproblems due to H is

$$\sum_{k=1}^{m} \binom{2m}{2k} \frac{(2k)!}{2^k} \le (2m)! \sum_{k=1}^{m} \frac{1}{(2m - 2k)!} \le e(2m)! \le e(4dr)^{4dr} = r^{O(r)}.$$

The dynamic programming algorithm traverses the quadtree in postorder. Assume that the current node visited is a leaf storing the hypercube H. Then, each subproblem for H is solved in the following way: If H does not contain any point of P, then the solution is $\sum_{i=1}^{k} |b_i b_i'|$. Otherwise, H contains exactly one point, say p, of P. In this case, the solution is

$$\min_{1 \leq j \leq k} \left(|b_j p| + |p b_j'| + \sum_{i \neq j} |b_i b_i'| \right).$$

Now assume that the current node visited in the postorder traversal is not a leaf. Let H be the hypercube stored in the current node, and consider any of its subproblems. The solution to this subproblem is computed by taking the best solution that is obtained by combining solutions to *compatible* subproblems for the 2^d children hypercubes of H. Here, we say that subproblems for two hypercubes are *compatible* if their common portals, if any, are paired in the two subproblems in a consistent manner.

The last node visited in the postorder traversal is the root of the quadtree. The hypercube H stored at the root generates only one problem, because there are no portals on the faces of H. Thus, by combining the solutions to all compatible subproblems of the 2^d children hypercubes of H, we obtain a minimum-weight tour of P in P' that satisfies conditions 4.(a)–(c) in the Structure Theorem. In this way, we obtain only the weight of this tour. It is, however, easy to extend the algorithm, such that the actual tour is obtained as well.

We estimate the running time of the dynamic programming algorithm. By Lemma 19.4.4, the quadtree has $O(n \log(n/\epsilon))$ nodes. Since each hypercube generates $r^{O(r)}$ subproblems, the algorithm spends $r^{O(r)}$ time at each node. Thus, the running time of the entire dynamic programming algorithm is

$$O\left(r^{O(r)} n \log(n/\epsilon)\right). \tag{19.9}$$

Let C be the tour of P in P' that is computed by the algorithm. By Lemma 19.6.10, C can be converted to a tour T of the original point set S, such that

$$wt(T) \leq \left((1 + \epsilon) \left(1 + \epsilon + O\left(\frac{1}{\epsilon^{2d} r^{1/(d-1)}} \right) \right) + \epsilon \right) \cdot wt(TSP(S)).$$

If we take

$$r = \frac{c}{\epsilon^{(2d-1)(d-1)}},$$

for an appropriate constant c (that depends on d), then

$$wt(T) \leq (1 + 6\epsilon) \cdot wt(TSP(S)).$$

Thus, if we replace ϵ by $\epsilon/6$ in the entire algorithm, and use Lemma 19.2.4, the Structure Theorem (Theorem 19.6.9), Lemma 19.6.10, and the bound in (19.9), then we obtain the main result of this chapter:

Theorem 19.7.1. *Let S be a set of n points in $\mathbb{R}^d$, and let $\epsilon > 0$ be a real number. In*

$$(1/\epsilon)^{O(1/\epsilon^{d^2})} n \log n$$

expected time, a tour of S can be computed, whose length is at most $(1 + \epsilon) \cdot wt(TSP(S))$.

Exercises

19.1. Prove Lemma 19.4.4.

19.2. Prove the first claim in Lemma 19.5.1.

19.3. Explain why in algorithm $\text{PATCH}(G, r)$ (see Section 19.6), the index j goes down from $1 + \log L$ to 0, rather than up from 0 to $1 + \log L$.

19.4. Consider the following modification to algorithm $\text{PATCH}(G, r)$ in Section 19.6: In the j-th iteration of the outer for-loop, we consider only grid hyperplanes h, whose level is equal to j. Prove that for this modified algorithm, the Patching Lemma (Lemmas 19.6.6 and 19.6.7) does not hold. In particular, show that, in the two-dimensional case,

$$\mathbb{E}(wt(G') - wt(G)) = O\left(\frac{wt(G)}{r} \log L\right) = O\left(\frac{wt(G)}{r} \log(n/\epsilon)\right).$$

19.5. Work out the details in the proof of Lemma 19.6.5.

19.6. The algorithm that computes a $(1 + \epsilon)$-approximation for the traveling salesperson problem uses the $(1 + \epsilon)$-spanner G as given by Lemma 19.3.2. Explain why it is essential that the weight of G is proportional to the weight of a minimum spanning tree of the point set P.

Bibliographic notes

This chapter is based on Rao and Smith [1998], who showed how to use spanners to speed up the polynomial-time approximation scheme of Arora [1998]. These authors also show how the generic PTAS of Section 19.1 can be used to design approximation algorithms for several other geometric optimization problems.

More information about approximation algorithms for the traveling salesperson problem is given in the bibliographic notes in Chapter 1.

20

Further Results and Open Problems

In this chapter, we give a brief overview of further results on geometric spanners. We also present several open problems.

20.1 Spanners of low degree

In this book, we have seen several algorithms that solve the following version of the spanner problem: Determine a "small" function $F(d, t)$, such that for any set S of n points in $\mathbb{R}^d$, a t-spanner for S with maximum degree at most $F(d, t)$ exists. We showed in Theorems 10.1.3 and 10.1.10 that $F(d, t) = O(1/(t - 1)^{2d-1})$. These theorems in fact show that such spanners can be computed in $O(n \log n)$ time.

Dobkin, Friedman, and Supowit [1990] posed a dual version of this spanner problem. That is, they asked for the smallest integer D_d, having the following property: There exists a real number t, such that for any finite set S of points in $\mathbb{R}^d$, a t-spanner for S with maximum degree at most D_d exists.

Dobkin, Friedman, and Supowit [1990] stated that $3 \leq D_2 \leq 7$. The following argument, due to Das and Heffernan [1996], shows that $D_2 \geq 3$. Assume that n is an even perfect square, and let S be the set of n points that are the vertices of a $\sqrt{n} \times \sqrt{n}$ grid, whose cells have sides of length 1. Let G be an arbitrary connected graph with vertex set S and having maximum degree 2. Then, G is either a path or a cycle. Hence, we can number the points according to their order along G as $p_1, p_2, \ldots, p_n$. Since each edge of G has length at least 1, the distance in G between p_1 and $p_{n/2}$ is at least $n/2 - 1$. On the other hand, the Euclidean distance between p_1 and $p_{n/2}$ is at most $\sqrt{2}(\sqrt{n} - 1)$. It follows that the stretch factor of G is at least

$$\frac{n/2 - 1}{\sqrt{2}(\sqrt{n} - 1)} = \Omega(\sqrt{n}).$$

This proves that, for every real number $t > 1$, there exists an integer n and a set S of n points in the plane, such that a t-spanner for S having maximum degree 2 does not exist.

The upper bound for D_2 was improved by Soares [1994], who proved that $D_2 \leq 5$. Salowe [1994] presented the following approach, which works for any constant dimension $d \geq 2$: Let S be a set of n points in $\mathbb{R}^d$, let $t > 1$ be a real number, let D be a positive integer, and let G be an arbitrary t-spanner for S having maximum degree D. Salowe proposed an algorithm that transforms G into a t'-spanner for S having maximum degree $\lfloor D/2 \rfloor + 2$, where $t' = 117t + 32 \cdot 3^{d+1}$. He did not provide an analysis of the running time, but the transformation can be implemented, such that it runs in $O(n \log n)$ time. Let G be one of the t-spanners in Theorems 10.1.3 and 10.1.10 with, say, $t = 2$. Observe that the maximum degree of G depends only on the dimension d. If we start with G, and apply Salowe's transformation $O(\log D) = O(1)$ times, then we obtain a t'-spanner for S having maximum degree 4. Thus, we have $D_d \leq 4$ for all $d \geq 2$. In fact, this result shows that a spanner of maximum degree 4 and constant stretch factor can be computed in $O(n \log n)$ time.

The problem of determining D_d was settled by Das and Heffernan [1996]; they proved that $D_d = 3$. In fact, they prove the following stronger result:

Theorem 20.1.1. *Let S be a set of n points in $\mathbb{R}^d$ and let $\epsilon > 0$ be a real number. In $O(n \log n)$ time, a t-spanner for S (where t depends on ϵ and d) can be constructed that has maximum degree 3 and at most $(1 + \epsilon)n$ edges, and whose weight is proportional to the weight of a minimum spanning tree of S.*

20.2 Spanners with few edges

Let S be a set of n points in $\mathbb{R}^d$, and let $t > 1$ be a real number. Since any t-spanner for S is a connected graph, it must have at least $n - 1$ edges. If the spanner has exactly $n - 1$ edges, then it is a tree, and we call it a *tree t-spanner* for S. Is there a constant t, such that a tree t-spanner exists for every point set S? The proof in Section 20.1 that $D_2 \geq 3$ suggests that the answer to this question is "no." We will prove in Theorem 20.2.1 below that this is indeed the case.

We first estimate the stretch factor of a minimum spanning tree T of S. Consider any two distinct points p and q of S, and let $p = p_1, p_2, p_3, \ldots, p_k = q$ be the path in T between p and q. We claim that the length of each edge $\{p_i, p_{i+1}\}$, $1 \leq i < k$, on this path is less than or equal to $|pq|$. Indeed, if this is not the case, then we replace any edge $\{p_i, p_{i+1}\}$ whose length is larger than $|pq|$ by the edge $\{p, q\}$, giving a spanning tree of lower weight. It follows that the length of the path between p and q is less than or equal to $(k - 1)|pq|$, which is at most $(n - 1)|pq|$, because $k \leq n$. Thus, any minimum spanning tree of any set of n points in $\mathbb{R}^d$ is an $(n - 1)$-spanner. Of course, this gives only an upper bound on the stretch factor. It is, however, not difficult to give an example of a set of n points in $\mathbb{R}^d$, whose minimum spanning tree has stretch factor $n - 1$. Hence, in general, minimum spanning trees do not have a bounded stretch factor. The following theorem, which is due to Eppstein [2000], states that there exist point sets S for which *every* spanning tree has stretch factor $\Omega(n)$. (Aronov et al. [2005] proved that a similar result even holds for Steiner trees of S.)

Theorem 20.2.1. *Let R be planar regular polygon with n vertices, where $n \equiv 0 \mod 4$, and let S be the vertex set of R. The stretch factor of every spanning tree of S is at least $(\sqrt{2}/\pi)n$.*

PROOF We may assume without loss of generality that the points of S are on the unit-circle. Let T be an arbitrary spanning tree of S, and let v be a centroid node of T (see Section 2.3.4). Hence, by removing v from T, we obtain subtrees, each of which contains at most $n/2$ points of S. We may assume without loss of generality that v is the north-pole of the unit-circle. Observe that more than half of the points of S are on or below the x-axis. Therefore, there are two points p and q in S that are (i) adjacent in R, (ii) in different subtrees of v, and (iii) on or below the x-axis. Let P be the path in T between p and q. Since P passes through v, the length of P is at least $2\sqrt{2}$. On the other hand, the Euclidean distance between p and q is at most $2\pi/n$. ∎

Thus, graphs with $n - 1$ edges can have unbounded stretch factor. What happens to the stretch factor if we allow $n - 1 + k$ edges, for some small integer k? Theorem 20.1.1 shows that a constant stretch factor can be obtained if $k = \epsilon n$, for any constant $\epsilon > 0$. The following theorem generalizes this result for all k with $0 \leq k \leq n$. This result was proved by Aronov et al. [2005] for point sets in the plane. The construction was generalized by Smid [2006] to any dimension $d \geq 2$.

Theorem 20.2.2. *Let S be a set of n points in $\mathbb{R}^d$, and let k be an integer with $0 \leq k \leq n$. In $O(n \log n)$ time, a graph with vertex set S can be computed that has the following properties:*

1. *The graph contains at most $n - 1 + k$ edges.*
2. *The graph has stretch factor $O(n/(k + 1))$.*
3. *Each vertex of the graph has degree at most 5.*

Aronov et al. [2005] extended the proof of Theorem 20.2.1 and gave an example of a set S of n points in the plane, such that every connected graph with vertex set S and consisting of $n - 1 + k$ edges has stretch factor $\Omega(n/(k + 1))$. Therefore, the result in Theorem 20.2.2 is optimal with respect to the number of edges and stretch factor.

> **Open problem 1:** Decrease the bound on the maximum degree in Theorem 20.2.2.

20.3 Plane spanners

In this section, we give a very brief overview of the large amount of research that has been devoted to the construction of plane spanners, that is, spanners for point sets in $\mathbb{R}^2$ whose embeddings are plane. In fact, the first publication on geometric spanners (see Chew [1986]) was on plane spanners.

Chew [1986] proved the following result: The L_1-Delaunay triangulation of a set S of points in $\mathbb{R}^2$, that is, the dual of the Voronoi diagram of S in the Manhattan metric, is a $\sqrt{10}$-spanner. (Observe that, even though the Delaunay triangulation is based on the L_1-metric, the stretch factor is measured in the Euclidean metric.) The journal version of this paper (see Chew [1989]) contains the following result: The Delaunay triangulation, based on a convex distance function defined by an equilateral triangle, is a 2-spanner.

Chew [1986] conjectured that, for any set S of points in $\mathbb{R}^2$, the Delaunay triangulation, based on the Euclidean metric, is a t-spanner, for some constant t. This conjecture was proved by Dobkin et al. [1990], who showed that $t \leq \pi(1 + \sqrt{5})/2$. The analysis was improved by Keil and Gutwin [1992], who showed that $t \leq \frac{2\pi}{3 \cos \pi/6}$. A more general result appears in Bose et al. [2004b]: For every two points p and q of S, the Delaunay triangulation contains a path between p and q of length at most $\frac{2\pi}{3 \cos \pi/6} \cdot |pq|$, all of whose edges have length at most $|pq|$.

If the points of S are (approximately) on the boundary of a circle, then the stretch factor of the Delaunay triangulation is at least $\pi/2$. It is widely believed that, for every set of points in $\mathbb{R}^2$, the Delaunay triangulation is a $(\pi/2)$-spanner.

> **Open problem 2:** Prove that, for every set S of points in $\mathbb{R}^2$, the Delaunay triangulation of S is a $(\pi/2)$-spanner.

Eppstein [2002] and Bose et al. [2006] proved that the stretch factors of the Gabriel graph, the relative neighborhood graph, and β-skeletons are not bounded by any constant.

Das and Joseph [1989] introduced a general approach for analyzing the stretch factor of plane graphs. Let α be a real number, such that $0 < \alpha < \pi/2$. The α-*diamond* of a line segment e is defined to be the union of the two isosceles triangles with base e and base angle α. A plane graph G with vertex set S is said to have the α-*diamond property*, if for every edge e of G, at least one of the triangles comprising the α-diamond of e does not contain any point of S in its interior. For a real number $\kappa \geq 1$, we say that G satisfies the κ-*good polygon property*, if for every face f of G, and for every two vertices p and q of G, such that p and q are on the boundary of f, and the line segment joining them is completely inside f, the shortest path between p and q along the boundary of f has length at most $\kappa|pq|$. Das and Joseph [1989] proved that the stretch factor of G is bounded by a function that depends only on α and κ, if G satisfies both the α-diamond property and the κ-good polygon property. A complete proof of this claim appears in Das [1990]. The analysis was improved slightly by Lee [2004]:

Theorem 20.3.1. *Let $\alpha \in (0, \pi/2)$ and $\kappa \geq 1$ be real numbers, and let G be a plane graph that satisfies the α-diamond property and the κ-good polygon property. Then, G is a t-spanner, where*

$$t \leq \frac{8(\pi - \alpha)^2 \kappa}{\alpha^2 \sin^2(\alpha/4)}.$$

Observe that every triangulation satisfies the κ-good polygon property with $\kappa = 1$. Several classes of triangulations satisfy the α-diamond property, for some α, and are, thus spanners. For example, it is obvious that this holds for the Delaunay triangulation with $\alpha = \pi/4$. (Observe, however, that Theorem 20.3.1 gives a stretch factor that is much worse than the result in Keil and Gutwin [1992].) In Drysdale, McElfresh, and Snoeyink [2001], this is shown for the minimum weight triangulation with $\alpha = \pi/4.6$. Finally, Lee [2004] shows this for the greedy triangulation with $\alpha = \pi/6$.

Plane spanners that satisfy the α-diamond property and the κ-good polygon property can be used to design competitive online routing algorithms that use a limited amount of memory. Some of these algorithms can be found in Bose and Morin [2004a,b].

Another general approach for estimating the stretch factor of triangulations appeared in Karavelas and Guibas [2001]: Let T be a triangle in $\mathbb{R}^2$, let ℓ be the length of a longest side of T, and let h be the corresponding height of T. The aspect ratio of T is defined to be ℓ/h. The aspect ratio of a triangulation on a set of points in $\mathbb{R}^2$ is defined to be the maximum aspect ratio of any triangle in the triangulation. Karavelas and Guibas [2001] proved that every triangulation with aspect ratio α is a (2α)-spanner.

As mentioned above, Chew [1989] showed that a plane 2-spanner exists for every set of points in the plane. It is clear that every plane graph on the four vertices of a square has stretch factor at least $\sqrt{2}$.

> **Open problem 3:** What is the smallest real number t, such that a plane t-spanner exists for every finite set of points in $\mathbb{R}^2$?

Levcopoulos and Lingas [1992] considered plane spanners of low weight. Using the result of Keil and Gutwin [1992], they showed that, given the Delaunay triangulation for a set S of n points in $\mathbb{R}^2$, and given any real number $r > 0$, a plane graph can be constructed in $O(n)$ time that is a t-spanner for $t = (1 + 1/r)\frac{2\pi}{3\cos\pi/6}$, and whose total weight is at most $2r + 1$ times the weight of a minimum spanning tree of S.

The problem of constructing plane t-spanners of bounded degree (for some constant t) was considered in Bose, Gudmundsson, and Smid [2005]. They present an algorithm that, when given a set S of n points in $\mathbb{R}^2$, computes a plane spanner for S, whose maximum degree is at most 27. The degree bound was improved to 23 by Li and Wang [2004]. Recently, Bose, Smid, and Xu [2006] gave an improved algorithm that constructs a plane spanner, whose maximum degree is at most 17. The spanners computed by all these algorithms are subgraphs of the Delaunay triangulation (and can be computed in $O(n \log n)$ time). In fact, Bose, Smid, and Xu [2006] show that every triangulation satisfying the α-diamond property contains a spanner, whose maximum degree is at most $14 + \lceil 2\pi/\alpha \rceil$.

> **Open problem 4:** What is the smallest real number D, such that, for some real number t that depends only on D, a plane t-spanner of maximum degree at most D exists, for every finite set of points in $\mathbb{R}^2$?

It is natural to try to generalize spanner results for triangulations to higher dimensional space. Unfortunately, not much is known. We mention the following result, which is due to Karavelas and Guibas [2001]. Let T be a tetrahedron in $\mathbb{R}^3$, let R be the radius of the smallest sphere that contains T, and let r be the radius of the largest sphere that is contained in T. The aspect ratio of T is defined to be R/r. Karavelas and Guibas [2001] proved that every triangulation of a set of points in $\mathbb{R}^3$, in which the aspect ratio of every tetrahedron is at most α, and in which the minimum interior angle is θ, is a t-spanner for $t = \max(4/\theta^2, \pi^2/4)$.

> **Open problem 5:** Does there exist a real constant t such that, for every finite set S of points in $\mathbb{R}^3$, the Delaunay triangulation of S is a t-spanner?

20.4 Spanners among obstacles

Consider a set of pairwise disjoint polyhedral objects, which we regard as obstacles. For a real number $t > 1$, a t-spanner for these obstacles is a graph G having the following properties: First, the vertex set of G includes the vertices of the polygons. Second, no edge of G intersects the interior of any polygon. Finally, for any two vertices p and q, there is a path in G between p and q, whose length is at most t times the length of a shortest obstacle-avoiding path between p and q.

Clarkson [1987] introduced the Θ-graph of Chapter 4, in order to construct such a spanner for the two- and three-dimensional cases. In his version of the Θ-graph, for each vertex p, space is covered using cones with apex p and having a fixed angular diameter. Then, for each cone C, the graph contains an edge between p and a closest vertex in C that can see p.

For the two-dimensional case, Das [1997] showed that a t-spanner of bounded degree can be computed in $O(n \log n)$ time, where n is the total number of vertices of the polygonal obstacles. Again for the two-dimensional case, Arikati et al. [1996] showed that by adding $O(n)$ Steiner points, a plane t-spanner can be constructed in $O(n \log n)$ time.

20.5 Single-source spanners

Given a set of n points in $\mathbb{R}^d$, a spanner is a network on this point set that would guarantee "short" paths between every pair of points. What if we do not desire a network with such stringent requirements? What if we have identified a "center" or "source" and we only require sufficiently "short" paths between this center and all other vertices? This is clearly a "single-source" equivalent of the spanner networks considered in this book. They are also an undirected version of the *sink spanners* presented in Section 4.2.1.

Definition 20.5.1 (Single-source spanner). *Let S be a set of n points in $\mathbb{R}^d$, let q be a point of S, and let $t > 1$ be a real number. A graph having the points of S as its vertices is called a t-spanner for S with source q, if for every point p of S there is a t-spanner path between p and q in this graph. The minimum value t for which the above definition holds is called the* single-source stretch factor *with respect to the source q.*

Khuller, Raghavachari, and Young [1995] showed that, given a weighted graph with n vertices and m edges (equivalently, given an arbitrary metric space), a specific *source* vertex, a stretch factor bound, and a (approximate) minimum spanning tree of the graph, it is possible to compute in $O(m + n)$ time a spanning tree for which the single-source stretch factor with respect to the source is bounded, and for which the total weight is within a constant factor of the weight of a minimum spanning tree. The resulting tree can be viewed as balancing the salubrious properties of minimum spanning trees (minimum weight) and shortest path trees (minimum distance from source) with respect to a given source.

How does the above algorithm fare for points in Euclidean space? Given n points in $\mathbb{R}^d$, we can use algorithm APPROXMST of Section 10.3.4 to compute an approximate minimum spanning tree in $O(n \log n)$ time. Given this spanning tree, the algorithm of Khuller, Raghavachari, and Young [1995] can compute the required tree for a specified source in $O(n)$ time. A related open problem is the following:

Open problem 6: Given a set S of n points in $\mathbb{R}^d$, design an efficient algorithm to find the best "source" vertex; that is, find the source vertex such that some spanning tree on S has the least single-source stretch factor (with respect to this source) among all the spanning trees.

If, instead of a point set, we are provided with a Euclidean graph G with n vertices and m edges, we can compute a minimum spanning tree of G in $O(n \log n + m)$ time. Thus, the required tree for a specified source can be computed in $O(n \log n + m)$ time, even if a minimum spanning tree is not available. The following open problem is closely related to the previous one.

Open problem 7: Given a Euclidean graph G with n vertices and m edges embedded in $\mathbb{R}^d$, design an efficient algorithm to find the best "source" vertex; that is, find the source vertex such that some spanning tree has the least single-source stretch factor (with respect to this source) among all the spanning trees.

20.6 Locating centers

Given a set of n points in $\mathbb{R}^d$, Eppstein and Wortman [2005] considered the problem of identifying the "star graph" with the least stretch factor. A *star graph* has exactly one internal vertex called its *center* with edges from the center to every other vertex; it has no other edges. Thus, the problem is that of identifying the star with the least stretch factor among the $n - 1$ star graphs. This problem has applications to various versions of the facility location problem.

The results of Eppstein and Wortman [2005] showed the following: (a) the stretch factor of any star graph can be computed in $O(n \log n)$ time; (b) for the case when the center can be any point in $\mathbb{R}^d$, the star graph with the least stretch factor can be identified in $O(n \log n)$ expected time; and (c) for the case when $d = 2$ and the center is constrained to be one of the input points, there exists a randomized algorithm to find the star graph with the least stretch factor in $O(n2^{\alpha(n)} \log^2 n)$ expected time, where $\alpha(n)$ is the inverse Ackermann function defined in Definition 12.1.20.

The following open problem is a natural extension to the above problem.

> **Open problem 8:** For a given positive integer k, define a k-*star* as a graph with k internal vertices called *hubs*, edges from the hubs to all other vertices, and with no other edges in the graph. Given a set of points in $\mathbb{R}^d$, design an algorithm to identify the k-star with the smallest stretch factor.

20.7 Decreasing the stretch factor

Given a geometric graph $G = (S, E)$ with n vertices and m edges, in Chapter 13, we saw how to approximate its stretch factor. It is clear that as we add edges to this graph, the stretch factor cannot increase. Supposing we were allowed to add a set of k edges to this graph, a useful question to ask is to determine which k edges to add in order to get the most gain, that is, to result in a graph with the least stretch factor. Farshi, Giannopoulos, and Gudmundsson [2005] considered this problem for $k = 1$. Their results include the following: (a) a $O(n^3 m + n^4 \log n)$–time and $O(n)$–space algorithm, (b) a $O(n^4)$–time and $O(n^2)$–space algorithm, (c) a 3-approximate algorithm running in $O(nm + n^2 \log n)$ time and $O(n)$ space, and (d) a $(2 + \epsilon)$-approximate algorithm running in $O(nm + n^2(\log n + 1/\epsilon^{3d}))$ time and space $O(n^2)$. No known results exist for $k > 1$. Two related open problems are proposed below.

> **Open problem 9:** Improve the time-space trade-off from Farshi, Giannopoulos, and Gudmundsson [2005]. Design an efficient algorithm to identify the $k > 1$ edges that minimizes (or approximately minimizes) the stretch factor of the resulting geometric graph.

If one thinks of every edge added as adding a "shortcut," then this leads naturally to the material presented in the next section.

20.8 Shortcuts

The concept of spanners is limited in the sense that it only guarantees reasonably "short" paths between vertices in a network. However, the concept can be put in a more general setting if one considers guaranteeing short paths between all points that lie "on" the network, whether the points correspond to vertices or to intermediate points lying on the edges of the network. When generalized appropriately, this leads us naturally to the concept of *geometric dilation* or *detour*, to be defined below (also see Exercise 13.6). In a railroad system, one may have access to the network only at stations (the vertices); however, if the network is a system of waterways or streets in an urban setting, access to the network may be possible at any point on any of its edges.

Let us suppose that we are given a polygonal chain C of total length $\ell(C)$ in the plane. Consider any pair of points, p and q, on C. Clearly, depending on how "winding" C is, the ratio of the distances between p and q along C may be considerably larger than the Euclidean distance between them. A simple question to ask is whether a small amount (of small total length) of *shortcuts* can be added to C so that any two points on C are within distance (along the curve and shortcuts) at most a constant factor away from their Euclidean distance.

Jones [1990] proved the existence of such shortcuts. Kenyon and Kenyon [1992] showed how to effectively construct such shortcuts for polygonal chains in the plane. To state their result precisely, assume that we are given 2-dimensional simple polygonal chain, which can be represented as a Euclidean graph $G = (S, E)$. Let $P(E)$ be the (infinite) set of points that compose the edges in E. The following is a restatement of a theorem from Kenyon and Kenyon [1992]:

Theorem 20.8.1. *Given a 2-dimensional simple polygonal chain C represented as a graph $G = (S, E)$, a (possibly infinite) set E' of new edges can be added connecting points in $P(E)$ such that, (1) in the new structure there is a path between any two points p and q in $P(E)$ of length at most $t_D \cdot |pq|$, and (2) $wt(E') \leq c_D \cdot \ell(C)$. Here $t_D > 1$ and $c_D > 0$ are two absolute constants.*

We highlight the interesting aspects of the work of Kenyon and Kenyon. First, though the number of segments added may be infinite, the algorithm outputs only a *finite length description* of the set of shortcuts. Second, we assume that the polygonal chain is simple; that is, the edges are noncrossing. If they do cross, then we have two points such that the Euclidean distance between them is zero, while the length along the chain is nonzero, resulting in a stretch factor of infinity. Third, if we are required only to provide shortcuts between pairs of points that are at least $\epsilon > 0$ distance apart, then the algorithm can be easily modified to only add a finite number of shortcut edges. This is perhaps justified since *finite precision* prevents us from distinguishing points that are too close to each other. Last but not the least, we note that the algorithm of Kenyon and Kenyon can be easily modified to achieve a property that has been referred to as *finite extendibility*. In other words, it is possible to obtain a structure with greater precision from one with a smaller precision by simply *adding* more segments, without having to remove the previous ones. The constant t_D will be defined precisely later and is referred to as *detour*.

More generally, the existence result of Jones, as well as the constructive result of Kenyon and Kenyon, are applicable to *rectifiable* curves in the plane. Das and Narasimhan [1995] extended the results to prove the following theorem:

Theorem 20.8.2. *Given a connected Euclidean graph $G = (V, E)$ in $\mathbb{R}^d$, and any $t_D > 1$, a (possibly infinite) set E' of shortcuts can be added between points in $P(E)$ such that, (1) in the new structure there is a path between any two points p and q in $P(E)$ of length* *at most $t_D \cdot |pq|$, and (2) $wt(E') \le c(t_D, d) \cdot wt(E)$, where $c(t_D, d) > 0$ is a constant depending only on t_D and d.*

Once again, we summarize the important aspects of the results by Das and Narasimhan [1995]. First, while Theorem 20.8.2 generalizes Theorem 20.8.1 to higher dimensions, it does more. It extends the results from polygonal chains to arbitrary connected Euclidean graphs. Second, while Theorem 20.8.1 proved the existence of a constant $t_D > 1$, Theorem 20.8.2 is true for any given stretch factor $t_D > 1$. Clearly, as t_D gets closer to 1, the constant factor $c(t_D, d)$ in the length bound of the shortcuts gets larger. Third, the algorithm achieves "finite precision" by only providing short paths between pairs of points that are not "too close." Fourth, both the finite extendibility and the finite description properties are satisfied. Finally, like the earlier planar version, it too can be generalized to smooth curves in higher dimensional space.

The running time of both algorithms were not analyzed since it depends on the values of the coordinates involved and not just on the number of vertices and edges in the input. For example, a pair of long, parallel edges will generate a lot of shortcuts.

20.9 Detour

The concept of detour was mentioned in the previous section. Here, we formalize this notion. Let $G = (S, E)$ be a geometric network in $\mathbb{R}^d$. We assume that the edges of the network do not intersect at any points other than the vertices. Let x and y be two points "on" the graph. In other words, each of the two points may be either a vertex of G or any point in the interior of an edge. Then the *detour* for the pair (x, y) is defined as the ratio $\delta_G(x, y)/|xy|$, where $\delta_G(x, y)$ denotes the length of a shortest path between x and y in G. The *detour* $t_D(G)$ of G is defined as the maximum value of $\delta_G(x, y)/|xy|$ over all distinct points $x \in G$ and $y \in G$. The definition of detour in its current form was first introduced by Ebbers-Baumann et al. [2001], although the basic idea may be found earlier in the work of Jones [1990].

The concept of detour has been found to be very useful. For example, Icking and Klein [1995] analyzed online navigation strategies by estimating the detour of curves. It was also used in proving results comparing the Fréchet and Hausdorff distance measures of plane curves [Alt et al., 2001, 2003].

Grüne [2002] proved a lower bound of $\Omega(n \log n)$ for computing the detour of any simple planar polygonal curve by extending Theorem 13.1.3. Ebbers-Baumann et al. [2001, 2004b] showed how to compute a $(1 - \epsilon)$-approximation of the detour of a polygonal chain in the plane in $O(\frac{n}{\epsilon} \log n)$ time. As shown by Grüne et al. [2002, 2003], it is also possible to compute a $(1 - \epsilon)$-approximation of the detour of a simple polygon in $O(n \log n)$ time. Agarwal et al. [2006] designed a number of algorithms to compute the (exact) detour of geometric networks. They showed how to compute the detour of a polygonal chain in the plane in $O(n \log n)$ expected time. A significantly different algorithm (with expected time complexity $O(n \log n)$) for the same problem can be found in a paper by Langerman et al. [2002], who also designed a $O(n \log^2 n)$–time algorithm for trees and cycles in the plane. Other algorithms to compute the exact detour by Agarwal et al. [2006] include a deterministic $O(n \log^4 n)$–time algorithm for polygonal chains and curves in the plane, a randomized $O(n \log^2 n)$–time algorithm for curves in the plane, and a deterministic $O(n^{16/9+\epsilon})$–time algorithm for chains in $\mathbb{R}^3$. Agarwal et al. also showed that computing the detour in the 3-dimensional case is as hard as *Hopcroft's problem*, for which it is strongly believed that a $\Omega(n^{4/3})$ lower bound applies [Erickson, 1996].

The problem of finding good bounds for the detour of any planar curve has been investigated by several researchers. Icking, Klein, and Langetepe [1999] and Aichholzer et al. [2001] have proved upper bounds on the detour of simple planar closed curves in terms of their oscillation width. It has been shown that given any simple planar closed curve C with minimum and maximum "caliper" distances (i.e., diameters) of w and D respectively, the detour of C is at least $\arcsin\left(\frac{w}{D}\right) + \sqrt{(\frac{D}{w})^2 - 1}$ [Ebbers-Baumann et al., 2004a], and at most $2\left(\frac{D}{w}\arcsin\left(\frac{w}{D}\right) + \sqrt{(\frac{D}{w})^2 - 1}\right)$ [Dumitrescu et al., 2005a].

Ebbers-Baumann, Grüne, and Klein [2003] also considered the problem of finding good bounds on the detour of any planar curve that contains a fixed point set S. They showed that the detour of a fixed, finite, planar point set has an upper bound of $1.67784\ldots$ and a lower bound of $\pi/2$. The lower bound was later improved to $(1 + 10^{-11})\pi/2$ by Dumitrescu, Grüne, and Rote [2005b]. Ebbers-Baumann et al. [2005] investigated the bounds when the given point set is embedded into a broader class of graphs than just planar curves. They showed that each finite point set can be embedded into the vertex set of a finite triangulation of detour at most 1.1247, and that each embedding on a closed convex curve has a detour of at least 1.00157.

For a detailed survey of results on detours, we refer to the paper by Gudmundsson and Knauer [2006].

20.10 External memory algorithms

Several algorithms that have been presented in this book have been later modified so that they lead to efficient implementations in the external memory model. In this model, efficiency is measured by the number of I/O-operations that an algorithm makes.

Govindarajan et al. [2000] gave an I/O-efficient algorithm that computes the well-separated pair decomposition of Chapter 9. This leads to I/O-efficient algorithms for computing a spanner with $O(n)$ edges (see Section 9.2) and a spanner with $O(n)$ edges and spanner diameter $O(\log n)$ (see Section 10.2).

Lukovszki, Maheshwari, and Zeh [2001] showed that the Θ-graph of Chapter 4 and the fault-tolerant Θ-graph of Section 18.5 can be constructed I/O-efficiently. They also generalized Clarkson's Θ-graph among obstacles (see Section 20.4) so that it can be constructed in an I/O-efficient way.

Maheshwari, Smid, and Zeh [2001] gave an I/O-efficient version of the algorithm of Arikati et al. [1996] to construct a plane Steiner spanner among obstacles.

A detailed overview of I/O-efficient algorithms for geometric spanner and proximity problems can be found in Zeh [2002].

20.11 Optimization problems

Throughout this book, we have been concerned only with uniform upper bounds on quantities such as the stretch factor, the number of edges, and the weight, that is, bounds that are valid for all point sets. In an optimization problem, we want to minimize such a quantity for a given point set. For example, given a set S of n points in $\mathbb{R}^d$, and given a real number $t > 1$, we want to compute a t-spanner for S with the minimum number of edges.

For general (non-geometric) graphs, the decision problems corresponding to most of such optimization problems for spanners are **NP**-complete; see Peleg and Schäffer [1989], Cai [1994], Brandes and Handke [1998], Handke [1999], and Chapter 16 in Peleg [2000]. Gudmundsson and Smid [2006] have shown that it is **NP**-hard to compute, when given any geometric graph G, a t-spanner of G with the minimum number of edges. Klein and Kutz [2006] showed this result for the case when G is the complete geometric graph. In other words, they showed that it is **NP**-hard to compute, when given any set S of points in $\mathbb{R}^d$, a t-spanner of S with the minimum number of edges. Cheong, Haverkort and Lee [2006] have shown that even the problem of deciding whether there exists a spanning tree of S whose stretch factor is at most t is **NP**-hard.

An interesting class of optimization problems is that of minimizing the stretch factor: Let $\mathcal{G}$ be a class of graphs, such as paths, cycles, trees, or plane graphs. Given a set S of n points in $\mathbb{R}^d$, compute a graph in $\mathcal{G}$ whose vertex set is S and whose stretch factor is minimum. As mentioned above, Cheong, Haverkort and Lee [2006] have proved that this problem is **NP**-hard if $\mathcal{G}$ is the class of trees. For other classes, the complexity status of such problems is not known.

> **Open problem 10:** For which classes $\mathcal{G}$ of graphs, does there exist a polynomial-time algorithm that, when given a set S of n points in $\mathbb{R}^d$, computes a graph in $\mathcal{G}$ whose vertex set is S and whose stretch factor is minimum?

If $\mathcal{G}$ is the class (or a subclass) of planar graphs (as opposed to plane graphs), then we can ask the question whether the graph with minimum stretch factor is non-crossing. Klein and Kutz [2006] have shown that there exists a set S of seven points in the plane, such that any tree with vertex set S and whose stretch factor is minimum has self-intersections. Cheong, Haverkort and Lee [2006] have given such a set S consisting of only five points. They also showed that for any set S of size at most four, the spanning tree of S whose stretch factor is minimum does not have self-intersections. Cheong, Haverkort and Lee [2006] have also shown that there exists a set S of points in the plane, such that any path (or cycle) with vertex set S and minimum stretch factor has self-intersections. Finally, they have given an example of a set of n points in the plane for which the minimum spanning tree has stretch factor $\Theta(n)$, and for which there exists a spanning tree whose stretch factor is bounded by a constant.

20.12 Experimental work

Here we report on a few publications that discuss experimental work related to spanners. Navarro and Paredes [2003] considered several algorithms for constructing t-spanners for points in a general metric space. They considered a recursive divide-and-conquer algorithm and a basic incremental greedy algorithm (which is the same as algorithm PATHGREEDY of Section 1.4). They also considered two variants of the PATHGREEDY algorithm, one that limits the propagation of an edge insertion, and another that inserts a lot of edges before recomputing the all-pairs distance matrix. They showed that three out of the four algorithms work well in practice. It has been reported that these algorithms compute t-spanners for graphs with several thousand nodes in a few minutes. Note that these experiments were not for the Euclidean metric, for which one would expect better performance than for general metrics.

Sigurd and Zachariasen [2004] report on an implementation of an exact algorithm to find the minimum-weight spanner and the comparison of its weight with that of the greedy spanner. Their algorithm for the exact minimum-weight spanner relies on an integer programming formulation, which they then solve using a branch-and-bound method using bounds from the LP-relaxations. They report that the greedy spanner (such as the one computed using the PATHGREEDY algorithm) is a surprisingly good approximation to a minimum-weight spanner and, for non-Euclidean inputs (i.e., points from an arbitrary metric space), had a weight roughly within 5% of that of the optimum. However, their experiments showed that the quality of the greedy spanner was much worse for Euclidean inputs. As the stretch factor was increased from 1.2 to 1.8, the difference between the weight of the greedy spanner and the optimal weight spanner increased from less than 5% to more than 20%. The conclusion for Euclidean inputs was that the greedy spanner was very close the optimum weight for small stretch factors, wildly off from the optimum weight for moderate stretch factors and eventually starts to get closer again as the stretch factor becomes large.

Finally, the only work comparing algorithms for computing Euclidean t-spanners is reported by Farshi and Gudmundsson [2005]. It is a comprehensive effort comparing the following algorithms: a modified version of the PATHGREEDY algorithm (that makes only $O(n)$ shortest path queries), a simplified version of the BUILDΘGRAPH algorithm (see Section 4.1.2) for constructing Θ-graphs, a variant for constructing ordered Θ-graphs (see Exercise 4.17), and WSPD-spanners using the COMPUTEWSPD algorithm of Section 9.4. They compared the algorithms on the basis of size, weight, degree, spanner diameter, and the number of crossings. Finally, they also experimented with point sets generated from different distributions. The greedy algorithm was found to be superior on all the reported measures except for the spanner diameter. It should be noted that a key measure, namely computation times, was not reported, for which the greedy algorithm is unlikely to perform very well. The Θ-graphs had small weight for nonclustered distributions, and surprisingly high degree for clustered distributions. The WSPD-based construction fared poorly except for clustered distributions, where it often produced spanners with size smaller than the ordered Θ-graph construction. Overall, the conclusion was that the quality of spanners produced (with a few exceptions) were in the following order: greedy spanners, Θ-graphs, ordered Θ-graphs, and WSPD-based spanners.

20.13 Two more open problems

In this book, we have seen several algorithms that compute, for any set S of n points in $\mathbb{R}^d$ and any real number $t > 1$, a t-spanner for S in $O(n \log n)$ time. Most of these algorithms work in the algebraic computation-tree model and are, therefore, optimal; see Theorem 3.4.4.

> **Open problem 11:** Is it possible to compute spanners in $o(n \log n)$ time, if the floor function, indirect addressing, and/or randomization are added to the algebraic computation-tree model?

The final open problem is that of designing a data structure that allows efficient updates of a spanner, when points are inserted and deleted from the point set. The only known nontrivial results are as follows. First, the ordered Θ-graph of Exercise 4.17 can be maintained in polylogarithmic time per insertion; it is not clear, however, how to efficiently support deletions. Second, it was shown in Arya, Mount, and Smid [1999] how to maintain the Θ-graph and the skip list spanner of Chapter 4 under insertions and deletions of points, in the model of random updates as defined in Chapter 4 of Mulmuley [1994]. (This model was introduced independently in Schwarzkopf [1991].) Intuitively, this model assumes that, after an insertion of a point, every point in the new set has the same probability of being the newly inserted point. Also, in a deletion, every point in the current point set has the same probability of being deleted. The reason that the Θ-graph and the skip list spanner can be maintained in this model is that the average degree in these spanners is bounded by a constant. Since the maximum degree can be linear in n, however, it is not clear how to obtain an efficient algorithm that maintains, say, the Θ-graph in polylogarithmic worst-case time per insertion and deletion. We finally mention a recent result of Gao, Guibas, and Nguyen [2006]. These authors have shown how to construct, in $O(n \log \alpha)$ time, a spanner with $O(n)$ edges and maximum degree $O(\log \alpha)$, that can be maintained under insertions and deletions of points, in $O(\log \alpha)$ time per update. Here, α is the aspect ratio of the point set, that is, the ratio of the diameter and the closest-pair distance.

> **Open problem 12:** Construct spanners that can be maintained under insertions and deletions of points, in $o(n)$ worst-case or amortized time per update.

20.14 Open problems from previous chapters

In previous chapters, many open problems have been presented. In this final section, we collect them in one list.

13. (from Section 3.4.2) Let $d \geq 2$ be an integer constant. For a given real number $t > 1$, prove a lower bound of $\Omega(n \log n)$ time in the algebraic computation-tree model for the problem of computing a Steiner t-spanner for a given set S of n points in IT^d in general position.

14. (from Section 4.1) The geographic neighborhood graph can be constructed in $O(n \log n)$ time for points in the plane. Unlike the Θ-graph, for dimensions larger than 2, it is not known whether the geographic neighborhood graph can be constructed within this time bound.

15. (from the exercises in Chapter 4) Let S be a set of n points in $\mathbb{R}^d$. In Exercise 4.17, we defined the ordered Θ-graph $\Theta(S, \kappa, \sigma)$ with respect to a permutation σ of S. Does there exist a permutation σ of S such that the degree of every vertex in $\Theta(S, \kappa, \sigma)$ is bounded by a function of κ only? Does there exist a permutation σ of S such that $\Theta(S, \kappa, \sigma)$ has both "small" degree and spanner diameter $O(\log n)$?

16. (from Section 6.5) What is the largest possible value of the ratio $wt(T_0)/wt(TSP(S))$, over all sets S of n points in $\mathbb{R}^d$ and all 2-optimal tours T_0 of S?

17. (from Section 9.6.2) Which metric spaces (S, δ) admit a well-separated pair decomposition of subquadratic size? Design efficient algorithms that compute such a well-separated pair decomposition.

18. (from the bibliographic notes in Chapter 11) Does there exist a set S of n points in $\mathbb{R}^d$, such that for any real constant $t > 1$, every t-spanner for S with spanner diameter $O(\log n)$ has weight $\Omega(\log n)$ times the weight of a minimum spanning tree of S?

19. (from Section 12.2) Let S be a set of n points in $\mathbb{R}^d$, let $t > 1$ be a real constant, and let $k \geq 4$ be an integer. Give a formal proof that there exists an algorithm that computes,

in $O(n \log n + kn\alpha_k(n))$ time, a t-spanner for S, having $O(kn\alpha_k(n))$ edges, and whose spanner diameter is less than or equal to k.

20. (from Section 12.2) Let $t > 1$ be a real constant, and let $k \geq 3$ be an integer. Prove that there exists a set S of n points in $\mathbb{R}^d$, such that every t-spanner for S, whose spanner diameter is less than or equal to k, contains $\Omega(kn\alpha_k(n))$ edges. (For $k = 2$, this is true; see Exercise 12.10.)

21. (from Section 12.2) Let $t > 1$ be a real constant. Prove that there exists a set S of n points in $\mathbb{R}^d$, such that every t-spanner for S, which consists of $O(n)$ edges, has spanner diameter $\Omega(\alpha(n))$.

22. (from Section 15.2.9) Is there an algebraic computation-tree algorithm that, when given a set S of n points in $\mathbb{R}^d$ and a real constant $t > 1$, computes, in $O(n \log n)$ time, a t-spanner for S, whose weight is proportional to the weight of a minimum spanning tree of S? Can such a spanner of bounded degree be computed in $O(n \log n)$ time?

23. (from Section 16.3.4) Given a set S of n points in $\mathbb{R}^d$, real numbers $t > 1$ and $\epsilon > 0$, and a t-spanner $G = (S, E)$ for S, is there an algorithm that computes, in $O(|E|)$ time, a $(1 + \epsilon)$-spanner G' of G with $O(n)$ edges? Of course, the constants in the Big-Oh bounds may depend on t and ϵ. Can such a spanner G' be computed without accessing every edge of G? In other words, can it be modified to run in $o(|E|)$ time?

24. (from Section 17.3.3) In Chapter 17, we have presented data structures that can be used to approximate the length of a shortest path between two query points in any spanner. Improve the preprocessing time, space requirement, and/or query time in Theorems 17.3.1, 17.3.3, and 17.3.4.

25. (from Section 17.3.3) The results in Chapter 17 give only an approximation to the length of a shortest path between two query points p and q in any spanner, not the approximate shortest path itself. Let k be the minimum number of edges on any $(1 + \epsilon)$-approximate shortest path between p and q. Is there an algorithm that computes a $(1 + \epsilon)$-approximate shortest path with $O(k)$ edges in $O(f(n) + k)$ time, where $f(n) = o(n)$?

26. (from Section 18.5) Is there an algorithm that constructs a k-fault-tolerant t-spanner with $O(kn)$ edges in $O(n \log n + kn)$ time?

27. (from Section 18.6.3) Is there an algorithm that constructs a k-fault-tolerant t-spanner of degree $O(k)$ in $O(n \log n + kn)$ time?

28. (from Section 18.6.3) Is there an algorithm that constructs, in $O(n \log n + kn)$ time, a k-fault-tolerant t-spanner, whose weight is bounded by $O(k^2)$ times the weight of a minimum spanning tree of S?

Exercises

20.1. Consider a simple polygonal chain with two edges and with a sharp acute angle θ between them. Show that, for a given $t > 1$, if the angle is sufficiently small, then it is necessary to add an infinite number of shortcuts to ensure a dilation of t.

20.2. Show with the help of a small example that the number of shortcuts generated by the algorithm of Das and Narasimhan [1995] depends on the values of the coordinates of the vertices and not just on the number of vertices and edges in the input.

20.3. Show that the detour of a closed simple polygonal planar curve P of length ℓ is attained by a pair of points (p, q) such that the distance between them along P is exactly $\ell/2$.

20.4. Show that the detour of a connected simple straight-line plane graph P is attained by a pair of covisible points.

20.5. Show that an exact minimum-weight spanner need not contain a minimum spanning tree.

20.6. Give an example of a set S of five points in the plane, such that any tree with vertex set S and whose stretch factor is minimum has self-intersections. Prove that for all sets S of at most four points in the plane, any spanning tree of S does not have self-intersections.

20.7. Give an example of a small set S of points in the plane, such that any path and any cycle with vertex set S and whose stretch factor is minimum has self-intersections.

20.8. Give an example of a set of n points in the plane for which the minimum spanning tree has stretch factor $\Theta(n)$, and for which there exists a spanning tree with stretch factor $O(1)$.

Bibliography

W. Ackermann. Zum Hilbertschen Aufbau der reellen Zahlen. *Mathematische Annalen*, 99: 118–133, 1928.

P. K. Agarwal. *Intersection and Decomposition Algorithms for Planar Arrangements*. Cambridge University Press, Cambridge, UK, 1991.

P. K. Agarwal. Range searching. In J. E. Goodman and J. O'Rourke, editors, *Handbook of Discrete and Computational Geometry*, pages 809–837. CRC Press, Boca Raton, FL, 2nd edition, 2004.

P. K. Agarwal, H. Edelsbrunner, O. Schwarzkopf, and E. Welzl. Euclidean minimum spanning trees and bichromatic closest pairs. *Discrete & Computational Geometry*, 6: 407–422, 1991.

P. K. Agarwal and J. Erickson. Geometric range searching and its relatives. In B. Chazelle, J. E. Goodman, and R. Pollack, editors, *Advances in Discrete and Computational Geometry*, volume 223 of *Contemporary Mathematics*, pages 1–56. American Mathematical Society, Providence, RI, 1999.

P. K. Agarwal, R. Klein, C. Knauer, S. Langerman, P. Morin, M. Sharir, and M. Soss. Computing the detour and spanning ratio of paths, trees and cycles in 2d and 3d. *Discrete & Computational Geometry*, 2006.

P. K. Agarwal, Y. Wang, and P. Yin. Lower bound for sparse Euclidean spanners. In *Proceedings of the 16th ACM-SIAM Symposium on Discrete Algorithms*, pages 670–671, 2005.

O. Aichholzer, F. Aurenhammer, C. Icking, R. Klein, E. Langetepe, and G. Rote. Generalized self-approaching curves. *Discrete Applied Mathematics*, 109:3–24, 2001.

M. Aigner and G. M. Ziegler. *Proofs From THE BOOK*. Springer-Verlag, Berlin, 3rd edition, 2004.

N. Alon and Y. Azar. On-line Steiner trees in the Euclidean plane. *Discrete & Computational Geometry*, 10:113–121, 1993.

N. Alon and B. Schieber. Optimal preprocessing for answering on-line product queries. Technical Report 71/87, Tel-Aviv University, 1987.

H. Alt, C. Knauer, and C. Wenk. Matching polygonal curves with respect to the Fréchet distance. In *Proceedings of the 18th Annual Symposium on Theoretical Aspects of Computer Science*, volume 2010 of *Lecture Notes in Computer Science*, pages 63–74, Berlin, 2001. Springer-Verlag.

H. Alt, C. Knauer, and C. Wenk. Comparison of distance measures for planar curves. *Algorithmica*, 38:45–58, 2003.

I. Althöfer, G. Das, D. P. Dobkin, D. Joseph, and J. Soares. On sparse spanners of weighted graphs. *Discrete & Computational Geometry*, 9:81–100, 1993.

S. Arikati, D. Z. Chen, L. P. Chew, G. Das, M. Smid, and C. D. Zaroliagis. Planar spanners and approximate shortest path queries among obstacles in the plane. In *Proceedings of the 4th European Symposium on Algorithms*, volume 1136 of *Lecture Notes in Computer Science*, pages 514–528, Berlin, 1996. Springer-Verlag.

B. Aronov, M. de Berg, O. Cheong, J. Gudmundsson, H. Haverkort, and A. Vigneron. Sparse geometric graphs with small dilation. In *Proceedings of the 16th International Symposium on Algorithms and Computation*, volume 3827 of *Lecture Notes in Computer Science*, pages 50–59, Berlin, 2005. Springer-Verlag.

S. Arora. Polynomial time approximation schemes for Euclidean traveling salesman and other geometric problems. *Journal of the ACM*, 45:753–782, 1998.

S. Arya, G. Das, D. M. Mount, J. S. Salowe, and M. Smid. Euclidean spanners: short, thin, and lanky. In *Proceedings of the 27th ACM Symposium on the Theory of Computing*, pages 489–498, 1995.

S. Arya and D. M. Mount. Approximate range searching. *Computational Geometry: Theory and Applications*, 17:135–152, 2000.

S. Arya, D. M. Mount, N. S. Netanyahu, R. Silverman, and A. Wu. An optimal algorithm for approximate nearest neighbor searching in fixed dimensions. *Journal of the ACM*, 45: 891–923, 1998.

S. Arya, D. M. Mount, and M. Smid. Randomized and deterministic algorithms for geometric spanners of small diameter. In *Proceedings of the 35th IEEE Symposium on Foundations of Computer Science*, pages 703–712, 1994.

S. Arya, D. M. Mount, and M. Smid. Dynamic algorithms for geometric spanners of small diameter: Randomized solutions. *Computational Geometry: Theory and Applications*, 13:91–107, 1999.

S. Arya and M. Smid. Efficient construction of a bounded-degree spanner with low weight. *Algorithmica*, 17:33–54, 1997.

P. Assouad. Plongements lipschitziens dans $\mathbb{R}^N$. *Bulletin de la Société Mathématique de France*, 111:429–448, 1983.

M. Ben-Or. Lower bounds for algebraic computation trees. In *Proceedings of the 15th ACM Symposium on the Theory of Computing*, pages 80–86, 1983.

M. A. Bender and M. Farach-Colton. The LCA problem revisited. In *Proceedings of the 4th Latin American Symposium on Theoretical Informatics*, volume 1776 of *Lecture Notes in Computer Science*, pages 88–94, Berlin, 2000. Springer-Verlag.

J. L. Bentley. Decomposable searching problems. *Information Processing Letters*, 8: 244–251, 1979.

J. L. Bentley. Fast algorithms for the geometric traveling salesperson problems. *ORSA Journal on Computing*, 4:387–411, 1992.

J. L. Bentley and J. H. Friedman. Fast algorithms for constructing minimal spanning trees in coordinate spaces. *IEEE Trans. Comput.*, C-27:97–105, 1978.

J. L. Bentley, B. W. Weide, and A. C. Yao. Optimal expected-time algorthms for closest point problems. *ACM Transactions on Mathematical Software*, 6:563–580, 1980.

M. Bern and D. Eppstein. Approximation algorithms for geometric problems. In D. S. Hochbaum, editor, *Approximation Algorithms for NP-Hard Problems*, pages 296–345. PWS Publishing Company, Boston, MA, 1997.

M. Bern, D. Eppstein, and J. Gilbert. Provably good mesh generation. *Journal of Computer and System Sciences*, 48:384–409, 1994.

S. Bespamyatnikh and M. Segal. Fast algorithms for approximating distances. *Algorithmica*, 33:263–269, 2002.

M. Blum, R. W. Floyd, V. Pratt, R. L. Rivest, and R. E. Tarjan. Time bounds for selection. *Journal of Computer and System Sciences*, 7:448–461, 1973.

H. L. Bodlaender, G. Tel, and N. Santoro. Tradeoffs in non-reversing diameter. *Nordic Journal of Computing*, 1:111–134, 1994.

J.-D. Boissonnat and M. Yvinec. *Algorithmic Geometry*. Cambridge University Press, Cambridge, UK, 1998.

B. Bollobás. *Modern Graph Theory*. Springer-Verlag, Berlin, 1998.

O. Borůvka. O jistém problému minimálním (About a certain minimal problem). *Práce Mor. Přírodověd. Spol. v Brně III (Acta Societ. Scient. Natur. Moravicae)*, 3:37–58, 1926a.

O. Borůvka. Příspěvek k řešení otázky ekonomické stavby electrovodných sítí (Contribution to the solution of a problem of economical construction of electrical networks). *Elektrotechnický obzor*, 15:153–154, 1926b.

P. Bose, L. Devroye, W. Evans, and D. Kirkpatrick. On the spanning ratio of Gabriel graphs and β-skeletons. *SIAM Journal on Discrete Mathematics*, 20:412–427, 2006.

P. Bose, J. Gudmundsson, and P. Morin. Ordered theta graphs. *Computational Geometry: Theory and Applications*, 28:11–18, 2004a.

P. Bose, J. Gudmundsson, and M. Smid. Constructing plane spanners of bounded degree and low weight. *Algorithmica*, 42:249–264, 2005.

P. Bose, A. Maheshwari, G. Narasimhan, M. Smid, and N. Zeh. Approximating geometric bottleneck shortest paths. *Computational Geometry: Theory and Applications*, 29:233–249, 2004b.

P. Bose and P. Morin. Competitive online routing in geometric graphs. *Theoretical Computer Science*, 324:273–288, 2004a.

P. Bose and P. Morin. Online routing in triangulations. *SIAM Journal on Computing*, 33: 937–951, 2004b.

P. Bose, M. Smid, and D. Xu. Diamond triangulations contain spanners of bounded degree.

Proceedings of the 17th International Symposium on Algorithms and Computation. Lecture Notes in Computer Science, Berlin, 2006. Springer-Verlag.

J. Bourgain. On Lipschitz embedding of finite metric spaces in Hilbert space. *Israel Journal of Mathematics*, 52:46–52, 1985.

U. Brandes and D. Handke. NP-completeness results for minimum planar spanners. *Discrete Mathematics and Theoretical Computer Science*, 3:1–10, 1998.

A. Brandstädt, V. Chepoi, and F. F. Dragan. Distance approximating trees for chordal and dually chordal graphs. *Journal of Algorithms*, 30:166–184, 1999.

P. Bürgisser, M. Clausen, and M. A. Shokrollahi. *Algebraic Complexity Theory.* Springer-Verlag, Berlin, 1997.

S. Cabello. Many distances in planar graphs. In *Proceedings of the 17th ACM-SIAM Symposium on Discrete Algorithms*, pages 1213–1220, 2006.

L. Cai. NP-completeness of minimum spanner problems. *Discrete Applied Mathematics*, 48: 187–194, 1994.

L. Cai and D. Corneil. Tree spanners: An overview. *Congressus Numerantium*, 88:65–76, 1992.

L. Cai and D. Corneil. Isomorphic tree spanner problems. *Algorithmica*, 14:138–153, 1995a.

L. Cai and D. Corneil. Tree spanners. *SIAM Journal on Discrete Mathematics*, 8:359–387, 1995b.

P. B. Callahan. Optimal parallel all-nearest-neighbors using the well-separated pair decomposition. In *Proceedings of the 34th IEEE Symposium on Foundations of Computer Science*, pages 332–340, 1993.

P. B. Callahan. *Dealing with Higher Dimensions: The Well-Separated Pair Decomposition and its Applications.* Ph.D. thesis, Department of Computer Science, Johns Hopkins University, Baltimore, MD, 1995.

P. B. Callahan and S. R. Kosaraju. A decomposition of multi-dimensional point-sets with applications to k-nearest-neighbors and n-body potential fields. In *Proceedings of the 24th ACM Symposium on the Theory of Computing*, pages 546–556, 1992.

P. B. Callahan and S. R. Kosaraju. Faster algorithms for some geometric graph problems in higher dimensions. In *Proceedings of the 4th ACM-SIAM Symposium on Discrete Algorithms*, pages 291–300, 1993.

P. B. Callahan and S. R. Kosaraju. Algorithms for dynamic closest-pair and n-body potential fields. In *Proceedings of the 6th ACM-SIAM Symposium on Discrete Algorithms*, pages 263–272, 1995a.

P. B. Callahan and S. R. Kosaraju. A decomposition of multidimensional point sets with applications to k-nearest-neighbors and n-body potential fields. *Journal of the ACM*, 42:67–90, 1995b.

T. M. Chan. Approximate nearest neighbor queries revisited. *Discrete & Computational Geometry*, 20:359–373, 1998.

T. M. Chan. On enumerating and selecting distances. *International Journal of Computational Geometry & Applications*, 11: 291–304, 2001.

B. Chandra. Constructing sparse spanners for most graphs in higher dimensions. *Information Processing Letters*, 51:289–294, 1994.

B. Chandra, G. Das, G. Narasimhan, and J. Soares. New sparseness results on graph spanners. *International Journal of Computational Geometry & Applications*, 5:125–144, 1995.

A. K. Chandra, S. Fortune, and R. J. Lipton. Unbounded fan-in circuits and associative functions. *Journal of Computer and System Sciences*, 30:222–234, 1985.

B. Chandra, H. Karloff, and C. Tovey. New results on the old k-opt algorithm for the traveling salesman problem. *SIAM Journal on Computing*, 28:1998–2029, 1999.

M. S. Chang, N.-F. Huang, and C.-Y. Tang. An optimal algorithm for constructing oriented Voronoi diagrams and geographic neighborhood graphs. *Information Processing Letters*, 35:255–260, 1990.

B. Chazelle. Computing on a free tree via complexity-preserving mappings. *Algorithmica*, 2:337–361, 1987.

B. Chazelle. *The Discrepancy Method.* Cambridge University Press, Cambridge, UK, 2000a.

B. Chazelle. A minimum spanning tree algorithm with inverse-Ackermann type complexity. *Journal of the ACM*, 47: 1028–1047, 2000b.

B. Chazelle and L. J. Guibas. Fractional cascading: I. A data structuring technique. *Algorithmica*, 1:133–162, 1986a.

B. Chazelle and L. J. Guibas. Fractional cascading: II. Applications. *Algorithmica*, 1: 163–191, 1986b.

O. Cheong and H. Haverkort and M. Lee. Computing a minimum-dilation spanning tree is *NP*-hard. 2006. Manuscript.

D. Z. Chen, G. Das, and M. Smid. Lower bounds for computing geometric spanners and approximate shortest paths. *Discrete Applied Mathematics*, 110:151–167, 2001.

D. Cheriton and R. E. Tarjan. Finding minimum spanning trees. *SIAM Journal on Computing*, 5:724–742, 1976.

H. Chernoff. A measure of asymptotic efficiency for tests of a hypothesis based on the sum of observations. *Annals of Mathematical Statistics*, 23:493–509, 1952.

L. P. Chew. There is a planar graph almost as good as the complete graph. In *Proceedings of the 2nd ACM Symposium on Computational Geometry*, pages 169–177, 1986.

L. P. Chew. There are planar graphs almost as good as the complete graph. *Journal of Computer and System Sciences*, 39:205–219, 1989.

N. Christofides. Worst-case analysis of a new heuristic for the traveling salesman problem. In J. F. Traub, editor, *Symposium on New Directions and Recent Results in Algorithms and Complexity*, page 441, New York, 1976. Academic Press.

K. L. Clarkson. Approximation algorithms for shortest path motion planning. In *Proceedings of the 19th ACM Symposium on the Theory of Computing*, pages 56–65, 1987.

K. L. Clarkson. An algorithm for geometric minimum spanning trees requiring nearly linear expected time. *Algorithmica*, 4: 461–469, 1989.

E. Cohen. Fast algorithms for constructing *t*-spanners and paths with stretch *t*. *SIAM Journal on Computing*, 28:210–236, 1998.

R. Cole and U. Vishkin. The accelerated centroid decomposition technique for optimal parallel tree evaluation in logarithmic time. *Algorithmica*, 3:329–346, 1988.

T. H. Cormen, C. E. Leiserson, R. L. Rivest, and C. Stein. *Introduction to Algorithms*. MIT Press, Cambridge, MA, 2nd edition, 2001.

A. Czumaj and H. Zhao. Fault-tolerant geometric spanners. *Discrete & Computational Geometry*, 32:207–230, 2004.

G. Das. *Approximation Schemes in Computational Geometry*. Ph.D. thesis, University of Wisconsin, 1990.

G. Das. The visibility graph contains a bounded-degree spanner. In *Proceedings of the 9th Canadian Conference on Computational Geometry*, pages 70–75, 1997.

G. Das and P. J. Heffernan. Constructing degree-3 spanners with other sparseness properties. *International Journal of Foundations of Computer Science*, 7:121–135, 1996.

G. Das, P. Heffernan, and G. Narasimhan. Optimally sparse spanners in 3-dimensional Euclidean space. In *Proceedings of the 9th ACM Symposium on Computational Geometry*, pages 53–62, 1993.

G. Das and D. Joseph. Which triangulations approximate the complete graph? In *Proceedings of the International Symposium on Optimal Algorithms*, volume 401 of *Lecture Notes in Computer Science*, pages 168–192, Berlin, 1989. Springer-Verlag.

G. Das, S. Kapoor, and M. Smid. On the complexity of approximating Euclidean traveling salesman tours and minimum spanning trees. *Algorithmica*, 19:447–460, 1997.

G. Das and G. Narasimhan. A fast algorithm for constructing sparse Euclidean spanners. *International Journal of Computational Geometry & Applications*, 7:297–315, 1997.

G. Das and G. Narasimhan. Short cuts in higher dimensional space. In *Proceedings of the 7th Canadian Conference on Computational Geometry*, pages 103–108, 1995.

G. Das, G. Narasimhan, and J. Salowe. A new way to weigh malnourished Euclidean graphs. In *Proceedings of the 6th ACM-SIAM Symposium on Discrete Algorithms*, pages 215–222, 1995.

A. Datta, H.-P. Lenhof, C. Schwarz, and M. Smid. Static and dynamic algorithms for *k*-point clustering problems. *Journal of Algorithms*, 19:474–503, 1995.

W. H. E. Day and H. Edelsbrunner. Efficient algorithms for agglomerative hierarchical clustering methods. *Journal of Classification*, 1:7–24, 1984.

M. de Berg, M. van Kreveld, M. Overmars, and O. Schwarzkopf. *Computational Geometry: Algorithms and Applications*. Springer-Verlag, Berlin, 2nd edition, 2000.

M. T. Dickerson, R. L. Drysdale, and J. R. Sack. Simple algorithms for enumerating interpoint distances and finding *k* nearest neighbors. *International Journal of Computational Geometry & Applications*, 2:221–239, 1992.

M. T. Dickerson and D. Eppstein. Algorithms for proximity problems in higher dimensions.

Computational Geometry: Theory and Applications, 5:277–291, 1996.

R. Diestel. *Graph Theory*. Springer-Verlag, Berlin, 2nd edition, 2000.

E. W. Dijkstra. A note on two problems in connexion with graphs. *Numerische Mathematik*, 1:269–271, 1959.

H. N. Djidjev. On-line algorithms for shortest path problems on planar digraphs. In *Proceedings of the 22nd Workshop on Graph-Theoretic Concepts in Computer Science*, volume 1197 of *Lecture Notes in Computer Science*, pages 151–165, Berlin, 1997. Springer-Verlag.

D. P. Dobkin, S. J. Friedman, and K. J. Supowit. Delaunay graphs are almost as good as complete graphs. *Discrete & Computational Geometry*, 5:399–407, 1990.

D. P. Dobkin and R. J. Lipton. On the complexity of computations under varying sets of primitives. *Journal of Computer and System Sciences*, 18:86–91, 1979.

R. L. Drysdale, S. McElfresh, and J. S. Snoeyink. On exclusion regions for optimal triangulations. *Discrete Applied Mathematics*, 109:49–65, 2001.

D.-Z. Du and F. K. Hwang. An approach for proving lower bounds: Solution of Gilbert-Pollak conjecture on Steiner ratio. In *Proceedings of the 31st IEEE Symposium on Foundations of Computer Science*, pages 76–85, 1990a.

D.-Z. Du and F. K. Hwang. A proof of Gilbert-Pollak's conjecture on the Steiner ratio. *Algorithmica*, 7:121–136, 1992.

D.-Z. Du and F. K. Hwang. The state of art on Steiner ratio problems. In D.-Z. Du and F. K. Hwang, editors, *Computing in Euclidean Geometry*, pages 195–224. World Scientific, Singapore, 2nd edition, 1995.

D. Z. Du and F. K. Hwang. The Steiner ratio conjecture of Gilbert and Pollak is true. *Proceedings of the National Academy of Sciences of the United States of America*, 87: 9464–9466, 1990b.

A. Dumitrescu, A. Ebbers-Baumann, A. Grüne, R. Klein, and G. Rote. On geometric dilation and halving chords. In *Proceedings of the 9th Workshop on Algorithms and Data Structures*, volume 3608 of *Lecture Notes in Computer Science*, pages 244–255, Berlin, 2005a. Springer-Verlag.

A. Dumitrescu, A. Grüne, and G. Rote. Improved lower bounds on the geometric

dilation of point sets. In *Abstracts of the 21st European Workshop on Computational Geometry*, pages 37–40, 2005b.

C. A. Duncan. *Balanced Aspect Ratio Trees*. Ph.D. thesis, Department of Computer Science, Johns Hopkins University, Baltimore, MD, 1999.

C. A. Duncan, M. T. Goodrich, and S. Kobourov. Balanced aspect ratio trees: Combining the advantages of k-d trees and octrees. *Journal of Algorithms*, 38:303–333, 2001.

A. Ebbers-Baumann, R. Klein, E. Langetepe, and A. Lingas. A fast algorithm for approximating the detour of a polygonal chain. In *Proceedings of the 9th European Symposium on Algorithms*, volume 2161 of *Lecture Notes in Computer Science*, pages 321–332, Berlin, 2001. Springer-Verlag.

A. Ebbers-Baumann, A. Grüne, and R. Klein. The geometric dilation of finite point sets. In *Proceedings of the 14th International Symposium on Algorithms and Computation*, volume 2906 of *Lecture Notes in Computer Science*, pages 250–259, Berlin, 2003. Springer-Verlag.

A. Ebbers-Baumann, A. Grüne, and R. Klein. Geometric dilation of closed planar curves: A new lower bound. In *Abstracts of the 20th European Workshop on Computational Geometry*, pages 123–126, 2004a.

A. Ebbers-Baumann, R. Klein, E. Langetepe, and A. Lingas. A fast algorithm for approximating the detour of a polygonal chain. *Computational Geometry: Theory and Applications*, 27:123–134, 2004b.

A. Ebbers-Baumann, A. Grüne, M. Karpinski, R. Klein, C. Knauer, and A. Lingas. Embedding point sets into plane graphs of small dilation. In *Proceedings of the 16th International Symposium on Algorithms and Computation*, volume 3827 of *Lecture Notes in Computer Science*, pages 5–16, Berlin, 2005. Springer-Verlag.

H. Edelsbrunner. *Algorithms in Combinatorial Geometry*. Springer-Verlag, Berlin, 1987.

D. Eppstein. Beta-skeletons have unbounded dilation. *Computational Geometry: Theory and Applications*, 23:43–52, 2002.

D. Eppstein. Spanning trees and spanners. In J.-R. Sack and J. Urrutia, editors, *Handbook of Computational Geometry*, pages 425–461. Elsevier Science, Amsterdam, 2000.

D. Eppstein and K. A. Wortman. Minimum dilation stars. In *Proceedings of the 21st*

ACM Symposium on Computational Geometry, pages 321–326, 2005.

J. Erickson. New lower bounds for Hopcroft's problem. *Discrete & Computational Geometry*, 16:389–418, 1996.

J. Erickson. On the relative complexities of some geometric problems. In *Proceedings of the 7th Canadian Conference on Computational Geometry*, pages 85–90, 1995.

S. Even. *Graph Algorithms*. W. H. Freeman, New York, 1979.

M. Farshi and J. Gudmundsson. Experimental study of geometric *t*-spanners. In *Proceedings of the 13th European Symposium on Algorithms*, volume 3669 of *Lecture Notes in Computer Science*, pages 556–567, Berlin, 2005. Springer-Verlag.

M. Farshi, P. Giannopoulos, and J. Gudmundsson. Finding the best shortcut in a geometric network. In *Proceedings of the 21st ACM Symposium on Computational Geometry*, pages 327–335, 2005.

L. Few. The shortest path and the shortest road through *n* points in a region. *Mathematika*, 2:141–144, 1955.

L. R. Ford and S. M. Johnson. A tournament problem. *The American Mathematical Monthly*, 66:387–389, 1959.

G. N. Frederickson. A data structure for dynamically maintaining rooted trees. *Journal of Algorithms*, 24:37–65, 1997.

G. N. Frederickson. Fast algorithms for shortest paths in planar graphs, with applications. *SIAM Journal on Computing*, 16:1004–1022, 1987.

M. L. Fredman and R. E. Tarjan. Fibonacci heaps and their uses in improved network optimization algorithms. *Journal of the ACM*, 34:596–615, 1987.

M. L. Fredman and D. E. Willard. Transdichotomous algorithms for minimum spanning trees and shortest paths. *Journal of Computer and System Sciences*, 48:533–551, 1994.

H. Freudenthal. Simplizialzerlegungen von beschränkter Flachheit. *Annals of Mathematics*, 43:580–582, 1942.

J. Gao, L. J. Guibas, and A. Nguyen. Deformable spanners and applications. *Computational Geometry: Theory and Applications*, 35:2–19, 2006.

J. Gao and L. Zhang. Well-separated pair decomposition for the unit-disk graph metric and its applications. *SIAM Journal on Computing*, 35:151–169, 2005.

M. R. Garey and D. S. Johnson. *Computers and Intractability: A Guide to the Theory of NP-Completeness*. W. H. Freeman, New York, 1979.

M. R. Garey, R. L. Graham, and D. S. Johnson. The complexity of computing Steiner minimal trees. *SIAM Journal on Applied Mathematics*, 32:835–859, 1977.

E. N. Gilbert and H. O. Pollak. Steiner minimal trees. *SIAM Journal on Applied Mathematics*, 16:1–29, 1968.

T. Gonzalez. Algorithms on sets and related problems. Technical Report, Department of Computer Science, University of Oklahoma, Norman, 1975.

J. E. Goodman and J. O'Rourke, editors. *Handbook of Discrete and Computational Geometry*. CRC Press, Boca Raton, FL, 2nd edition, 2004.

S. Govindarajan, T. Lukovszki, A. Maheshwari, and N. Zeh. I/O-efficient well-separated pair decomposition and its applications. [See notes] Algorithmica, 45:585–614, 2006.

R. L. Graham and P. Hell. On the history of the minimum spanning tree problem. *Annals of the History of Computing*, 7:43–57, 1985.

L. F. Greengard. *The Rapid Evaluation of Potential Fields in Particle Systems*. MIT Press, Cambridge, MA, 1988.

A. Grüne. *Umwege in Polygonen*. Master's thesis, Universität Bonn, Germany, 2002.

A. Grüne, R. Klein, and E. Langetepe. Computing the detour of polygons. In *Abstracts of the 19th European Workshop on Computational Geometry*, pages 61–64, 2003.

M. Grünewald, T. Lukovszki, C. Schindelhauer, and K. Volbert. Distributed maintenance of resource efficient wireless network topologies. In *Proceedings of the 8th Euro-Par Conference*, volume 2400 of *Lecture Notes in Computer Science*, pages 935–946, Berlin, 2002. Springer-Verlag.

J. Gudmundsson and C. Knauer. Dilation and detours in geometric networks. In T. F. Gonzalez, editor, *Handbook on Approximation Algorithms and Metaheuristics*. Chapman & Hall/CRC, Boca Raton, FL, 2006.

J. Gudmundsson and M. Smid. On spanners of geometric graphs. In *Proceedings of the 10th Scandinavian Workshop on Algorithm*

Theory, volume 4059 of *Lecture Notes in Computer Science*, pages 388–399, Berlin, 2006. Springer-Verlag.

J. Gudmundsson, C. Levcopoulos, and G. Narasimhan. Fast greedy algorithms for constructing sparse geometric spanners. *SIAM Journal on Computing*, 31:1479–1500, 2002a.

J. Gudmundsson, C. Levcopoulos, G. Narasimhan, and M. Smid. Approximate distance oracles for geometric graphs. In *Proceedings of the 13th ACM-SIAM Symposium on Discrete Algorithms*, pages 828–837, 2002b.

J. Gudmundsson, C. Levcopoulos, G. Narasimhan, and M. Smid. Approximate distance oracles revisited. In *Proceedings of the 13th International Symposium on Algorithms and Computation*, volume 2518 of *Lecture Notes in Computer Science*, pages 357–368, Berlin, 2002c. Springer-Verlag.

J. Gudmundsson, C. Levcopoulos, G. Narasimhan, and M. Smid. Approximate distance oracles for geometric spanners. Manuscript, 2004.

J. Gudmundsson, G. Narasimhan, and M. Smid. Fast pruning of geometric spanners. In *Proceedings of the 22nd Symposium on Theoretical Aspects of Computer Science*, volume 3404 of *Lecture Notes in Computer Science*, pages 508–520, Berlin, 2005. Springer-Verlag.

A. Gupta, R. Krauthgamer, and J. R. Lee. Bounded geometries, fractals, and low-distortion embeddings. In *Proceedings of the 44th IEEE Symposium on Foundations of Computer Science*, pages 534–543, 2003.

D. Gusfield. *Algorithms on Strings, Trees and Sequences*. Cambridge University Press, Cambridge, UK, 1997.

D. Handke. *Graphs with Distance Guarantees*. Ph.D. thesis, Fakultät für Mathematik und Informatik, Universität Konstanz, Konstanz, Germany, 1999.

S. Har-Peled and M. Mendel. Fast construction of nets in low-dimensional metrics and their applications. *SIAM Journal on Computing*, 35:1148–1184, 2006.

F. Harary. *Graph Theory*. Addison-Wesley, Reading, MA, 1972.

D. Harel and R. E. Tarjan. Fast algorithms for finding nearest common ancestors. *SIAM Journal on Computing*, 13:338–355, 1984.

J. Heinonen. *Lectures on Analysis on Metric Spaces*. Springer-Verlag, Berlin, 2001.

K. Hildrum, J. Kubiatowicz, S. Ma, and S. Rao. A note on the nearest neighbor in growth-restricted metrics. In *Proceedings of the 15th ACM-SIAM Symposium on Discrete Algorithms*, pages 560–561, 2004.

F. K. Hwang, D. S. Richards, and P. Winter. *The Steiner Tree Problem*. Elsevier Science, Amsterdam, 1992.

C. Icking and R. Klein. Searching for the kernel of a polygon: A competitive strategy. In *Proceedings of the 11th ACM Symposium on Computational Geometry*, pages 258–266, 1995.

C. Icking, R. Klein, and E. Langetepe. Self-approaching curves. *Mathematical Proceedings of the Cambridge Philosophical Society*, 125:441–453, 1999.

H. Imai and Ta. Asano. Dynamic orthogonal segment intersection search. *Journal of Algorithms*, 8:1–18, 1987.

V. Jarník. O jistém problému minimálním. *Práce Moravské Přírodovědecké Společnosti*, 6:57–63, 1930.

D. B. Johnson and T. Mizoguchi. Selecting the Kth element in $X + Y$ and $X_1 + X_2 + \cdots + X_m$. *SIAM Journal on Computing*, 7:147–153, 1978.

D. S. Johnson and C. H. Papadimitriou. Computational complexity and the traveling salesman problem. In E. L. Lawler, J. K. Lenstra, A. H. G. Rinnooy Kan, and D. B. Shmoys, editors, *The Traveling Salesman Problem*, pages 68–74. John Wiley & Sons, New York, 1985.

P. Jones. Rectifiable sets and the traveling salesman problem. *Inventiones Mathematicae*, 102:1–15, 1990.

C. Jordan. Sur les assemblages de lignes. *Journal für die reine und angewandte Mathematik*, 70:185–190, 1869.

M. I. Karavelas and L. J. Guibas. Static and kinetic geometric spanners with applications. In *Proceedings of the 12th ACM-SIAM Symposium on Discrete Algorithms*, pages 168–176, 2001.

D. R. Karger and M. Ruhl. Finding nearest neighbors in growth-restricted metrics. In *Proceedings of the 34th ACM Symposium on the Theory of Computing*, pages 741–750, 2002.

D. R. Karger, P. N. Klein, and R. E. Tarjan. A randomized linear-time algorithm to find minimum spanning trees. *Journal of the ACM*, 42:321–328, 1995.

R. M. Karp. Reducibility among combinatorial problems. In R. E. Miller and J. W. Thatcher, editors, *Complexity of Computer Computations*, Advances in Computing Research, pages 85–103. Plenum Press, 1972.

R. M. Karp and J. M. Steele. Probabilistic analysis of heuristics. In E. L. Lawler, J. K. Lenstra, A. H. G. Rinnooy Kan, and D. B. Shmoys, editors, *The Traveling Salesman Problem*, pages 181–205. John Wiley & Sons, New York, 1985.

J. M. Keil. Approximating the complete Euclidean graph. In *Proceedings of the 1st Scandinavian Workshop on Algorithm Theory*, volume 318 of *Lecture Notes in Computer Science*, pages 208–213, Berlin, 1988. Springer-Verlag.

J. M. Keil and C. A. Gutwin. Classes of graphs which approximate the complete Euclidean graph. *Discrete & Computational Geometry*, 7:13–28, 1992.

C. Kenyon and R. Kenyon. How to take short cuts. *Discrete & Computational Geometry*, 8:251–264, 1992.

S. Khuller, B. Raghavachari, and N. E. Young. Balancing minimum spanning trees and shortest-path trees. *Algorithmica*, 14: 305–321, 1995.

R. Klein, C. Knauer, G. Narasimhan, and M. Smid. Exact and approximation algorithms for computing the dilation spectrum of paths, trees, and cycles. In *Proceedings of the 16th International Symposium on Algorithms and Computation*, volume 3827 of *Lecture Notes in Computer Science*, pages 849–858, Berlin, 2005. Springer-Verlag.

R. Klein and M. Kutz. Computing geometric minimum-dilation graphs is *NP*-hard. *Proceedings of the 14th International Symposium on Graph Drawing*. Lecture Notes in Computer Science, Berlin, 2006. Springer-Verlag.

D. E. Knuth. *Fundamental Algorithms*, volume 1 of *The Art of Computer Programming*. Addison-Wesley, Reading, MA, 3rd edition, 1997.

D. E. Knuth. *Sorting and Searching*, volume 3 of *The Art of Computer Programming*. Addison-Wesley, Reading, MA, 1973.

R. Krauthgamer and J. R. Lee. The black-box complexity of nearest neighbor search. In *Proceedings of the 31st International Colloquium on Automata, Languages and*

Programming, volume 3142 of *Lecture Notes in Computer Science*, pages 858–869, Berlin, 2004a. Springer-Verlag.

R. Krauthgamer and J. R. Lee. Navigating nets: simple algorithms for proximity search. In *Proceedings of the 15th ACM-SIAM Symposium on Discrete Algorithms*, pages 798–807, 2004b.

R. Krauthgamer, J. R. Lee, M. Mendel, and A. Naor. Measured descent: a new embedding method for finite metrics. *Geometric and Functional Analysis*, 15:839–858, 2005.

J. B. Kruskal. On the shortest spanning subtree of a graph and the traveling salesman problem. *Proceedings of the American Mathematical Society*, 7:48–50, 1956.

D. Krznaric. *Progress in Hierarchical Clustering & Minimum Weight Triangulation*. Ph.D. thesis, Department of Computer Science, Lund University, Lund, Sweden, 1997.

D. Krznaric, C. Levcopoulos, and B. J. Nilsson. Minimum spanning trees in *d* dimensions. *Nordic Journal of Computing*, 6:446–461, 1999.

H. W. Kuhn. Some combinatorial lemmas in topology. *IBM Journal of Research and Development*, 4:518–524, 1960.

J. A. La Poutré. New techniques for the Union-Find problem. In *Proceedings of the 1st ACM-SIAM Symposium on Discrete Algorithms*, pages 54–63, 1990.

T. J. Laakso. Plane with A_∞-weighted metric not bilipschitz embeddable to $\mathbb{R}^n$. *Bulletin of the London Mathematical Society*, 34:667–676, 2002.

S. Langerman, P. Morin, and M. Soss. Computing the maximum detour and spanning ratio of planar paths, trees and cycles. In *Proceedings of the 19th Symposium on Theoretical Aspects of Computer Science*, volume 2285 of *Lecture Notes in Computer Science*, pages 250–261, Berlin, 2002. Springer-Verlag.

E. L. Lawler, J. K. Lenstra, A. H. G. Rinnooy Kan, and D. B. Shmoys, editors. *The Traveling Salesman Problem*. John Wiley & Sons, New York, 1985.

H.-O. Le and V. B. Le. Optimal tree 3-spanners in directed path graphs. *Networks*, 34:81–87, 1999.

A. W. Lee. *Diamonds are a Plane Graph's Best Friend*. Master's thesis, School of Computer Science, Carleton University, Ottawa, 2004.

D. T. Lee and B. J. Schachter. Two algorithms for constructing Delaunay triangulations. *International Journal of Computer and Information Sciences*, 9:219–242, 1980.

D. T. Lee and C. K. Wong. Quintary trees: A file structure for multidimensional database systems. *ACM Transactions on Database Systems*, 5:339–353, 1980.

D. T. Lee and Y. F. Wu. Geometric complexity of some location problems. *Algorithmica*, 1:193–211, 1986.

H.-P. Lenhof and M. Smid. Sequential and parallel algorithms for the k closest pairs problem. *International Journal of Computational Geometry & Applications*, 5:273–288, 1995.

C. Levcopoulos and A. Lingas. There are planar graphs almost as good as the complete graphs and almost as cheap as minimum spanning trees. *Algorithmica*, 8:251–256, 1992.

C. Levcopoulos, G. Narasimhan, and M. Smid. Efficient algorithms for constructing fault-tolerant geometric spanners. In *Proceedings of the 30th ACM Symposium on the Theory of Computing*, pages 186–195, 1998.

C. Levcopoulos, G. Narasimhan, and M. Smid. Improved algorithms for constructing fault-tolerant spanners. *Algorithmica*, 32:144–156, 2002.

X.-Y. Li and Y. Wang. Efficient construction of low weighted bounded degree planar spanner. *International Journal of Computational Geometry & Applications*, 14:69–84, 2004.

S. Lin. Computer solutions of the traveling salesman problem. *Bell Systems Technical Journal*, 44:2245–2269, 1965.

S. Lin and B. Kernighan. An effective heuristic algorithm for the traveling salesman problem. *Operations Research*, 21:498–516, 1973.

N. Linial, E. London, and Y. Rabinovich. The geometry of graphs and some of its algorithmic applications. *Combinatorica*, 15:215–245, 1995.

R. J. Lipton and R. E. Tarjan. Applications of a planar separator theorem. *SIAM Journal on Computing*, 9:615–627, 1980.

R. J. Lipton and R. E. Tarjan. A separator theorem for planar graphs. *SIAM Journal on Applied Mathematics*, 36:177–189, 1979.

G. S. Lueker. A data structure for orthogonal range queries. In *Proceedings of the 19th IEEE Symposium on Foundations of Computer Science*, pages 28–34, 1978.

T. Lukovszki. New results on fault tolerant geometric spanners. In *Proceedings of the 6th Workshop on Algorithms and Data Structures*, volume 1663 of *Lecture Notes in Computer Science*, pages 193–204, Berlin, 1999a. Springer-Verlag.

T. Lukovszki. *New Results on Geometric Spanners and Their Applications*. Ph.D. thesis, Department of Computer Science, University of Paderborn, Paderborn, Germany, 1999b.

T. Lukovszki, A. Maheshwari, and N. Zeh. I/O-efficient batched range counting and its applications to proximity problems. In *Proceedings of the 21st Conference on the Foundations of Software Technology and Theoretical Computer Science*, volume 2245 of *Lecture Notes in Computer Science*, pages 244–255, Berlin, 2001. Springer-Verlag.

M. S. Madanlal, G. Venkatesan, and C. Pandu Rangan. Tree 3-spanners on interval, permutation and regular bipartite graphs. *Information Processing Letters*, 59:97–102, 1996.

A. Maheshwari, M. Smid, and N. Zeh. I/O-efficient shortest-path queries in geometric spanners. In *Proceedings of the 7th Workshop on Algorithms and Data Structures*, volume 2125 of *Lecture Notes in Computer Science*, pages 287–299, Berlin, 2001. Springer-Verlag.

U. Manber. *Introduction to Algorithms: A Creative Approach*. Addison-Wesley, Reading, MA, 1989.

U. Manber and M. Tompa. The complexity of problems on probabilistic, nondeterministic, and alternating decision trees. *Journal of the ACM*, 32:720–732, 1985.

J. Matoušek. *Geometric Discrepancy: An Illustrated Guide*. Springer-Verlag, Berlin, 1999.

J. Matoušek. *Lectures on Discrete Geometry*. Springer-Verlag, Berlin, 2002.

K. Mehlhorn. *Data Structures and Algorithms 3: Multi-dimensional Searching and Computational Geometry*. Springer-Verlag, Berlin, 1984a.

K. Mehlhorn. *Data Structures and Algorithms 1: Sorting and Searching*. Springer-Verlag, Berlin, 1984b.

K. Mehlhorn and S. Näher. Dynamic fractional cascading. *Algorithmica*, 5:215–241, 1990.

K. Menger. Zur allgemeinen Kurventheorie. *Fundamenta Mathematicae*, 10:96–115, 1927.

J. W. Milnor. On the Betti numbers of real algebraic varieties. *Proceedings of the American Mathematical Society*, 15:275–280, 1964.

J. W. Milnor. *Singular Points of Complex Hypersurfaces*. Princeton University Press, Princeton, NJ, 1968.

J. S. B. Mitchell. Guillotine subdivisions approximate polygonal subdivisions: A simple polynomial-time approximation scheme for geometric TSP, *k*-MST, and related problems. *SIAM Journal on Computing*, 28: 1298–1309, 1999.

J. S. B. Mitchell. Geometric shortest paths and network optimization. In J.-R. Sack and J. Urrutia, editors, *Handbook of Computational Geometry*, pages 633–701. Elsevier Science, Amsterdam, 2000.

M. Mitzenmacher and E. Upfal. *Probability and Computing*. Cambridge University Press, Cambridge, UK, 2005.

L. Monier. Combinatorial solutions of multidimensional divide-and-conquer recurrences. *Journal of Algorithms*, 1:60–74, 1980.

R. Motwani and P. Raghavan. *Randomized Algorithms*. Cambridge University Press, Cambridge, UK, 1995.

D. M. Mount. Dumbbell trees. Unpublished manuscript, 1994.

K. Mulmuley. *Computational Geometry: An Introduction Through Randomized Algorithms*. Prentice-Hall, Englewood Cliffs, NJ, 1994.

W. Mulzer and G. Rote. Minimum weight triangulation is **NP**-hard. *Proceedings of the 22nd ACM Symposium on Computational Geometry*, 1–10, 2006.

G. Narasimhan and M. Smid. Approximation algorithms for the bottleneck stretch factor problem. *Nordic Journal of Computing*, 9: 13–31, 2002.

G. Narasimhan and M. Smid. Approximating the stretch factor of Euclidean graphs. *SIAM Journal on Computing*, 30:978–989, 2000.

G. Narasimhan and M. Smid. Approximating the stretch factor of Euclidean paths, cycles and trees. Technical Report 9, Department of Computer Science, University of Magdeburg, Magdeburg, Germany, 1999.

G. Narasimhan and M. Zachariasen. Geometric minimum spanning trees via well-separated pair decompositions. *ACM Journal of Experimental Algorithmics*, 6, 2001. Article 6.

G. Narasimhan, J. Zhu, and M. Zachariasen. Experiments with computing geometric minimum spanning trees. In *Proceedings of the 2nd Workshop on Algorithm Engineering and Experiments*, pages 183–196, 2000.

G. Navarro and R. Paredes. Practical construction of metric *t*-spanners. In *Proceedings of the 5th Workshop on Algorithm Engineering and Experiments*, pages 69–81, 2003.

J. Nešetřil. Some remarks on the history of MST-problem. *Archivum Mathematicum*, 33:15–22, 1997.

J. Nievergelt and F. P. Preparata. Plane-sweep algorithms for intersecting geometric figures. *Communications of the ACM*, 25:739–747, 1982.

J. O'Rourke. *Computational Geometry in C*. Cambridge University Press, Cambridge, UK, 2nd edition, 1998.

C. H. Papadimitriou. The Euclidean traveling salesman problem is NP-complete. *Theoretical Computer Science*, 4:237–244, 1977.

D. Peleg. *Distributed Computing: A Locality-Sensitive Approach*. Monographs on Discrete Mathematics and Applications. Society for Industrial and Applied Mathematics, Philadelphia, 2000.

D. Peleg and A. A. Schäffer. Graph spanners. *Journal of Graph Theory*, 13:99–116, 1989.

D. Peleg and J. D. Ullman. An optimal synchronizer for the hypercube. In *Proceedings of the 8th ACM Symposium on Principles of Distributed Computing*, pages 77–85, 1987.

D. Peleg and J. D. Ullman. An optimal synchronizer for the hypercube. *SIAM Journal on Computing*, 18:740–747, 1989.

S. Pettie and V. Ramachandran. An optimal minimum spanning tree algorithm. *Journal of the ACM*, 49:16–34, 2002.

F. P. Preparata and M. I. Shamos. *Computational Geometry: An Introduction*. Springer-Verlag, Berlin, 1988.

R. C. Prim. Shortest connection networks and some generalizations. *Bell Systems Technical Journal*, 36:1389–1401, 1957.

E. Prisner. Distance approximating spanning trees. In *Proceedings of the 14th Symposium on Theoretical Aspects of Computer Science*, volume 1200 of *Lecture Notes in Computer Science*, pages 499–510, Berlin, 1997. Springer-Verlag.

W. Pugh. Skip lists: A probabilistic alternative to balanced trees. *Communications of the ACM*, 35:668–676, 1990.

M. O. Rabin. Proving simultaneous positivity of linear forms. *Journal of Computer and System Sciences*, 6:639–650, 1972.

S. B. Rao and W. D. Smith. Approximating geometrical graphs via "spanners" and "banyans." In *Proceedings of the 30th ACM Symposium on the Theory of Computing*, pages 540–550, 1998.

E. M. Reingold. On the optimality of some set algorithms. *Journal of the ACM*, 19: 649–659, 1972.

D. J. Rosenkrantz, R. E. Stearns, and P. M. Lewis. An analysis of several heuristics for the traveling salesman problem. *SIAM Journal on Computing*, 6:563–581, 1977.

J. Ruppert and R. Seidel. Approximating the d-dimensional complete Euclidean graph. In *Proceedings of the 3rd Canadian Conference on Computational Geometry*, pages 207–210, 1991.

J.-R. Sack and J. Urrutia, editors. *Handbook of Computational Geometry*. Elsevier Science, Amsterdam, 2000.

S. Sahni and T. Gonzalez. P-complete approximation problems. *Journal of the ACM*, 23:555–565, 1976.

J. S. Salowe. Constructing multidimensional spanner graphs. *International Journal of Computational Geometry & Applications*, 1: 99–107, 1991.

J. S. Salowe. Enumerating interdistances in space. *International Journal of Computational Geometry & Applications*, 2:49–59, 1992.

J. S. Salowe. Euclidean spanner graphs with degree four. *Discrete Applied Mathematics*, 54:55–66, 1994.

F. Santos and R. Seidel. A better upper bound on the number of triangulations of a planar point set. *Journal of Combinatorial Theory, Series A*, 102:186–193, 2003.

B. Schieber and U. Vishkin. On finding lowest common ancestors: Simplifications and parallelisations. *SIAM Journal on Computing*, 17:327–334, 1988.

O. Schwarzkopf. Dynamic maintenance of geometric structures made easy. In *Proceedings of the 32nd IEEE Symposium on Foundations of Computer Science*, pages 197–206, 1991.

S. Semmes. On the nonexistence of bi-Lipschitz parameterizations and geometric problems about A_∞-weights. *Revista Matemática Iberoamericana*, 12:337–410, 1996.

M. I. Shamos and D. Hoey. Closest-point problems. In *Proceedings of the 16th IEEE Symposium on Foundations of Computer Science*, pages 151–162, 1975.

M. Sharir and P. K. Agarwal. *Davenport-Schinzel Sequences and Their Geometric Applications*. Cambridge University Press, Cambridge, UK, 1995.

M. Sigurd and M. Zachariasen. Construction of minimum-weight spanners. In *Proceedings of the 12th European Symposium on Algorithms*, volume 3221 of *Lecture Notes in Computer Science*, pages 797–808, Berlin, 2004. Springer-Verlag.

M. Smid. Closest-point problems in computational geometry. In J.-R. Sack and J. Urrutia, editors, *Handbook of Computational Geometry*, pages 877–935. Elsevier Science, Amsterdam, 2000.

M. Smid. Geometric spanners with few edges and degree five. In *Proceedings of the 12th Computing: The Australasian Theory Symposium*, volume 51 of *Conferences in Research and Practice in Information Technology*, pages 7–9, Sydney, 2006. Australian Computer Society Inc.

M. Smid. Maintaining the minimal distance of a point set in polylogarithmic time. *Discrete & Computational Geometry*, 7:415–431, 1992.

W. D. Smith. *Studies in Computational Geometry Motivated by Mesh Generation*. Ph.D. thesis, Priceton University, Princeton, NJ, 1988.

J. Soares. Approximating Euclidean distances by small degree graphs. *Discrete & Computational Geometry*, 11:213–233, 1994.

J. Soares. Graph spanners: A survey. *Congressus Numerantium*, 89:225–238, 1992.

J. M. Steele and T. L. Snyder. Worst-case growth rates of some classical problems of combinatorial optimization. *SIAM Journal on Computing*, 18:278–287, 1989.

J. M. Steele and A. C. Yao. Lower bounds for algebraic decision trees. *Journal of Algorithms*, 3:1–8, 1982.

H.-H. Stølum. River meandering as a self-organizational process. *Science*, 271: 1710–1713, 1996.

K. Talwar. Bypassing the embedding: Approximation schemes and compact representations of low dimensional metrics. In *Proceedings of the 36th ACM Symposium on the Theory of Computing*, pages 281–290, 2004.

R. E. Tarjan. Efficiency of a good but not linear set-union algorithm. *Journal of the ACM*, 22:215–225, 1975.

S. R. Tate and K. Xu. General-purpose spatial decomposition algorithms: Experimental results. In *Proceedings of the 2nd Workshop on Algorithm Engineering and Experiments*, pages 197–215, 2000.

R. Thom. Sur l'homologie des variétés algébriques reélles. In S. S. Cairns, editor, *Differential and Combinatorial Topology*, pages 255–265. Princeton University Press, Princeton, NJ, 1965.

M. Thorup. Parallel shortcutting of rooted trees. *Journal of Algorithms*, 23:139–159, 1997.

P. M. Vaidya. Minimum spanning trees in k-dimensional space. *SIAM Journal on Computing*, 17:572–582, 1988.

P. M. Vaidya. An $O(n \log n)$ algorithm for the all-nearest-neighbors problem. *Discrete & Computational Geometry*, 4:101–115, 1989.

P. M. Vaidya. A sparse graph almost as good as the complete graph on points in K dimensions. *Discrete & Computational Geometry*, 6:369–381, 1991.

J. H. van Lint and R. M. Wilson. *A Course in Combinatorics*. Cambridge University Press, Cambridge, UK, 1992.

K. R. Varadarajan. A divide-and-conquer algorithm for min-cost perfect matching in the plane. In *Proceedings of the 39th IEEE Symposium on Foundations of Computer Science*, pages 320–329, 1998.

D. E. Willard. *Predicate-oriented database search algorithms*. Ph.D. thesis, Harvard Computation Laboratory, Harvard University, Cambridge, MA, 1978. Report TR-20-78.

D. E. Willard. The super-b-tree algorithm. Report TR-03-79, Harvard Computation Laboratory, Harvard University, Cambridge, MA, 1979.

D. E. Willard and G. S. Lueker. Adding range restriction capability to dynamic data structures. *Journal of the ACM*, 32:597–617, 1985.

A. C. Yao. On constructing minimum spanning trees in k-dimensional spaces and related problems. *SIAM Journal on Computing*, 11: 721–736, 1982a.

A. C. Yao. Lower bounds for algebraic computation trees with integer inputs. *SIAM Journal on Computing*, 20:655–668, 1991.

A. C. Yao. Probabilistic computation: Towards a unified measure of complexity. In *Proceedings of the 18th IEEE Symposium on Foundations of Computer Science*, pages 222–227, 1977.

A. C. Yao. Space-time trade-off for answering range queries. In *Proceedings of the 14th ACM Symposium on the Theory of Computing*, pages 128–136, 1982b.

N. R. Zeh. *I/O-Efficient Algorithms for Shortest Path Related Problems*. Ph.D. thesis, School of Computer Science, Carleton University, Ottawa, Canada, 2002.

Algorithms Index

Index

Printed in the United States
by Baker & Taylor Publisher Services